HAMISH'S MOUNTAIN WALK
and
CLIMBING THE CORBETTS

HAMISH'S MOUNTAIN WALK

and

CLIMBING THE CORBETTS

by HAMISH M. BROWN

HIS TWO ACCLAIMED MOUNTAIN-WALKING
BOOKS ON THE MUNROS AND THE CORBETTS

Bâton Wicks Publications

Hamish's Mountain Walk was first published by Victor Gollancz Ltd., London
in 1978 © Hamish M. Brown 1978

Climbing the Corbetts was first published by Victor Gollancz Ltd., London, in 1988
© Hamish M. Brown 1988

This combined edition of *Hamish's Mountain Walk* and *Climbing the Corbetts* was first
published by Bâton Wicks Publications, London in 1997
© Hamish M. Brown 1997
ISBN 1-898573-08-5
A CIP catalogue record for this title is available from the British Library

Printed and bound in Great Britain by
Mackays of Chatham PLC, Chatham, Kent

Bâton Wicks Publications, London
all trade enquiries to:
Cordee, 3a De Montfort Street, Leicester LE1 7HD

AUTHOR'S ACKNOWLEDGEMENTS (for *Hamish's Mountain Walk*): The maps for this book
were drawn by Jim Renny, to whom I am most grateful. Beryl Luke, Mrs Brown of Glasgow and
Osborne House in Kirkcaldy valiantly typed my scribbled notes into something legible. The
photographs are my own, except the historical ones which came largely from Scottish
Mountaineering Club sources and I was also allowed to quote freely from its journal. Thanks also
to Mr Lovat Dickson for permission to quote from Richard Hillary's *The Last Enemy*. Robin
Campbell, Tom Weir, Jim Donaldson, John Hinde, Sandy Cousins and Tom Waghorn all provided
material, and without the support of family and friends there would be no book. The Walk was
much easier than the writing of the book! To all who appear in it I am indebted. I used a Rollei 35
camera which gave good results. Kodak film was used – also for the cover illustration enlarged
from a Kodachrome 25 transparency. (for *Climbing the Corbetts*): I am indebted to Jim Renny
for providing another fine set of maps. The short extract from Torridon Highlands by Brenda
Macrow is reprint on page 265 by permission from the author and publisher, Robert Hale Ltd.

HAMISH'S MOUNTAIN WALK

*The First Traverse of all the Scottish Munros
in One Journey*

by

HAMISH M. BROWN

All men are free under the stars
Yet we bolt our doors and creep to bed,
All men are kings upon the earth
But some have sold their thrones, despaired and fled;
All men, in Adam, walked with God,
Now God, and walking, both are odd.

We were dreamers, dreaming greatly, in the man-stifled town:
We yearned beyond the sky-line where the strange roads go down
KIPLING

That is the difference between age and youth. Boys do things
for no reason. I wonder do we get old because we do things
by reason instead of instinct . . . ? A married man looks
comfortable and settled: he looks finished if you understand
me, and a bachelor looks unsettled and funny and he always
wants to be running round seeing things
JAMES STEPHENS *The Crock of Gold*

CONTENTS

PHOTOS IN THE TEXT

between pages 164 and 165

1. Sir Hugh Munro and friends "on the hill"; 2. Rev. A.E. Robertson;
3. Brian Ripley; 4. Blackrock Cottage and Buachaille Etive Mor;
5. John Hinde; 6. Sandy Cousins; 7. "Kitchie" – Hamish's dog;
8. Glen Dessary; 9. Camp by Loch Hourn; 10. Beinn Sgriol;
11. Garbh Chioch Mhor; 12. A Scottish Mountaineering Club meet;
13. Maol Chean-dearg; 14. Sgurr nan Gillean from Garbh-bheinn;
15. Braehead School's last Munro; 16. Seana Bhraigh;
17. On the summit of Ben Hope.

LIST OF MAPS

BY WAY OF INTRODUCTION

IT WAS A hot, stuffy day in the office: no ventilation, no windows, and monotonous work. After having spent twelve happy years in the field, pioneering outdoor education at Braehead School in Fife (only leaving when the school itself closed), I was now County Adviser on Mountain Activities. Every fibre rebelled at the incarceration. For the first time in my varied life I felt as caged as a poor lion in a den of Daniels. What was I doing tied to a desk with no view of sky and hill, no sound of bird or sea?

My eye fell on a map of Scotland. I spread it out on the floor and knelt over it. Immediately I received a wallop on the backside as a colleague banged through the door bearing one vital aspect of bureaucracy—the tea.

I sat sipping the tea (they never can drum-up properly) and gazed at the map on the floor. "God, how I love this land," I thought. With three rounds of the Munros done, and some of the summits ascended scores of times over decades of wandering in the highlands and islands, it needed little to set the memories dancing like heat-shimmers on the hill. Oh, to be tramping a far hill right then!

What could be new? different? demanding?

What about all the Munros? Those 279 summits over 3,000 feet?

But!

But I did no more work that afternoon. The seed was sown and no farmer eyed his unbroken ground more keenly than I the map at my feet. When I eventually folded it up I really folded up my job as well—burning my boots so to speak. I could hear the objections. Why risk security? You are forty now. What will you do afterwards? How can you afford it? It would be far too difficult to organise. Someone else might do it meantime.

So I said nothing—and worked the happier knowing the day appointed. The French have a saying: "The young aren't on to it, and the old aren't up to it." As far as I was concerned it was just the right time. The silence was also a necessity; it *is* a competitive world, and being second is not as good as being first. There are few enough things where I, Mr Average, might find the priority.

Of course there would be sacrifices: comfort and companionship, the ease of "normal" work and the indulgence of normal enjoyments. Unlike a condemned man, my privations were self-inflicted, so there could really be no complaint and no self pity. You need to be a bit older to realise the implications, old enough to know better in fact—and then to ignore them all and go for the joy of it. We are given only one life. Surely its days are to be spent rather than hoarded, and given rather than spent? Everything should go to grasp what is best while it can be meaningful. What use is "security" twenty years hence if that is *all* those years give? Life should be lived greatly from day to day.

At this period I had been doing a great deal of reading about sea voyages. I had had voyages as an instructor on the schooner, *Captain Scott*. The lure of sea is very similar to that of hills. Strange, though, that solitary sailors are hailed as heroes whereas the safer solo land-lubber is condemned.

One of the reasons we climb is the challenge—which can be as varied as the sizes and shapes and psyches of *homo sapiens*. My own interests are many: I am happy bird-watching, or merely Munro-bagging, canoeing, ski-ing, or on the sea, climbing, taking pictures; too many interests to excel at any. On rock the spirit is not what it used to be, but any walking challenge had to be as great. Rob Collister, in telling of a ski traverse from Zermatt to Verbier (in one day), puts it clearly: "If mountain travel is to be as enjoyable as mountain climbing, it must, in its own way, be equally demanding." So you make it so.

The idea had long been there but the shock was suddenly seeing oneself stepping forward to try it. Thus must a four-year-old feel when thrust out in public to compete in his first egg-and-spoon race.

This book has been written twice. Following all the interests my logs swelled into a mighty tome which would be beyond reason these days of economy. So it had to be hacked down like an unruly garden. It is still a patchwork; but that is what the Walk was—a thing of shreds and patches. It is not a guide book, yet you will really need the maps to follow it and it gives away quite a bit to the discerning reader. It is given largely from a walker's point of view. Some favoured spots are passed over quickly for elitist reasoning and the best and rarest of the wildlife is not described: osprey eyrie or snow bunting nest are more precious to me with the eggs left untouched!

Equipment and food notes are added at the back, for a trip like this is a logistical exercise—a part of the game which can keep participants talking till all hours. Planning is crucial: a message perhaps most needed to be learnt by the young, though the whole reason of the game must never be lost: we go because it is fun—and not just in retrospect! Recently a group of teenage girls came to me asking if I would take them hill-walking and what did they need to begin? Resisting an easy, "Yes, I'll take you" (they were not unattractive), I said, "You can take yourselves, and all you need is a bus ticket to the Lomonds." I still believe that is how we should start—wanting enough to go, regardless. The beginner needs little else. That this trip took as much planning as any to the Andes or Himalayas was for the reason it was not a beginner's one.

Sandy Cousins, who did a Munro trip from Cape Wrath to Glasgow, was telling me how he had had requests from walkers from England who wanted all the details so they could do the same, often on their first trip north. Sandy's answers were not encouraging! You cannot become an instant mountaineer, no matter how firm a belief in a platter-existence you have. It does not come on a plate. Long Walks like this, or Sandy's, or John Hinde's, were the outcome of decades of knocking about in the highlands. We sinned with our eyes open!

Certainly dream dreams, that is the birthright of youth, but you cannot grow vegetables without digging the soil. *My* preparation was almost two thousand Munros long.

Do not funk the Gaelic names; they can become quite a fascination in time, giving all sorts of information—or puzzles—which enrich experience. Some help is given at the back of this book, though as a non-expert, I do not claim great accuracy. The experts only argue anyway.

I have a great many people to thank, obviously: all the family and members of my club, the Braes o' Fife, who assisted in so many ways— it is their story as much as mine. Robert Louis Stevenson wrote, "Every book is, in an intimate sense, a circular letter to the friends of him who writes it." This is particularly so with this tale.

It is, of necessity, much in the first person singular. It is a very personal narrative, yet I hope shows something of this great land of ours. The trip gave a marvellous intimacy with that land, such as cannot be found just on weekends and holidays. I feel somewhere along the line, man has gone astray. Perhaps the break came when we stopped leading sheep and began to drive them, when we turned from the hand loom to the machine, from foot and field and home to vehicles and railways and factory. We have rushed off after the good life—and have overshot the mark. This was a return to rock-reality, the womb-comfort, the joy of untrammelled simplicity. It is really the walking of years with the kernel of the three months of the Long Walk.

Both the Walk and this book were done, using the One Inch map with its individuality, spellings and heights. We had all grown so accustomed to its face—yet by the time this book is published we will be accepting the metrication of our mountains (force-feeding for some!) and future books will be in the new idiom. Eventually at least we can have really definitive Tables—of heights over 914 metres. The Munro game goes merrily on, however. I have tried to note some of the changes sprung upon us. What would Munro think of it all?

THE HISTORICAL SETTING

WE TEND TO regard hard walking as a modern phenomenon but the opposite is probably correct; we have largely forgotten how to walk. The drovers who brought beasts from the Hebrides to the Falkirk Tryst, or those who took them on to Smithfield, knew what walking was; *any* Highlander did, and so did any one not gentry enough to own a horse. We even read of the regular tramping done by academics between London and Oxford or Cambridge.

There were next to no Highland roads before Wade and Caulfield built theirs during the eighteenth century. William Taylor's book, *The Military Roads in Scotland* (David and Charles), tells their story. Next time you take a day off from climbing in Glencoe and go bombing off up to Fort William, remember that the road was built as recently as 1786.

The aftermath of the 1745 Jacobite rising brought great social changes; people were more tied down locally, urban life was spreading—and at once we have the "escapist" reaction, which continues to this day. The end of the eighteenth century began a great period of "Tours" in the Highlands. Several of these are described in Maurice Lindsay's books, for which we should be grateful as the originals are often great tomes. Though most of these tourists made maximum use of ponies some great things were done on foot. The poet Keats for instance, hardly an athletic type, along with a friend, Brown, walked the 642 miles from Lancaster to Inverness in 42 days.

Some travellers seemed to revel in the roughness but it took a long time for mountains to be enjoyed simply for themselves. In 1767 an Edinburgh botanist, James Robertson, had quite happily wandered over Klibreck, Wyvis, and other hills in the north, taking river-crossings, snow storms and hill-cloud very much for granted. In 1771 he had a real Munro-bagging spree: Clova, Lochnagar, Ben Avon, Cairngorm, the Sgoran Dubhs, Nevis, the Killin hills, Rannoch ridges and the Monadh Liath. The acceptance was complete, even if under the banner of science.

Professor Forbes, "the discoverer of the Alps", was an important figure both in climbing and geographical terms yet, strangely, left little mark on Scotland. He covered vast distances on foot: in 1836 he included the first ascent of Sgurr nan Gillean, and in 1845 began six successive summers in the Highlands. A Michel de Bernhoff (who tramped from St Petersburg to Paris) considered thirty miles a day a fair average.

We should not overlook the early work of the surveyors: the Ordnance Survey did much on foot from necessity. Thomas Colby, the Director General from 1820 to 1846, cheerfully covered 513 miles in 22 days, had one day off, then did another 22 days over 586 miles. That was primarily exploratory rambling, the hard grind of carrying heavy camps and equipment was the main work, when several months might be spent on one mountain alone. The whole story would be quite a saga and one about which I wish the O.S. would give us a popular account.

In that pre-train, pre-car period the Highlands and Islands were incredibly remote of access and difficult to move about in, and they had seen a drastic fall in population. Today we are apt to question the deer forests as the sacred preserve of the rich, forgetting that these estates were carved out of a wilderness already created by the Clearances and the sheep. The Highland economy had collapsed. Deer for sport created jobs, as remote corners were opened up, roads constructed and houses built.

The general ignorance of the hills was remarkable. If we did not quite have the Alpine idea of dragons and demons (these we put in the lochs) the high summits were regarded as not worth visiting. We can hardly blame the O.S. for the cursory nature of some of its surveying of the more remote areas in this impossible terrain. Mountaineering had not been invented.

As a sport it was a nineteenth-century creation. The Highlanders, as ever, lived in and tramped over the hills, already perhaps as the servants of landed gentry up for the stalking. They had no real influence on mountaineering as we know it now, though for a while they did form a loose body of "guides" for tourists who desired Ben Lomond or Lochnagar or other "fabulous adventures". There were the odd scientists who were also out with the main flow—men such as the hectic Dr John Macculloch, who, in his geological wanderings which began in 1811, covered vast distances on foot, on pony, and by boat and could justly, for his day, claim to have ascended "almost every principal summit".

It was really the professional, middle class—lawyers, clerics, professors (including scientists)—who, bursting out of their urban strait-jackets, created the sport of recreational mountaineering. The Alpine Club was founded during the winter of 1857–58. Its members often enjoyed activities in the hills of Wales and Lakeland, and, to a lesser extent, Scotland. When the Scottish Mountaineering Club was formed in 1889, its membership included, or contributed, many members of the Alpine Club.

Between the dates of formation of the two clubs quite a few other small clubs or bodies had come into being, often local, which included the hills in their activities. Some people today have expressed surprise that no lead came from north of the Highland boundary, but in those regions practical experience of the hills was just a fact of life—mountaineering is basically a flight from urban pressures, escapism again, which becomes the more frantic and global, as the burden of civilisation grows heavier year by year. You do not find many keepers or shepherds indulging in recreational hill days, though probably the earliest British rock-climbers were the wildfowlers of St Kilda and the Hebrides, who climbed not only to obtain food but for pleasure.

Before Sir Hugh Munro brought out his *Tables of Heights over 3000 feet* (1891), it was generally believed only some thirty hills were of that height. A few of these were popular expeditions even in the eighteenth century, but suddenly to be given a tenfold inheritance was almost overwhelming. The formation of the Scottish Mountaineering Club played an important role in consolidating and expanding the trend. It began a systematic covering of the Scottish hills, soon discovering in them a playground as satisfying as the Alps and not just a poor substitute. The first journal appeared in 1890. Its preface starts with the curious quote: "Let thy words be few". (That was thirty volumes ago.) It then gave away the riches in store: there were possibly three hundred mountains over 3,000 feet, "some perhaps never ascended". What more natural than to list these? What more natural than to try and climb them? The list duly appeared in the second volume of the Journal and in a few years the "Munros" were an established game.

Munro's Tables are today a separate volume, periodically revised, published by the Scottish Mountaineering Trust and full of photographs, maps, references—and now, metric equivalents. Little did Sir Hugh know what he began. He was in the process of revising his list when he died, so we will never know if he intended a fuller definition

of a "Munro". Of his list of tops some were elevated to the peerage of
"separate mountains" and these took on the name of "Munros", the
others remained "Tops", or "subsidiary summits"; which is all we have
to go on. His reason for this classification has always been a fruitful
source of debate.

A stricter definition was given to another series of hills more recently
listed by J. R. Corbett, and named after him, the "Corbetts": hills
over 2,500 feet, with a re-ascent all round of 500 feet (which is often
erroneously thought to apply to Munros).

A brief look at Munro, the man, shows a warm personality and an
enthusiast with many interests. He was an original member of the
Scottish Mountaineering Club and its third President (1894–1897).

Hugh Thomas Munro was born in London in 1856, eldest of nine
children, and much of his life was spent there or in the family's native
Scotland, where he first managed and then inherited the estate of
Lindertis near Kirriemuir. He was a great collector as a child: fossils,
shells, eggs, butterflies; even as a young man, after a spell in South
Africa, he returned with a collection of Basuto curios, antelope heads,
a black boy, and a monkey.

He came to the mountains when a student in Stuttgart in his late
teens. Travel could almost be regarded as a collecting activity with
Munro, a game played all through his life, both professionally and for
pleasure. He had a business training in London, but was also known as
a good musician and dancer, and he had a flow of "capital talk".
(When he and another great talker had a day on the hills together they
both returned complaining they had been silent all day as each was
unable to get a word in edgeways.)

Several years of this good life of business, travel and pleasure ended
with pleurisy and in 1880 he went as Private Secretary to join Sir
George Colley, Governor of Natal. During the Basuto War he served
with an irregular cavalry corps and saw exciting times. Once back in
Britain he spent more time at Lindertis, and the hills came to play an
important part in his life. In 1885 he stood as parliamentary candidate
for Kirkcaldy Burghs in Fife, as forlorn a Tory hope then as now, but
nobody else would come forward to do battle. He never stood for his
local Forfar seat, though active behind the scenes.

When his children were old enough they were dragged off to
Germany, Greece, Morocco, the States, Japan, Ceylon and other lands
near and far. Munro in Yosemite is a nice thought. He was a natural

choice for a King's Messenger—an official courier bearing documents about the world. It is a pity that photography was still in the frozen pose state in those days, for we have few pictures of the man as he must have been; he was certainly no bog-bound laird but a man of wide experience, talents and knowledge, and he enlivened any company. He would travel back from the ends of the earth for an S.M.C. Meet and the Journal published over eighty of his articles and notes.

In 1914 he was past military age but went out to Malta to work, and in 1918 he organised a canteen in the castle town of Tarascon. The following spring a chill developed into pneumonia and he died, at the age of sixty-three.

This is the man who gave us the Tables which we gave back as "Munros" (he disliked eponymous mountain names), to make surely one of the oddest of best-selling books.

Munro loved nothing better than to undertake long through-routes, often in winter, often alone, and clad in uniform of cape, knicker-bockers (or kilt), and Balmoral bunnet, with a long ice axe. He was a skilled all-rounder but was less enthusiastic about rock-climbing. Aneroid and notebook ensured the Journal was peppered with obser-vations and corrections to the map. He was a Survey in himself, and a deal more accurate, and this before railways or motor cars. When these new modes of travel appeared, he actually wrote articles to show how they could open up new approaches to the hills. Nobody used the new-fangled machinery to better advantage.

I mention one or two of his trips later, but just one example here. In 1891 he crossed from Blair Atholl to near Kirkmichael, "heavy walking all day in soft snow. . . . At Diranean they had to scrape me down with a knife to get the frozen snow off." On Beinn a' Ghlo the snow was blowing "in spiral columns several hundred feet high, penetrating everything, filling pockets and drifting between waistcoat and shirt, where it melted and then froze into a solid wedge of ice. . . . I never suffered so severely from the cold."

Munro never completed the ascent of the Munros and Tops he had listed. He had kept for last the easy Carn Clioch Mhuillin above the Dee as it was near home and would make a good celebratory summit— ponies carrying up the champagne—and then there was the Inaccessible Pinnacle, the end to many Munroist hopes. He was driven out of Skye by atrocious weather in 1895; in 1897 a Yachting Meet could not even anchor safely; in 1905 arrangements with Harold Raeburn (the

MacInnes of his day) fell through. He was there as late as 1915, but without success.

In 1901 the Rev. A. E. Robertson was the first man to complete the Munros, and it was twenty-two years before the second round was made—by another Reverend. "A. E. R." was a colourful personality, too, and also President of the Scottish Mountaineering Club (1930–1932). He was more of a climber than Sir Hugh, a trait marked on his first, solo, ascent, Goatfell on Arran, when he chose to scramble the last thousand feet to the summit. He was then twelve or so. One of the surprises following my own trip was to be introduced to his spry widow, sadly now no longer with us. He married twice (Munro, on the other hand, was a widower most of his life) and died in 1958, aged 88.

Archibald Eneas Robertson's parish was at Rannoch, an appropriate hill setting. In two successive years he thought nothing of knocking off 72 or 75 Munros in three-month holiday blitzes. What he called "a desultory campaign of about ten years" saw the task accomplished. Pony-trap and boat helped, and above all a push bike, for he was a great cyclist. For the rest he walked, and found accommodation in the wilds, usually with shepherds or keepers for, speaking their language as he did, and with so many common interests, he was always a welcome guest—even when he appeared with no warning. He stayed with the McCooks at Ben Alder on many occasions after dropping in there for the first time in 1893. The Aonach Eagach, with his wife and his oldest friend, Alexander (later Lord) Moncrieff, gave A. E. R. his final Munro. He kissed both the cairn and his wife—in that order.

Good gear and meticulous planning was part of his success. He often carried a whole-plate camera into the wilds and produced some superb pictures, and he was also a historian of note, an interest shown in an article on "coffin" roads and tracks in the North West, which appeared in the S.M.C. Journal in 1941. There are extracts from his diaries in the Journals of 1948 and 1949. In connection with this interest he rose to high position in both the Scottish Rights of Way Society and the Royal Scottish Geographical Society. A bridge over the Elchaig below the Falls of Glomach was built as a memorial to Robertson. He was a skilled man with his hands, making a table for the C.I.C. Hut for instance.

The Rev. A. R. G. Burn not only repeated the Munros in 1923, but added the subsidiary Tops. J. A. Parker, Munroist number three in 1929, added the "Furth of Scotland"—the resonant term for the

3,oooers of England, Wales and Ireland. The first "grand slam" of Munros, Tops and Furth fell to W. Docherty in 1949, a surprisingly late date. Munroist number four was Corbett, of that ilk, in 1930. In 1947 Mrs John Hirst completed the first female round, and also a husband-wife combination. The Macdonalds in 1958 saw a father-and-son Munro effort, and in 1974 a father-and-son Munro and Tops success went to the Lawsons. The "grand slam" was made by Anne Littlejohn in 1960. There are fifteen females in a 1977 list of 143 Munroists which now grows at an annual average rate of five people.

In 1964 Philip Tranter did them all again and in 1966 Eric Maxwell repeated not just the Munros but Tops as well. George Smith and I repeated in 1969 and I did a third round while with Braehead School. The School was after a "school's round" before it closed down and was demolished. The pupils succeeded—and so did Kitchy, my dog, in 1971. The trip recorded in this book gave a round in a single expedition, and not so long after it a fifth personal round slipped in. Basically I am not a Munro-bagger, at least no more than anyone else; as I ski, climb, canoe, go abroad a great deal, my proportion of Munro-days to others could well be less than that of most people. I just happen to have had a vast number of happy days in the hills.

Doing the Munros has become an immensely popular activity. And why not? Metrication will soon give the list a certain archaic charm, but a new substitute list of 1,000 metre summits is not likely to take over as there would be too few to make a worthwhile challenge. The Munros are a perfect target. Even allowing for the Great War it seems surprising that only eight people had done the Munros before the Second War. Our new ease of travel, and longer holidays and affluence, has changed things dramatically. The S.M.C. Journal keeps the list up to date and at present those within (or is it without?) the pale number 143. Only fifteen have done the "grand slam", perhaps showing a tendency to be content with minimal standards. A high proportion of English Munroists are in the list and though many are claimed by the S.M.C., they are basically Rucksackers or Fell and Rockers. The Grampian Club has provided a large number too. Perhaps a score of modest(?) walkers have kept their success private; a pity, as it leaves records incomplete. A name in a list means little enough and anyway the whole game is played by a small and suspect section of the population. The S.M.C. Journal briefly notes new additions to the list each year and welcomes information.

I was not really conscious of Munros until I went to Braehead School, but my post there, the first to organise outdoor pursuits in a state school in Scotland, soon led to the discovery. Kids are competitive and when we formed a club, an entry qualification of ten Munros was a safeguard: each member would have been away several times by then—and was usually hooked. I kept a careful log from that time onwards, a habit maintained on this Walk. From its notes has come this book.

Two developments made the Walk a goal to aim for after Braehead closed down. In the sixties the R.A.F. Rescue teams made several north–south and east–west expeditions over numerous Munros. I met John Hinde, who was involved and whose accounts had stirred up readers; he was not the first in either direction, but has done both and led the biggest expedition in 1968. He stresses it is not a competitive game, any cutting corners leads to lack of safety. These R.A.F. trips were very much team-work and part of training. Few civilians had the time or the organisational support to try it and the statistics were frightening. Pete McGowan (Valley Team leader) ran up 100,000 feet of ascent in 19 days, 350 miles for 58 Munros. Here is the development of the traverses in the sixties:

Nov. 1962	East–West	(K. Shaw, McKerron, Ballantyne)	11 Munros
Summer 1964	North–South	(Armstrong, Golton, Raven)	37 Munros
Summer 1966	North–South	(Ward, Morrison, Bradshaw)	32 Munros
Summer 1966	West–East	(Hinde, R. Shaw)	30 Munros
Summer 1967	South–North	(Gilligan, Ward, Wagg)	26 Munros
Nov. 1968	North–South	(McGowan, Tomlinson, Hinde, Blyth)	58, 49, 48, 45 Munros

John Hinde said he lost weight but gained fitness on this last trek. Ben Humble, a veteran S.M.C. member who met the party on Ben Lomond, thought John looked older with the strain, but then their last days had been continuously wild and wet. Another civilian who was in at the end was a younger Munro enthusiast Sandy Cousins who, three years later, in 1971, was to make a big trek, north–south, from Cape Wrath home to Glasgow, over 47 Munros, 370 miles and 90,000 feet of ascent. A full account of this journey can be found in the 1972 S.M.C. Journal.

I followed these trips with interest, and dreamed dreams, but the other development, even more daring, came in 1967 when Brian and Alan Ripley made an attempt on all the Munros in a single walk. They were Karabiner Mountaineering Club members with little Scottish tradition, so their effort of 230 Munros, 1,325 miles and 337,850 feet was phenomenal. I read Tom Waghorn's article in *The Climber and Rambler* at the time and marvelled.

The Ripley brothers did not succeed on account of several factors, many of which stemmed from not really knowing beforehand just what they were in for: the midges in August and September, wet and wind and snow later, the persistent strain of clashing with stalking interests, worries about food (their base being in Manchester), packs weighing fifty pounds or more at times, difficult rivers, blisters and sores, ever-shortening hours of daylight. Brian's log reads like a graph: ups and downs but each down just that bit lower than the last as the burden grew heavier. The environment was hostile yet often they were bored and had to bully themselves on. Few can appreciate what these young lads went through. Their youth was against them I suppose; powerful all-round hillmen as they were, Scotland was not known to them as it was to, say, John, Sandy or me—who were all a score of years older—on our trips. The August start alone was a vital mistake.

The starting date was dictated largely by other engagements, and Brian was off to the Himalayas the following summer. He was a strong mountaineer with such ascents as the Bonatti Pillar on the Dru, for instance, to his name. He was tragically killed by stonefall on Malubiting, 25,451 feet. This trip of mine could so easily have been his, or Philip Tranter's, a powerful Scottish all-rounder, who died in a car crash on the way back from climbing in Turkey, much more worthy lads.

Sandy's Walk was much more in mind when I was planning mine, but two things were remembered from the Ripleys' attempt: first, they had had dietary troubles and secondly, they took lifts. The former gave me some concern but I could not make too many enquiries for fear of giving the game away; the latter I felt was unaesthetic, the only "rule" I made was that the journey should be all self-propelled. I loathe walking on tarred roads so decided I could, morally, use a push bike—especially for the long hauls to and from the island Munros on Skye and

Mull and also round the A9. I toyed with the idea of canoeing to and from these islands but reluctantly decided it was too chancy and too much of an imposition on others. An island became the starting point to save one diversion. Off-duty travel would be legitimate, I thought, but in practice was a rare indulgence. And I knew I had to finish by the start of the stalking season.

Reading the Ripleys' log I feel they first bent and then broke the idea of self-propulsion; the odd bus or car, the runs on Skye, and then to and from Mull from Glencoe—and another factor consciously or unconsciously was added to the mental burden. Time and finance were problems, perhaps undermining body as well as soul. You can only take so much. Brian's log is brief and often cryptic; it reads like a thriller. They began on August 13th, and ended on November 10th on Beinn Dorain, when they were beaten off by the worst weather of all. Alan's ankles were swelling badly at the end and Brian had slit the back of his boots to make them bearable. A doctor said Alan was suffering from iron deficiencies. David Summerfield, another Karabiner Mountaineering Club member, was with them for about half of the trip but had to drop out. The early days saw an agony of sore feet, sore shoulders and a communal collection of 25 blisters.

They had great days, of course, and even some of the poor weather days did not deter from fine things—such as a traverse of the Cuillin Ridge. Ironically they had a succession of fine days in the Blackmount just before the end.

These, then, were my influences. They were all from the mountaineering tradition. It was only after the Walk I read books or articles by Hillaby, Merrill or Snow, and they rather frightened me with their disciplined, clockwork routine. I prefer Eric Newby—or Shipton and Tilman who are perhaps my oldest mentors. They are in line with the most traditional means of travel. Adam and Eve walked. Amazingly, despite all man has done to himself, he still can walk. The greatest feats are all unrecorded, lost in anonymous treks of Boers or Americans, of Bushmen or Asians, of Aborigines or Russians. Our self-conscious efforts are mere self-indulgence, irrational and unnecessary. I have no guilty feeling, however, for if we did not, "whiles, dance, we would aye greet."

HAMISH'S MOUNTAIN WALK

GENESIS

GENESIS IS GOOD for you! The decision to do this trip certainly was refreshing and though it was a snap decision in some ways I had no illusions about what was involved. So much of my reading at this time was of others *doing* things yet I was desk-bound and frustrated, kept from action even at my job.

It was around Hallowe'en 1972 that I spread the map on the office floor—and knew just what I would do in 1974. The period between *was* the Walk in some ways, the toil was there, not in the actual walking. Right from the start I knew it would be a largely solo trip. It would simplify a whole host of problems—not even a committee of two to delay things and, God knows, I'd had my fill of committees. Tentage, the doubling of every bit of food, finding a second cycle or canoe, the difficulty of back-up and above all finding the right person—all these problems just did not happen. Close proximity with anyone over a long period, especially under stress, can be unhappy if not worse. Simplicity is the forgotten virtue.

I cannot recall when the actual timings were decided but obviously not immediately, as 1974 and not 1973 was chosen. I had some obligations to my job! That first winter, though, I doodled maps endlessly as I tried to link up the best line between the 277 summits. They even grew to 279 before I set off, as the O.S. caught up on their inadequate surveying of our North West. A mapboard faced desk/bed at home but of course much of it could be done in my head anyway. This gave me a pre-occupied air which some took for avid concentration on work in hand. One obvious joy would be to do endless days activating what an old friend Willie Docherty called "the creed of the long traverse".

The route clarified in general, though it was never static and in points altered even in the course of doing the trip. Sanely, not racing, how long would it take? I tackled this in various ways and the answer always seemed to be 3½–4 months. May and June are usually the best months. There was the Stalking after July. That would suggest a start in early April; in fact the first of April seemed the obvious choice.

I went south–north both for romantic and practical reasons. I hoped for the better weather in the north and west. By starting on Mull I cut out one long arm. Bothies and huts in the north would help once into the midgy months, when the enjoyment of camping is apt to wear thin. All previous trips had been done north–south so perhaps there was an element of cussedness too.

The costing was approached from various angles and gave £400.

The route eventually was worked out on ½-inch maps which went to my brother so that he could follow my doings, and then the 1-inch which I used. I needed 22 maps in all. Both Dollar and I would have identical route-books with the day-to-day plans and a list of places where I would phone, a safety factor. I began to accumulate gear for the trip, selecting and testing—breaking in three new pairs of boots till I knew they were comfortable—over Christmas–New Year doing two weeks' non-stop to see how the unfit body would take it. In January I began bringing in S.M.C. and B.F.M.C. friends who could act as weekend support and, when David (my brother) and his wife, Marina, agreed to act as "base" and even come as field support for the first part, I really felt a surge of faith that it would "go". Later Mike Keates agreed to come out for the last two weeks in the north. David lived at Dollar in Clackmannanshire, Mike at Inverness, so this really covered the land.

I thought of sponsorship but as I had saved enough, it was not a desperate essential. If the Walk succeeded I could cash in a bit after-wards; but I wanted to enjoy it as my journey, untrammelled, and not as a public stunt. There was also the lure of the priority. This was not just my dream. Being first has its place, transient though it be; someone can always do it faster or shorter, cleaner or bolder, backwards or on their heads. The vital thing is to enjoy the doing of it.

As a keen canoeist I thought of canoeing to and from the islands (Mull and Skye) but this would be too great a risk of precious time. Later I did bring in the canoe for Loch Lomond. A cycle too could be used on the long, dull, tarred roads which could not easily be avoided. So long as it was *all* self-propelled it was valid.

I started using lunch breaks for wee jobs: mosaic-ing the maps to suit, trimming candles, preparing labels, making lists; at weekends in the north I would note the sites of telephone boxes and nibble away at the weight problem, endlessly trying variations of gear. I could not afford to buy much new stuff, so expediency played its part. My major worry was a tent. I had a good Vango featherweight but it had so many guys and bits and pieces—and it was nylon which meant condensation problems. This became almost an obsession, but when Dave Challis heard he offered me a tent, also nylon, 3½ lb weight, with, he said, no problem. I was sceptical! He brought it to a conference later and pitched it on display. It was not even new. It was all mine. A few filthy weekends persuaded me he had been correct. There was condensation, but it did not matter; by the simple method of keeping the tray-shaped groundsheet away from the walls with elastic the condensation just ran into the ground.

Various courses and a season in the Alps gave a pause in the summer, and once back I handed in my notice so was free to *do* again: a Hebridean trip in November, a month on the schooner *Captain Scott*, then the usual holiday courses in the North West. Time suddenly was running out.

Back home it was already mid-January 1974. The stockpile came down from the loft, a last big shopping to the Alliance Cash and Carry (could I eat all that?), and from Hughes, our local grocer. The dates of a proposed visit to the Polish Tatras eventually became known and put the starting date back a few days.

On the fourth of February we had an unusual wine and cheese party. We looked at slides of the Alps and various odd club doings but the main activity, saving me a 100 man-hours, was breaking down bulk food into one-man size pokes. Chaos: Ian and Mary in a bedroom dealing with a seven-pound bag of curry (one beer for every pound, it took), John and Penny in the kitchen with a sack of raisins (busy adding wisecrack comments on slips of paper), Val, Ian Mitchell and Patrick were in the front room and Bob and Liz Wallace, George and Beryl slaved in the hall, with peas, carrots, beans, coffee, tea, cocoa and so on. John Dunnett and Mike Duncan came in later and wondered what was going on—not being in the secret. Mother had wisely gone out to visit friends.

Not all even then knew the whole truth, which was disguised simply as a "marathon walk through the Highlands and Islands". It says something for the dream that quite a few people at once suggested the truth. I even had two telephone calls from people thinking about such a project and wanting advice. As they hoped it would take two or three weeks of a summer holiday, a few statistics ended their hopes.

Many food parcels were going to be required along the way. I had worked out three motor itineraries to lay these caches, entailing a thousand miles of motoring. The physical work of parcelling was immense. Cards were prepared for each parcel, for no two were the same, and these were scattered throughout the house. A sample card might look like this:

The translation: "Loch Duich cache site, food for four days plus reserves to see me to Affric Lodge. Map 18 to go into this parcel and it was to go to Mike Keates who would deliver it." There were 42 of these labels. Each type of food, plus things like candles, matches, toilet paper, film, books had to be taken round, in turn, from label to label and the right estimate left. This game was played by mother and I; you can imagine what the house looked like at the end of it.

The worst job of all came next—doing it all up. Again, no standardisation was possible, some were going to be actually buried in the hills, others would be safe indoors, most were going to destinations as yet unknown. We used 2,000 polybags from tiny to sack-size. Friends had been hoarding cartons and string for a year. A parcel took a good half-hour usually; each was double-checked against a "standard" list, and only a packet of Vitawheat was missed, all through. I reckon there are few mothers (never mind being an O.A.P. grannie too) who would take to grovelling on the floor for days playing this mad Father Christmas game.

The three car trips were made. It shows the highlander at his normal best that only once did the first person asked refuse to take in a parcel, and their jobs varied from forester to doctor to railway linesman to hotelier, roadman to policeman.

Caches contained a mixture of tinned food, for immediate use, and dehydrated for carrying on the way. As a supplement I would eat in hotels, buy fresh stuff, and at weekends various friends came up via Dollar, where Marina produced weekly treats of fresh meat, fruit, home baking and so on.

My Dormobile was finally packed as a mobile base store with reserves of all kinds and delivered to Dollar.

It was time for a holiday—the Tatras.

I

MULL, ETIVE AND GLENCOE

"I lived for the day when I could get out with my ship, and stay away."

ALAN VILLIERS

Wednesday 3 April THE ROAD TO MOOLA

We left Dollar in fog—which began to thin only near Lix Toll—steaming off the fields and holding to the line of the river. The whooper swans were dabbling at their reflections in Loch Dochart. Ben More thrust through like Fuji Yama: a snowy cone reaching up from bountiful spring. The gift of such anticyclonic conditions was a blessing indeed for the start of the venture.

Oban was urbane and peaceful in pre-season quietude. We drove on to the ferry *Columba*. Every craft in the harbour had its inverted twin until our wake washed them all away as we steamed off for Mull. The bar had only one customer; everyone else sprawled on deck in the sun. Duart Castle welcomed to the island; lying dark in the eye of the sun it translated itself for us, the *black height*. It is the clan Maclean seat and goes back to the thirteenth century, now the home of Sir Charles Maclean, 27th chief, and also recently Chief Scout.

We stopped to change nephew Kenneth's nappies by Lochdonhead, then ran up the slicing Glen More. The hills were hazy with the sweet reek of burning and when we passed the source of the scent, by Loch Scridain, it was replaced by the tang of the sea. There had been curlews and wheatears in the glen, here oystercatchers and redshank added their calls. It was full spring. The rushed days in Kinghorn and Dollar had only been stations on the way back from Poland; suddenly this felt home—where sun and sea and mountains meet, westwards where all dreams lie.

I should have been "psyched-up" no doubt but found myself calm. There was nothing to do—except savour the scene. Just the walking to do now, and that was not in my control. I had planned and prepared.

B

I could do no more. So Mull was consciously savoured, its perfection an intoxicating joy.

Kenneth spent hours throwing stones, and himself, into the water. A gentlemanly heron watched from a boulder beyond, a perch he maintained while the tide turned and flowed and the sun dipped to halo his shape in gold. Sheep came and "scarted" themselves on the Dormobile and their lambs tripped over the guy lines of my tent. It was a bare feet and bare torsos day, doing nothing and then resting afterwards. I lay reading *Travels with a Donkey*—which might have been significant.

I had, actually, been re-reading much of Stevenson, a sadly-neglected author. Few have captured our landscape so well. In *Kidnapped* for instance, the shipwreck on Mull, the crossing of Rannoch Moor, the Ben Alder days at Cluny's Cage—these are gems of description. Every word of Stevenson is precise and right, truly a man who knew how to live.

We had established ourselves a diplomatic Kenneth-distance away from the tents of our B.F.M.C. friends, Lorna and Carol, Bob and Ian, who rolled in later, brosy with sun and good doings.

I was banned from cooking even, so sat by the shore, after removing a dead polecat. Kenneth was sent, protesting, to his Dormobile bed. The smoke of burning still veiled the hills at the head of the loch. The waters were purply bright. The ponderous heron and two struggling cormorants flew across, the eiders dodged among the weeds, commenting "Oh! Oh!" Curlews called on the hill, a pheasant honked in the wood, a buzzard mewed overhead. Lambs bleated. Two miles across the loch came children's laughter. These are the magic sounds of silence, the magic colours of content.

After supper we piled wreaths of seaweed on the bonfire so it belched out a great column of smoke and rattled away like musketry. A seal edged in to eavesdrop on our talk. Some deer crossed the road, white caudal patches showing in the moonlight. A big moon seemed to swell gradually, and spent its hours blowing stars across the chill sky. The dew fell. The burn talked in its sleep. . . .

And on the morrow the Long Walk would begin.

It might have been otherwise if David had not seen us gaily distributing "Napisan" instead of milk powder for the fireside brew.

Thursday 4 April THE BEN MORE GATHERING
Mull is one of the two islands which have Munros, but whereas Skye
has a whole extravagant ridge of them, Ben More in Mull is the only
other. The whole of Mull is worth exploring, the longer you spend on
it after all, the less sore you will feel at the penal ferry cost of reaching it.
It has a fascinating coast and the attached islands are all interesting:
Iona, Ulva, Gometra, the Treshnish, Staffa of Fingal's Cave fame. . . .
Not far from the camp, round the Gribun, the sea cliffs tower over the
road, and the houses fit tight in between road and sea, spaced regularly
along, except, in one place there is no house but a big boulder. There
was a cottage originally but the boulder crashed on to it, killing a
newly wed couple within. The wedding guests were dancing in the
barn and did not even know.

Along the Gribun is MacKinnon's Cave, one of the biggest in the
country, over two hundred yards long; along again lie the miles of the
Wilderness, a devastated area of boulders and 1,000-foot basalt cliffs.
There is a 40-foot fossil tree.

Ben More queens it over all as the *big hill* should: a grey, saddle-
backed peak, which can be seen from all directions on land or at sea. It
radiates ridges in several directions from the summit which can cause
confusion in the mist for the top is highly magnetic and the compass
can be 180° out—which is always off-putting to those who have been
taught always to trust the compass.

The finest approaches all converge on A'Choich first. This 2,730-foot
top then allows a fine connecting ridge to the Munro. The best route is
the most direct. We reached it up the Allt a' Ghlinne Dhuibhe—
hugging shade and needing little excuse to stop. White hares and deer
were more easily watched from a sitting position—and we could always
take another picture of the girls in their bikinis. Bob gave us a cheerful
dissertation on sheep's liver flukes.

In turn I told of Alex, an ex-pupil of mine who was reprimanded in
the Cairngorms, on a course, for drinking the water straight. Did he
not know of this hazard? "It is what all the old shepherds die of,"
came the dire warning. "You must boil it for twenty minutes." Alex
took the line that as long as it was *old* shepherds dying of it, he was
prepared to take the risk!

Romping back down to camp Bob managed to set some boulders
bouncing down on top of me. I was a hundred yards ahead. I stopped

one on my rucksack and another took the legs from under me. This was the most serious "accident" of the trip. Had I been facing uphill and got it on the front instead of the back of the knee there would have been a different tale. As it was I had grand itchy scabs to crinkle at every step for the next week.

The family were off to Iona in the Dormobile so I joined Lorna and Carol for tea. They were very touchy. Lay a finger on them and they leapt. Bikinis were a mistake. They were now in the pink—literally. Even a swim in the sea did not help. I wore my pyjamas (last time for three months) as protection against the sun. It was a long day of ease really. The traces had been freed.

Friday 5 April   BY THE SWEAT OF YOUR BROW

"Only 357,000 feet to go," I had joked on top of Ben More, little knowing this was 90,000 feet short of the reality, but such figures are meaningless anyway; in fifteen Everests, what's a Munro here and there? I underestimated the mileage too—but it had only been guessed at (1,200 miles) by using a piece of string on a small scale map. The detail that did matter was the daily "staging" which had been carefully worked out. The original 112-day estimate came out at 112 days. The strategy, if you like, was clear, the tactics were often decided on the spot.

Previous, extensive knowledge of the ground made this much easier. I could envisage the ground, a great asset, though not fully realised till looking back. John Hinde and his R.A.F. gangs, Sandy Cousins, all owed a lot to this too; in contrast, many of the failures on such efforts were younger, inexperienced lads. (The Ripley brothers were an exception. I did not consider myself in their class, so their failure was both a warning and a spur to which I paid great heed.)

The sheer scale and loneliness of the Scottish hills can prove a mental as well as a physical barrier. At Aultguish Inn I was told of one "Walk" which ended simply from the demoralising effect of rain. Flooded rivers had not been expected and the route and meeting points all went haywire. It became a nightmare of impracticability—and all the time the rain and wind pummelled and battered till the world became one great wetness and despair. It took only a few days to break the spirit.

Experience would have dealt with that, but experience takes time I suppose. Sandy and John had had years of soaking—maturing—and so, I suppose, had I. It all relates not only to a scheme like this, but also on the prickly topic of "Leadership". I find it horrifying for instance that people are leaving school intending to become mountain instructors. What can they know about it at that age? Experience is a key factor for success, though failure can be rewarding, giving as it does the most emphatic of all experience. So long as mistakes are not fatal, they are useful! "We are all, in a sense, survivors" as I once heard; but again, listening to a radio panel discussing climbing, the chairman drew it all together with the profound remark that "climbing is not for the beginner".

Today's circuitous route gave not even one Munro though I sweated as I have seldom done in Scotland—or elsewhere. It began gently.

I was off at 6.30 on a dewy morning when the only stir was the wild-life. I left the Broons sleeping, and Lorna and Carol breakfasting, for we were all catching the early ferry. I was using a Raleigh "Stowaway" cycle, as I would for several longer reaches of unavoidable tarred road. Walking hard roads is not my idea of fun. Legally, a bike is "an aid to pedestrianism" and not a vehicle or machine, and it kept my basic rule of self-propulsion. If you object, the solution is obvious! (But then you would have to swim to and from the islands, or go barefoot, or without food. You can soon reduce it to absurdity. The prime aim was enjoyment, after all.)

Six sorry sheep had marooned themselves on an islet at the head of the loch and a lamb in the black burnt area was bleating its woe at being born in such surroundings. Push bike was an apt description for the haul up Glen More. The girls bombed past on the pass. A redwing flew along with me for a while. At Ishriff I raced through a party of red deer (frightening) and at Loch Don a roe buck watched me pass. I suddenly realised it was still some way to Craignure and the boat left in thirteen minutes: intriguing possibilities, as the car had my rucksack with everything, including money, in it.

You cannot hurry cows, or heavy bikes. When I clattered on to the *Columba* with three minutes to spare I was quivering with the effort. Half an hour later she sailed.

We had a second breakfast while my clammy shirt dried, then prowled the deck, too aware of action ahead to play the placid tourist. Lorna and Carol were off for Glendessary which I would only reach in June.

Oban again, the bay full of eiders and reflections, the pier all bustle and calling voices. I made an inauspicious start by going over the handlebars. The pier planks are carefully laid with cycle-wheel-size gaps between!

There was a long brae out of town but I had stocked up, and on top of the hills found a nook among the primroses and celandine and consumed milk and hot-cross-buns. This was about the richest landscape I would ever see—which is why it is so full of the earliest marks of Scottish history.

I have never trained, as such; life is too hectic otherwise, even if the physical laziness could be overcome. Since much of my time is spent on the hill, I suppose some fitness carries over. The climbing and long ski trip in Poland had removed any surplus weight. I did not lose any more on the Walk.

Glen Lonan was pleasant going but lacked water, so at Taynuilt, on the main road again, I bought ice cream and peaches. Wayside indulgence became a principle in the months ahead. It was interesting to see what was chosen when faced with all the wealth of a grocery shop. I did not develop a chocolate craving as others seemed to have done but sweet, juicy things were top desires.

Taynuilt has a monument to Lord Nelson erected in 1805 by the Lorn furnacemen—thirty-seven years before the one in Trafalgar Square. The main road through the jaws of the Pass of Brander was quiet. Road, rail and river squeeze through here in promiscuous ribbons. The small dam on the river has an electric lift instead of a fish ladder. Brander is famed for fights by both Wallace and Bruce, the latter here clashing with the MacDougalls in 1308, a fray from which the Campbells gained. The main Campbell castle was on Innis Chonnail, down Loch Awe. Kilchurn was also theirs and inspired Wordsworth and others to versify. The clan only moved south to Inveraray in the late fifteenth century. Their motto is still "Cruachan" and the phrase, "It's a far cry to Lochow" (Loch Awe) has much of history in it beyond the pages of Neil Munro.

Neil Munro is another of the superb painters of the highland scene. His book, *The New Road*, is one of the best. He is probably better known as the creator of *Para Handy*, which he wrote under the name of Hugh Foulis.

For years Hydro and road works had been active along Loch Awe but now one can speed by—at twice the speed of seeing anything. A new tourist attraction is to take a minibus tour into the heart of the mountain to see the power station which is part of the second-largest pumped storage scheme in the world. The reservoir is 1,200 feet above the turbines, held in a corrie of Cruachan, whence I was bound after leaving the bike and collecting a parcel from Mrs Moyes at one of the Hydro houses. I also had a look at St Conan's.

This church is an odd hotch-pot architecturally but its setting by the loch makes it worth seeing. Plain glass windows sweep round the front of the church—nature giving a view no stained glass could match. A rib of Robert the Bruce is preserved here, the rest of him being home in Fife at Dunfermline Abbey.

Cruachan is really an array of summits, eight in all. Sir Hugh gave it two Munros and one of the anomalies of his Tables is that the Taynuilt Peak, 3,611 feet, a subsidiary summit of the Main Munro, 3,689 feet, is higher than the other Munro, Stob Diamh, 3,272 feet.

The toil up on to Cruachan was memorable for the intolerable heat. Every trickle of water was pounced on. Collapsing on the second day with heatstroke would be an odd ending to the Walk! There was a view down Loch Awe as far as New York. It is the longest loch in Scotland, though Loch Ness and Loch Lomond are bigger.

I passed the shapely dam and contoured round into the burn behind Beinn a' Bhuiridh. Glorious shade! I splashed in a pool with the gusto of a dipper, then followed beside or in the burn to pitch the tent near the col above—at about 2,300 feet. After a brew I went up Beinn a' Bhuiridh, 2,941 feet, a summit which was all lumps and bumps and pools of melt-water. This is a "Corbett", a mountain of over 2,500 feet, having a drop all round of 500 feet. A list made by their eponymous creator is now printed in with Munro's Tables. People often think the 500-foot clearance also applies to Munros, but this is not so. Corbetts are much better disciplined, and often much more satisfying besides being better viewpoints. Quinag, Beinn Dearg Mhor, Allival and Askival, The Cobbler—these are all Corbetts. Stac Polly or Suilven do not even reach that height; all of which shows what a daft game this is.

Sunset seemed quick: the burnished loch went out leaving a dull, raw world. A lone bird cried. It was gloriously lonely.

Saturday 6 April SMITTEN BY THE SUN AND ADDICTED

Beira, Queen of Winter in Scottish mythology, who built the hills with her magic hammer, once forgot to cover a well on Cruachan, and overnight it flowed down to fill the valley below—hence Loch Awe. Now her well's overflow has a dam, and other powerful hammers have hollowed out her mountain. The reservoir for the power station has done little damage to the surroundings; so often in the months ahead I was to see others with disfiguring shorelines—like dirty bath rims.

As the weather still looked good I set off early to make use of the cool hours. Having the whole day and no base to return to gave a great freedom. I could hurry or dawdle as I saw fit. I averaged about a mile an hour this first hard day of carrying a pack; but the real enemy was the sun which gave a physical battering. At the end of the day it was interesting to see how the pace shot up—uphill—simply because there was shade again. I was quite sorry to leave my "nest among the stars" (Obadiah), and one outcome of the Walk has been a taste for high camping, even at weekends. The rewards make the effort worth while. You cannot know a mountain till you have slept on it.

A long ridge, snow edged, led to Stob Diamh (Stob Daff) from which I made the longer traverse to the Main Summit and back. Drochaid Glas had crags which looked like the Inca altar at Ollantaytambo. Litter today included such diverse objects as an egg-cosy, a U.S. coin, a watch glass and a usable biro. Good winter climbing is to be had in the northern corries but the only account I have read is in J. H. B. Bell's *A Progress in Mountaineering*. There was a lot of snow still. Stob Dearg is better known as the "Taynuilt Peak", and it was the poet W. P. Ker who whimsically, aptly, referred to the Nordend of Monte Rosa as its Taynuilt Peak.

I did not linger on Cruachan Beann, the *mountain of peaks*, but retraced with hopeful, but fruitless, diversions in search of water. I had to go past the last horn of Sron an Isean, the *nose of the imps*, before it was safe to drop down. With an ice axe there could have been a good glissade. The Lairig Noe was a lonely col but by traversing up and across I reached a good burn. The bliss of a hill brew! The purple saxifrages were wilting in the heat and deer let you pass twenty yards off as they were too done to move.

I followed up the burn which gave a noisy rush of coolness. The summit of Beinn a' Chochuill was pleasantly draughty. I left a question-naire on the cairn—which was found the following weekend. This was a brief series of questions, which could give some idea of the usage Munros received, and I left them only on what were relatively remote summits. The results are given in an appendix. An Oban couple were on top and we met several times on the dip and rise to Beinn Eunaich.

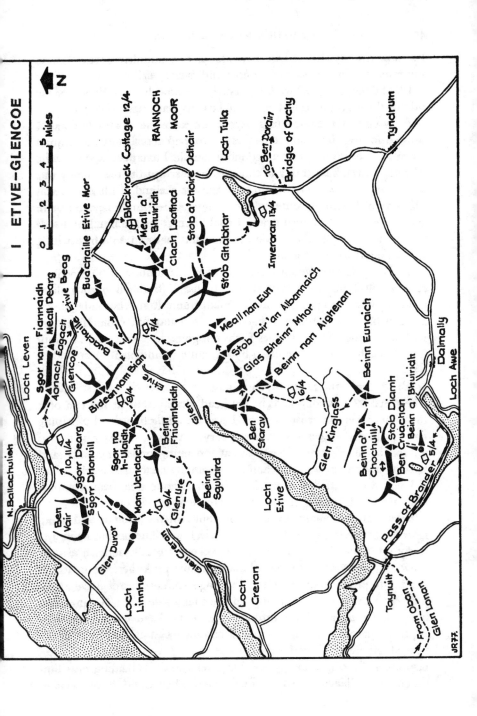

1 ETIVE-GLENCOE

N

0 1 2 3 4 5 Miles

N. Ballachulish

Loch Leven

Sgor nam Fiannaidh
Meall Dearg
Aonach Eagach
Glencoe
Buachaill
Etive Beag

Buachaille Etive Mor

Blackrock Cottage 12/4

Meall a' Bhuiridh

RANNOCH
MOOR

Clach Leathad

Stob a' Choire Odhair

Loch Tulla

Stob Ghabhar

To Ben Dorain

Inveroran 13/4

Bridge of Orchy

Tyndrum

Ben Vair

Sgorr Dhearg
Sgorr Dhonuill

10, 11/4

Sgor na h-Ulaidh

Bidean nam Bian 8/4

Beinn Fhionnlaidh

Meall nan Eun

Stob coir'an Albannaich

Glas Bheinn Mhor

Beinn nan Aighenan

Beinn Eunaich

Mam Uchdach

Glen Ure 9/4

Beinn Sgulaird

Glen Duror

Loch Linnhe

Ben Starav

Glen Etive

7/4

6/4

Glen Kinglass

Beinn a' Chochuill

Stob Diamh
Ben Cruachan
Beinn a' Bhuiridh 5/4

Dalmally

Loch Awe

Pass of Brander

Loch Creran

Glen Creran

Loch Etive

Taynuilt

From Oban

Glen Lonan

JR 77.

Its snow rim was littered with thousands of small olive beetles. These summits translate as *peak of the hood* and *fowling hill.*

I had done two days' walking in one, and now dropped down the far side of these groups into Glen Kinglass, a glen many look down on, but few visit. The Starav hills beyond were the morrow's effort and I wanted to sleep high on them. First I dropped down to 200 feet, quite a brutal descent with the ground more complex than the map indicates. The glen was a heat-trap and though I had stripped to just underpants and boots, the sweat poured down. The potentially difficult river was a highway of blazing granite cobbles. I lay under the alders, actually in the water, while I brewed again. I could almost see the bracken fronds unrolling. An eagle spiralled in the sun till it mewed into a buzzard. It was an effort to go on again.

The Allt Hallater was a succession of granite slabs and blue pools—resisted till I pitched camp after a thousand feet had been gained, suddenly easy going as the sun was sinking and there was shade. It was another fine site with a view back to the Kinglass Rubicon. If the day had been almost grim at times I was not going to complain and tempt fate. I was happy to be smitten by the sun and addicted.

Sunday 7 April HALLELUJAH, I'M A BUM
The words of this song kept in my head all day; but at the end of it there was a certain twist to them. I was waddling like a jockey, trying not to rub my cheeks—Marina's cheery, "Ah, yes, nappy rash!" was all too accurate. Days of salt sweat streaming down my back and soaking my pants were the cause, an unusual one for Scotland.

I was a bit stiff and slow off the mark. Eating rice crispies with a knife was a frustrating game. Memo: remember a spoon next time!

Beinn nan Aighenan was just above but I went up to the col linking it to the Starav range so I could dump the sack a while and enjoy the rocky scramble. If you play it right you need hardly touch grass, or snow as it was today. It is one of many granite peaks hereabouts which just fail to produce anything for climbing. No more secret Etive Slabs. I reached the summit climbing up the shady side of everything. The fangs of Cruachan rising through the gentle haze tones were very Alpine. There was no sign of man's handiwork at all and hills simply ranged off in all directions. In some ways I was taking a chance, beginning the trip among these fairly hefty and demanding hills that range from Glencoe down to Loch Awe. They could have been in winter condition, instead of sun-beaten. Aighenan is *peak of the hinds* but I saw none. Starav is unhappily the *stout* (or *strong*) *hill* and Glas Bheinn Mhor just the *big grey lump.*

Back on the col I found the area teeming with frogs, something I had seen before. There were scores of them; a great moving and croaking. My steps set them leaping for the pools but as these had skimmed over with the night's frost the result was quite a pantomime as they skidded across the ice or went splintering through it.

Starav is king of the Etive hills, a bold shape with a tent-shaped summit. It rises straight from sea-level and makes you feel its 3,541 feet. It is a good winter peak with narrow ridges and deep corries. My east ridge of today is knife-edged in places and leads to a top which is often taken for the summit if it is cloudy. The highest point is round the rim to the north. It has a summit to linger on. I wandered about looking down the various sides. It has a commanding view down Loch Etive, a real fiord of a Loch. I thought of the words of Deirdre's "Farewell to Alban":

> "O Loch Etive, where the brothers
> Built our Doune for me, a bride;
> Joy to rise and there behold
> My fold of sunbeams—Etiveside."

Deirdre of the Sorrows was a first century Pictish princess who was married to a King of Ulster; there are several legends about her connected with Etive.

Glas Bheinn Mhor was a bit of a plod after Starav. Stob Coir' an Albanaich, the *peak of the Scotsman's corrie,* has a big cairn on top of which a smaller one had sprouted. The Ceitlein Glen is the best of those up Etive. One branch leads to a considerable gorge and there are areas of granite which will give some climbing. One pinnacle has the following guide-book description:

Patey's Old Man. 70ft. Unclassifiable. I.Rowe, W.Sproul May 1967. Protrudes from left wall of gorge. Lasso the top and climb the rope. Treat gently.

I had pulled on waterproof trousers to enjoy a good bum-slide from Albanaich, when its north-east corrie rumbled down an avalanche of rock and snow. Meall Tarsuinn beyond, was an annoying whaleback, which, like many Tarsuinns (the name means *transverse* or *cross peak*), lies between desired Munros. Almost always they should be traversed, not flanked. The col before the wet, grassy dome of Meall nan Eun, *hill of the birds,* is an unusual slot. The Ceitlein approach can be made up granite slabs unless the burn is in spate. This fifth Munro for the day was saturated with melting snow. It is a contender for the prize for the dullest Munro, so I left a questionnaire in the cairn. An Edinburgh lad found it next day.

Instead of going down the Ceitlein to Glen Etive and then up the Glen, I kept to the hill, cutting through behind Stob Dubh, 2,897 feet, to descend direct to camp. This summit dominates the Glen and is as fine as anything which happens just to be 103 feet higher. Very red deer were milling about in the pass, a mile of level-going. I took off my pants (all I'd had on all day again) in the hope that the rubbing would ease. I hoped the deer would not mind. There were a surprising number of dead ones, some recent and some just smell and bones. Scots pine, holly and so on grew in the gorge where grazing was not possible by the deer. It is sad to reflect that trees once covered the land from here to Deeside and north to Loch Maree. Man has made a right mess of his earth.

Stob Dubh's shadow was reaching out across my bows but I beat it to the first of the big pools in the river and, having only boots to remove, was soon splashing in the gasping cold of its melted snow water. My rolled-up shirt which had been stuffed up my back to let air in under the rucksack was as wet as if I'd thrown it in the pool, yet during the time taken by a few dives and lengths, it dried completely. I hung myself up, like a cormorant, to drip dry too.

The path led into shade—and there, ahead, was the Broon establishment: Dormobile and tents. I paddled straight over and joined Kenneth for Ribena. They were very pink Browns by now. Marina produced a tin of pears—and a spoon.

Monday 8 April B. AND B. AND B.
Which stands for Buachaille, Buachaille and Bidean: a day of nearly 8,000 feet. Marina had slipped the late night forecast into the tent after I was asleep. It said "dry, but cooler"—so we had an even hotter day. I did not see them in the morning as their holiday hours and my early rising times were very different.

I went down to Dalness and up to the top of the Lairig Gartain, which is a text book example of a U-shaped glaciated pass. Its flanks were smooth grass, and twice sheep above sent stones bouncing past. The col was 1,600 feet, and rather than lose height I fought along a poor traverse on the Buachaille Etive Mor. This was not a good line and in the end I only climbed on to the crest after cutting steps up a snow slope—using an improvised porphyritic ice-axe. I discarded most of my clothes again to walk along to the Munro, Stob Dearg, the *red top*, at the far end. Not a soul was in sight on this most popular of hills. Rannoch Moor lay spread like a map over the notch of the Crowberry Tower, vanishing into haze, out of which Schiehallion rose in familiar conical shape.

I can still remember clearly the thrill of seeing the Buachaille with climber's eyes for the first time as we came over the Moor. I had walked and cycled in view of it often enough but I was out of my teens before really taking up rock climbing "properly"—with ropes and all the junk.

I was a missionary assistant in a Paisley parish (Martyrs' Memorial) at the time. It took the Asian 'flu epidemic to procure a rope. That virus was particularly lethal to old people; and when many of the ministers went down with it, I found myself having to conduct a number of funerals at the crematorium. You actually received a fee for that, so after a couple of weeks I was able to cycle off to Glasgow and purchase one of the new-fangled nylon, hawser-laid ropes. A hundred feet of it cost under £5. The next weekend it was used on the Buachaille, climbing Agag's Groove, the Rannoch Wall test-piece, before going on over the Tower to the top. It was a day just like today.

Often, though, you may have to queue for Agag's. Last time on it we found a notice affixed, which read: "Road narrows, no overtaking"! We have come a long way from the outlook of an English traveller in 1792 who called the Buachaille "the carcass of a mountain, peeled, sore and hideously disgustful".

I retreated back along the long crest and down to the glare and heat of the pass. The Buachaille Etive Beag's *black top*, Stob Dubh, is happily immediately above the col. It was still a sweaty pull up. The deer were much too weary to move; heads simply swivelled to watch and I half wondered what the result would be if I walked right round them a few times. . . .

The wee Buachaille once gave us the coldest cold I have ever met on the hills. We were traversing the crest in a spell of clear, winter weather which was most enjoyable. Suddenly, with nothing visibly different, we walked into a block of air that was super-cooled. It left us gasping. It was as easily left, and we went back and forth several times into it from sheer fascination before going on. One of the party had wet boots which froze at once, and he ended with frostbite.

Back down at the rucksack I was hot, tired and dusty. I took all the sweaty clothes, and boots, off to let them dry out. The Meta stove managed to set the grass alight and in seconds flames were darting among my scattered gear. By the time I had dealt with that I was even hotter and dirtier. I went across to the next pass to where there were pools and plunged into the freezing water. Bliss! The Lairig Eilde is also about 1,600 feet and cuts off the Bidean massif from the Buachailles. A creeping line of shadow drove me on upwards eventually. The broken crags above were covered in hard snow and no outflanking was possible, so a pole section from the tent this time had to do the work of an ice-axe.

I was soon up into the golden glow again and thankfully the slopes along and up to Stob Coire Sgreamhach were mossy and full of melt-runnels. There was a great temptation to camp. I drank again and again and went on for Bidean, outflanking a bit on a line I had picked out yesterday. Bidean was quite a thank-God summit, at 3,766 feet it is the highest in Argyll, and the highest of the trip to date.

The only other time I had done the combination of these three Munros was with the unlikely mixture of Marlborough, Eton, and Braehead schoolboys. It was unintentional, as we had only gone up to see Ossian's Cave, but one thing led to another. We were not provisioned for a long day, though, and were a bit weary by the Lairig Gartain. I discovered a mush of old raisins in a pocket and just a few of these each soon produced the zoom needed to do the last slope.

Bidean nam Bian's summit is hidden away behind an array of satellite peaks and corries and ridges. The Three Sisters which dominate Glencoe are merely the ends of spoke-like ridges which eventually lead to the top. The name means the *spiky summits of the skins or hides*; an old S.M.C. Journal suggests this is because of the quantity of epidermis lost on the rocks by generations of climbers.

I set off west over a subsidiary top we have always known as Ossian's Seat, then turned to drop down to one of the "Windows of Etive", a col separating Gleann Fhaolain leading to Etive, and the Fionn Ghleann leading to the Coe. The slope seemed to be made of loose boulders set on the vertical. They had a nasty feeling of impermanence.

The sun was dipping again, and I hurried to find a good site before it became too dark for a photograph. The procedure was becoming established: stove on while tent up, then while tea "mashed", a quick photo, then fill the gallon container and crawl in if need be till the next day. I could seal myself in, safe from rain or midges. These days it was the cold that drove indoors. I would linger outside till the sun went, then would escape the freezing shadows into the warm sleeping bag, the joy of simple, good food—and endless brews.

Tuesday 9 April NAKED BEFORE THE MOUNTAIN

Yesterday the actual glen of the Coe had hardly been noticed. All the days so far had been dominated by the glen and loch of Etive, which is how it was in the past when the sea approaches were the vital ones. South of a line from Etive to Iona the influence of Ireland long remained, while north and west of that the Norse influence was the main one.

I rose at five simply to relish the breathless cool and quiet. I have had several spells like this, even in Glencoe, which has the reputation of first filtering Scotland's weather before distributing it elsewhere. It can be worse on Rhum or in the Skye Cuillin, where the rocky landscape can make a shimmering oven which is overbearing. Not that you risk complaining about heat in Scotland. That would be tempting fate. Wordsworth wrote some lines about Glen Etive and its "playful waterfalls". He must have had it in its normal state.

I began the day with a descent, flanking under cliffs to reach the Bealach Fhionnghaill. Red rock changed to schisty grey and later in the day was to change again to golden granite. This bealach (*pass*) must have seen the flight of fugitives from the 1692 Massacre—of which more later. We once fled over it to avoid being devoured by the Etive midges, packing up a camp at dawn and heading for the safety and sanity of Ingrid's hostel. In the dark we had rubbed on stinking repellant and only daylight revealed the jaundiced result. We had used the wrong stuff—iodine. We had also fled this glen when a lad in our party complained of pains in his side. Appendicitis was our suspicion and was verified at the hospital, but he had had it out only about ten days before. The culprit was most indignant when he discovered we had hustled him to the local maternity hospital.

I did not recognise the col.

The *Peak of the Treasure*, Sgòr na h-Ulaidh, lay a couple of miles on along a ridge past it and gave some scrambling up "wee wa's" and lots of deer stumbling through the snow patches. The pools were full of frogs again. From the notched summit the Ben stood out in clear morning light.

I slid off down on the rims of snow.

Gaelic names are often far from straightforward. Cairnwell for instance should be An Carn Bhlag, the *hill of blisters*, A'Chralaig is Garbh-leac, Lawers is from labhar (the sound of rushing waters). Beinn Achaladair is corrupted from Beinn Achadh-Fhaladair—the aspirants simply dropped. Ben Vorlich is Ard Mhur'laig, *height of the sea bag*. An appendix is given at the end of this book to try to help a little.

Ulaidh is not often visited, being four miles from any road; but it has good ridge walking, good winter climbing and a commanding view. The glaciated pass between it and Beinn Fhionnlaidh (pronounced "Ula") has a strangely lost-world feeling. Plantings on both sides make it difficult to reach with its moraine humps and bumps. The north-east end of Fhionnlaidh has some intimidating, virgin, cliffs.

I took a slow-rising traverse line across its north flank, hugging the shade. The trig point lies a bit to the west on the flattish top. I baled off the quartz crest on the south side already knowing I had lost the race against the heat. *Finlay's mountain* was not mine.

The grilling below was the worst of the whole trip—and it was an odd repetition. Tom Izatt, my dog Kitchy, and I had done Sgulaird (where I was heading now) and Fhionnlaidh from Etiveside—an approach I would recommend only to my enemies. "The appearance is that of matter, incapable of form or usefulness, dismissed by Nature from her care, disinherited of her favours, left in its original elemental state, or quickened only with one sullen power of useless vegetation" (Dr Johnson). It was a close, hot, midgy day and the vegetatious descent to Etive almost reduced us to tears of vexation. Memorable of course.

Today it was simply sizzling hot. To prevent another dose of nappy rash I stripped off completely and wedged a sponge in the small of my back. Every ten minutes I had to wring it out. My rucksack soaked right through.

Pathetic dollops of dry spawn lay on the cracked, dried peatholes. A deer skull protruded from the dusty heather. The air smelt stale. In contrast, the lochans felt icy cold and I just could not bear to swim, I was too weary with the heat. At the lochan at the head of Glen Ure it was tempting just to camp. There was a delectable site. Tomorrow I could go on. However a drum-up restored initiative enough and on I went for the ridge of Beinn Sgulaird, the *mountain of yelping*. By the time I flopped on the summit I thought it well named. The Ripley brothers had commented too on the seeming length of this approach.

This is subjective of course: Sgulaird is a fine double-humped camel of a hill, looking over Appin and the West, built of sturdy granite with some slabs on the north flank. The east ridge is an endless succession of bumps which nearly drove me to distraction this day, adding to the toil and time. It was a dour ascent. I traversed into the east corrie and found it perversely wet. The summit proved not to be the summit—there was another beyond. It was one of those days. I descended gingerly to the rucksack and had yet another brew. The descent to sea-level down Glen Ure looked tough but a stalker's path simply led down into its sweltering depths. Buzzards were swooping and calling along the crags—far too like bloody vultures for comfort, I thought.

Glenure House at the foot was white and tidy looking but there was no sign of life. At Elleric across the valley I received a cheery wave from the occupants of deck chairs who sprawled with iced drinks in their hands. It was tempting to wave back, differently.

I turned up the glen, instead of down to Loch Creran, and a couple of miles of forestry track was enough. I was blown. A burn, and a litter of dry oak leaves to bed on, gave a fine site for the night. The Meta stove, which I used at some parts of the trip instead of Gaz, had to be perched on a stone for safety. Seldom can fire risk have been greater than during these few days past.

The site was noisy with wrens, tits and chaffinches. Long-tailed tits passed through. The blackthorn was out. It was good after all. I drank and drank and ate and drank and drank again. "Fresh food tomorrow" my log noted in expectation.

I quote it direct: "Survival today, not fun. A bit stiff, all over. Tendons tender; lighter boots take less effort but the feet have a harder hammering if there is a pack carried—bruising, not blisters. Both these days a bit too much, but able to force the body on. Still enjoyed. Nice to stop! Bare feet bliss. Primroses out. Sgulaird through a frieze of branches. About 6,000 feet today. 13 hours. Who wrote of the sun their undoing? Or being naked before the mountain?"

Wednesday 10 April THE VAIR PAIR

Today, I reckon, ended the breaking-in period and, out of the heat and effort of the days so far, a fit body now crawled forth—rather like a dragonfly from its old shell. We pay for civilisation so called, with body as much as with soul. I am a bit scornful about the hardship aspect. Who is facing it in fact? Experiments with rats showed you could overwork them, starve them, freeze them, in general make life hell for them—and they thrived; but give them endless food and luxury, crowd them together in urban opulence—and they went mad.

The birds were still in full song when I woke. A yaffle was loudly calling nearby. Just a touch of rain was needed to set full spring racing through the lacework of branches. The oak wood ran out soon after I set off, and the miles of path above Salachail rose through dull plantations of fir, though still young enough to see over. An odd incident happened. I was deep in daydreams, thinking about youthful African days, when suddenly there was a coughing bark which made the hair on my neck stand upright. A lion! Of course it was nothing of the sort; just a wee roe deer which continued to roar away until I was out of hearing. Marvellous sound, all wild challenge.

This path is a marked forest trail over to Ballachulish village, and worth doing before the trees grow higher. The col is 1,400 ft. An old S.M.C. Journal tells of a crossing in 1913 when a party left Taynuilt for Glencoe, crossing Loch Etive, up the glen here and over direct: 22 miles, in nonstop rain. The Salachail stream nearly turned them back as the bridge had disintegrated into a length of rotting fir covered in nails "business end uppermost". The young bachelor of the party was made to straddle across first! At Glencoe they were told it had been raining for 72 hours. At the Clachaig they admitted "we did not despise a change and some warm food".

From the stile on the pass the Bheithir pair looked very dull; the circuit from the north is much better, and all of it from Beinn Bhan to Creag Ghorm should be done, the western arm is not boggy as the map might imply, the pools are due to the strata. I angled down to the forest that crept over the watershed from Glen Dura and lit the stove. A sheep made a wild dash from inside the forest and I winced as it reached the fence—but it simply broke through as though the wires did not exist. Even more amazing are stags, with full antlers, who wiggle themselves through such fences if the wires are not tight or close—or the fence simply low enough to jump over. They will clear a fence as high as a man can reach.

My earliest wanderings in hills were in South Africa, where we had landed as War refugees from Singapore. Hence my daydreams earlier. The Valley of the Thousand Hills is as beautiful as it sounds. The opening of Alan Paton's novel, *Cry the Beloved Country*, has the feel of it: "There is a lovely road that runs from Ixopo into the hills. These hills are grass-covered and rolling, and they are lovely beyond any singing of it. . . . About you there is grass and bracken and you may hear the forlorn crying of the birds of the veld. Below you is the valley of the Umzimkulu on its way from the Drakensberg to the sea; and beyond and behind the river, great hill after great hill . . ." Among those blue *kloofs* and *bergs*, in the eternal sun of youth, I had a passion for following streams, ever upwards, to the source if possible. Not having grown up, the habit persists—and was applied on Sgorr Dearg now.

The burn gave good scrambling on rock which resembled compressed raisins. Young, climbing on magical Brandon, aptly described climbing on fingers and toes what he held together with elbows and knees—it was that sort of fun. Little valour and much discretion drove me out from one pitch and I sat puffing and eating damp sandwiches for a while. A windcuffer hovered overhead. The gut ended with a tunnel under a wedge of old snow; scree led to the ridge above. East of Dearg, in winter, lies one of the most graceful arcs of snow-rim you will ever see, the perfect curve. Today it was an edge merely with a necklace of steps up it. These led to the stark, beckoning trig point.

I romped and glissaded down to the gale-battered fence on the col to Sgorr Dhonuill, the next Munro. It is a fine hill with a sweeping coastal view—and a long northern ridge with a prow pointing down to the new Ballachulish Bridge. The racket of its construction, even individual voices, came up with remarkable clarity. The cairn was stuffed with tins; full, they would have made a meal: orange juice, sardines, pork and beans, strawberries or pears, beer or coke. Wishful thinking! It is *Donald's peak* for reasons unknown.

I returned to the col, cut down steeply to the edge of the wood, picked up the sack and went singing off for civilisation accompanied by a bucking, bounding herd of cows.

I had dithered for the shops to open after lunch, but found it was half day. Ballachulish, being the ugliest village in Scotland, was soon left.

It reminds of some parts of Wales with its derelict quarries and abandoned station. Slate began to be quarried there in 1697.

On the footpath to the forest camp-site I met the Dollar Broons. Kenneth must have been puzzled by his vanishing and appearing uncle, a right peripatetic Jack-in-the-box. At the Dormobile I slowly unwound: washed clothes and self, ate and drank treats (fresh rolls and Kenneth's Ribena), did some more logistics . . . even the relaxing was quite hard work!

Thursday 11 April   GLENCOE REST DAY

I lay in bed till nine o'clock, aware that the wind had risen and the weather had turned cold and raw. It had to happen, I suppose. David, Marina and Kenneth went off to be tourists in the Dormobile. I wandered down to the Hotel at the crossroads and used it as an office. Quite a stack of mail to deal with as ever. I ordered some lightweight waterproofs from Tiso. The banter of a cheery waitress rounded off a pleasant lunch.

I had covered 112 miles and 38,000 feet, so my estimates were already out. The body was all right but needed to be treated gently a bit. The sore tendons were the only niggle, a common complaint of hard carrying. Miles and feet were obviously going to be a perpetual erratic equation.

After lunch I did a circuit of the valley which held so many happy memories. I wonder how many remember Ingrid at the Youth Hostel?

Ingrid and Jim Feeney were the wardens there for years and created a unique climbers' hostel. She was "aunty Ingrid" to all our Braehead kids, who loved her. One of them described her as "six foot—in every direction". It was marvellous to come off the hill to find tea ready and something cooking away for us in the oven, or to gather in the Clachaig, singing the evening out. They don't seem to make wardens like that any more, nor hostels. Names echo down the years: Mike McMullen, a young army officer, who was taken round the Ben Vair pair one winter by Mike Smith, one of my fourteen-year-olds. Later McMullen was to become an internationally famous yachtsman, then, tragically lost his wife—and then himself in a solo Atlantic race. Pete Thomas, now the old man of Skye, was a youngster then, foot-loose and Scotland free. Ian Clough was there often with R.A.F. gangs and Hamish MacInnes and Terry Sullivan ran their courses from Ingrid's. It was a smaller world then.

Last time I saw Ingrid was in Fort William in the height of the tourist season. From eighty yards away she spied me, and a great screech of "Hamish" had a hundred eyes turning. Faced with this, I too turned to look along the street. Heads were probably turning at Ballachulish. I was seized in a bear hug from behind. . . .

On up to the Clachaig Hotel. In the woody grounds before it, there used to be a fine little pond which acted as a reflecting pool to the walls of Bidean.

> I desire the high place,
> The place of sun-touched night,
> Of the veil of mist arising
> And eagled wings of light;
> Of red crags of Bidean,
> The blackness of the ridge,
> And a late splash in the river
> Below the bridge.

Years ago, some unimaginative person drained this pond. Today you would hardly know its site, a dream covered over with scrub and willow herb. . . .

One afternoon we were coming out of the Clachaig when Ingrid twisted her ankle on a pebble. We had been having afternoon tea. It took hours to return to the hostel, and the next day we took Ingrid to the old Belford Hospital in Fort William. Ingrid was well known there, as she often delivered injured climbers, so when we staggered in at the door together, the staff rushed up and grabbed me, leaving Ingrid perched on one leg crying, "It's me! it's me!"

By the Green a plaque commemorates the Massacre of Glencoe. In 1691 William of Orange proclaimed a pardon for all rebel clans provided they took an oath of allegiance before the year ran out. Many of the chiefs, loyal to the Stuarts, sought their exiled monarch's permission before acting. MacIan had procrastinated and obtained clearance only near the end of the year; the same day he reported to Colonel Hill, the Governor, at Fort William, to tender his submission.

As the oath had to be administered before the Sheriff of Argyll, Colonel Hill gave MacIan a covering letter and sent him south to Inveraray. Delays, unavoidable, meant the oath was not administered till January 6th. As a matter of routine, the documents were sent on to Edinburgh; but already plans were afoot to harry the clan, and doubtless to the bureaucratic bosses the letter of the law was an added convenience.

It was perhaps unfortunate that the Secretary of State, the ill-remembered Master of Stair, was in London, as were the two great Campbell earls: Argyll and Breadalbane. A month before the amnesty offer lapsed, Breadalbane and Stair were planning the massacre. (The former's lands had suffered at MacIan's hands, so there was no love lost.)

Stair wrote to Livingstone, the officer commanding the army in Scotland: "I hope the soldiers will not trouble the government with prisoners," and later, "I believe you will be satisfied it were a great advantage to the nation that thieving tribe were rooted out and cut off. It must be quietly done. . . ."

So the plans were laid. Colonel Hill was regarded as too sympathetic, and the second in command at Fort William took over.

On February 1st, 120 men were billeted on the people of the glen, a move not unusual when the garrison of Fort William was overbig. The MacDonalds were given promises of safety.

Campbell of Glenlyon was uncle to the wife of Alexander MacDonald, MacIan's second son, and blatant socialising continued even on the eve of betrayal, when they sat playing cards together.

It was a nasty business and, where officers were present, a barbarous one. MacIan was shot in the back as he rose from bed, his wife died after being stripped and mauled; babes and old men of eighty were butchered, while semi-naked wives and children fled into the howling blizzard. The soldiers obviously had no liking for their orders, and to this day the tradition is kind to them. Certainly only 40 corpses were produced from a population of 150, though the like number probably died of exposure. All the hamlets were pillaged and destroyed, the remnant left in desperate straits.

It was this aspect of "murder under trust" which horrified the highlander. This was actually a crime, in Scots law, second only to treason. In the resulting furore, a commission of enquiry was appointed—of course. In the end it did little and the instigators suffered little, or not at all. The name Campbell, however, had taken on an eternal tarnish.

The remnant resettled in the glen, coming "out" in the 1715 and 1745 Stuart risings, growing and multiplying in the years that followed, until the glen, like much of the highlands, was overpopulated. Then came the sheep and the clearances: the people were evicted, the clachans destroyed, the fields reverted to grass.

Dorothy Wordsworth noted the dereliction in her diary in 1803, and not many years later, another traveller noted: "The sheep-farming system has done the work of extirpation more effectually than the Secretary's massacre."

Various books tell the story in great detail. For those wanting to know more of highland history from the seventeenth to nineteenth centuries, John Prebble's three books—*The Massacre of Glencoe, Culloden*, and *The Clearances*—are easily found (Penguin paperbacks), and though slightly journalistic, they quote sources and give facts. "An' facts are chiels that winna ding."

Friday 12 April AONACH EAGACH
This famous tongue-twister probably gives the finest ridge to be found outwith the Cuillin of Skye. The name applies now to the three miles or so of wall enclosing Glencoe on the north. There are two Munros involved: Meall Dearg and Sgor nam Fiannaidh—the *peak of the Fianns* (Fingalians).

Running up the latter, the western end of the ridge, is the Clachaig Gully. It would have been a superb day for climbing what is reckoned as one of the really great gully routes. I have never seen it so dry, the rainfall here is, after all, ninety inches. Coming out at the top after climbing it once we heard a father check an offspring with the warning, "Ah wouldna go down there lad; looks like a dirty big 'ole."

It is a magnificent dirty big hole. On one wet ascent I remember happily sitting right in the slot at the top of a red chimney to belay; the water piled up behind me so tightly was I wedged. When my second was sufficiently gripped I stood up and let the flood go! . . . A friend once recently asked one of the first ascensionists, W. H. Murray (the story is in his *Mountaineering in Scotland*), about the gully. "Try and climb it in June," came the reply. "The flowers are really at their best then."

Too many feet have worn a groove down its banks, now, as they race for "the other Clachaig", so a rising traverse taking in many little crags gave me the ascent I wanted. The top of Sgor nam Fiannaidh (Feen) was bitter cold in a north wind and there had been an overnight sprinkling of snow. The weather kept dry still.

The first half-mile undulates, then, at a stride, you are on to inescapable, worn, crampon-scratched rock—all the rest of the merry way. The worn appearance testifies to its popularity, but it is as a winter climb that it comes into its own, an Alpine delight. There are some pinnacles (which walkers who never scramble will find daunting) where, one Hogmanay, two of us were blown off our holds again and again during a ten-hour, desperate traverse—an exhausting and frustrating way of playing yo-yo. Today the familiar details were welcomed like old friends and the fit body relished the succession of bumps, spikes, gullies, wee wa's that is the Aonach Eagach. At Meall Dearg the clouds came and went. A tin of pears just went. The gap beyond was wickedly cold, as cold as Sgulaird had been the opposite. The high-stepping scramble up Am Bodach, which finished the ridge, brought me to the first of the Good Friday pilgrims. There were scores coming up, so I blessed the early start that gave me the ridge in solitude. I reached the road in forty minutes. Twenty Munros. Twenty views. It was incredible. I sat looking at the marvellous post-card view down the glen.

It is justly famous, though as late a writer as Dickens could produce this: "Glen Coe itself is perfectly terrible . . . an awful place . . . scores of glens high up, which form such haunts as you might imagine yourself wandering in, in the very height and madness of a fever." Queen Victoria made one of her typical "excursions" to this spot in 1873, a visit notable for the cleg-like attention of a newspaper reporter—whom John Brown was rather itching to deal with.

David had dropped off the bike, and I used it to pech up to the Ladies Scottish Climbing Club hut at Blackrock. A tussle against the wind, as usual, gave ample time to study the filthy mess deposited by the lemming-like motorists. The waterfall in the gorge was just a trickle. Easter tents clustered round the cairn of the fold of Meannar-clach where in the old days the plundered cattle were gathered. Lochan na Fola, as you pull on to Rannoch Moor, is the *loch of blood*; tradition tells of a local squabble over the sharing of cheese in which the fray was so vicious that all the participants perished!

The Buachailles were set on the right and on the left the Devil's Staircase took the old road to Fort William over the hills to Loch Leven. This is a Caulfield Road (*c.* 1750) *not* a Wade Road as everyone thinks. The Kingshouse was the old changing house. The road through the glen was made only in 1786 and the present motor road, a wonder in its day, in 1932.

Blackrock is very old, its walls six-foot thick, deepset in the Moor. Past it runs the old military road, above it, the paraphernalia of ski facilities. The Dollar crew were parked outside and the Northumberland Climbing Club within. The *Light Brown* seemed to have run out, though, for they vanished off to the Kingshouse, Scotland's oldest licensed establishment.

Kenneth's nappies hanging on the line had frozen solid before we turned in.

Saturday 13 April THE END OF THE BEGINNING

"An inconceivable solitude, a dreary and joyless land of bogs, a land of desolation and grey darkness . . . a world before chaos . . . its elements only rock and bogs with a few pools of water."

So Dr John Macculloch described Rannoch Moor, but he libels it a bit. I love its wide emptiness, its wild skyscapes and crying birds, and have criss-crossed it many times: on foot, ski, canoe and skates! Much of it lies about the 1,000-foot level and in size it would take the Lake District nicely—not that any such swop would be contemplated by either side's advocates. The Moor drains partly east and partly southwest.

The peaks I would traverse today form an odd watershed, for one side of them drains to the Etive complex while a few feet away the drainage eastward takes waters through Loch Ba, Loch Laidon to Loch Rannoch and the Tay, and eventually the North Sea. Yet these hills perch above the sea waters of Loch Etive. There is quite a drop to the south where the Achallader hills form a big barrier and this trough takes waters from the east of the Moor to Loch Tulla down Glen Orchy, to Loch Awe and so to the sea on the west coast. The West Highland Railway swings up to skirt the east of the Moor by this natural line but so difficult was it in places to find a bottom for the railway that it is floated on rafts of brushwood. You may catch a glimpse of a sign saying "Soldiers' Trenches 1745", which refers to a reclamation scheme—but the soldiers suddenly found some fighting to do that year and never returned.

Loch Tulla is a beautiful loch. But enjoy your view of it from the road just now for there has been planting between road and loch, with sad lack of imagination, and all you will see ten years hence will be a barrier of trees. Old roots in the bog show that once the Moor was forest—the old Caledonian Forest which our forefathers destroyed.

Loch Ba, on the Moor, appeared in one early map as Loch Ball, which told where the cartographer came from. Coire Ba is one of the largest corries in Scotland. My cluster of Munros today rimmed it.

As you pull up on to the Moor from the south you will notice "the Rannoch Rowan"—a sturdy tree to the left of the road which grows out of a big rock like a flower pot. No doubt a bird dropped a seed in the cracked rock and ever since it has thrived, safe from deer and sheep. None of us would dream of passing without giving our friend a wave. Many old sheiling ruins still have a struggling rowan beside them, planted for luck, to keep away bad spirits. "The Rannoch Rowan" always seems to me to be the spirit not only of the Moor and Glencoe but of all hill adventures.

The old military road skirts the moor to the west and heads from Blackrock to Kingshouse. Blackrock is a "hut" of character. From its door I looked out to a moonlit, frozen dawning, loud with grouse and with the shadowy passing of deer. The custodian was Mora McCallum, a name from the Munro list—but more regarded as a hard-person equally at home on the Etive Slabs. Having watched her on Rhum I only hope she realises how bad she is for male egos. I thawed a hole in the frost of the Dormobile windows but every one was asleep so I wended off up to the ski slopes. For the only day of the trip, I had an ice axe.

Meall a' Bhuiridh gives good ski-ing (weekends and holidays) and my day's route is sometimes done on the boards by the ski-mountaineers. The *hill of the roaring* is perhaps not inappropriate for a ski mountain.

I pulled up under the lift, frozen footprints in the mud making a staircase. Coire Pollach (porridge!) was happily frozen too. I relished cutting steps straight up the snow to the summit. Eight o'clock with a silver *peso* of sun shining through the smokey-cold Moor. Another superb day, almost frightening, much too good to be true. I set the far corries ringing with a yell of glee and slid off down to the col and the hoary ridge up to Clachlet's corniced flank. Clach Leathad is a big whaleback; the new metric tables have switched the highest point to Creise, though. I chose a spot in the mile of cornice, chopped up to it and had fun beating a way through. Snow bunting seemed to be fascinated by the glittering chips, chasing them down the slope below where the lochan was frozen, and those on the Moor, hundreds of them, glittered like sequins.

I glissaded down to 2,300 feet again. Before the pull up Stob Ghabhar
I had a break and lay sunbathing. A tumbling array of icicles set off a
complaining ptarmigan who had been sunbathing in the line of fire.
Stob Ghabhar was still in winter array, very imposing today, leering
over its corrie loch which was half frozen, and cracked like glass. Four
lads from East Kilbride were on top—only the second lot of people I'd
met since Chocuill. Stob Ghabhar is the *peak of the goats*. Shepherds
encourage goats in the hope that their presence on the crags will help
keep the sheep off them. Later we would add Carn nan Gabhar by the
Tilt, Lochnagar above Deeside, Sgor Gaibhre of Loch Ossian, and two
called Carn nan Gobhar overlooking Strathfarrar—all Munros. I left
this goaty hill in a 1,000-foot bum-slide.

Stob a' Choire Odhair (Corrour) is a sort of afterthought but like
many lesser hills next to big brothers it has the finer view. From it I
could see four parties all labouring up to the summit I had just left.
The early start again. You cannot lose with it: if it is a foul day and
becomes worse at least you might gain one summit before being driven
off, if it improves you are high, ready to make a day of it. I have
never seen the sense or fun in boozing stupid at nights and missing
the best the next day. There is a certain malicious joy in being clear-
headed and happy when everyone else feels as foul as they look. It is a
good time to sing, bash about in boots, or drop the pans down the
stairs. . . .

I was torn between desires to linger or to descend quickly. No rucksack, fit at last and not overhot, it was a day all joy. I had a good look
at tomorrow's array and set off at a trot. A stalker's path (not on the
O.S. map) drops quickly to join the main path down the Allt Toaig
(not on the O.S. map either) and I was soon at Victoria Bridge where
I had seen the V.W. from a long way off. There was nobody there but
as soon as the tea was ready they rolled up. Such timing takes years of
practice, or a natural talent. Nearer Inveroran we set up camp by a
meandering stream.

I padded about in bare feet. The final hectic planning. From
tomorrow I was on my own; the back-up of Dormobile and family
ended. It had worked out very well and if the sun had been hard on me
it made life easy for Marina and David—Kenneth only needed to be
dumped in the nearest river or sea!

The statistics of Section I could finally be totted up: 142 miles,
49,050 feet, which averaged 2,050 feet per Munro per 6 miles. These

11 days had taken me over big brutes, often starting from sea-level, so any "average" was misleading; east of the A9 the miles would increase but the footage drop considerably.

Ben Dorain, across Loch Tulla, where I would set off tomorrow is a hill forever associated with Duncan Bàn MacIntyre, one of the great Gaelic poets. It was the subject of "Farewell to the Bens", written after his last ascent—when 78—one of the most famous of all songs of the hill. It had over 550 lines and yet Donnachadh Ban (*Duncan of the Fair Hair*) could not write, his work being dictated to the Rev. Dr Stuart of Luss, and published in 1768.

MacIntyre was born poor and served as gamekeeper or forester; in Glen Etive he wooed and won the bailiff's beautiful daughter; in the '45 he, perforce, served Campbell interests rather than those of the heart—and ended in the cookhouse. He was to retire ultimately from the Edinburgh City Guard. All the time, he had been composing: songs of hunting, of loving, drinking songs, soldier songs, lampoons and eulogies. At a ceilidh, he could recite thousands of lines of verse by heart. Burns or Scott never met him in Edinburgh, yet, in Gaelic tradition, he is every bit their equal. We've had stamps for Burns and Scott, yet 1974, the 250th anniversary of the birth of Duncan Bàn MacIntyre, could hardly have been less noticed.

He was one of the earliest to *express* feelings for the mountains. He toured to help sell his books; and was noticed in Fort William singing from a volume held upside down! He died aged 88 and is buried in Greyfriars' Churchyard in Edinburgh, but his real monument is this landscape: the soft waters of Loch Tulla, the red-barked pines and the yellow cone of Ben Dorain.

I went to give mother a ring from Inveroran Inn, one with a history going back to droving times, when the route from Skye and Lochaber came down over the Blackmount. William and Dorothy Wordsworth had a second breakfast there after coming from Kingshouse. "The butter not eatable, the barley-cakes fusty, the oatbread so hard I could not chew it, and there were only four eggs in the house which they boiled as hard as stones."

After a supper brew at the Dormobile I gave a casual goodnight and goodbye and crawled into the tent. It seemed so undemonstrative, yet I was bubbling inside. Excitement kept me from sleep and I lay reading till all hours, snug inside the sleeping bag though my hands froze. Frost-pollen dusted the walls of the tent. Even when I blew out the candles and lay in the moon glow I was still aware of the tingling world without: a coot calling and the throbbing pulse of snipe drumming.

"Spring is come home with her world-wandering feet
And all things are made young with her young desires."

FRANCIS THOMPSON

II

LYON AND LOCHAY

" . . . . alone I climb
The rugged path that leads me out of time—
Out of time and out of all,
Singing yet in sun and rain,
'Heel and toe from dawn to dusk,
Round the world and home again.' "

JOHN DAVIDSON

Sunday 14 April A SABBATH DAY'S JOURNEY

The cold had really battened down overnight and the tent was furry
with frost crystals both inside and out. The ice rattled in the watercarrier. I made the last meal in luxury: from now on it was the small
tent and minimal gear. There was no sign of life from the Dormobile
as I patted it goodbye and set off for Bridge of Orchy. The thousand
eyes of night had closed, so nobody saw me steal away to my solitary
hills. C. S. Lewis writes: "Most of us, I suppose, have a secret country."
Mine might not be so adventurous as Narnia; but at least I was gloriously free to set off into it.

The hotel and station were both silent. Yet what memories! Two
friends of mine once slept in the station "Gents" (carefully going outside to pee) and gave the station master heart-failure in the morning.
Three of my kids once were allowed to use the "Ladies" when their
tent had gone up in flames, an accident due to the primus being
outside the tent. Stoves, Gaz ones especially, are one of the biggest hill
hazards and they were all thoroughly trained in primus procedures. As
a last resort they had been told simply to put a hand under the stove
and throw it outside. I only saw this done once, at Bridge of Orchy.
The flaming missile came flying out the door of a tent—and went
straight into the tent opposite.

Here too we once endured 80 hours of deluge (three days and nights),
the worst I think I have ever known. Mr Macdonald came over from
the hotel to offer help only to find everyone all right: two snoozing in
the first tent, two playing chess in the next, two brewing in the next—

who offered him a cup of tea. We all went over to the hotel kitchen later and sat watching "Dr Who" while we supped bowls of soup. It is touches like this which make or mar hotel reputations. I have a very definite list of those I recommend and those I most certainly do not. I recommend Bridge of Orchy.

Beinn Dorain is seen as a fine cone rising above the railway as you come over the pass from Tyndrum. A gate leads from the station right on to its lower slopes. The name is *hill of the otter*—a beast found throughout the hills, much more than people realise. We once met one on Christmas Day on Beinn a' Ghlo—undulating through deep snow at 2,000 feet up. Ravens are resident here on the crags and were calling as I passed on up the north ridge. The hard snow patches and rims made for easy walking and the lochan was a perfect mirror of Sellotape-tin blue. Last time on the summit three of us had fallen asleep watching a sunset.

The view today was outstanding; among the very best ever, anywhere. I named over a hundred peaks and apart from the Buachailles and Aonach Eagach all the Munros to date seemed visible, even the tent-shaped summit of Ben More. In the sun and cold everything was bright as crockery.

This was a great contrast to the Ripleys' trip. Alan had gone to the doctor from Bridge of Orchy. It was suggested that swelling ankles were caused by iron deficiency. Brian wrote on November 11th: "We had decided earlier that if we couldn't do these five peaks today, we would have to pack in as we were getting too far behind schedule." Their log was brief: "Tried to get up Beinn Dorain. Turned back at 3,000 feet. Wind gusts must have been up to 80 m.p.h.—and hailing heavily." They gave up even trying to crawl, and once down pitched their tent inside a sheep shelter. 1,325 miles, 377,850 feet, 13 weeks and 230 Munros lay behind them. It must have been heart-breaking. It was as well not to have known these details as I sat on my sunny peak.

Beinn an Dothaidh (Doe), *hill of scorching*, all too literal today: I have never been sure whether the summit is as shown on the map or the point along the rim. The north side has some good hidden winter routes. There is a wide view out over the Moor of Rannoch, and Loch Tulla today was burnished from weeks of sunshine. The next peak along, Achaladair, and the next again, Chreachain, have two tops each, both facing boldy out to the Moor. Behind them, like a ball held in a

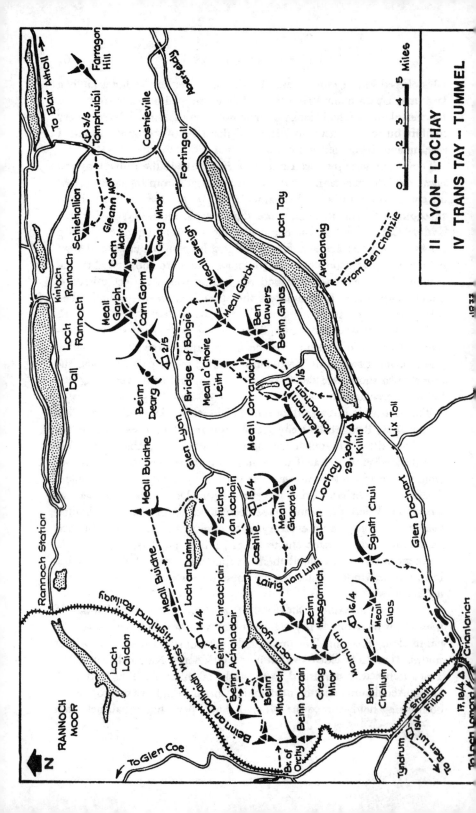

II LYON – LOCHAY
IV TRANS TAY – TUMMEL

fist, is Mhanach (Vannoch) which also has two summits the statutory mile apart. This awkward outlier was my aim first, then Chreachain, and Achaladair. Contouring to the col for Mhanach was too steep for comfort but at the peaty col I could at least leave the sack—with a label saying the owner was returning, please do not remove.

The ascent was up slopes running with melt water. Beinn Mhanach, *monk's hill* (which is perhaps why there is a large white quartz cross near the cairn), is most easily done up the Auch Glen, since Gorton Station on the Moor is no more and the Glen Lyon side is moated with a Hydro loch.

I had a brew at the sack, for the softer snow was tiring. Wending on up the burn I had a session of most erotic imaginings—reaction perhaps to the monastic existence, but one which was never repeated. We are adaptable creatures I suppose.

It took sweaty contouring and much burn-crossing to lodge on Chreachain's western top, a Meall Buidhe, one of three such named that I was to cross in 24 hours. Figures on the prow of Achaladair had a Bonington-like *contra jour* brightness. The Moor was bright with the glitter of a thousand pools. Chreachain, 3,540 feet, was the day's highest, a cone which can be seen from afar. A deep bite of corrie on the north side has a textbook lochan at its foot, a campsite for the dreamer with the cliffs above it, a view over the Moor and old Crannoch Wood and the toy-town railway below.

I overhauled two lads from a Glasgow youth group whose tents could just be seen near Gorton bothy. They had been swarming all over the hills but these two had lingered on high. They were puzzled at the derivation of Beinn a' Chreachain which is the *hill of the drinking shell*. Alas, so much like this has vanished into the past. It needs a resident community to maintain traditions.

I mentioned an odd accident I had had, not very far from their camp down on the Moor. I tripped over a guy line and a wee toe "snapped just like a twig" (so I was told). It was a bit of a nuisance as we had just arrived there to explore the Moor (the Rannoch Rush, *Scheuchzeria palustris*, grows here and in Poland and nowhere else in the world), so it was simply ignored—a hole cut in a gymshoe gave it freedom, and thus shod, I crossed the Moor twice and climbed this group of hills. A week later I hobbled into hospital back home and was immediately told to "Sit down, sir, no walking on it, just rest! . . ."

It was too hard to explain; but a real row came later when I pleaded

c

not to have it plastered as I was off to the Pyrenees for five weeks' climbing. It rapidly developed into a—"you must"—"you mustn't"— "you must" confrontation. Compromise: I went off with a bandage sprayed with something to make it firm (but not bulky) and this could come off once there—after all, a boot was as good as anything to hold the toe in place. It worked quite well.

A chunter down again, then up the very edge of Beinn Achaladair, *hill of the mower*, which gave some scrambling on bulging granite, happily in the shade. Carpets of purple saxifrage and a mountain blackbird nest were interesting. I descended Gleann Cailliche, the *glen of the old woman*, which drains these hills into Loch Lyon. An eerie passage or two about this glen can be found in Duncan Fraser's *Highland Perthshire*.

I wish I had read it beforehand; perhaps I too could have paid my respects to the eternal lady and her never-ageing family. I innocently passed Tigh-nam-Bodach, though I did notice the evidence of the old shielings: sad stones that told of summer songs long gone before the assault of the sheep. The sheep were obviously still there: the whole glen had been burnt, so I walked through a dirty, dry cloud of dust. Groups of deer went crackling off along the brittle, charred slopes.

Each spring and autumn in the eighteenth century, the people of Meggernie and latterly Chesthill came and went the score of miles from these high pastures, as folk did to the upper glens all through the Highlands. Then the pattern broke and the blackface sheep came. The lowland cities and Canadian prairies received the exiles, and the landlords grew rich from their people-cleared glens.

The only person remaining is the old Caillich who gave her name to the glen unknown centuries before. . . .

> "Tigh-nam-Bodach, living all her lone,
> Born of water, turned to stone."

I soon left the Allt Cailliche to contour—rather endlessly across those dirty slopes—round into Gleann Mhearan, a gateway glen, east of Beinn a' Chreachain. In the old days this was quite an important through route from Glen Lyon to Rannoch Moor. It was easy to envisage "caterans and raiders, drovers and packmen, Prince Charlie's men and Hanovarians passing through the defile" (A. E. Robertson).

In 1810 Thomas Telford proposed a road from Killin to Glen Spean (estimated cost, £15,360) which would use this pass—70 years before the railway was to snake round under today's hills and on by the same route to Loch Treig and the Spean.

I pitched my tent by the dwindling Mhearan burn at the junction with the Eas Fhiuran which would give my continuation east tomorrow. Today had been quite enough: 7,400 feet and 13 miles, a scorching Sabbath day's journey. Since it was Easter Sunday I broke from my daily Bible readings to go through the Easter accounts in the Gospels. Very vivid. And vital. Above the camp was an area full of hundreds of splayed roots and white, dead trunks. They rose out of the black peat like something out of C. S. Lewis: sculptures come alive, contorted and groping like starved memories of far off times reaching for the pitying sun of today. I dreamed of them under my frosty shroud that night.

Monday 15 April BUIDHE, BUIDHE AND STUI

As soon as the sun left Gleann Mhearan the cold swept in like a tide. I took the Gaz stove to bed and soon had tea and porridge ready while still comfy—so much for roughing it. Fingers stuck to the tent pegs and the tent folded like stiff cardboard. Wordsworth could have been thinking of this hushed and secret place when he penned

> The silence that is in the starry sky,
> The sleep that is among the lonely hills.

The only sound was the dawn chatter of grouse, the very epitome of peace.

The first Munro, Meall Buidhe (Boo-ee) lay seven miles off, as the craw flees, but a wheen loner as the gangrel gangs, for another Meall Buidhe lay between. It was a Corbett which I had not been on, so was a bonus. A corkscrew route beside the wren-loud burn took me up out of the deep freeze and at once I found long-johns impossible. Changing out of them I knocked over my brew. The high moor teemed with deer —which came galloping past. Frozen bogs and snow again made for good going to the Corbett, where I snuggled in beside the cairn for a lazy hour.

Golden plovers were calling and there was the incessant summer *twee twee* of pipits. Long streamers of cloud were escaping from Loch Rannoch up on to the Moor. Ben Nevis was clear, and never have I seen it day after day like this. One day clear in ten is the usual. I heard, and then saw, a train caterpillaring round the edge of the Moor: the morning down-train for Mallaig. For once the sight did not give me itchy feet. A snipe began drumming and a brace of ptarmigan dawdled past. It was full spring "come laughing to the hills at last" (W. K. Holmes). A grinning dog fox trotted by only twenty yards off and never even noticed me. The train pulled out of Rannoch Station and became a faint grumble in the distance.

I roused myself from the lethargy of my perch and went down by an odd, deep slot, choked and overhung with snow, then pulled up the emptiness beyond. In the middle of nowhere I picked up the tracks of a vehicle—not even ghillies walk now it seems—and later I heard a vehicle coming but when I breasted a shoulder and could see for miles, there was no sign of it, and nothing appeared. A phantom vehicle? Nonsense! Or was it?

In a glen I could name there is a house set back from the road and reached by a narrow, fenced-in track on which you could neither turn nor pass another vehicle. The farm folk were expecting visitors and sat looking out into the winter night for their arrival. At last a car pulled off into their half-mile drive, headlights weaving through the trees. Then the lights vanished; and no friends arrived. They felt a bit worried, yet if anything had happened surely someone would have walked up for help. Before they could do anything another car swung into the drive and they watched its lights come steadily all the way up. It was the expected friends—and they had seen no other car. Twice more that winter they spotted lights turn into their drive yet nobody arrived. A neighbouring house also saw them, asking who had visited, when nobody had. No tracks were left on the muddy track. Explain it who will.

At one o'clock I reached Meall Buidhe, busy chanting French vocabularies, another intended regular activity which never succeeded —there was always too much of interest. Two unsuspecting lines of deer crossed ahead, stopped, sniffed and then took to their heels. A second later a fox trotted into view. He saw me, gave a splendid double take, and also shot off.

The Munro Buidhe I remember from a tough trip in poverty days. Joe and I hitched to Bridge of Orchy station one Friday night, then took the morning train to Gorton and reached the summit by a long flog over the Moor. We dropped down to Glen Lyon and after rescuing a lamb from a cattle grid, spent a miserable night, soaked through in a sopping tent. On the Sunday we crossed to Glen Lochay and traversed Beinn Chaluim to Crianlarich, then hitched home to Fife. Car-bound days cannot equal such doings. The sheer hell of that night. The look on the girl's face in the Crianlarich Hotel when we asked for second afternoon teas. Such weather was the normal for April.

I dropped down Coire Pharlain to the loch but it was oven hot in the corrie and a golden pool in the burn was irresistible. I struggled out of clammy garments for a real bath: soaping and diving in several times and drip-drying in the sun. Some April! Pink pincushions were on the larches which framed the loch. The Stui rose across the dam, seamed with shadows I was glad to see. There was no passage across the top, so it was down and up. A Glasgow family yelled something about it being "a grand day for a wee walk . . .".

Stuchd an Lochain (The Stui) is a well-scalloped peak which fills the view looking up Glen Lyon. An ink-spot lochan lies hidden in a northern corrie. The mile round its rim was grassy and soft so I left my boots behind with the rucksack and enjoyed a barefoot romp. What anyone would make of the tracks across the snow patches. . . .

One of Scotland's earliest recorded hill ascents was of the Stui in 1590 when mad Colin Campbell of Glen Lyon ascended it. The description of the corrie rim "beetling over a deep circular mountain tarn" (Lochan nan Cat) is accurate. One wonders at the rest. Having driven a herd of goats over the cliffs, the Campbell tried the same game with one of his attendants, who only escaped by his quick wits.

I left the cairn at 6.30, yet at the back of seven was knocking at the keeper's door at Cashlie, in Glen Lyon, to the south. Glen Lyon is steeped in history as befits the longest glen in the country. It gives a cross-section, almost, of all history, geography and everything else. From my route down I could see the sites of at least four of the many ancient forts which tradition associates with Fionn, whose legendary home was here in the days before history.

Here too is the Bhacain, a stone shaped like the head of a hound, to which Fionn tied his great hunter Bran: Bran of yellow paws and black flanks and a chain of pure gold. Here too one of the several "testing stones"—to prove an aspirant warrior's strength. The Bhacain had another use they say, for under it would creep the young lassies of the glen, seeking its mysterious powers before heading to the fearful lowlands for the harvest time. They did not have The Pill in those days.

The terriers brought out the keeper and I thankfully received my parcel. I mentioned the odd coincidence of two Buidhes in the day, each with a fox; Mr MacDougall was, I'm sure, glad they were not his concern, but no doubt the word would be passed on.

Half a mile down the road lay tiny Stronuich Reservoir, and a swaying, slatted bridge let me round it to where the Allt Laoisich came down in a noisy waterfall. As so often, there was only just time to whip the tent up and take a photo of the site before the light faded. A gargantuan meal followed, for most caches had one tinned meal at least. Tonight it was hamburgers, carrots and sweetcorn—plus pears and creamed rice, plus the usual soup and coffee. "Roughing it"?

Many years ago, a gang of us were tramping home down all the miles of Glencoe to the hostel, when we were stopped at a lay-by. A card table had been spread with a lace tablecloth and on it was arranged a dainty afternoon tea: delicate china, silver teapot, cake-stand—the lot. Enjoying this was a minute, ancient aristocrat of a figure, dressed in black in the style of Queen Victoria herself, watched over by a uniformed chauffeur. We chatted away amicably and did not refuse the offered sandwiches. The crusts had been cut off, naturally, and a frilly doily edged the pile. As we parted, she said, "Well, it was so nice talking to you boys. I do so enjoy roughing it."

It became a bit of a catch phrase.

Tuesday 16 April   THE FOREST OF MAMLORN

"Forest" perhaps needs explaining, for you will find few trees on these hills. A thousand years ago, yes; it was all forest, the great wood of Caledon. Now only a few tatty remnants of it survive: the Black Wood of Rannoch, Crannach Wood, bits of Speyside and Dee, by Loch Maree. . . . For the rest, skeleton branches rising from the peat bogs are all the signs remaining. With the destruction of the woods went the last wolves and robbers; though it might be argued that these survive now in the cities under cover of the concrete jungles.

The sporting estates of the Victorian era used the term "deer forest" and because these often followed natural boundaries, such as groups of mountains, the term has stuck: you have the Mamore Forest, the Forest of Atholl, the Forest of Mamlorn and so on, which may, or may not, have trees and may, or may not, have deer.

"Maim Laerne is the King's Forest—very rich in deer, lying upon Brae Urchay, Brae Lyon and Brae Lochay" an old account tells. These braes were, and are, a tangle of peaks, steep and broken, threaded by deep passes and tricky rivers but access is easy by car now, from the east, up Glen Lochay or Glen Lyon. A Hydro road links them over the pass of the Lairig nan Lunn but is kept inviolate by locked gates. It would not do to let the public, whose taxes built it, enjoy a natural round drive!

I woke to a clammy world of fog and set off up my river in a dewy wetness. Sheep loomed large as elephants and deer "broke, and went outraged and sniffing into the dark wind". After an hour, however, I broke through the cloud into the sun. I left the tent spread to dry and gradually discarded garments on the way up Meall Ghaordie which is generally a lumpy and unimpressive hill. A quartz vein breaks through near the summit. I could hear the dogs at Cashlie giving tongue, the noise filtering up through the valley cloud.

After fetching the tent, the seven miles west to Heasgarnich probably gave the hardest going so far: very rough, deep heather with endless peat bogs and schisty crags—and hares and ptarmigan forever exploding at my feet. At one stage I sat for a long time watching deer which were browsing just below me, and then spent half an hour at a pool which seemed 10 per cent water and 90 per cent frog spawn. It was teeming with frogs, but at my first step they vanished. Slowly, eyes would rise above the water, but it took twenty minutes of immobility before they ventured forth again. For days, now, the dried-up peat pools had held shiny dollops of spawn. Mating was in full swing here. Two, gripped tightly together, went swimming off with legs kicking in perfect co-ordination. I finally scattered them all again when I could no longer contain my laughter at one frog which simply could not co-ordinate its legs into a breast stroke.

This happy procrastination could not put off the next pull, but again it was for a bonus Corbett, Meall nan Subh, 2,638 feet, a frustrating series of knolls, bogs and detours. How you could be sure of it in mist, I don't know. It had gone noon, so after crossing the Hydro road (Lairig nan Lunn) I lunched on Beinn Heasgarnich's massive slopes.

I paddled in the burn happily; then created a David Livingstone sort of hat to protect my ears which were slowly frying in the sun. Heasgarnich is a big brute of a hill, a heartbreak sometimes, but I have always been lucky with weather and company.

I first plodded up it during an S.M.C. Meet along with Messrs Gorrie, Fraser and Hartog. The last was recovering from frostbite acquired on the Mustagh Tower trip, Barclay Fraser was to climb with me in many foreign countries, and Charlie Gorrie was soon to teach at the same school where he was nicknamed Beinn a' Chlachair—because it sounded like a single malt. We had taken in this hill from Braehead on a Killin to Skye trek and also on several day trips.

The whole hill is a gentle-sloping chaos: peat bogs and fast streams. I followed up the Allt Tarsuinn. It was lined with perfect camping swards and I passed on sadly. A scarp turned the river into tumbling falls. It was cruelly hot. The burn rose in a lochan only 200 feet below the summit so must be one of the highest, and the glaciers of Heasgarnich must have been among the last to disappear. It was a relief to break over the snow rim to the cairn.

I wrung out the sponge pad from my back and dealt with a melted mess of chocolate. Ghaordie looked a thousand miles away. Chreachain dominated the other side. The sun glared into my eyes as I walked off round the rim.

I left a questionnaire. It was found the next weekend by Erland Flett who had just moved into the flat of another friend, Robert Aitken, who himself was to find a questionnaire in July on Lurg Mhor. Erland I later met in the Atlas and we shared a flooded Dormobile refuge in Marrakech. Scotland is still a comparatively small world. There are more climbers in Manchester, for instance.

The ridge down was steep and solid. The col had the name Loch na Baintighearna on it but there was no loch—just an excess of peat hags. They were dry and easy to cross. I brewed and spied out Creag Mhor above. Could I do one more Munro?

Several years ago when Ian and Mary McLeod had just started climbing we had climbed Heasgarnich out of valley cloud, rather like today. It was in January, but so mild for weeks that we left axes behind. We came down to the col to add Creag Mhor. Its north-east flank is usually a sopping, hanging garden in summer. In those inversion conditions we soon found the wet had turned to ice and the very steep, mixed ground was highly dangerous for novices. To climb down was the more dangerous alternative so we went on up, right cannily, till we found our way barred completely by a band of rock-hard snow, the remnant of a cornice. There were rude remarks about the value of certain mountain certificates!

When in doubt, eat. My jammy knife gave me the answer and I turned to work on the snow band with it. It was easier than expected and I soon had a staircase spiralling up to the ridge. I crept down again to carry up the dog and the other two gaily ascended after, with all the confidence of ignorance. They would not do it so casually now!

Having avoided supplying Benny Humble with some statistics that day I was a bit cautious now, as I sat, again with no ice-axe. But I was up and down in an hour. The snow was soft, the crags illusory, and without the pack the going just felt blissful. I landed right at the slim cairn, circled north to the first snow gully and bumslid down a thousand feet to end 50 yards from the gear.

I followed down the Allt Bad a' Mhaim, contoured and finally pitched on the 1,000-foot contour which I hoped would keep me above valley clouds. It was another delectable camp. (Did I ever have one that was not?) By the wending River Lochay curlews were bubbling, one of the greatest of all wild sounds. Pied pipers and snipe added their contribution and wheatears were about. This was perhaps the "essential silence" that Stevenson mentions.

Wednesday 17 April A ROOF OVER MY HEAD
Peewits and curlews woke me in the morning again, disembodied voices calling through a clammy mist. I could hear the birds' wings as they went off from my route up the river into the folds of the hill. The grey stones of a dead village seemed unspeakably sad in that shrouded emptiness. History is a long tale of the many imposed upon by the few and the tragedy is that so many of the many do not care.

I hoped for three Munros today: *Malcolm's peak*—Beinn Chaluim— to the west of this pass, then Meall Glas and Sgiath Chuil to the east. It would be a real challenge to do Ghaordie to Sgiath Chuil in a day. It would be much harder than the Mamores for instance. Any takers?

Chaluim is a finer peak than most descriptions would hint at. As a winter hill it is at its best. Again I suppose I have been lucky with the day and the company. If you want to be different do it from Auch; oddly enough you see it to advantage from near Bridge of Orchy. I left my rucksack among a dead forest of pine stumps behind the dead village and climbed up into the mist. The crags of Stob a' Bhiora might repay winter exploration; today they were a barrier which I tried to outflank but ended by climbing on the easy side. The weather became lighter and warmer, and on the eastern prow of Chaluim it cleared.

The view was fantastic! Yesterday's cloud had been merely ankle deep, today the thick whiteness wrapped up to the very throats of the hills. A blazing, pulsing, cloud sea reached as far as eye could see at about the 2,000 ft level, the inversion to end them all. Out of this white world rose the detached heads of all the great hills. I raced to the summit in a panic of disbelief and then sat to marvel.

Perhaps it would last till Meall Glas! I did some rapid christies down the snow flanks and plunged into the clammy clouds again. The compass seemed a sad thing in that romantic setting and it was used impatiently, if dourly, to find my gear. I followed a burn up Meall Glas but it was a doubtful navigation aid as it had innumerable forks not on the map. However, after a scramble up some garnet-splattered rocks the cairn broke from the cloud a hundred yards off. I was just too late. Patches of blue appeared overhead but even a long meal stop failed to stay the steaming, rising flow.

I went along to a minor top, then down and across the sea of bog which forms the watershed. Somewhere in the mist a shepherd was calling to his dog. It cleared on the way up Sgiath Chuil, the *back wing*, but the view was quite tame and ordinary. I sat on the knuckle of summit rocks and wrote some letters, brought my log up to date and left a questionnaire again. It was not found for over two weeks which is perhaps judgement enough on this dull hill.

My first visit to it was anything but dull. Robert and I were young and ignorant then, which is my only excuse for our day of fiascos. His mother had dropped us up Glen Lochay and fixed a tea-time meeting in Glen Dochart. We made our way up Sgiath Chuil without difficulty. The O.S. unhelpfully cut off our map not far to the south but going that way we could hardly miss the River Dochart so this did not really matter. (I was using the same map today. The price on the front said 1/6d.)

Not long after leaving the gale-blown summit shots rang out (it was October) and a bullet passed so close that we threw ourselves flat. We did not "hit the dust" so much as the mud—black, slimy, peaty stuff. We carried a fair quantity of it on with us, as we made a cautious, C.C.F. trained right-flanking movement to get behind the enemy. Eventually we hit some scrub. There were people on a zig-zag new road, so we had some more crawling about. At last it seemed clear. We felt we had done not badly for the first time under fire. We did an "over the top" sort of charge down a shaly cutting, on to the road, giggling and tumbling down—to land at the brogued feet of an imposing woman who bulged and bristled all the way up to her deerstalker hat.

Her immaculate tweeds contrasted somewhat with our grimy army surplus.

Her eye alighted on my trailing length of scarf.

"Is that a Dollar scarf, boy?"

It was either that or St Mirren, and as soon as I opened my mouth I would betray which; I confessed it was.

"Ah! My children go to Dollar . . ."

We parted most amicably. War games over, we cut corners down to the Dochart which here does a fair imitation of the Limpopo. After casting up and down we had found neither bridge nor shallows. After an hour we gave up and reverted to the C.C.F. stuff. Carrying our boots and clothes aloft we made a chilly, bellybutton-deep crossing. From the other side we could see round the next bend; there, to be sure, was a bridge.

Still only half dressed we were distracted by a thrashing among the whin bushes on the bank, and found a ram stuck with its horns entwined in the fence. It had bled its forehead. We struggled with no success and retreated much pricked and battered. Still in bare feet I set off across two fields to call at what looked like a shepherd's cottage. The fields had recently held cattle. They also grew ambushing rosettes of thistles.

Fortunately there was a shepherd so we gave him that problem and turned to ours which we now decided was to forestall Robert's mother calling out a search for two overdue walkers. We thumbed like mad. A lorry stopped almost at once.

We babbled out our story over the next mile or two as we charged along.

"What hotel was it you were meeting in for tea?" the driver asked.

"Luib. Why?"

"Ah weel now, Luib's back the way. Yon's the Lix Toll."

We did not receive any further lifts however hard we exercised our thumbs and Robert's mother, like Queen Victoria, was "not amused".

History, fortunately, only repeated itself in broad outline today. I could see perfectly clearly where Auchessan lay, with a bridge over to the main road, but even from a distance I could hear the bustle of heavy traffic on the road. I did not fancy dodging along it for five miles. I would stay on this side of the valley.

That was a mistake. First I had a temper-fraying tramp through dusty, clawing heather, then a new track led away *uphill* again, directly into the hot sun, only to hand me over to the purgatory of new forest plantings. I was above Loch Iubhair (*Loch of the yews*, another site of Fingalian legends) and between it and Loch Dochart there seemed to be a chance of crossing; the stinking, dangerous road suddenly appearing benign and welcoming. I struggled down only to find the linking river was twenty yards wide and about as deep. To add to the torture a boat lay on the bank—the other bank. I could not see if it had oars. I was quite prepared to swim over for it, then fetch my clothes and rucksack. But my problem solved itself. A shepherd began gathering in the field opposite. I slunk away. I would not appeal to him; like most I was readier to be taken for a thief than a fool.

I went through my repertoire of invective, which spans from Arabic to Zulu (they say travel broadens the mind). I passed a ruined house. Out in the loch was a ruined castle. It had been captured once by the MacGregors in mid winter when they simply walked out over the ice and surprised the occupants. Each winter whooper swans return to it. It is an idyllic spot, especially on the other side. I battered through decaying woods, then climbed a small hill, then crossed a last marshy mile to the viaduct for Crianlarich.

It was a weary and sun-battered traveller who reported to police constable Kaye who had a parcel of goodies. I staggered up to the hostel with it—a juicy meal: tea, milk, fruit, coffee went with the actual food, all quickly made out of tins. The hostel was an old barracks of a place, the military atmosphere maintained by the temporary warden. He had the pots sized off from the left even, and he tested the heat of the range by spitting on it.

There were several hitching Aussies and South Africans, three noisy lads planning Ben More, a quiet couple and Peter and his Paw from Lanark. It had an old-fashioned hostel atmosphere. I washed my underwear and went out to watch the sun setting on Chaluim. I gave it a wave—only it was not a wave . . .

Thursday 18 April   CRIANLARICH STILL
I was first up, at eight o'clock, which was after all a long lie for me. Mops were duly issued by numbers and I was paraded off to swab the ablutions. I was given permission to hang my washing on the line while away for the day. With my flannels rolled down and a pullover on I could pass as a tourist. The shop was helpful and kept my purchases

till 4 p.m. when the barracks would reopen. I had a day free. A twelve-hour pass.

At the station I sat in the café and read the paper. A train came in and there was a brief bedlam. I went down to the hotel for further festering. I had given David a ring the night before to fix up meeting Barclay and give a list of "wants". This was a statutory rest day and tomorrow was an easy day too. I was half tempted to add Ben More and Stobinian, but the left tendon was playing up a bit. A rest would ease it, which it did; I had no further complaints—apart from a pair of fried ears. I do not think I have ever been so sunburnt. I had lunch in the hotel and then lazed the afternoon away by the river, reading. Morale was fine and there was little to do. Section two was over, the tally now 74,000 feet climbed and about 207 miles walked.

Grapefruit juice; fried steak with onions, tomatoes, spuds and corn; gooseberries and creamed rice; real coffee . . .

The trio had done Ben More all right, Peter and his Paw had been up An Caisteall—in self defence I told something of my recent doings. A Kenya medic and girl friend swelled the ranks. At ten to eleven the lights flashed. A Scots voice muttered something about Barlinnie. At eleven the patrol came round and the lights went out.

III

FURTHEST SOUTH

"To every man there openeth
A way and ways and a way.
And the high soul climbs the high way
And the low soul gropes the low
And in between on the misty flats
The rest drift to and fro.
But to every man there openeth
A high way and a low
And every man decideth the way his soul shall go."

JOHN OXENHAM

Friday 19 April CAMP IN THE KING'S FIELD

The walk from Crianlarich west along Strath Fillan was on tarred roads, so I rose early to make the trip before traffic took away any of its enjoyment. This really gave me an extra lazy day, as Barclay Fraser was coming up and I wanted to do the Laoigh group with him.

The glen is named after the seventh-century saint who completed the work of conversion here. A piece of his crozier (the quigrich) and a bell from the priory (the bernane) are two of the priceless relics in the National Museum of Antiquities in Edinburgh. The bell was stolen by an English traveller in the seventeenth century and the crozier ended in Canada with the last of the hereditary custodian's descendants; so their survival is something of a miracle.

This and some fourteenth century history filled my mind as I walked along enjoying the prosperous strath scenery—something I was not to see much of in the weeks ahead. The bridge was in its usual battered state. It seems that some motorist is always knocking it down quicker than the squad can repair it. I crossed and turned up to camp in the King's Field—Dail Righ. The O.S., as with many historic sites, keeps this one a secret. It was annoying to find local litter dumped there but even that turned to the good when I found some interesting old bottles which were collectors' pieces.

Robert the Bruce retreated this way after his defeat at the battle of Methven (near Perth) in 1306, but then met the MacDougalls of Lorn who turned him back to Crianlarich. Somewhere near Loch Dochart he was ambushed by three scouts while protecting the rear of his small party. He managed to kill all three foes, quite a feat in itself, but had to part with his plaid in doing so. Its brooch became a MacDougall family heirloom till they were burnt out, in 1647, during Covenanting troubles. It vanished, but turned up 178 years later in Campbell hands! Bruce made many journeys among the Highlands and Islands and is a really great figure of history, despite the tarnish of popular legends.

Barclay rolled up in the afternoon in his V.W. conversion—which had previously helped provide a base for a fine climbing trip to Corsica. We had climbed together in the Atlas and Andes as well, all since Barclay had "retired". He brewed, and then acted as chef while I ploughed through the mail, glanced at the newspapers, looked at Tatras slides and decided I could not really accept a wedding invitation for the next day.

I was up late by candle light, still nibbling away at little things. The new lightweight trousers and jacket had come from Tiso, which took away a few more pounds of the weight that went everywhere with me. It was Chay Blyth who said: "My formula was simple—careful planning, attention to detail, hard work, the right tools for the job, and a big slice of help from Up Above."

With which I would agree entirely.

Saturday 20 April QUEEN LAOIGH

A friend of mine who has an odd habit of sexing his hills always talks of Beinn Laoigh (Lui) as female. If this is so, then she is a queen among hills. It might also explain why for the first time on the trip the hills were clouded thickly—but perhaps this change was retribution for sweeping the extreme south anti-clockwise, since it is always more propitious to progress *car deseil*, or clockwise.

I had risen at six to dash off the odd letter while Barclay dealt with breakfast. We set off at the back of nine, crossing to join the Allt Coire Dubhchraig at a remnant of old Scots pine wood. There is a great deal of planting all round this group of hills. There was once quite a settlement by the Eas Anie but it has gone completely. The scars on the hillside are old lead mines. Several companies made and lost fortunes mining here before the workings finally closed in 1923. The Campbells once wrecked the mines in 1745 as they were then run by an English

Jacobite, Sir Robert Clifton, but you can still pan for gold by the King's Field.

Apart from one waterfall our route held little of note, and the melt water and snow soon soaked our feet. It was an easy plod, apart from trying to keep up with the galloping Fraser. Beinn Dubhchraig failed to give a view though it stayed dry. We headed for Beinn Oss, *hill of the elk*, which hints at the antiquity of our hill names. It is a rockier hill: mica schist country again. The top just failed to clear so we ate on the col before Laoigh. I left my rucksack there too before the climb up to 3,708 feet, which makes Laoigh queen indeed over this corner of the kingdom.

Laoigh is a double headed peak with a rim edging the glaciated *corrie of the winds*, Coire Gaothaich, to the north east. This has been a popular winter climbing peak since the 1890's when every slight rib and gully was dutifully pioneered.

After some conversation, we had to "twine"—Barclay off down the north and I to the south—after adding Beinn a' Chleibh, a small afterthought to Laoigh, being just 3,008 feet. It deserves its name, *hill of the basket*. It is a real outlier if you have come from Cononich side yet hardly worth a trip on its own. The Oban road approaches are well defended by plantings. The summit has several cairns to confuse you in mist. After this pilgrimage I flanked back across Laoigh's skirts to my rucksack on the other col and set off on to new ground—something which always raised fresh enthusiasm.

I was soon below cloud level and having to take off my shirt again. To the south lay an area of gentle watersheds and a maze of bog and stream which the Hydro have tapped and led into a complex scheme. Despite these man-made incursions it is an area with a feel of wilderness. The bogs were dry for once and made walking easy on the fibrous hags. The whole area was alive with deer. I have an African cousin who once doubted if Scotland had any "wide, open spaces". I wished he was there to watch one herd charge off, scattering some silly sheep, splashing through a sparkle of river and streaming into the far distance until they became a mere feel of movement. As most of the herds had hardly bothered to move to let me by, I was quite puzzled at this obvious panic and its cause.

I had intended to drop down to Glen Fyne and do a sackless ascent of Argyll's Beinn Buidhe the next day, but the lure of a high camp was too great, and as by now fitness was so built-in that weight did not

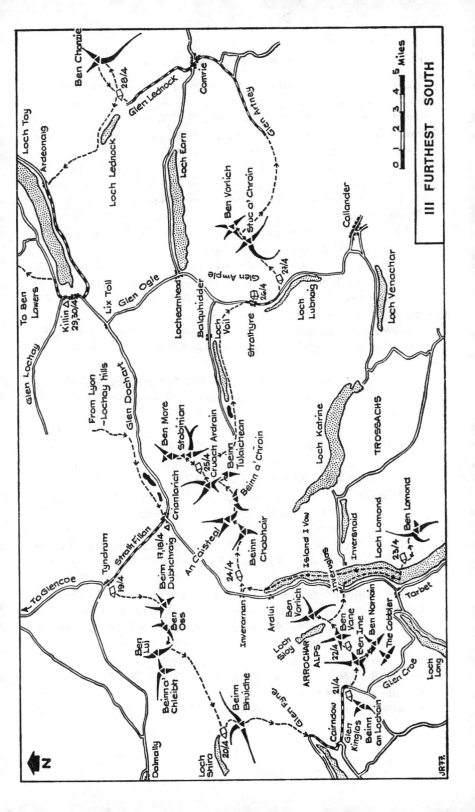

III FURTHEST SOUTH

0 1 2 3 4 5 Miles

matter, I decided to stay up. I followed an aqueduct which was tapping all the side streams of a glen and actually taking the water back over the glen's watershed to drain into Loch Shira. Near the loch I saw what looked like a cave but proved to be a split boulder. In its lee I pitched the tent and thankfully got into bare feet while the billy boiled.

Glen Shira was once home for Rob Roy when the rest of Scotland was made too hot for him. Neil Munro set his novel *Gillian the Dreamer* in the Glen too. At its foot is the castle which is the seat of Clan Campbell.

I had not seen a soul since parting from Barclay but the loneliness was no hardship as some warned it would be. It led to a quiet routine and a blissful contentment. I usually had tea ready by the time the tent was up. At the lunch stop I soaked dried vegetables and these would go on to cook along with potato, macaroni, rice or some other stodge, plus the meat, usually tinned for value. Soup would clean out the dish and I would finish with apple flakes or some other fruit. This night I had a mix of eggs, cheese, chicken, macaroni and three veg—so skipped the soup.

I watched the sun down behind the *hill of the fairy*, Beinn an Sithein— grey shafts of light and banners of cloud. Gillian was not the only dreamer in these parts . . .

Sunday 21 April   REST AND BE THANKFUL
Six o'clock seemed too raw to rise so I slept on a bit. A sneaky wind "annoyed the stove" as my log put it. The hills were cloud-capped. A big burn gave a pleasant scramble up through the shambolic schisty landscape. A nesting pair of dippers scolded me out of their territory. Above a lonely corrie the north-east summit poked through the mist so I skirted it to gain the ridge beyond. Everything was exaggerated in the billowing vapours and I had an enjoyable plod up to the trig point, though, sadly, no vuidhe.

Beinn Buidhe has quite a personality and is not a bad wee hill. Glen Fyne and Glen Shira are more normal routes in to it, but the way from the Lochy to the north should now be avoided owing to plantings.

I retraced a bit, then broke down the steep, craggy slopes of the summit ridge to gain the extensive upland boggy miles. The black peat was marked by thousands of deer tracks and the beasts were mincing about as I walked through their area. I followed the glen down behind

Newton Hill to reach Glen Fyne—which runs down to the loch of the same name. I stopped at the upper limit of the trees in the burn to delight in the view. The spring flowers were all out now: primroses, violets, celandine. An eagle was working the high slopes and later, below, I saw three buzzards.

There was also a field of cows to go through; these I did not mind but I was not so sure about the big black bull with a ring in his nose. Loch Fyne was a return to sea level, which I had left at Loch Leven, Glencoe, and would not meet again for many weeks—not until Knoydart. Even working up the North West I saw remarkably little of the sea. Some day I will have to go on a coastal journey to make up for it.

I had a pleasant lunch at Cairndow Inn, with its cosy atmosphere. Keats and his friend Charles Brown had been there in 1818. The poet was then 23 and had less than three years to live, yet did a tramp of 642 miles in 42 days from Lancaster to Inverness via the Burns Country, Loch Lomond, Inveraray, Mull, Iona, Ben Nevis and Loch Ness. Coming here they had already done fifteen miles before breakfast, hoping to stop at an inn called "Rest and Be Thankful". They found this was only the top of a pass, not an Inn, which lay here, five miles on. Ben Nevis was quite a good effort for the period. You can guess the weather from the lines Keats wrote about it: "I will climb through the clouds and exist."

My walk was a lingering one for Kilmorich Church, white and clean-lined, delayed me; it is octagonal in shape. Then the gardens of Strone House needed to be looked at. They were a fabulous explosion to my moorland eyes: spring bulbs, geans, azaleas. I walked up lengthy Glen Kinglas. The old road ran parallel with the new and gave safer walking.

I once acted as a courier on tourist buses laid on for the American navy which was visiting Oban. The circular tour brought them here, and a stop was made for the men to photograph some highland cattle. ("Say bud, why do all your cows wear winter woollies?") I assured them that the beasts were quite docile despite appearances and a few hardy souls went up the hillside to take close-ups. Highlanders are docile. They are also curious; so ambled forward to meet the sailors who paused, then retreated a bit—which only encouraged the cows to come on. In no time at all the sailors were running pell-mell for the fence with the cows lumbering after. Nothing I could say would convince them I had not deliberately fixed the whole thing.

At Butterbridge near the head of Glenkinglas I pitched the tent in the lee of the old bridge, brewed—and fell asleep. It was the Rest and Be Thankful after all. The shepherd was not at home so I set off at 5 p.m. to add Beinn an Lochain, another Munro. It overlooks Loch Restil and is a craggy, twisted peak with a double summit. There are some quite big crags and, on the north side, debris from a colossal rockfall like the one which holds the famous Shelter Stone in the Cairngorms. I wended off across the face to make some fun and came upon the decapitated body of a lamb. A fox had been before me. The view on top was dreich and grey for once and the restless buzz of traffic hauling through the pass of the A83 was a constant reminder of things I had almost forgotten. I had a look to the Arran hills and the Paps of Jura before running down in one fell swoop—delighted to see a smoking chimney.

The Beatons had been away fishing. "Too dry" was the complaint for that game. He was not too pleased to hear of the fox. I retreated with my parcel to enjoy the goodies of a tinned meal. The first soup was a bit of a disaster for I made it, not with mushroom, but Horlicks' powder.

Big Ben Ime made a bold shape in the night sky. Headlights waved across its lower slopes like feelers as the weekenders poured off back to Glasgow. And still it had not rained this trip! The cars thinned and the valley bottom became gruey cold and dead—as dead as the dead sheep by the roadside.

Monday 22 April THE ARROCHAR ALPS

I had a short and easy day as I particularly wanted to spend the night at a beautiful spot I had seen years ago. I left camp in a brittle blue morning, and had walked on the road for only a few minutes when I was offered a lift.

There were lay-bys in plenty but no litter bins and in the end I had to bury my things deep in the wood, piling on stones to ensure that they were not dug up by animals. A Land-Rover was going off up to Abyssinia and I gave the driver a bag of extra food to leave with the Beatons. I found a cool channel to "burn-up" again and eventually left it with a nice back and knee climb: back on rock, and knees on old snow wedged in the gully. I left my rucksack below Ime and went off to do Narnain first. It is a hill with some climbing but is overshadowed by the scope on the Cobbler across the valley. For wet days, though, it can offer some titillating subterranean routes. You can actually climb right through the hill. In one of its tighter spots one of my lads once managed to jam his climbing helmet and in his struggles ended up dangling from this rather unusual "chock".

The Arrochar Alps are riddled with caves and howffs of all sizes. Some overgrown gashes can provide booby-traps every bit as dangerous as crevasses. A night in a cave here is admirably described by Alastair Borthwick in *Always a Little Further*, possibly the funniest book ever written about the hills. These hills were very much the playground of the Glasgow lads in the hard days of the depression. Keats' cry: "I will climb through the clouds and exist" would have found an echo of sentiment round their howff fires.

This group provided a surge in climbing standards, and in the whole outlook of climbing, which is all too often missed in the histories of the game. John Cunningham was doing hard climbs here before certain folk-heroes down south were ever heard of. Jock Nimlin was the main pre-war pioneer, then later names like Cunningham, Smith, MacInnes appeared. They seem to have a remarkable survival record.

It was possible to make Narnain's truncated plateau by climbing on the flanks a bit. The Cobbler stood across the way in dramatic shadows. Its earlier name was Ben Arthur, for this is yet another area which lays claim to the Arthurian legends. At the cairn I found a clean hanky and a pair of woollen socks. Some one must have known my needs exactly.

In pre-nylon days four of us once took an awful pasting on these hills. Our tents were at Loch Restil, and back at them we stripped and dived into sleeping bags, dumping all our clothes into a blanket. This sodden bundle we weighed at home the next day. It averaged that we had each carried down ten pounds of water, and in those days any child could tell you a gallon of water weighs ten pounds.

Beinn Ime, the *butter mountain*—perhaps to balance the Buttermilk Burn which flows down to the torpedo station on Loch Long—is the highest in the group, though it fails to produce anything exceptional. Its best feature is a stepped east ridge down which I had once taken a party from Ardroy, our county's Outdoor Centre at Lochgoilhead. Another group had been camping at its foot and I said then that I would do likewise some day. I set off for it now.

I managed to find a good place for a standing glissade off the north ridge and left a swinging track of eight linked turns like some giant skier. I pitched my tent in a nook, up above the valley, so it was part of the view: an ochreous, secret place that looked out to the knobbly hill of A' Chrois. It was only midday.

Sun and shadow battled it out and I moved in and out of the tent to match, like an alpine weatherpiece. My log entry ended: "Little new this section as so well known of old. Write home. Wash undies. Go through the Route Book changing odd things for the better—lots of time walking to think about it. Feet fine, tendons no bother now. Ears like fried spam though! A bath would be a treat. Sponge over chilly. A slow chicken and rice meal. Day just goes."

Tuesday 23 April   DOON THE WATER

Ben Vane was a mere 1,400 feet above the camp, which I left rather thankfully. It had been a lumpy, sloping site and I seemed only to fall deeply asleep when it was time to get up. I went round over the north flank so that I could leave the rucksack and then nip up and down the peak. A little reedy pool reflected the snowy bulk of Beinn Ime like a galleon half seen through bottle-glass, a bronchial redstart was praising the sunshine; altogether superb—and morale reacted accordingly. From the summit Buidhe looked just like the Fife Lomonds in outline; the Cobbler appeared to have an elephant standing on top; Loch Lomond was smitten into silver. Ben Vane may only scrape home as a Munro by three feet but like many a Corbett or lesser peak the view is all the better for that. Very seldom do the big hill summits give the best views. Here, there had been interesting folds in the mica, and the summit is littered with wavy plates of it. I've seen inferior sculpture at the Academy!

I collected the sack and bundled down to Loch Sloy with its soiled, man-made alterations: a dam with a drought-lined loch, double rows of pylons, scrap concrete. . . . The water is led through to the Inveruglas power station above Loch Lomond, a scheme opened in 1950, the Hydro's first.

The heat of the concrete in the sun seemed to be attracting a plague of black flies, and crossing the dam was like something out of a horror film. I was waving my hat in front of my face in an effort to see. The gutter was half an inch deep in dead flies. At least they did not bite and they soon dropped off once I was on the slope beyond.

I left my tent tied to a pylon to dry, then set off up Ben Vorlich. To distinguish it from the Perthshire Vorlich, near Lochearnhead, it is referred to as "Argyll's Ben Vorlich" though it is in Dunbartonshire and both names, I suppose, will go with regional changes. W. K. Holmes in his gentle book *Tramping Scottish Hills* has a chapter headed "Argyll's Ben Vorlich". W. K. H. was an old man who befriended our gang of enthusiasts when we were youngsters roaming the Ochils from Dollar. Our outlook owes a lot to his teaching.

The way up from the dam leads to some areas of fallen rock which are a weird sight. The Shelter Stone is a pebble in comparison; here, you can climb right into the bowels of the earth it seems. The final slope is a real contrast, the trig point standing almost indecently stark from the green slope of grass. There is another summit 100 yards to the north. Take your pick.

The eastern approaches are long—and beware of the Little Hills; they are an endless succession of bumps and tops. From the dam Vorlich was just two hours up and down, even with some fun among the "Narnia Boulders". There was nothing left to make a brew so I set off down the Hydro road to the banks of Loch Lomond. The glen was full of displaying wheatears, bobbing and flitting their white rumps and darting up into the air for love. Interesting that the old English for this bird is the apt "white arse" but the Victorians changed it when that word had slid down the scale of propriety. In Gaelic it is *clachoran*— little one of the stones.

On the heights the only sign of spring had been the posturings of the ptarmigan, but walking down Coiregrogain it was flaunted in the vivid larch, the uncurling bracken fronds and the extravagance of flowers.

I reached the road at Inveruglas. In 1753 James Wolfe (of Quebec fame) spent some miserable weeks building the road here. He had little good to say of place or people. The tourist boom was still to come, soon enough for Smollett in *Humphrey Clinker* to write, "This is justly stiled the Arcadia of Scotland; and I don't doubt it may vie with Arcadia in everything but climate." Today it was Arcadia, even in climate.

I went down to the Caravan Park and of course the McNivens were at lunch, but he kindly came and showed me where the canoe was waiting. When we turned it over there was some confetti which boded ill for the parcel. It was a mess of polythene and string with only the tins surviving. So no brewing there. A can of coke soon went, though!

I sat by the loch to tidy things up and do some food planning, then paddled off for Tarbet at 1.30. An unwanted jar of jam I donated to the nearest caravan. The commuting owner took my mail to post in Glasgow, which would puzzle the recipients. The paddle down the loch was enjoyable though very hot and the glare off the water was as bad as sun off snow. Although only 20 feet above sea level, Loch Lomond is over 600 feet deep off Tarbet, and has the largest surface area of any British loch.

It is strangely divided into a highland and a lowland section: the former fiord-like, narrow and long, the latter open and covered with woody islands—which gave rise to legends about "floating islands". Its waters supply a whole range of needs—even as far away as Grangemouth on the Forth.

I looked at Wallace's Isle and Inveruglas Isle—the latter has the ruins of a MacFarlane stronghold which was sacked by Cromwell. This was MacFarlane land in the olden days when they had a reputation akin to Rob Roy's, and the moon was known as "MacFarlane's Lantern".

Neil Munro once wrote a description of pulling an oar that went something like "at the end of the first mile you think you are going to die, at the end of the second you decide to keep on till you do die, at the end of the third you find yourself looking round and enjoying the scenery." At that stage I was nearing Tarbet, and pulled in to the slip.

Fruit, milk and rolls were the tit-bits. I stocked up well to replace the mousey items. I also spent a very hot and bad-tempered hour trying to contact Dollar on the phone. Our vaunted G.P.O. improved services at one time gave me an engaged and ringing tone simultaneously.

Tarbet implies a town on a narrow neck between lochs; here it is the neck to the sea at Loch Long. In 1263 Haakon made good use of this position. His son-in-law, Magnus, sailed up Loch Long (the *ship loch*), dragged his longships to Loch Lomond, then went plundering south back to the Clyde. The subsequent Battle of Largs ended the Norse expansion. Haakon retreated to Orkney and died the same year. The Hebrides were ceded to Scotland's Alexander III.

The south end of the loch was rich even then, so was always a target. In the seventeenth century the MacGregor raids on Colquhoun lands were so vicious that they were finally proscribed. In the eighteenth century the famous Rob Roy had a house at Craigrostan until ousted by the Grahams and forced into lawlessness. Rob Roy was at the Battles of Killiecrankie, Glenshiel and Sherrifmuir but died before the "45". He travelled beyond Rannoch, even raided in the far Buchan lands, and also lived in Glen Shira under Campbell protection. He actually died in his bed—but he had taken out an insurance of seven sons.

The canoe was well-loaded when I left: sleeping bag and tent aft, food in front, rucker between my legs, and camera and boots down the side. It was an old canvas kit construction which I had bought for a fiver ten years before. It had been off the West Highlands many times (a great aid in Munro-bagging too) and survived rivers like the Tay and Tweed. I would not swop it for the best of new plastic models. The change in routine was enjoyed and the canoe cheerfully went slap-slap-slap into the hurrying waves as I crossed to Rowchoish on the east shore.

The Ferris Bothy had no water handy so I chose an enchanted spot by the shore to camp. The air was loud with bees, for gean, gooseberry, sycamore and blaeberry were all in flower.

I washed the tins again before opening them. The cream had gone off with the weeks' cooking in the canoe. The strawberries were all right! It would be interesting to see what became of the parcels which had been simply buried in the wilds. I had presumed polythene would have discouraged mice. I had forgotten to buy tea at Tarbet.

I lay only in undies to watch the sun set behind the Cobbler. A quivering highway of gold led across the water. A pair of merganser were briefly shadowed in it. A child's voice came clear across the loch. A train pulsed and died. My daily portion was Romans VIII with its great closing affirmation; the perfect rounding off to a perfect day.

Wednesday 24 April AND UP AGAIN
Colonel Hawker in 1813 noted that ladies making the ascent of Ben Lomond sometimes took a piper with them so as to dance on the summit. Perhaps Sir Hugh Munro took his flute.

Lapping instead of running water was a novel sound on waking. There was a riot of woodland birds calling, too, and I thought I might just hear the first cuckoo. No sooner the thought than the familiar pirate call came across the loch. It was summer!

New roads and plantings were not on my map; but then dealing with plantings is one of the games walkers play. It is a game with a high frustration content and should be in the M.L.C. syllabus. I used a craggy bit where the trees could not grow. A dead goat was discouraging—and a dead woodpecker a delight, or at least its feathers were with their polka dots. I took three feathers back to sew on my hat, so they

did the furthest south to furthest north and were duly left on Ben Hope
to puzzle northern ornithologists.

Ben Lomond is one of the most popular hills in Scotland and has
long been so, though it is no longer regarded as the second highest, as
it once was. From some of the accounts of early ascents one wonders
why it was attempted. Stoddart accorded it "surprise, arising almost to
terror . . . one side forcibly torn off, leaving a stupendous precipice".
Can this be the same douce hill up which Tom Weir, like some cherubic
Pied Piper, led his laughing gangs of local school children?

Thomas Wilkinson describing his tour of 1824 was obviously a convert. "Mountains and their accompaniments are among the finest
specimens of the sublime." Writing of Lomondside, he describes "a
female who was reaping alone; she sang in Erse as she bended over her
sickle; the sweetest human voice I ever heard; her strains were tenderly
melancholy and felt delicious, long after they were heard no more."
Wilkinson sailed across the loch and arrived on the summit with six
men, six women, a black servant and a pony with provisions. Hardy
John Macculloch, 10 years later, brought the hill down to reality: "its
ascent is without toil or difficulty, a mere walk of pleasure." That was
obviously pre-Forestry Commission days. He met two lassies who had
gone up alone—and enthused about their shapely legs.

The favourite speculation concerning the name is the old British
"Llummon", meaning *beacon hill*, which would be appropriate both
for it and the Fife Lomonds. Odd that a Loch Leven lies below the Fife
Lomonds and that that was the older name for Loch Lomond—which
still drains to the Clyde by the River Leven.

Rowardennan gives the great trade route; but I perforce was doing it
from the north side of Ptarmigan Hill, a bloody-minded sort of ascent:
sweating up fire-breaks and with a melancholy cuckoo going like a
perpetual clock. The view was soft—as if seen through a Victorian
varnish-tinted spyglass. The fourth top was the summit.

Back at the tent I procrastinated: wrote up the log, watched a coal
tit, found lots of reasons for lingering. However, the good book is
adamant: "Ye have compassed this mountain long enough: turn you
northward" (Deut. 2:3). The same writer mentions "that goodly
mountain"—perhaps he had the Ben in mind, this southmost of the
Munros. It had a certain milestone quality: I was now embarked on the
south–north trip as well as the larger.

I paddled off with heaven "a fair blue stretch of sky" again, beyond surprise at good days, now. The dazzle was almost soporific. I kept in the middle of the loch. Inversnaid was a landmark with the white hotel bright in the sun. Of Inversnaid were written some of the most quoted of all lines about the Scottish hills; unexpectedly by Gerard Manley Hopkins:

"What would the world be, once bereft
Of wet and wildness? Let them be left,
O let them be left, wildness and wet;
Long live the weeds and the wilderness yet."

Hans Christian Andersen came through to Inversnaid from the Trossachs to sail up and down the loch. The Wordsworths and Coleridge went in reverse order—and called on Scott going home. This was before *The Lady of the Lake* and all that, so gives interesting literary speculations.

A bit along from Inversnaid there was a bold CAVE painted on the rock. This was not a Latin imperative but a crude signposting of Rob Roy's Cave. Bruce had used it in 1306. I went on to land on Island I Vow, a name which had long fascinated. Later Ronald Laing wrote me to say it was murdered Gaelic: Eileann a' Bhogha, *island of the bow*.

It was a small islet—about a bowshot from the shore. Orchids and hyacinth made a scented carpet under the jungle of trees. A chilly barrel-vaulted cell was all that remained of the castle, built by Mac-Farlane of Arrochar who was rewarded for leading 300 Highlanders to the battle of Langside against Mary Queen of Scots. They used this castle when the one at Inveruglas was sacked by Cromwell's troops. The isle was girt by a sandy shore due to the low level of the loch. It would have been a perfect camp site but I had to push on: the next reach is a memory of cows and cuckoos calling from opposing shores.

I put in to collect a parcel from the Ardlui Hotel. It was lunch time so I went into the bar. A lanky lad in a deerstalker was the only other occupant. He had been there in February when I delivered the parcel.

Loch merged imperceptibly into river, the Falloch. Oss and Dubh-craig rose ahead. The holiday paddle was over. I was in the highlands again. I managed to end just one field away from the Inverarnan Hotel where I had arranged to leave the canoe with the Campbells. They were in the throes of re-opening after big alterations—and hoping to build up a climbing clientele again, for the hotel had been a famous one under the long rule of the Girvans.

I ate a colossal meal before starting uphill, and relished the first tea

I had had since camping under Ben Vane. Ben Vorlich was a pleasing peak through a screen of trees. The browns of winter were passing.

> A sudden shout of white
> In Winter's waiting wood:
> Come Spring and see—
> The blackthorn out.

The Ben Glas Burn was reduced to straggly strands, its falls bearing little of the suggested resemblance to the Grey Mare's Tail. The sun was hard in the west; Laoigh's cone split the rays into streamers of silky light. The slope eased and Glen Falloch vanished; instead, ahead, the peaks of tomorrow circled a valley warm with evening. I pitched the tent quickly by the brand mark of an old sheiling: a grey rectangle in the brown hide of heather. A wing of over a hundred geese flew across the yellow sky, straining and calling for the lonely north. Tomorrow they would fly over Ben Hope. In the last light I sewed the Ben Lomond woodpecker feathers to my hat.

Thursday 25 April   THE FIRST HUNDRED THOUSAND

That was the footage total by the day's end. I was now thoroughly fit, and deeply content. Not since childhood had I so relished a spring season. The magic of the sun almost swallowed me whole. It no longer burnt. Perhaps the whole joy lay in being untrammelled; for we so seldom know that freedom these days. Just opening one's eyes, and ears, first thing in the morning, became important. How familiar the sound of water; the erratic burble of grouse. Man is so often an alien in his own country.

Strangely, the notes I read that morning, written by dear Rev. William Still of Aberdeen, took this theme too: "alienation is theological, between God and man; sociological, between man and other men; psychological, between man and himself; and ecological, between man and nature. . . . The first Western man to speak of alienation was not Rousseau, nor Hegel. It was Augustine, and then Calvin who used the concept to emphasize that the problem of sin and evil was not just theological but rational—a breach of man's relationship with God entailing a breach of all other relationships." God so often chooses to speak from the mountain tops; but He will never shout.

When I poked my head out of the tent it was to see the valley white-washed with hoar. Day exploded over Chabhair and I was off at seven into the brightness. Lochan Chabhair was reedy and on the castled ridge above another turquoise pool reflected the clear sky. Beinn Chabhair (Havar), *peak of the antler*, is a rough pile of minor crags and bumps. The purple saxifrage was over: lying tatty as a discarded garment. From the summit I could see eastwards: the only new ground, the rest had all been done—quite a daunting thought.

I went on down to the col beyond; one with a Coire a' Chuilinn on both sides. Near ridges framed Queen Laoigh. I skirted some quite big crags to gain the col the other side of the next Munro where I pitched the tent to dry off the hoar, brewed, then went up *the castle*, An Caisteal. Twistin Hill from Derrydaroch is the most popular route of ascent, but it is a long way over many bumps. All this group need respect in mist or winter. They have some good things but just fail to fire the imagination.

The weather was chilly and breezy back at the tent so I hurried on over Beinn a' Chroin, which is double topped (the name means *hill of the cloven hoof*), with its east summit the higher. On it, years ago, Derry Dunsire won his 102 Munros, the most by any Braeheader before leaving at 15. Ali Smith had 100. A score or more left with 50 plus, always an ambition and resulting in a presentation and various things at school, and from me, a dinner in a luxury hotel. Who says Munro-bagging is not competitive? If two kids had the same number of Munros they would count "Tops", rather as football teams counted goal averages, to fix their league positions.

The east side of Beinn a' Chroin is twisted, so the burns overlap rather than set off from a single col. The Ishag, going south, is another that changes its name perpetually: Ishag, Lochlarig, L. Doine, L. Voil, Balvaig, L. Lubnaig, Leny, Teith and finally Forth. North flows the Falloch to double round to Loch Lomond and the Clyde, while just over Cruach Ardrain, the next Munro, the streams join the long chain ending in the Tay. Three great estuaries all start in this group. Being in the heart of things I stopped for lunch and an hour lying in the sun.

I have read of several dedicated long-distance men, who would all have had a fit at this sort of behaviour. They set themselves rigorous miles per day and nibble chocolate as they walk rather than break the rhythm. They are welcome to their approach! I cannot afford eight bars of chocolate a day, anyway. My spot was so quiet that the wind in the grass sounded quite noisy. (Civilisation's decibel level was hard to bear at the end of the trip.) A beetle crawling up the rock beside me was noticed because it was *heard*.

It was too early to stop for the day so I went on again. There was never a shortage of further hills. The three I had done form a natural trio and the next two were a natural pair: Cruach Ardrain and Beinn Tulaichean. I reached the saddle between them by cutting round under Stob Glas which is quite a craggy bulk, with winter, if not summer, routes on it. I went up the Cruach, the *high slopes*, first.

It is a "goodly mountain" from any angle; the horseshoe on the Crianlarich side being the popular circle of route, though the start is made difficult by plantings of trees.

I met people on top. We chatted, and finding one lad had worked with the Hydro at Rannoch, we revelled in mutual enthusiasm for that area. This led him to ask if I, by chance, knew Hamish Brown.

We repassed going to and from Tulaichean and my wee Rollei had some foreground for once. I half thought of going on for Ben More and Stobinian but was content to rest below them on the col. A flash flood had gouged out a great gash down the hillside under the cliffs of Creagan Dubha. The *black cliff* was well named, a deep cleft in it would make a winter route. I did not linger under it: there was a nice, clean big boulder among all the old mossy ones.

I pitched the tent twice, for as soon as it was up the wind changed 180°, a dirty trick. It was a site remembered for its tipsy wheatears. For the first day in ages I had seen no deer. Just sheep. As I was in early (5 p.m.) there was ample festering.

Slowly the hills had clouded and the weather felt warm and muggy. The early cirrus had become hill cloud. It looked like rain, as Noah said.

Friday 26 April   TO BONNY STRATHYRE

It did not rain that night as expected. However, I was not far above the camp before I was into swirling cloud, so followed the snow edge of the south-west ridge to the cone of Am Binnean or Stobinian as it is more often called. Even with a cagoule on, the wind felt bitterly cold. Blue glimpses tempted me to linger but eventually I went shivering off in self-defence. No navigation problems, the ridge down was rimmed with iron-hard snow. Stobinian, I have noticed in several winter visits, is always much more icy than Ben More, its twin to the north. Stobinian's cone has a sliced-off look which makes the pair unmistakable when seen from elsewhere.

Ben More is just the *big hill* (it is 3,843 feet) and the col between it and Stobinian is merely Bealach-eadar-dha-Bheinn, the *pass between the hills*. Ben More was clear, but Stobinian stayed in cloud longer. It is a thrawn hill, but obviously popular, for it was the dirtiest I had met—every cranny stuffed with papers and cans.

It had been one of my first Scottish hills. On it that day I had found some white heather, seen my first long-tailed tits, and, in a wood, had the alarming experience of being mixed up in a herd of deer who had winded, but not seen, me, and who went charging off to leap right over my head where I lay on a bank. The normal way up, from near Ben More Farm, takes the north-west ridge which is bounded by a corrie which holds snow well into summer. In the 1890's a climber slipped on hard snow down this corrie and was killed—one of the first recorded climbing accidents. The hill produces some big avalanches at times.

The worst accident on Ben More was an aircraft crash one winter. The plane hit just below the summit—fifty feet up or to either side would have cleared it. There are still tiny fragments lying about. I picked up three links from a metal watch-strap.

Scott wrote, "On high Ben More green mosses grow", and cutting down from the bealach between the hills I found myself bogged in some of them. After a brew I took the burn down to Inverlochlarig, where I arrived among a scattering of guinea fowl. Not long after, cutting across fields, I came on a shiny black bird standing by a burn. It seemed to have no head, till after some yelling on my part, it unfolded and became a cormorant. It must have been tired for it sat tight.

I was following the south shore of the two lochs leading to Balquidder, to avoid the tarred road on the north shore. Loch Doine was boggy and plantings had destroyed the old path—it is high time we had legislation to control *all* changes of land use. The path still ran along by Loch Voil, a delectable reach with the Braes of Balquidder across the water. I crossed the hump bridge to visit the shop; and to pay respects to Rob Roy who is buried here, at the old churchyard.

I left the village in a gaggle of kids quarrelling their way home from school, but they slowly dropped away as I walked the old back road to Strathyre, through the woods that ring another *hill of the fairies* (Beinn an-t-Shithein).

The Ben Sheann Hotel made me welcome. They had a parcel. Suddenly life became hectic again. I rang Robert Elton, due to bring mail, to see if he could come 24 hours earlier than planned. I then rang my brother David to fix up delivering the wanted supplies. I repacked a bit—and washed everything I could. (Washing and wearing everything at once presented certain problems.) Finally I splashed, happy as an otter, in a bath. Hotels do have some good points after all.

I carried out food from the parcel and ate in the woods. Since the camp in the King's Field another week had given eighteen further Munros. Now I would begin to work into the heart of the land, up to the Cairngorms, then the Lochaber sweep, then on to the Great Glen. It was a bit frightening. There was such a long way still to go.

IV

TRANS TAY AND TUMMEL

I'm just a donnert gangerel
On a by-way through the murk
But I ken the yett that's best, ma bairn,
An' its toll I dinna shirk.

It'll tak ye ower some muckle braes
And ower wi snaws an' frost
But in the back end o' yer days, ma bairn,
Nae guid thing ye'll hae lost.

Aye, there's mony paths tae tempt ye
But only yin be best;
So tak the ane ma bonnie bairn—
'Tis a hunner o' the rest.

Saturday 27 April AND THE RAINS CAME TUMBLING DOWN
Tea in bed was quite normal I reflected, even if eight o'clock was not, and the bonny lassie bringing it in was a decided improvement. Most of my clothes were hanging out of the window. I had had quite a bath the night before. Being above the kitchen and the room being blessed with conversational piping I wondered what they had made of my exuberant use of hot water. The smell of bacon and eggs lured me down after some packing and a hack at the growing beard. It was a pattern of hotel use that was to become familiar.

Strathyre is a pleasant corner, at its best today in the spring sun with the chestnut spires dropping petals like snow. The village used to have the odd name of "Nineveh" when it was just a crofting community. It changed with the coming of the railway. Now the railway has gone. The west side of Loch Lubnaig is good walking—away from the rat-race of the road. I wandered about taking photographs, and in the shop could not resist buying a tea called "Green Gunpowder" as it was one we had often drunk in Morocco. The Inn provided conversation and coffee; recently redecorated by the Betteridges, it had appliqué-work pictures of the planets, done by a school girl, which I really liked. The

D

antique shop was hard to resist. Mr King had pinned a notice on the door requesting visitors to "call at the wee cottage if out".

I had just returned to the Ben Sheann Hotel when Robert Elton arrived: another old S.M.C. worthy. In Morocco, at 69, he knocked-off five 4,000-metre peaks in a week, and I was recently reading of a route of his done in Ardgour in 1927! He was to leave for Crete in three days' time. We lunched together and then while he went for a walk I used his Dormobile as an office to deal with the mail. The first slides of the trip, from Mull, showed that the new Rollei worked well. The replies to three questionnaires came too, and I suddenly felt I had been away some time.

The Walk started again in the afternoon with a wander down Loch Lubnaig, a pretty loch: a bend in the middle gives two views for the price of one. Even with a tarred road alongside, it was quiet, and I felt "Healthy, free and the world before me", in Walt Whitman's phrase. Which is why I walked so innocently into a meteorological ambush. Just before I left the road, lined with blackthorn and primroses, Robert drove up, his car full of pussy willows and new larch branches.

The forestry folk as usual had kept their doings secret from the O.S., and I had a bit of scrabbling about before gaining the right of way through to Glen Ample. Some hens in plus-fours told me I was trespassing. There now "went up a mist from the earth and watered the whole face of the ground". It rained in a very determinedly damp and dreary manner, which later turned to a porridgy sleet. Just short of the col I found a corner tucked in beside the burn, so quickly pitched the tent and piled into bed. There was a certain novelty watching the sleet sway and dance across the landscape. Later in the trip rain became a dominant feature, terribly depressing at times, but ultimately accepted and in the end just ignored if need be. The trip finished with as long a run of pernicious weather as it had started fair.

Robert had brought fresh food, so steak and onions, Marina's weekly baking, spinach, and fruit were relished. I also found I had brought on a bit of cast iron decoration which I had meant to leave in the car. Here it was as useful as an ashtray on a motorbike, so was dumped, sadly. There were odd things found, or hidden, all through the trip, which may or may not be collected in the future. When I blew the candle out the rain was still coming down hard and a poor moon was hirpling among the clouds, hurrying the day away.

Sunday 28 April AND THE SNOWS CAME FALLING AFTER

I was as cosy in the sleeping bag as a cat inside its fur but as there was no pretty maid to bring tea I perforce had to uncurl and stretch. When I stuck my nose out the tent it was to find it had snowed overnight. As my last memory had been of accelerating rain, like horses breaking from trot to canter to gallop, the snow was a surprise. The walls of the tent were streaming, but it all ran into the ground. I blessed Dave's ingenious tent design.

I had a long, contouring rise to follow, with odd crags to go round. The sheep had broken trail quite often. I was still walking with eyes in pockets—one brief glimpse down to Loch Earn was all the view I had. I was sorry Stuc a' Chroin could not offer better, for as an opportunist youth it had been my first ski Munro.

I had planned to meet a friend in Glencoe on the Friday night, but got as far as Glen Ogle to find the road blocked and had walked back to Strathyre before giving up and crawling into the woods to sleep under the trees. It snowed all night. I remember the brilliance which one candle on a tree-stump produced on the silent, delectable bivy. On the Saturday I thumbed a lift to Edinburgh and trained home. I knew the local climbing club had a bus trip the next day, so joined them, taking skis. These were a new toy, and having done Largo Law and then White Wisp it seemed a natural progression, for the third day on the planks, to do a Munro. We all set off from Lochearnhead for Stuc a' Chroin, myself with the climbers' rude remarks about skis chasing me ahead. They found me asleep by the cairn, fair trakit, but there three hours ahead of the plodders. I had only had piste bindings and shudder at the memory. We must have been fit once. As all I could do was traverse and "sit-down turns", the descent was quite hilarious. The long traverse down Glen Ample still let me in hours ahead again. There and then I became a convert to ski mountaineering.

There was no sunbathing on the top today. I was forced well along above Coire Fhuadaraich before it was safe to cut down to the col. The new snow and the old cornice-rim barred progress earlier. My hands froze as soon as I took them out of my pockets and my eyes streamed in the cold wind. I dropped down the lee side and left the rucksack, then went up a sheltered rake and along the fence to the top of Ben Vorlich. As the next storm seemed due it was a case of walking round the trig point and off down again.

At the rucksack I cowered in a cranny to eat while the storm blew past. I could see a line of figures on the slopes of the Stuc, at odd moments their voices came loud and clear down the wind. Most ascents are made from Loch Earn so I was looking down the wrong side, so to speak, not that I could see much of the well-named Gleann an Dubh Choirein. It runs down for five miles then curves round east to become Glen Artney, scenery Ochil-like and douce, though once a royal hunting forest. Scott's *The Lady of the Lake* begins here with the well known lines, "The stag at eve had drunk his fill . . . in lone Glen Artney's hazel shade."

The clouds followed me down the glen, the rain forcing me into sweaty "skins". Ruins galore told of past life in the valley. A right of way leads over to Callander—one I had followed as a schoolboy on a cycle and not seen since. The tracks grew surer and after stark Glen Artney Lodge the landscape became tamer. I had a brew where a bridge crossed the Water of Ruchill, sheltering under it until the rain stopped.

My log cried that "down the glen seemed all uphills", but the nine miles of tarred road were quite enjoyable. Fields of pampered sheep gave way to fields of pampered cows. Cultybraggan camp brought back memories of C.C.F. days. Comrie was very welcome. A new bungalow suburb had house-names like "Fairhaven" and "Dunroamin". I went into the Royal Hotel for an hour's break over a vast pot of tea. The village was Sabbath-quiet.

I wandered on up a brae towards Glen Lednock: up past Twenty Shilling Wood and Pollyrigg. The road is squeezed in between hill (topped by the Melville Monument) and gorge (pot holes, The Devil's Cauldron). Above this wooded slice of country the glen opens up into a noisy strath, with cushies in the trees, pheasants honking, curlews chasing and yelping, redshanks, peewits and pied pipers—a real cacophony. The glen had a prosperous air. The school was newly painted white. From Invergeldie I followed the old track up the side burn. One cow turned out to be a bull and I nearly went screw-eyed trying to keep one eye on him and one on my feet on the gooey path.

I tucked my tent in by the burn and was glad to take the boots off; today and tomorrow gave about forty miles, half of it on tarred roads, the longest I would have to face. My feet were unmarked. It snowed hard for an hour and then for the rest of the night gave a right *helm o' weet*. I was reminded of a lad on Rhum who declared that if the rain

was custard and the rock was pudding, he would happily eat his way up
the hills.

Monday 29 April   A PEAK AND A PASS

I had little encouragement in the morning. Storms chased each other's
tails down the funnel of glen. Dennis Gray writes in his autobiography:
"Climbing is not easily analysed, partly because both its motivations
and its rewards are so variable." I went off into the snow showers quite
happily, though I am sure others without the motivation or reward
would have thought it daft. Churchill climbed Monte Rosa—and
never went near a hill again; yet we see severely handicapped people
driven to them compulsively. John Emery, who had lost his toes from
frostbite in the Himalayas, told how it "moved and excited beyond
description". The basic thing is that it does do just this, at all levels
and skills and in all the variations climbers play. Let all respect each
other.

My game satisfied me today. It sometimes felt like snakes and ladders
with its ups and downs, but provided I played on I had no doubt the
square marked END would come. A track up the glen helped, then the
hollow of a burn let me sneak up out of the wind. Once on the heights
I blew along in great style.

Innumerable hares would break and run, spraying up the powdery
snow from the heather. We wrote brown tracks through the grey
wilderness. Ben Chonzie (or Ben-y-Hone as it is pronounced) teems
with hares as few other places—I have counted fifty at one time. There
were a lot of grouse too. I met a mountain blackbird (or ring ouzel), a
species which seems to be increasing. This is the *hill of the deer cry*.

The toil of snow-covered heather gave way to blaeberry and then
moss and stone. A hoary cairn turned out to be a grouse butt, but a
fence led to the top. A cross of old fence stabs, stones and posts, all
hoary and glowing, looked just like a Friedrich painting. There was no
view down Loch Turret, nor to Lawers, which is seen at its best from
here. Previous knowledge was welcome as I scurried off.

My hat was pulled down and a hanky tied over my nose to keep off
the stinging icy particles. I went along the plateau and down the
long flank to another new track. As I trotted down it eased off. A
skylark was singing its heart out in the mist, very much the "unbodied
joy" of Shelley's poem.

Plans to keep to the tops and traverse them to Loch Tay were abandoned. I brewed at the tent and then took the pass I had once used with a bike twenty years before: up by Sput Rollo to a reservoir. The fall was lowly, humbled by the weeks of no rain. Sandpipers, the singing heralds of summer, went past silently—probably wishing they had stayed in sunny Morocco. The loch in some ways improved the view. I nearly stood on a grouse nest: eight grey eggs and one ruddy one.

I have always maintained passes are as satisfying as peaks (and more rational) and this one, with its feeling of being a portal to the Tay, is a good example. Its descent by the Finglen had many tempting camp spots. Woodcock and cuckoo flew past as I descended to the Inn at Ardeonaig. The setting has a rich, English quality to it, a contrast to the heather above and to the many ruins left from the evictions in the 1820's.

Tenpence produced five big cups of tea. The room was a collector's den: carved iron tables with brass tops, an old gun, real and converted paraffin lamps, a miner's lamp, prints, an array of stoneware including several "pigs". I set out again at 5.30 for the eight miles of road to Killin, arriving at seven, without any aches or pains. A roadside notice said: "No fishing beyond this fence." As the loch lay half a mile away it conjured up images of mighty castings. Firbush Point and Fiddler's Bay were two nice names. Lawers showed white in a brief clearance and Tarmachan made a backcloth to the falls at the west end of the town. The island below the bridge is the burial ground of the Clan McNab.

McNab of McNab at once conjures up a painting by Raeburn. This chief, Francis, *b.* 1734, stood six-foot three and his hat another foot. He backed up a wedding proposal with the enticement that he owned the most beautiful burial ground in Scotland. He never did marry, but his numerous progeny fought on many a battlefield. (Three at Waterloo.) When he died in 1816 he left debts of £35,000. The Highlands were bled to try to maintain the chief's show in fashionable Edinburgh or London, the people were cleared for sheep or deer—a state which remains to today, financial gain for a few owners being still maintained as right and proper. The people were betrayed, their land stolen—and they do not forget, though, tied into a feudal system, they can do little about it.

To revert to the McNabs. One tale tells how a party was robbed as they returned from Crieff, by the McNish of Loch Earn. The McNab had twelve sons, so he gathered them all, and hinted darkly: "The night is the night if the lads were the lads." They scurried off with a boat to Loch Earn and rowed out to the enemy stronghold to slaughter all there and return with the chief's head. A bearded head appears in the McNab arms.

It was a Killin minister who first translated the New Testament into Gaelic, his son, and successor, translating the Old Testament. The church and hotel stand in a corner of the sleepy town (main industry, tourism). The church was built in 1744 but replaces an older one. Its seven-sided font is unique and could be a thousand years old. The most interesting relics are the "Healing Stones" of St Fillan (now in the old tweed mill) which are very ancient and said to have unusual powers. From here, westwards, the whole valley is steeped in religious lore.

I went into the Youth Hostel and had it almost to myself. The Peevors had a parcel for me. They lit a fire and we sat before it and set the world right. I was glad to have the road bit over. Its saddest element had been the toll of wildlife: I had seen a slaughtered squirrel, mole, several hares, various mice, a shrew, a pheasant, a lamb, a hedgehog, a grouse, a frog and any number of unidentifiable bits of fluff and feather. At eleven we took our yawning ways to bed. In the food locker I found a slip of paper giving a curious example of racial prejudice. Perhaps it was left by an American. It analysed us all: "The Scots, who will keep the Sabbath, and anything else they can get their hands on; the Welsh, who pray on their knees, and on their neighbours; the Irish, who don't know what they want but will fight each other to get it; the English, who consider themselves a race of self-made men, thereby absolving the Almighty of a great responsibility."

Tuesday 30 April KILLIN TIME
A day when I was quite glad to do nothing and rest afterwards. A writer in 1799 used the term "a gloom of settled vapour", which described the weather well. Another writer declared "as for climate, there are nine months of winter, three months of spring, and there is no summer at all." Which just shows how little things change; an article in a recent Swiss magazine about climbing in Skye ended, "Hélas! la réputation de l'île ne ment pas: il pleut!"

Killin is an old site. "Cill Fhinn", the cell or burial place of Fingal, some would have it, with a stone behind the town marking the spot. The

Campbells arrived in the fifteenth century when the king rewarded Sir Colin with the Barony of Lawers for helping capture his predecessor's assassins. Finlarig was added in 1503 and the Campbells flourished as they were wont. Black Duncan "causit saw akornes and seid of fir therein, and plantit in the samen young fir and birk anno 1613 and 1614", for which we are grateful to this day, Tayside being leafy rather than barren. Just to the north, in Glen Lyon, in the eighteenth century, the first larch in Scotland was planted. So were beeches, and Glen Lyon remains a specially fine sight in its autumn colours. The Campbell power has now gone, the last Earl of Breadalbane sold much to the Hydro Board. The McNabs are named back to the time of David I, but gained some notoriety at the field of Dalrigh where they tried to capture Robert the Bruce. All good stuff for the tourists.

I was brought back to earth by hearing my name yelled. It was Brian Hall who had once been at Glenmore Lodge and was now Warden of Stirling University's centre on Loch Rannoch. I lunched at the hotel which reflects the importance of Killin as a fishing centre. Inertia led me back to the hostel. In the school porch some girls were trying out dance steps while others produced "mouth music"—quite oblivious of the spectator.

Chris Peevor and I sat by the fire and talked the night away. Solitude can be sweet as honey—but try living on honey only all the time!

Wednesday 1 May   CIRCUITS AND BUMPS

> "We shall grow old apace and die
> Before we know our liberty. . . .
> Come, let us goe, while we are in our prime;
> And take the harmlesse follie of the time"
>
> HERRICK

That came over the radio in a May day selection! The local cuckoo had roused me at seven. I went off, down by the lochside, passing the Campbell ruin of Finlarig shrouded and greened over on a knoll. There is even a hanging tree. The local courting couples alone go near it.

Paddle steamers used to ply up and down the loch but they and the railway station are all gone. Finlarig Power Station alone was new to me and I followed its pipeline up the hillside. The map happily showed a path but there were so many animal tracks that I was not certain whether I found it. I cut up through small crags and over boggy wet to gain the contouring Hydro road. I went into the mist which swirled and scattered like water stirred up by passing oars. Killin through the clouds was like Keswick seen from Latrigg.

I followed the road round to the lairig where the public road cuts over to Glen Lyon and found a tailor-made camp site of a tiny sward in the loop of a burn. A notice about stalking on Tarmachan asked walkers to contact the factor—at Brechin. The other side of the road is National Trust land: the Lawers range which I would nibble at today and go over tomorrow. The Trust, with its honeypot ideas, has brought thousands to the hills here, with the result we have the country's only paint-spotted route along the hilltops. There is an unsightly eroded track, sleepers over the bogs, a visitor centre . . . an incredible lack of conservation from a body given land to keep for the nation. Lawers is famed for its Alpine flowers so on the summit is a notice to this effect and people, with no botanical interest, go off to see! It makes one shudder. The same approach is seen in Torridon and Glencoe.

The western arm of Lawers has a couple of Munros and after a brew I headed off for them, with the idea of circling round to Meall nan Tarmarchan. Meall Corranaich is the *bracken corrie hill*. As I went straight up it, the cloud scampered ahead and it was actually clear on top. I arrived dripping. Lawers was very white, with its height of just under 4,000 feet. I rimmed on old snow, along and down to the col, and on an easy pull up Meall a' Choire Leith. Azalea was in flower. An asthmatic golden plover wheezed ahead. This is a peak only the wayward Munro-bagger is apt to go for, but it has a good view being out on a limb over Glen Lyon. There is a great deal of Ben Lawers facing north and few walkers know it.

My first-ever juvenile trip brought me here. From my home at Dollar I had cycled through the Trossachs and crossed Loch Lomond to the Arrochar Alps, then pushed up to Crianlarich (Ben More) and on to Killin. I did Meall nan Tarmachan from the lairig then started off down to Glen Lyon, at that time on an unsurfaced road; no dam either. A tyre blew out but I was welcomed to a Scripture Union camp at Bridge of Balgie and the next day, while the bus brought a new tyre from Aberfeldy, I joined a mass assault on Lawers up these golden shoulders on the Glen Lyon side. The next day Schiehallion was done on the way to my own camp at Blair Atholl—and another Munro-bagging addict had been born.

Heading for the lairig road I found a delightful waterfall that made a picnic spot. I happily fell asleep there so had to go skelping on when I woke as I was expecting visitors at 5.30 at the tent. On the ridge up to Tarmachan I found a broken Stevenson's Frame which was odd. The way up was all lumps and hollows, lochans and snow flanks—some steep enough to need dodging. Bad weather had been blowing in again from the west and the fangs of the fine western reaches of Tarmachan soon vanished. The summit was bleak; streaming mist, which silvered garments at once. The snow rims forced me well round before I could break down. The tent was reached at 4.30. At 5.20 Ann Winning, Peter Miller and "Bramble" arrived, having driven along from Aberfeldy after school. We sat in the car in the rain drinking chocolate, recalling many familiar situations.

Ann had taught at Braehead for several years. Peter was one of her Breadalbane climbing protégés. Could he join me for Skye? Knowing them both, I was happy enough, though I had hoped for a solo trip of the Cuillins, but that would depend so much on weather: *la réputation de l'île*, etc. "Bramble" was Ann's new Jack Russell puppy: still at the stage of being all prickles and piddles. . . . When they drove off I demolished the fresh food they had brought, then read their Sunday papers. Ann had been asked if she could let me have an old pullover and took me at my word, delivering one liberally splattered with paint. Worn outside-in it looked respectable, I hoped. Daylight fizzled out like a dying candle.

Thursday 2 May   LAWERS TUSSLE

The wild night led into a wild day but eventually I packed up the camp and squelched off. Beinn Ghlas had a deal of slobbery snow on it but it was from the col beyond, for the Lawers ascent, that it became deeper, and conditions quite vile. I slithered or slipped often enough, and now and then hail showers would have me withdrawing into my waterproofs like a tortoise. The cairn felt an unhealthy place to linger, as my hair tingled with electricity. I took a bearing and slithered off quickly.

After crossing an unimportant bump I headed up the sharp, pointed, Top of An Stuc, a summit for which I already had a healthy respect. Years before we had crossed it after days of rain, when it had suddenly frozen to become lethally slippery. It is steep and shoots off into flanking corries. To the south is the finest rock face profile I know, much better than the Merrick one. From yesterday's western arm I had

seen a rake flanking An Stuc which I was able to find even in today's
storm. It led to a feared problem: the snow rim of the corrie head of the
Fin Glen. This was so wide that it was not possible to look over without
going to the edge and that was not on, as there could have been a
soggy cornice. The light had the dazzling white quality associated with
conditions of white-out. Seeing anything was difficult.

I said rude things and began to grope upwards, vibrams proving
most insecure on schisty slabs all plastered in slobbery snow and the
tent pole making a rather poor alpenstock. Each step had to be gingerly
tested. In the cutting wind it was not pleasant work. Gusts would swing
me round violently. The heavy pack seemed twice its weight. Willy-
nilly I climbed An Stuc.

I took a bearing and set off again. The descent was steeper and gave
another tussle. Despite the wind, bare hands had to be used to deal with
the mixture of rotten schist, ice, mud and snow. The slope ran away
down into the glaring white, but, visible or not, I knew too well how
far I would go if I slipped. In these circumstances you just don't!
With hindsight I reckon it was the most dangerous bit of the whole trip.

On the col I went through that peculiar sensation of bringing life
back to frozen fingers and then used them to stuff food into my mouth.
I felt so bloody I decided I might as well go on—conditions could
hardly become worse. Meall Garbh was reached over its endless
rough bumps. Meall Greigh lay away south, and my descent to Glen
Lyon was northwards, but the rucksack could not be left or it might
never be found again. So I had more dogged compass work and even
felt satisfied to end bang on the desired cairn. I back-tracked and swung
round and down till I could stuff the compass away knowing the water
I splashed through could only lead to Glen Lyon. I came out of the
cloud at 5.30. It broke up, and a bold patch of blue appeared. Wet feet
pounded down soft, wet slopes, the route all blissfully downhill. I
paused on a knoll with a glittering view right up the glen: silver snake
of river and rich green of fields running west to vanish in an explosion
of cloud and sun triggered off by sunset colours.

At Rorromore I greeted a shepherd and collected two ewes who
would walk on ahead and not let me pass. At Balnahanaid I collected a
great flock of rams who were plainly hoping for a hand-out. When the
shepherd drove up they soon swopped their affection. I crossed the
bridge to Camusvrachan.

Dr Fulton had converted an old church into an attractive house and garden: Cille Fionn. She was at home, luckily, though my first greeting came from a Yorkshire terrier and a Dachshund with one eye. (In my log I wrote it down as a Dachstein with one eye!) I collected my parcel and was let out by a gate at the back which led straight on to the hillside.

I wandered up through a larch forest until I found a perfect ledge perched above the burn. But I had little time to relish it: I was over 1,000 feet and the cloud base was at 2,000 feet. Darkness came pressing down with the clouds. I soon crawled in and started a glorious feed. Weight would be easiest carried internally, I decided.

Friday 3 May   LAID DOWN MY HEAD, TOMPHUIBIL

A junction in the burn just above the camp tempted me to take the west fork, hoping to add a Corbett before turning east along the run of Rannoch Munros, but a real lashing of hail and snow was easiest dealt with by turning my back on it so I was battered up on to Carn Gorm. There were big herds of deer everywhere.

This group of hills I knew well because their northern slopes drop down to the Black Wood of Rannoch where Braehead School had had a bothy at which scores of boys and girls were first introduced to camping and the hills. The Black Wood is a superb remnant of the old forests that covered Scotland once. Some of the pines are 200 years old. Much was burnt to try to displace the lawless men who took refuge in it, such as the local "Rob Roy", a Cameron known as "Sergeant Mor". After Culloden he had gathered a band and they had refused to surrender themselves, their arms or their tartan. The old mansion at Dall is now Rannoch School, originally modelled on Gordonstoun. To the east is Carie where the Jacobite Robertson chief, in 1746, had his house—and brought to it General Cope's carriage after Prestonpans. As there were no roads west of the A9 it had to be carried bodily over rivers and bogs and braes.

The previous knowledge was useful again and I was able to keep going even when the icy showers came whipping in. The first week in May is rather known for being dirty—thereafter the best weather of the year normally follows. The next Munro was another *rough hill*, Meall Garbh, it was followed by a long, rocky waste. The fences are not navigational aids. Carn Mairg is the group's highest summit, a rocky one. An old iron ladder stood over the wreck of a fence, an odd reminder of the wealthy days in the past. I skirted Meall Liath to slope down to the col for Creag Mhor, the southern outlier which so dominates lower Glen Lyon. It has two tops and provides the usual doubts, for whichever you are on the other appears higher.

Many snow patches, contourings and flounderings later I was dropping into Gleann Mor, the secret valley moating Schiehallion to the south. The peak showed as a long ridge, not the classic cone as seen along Loch Rannoch. The peak's symmetry tempted the Astronomer Royal, Maskelyne, to conduct experiments on it in 1774 to try to determine the earth's weight and mass.

Isaac Newton had suggested experimenting with a peak whose mass would exert a pull on a plumb line held nearby. Several decades passed before the Royal Society backed the experiment in Britain. Finding the right mountain was the first task. There were no maps to help. The technical details are beyond me, but the experiment needed 43 different sightings on stars, and the measuring of angles to one three-thousandth of a degree of accuracy. The ten-foot telescope would take a week's work for twelve men to shift round the hill. Two years of surveying went into determining the hill's shape—then the calculations began. Their astronomical clock, after adventures in St Helena, Schiehallion, the U.S.A. and in the Ben Nevis Observatory, now resides in the Edinburgh Met. Office. Hutton, another F.R.S., one of the surveyors, was the first person to link similar heights on a map by lines—so Schiehallion saw the birth of contours which are now taken for granted.

Gleann Mor has some limestone so shows up as bright green among the heathery browns. The river has carved out weird channels, and I nearly fell into Uamh Tom a' Mhor—Big Tom's cave. I pitched the tent to dry it off in the breeze. Deer, very grey in colour, moved past on stilted legs. I set off at four o'clock to add Schiehallion, and at six I was off again, having been up and down, brewed and packed up. It was a real treat to romp up unladen—and without contending with vile conditions.

Schiehallion is the *fairy hill of the Caledonians*. It is Rannoch's local showpeak so we from Braehead had been up it with many school gangs. Its north flank is a great sweep which in winter can give good practice in crampon use. The view today petered out before the hills of Glencoe but the loch winked a friendly eye. Dunalasdair Reservoir was low and I hoped rain would not cause it to rise suddenly, for this often wiped out many birds' nests. Kinloch Rannoch is misnamed, for Kinloch means *head of*, yet it sits at the foot of Loch Rannoch. On a clear day you can see from North Berwick Law to Lochnagar to Ben Nevis from the summit of Schiehallion.

Descending the glen the deer gave way to sheep. I hit the old Wade road at White Bridge and collected another parcel from Mr Forest, the roadman, who has created a fine garden beside the high and lonely miles he maintains. We chatted till hunger drove me to excuse myself. Near the top of the pass at Tomphuibil I found a secluded spot among disused quarry workings. There is an old ice-house nearby. I pitched with the door facing Schiehallion. The poet Thomas Gray had the cheek to call it "that monstrous creature". It was after eight when I began brewing and I was lying there in blissful ease when a roar and pounding feet betrayed a visitor. David grinned in at the door.

He dumped a pile of mail on me and said to come along to the Dormobile for coffee. This was an unscheduled meeting. He and Marina were taking the bike to Kincraig so that I could have it to get over some dull A9 road stretches later on. Always an opportunist, I said I would be happy to use it on the morrow. At the Dormobile I scrounged fresh bread, bacon and eggs. Kenneth was in the back "sleeping". Marina produced coffee and Turkish Delight. They had gone to leave mail with Mr Forest, only to find I had just been—a day early. David soon guessed where I would be camping.

They had come up through Aberfeldy which has the most famous of all Wade bridges. It has even appeared on a British stamp. This pass is at 1,270 feet, then drops to the single arch of Tummel Bridge before heading over by Dalnacardoch to the A9 line. I walked home to the coldest night of the trip. The stars were pulsing in massed array and there was a big, blowing moon. The black-headed gulls called all night on the loch.

Marina wrote later to say the next night they were back at Rannoch. Kenneth refused to go to sleep and kept pulling the curtain aside to look along the road for his uncle who appeared at the oddest times. "Eesh-eesh" was as near as he could get to Hamish and this he kept repeating. At home, too, a telephone call would have him grabbing my map board and tracing along the magic pins that marked the route.

Saturday 4 May   CAM' YE BY KILLIECRANKIE, O?
I was brewing early in self defence, for the cold was dagger sharp. The tent pegs stuck to fingers—not usual in May. A gigantic sun soon throbbed in the haze and before most folk were awake I was spinning

down to Foss and Loch Tummel. Boats were moored on top of their reflections. Schiehallion took on its cone shape, trailing a cloud like a volcano.

Beyond the mirror of loch I crossed the Coronation Footbridge. This whole area has been laid out with paths and tracks and the Hydro have created lochs which look fine in the woodland setting. Ben Vrackie and Ben-y-Ghlo form a mountain backcloth, well seen from the 130-foot-high new bridge over the Garry. It cost £300,000 in 1968. The railway viaduct, over 500 feet long, cost £5,730 when it was built.

The nature trail (N.T.S.) showed a ruined chimney where Robert the Bruce rested after the rout at Methven—a day lost partly by Pembroke breaking a sacred tradition and attacking the newly-crowned king on a Sunday. They went on to capture and kill Bruce's brother and they grabbed his wife, daughter and sisters from the sanctuary of St Duthac. Two of these royal ladies were hung in a cage from the walls of Berwick.

Gilpin called Killiecrankie "an ample specimen of the sublime", the sort of praise it has endured ever since. With an ever-changing A9, Wade's old road, the railway and pylons all squeezed into the defile, besides the river, it holds its sublimity wondrously well. The N.T.S. have a small centre with a display on the Battle of Killiecrankie—another where a dead man won the day. Dundee's highlanders routed Mackay's troops, winning the day for James II, but Claverhouse himself was mortally wounded. Macaulay has described the battle, and Scott of course. Rob Roy was taken along by his father and had his first taste of fighting there. The highlanders were unable to pass Dunkeld despite their victory, and the loss of their leader resulted in the campaign fizzling out. Only a haunting song remains—and up in Blair Castle you can see Bonnie Dundee's breastplate, with a hole in it.

I collected a parcel at Killiecrankie Hotel and waited there for the Broons to catch up. I was chatting to a couple who turned out to be from Dollar, and who knew us as schoolkids. The miles up the A9 to Blair Atholl were not enjoyable. I booked in at the Tilt Hotel and started the usual game of trying to wash and wear things at the same time. I spent the evening with Dewi and Maggi Jones who had once worked at Fife's outdoor centre and now lived at Blair Atholl.

The Atholl estate is another which has a long tradition of tree-planting, one duke being known as "the Planting Duke". Timber for shipbuilding was important to the area and the introduction of iron hulls a disaster until the railways came with their call for sleepers. By 1830 over 140 million larches had been planted. The trees at Bruar Falls had been planted following a visit from Robert Burns. The poet had left some verses, speaking through the Bruar Water, pleading for trees. The castle is open to the public, and is interesting. On our first visit six of us, kids, were thoroughly spoilt by a nice old guide (rather to the resentment of a bus group he was meant to be leading) and it was only later we found that he was the Duke of Atholl himself. During the "45" the castle suffered what was to be the last ever siege in Great Britain, an odd one as the Jacobite leader Lord George Murray was besieging his brother, the earl. The Dukedom was conferred in Queen Anne's day.

I had my usual mail-and-logistics evening till late. I wrote to Mike Keates with new ideas which would allow the last two weeks to be done without having to carry the tent. Whatever people like to believe, attention to detail is one of the essentials of success. The slog before this trip repaid that care by giving freedom from care. If the human animal could just keep on walking, all would be well. This section had given a stormy 26,000 feet in its 94 miles.

V

THE SOUTHERN CAIRNGORMS

"Let the mountains bear prosperity. . . ."
PSALM 72:3

Sunday 5 May BRAIGH COIRE CHRUINN-BHALGAIN
I finished off *The Story of San Michele* over tea in bed and for the early walk had a Flashman tale. Tea in bed was not what it could be with the A9 traffic snorting past twenty yards away. Nor was the breakfast up to tent standard. The greatest pleasure was dry, snug, clean clothes.

I read up the Tilt and Fender roads. The rich landscape of greens and browns was one I knew well. Flashman was deposited in a bothy where I left the tarmac. I had bought *Weir of Hermiston* in the village. I was having a snack in the hut and watching a peewit bowing his rufous rump at me when I slowly realised the hill above was crawling with people: pinpricks of colour, those polluting identikit colours, that stood out against the burnt hillside darkness.

I crossed bogs and ascended by a line of grouse butts. The slopes were a grey and brown jig-saw of heather, burnt over the years to encourage new growth. There is a false summit to Carn Liath and as I topped it I found a female squatting before me. Movement being the thing one notices, I simply turned and admired the view for a few minutes. The true summit had a bus load of visitors from the old "Scotsman" club, now the "Ptarmigan Club", out on their first-Sunday-in-the-month trip from Edinburgh. I regretted my late start, another hotel drawback, for with so many people on the hill the sense of solitude vanished—and so did any chance of seeing much in the way of wildlife.

I had forgotten what a fine group this was: big brown and grey domes, clean-honed by the wind, runny with screes and seamed with deer tracks. It was a hill group I had been on more often in winter. Once the wind was so powerful that I took a photograph of our party "leaning" on it. Another intensely cold Christmas Day our eggs froze solid at camp, and at 2,000 feet up we met an otter out for a bit of tobogganing. The farmer was on skis.

Today was bitter cold so I soon went on. There were people all along the ridges: some had taken only single tickets up Carn Liath, but others went on for the other Munros: Braigh Coire Chruinn-Bhalgain, the *slope of the round, bag-shaped corrie*, and Carn nan Gabhar, the highest, at 3,671 feet. Beinn a' Ghlo (or Ben-y-Gloe) covers all three in a group name. They stand as a solitary bulk bordering on the lowlands. B.C.C.B. had quite a picnic collection of folk but the atmosphere was rather from Jerome K. Jerome as people cringed behind the cairn, or each other, in an effort to avoid the searing wind. The last Munro lies beyond a substantial col so I left the sack by a long and very visible snow runnel and went off for it. As the group name means *hill of the mist* I was taking no chances. Never leave a sack without some sure marker.

I came back over B.C.C.B. Always another Munro after all—and the shortest way down. (1974 ended with 344 Munros, a yearly tally I am never likely to equal again; the figure for 1969 was 206 and most years straggle to the 100.) I suddenly had the hill to myself, and almost breathed a sigh of relief. Though the company had been enjoyable one of the loved aspects of Scottish hill-going is the solitude. Our own Braes o' Fife Club tries not to go in a party of more than four or five. Above that number all sorts of dissatisfactions creep in. We also try to discourage the hideous belisha-beacon clothing which we are conned into wearing. (I know it is in the name of safety, but you can have a bright poly bag hidden in your sack till you want to be seen instead of becoming part of the human pollution problem. The same criticism goes for tents in the wilderness.)

Several hundred feet of standing glissade took me well on my way down to the great cleft of Glen Tilt. The rest was brutally steep grass. For once the River Tilt gave no problems and I hopped over to the road. A rainbow spanned the vee of the fault line. I crept under a bridge for a shower, left the sack there and went a couple of miles down to Forest Lodge.

The keeper, Mr McGregor, benign and unshaven, had a food parcel. We had a wee crack, then I went up the glen again. Many are the tales of this stalwart figure confronting unauthorised motorists who have dared the potholes of the private road up the glen. Once we were brewing at the Dormobile after a day on the hill when he stopped to check on us. (We had permission.) I had fished some nice red granite stones out of the river for a garden dry-stane-dyke. These were eyed. "Aye, aye, there's some folk just climb hills but others now, mun tak' the hill home with them!"

Fitness allowed the addition of a heavy parcel to go unnoticed though I lightened the load by the weight of mandarins and cream. A fit body is a marvellously casual thing. I ate up the miles to the head of the main glen to camp by the Falls of Tarff on a bright sward. Last time up there I had led a cycling gang through to Braemar. Where the track became a mere slot I caught a pedal and fell down the bank, bouncing alternately with the bike, till it landed splash in the river; I stopped one bounce short.

Today I was furious to find the site disfigured with litter, half-buried compo tins, bare stone marks and stove burns—all the signs of Army activity. Tins had been pushed into molehills, hidden under the nearest stones, or simply thrown into the river. It took an hour to clean up the place before I could feel relaxed in it. I threw dozens of boulders back into the river: campers should never leave them where tents have been: the grass looks as if it had chicken-pox after a few years. I like my camping to be as secretive as possible: known to none at the time or after.

Craig Dhearg caught the evening sun, lighting the translation of its name in almost neon extravagance. The sound of the big river dominated the site: river and falls. I concocted the first curry of the trip. A quarter of the tally had been done. A month had gone by as casually as river flow.

The Tilt is one of the oldest of through routes. It narrowly missed being linked up with the Lairig Ghru in an English-type long-distance jamboree track, the brain-child of the Scottish Countryside Commission. The route was all worked out, and a massive report issued with all the details, before any users heard about it. After a terrific outcry the scheme was dropped. Some consultation *first* could have saved a great deal of money and effort. It was even suggested that sometimes the path would have to be closed in the interests of stalking. It would have been fun seeing the Commission trying to "close" a right-of-way as old as any in the land.

In 1847 a botanical professor had had the Tilt barred to him and the ensuing lawsuit clearly showed the right of way. In Scotland we try to keep a sane balance, respecting each other's interests and rights. We

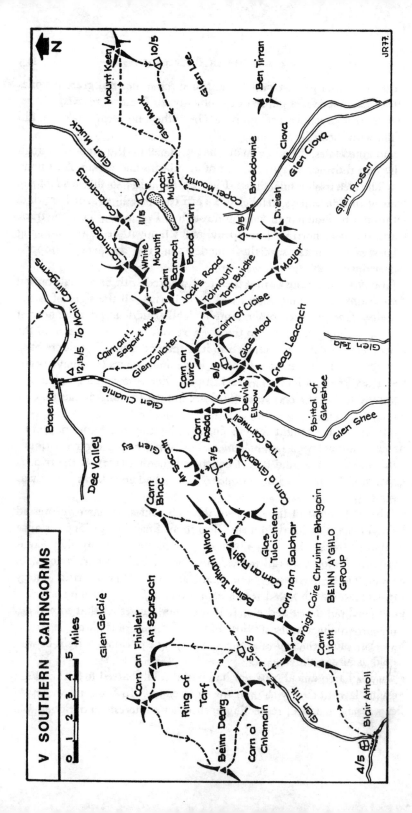

V SOUTHERN CAIRNGORMS

Miles
0 1 2 3 4 5

Dee Valley

Braemar

Glen Geldie

Carn an Fhidleir
An Sgarsoch

Ring of Tarf

Beinn Dearg

Carn a' Chlamain

Glen Tilt

Blair Atholl 4/5

5,6/5

Beinn Iutharn Mhor

Carn an Righ

Glas Tulaichean

Carn nan Gabhar

Braigh Coire Chruinn - Bholgain
BEINN A'GHLO GROUP

Carn Liath

Carn Bhac

An Socath

Glen Ey

7/5

Carn Aosda

Devils Elbow

The Cairnwell

Carn a' Gheoidh

Spittal of Glenshee

Glen Shee

Glen Isla

Creag Leacach

Glas Maol

8/5

Cairn of Claise

Carn an Tuirc

Glen Callater

Cairn an t-Sagairt Mor

12,13/5 To Main Cairngorms

Jock's Road

Tolmount

Tom Buidhe

Mayar

Dreish

9/5

Cairn Bannoch

Broad Cairn

White Mounth

Lochnagar

Conachraig

11/5

Loch Muick

Capel Mounth

Braedownie

Clova

Ben Tirran

Glen Clova

Glen Prosen

Glen Muick

Glen Doll

Glen Lee

Mount Keen

10/5

N

JR77.

do not register rights-of-way as in England but are given freedoms which we value. Were they all cut and dried everyone would lose a great deal. So there have been very few cases like the "Battle of the Tilt". The 1975 Scottish Mountaineering Club Journal had an article on this and allied tales, "Stravagers and Marauders" by Robert Aitken, which is good reading.

The glen itself is full of history and old ruins: whole villages lie tucked away in side valleys, telling of what past? Pennant on his tour went through to Braemar in 1769 and called the glen "the most dangerous and the most horrible I ever travelled". James VI stayed there as the guest of honour at a specially-built wooden lodge and enjoyed a massive deer drive. Pools for fish were created. As a final flourish, on his departure, the lodge was burned to make a huge bonfire. One hears little snippits like this and longs to know more. The glens were not always empty.

Monday 6 May THE RING OF TARFF

"Willy-needy, willy-needy, willy-needy . . ."

The call of a summer piper woke me to a cold morning—cold enough for me to take the Gaz stove into bed and read *Weir of Hermiston* for an hour before starting to brew. Long day or not, it was nine before I set off.

I scrambled about taking photographs of the falls as they foamed in the sun. The Tarff supplies the bulk of water for the Tilt which beyond here lies in a remarkable slot of trench. The falls are among the best in the land but seldom seen, as they are far from any road. It has been suggested that the upper Tilt flow has been reversed and that the Tarff waters once flowed to the Dee. The Tarff, crashing out of its gorge, has always been a hazard to travellers between Atholl and Deeside: the Belford Bridge was erected in memory of a drowning in Victorian times. The bridge is a perfect period piece, spanning the pool into which the double fall tumbles. It is a great spot.

I explored upstream—where there is a higher fall—and then flanked upwards along a series of "little hills". The country is misleading: small and simple on the face of map and landscape, but the miles contort and the hours pass in remarkable fashion. Heather braes and black bogs ensure the Ring of Tarff is no stroll. It is wild mistmoor, unlived-in, lonely as a sad heart, the silence more crashing than any sound could be.

An Sgarsoch and Carn Ealar, the *fiddler* (Fhidleir), are not among the more exciting of Munros, though their isolation will probably add something to their acquisition. For instance, in 1908 Munro and Walter Garden dined at Blair Atholl, then drove and walked up to the Belford Bridge, which they left, already well soaked, at 9.40 p.m. The Tarff was in spate. To read a compass they had to shelter under a coat. Sgarsoch's summit dome was chaotic, the cairn hard to find in the rain, dark and cloud. As they were "unable to keep their powder dry" they could see neither map nor compass. Ealar was abandoned and they simply steered into the wild north wind to drop down to the Geldie. It was unfordable for many miles and they staggered into Braemar at 10.20 a.m. They had a certain style in those days. Another S.M.C. party in 1903 did this pair and Chlamain starting at 2.30 a.m.—so as to be sure of being "back for dinner" at Blair Atholl. They walked on dried peat bogs, all too glad of such conditions.

Today I had it not bad myself. The hills are a good pair from which to view the Cairngorms. The valley mists had streamed off into invisibility. Only Nevis remained hidden. The hills of Glen Etive could be named. A day of infinite things: glossy, moleskin mountains and happy animal activity. Surely too good to last.

Ealar is the meeting place of three counties: Perth, Aberdeen and Inverness, or as would be on the morrow, three regions: Tayside, Grampian and Highland. There were large herds of deer all day. They trailed muddy tracks across the snow patches. By the time I had followed down to and then trekked up the Tarff I was ready to envy them as they lay on the snow. I paddled and rested a while, then pushed on for Beinn Dearg, a granite-pink cone which takes a bit of coming-at from any direction. Combined with Chlamain it gives an excellent introduction to bumps and bogs, about which the map retains a coy reticence.

Both Ealar and Dearg received questionnaires. Alan Smith of Glasgow found the Ealar one three weeks later, and also one to the north, on Carn Cloich-Mhuillin, which is comment enough on these hills. He had tramped up from a camp at White Bridge, wearing swimming trunks. Dearg's was found after a week by a gang with Eddie McCulloch from Dundee. He made rude comments about bogs too.

Carn a' Chlamain remained. It was Queen Victoria's first Munro— the first of quite a bag. She would have made a notable patron for the

L.S.C.C. I reckon. Her journals and letters written in Scotland are well worth reading; she ranged widely and did more than any one else to remove the old wounds of 1745. In 1842 she was the first monarch to visit the highlands voluntarily and freely since Jamie Six beat it off to London.

Carn a' Chlamain is the *cairn of the gled* or *kite*. From Dearg it is reached by devious means, ease of approach being in proportion to cunning employed. I did not linger on top as the weather was sneakily turning raw. I was eventually caught by the bogs—flying off like the victim of a judo expert and thump'ng into a gooey spot. I carried a fair bit of it away on my clothes.

The yellow strath rang with the crying of plover and curlew, giving a loneliness to the one building standing, the Tarff Bothy—a man-made, geometrical shape among the flowing river and brae curves. An old A.A. Hotel sign hung on a gable. I brewed, and had a dram, signed in the register, and went down for a wash, removing the mud. The clothes dried before I was back "home". I deposited my Stevenson and took a blood-and-thunder. Still, a two-star howff.

I read most of the way back, walking down, or tripping out of, deer tracks. The path shown was illusory. The new dirt road came over a gap to end at a stable. The Ring of Tarff is a fine round largely in retrospect.

Tuesday 7 May THE GREY WASTELAND

If no hill is dull, some are certainly less entertaining than others. This section of the Walk would probably have my vote as the least notable of all. Luckily the animal spirits seemed high during the long, grey miles.

The upper Tilt gave a trouble-free crossing. I read my way up the slopes on to the ridge above Fealar Lodge, the highest and one of the most remote in Scotland. In 1822 the shooting tenant won a remarkable wager: midnight to midnight to shoot 40 brace of grouse, to ride to his home at Dunnottar (near Stonehaven on the east coast) and back again. The shooting took four and a half hours, then the 140-mile ride was accomplished, with time enough to descend at the end to Braemar again for 10 p.m.

The cropped heather led easily up to Carn Bhac which has an area of graded chips and blocks of quartz that look as if they have been combed. From there Beinn Iutharn Mhor was an unexpectedly fine sight:

a snow-filled corrie topped by an almost-perfect cornice. Just one portion had fallen to streak down to the lochan—the sort of flaw a child weeps over when building the dream sandcastle, and a bit falls down. Iutharn may mean *hell*. Bhac is *peat banks*.

The dip between the two Munros is very boggy. The ascent was runny-nose cold. I ran down the other side and flanked to reach the col for the *king's cairn*: Carn an Righ. It was such an easy ascent that I went off into a day-dream and, when I reached the summit stood completely disorientated as I was faced with a massive Beinn a' Ghlo which I did not recognise at once. I have had the same feeling in a tent, waking, and for a moment not knowing where I was.

I traversed deer tracks up Gleann Mhor, made some chicken drinks and then went up and down Glas Tulaichean, the *grey hummock*, at 3,445 feet the highest of these plain hills. The clouds were rolling in so I took a bit of old fence iron and descended direct back to the sack. The top few hundred feet gave a standing glissade, the rest a glorious bumslide—the nether regions kept dry by a bit of polythene sacking, which also reduced the coefficient of friction considerably. Two ptarmigan stood resolutely in my line of fire, trusting in their camouflage no doubt, but while they had changed to summer the hillside had not. They only burped off in the nick of time. At the foot of the slope I nearly had a repeat—with a hare. Obviously the speed of sliding humans was not easily judged.

There are some extensive bogs at the head of the glen and an odd, round, dug, pool which puzzles as to why it is there. Over the watershed lies Loch nan Eun, a favourite wilderness campsite of mine. Several of us from Braehead once met there coming in from different routes, quite a good night exercise. On another occasion Edi Crooks and I had to dig through eighteen inches of ice to reach water. Today a ring of acid-whitened stones showed where someone had pitched a tent on the peat itself; flat ground is hard to find, I suppose. The loch's name means the *loch of the birds* and its two islands were raucous with nesting gulls—2,550 feet above sea level. At 3,050 feet a few days later oyster-catchers were calling by Loch Etchachan, and under Bhrotain lies the *loch of the black-headed gulls*. Hardy birds all.

Sadly I left the chance of camping by *lapping* water (Loch Lomond was the last such site) and went on another couple of miles to lodge by the usual *running* water of a burn under An Socath. The sky paled to a delicate blue and the bovine bulk of Gheoidh and its odd "horn" of

Carn Bhinnean glowed in the sunset. The grey wasteland glowed. It is a country of browns and ochres and blues often, with great sky character. When it is grey, it can be in tones that no camera could ever touch. They are hills to camp on and see at dawn or dusk.

My lonely spot was at 2,425 feet, set in a slot by a burn which flowed underground for much of its length. There was just time to pitch and eat—a big hoosh of everything thrown in together, a meal spiced only with need. The company and setting were both agreeable.

A transistor radio had tempted me as an extra but it was a gadget, so was left. A book did not depend on dodgy mountain reception. I did miss music though. (Between trips I drive everyone mad at home by making up the loss.) Braehead gangs were quite likely to come stomping back to camp singing a chorus from *Aida* and on trips to Ireland we sang and climbed equally, thanks to Kirsty Adam. A photograph of us with the kids on a summit found its way to Morocco one winter there, local friends saw it and jumped to the conclusion this was my wife and family. Such fecundity, of males especially, made my reputation soar in their Islamic regard. I have not had the heart to shatter the illusion.

Alas, music on the Walk was limited. Water Music all too often. Sometimes one dreamed of Handel's Lager or Bach's Bass in B. Minor . . .

Wednesday 8 May THE DEVIL'S ELBOW
An Socath was just above and gave an airy ridge walk. The new Tables have switched the Munro from one end to the other. A *south* wind was so bitter that I had to don a cagoule on top of all my garments to keep bearably warm. It was an excuse for a second breakfast before striking camp, then a burn down and a burn up gave me Carn a' Gheoidh, the *cairn of the goose.*

A small lochan had been blown nearly dry, and Loch Vrotachan had white horses and the spray sheeting off over the heather for a hundred yards. The wind rushing out of the corries to the south made it quite a tussle to rim round. Years ago I had an unforgettable experience here. It was a day of big, billowing clouds—explosions in slow motion. The clouds suddenly parted and a long corridor of clarity led the eye down glens and ridges southwards to the Lomonds of Fife and Arthur's Seat. The corridor was only a quarter of a mile wide, yet I could see seventy miles. While still marvelling at the view a flock of about thirty white ptarmigan burst from one wall, went sweeping round in the sun, then swooshed over my head to vanish in the cloud again. When I turned from following their flight, the corridor had closed.

On the Cairnwell (Scotland's easiest Munro with, or without, the chairlift) the anemometer was "fair going its dinger" and everything was well guyed down. This is Penguin Country and nothing looks so soiled and sorry as ski machinery and markings in their summer nakedness. Ski-ing has its valid claim but needs careful management. So much had to be learnt the hard way in Scotland. So much does not seem to have been learnt at all. The grim scraping of bulldozed tracks over the hills with little thought of the result is typical; there are some dreadful eyesores, not just the tracks but erosion caused by bad siting. Nor is any planning needed for tree planting, so views of great beauty, and importance as a tourist attraction, are wiped out by unthinking afforestation. It seems quite fantastic that there is no control over the drastic change of landscape use. The machinery for planning control exists, but it seems the vision does not.

Our mountain heritage in Scotland is both precious and fragile. Even bodies like the National Trust who have been given parts of it to protect seem unable to resist the "development" urge. At times I am tempted to say "to hell"—"I've had it good"—"there are limits to one's fighting powers". But can we allow the future to blame us for the loss? This is every man's fight, and in particular, it is a fight for the young; but then, I wonder if they know how to fight. We have all been trained to hold our hands out with open palms.

I came back down the Cairnwell along the snow fences, full of past memories. Most of our girls' parties learnt to ski here. The area I had been over in the last two days is all great ski-touring country, a side of mountaineering that deserves to be far more popular.

Two fishermen were battling through to Loch Vrotachan: the *loch of the lost skiers*. We yelled a greeting and I blew on up Carn Aosda, an unpronounceable Munro (try "Carn Oosh"), which is in danger of being demoted as the skiers wear it down. It is only 3,003 feet: bottom of the class. Down on the road I went into the café and indulged in three hot pies and three cups of coffee. The manager, Mr Patterson, had a parcel, quite a bit of which I left as a thank offering. I rang Jim Donaldson at Braemar and then Marina at Dollar. Kenneth, aged two, answered first as usual with his gurgly conversation but I managed to get my message through: "At Cairnwell. Next phone from Braemar

Sunday or Monday. Alarm if not, Tuesday. Checks: Thursday, Glendoll
Y.H., Saturday, Mr Robertson, Spittal of Glenmuick where also John
Lawton meeting noon, Saturday. If I do not arrive, pass things to Mr
Robertson. Wants: new anklets, Suppletect, a book, writing materials."
Peep-peep-peep went the machine. "O.K.? Ta! Cheers."

That was typical of the safety system operating. I fled the sound of a
juke box but on the hill was overtaken by a Caterpillar and Land-
Rover going up in tandem. Some hills is definitely not lonely.

The Cairnwell pass is 2,199 feet, our highest main road. The famous
Devil's Elbow just below it is, alas, no more, being superseded by a
foul, steep brae which is much harder on cars. This has been a major
route to Deeside from time unrecorded. It was built as a military road
in 1749–50. St Rule, with the relics of St Andrew, crossed it to join the
Pictish king Angus I Mac Fergus in the eighth century. Legend is even
older.

Down Gleann Beag, above the Spittal of Glenshee (an old hospice),
lies Ben Gulabin, a hill connected with the Fingalian hero Diarmid Mac
O'duine. He slew a monster boar on the hill but chanced to knock his
foot on a bristle, which tiny wound led, eventually, to his death. If this
sounds a bit like the Achilles story, it probably is; Celtic and Classical
mythology have several links. In 1644 the Cairnwell saw a battle
against a cattle-lifting party from Argyll. A famous Braemar archer
became the hero of the fray but had the misfortune to return home with
an arrow sticking from his own posterior.

I could see the Elbow as I flanked out to Creag Leacach. A band of
snow had frozen in the sharp south wind and I had to cut steps with a
slice of schisty rock to cross it. A wall undulates along to the top. In the
mist the summit bump can be difficult to be sure of; they all look the
same. The wind bullied me along and up Glas Maol. A mitt on a stick
decorated the cairn. (One time it was an onion on a stick.) I dropped
down to collect my sack, left before Leachach, then contoured into
the lee-side corrie to look for a camp-site.

I crossed several burns and in the end pulled up, crossed the Monega
Pass track, and dropped down into the next corrie. It proved a veritable
wind tunnel. The next again was less draughty. I chased some deer
away and pitched by a burn. It proved a noisy, uncomfortable night:
the tent sloping, the ground lumpy and the wind scratching endlessly
at this poor bellyfold among the hills.

Thursday 9 May DRIESH AND NOT SO DREICH

The tent proved itself overnight. The wind was very wild, giving it periodic thumps while careering down the corrie. I cringed as I heard them coming. Previous disasters with nylon tents were still much on my mind.

I had had two epics of high camping with the water pouring in at about a pint per hour, and winter has many hours of darkness. The sewn-in ground-sheet had been very effective; it had let none of this water out. I might as well have slept in a bath. I took the present tent with great scepticism, but came to have great faith in it. Sure, there was condensation, but it ran down into the ground, for the tray-shaped groundsheet was held off the walls by elastics. Simple and effective. (This also meant one could pee without going out; a vital benefit once sealed inside on a midgy night.) The only thing I took a long time to become used to was the noise; a breeze rattled it, sounding like a gale.

Here though there was a gale, and a dreich, grey morning when I crawled out. Not far up the burn I passed a much better site.

Once over the corrie rim it was really wintry, the wet far colder in feeling than any of the hard frosts of April. From Cairn of Claise I set off into featureless country, gentle-sloping, streaked with snow, milky with mist. Contrary to opinion it is easy ground like this that is hardest for navigation. Anybody can navigate along the Aonach Eagach; but try the Cairngorms, or here, or Kinder. That is where you really have to be accurate, just when the mind is dulled.

A corrie rim came on schedule, and another bearing took me past a ruin to the top of Carn an Tuirc, within a minute of the estimate. Such accuracy always gives a certain element of wonder that navigation actually works. The wilderness beyond was treated with simplicity: minimal bearings: the first one beastly cold as it led into the wind, the second a long leg of forty minutes to a fence I had marked, then along it through a lunar landscape of tussock, snow, bog and brae. Dotterel crouched or scampered off, a snipe went like a squib, ptarmigan sat stolidly and pipits flitted past, slicing sideways in the gale—a strangely animated, avian wilderness.

The fence came four minutes ahead of schedule, then a clearance showed me the paps of Tolmount and Tom Buidhe. There can be few pairs of Munros so easily collected as this couple of Siamese twins, yet they are not to be scorned either. Jock's Road, the famous pass from Glen Clova to Braemar, lies just beyond, and twice during my lifetime, groups have died struggling over it in winter blizzards. Easy is a relative term.

So much is relative. I happily left my rucksack on a fencepost to do Tolmount, something I often did. Yet I have seen categorical "Never leave your rucksack"—just as I have seen "Never go alone"—statements which are, when unqualified, highly irresponsible. It is quite wrong to lay down *rules* for the hills; basically the hills don't play by the rules and their evil has to be matched with cunning, with gumption, not a set of procedures which ultimately fail. Common sense is not part of the M.L.C., though. Experience is still the sum total of our near misses.

The miles beyond Tom Buidhe are savannah-like, a comparison I found apt with the deer streaming off like antelope. There were brief clearances of weather so I hurried along to cash in on them in case it clamped down. I ate up the miles to the Fee burn, then, with Mayar ahead, relaxed. I actually dropped right down into a peaty hole where a burn ran underground and in that shelter had a cosy brew. The map showed some fine names: I'd passed Kilrannoch, the Burn of Fialzioch and the Dun Hillocks, while west lay Finalty Hill. Unfolding the map I found even more speculative names: Dog Hillock, Horse Holme, Shank of Inchgrundle, Loch Brandy, Naked Hill, Meg Swerie, Bad-happies, The Witter, Hill of Saughs, Trusty Burn, Boustie Ley and Watery Hill—and that is but a sample.

A party passed over Mayar just before I reached it. Navigation had not been difficult. Helpful fences more or less linked on to Driesh. I added it and returned, dropping down to the valley by the Shank of Drumfollow, into the forest and over a fallen tree which is now highly polished by the passing of many walkers' breeches as they take its short-cut to the youth hostel. There I found my parcel, and a store, and the Browns at the farm sold me creamy milk and fresh brown eggs. Life felt good. There was also a one-inch map of the way to Mount Keen, which I had posted as I had found it only at the last minute. I was to be glad of it.

A gang of Alyth boys and girls came in to see the hostel, having crossed Jock's Road. Dan Smith, the warden, sounded like a guide to a stately home—which to an extent he is. The hostel is a white shooting lodge set among vivid forest. It was built at the turn of the century. An early owner had tried to close Jock's Road to the public (and the

Mounth path to Ballater) but ran up such a bill over the litigation that he had to sell out.

I had the hostel to myself, so Dan and I had a good blether, he being a hillman too. He leant me a *Climber and Rambler* (always makes me think of a rose-grower's magazine) which had one gem, describing hut life: "We seemed to do nothing but saw up wood to keep the fire going to dry out clothes we got wet sawing up wood."

I slept poorly, all too aware of a growing roar of river as the rain poured down in the night.

Friday 10 May FURTHEST EAST

It was a bleak dawning. A curtain of rain fell in front of the window; giving a feeling of despair. Only well on in the walk did I learn not to be depressed by filthy weather messing up my plans. I think it was the wearing return to more logistics when things could not go to plan that drained me; at least I had a clear decision here: I was staying. A huge breakfast and an hour with a needle, then at 10.30 the rain switched off and the valley choked itself with clouds of steam. Perhaps I should go.

I left at noon. The Bachnagairn road was all washed-out worms. A redstart grated beside the turn off for the Capel Mounth path but I went on to pass the Capel Burn by the bridge, as the path would certainly give no ford in that spate. I followed this old drove road of zig-zags up into the cloudy tops. A county boundary led all the way to Mount Keen and I hoped there just might be a fence along it. There was no fence. A new bulldozed track simply led me a hundred yards into the murk and left me there on the edge of the bogs.

I floundered through them, then took the Allt Darrarie west of the aptly-named Watery Hill, deciding this would be better than heather and bog bashing. It was. I crossed it at once as it was in spate and soon became quite deep. After two miles following it down gently, I turned up a side stream (when it swept off for the Spittal) then a fork—and I was well committed to the moors of madness. I had read "to navigate up there you're either a fool or an expert". I did not have much doubt of the former. I had better become the latter.

At the last shelter I ate egg rolls, brewed and had a tin of oranges as morale-booster. My cutting was like a trench on a battlefront. It sounded nasty overhead. My gully petered out later and left me by a green and slimy pool. This bit of countryside is full of great holes and sinks, ditches and mounds, hollows and hags; and the constituent peat itself ranges from firm cutting-cake, to meringue glacé, to watery Chantilly. It is as if two giants have had a battle, their only weapons being an inexhaustible supply of Christmas pudding, then having tired of fighting they had taken hoses and given the scene a good wash down.

While I had brewed I had reduced the required bearings to two. It was not a day for the niceties or finer points of navigation. The first leg was three miles, the second a shade less and should bring me to the cone of Mount Keen. Even the fool could see it was going to be fun— you could not take more than a dozen steps in a straight line. You would have to go to the Ruwenzori to find bog like this.

I aimed for a nick on the skyline, at the limit of visibility, but am unaware of having reached it. The cloud came down and it began to rain, hard, as it did to the end of the day—except when it was sleeting and snowing—a biting horizontal battering from the flank, just the thing to cause navigational "drift". I played the endlessly repetitive game of taking a bearing of something on the verge of visibility (edge of hag, boulder, tuft of grass), then making for it round, through or over any obstacles that lay between. These were often considerable, and always slaistery. (The Scots often have a word for it.)

Somewhere in this Bunyan bog I found a Met. balloon and while trying to collect it the ground caved in and I landed in a stream ten foot underground, all tied up in balloon, guys and bits and pieces. I climbed up out of my crevasse with the recording label which was duly dispatched. The balloon had left Shanwell in September 1973. I described the incident so was a bit put out later to receive a massive box asking would I be so kind as to send the whole caboodle to them. I was tempted to send them a six figure reference and a spade.

The day was unique. I actually revelled in it, even at the time. Only the irrationality of my ploy was justification for being there at all. It would have been easy to escape down to the Water of Mark and then up to Keen tomorrow, but having taken up the fight, I was determined to stick to it. What climber likes to waste height already gained?

The variety of bog was amazing: solid or oozing, smooth peat and broken hags, hillocks, banks, deep-cut burns, swamps, lochans, even dry rocky sections. There seemed to be little life—and most of it dead, so to speak, the bleached bones and scraps of hares and ptarmigan. Such landmarks as there were (the Burn of Fasheilach one) came as expected, then, after hours of teasing away, the new bearing which made only one difference, the sleet battered on the starboard bow instead of abeam. Bogs. Bogs. Bogs. Some were deeply worn. The ground began to rise steadily, gravels broke through a bit, and a cairn, the first man-made object apart from the stray balloon, was strangely evocative.

The last bit seemed interminable. There were some very gooey bits, black lochans almost. A pair of hare's legs, furry and obscene, perched on a tussock. A post appeared on my casting line, then several more. They marked nothing in way of a path but after rising on to heather slopes I found the Mounth track to Glen Tanar.

It began to snow properly. The wind was bitter—and from the south again (deflected by the summit cone, perhaps). I became white with hoar. The summit granite jumble was very welcome. I rammed down a bar of chocolate and left a note on the wrapper at the cairn, the eastmost Munro. I ran like a madman off the summit to regain some warmth. I had reached the summit within ten minutes of the time guessed back at the hostel, which, in retrospect, rather pleased me.

The old path, called *The Ladder*, had been smashed up into a vile Land-Rover track but I was soon down into Glen Mark and pitched in the lee of a dyke. I just got the meal on when dusk came down like a curfew. As I had no candles I lay snug in the flea bag cooking by the light of the stove. The rain and hail battered the fabric an inch above my head. There was almost something of arrogance in being there. The margins are never wide and sometimes they are very narrow. It was an arrogance mingled with humility.

Somewhere in the day's madness I had clocked up the first 500 miles, and I had made a west–east traverse, though the purist might argue for Banachdich and Skye, Ben More and Mull being slightly east. But I was now on the way for Keen-Banachdich, in any case.

Mount Keen has one of the earliest recorded ascents of a Munro: July 1618. The Mounth path was then in use, and no doubt there had been scores of ascents; however, it fell to the Water Poet, John Taylor, is his *Pennyless Pilgrimage*, to record one: ". . . when I came to the top of it, my teeth beganne to dance in my head with cold, like virginal's jacks; and withall, a most familiar mist embraced me round . . . withall it yielded so friendly a deaw, that it did moysten throw all my clothes." I knew exactly what he meant.

Saturday 11 May   VISITORS FROM DOWN UNDER
I started the wettish, westish wending early the next day. The journey up the Water of Mark was enjoyable. I cut one loop of river by the

Earn Stone from where I could see up to the cloud-capped dome of
yesterday. Maybe it never clears up there, a perpetual Wuthering
Height. From a side stream I joined my starting point of yesterday.
The nick lay on the skyline. My footsteps marked across a black mud
patch. A good stalkers' path criss-crossed the stream down by Creag na
Slowrie to the Spittal of Glenmuick where I had a meeting planned
with John and Penny Lawton. He was an Australian doctor whom I had
first met in the Alps. A spell at Edinburgh was giving him the freedom
of Scotland.

I hung the tent from a tree and went off to Mr Robertson, the
keeper, to collect a parcel. John Hinde had done the same on one of
his long treks. John, Penny and a Chinese friend arrived at 3 p.m.
They were off for a holiday in the north. A shower saw them on their
way. The kids watched fascinated as a line of stags stuttered its way
through the pines. Later the herd passed my camp in the wood opposite,
grazing their way slowly past and out of sight. I lay reading my mail all
the while. Marina wrote saying that the telephone only needed to ring
and Kenneth would rush to my itinerary board calling out my name.
My log mentioned an orgy of fresh food again. The bubble and squeak
of roding woodcock was the last sound coming through the hush of
mist.

Sunday 12 May   NO CLOTHES, SORRY CAN'T COME
"Up at six and off at seven" was almost automatic by now. The fair
dawn spluttered out all too soon. I went up Conachraig hoping the
clouds would clear and give me a view of Lochnagar. No luck.

On the path I overhauled two lads dressed like lost fishermen in
oilskins and big boots. Fifty yards at a time was all they could manage
before steaming up and stalling. Did I know where the Red Spout
was? They sounded sceptical when I said it would be full of snow. I
hastened on into the clouds speculating that their errant way was a
more valid experience than that of assembly-line production. Being
lost is a much more effective way of learning than being led, or being
churned out by the instant mountaineering industry with its question-
able practices. It is not unknown for teachers to do the M.L.C. merely
as a bit of paper which might give them an edge in job-hunting, or to
get more money. Their mentors play musical chairs, juggling salaries
and scales, creating departments and bumf. The whole system is open
to question. I remember meeting a gang of trainee teachers on a hill
E

above Rannoch Moor. The view was superb yet they arrived and slumped down with all the enthusiasm of potato sacks. Nobody commented on the scene. Nobody looked at a map. Nobody said much. Nobody trained anybody in anything. After a statutory five minutes they filed off in their identi-kit rigs. And these were the potential leaders of kids.

The ascent to the plateau was quite an icy scramble. On top, tracks led through snow and melt to Cac Carn Mor, whose cairn many take for the summit, which is actually on a bit, Cac Carn Beag (the Mor and Beag are the wrong way round). I installed myself in the summit rocks and was just tucking into bacon butties when another boarding party scrambled up, a couple plus an older gangrel who seemed all artificial limbs, and blind. I can hardly think of anything more remote from the institutionalised mountaineer than Syd Scroggie. They had come up from overnighting at the Glas Allt Shiel, once a favourite haunt of the mourning Queen Victoria.

Some years before, three of us had met Syd on the long road up to Derry Lodge. He was alone. We chatted a while, a conversation punctuated by his comments on this and that bird which he heard, and which we neither saw nor heard. Now on Lochnagar he was able to describe the view though we could see nothing but mist. And he trotted out all the bearings while we were still groping for compasses. Only when well away from the summit did it clear so that I could see down to Deeside, and the lochs and woods that Queen Victoria knew as "the bonniest plaid in all Scotland".

White Mounth is a dull dome of a Munro: a snow-soggy bump today. Next comes Carn an t-Sagairt Mor which has two cairns on top, fifty yards apart and both decorated with pieces of crashed aircraft. I went on round the deep trough of the Dubh Loch to add Cairn Bannoch and Broad Cairn—almost back to Jock's Road in my sweep. It is all rolling granite plateau country, great on ski. The Dubh Loch reminds of Loch Avon, a deep-set, crag-bound, black ribbon of water. Instead of the Shelter Stone Crag there is Creag an Dubh Loch (with climbs as hard), instead of the Feith Buidhe, the Allt an Dubh Loch and instead of the Stag Rocks there are the Eagle Rocks. Climbers must enjoy the old S.M.C. comment on the cliffs as "overhanging rocks which are manifestly impossible".

I rewound my route over "Taggart" and dropped down to Loch Callater. Gulls blew like confetti up the loch, nesting safe on an island as usual. The road was covered in stinking diesel oil and two caterpillar vehicles came up, one driven by a lad who must have been all of fifteen. I passed the miles singing hymns and psalms—it was the Sabbath after all. The golfers and cuckoos on the golf course eventually shamed me into self-conscious silence. The Youth Hostel, a fine granite building, stood on the edge of the town, very welcome.

Seeing it nestling in the trees reminded me of a sermon we once had under the pines there. The Rev. William Still from Aberdeen talked to our youngsters for an hour and a half—and held them enthralled. Reality, in any aspect, can only kindle. It is today's tragedy that reality is so glossed over by the puerile, the facile and the plastic.

Mrs Ewan has been the happy warden at Braemar for so long as I can recall. I had a shower and then went round to spend the evening with Jim and Sheila Donaldson. A dainty meal in a house seemed an incredible luxury. Mountain pictures by Alf Gregory and Tom Weir were on the wall, pages of the latest Munros Tables lay ready for revising. Jim is the keeper of the facts and figures. They had a parcel for me. Jim did the Munros back in 1961 and has probably skied more of them than anyone. When I had left the parcel in February he had a leg in plaster to prove it. Their hospitality was much appreciated.

I had a gigantic washing of everything, once back at the hostel, so retired to the dorm draped in a blanket. An hour later Mrs Ewan crept in and shook me awake. Jim was on the telephone asking if I would like to go out on a search for some folk missing on the Feughside hills. I whispered my apologies. I had no clothes—I had washed every stitch to the extent that I "lay between the lily white sheets with nothing on at all".

Monday 13 May QUIETLY FLOWS THE DEE

The missing trio had been found, suffering a bit from exposure, but Jim was back for breakfast. A large gang from Inverness Academy were in at the hostel last night. They, Gordonstoun, and Braehead used at one time to be the gangs one met on the hill—in the good old days. The tradition still lingers it seems. The type of noise was familiar. Youth is certainly the time to start.

I prowled about Braemar a bit then reccied the Dee down to Braemar Castle without finding any spot for easy wading. The river was still high, so I would have to make the detour to the bridge. The castle sat sunnily among the larches by the river, quite an historical place, it is open to the public. The Invercauld Arms now occupies the site where the standard was raised in 1715. A garrison was maintained at Braemar up till 1831.

Back in the village I watched a craftsman working with horn. Braemar is a prime tourist spot in summer, of course. The Aberdeen accents were still obvious, not yet overwhelmed in the babel of summer tongues. I once heard a local climber query, "Fa' did ah fa' fa' times?" And had I not come in past fields loud with teuchats calling? A house had a plaque mentioning that it was here Robert Louis Stevenson had stayed as an invalid in 1881, and written *Treasure Island*, which made his name. Reasons of health brought Queen Victoria to Deeside, too; she had considered Lagganside but a summer monsoon there, and word of the drier clime of Deeside, brought Albert prospecting to the east.

I had intended an early night but two Tasmanian lassies easily prevented that. It was a calm evening and we only fell silent as dusk shuttered down on its silver glow. Looking back, what could have been a dull section of the walk had gone quite pleasantly if not quite without incident. The plateau-like landscape had brought the average height per Munro down to about 1,400 feet, compared to over 2,000 feet at the start. Braemar itself is over a thousand feet up. It would be interesting to see what the main Cairgorms would give.

VI

THE MONADH RUADH

"But we sleep by the ropes of the camp, and we rise with a shout
    and we tramp
    With the sun or the moon for a lamp, and the spray of the wind in
    our hair "

JAMES ELROY FLECKER

Tuesday 14 May BACK TO THE SINGING HEIGHTS

"Say, is that an English breakfast?" The hitch-hikers watched, all
eyes, as I ploughed through cereal, a mixed grill, fruit, tea, toast and
marmalade.

The morning had a glitter like crystal at a banquet and for once kept
its splendour. The clean town and tidy landscape seemed as if it had
just had a spring clean. Braemar Castle had obviously been painted
in to complete the filming of some romance. The eye led from the valley
richness and the brightness of the Dee up to the combed greys and
browns of the vast moines and mountains. The Cairngorms. The
Monadh Ruadh.

I had picked up one of Molly Weir's books, *Shoes Were For Sunday*, and
read it walking down the miles of road to the Invercauld Bridge and on
up beyond. At one stage I walked straight into a gate (and apologised)!
After the walk I was doing a programme with Tom Weir and mentioned
reading while walking and my apologising to a gate. He at once asked
what book I'd been reading and of the scores I did read it had to be one
by his sister.

The old bridge over the Dee had its postcard backcloth of Lochnagar,
the Byron image of

". . . the crags that are wild and majestic!
    The steep frowning glories of dark Lochnagar!"

Patey parodied this into a song,

"Gasherbrum, Masherbrum, Distigal Sar,
    Are all good training for dark Lochnagar"

which became set in my mind all the way up the Slugain path. I had
a brew once past the ruins of the old lodge. A pool reflected the snowy
rims of the high hills. I had a last look back down the secretive path to
the feudal landscape and went on into the folds of the hills.

Cairn Toul was a familiar shape. In the south the snow corrie of
Iutharn Mor stood out. The path led on under the big corries of
Beinn a' Bhuird. Coire na Ciche comes first, only losing impressiveness
when Coire nan Clach, the *corrie of the boulders*, appears beyond. I put
a foot in a bog. Washing the stocking at a burn, I saw the glitter of an
eye and found a pipit nesting under a tuft of grass. It had five eggs of
warm, spotted loveliness. I hurried on. Deer were lying along a snow
rim above. Somewhere above Clach a' Chleirich, the *Clergyman's stone*,
the path ran out and it seemed a hard haul up to the Sneck, the
3,200-foot col between these two eastern giants. Once I left the rucksack
progress was like levitation. The sun glinted on a vehicle down by the
Avon river below the Slochd Mor, as the valley on the other side is
called. The col had a cluster of wind-sculptured rocks which could
have been quite at home in a modern art collection.

North from here is some of the emptiest landscape in Britain. Go
astray and you will go twenty miles possibly before seeing a habitation.
I doubt if that could be done elsewhere. The name Avon derives from
Ath-Fhinn meaning *Fingal's ford*. The hero's wife is supposed to have
been swept away and drowned near Inchrory. The point at which
the Lairig an Laoigh path crosses the Avon is still called Ath nam
Fiann.

Ben Avon, though 3,843 feet, is soon reached from the Sneck. It is a
great plateau with many strange "warts" or "barns" of granite. The
summit is one, Leabaidh an Daimh Bhuidhe, meaning the *couch of the
tawny stag*, though if you search, all you will find is two wind-carved sea-
lions, one with a basin in its head. Several of the tors have these hollows
carved out by the swirl of grit and water. (On Ben Loyal in Sutherland
I have actually had a bath in one.) I spent half an hour clambering on
the Henry Moore shapes, then sat on top enjoying sun and view.
Lochnagar looked a bit further off now. Morven to the east and Ben
Rinnes to the north act as outriders to the big hills, the better viewpoints
for not being Munros.

I went down, collected my sack, and up the other side to rim round
the big *table* of Beinn a' Bhuird. The Dubh Lochan was a white lie to
its name as it reflected the snowy cliffs. The summit, 3,924 feet, was at

my end. These two big hills plus the four of over 4,000 feet form the "Big Six" of the Cairngorms. They have been done on skis and they are a pretty good summer walk.

The south summit lies two miles on, with the wound of a Land-Rover track up it; just one of many inflictions disfiguring these clean heights in the name of ski-ing, which the snowless winters have shown for folly. I suppose these two hills have the best of defences in a lazy society—long miles of necessary self-propulsion.

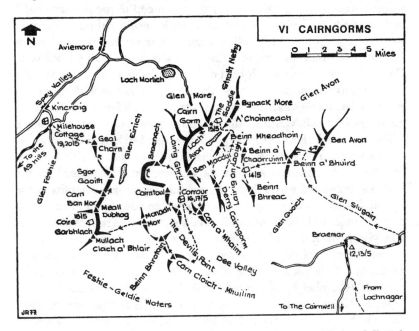

From Beinn a' Bhuird I could see the warts on top of Beinn Mhead-hoin and also the Barns of Bynack, two other areas of weathered granite. I dipped to 2,750 feet on the Moine Bhealaidh, the *Pass of the moss,* and on its vast, ochreous, flat sweep, pitched the tent. It was another site I had dreamed of for years. Instead of dashing off for the Munros at either end of it, I sat to enjoy the sunny hours of evening. The hot day had caused some sweaty chafe again. To sit was bliss. The deer browsed towards me unconcerned, grouse came noisily down like distended helicopters to pitch in the heather, and the saddest song of the hills, the golden plovers' call, was a constant background. It had been a day with the gathered perfection of a symphony.

Alas, contrasts come in all ways, the night was made foul by something I had eaten. In our local dialect I was "minging" and did not enjoy the company one little bit, however fine the setting.

Wednesday 15 May   A WINDY WINDAE

I was up early, in self-defence. I buried deep a suspect packet of dried onions. It was back to raw winds, but thankfully dry. I had heard a skylark singing above the tent long before six-thirty, when I set off. Beinn Bhreac was a gentle walk to the south end of my plateau, but I had not gone far before the tent was simply swallowed up in the vast sweep of this empty reach. What a contrast say to the site under Ben Lomond! I tried to capture the atmosphere on slides. Beinn a' Chaoruinn lay to the north of the site and I did both these Munros before returning for breakfast. By then I was fit to live with again.

I had left a questionnaire on the latter. It was found by a fellow-member of the A.B.M.S.A.C. the next day, James Walmsley, who wrote a kind note back. He mentioned the late Willie Docherty in it, a person known now to a decreasing circle of friends, one of that passing breed of "gentle giants", modest and kindly who yet did mighty deeds in the hills. He published privately a trilogy listing some 900 summits in the British Isles and including dozens of large, pullout panoramas which must be unique. Having heard of our Braehead doings, he very kindly had given me a set. We became friends. He had an encyclopaedic knowledge of the hills, despite having nearly lost a leg in the war and having a wife helplessly bed-ridden. At the top of his house he had a prophet's chamber lined throughout with framed panoramas.

W. K. Holmes (author of *Tramping Scottish Hills* and volumes of verse) was another of this sort who had befriended our gang when we were kids at Dollar. He was the only adult we met in the Ochils, we thought him rather fine, though goodness knows what he thought of us banging in six-inch nails for pitons on routes in the out-of-bounds quarry. He came and watched, though—his example meant a great deal, I can see now.

The hills are peopled with all these past memories, enriching, encouraging. How could I possibly be bored? Oh, can I plead, for the taking of the heritage in full; do not be a specialist, the mountains are worth so much more. Read, and look, and go and go to the very end. It is all joy.

The Cairngorms are divided north–south by two great passes, the eastern, the Lairig an Laoigh, the *Pass of the calves*, lay just below this moine, at this stage a deep trench across which I looked to Coire Etchachan. North and south of this corrie lay my next two Munros; I therefore had to drop steeply down into the pass before starting the day again, so to speak.

On the slopes of warty Beinn Mheadhoin I found a hole which looked as if it had been caused by lightning or by a meteorite, for it was too fresh for the work of Cairngorm hunters. The barns were like piles of platters—fascinating weathering. A ptarmigan flopped off its nest at my feet and tried to lead me away with a mock-injury display. I hurried on for the wind was icy cold and the eggs would soon chill. Sometimes I have only been saved from standing on nests by the sitting bird's blinking eye. The camouflage is perfect. Dotterel, too, sit tight, often to their grief, rarity making them prey to the inane egg-collecting mania.

Mheadhoin's summit is another barn, and not for the first time I reached it on hands and knees, the wind making balance difficult. From it I could look straight down on Loch Avon. The scene was still like something from the arctic. I was sad not to be using the famous Shelter Stone (by the next morning I was to be doubly sorry), probably the most famous howff of all. There used to be a visitors' book. One brief entry took our interest; it said, "It moved"! Nearby the Cairngorm Club was founded—the first club in Scotland.

Not so long ago a body was found near the Shelter Stone. It had lain for some months, yet nobody knows who or why. Forty years ago, on Ben Avon, another body was found in a burn, and its presence there is still unexplained. On a rock upstream was laid out a razor, brush and other toilet items; an attaché-case held pyjama trousers and the like. His identity was never discovered, nor why he should have been up there dressed in city suit and bowler hat. There have been something like sixty unexplained bodies or vanished persons in the Scottish hills, since records have been kept.

The Cairngorms are among the most-used hills now, yet off the beaten tracks you can still be very much alone. From Mheadhoin down to Loch Etchachan there is now a path. This loch, sited at 3,050 feet, is the highest large spread of water in the country. Lean trout survive in it and pied pipers were calling round it today. My first acquaintance with it had nearly been my last for I had managed to get adrift on an ice floe. In winter it can be iced over for weeks—I have crossed it on ski. Today the ice still rimmed it and the wind was throwing the spray far up the slopes round it, reminding me just how wild and inhospitable these hills can be, modest though they may seem in area or height when compared with foreign ranges.

Derry Cairngorm lies out on a limb and gives some good boulder-hopping practice. It is probably the least-visited Cairngorm summit, and one of the best with its view of the Lairig an Laoigh, Glen Derry, and the cliffs of Sputan Dearg and Lochain Uaine. Every other loch seems to be a *green loch* in these hills.

I hopped my way back off Derry Cairngorm and dropped into Coire Etchachan where there is a small concrete memorial hut built in 1954. In the book I found the name of a local lad, Pat Heneghan, and of Gordon Mackenzie who had been with me in the Alps a year previously. A mouse was often mentioned—or was it a shrew? From there I dropped down into the Lairig and followed it through to the Fords of Avon where there is another wee shelter with a book. Syd Scroggie, met on Lochnagar, had been there. So had Robert Aitken, an old climbing partner.

The ford was just a ford, fortunately, and I crossed dry. The shelter was welcome and I sat out of the wind relishing a brew. The howff has a garden of compo ration tins.

I was tempted to stay the night but, high wind or not, the call to push on was stronger than sanity. I pinched a candle, left two paperbacks and wended up to Loch Avon, which I could hear long before it came into view: the waves were crashing on its red sands like a sea. A toil up boulders, heather and juniper took me to the Saddle and I dropped down the Strath Nethy side hoping for a lee. There was none, but after eleven hours on the go tendons had had enough, and I pitched the tent.

Thursday 16 May WIND ON THE LEFT
The night produced a Cairngorm roarer, the big wind whamming up the glen into the tent which cracked and banged so that sleep was really impossible. A bivy bag would have been much less noisy. The night stayed dry, mercifully, though, after midnight, it blew so hard that I half-dressed and half-packed in case of an emergency exodus. At 5.45 I rose thankfully. Neither candle nor stove could cope with the wind inside the tent, so after a tepid breakfast I crawled out again to battle the flailing canvas into a packable bundle. Leaving the gear I staggered up the slope above for A'Choinneach, a minor Munro.

My course up the slopes was erratic as the wind landed blow after blow, eventually sprawling me on to the granite gravel with an unexpected lull. Loch Avon, below, looked like a sea torn by a storm from some unlikely film. A'Choinneach was dull enough to merit a questionnaire. It was picked up two days later by Peter Mackay from Alva (like Dollar, an Ochils hillfoot town), who was then on Munro 100. He climbed, he said, to get away from people who ask him to fill in forms.

Bynack More, a better Munro, was reached almost at a trot, the wind pushing me up its flank. Cairn Gorm was spouting smoke-like clouds of its own making. I had wanted to visit the Barns of Bynack, a group of tors big enough for some climbing, but decided I had plenty to do as it was. I reckon it took twice the calories to fight my way down to the Saddle again, into the wind, than it had to sail uphill with the storm. A roof over my head was a dream. Two nights without sleep had me yawning like a zombie.

It would be easy to believe in the *each uisge* on a day like this, for the loch had a hundred wild horses kicking on its black surface. Toiling up the slope on the other side of the Saddle, even with the extra weight of the rucksack, I was twice knocked over. I traversed above a shallow corrie to leave my burden on the slopes of Coire Raibeirt, then spread my jacket like a sail to help me up Cairn Gorm. Two dotterel with flickering legs went speeding off, and just a minute before reaching this most popular of summits I found a fine cluster of Cairngorm stones in a block of granite. I hid it, took a bearing and paced the distance from the cairn. Months later I returned for it—and could not find it.

The largest Cairngorm ever found—two feet long—can be seen at Braemar Castle. It was found in the eighteenth century on Beinn a' Bhuird after the Cailleach nan Clach, the *old woman of the stones*, had dreamed about it. A 50 lb monster was found by the Feith Buidhe by John Grant of Ryvoan. It went to Queen Victoria, Grant receiving £1 per lb for it, quite a sum in those days.

Cairn Gorm is one of the most visited of summits. It now has an erosion problem, a chair-lift, a café and such like. The name has come to be given to all the hills, replacing the kindlier Monadh Ruadh—the *blue hills* replacing the *red*. Speyside is the tourist magnet. On the A9 at Aviemore there is even a road sign marked "Cairn Gorm". This is a corner of Scotland I try to visit only during the odd days of the off season. There are worn paths connecting all the popular tops and routes, as in the Lakes, but equally, go aside a wee, and it is all yours. The Monadh Ruadh is still finer than the sum of the ants who crawl over it.

The tourists are not new. One of the attractions used to be that Macdhui was regarded as the highest point in the British Isles. While working on notes recently I was glad to see that a new book by Campbell Steven had come out, for it tells quite a bit about early visitors to Cairngorm. *The Story of Scotland's Hills* (Hale) gives many fascinating historical accounts and is a must for anyone wanting more than just topographical information. Another comprehensive book is that by Adam Watson and Nethersole-Thomson, *The Cairngorms* (Collins). Doing courses in the hills I am for ever recommending books and am usually saddened to see nobody at once note the titles. Any book can be ordered from the local library where a whole world of vicarious fun lies ready to hand. Few seem to use it!

I cringed in the doorway of the radio relay station only to cram in a Lee's Macaroon Bar, then fought back down to my rucksack. A refreshing high traverse followed, taking me round to Lochan Buidhe, the highest small lochan in the country (3,683 feet), where I went into the Curran Bothy for a brew. The floor was inches deep in ice, covered in melt and a malodorous collection of refuse. It was the first and last time I would use the place. It has since been knocked down. Hateful place, it had been the fatal loadstone of a Cairngorm tragedy. It was while trying to make for it that an Edinburgh school party had been overwhelmed by a blizzard and died on this wild plateau.

As with so many tragedies it drove many into ridiculous extremes of attitude. Climbers too readily cry "keep all kids out", yet most of them first went on the hills as kids themselves, and probably a deal more dangerously. All of us who have been at this game a long time are survivors in a way and in no position to throw stones. Yet safety has been made the latest sacred cow and the hills roped down with a load of rules and regulations. One authority had the following orders worked out: the Cairngorm plateau banned from October to April; parties to go up a hill only so long as they return by the same route; in winter they must not go above 2,000 feet; climbing, only up what they can climb down; through routes and treks forbidden, and areas beyond the Great Glen are not to be used because too remote.

The hills cannot be made completely safe. It is a pity that the M.L.C. has been regarded as a magic wand that ensures safety. It merely shows a basic hill competence, nothing more. Yet the experience and competence of climbers is seldom called upon to help head-masters assess a teacher's potential on the hill with kids. It is easier, I suppose, to rely on a bit of paper. Some naughty people, too, have proclaimed that one type of mountain activity is more "worthy" or "right" than another. But you cannot separate values, ideals, dreams, motivations, nor grade them. The hills are not there for climbers, for walkers, for skiers, for mountain rescuers, for bird watchers, for tourists, for committees, for school kids, for grannies, or even for educationists. They are there for fun—for the rising of any man's heart, whatever the game he plays. Answer only to your own heart.

These were no doubt gloomy thoughts, appropriate for the midden of the Curran, perhaps. The shelter gave a wind-free brew. I had coffee and soup and then went off still supping a bowl of porridge in an effort to gain Macdhui ahead of the mist. The mist won. By a ruined gable I donned waterproofs—it was bitter cold in the cloud. The whole region of this summit is a mess of holes and bothy ruins and the like—a reminder of the days of searching for Cairngorms. We were mercifully spared the erection of a massive cairn to raise Macdhui above the Ben, a scheme which failed due to cash shortage.

Circling down and round I came on three figures in the familiar colours of Glenmore Lodge. We loomed up on each other, passed, and vanished like ghosts. Naturally the mind turned to the tales of the Great Grey Man. Sadly I have nothing personal to relate, despite many visits in misty weather, despite even sleeping on the haunted mountain. The Lodge staff do not tell tales and the locals keep quiet on the topic. Persistent puzzles could be largely due to our ignorance, yet it is easy to joke. One wonders just what Collie, famous scientist, but also famous joker, was up to when he first admitted taking to his heels on Macdhui. That was in 1891. Since then there have been other admissions of terrifying phenomena. Borthwick touches on it in *Always a Little Further*; John Buchan (a fine climber) has a story of a similar experience in Bavaria entitled "Pan" (in the S.M.C. Journal, vol. 22, p. 41). Why, of all Scotland's likely hills, is this one singled out for such persistent tales?

Beyond the Tailors' Burn I turned down and came out of the blowing cloud. Rising in a succession of bumps the only real ridge in the Cairngorms led on to Carn a' Mhaim, the day's fifth Munro. On the col, the Ceann Caol, I found a white azalea among the many pink ones. I blew along to the summit which has a great view down into the Lairig

Ghru and to Braeriach. Below I could see the Corrour Bothy which squatted like a spider in a web of radiating paths. It was to be my shelter for the night, eventually.

First I went on to the end of the ridge which always looks higher than the real summit, then dropped down to cross the Glen Derry path to gain the Lairig Ghru well to the south of the bothy. I had a brew and emptied my rucksack. A lochan above me actually drains both ways, to Dee and Derry. I carried on down the Lairig path till opposite the Allt Garbh where I boulder-hopped the Dee rather cheekily, then once I had added a heavy load to my rucksack I more cannily chose to paddle back.

This load was a food parcel which I had buried, back in February, among a jumble of granite boulders; it proved to be in perfect condition. The sugar ran out of its bag freely. No damp at all. Untouched.

The way across to the bothy was signposted and the Dee has a bridge; after all this is the country's premier pedestrian motorway, so to speak, and the "services" have to be provided. Being about the busiest of all bothies it is often also the dirtiest. Even the deer know this and you can lie listening to them clattering among the tins and rubbish at night. The bothy was originally built in 1877, but in 1950 had to be virtually rebuilt in unfriendly concrete and non-combustible materials, a testimony to vandalism. Seton Gordon, the grand-master writer on the Cairngorms, tells a story of being in the bothy during a blizzard when his friend went out to fetch water from the burn and did not return. In the storm he had lost the bothy, and only found it again by following the sound of the bagpipes which Seton Gordon was playing for the purpose.

This great pass, which rises to 2,700 feet, is an old through route—as old as man himself no doubt. Cattle were regularly driven through it to southern markets. Raiders used it. The Tailors' Stone marks the spot of one tragedy. It is as well that the idea of creating the glorified "Grampian Way" through here has been dropped, or we no doubt would have a few more.

I joined an older man in the bothy. The statutory brew was welcome. I was bleary with the wind. R. L. Stevenson I think it was who talked about "the flaws of fine weather we call our summer". It cleared for a blink of sunset sun. A mountain blackbird was tugging at a worm on the lawn outside, just like his urban counterpart. In the middle of the night I went out and sent off a startled stag. By then the night was impressively wild, with weird clouds towering and a single beacon star bright in the vee of the Lairig. Some things you cannot spoil.

Friday 17 May WIND ON THE RIGHT

Sleep can be either consciously relished or a deep oblivion. It was from the latter I woke at 7.30. My bothy companion packed and even washed before going off to Loch Morlich, hoping to return later to go down the Tilt. I merely ate. It was nearly ten before we went our ways.

Devil's Point looms over the bothy, a thrust of crag and slab that sticks out in any view down the Lairig. The slab was not to be resisted, and rather than go up the corrie path I simply scrambled up direct. On top I nearly stood on a ptarmigan brooding her seven eggs. Dodging wet and boulder areas I gained the rim for Cairn Toul, the *barn hill*, which was again very windy. Angel's Peak beyond is another thrusting shape; Sgor an Lochain Uaine, its older name, tells that it sits above yet another lochan of common name. The loch was like a cauldron, all spume and motion. Braeriach, across the fastness of the Garbh Choire, had a weird cloud formation above it.

The Garbh Choire is one of the wildest in Scotland, a huge bite, or bites rather, taken out of the plateau which is all near or over the 4,000-foot mark. The whole rim was still corniced. Many times on the plateau I was forced into a run by the push of the wind. The infant Dee falls from the plateau, usually in a string of white which today was oddly missing. I found out why when I went over to see the fall—and received most of it in my face. The wind several times knocked me down or threw stinging gravel at me. Progression had a drunken look about it as I would stagger first one way, then rush off in another, then lean on nothing, then fall down. Approaching gusts could be seen in the spray they picked up, like miniature waterspouts. It was an entertaining way of gaining Braeriach.

The summit itself was quite without wind, but it was not quiet. A roar like the sea came from only a few feet away and the fantastic upward thrust of wind out of the corrie was creating the cloud paintings overhead. It was eerie and impressive, but a glower of grey was a warning not to linger.

It was on the cliffs where the infant Dee plunges down into the corries that one of the earliest rock-climbs was recorded in Scotland, in 1810. The Rev. George Keith Skene was tracing that river to its source and no bit of cliff was going to divert the enthusiastic scientist. The route is still in the climbers' guidebook. It was the same gentleman who finally destroyed Macdhui's claim to be the highest. His measurements gave it 4,300 feet (four feet out from the present) but his son came back with an upsetting 4,406 feet for Ben Nevis.

I returned to the Lairig by the Sron, meeting a vertical wind at the first nick on the rim and later stopping to look at bits of old wreckage from a wartime air crash. As a kid I took home from there an old flying boot with some bones in it; a precious souvenir which my parents managed to lose rather quickly. On another occasion I broke an ice-axe trying to gain some mechanical parts.

The latest two trips had been with Assessment candidates for the Instructor's Certificate, overnight exercises from Glenmore Lodge, the latter memorable in full moon on new snow that made a wonderland out of winter. You could read the map without a torch and see for miles. Not the most testing of conditions for assessing navigation, but a night the victims will not forget. My group of Instructors crossed from Glen Feshie, walked up Glen Einich and then over the plateau, bivying on Braeriach before going out via the Sron to Loch Morlich.

Today the Sron na Lairig col was devilish, and it took a real tussle to drop the 200 feet off it to the forgotten zig-zag of a path. After that it was a romp. Wreckage was strewn right down to the burn in the Lairig and if you went up Macdhui by the slope opposite you could follow wreckage there too, for another plane had crashed on that side. The Devil's Point and Carn a' Mhaim are nicely balanced seen from here and the loops of the Dee were glittering and silver; Poussin could not have arranged it better.

An hour of boulder-hopping saw me back at the bothy. I crossed well up from the bridge, which is cunningly placed to land one right in a big peat bog which has been well ploughed with a million feet. Be warned of Cairngorm bothies, they are often full, and at the best grimy, sweaty, concrete boxes. Earlier I mentioned the tragedy of the tailors: they had set out on a wager to dance, in one day, in the dells of Abernethy, Rothiemurchus (Speyside) and Dalmore (Deeside). The worst of the pass over, they perished at the spot known as Clach nan Taillear. Even the doucer Lairig an Laoigh had a group tragedy, in 1805, when five out of seven soldiers died in a storm while walking from Edinburgh home to Speyside. I have been pinned down at Corrour in a blizzard in which it was impossible to move. The bothy was a real haven then.

I kept a candle in the window and periodically warmed soup and tea water. Weekenders were expected. At midnight two winking lights appeared miles off. There was a sensation of excitement and unreality watching their approach. Figures evolved out of the glowing patches. Ian and Mary McLeod and a German teacher friend, Wolfgang, burst in; our high-spirited reunion was no doubt a puzzle to two quiet French girls who had arrived a bit earlier. Brews, beer, soup and much chatter ensured I had my latest bedding of the trip. We drifted into a silence lapped with the sound of rain.

Saturday 18 May TENT IN THE CLOUDS
The French girls snored, but they were away first. In sawn-off jeans we reckoned they would have delicately blue knees on top of Braeriach. It still rained steadily though the cloud cleared off the tops. I was telling the others of our last Braehead trip at Corrour when we had had the Army encamped about us. We had stayed on for two extra days living off their left-overs. Every boulder seemed to be hiding a steamed pudding or tube of gooseberry jam, quite apart from what we were officially given. If the Army chose not to march on its stomach, we did!

Eventually the rain turned off, so there was no excuse for prolonging our fester. Ian, Mary and Wolfi set off to traverse Macdhui while I turned for the Bhrotain group. They had the more interesting day, for they had no sooner settled into the Etchachan Hut than Wolfi spotted someone "humbling" down from the near crags: a young Marine who had completed a V.S. route and then fallen on a loose boulder. They had to evacuate him to Derry Lodge.

The Dee sang bonnily—and deeper than before. I had to paddle again at the same easy spot near the cache site. The blue milkwort was out and suddenly there seemed to be butterwort stars everywhere—as if they had crawled out like starfish from the pools. I followed the Allt Garbh which joins the Dee there, its deer-tracked gorge or the slabby burn itself giving better walking than the deep, clawing heather. Close-cropped heather above was better and took me up Carn Cloich-mhuillin, the *cairn of the mill*, the hill Sir Hugh had intended for his last as it was easy to ascend with ponies bearing the appropriate celebration-day libations.

Tramping up Bhrotain beyond, I entered cloud—and that was that for the rest of the day. My steering led to the knobbly cairn and the nearby trig point. Bhrotain and Bhrodainn, a loch in the Gaick Pass, probably derive from Brodan, the hound of Celtic lore, which chased the white stag of Ben Alder into the loch where both vanished for ever. The corrie between Bhrotain and Monadh Mor (the *big dumpy hill*), the next along, is Coire Cath nam Fiann, the *corrie of the battle of the Fianns* (Fingalians). It is sad that so many legends only linger in mysterious place names.

Both are unshapely lumps of hill, part of an empty quarter only visited I reckon by working keepers, filthy Munro-baggers, and a few other aberrant walkers. In quite a number of visits I have never met anyone up there, though I have still to go on a day with decent visibility.

Between these hills and the Devil's Point runs Glen Geusachan, once a deer sanctuary, a long glen, with slabby flanks (which might repay climbing on) and only lacking a loch to give it full splendour. An interesting lochan lies above its head, Loch na Stuirteag, which at 2,840 feet must be the highest site for nesting gulls in Britain, nor could they be much further from the sea. The name means *loch of the black headed gulls*—which certainly do make a stuirteag of a noise. The gulls nesting now are common gulls, but the name was given about eighty years ago. Before that it was the "Insignificant Loch".

Monadh Mor was reached over a bouldery col and gave typical map, watch, and compass navigation, both to reach it and for the continuation, until the snow banked down to the Allt Luineag, a mess of river dawdling in the puddles and melt. It is a wonderfully empty desolation, the home of haunting birds and wet winds. I crossed the river and cut through between a Top of 3,009 feet and lonely Loch nan Cnapan, both faintly discernible. A path of sorts (deer?) led to the Allt Sgairnich which led to a new bulldozed track. I took it for a while but then reverted to map and compass to make sure of hitting the strong, if infant, River Eidart, here known as the Caochan Dubh. The ground was very *dubh*. I found the river and followed it down to where it made a marked swing to the south-east—which let me know exactly where I was. Not for nothing is this the Moine Mhor, the *big moss*; broken country of peat hags and, higher, grassy sweeps now scarred by man's new tracks. I ran into the Land-Rover track again and as I knew where it left the plateau to drop to Glen Feshie, I gave up map and compass to follow it. A fork of the track soon landed me on Mulloch Clach a'

Bhlair just after 7 p.m. As it had rained for several hours I decided it was time to stop. In the conditions it would have been a tricky night descent to reach the Feshie. I might be a "spoilt child of adventure" in the words of Roger Duplat, but I was a canny one withal. I pitched the tent within sight of a corrie rim which bubbled over with cloud. It was crying plover country, a desolation I love. One by one four candle stumps burnt out as I scribbled the day's log. At 3,025 feet the site was to prove the highest of the Walk.

Sunday 19 May   REWARDS AND THE FESHIE

Some days are good from the opening of eyes. This was one such, no doubt helped by being at over 3,000 feet already. The first brew was made while still cosy in the sleeping bag, and eating and reading made for a lazy start. Stones went into the burn and I left no sign of my stay beyond a temporary depression in the soggy grass. The cloud was tense and bright with the promise of clearing.

I groped round the rim of Coire Garbhlach, a gravelly, floral place seldom visited by walkers. The cloud teased off like cotton wool pulled from an aspirin bottle. I stood on the dome of Meall Dubhag. A ptarmigan sat in the confidence of its camouflage. Perhaps it should be my symbol of the summits, this gentle bird of the mists and snow, of bog and ridge and dew-glitter. I sat watching it a while, then read a bit, willing the weather to clear up and the sun to shine again. Impatiently I stormed over Carn Ban Mor.

Only then it cleared. Like surf sucking seaward, breaking, ebbing, clear. I gazed about the casual complex of the Cairngorms, over the green richness of Speyside, to western dream hills that were still to come. It was very good. I romped on, singing as only optimism in the sun can sing.

> "Where lies the land to which the ship would go?
> Far, far ahead, is all her seamen know."
>   A. H. CLOUGH

Today was a day of holiday! Sailing free!

If I have dwelt on this feeling of elation, it is on purpose. The feeling of being in tune, both with the finite and the Infinite, is a vital part of the game of hills we play. We suppress the romantic only to our hurt. If I had my ups and downs, usually related to the weather, then, overall, the ups far outnumbered the downs. There would be no sense in it otherwise. The bad days of course make better copy (disasters sell best of all), and we British are so loath to appear enthusiastic about anything.

One winter, back in the days when perforce we had to exercise our thumbs, Mike Smith and I hitched up from Fife one Friday night. We had agreed to meet at a certain bridge at midnight, which, despite blizzards and one lorry arguing with a telegraph pole, we did. We walked to Glen Feshie and camped. It was freezing-the-eggs cold but gave a swinging day over these hills in just the way today was doing—except we were one Munro on that day. Looking to Sgor Gaoith today I had a feeling of disbelief. On those gentle slopes we had got lost, Mike and I, in classic fashion too. It was obviously going to clear so we were lazy about steering by compass, and tramped on in the mist. We found two more tracks, newly made, which was surprising at that early winter hour. When we joined an even bigger track we at last became suspicious and at that moment the cloud blew away to reveal every-thing written in the snow. It was quite amazing what a small circum-ference our circling track marked out, while we were quite sure we had been going in a straight line. We hurried on from the displayed track of our sinning.

Later in the year Mike and I and a teacher friend had a similar experience on a narrow ridge above the Great Glen. On such a defined ridge we were only checking every now and then as there was so little chance of straying. Yet on one check we found ourselves 180° out. We turned in obedience to the compass but our friend raised hell—he was for on. There was a right old argument until, left with no supporters, he came with the compass. Mike had just stood by grinning and saying nothing—a change for him. As we set off he whispered to me as I passed: "the Feshie hills, eh?"

Sgor Gaoith, 3,658 feet, is the *peak of wind*, a dramatic perch of a summit being a prow overlooking the long line of cliffs above Loch Einich. The group is usuallly known as the Sgoran Dubhs, for Sgoran Dubh Mor, the next bump on, though 3,635 feet, and therefore only a Top, is the dominating piece of dark architecture seen from Glen Einich. The cliffs give long ridge climbs, grand in setting, on nervy granite, pioneered by a regular Who's Who of the far off times: Naismith, the father of the S.M.C., Mackay, Raeburn the Great, Solly, Maylard, King, Glover, welcome Sassenachs, arch-Munroist A. E. Robertson—and from less distant times names like J. H. B. Bell,

H. I. Ogilvy, who was killed here, Richard Frere the writer, George Ritchie and Alistair Cram, who I was to meet on the Walk.

Pennant, in his 1794 *Tour* mentions "Sgorgave in Rothiemurchus" which is probably Sgor Gaoith. It has a "Cailleach" pinnacle to match the "Bodach" across on Braeriach opposite. The flesh and blood people of Glen Einich and of the sheilings at the head of the loch have long gone.

I pitched the tent to dry in the sun and breeze on top of the peak, and lay looking over the edge. The loch was brilliant silver—for a change. Ptarmigan were making noisy and erratic flights among the arêtes of grey rock and a herd of deer browsed all unaware not far below my eyrie. Opposite the bulk of Braeriach blocked the view, but to the south I could see Beinn a' Ghlo and the Ring of Tarff beyond the rim of the snow-patched wilderness I had stravaiged over yesterday.

In the 1780's Colonel Thornton, the famous (or infamous) sportsman, had flown his falcons at ptarmigan up here. Dotterel too. One of my joys this trip was to see rare birds, not just in the known places; but that is not something I will be mentioning. The first snow bunting nest discovered in Scotland now sits in the British Museum!

Munro-baggers are driven off the rim to descend out for a measly Geal Charn, 3,019 feet only, but on the sacred list. A group sat eating by its cairn but the finer view is over at some cairns on the rim so I paused there instead. As I continued I noticed that Schiehallion away to the south and Ben Rinnes to the north are perfect mirror images with long and short sides matching. The eye also went to the gash of Loch Ericht and its guardian, Ben Alder. It then struck me that this was the next section. The way to the west was opening. Lochaber would see the half way, mathematically, and the Great Glen the half way, psychologically. . . .

The descent to Glen Feshie takes one down through zones of boulders and deep heather—inescapable. The remnants of old pines were douce after the arid heights. I had a brew just to revel in the richness of the setting. Brewing was always an excuse for a stop—or vice versa. Wood ants were rather active and there were flying insects, while a cuckoo with a sticky "ooh" kept up its monotonous call. Nature-loving has moments when one feels like putting in for a divorce, but with siskin, coal and crested tits, chaffinch and warblers all flitting and chitting it was a delightful change. I ate the last of my food and scattered thank-you crumbs in best Stevenson tradition.

The River Feshie was bouldery and low, a mere paddle. A roe deer barked as I set out across it. The Ripleys had a more exciting crossing a bit higher up the river. Brian wrote: "As I was crossing the swing bridge I very dreamily let the map slip from my grasp. It fell into the fast-flowing waters and floated merrily away. A mad dash followed . . . after about half a mile Alan made a spectacular dive, grabbing the precious map but getting thoroughly soaked." All I did was nearly stand on a clutch of large pied piper's eggs. Camouflage can be too good! Then, once I had booted-up again, I nearly had a heart attack—a capercailzie went clattering off.

The Dell Hotel at Rothiemurchus often has enthusiastic ornithologists staying and one guest had spent most of his time happily watching a brooding caper in the bushes opposite his bedroom window. Only on his morning of departure did he confide his find to the hostess. She promised to keep quiet—and did as far as the kitchen . . . "and that bird-watcher has spent a happy holiday doing little else but watch our broody turkey!" It could easily be done; but turkeys do not rise at your feet and racket off through the trees half scaring the wits out of you.

Our native capercailzies had been wiped out by about 1771 (the last was recorded in Glenmoriston), and reintroduction at Mar Lodge in 1827 failed. In 1837 efforts at Taymouth Castle by Loch Tay succeeded, the original 32 becoming over 1,000 a quarter of a century later, on that estate. The Black Wood of Rannoch birds no doubt came from there. Introductions east of Inverness were made in 1894 and now the bird is fairly common in coniferous woodlands.

As I stepped it out for Milehouse I was surrounded by new plantings, trees being Speyside's other industry. Over the whole country our treatment of trees has a poor history. Romans, Vikings, raiders and lawmen, all down history, burnt and cut at this precious covering. Bare Rannoch Moor has the old bones of skeleton trees across it. Only on the islands are there remnants, safe from sheep and deer—which man drove on to the hills (the deer's natural habitat is forest). Commercial greed just about destroyed all that was left: shipbuilding and iron smelting decimated the Speyside, Argyll and Loch Maree forests. After the 1745 money was urgently needed by clan chiefs aping the good life in London. They sold their woods for cash as they sold their people for sheep. Names such as the York Building Company and the Duke of Sutherland were synonymous with blatant exploitation. The ravaged landscape has been starved, burnt uncontrollably, and overgrazed ever since. It has taken writers like Fraser Darling to stir the public conscience.

The old ways of pre-1745 were changing, but the forced peace after that date, together with the introduction of the potato, helped to create a population explosion which only the export of people could relieve. Some landlords beggared themselves trying to help their tenants, and some of the present scenic gems owe their green beauty to sportsmen who had bought their acres with cotton-spun sterling. Have a look in the deep gorges and ravines in the wilds where no fire or beast has ever destroyed. There you will find the secret, old Scotland: Scots pine, birch, rowan, holly, willow, hazel and so on.

On Rhum they are re-creating the original woodland—with results we will not see for generations. The first thing the Conservancy did on the island was get rid of the sheep. At Kinloch you can see, next to each other, areas where deer are allowed and excluded. On the latter good soil and ground cover is found.

Forgive me if I have flown off into the trees after my caper—but wildlife matters and trees matter. They are part of our mountain heritage, and as man-dependent as the rest. I would almost stick my neck out to say the Irish Munros have a beauty ours lack, for where ours rise almost always from a sterile desert of our past creating, in Ireland the hills rise from a patchwork of bright green fields. You look down on a landscape blue with smoke (you can smell it even on the tops), dotted with homes, stitched with wending roads and hedgerows and trees. Come down off our tops and you pass the refugee deer to find glens of sheep and broken walls of houses, treeless, empty. Men betray themselves in the way they have treated trees and soil.

I collected my cycle from Clive Freshwater who runs the sailing/canoe school on Loch Insh and lives next door to the Ladies Scottish Climbing Club cottage of Milehouse. He was in the throes of litigation over canoeing on the Spey, a case he was to win, though appeals went to the House of Lords. Landowners are slow to see that co-operation is the best policy. Clashing with the masses can only lead to one thing.

The shop was shut so I went up to the Ossian Hotel and treated the inner man. The contrast was savoured: there over the trees and the crying gulls were my hills, and here was I having buttered scones and cakes sitting on the lawn and throwing stones for the dog to fetch.

The girl who made the tea had the west-country surname of Rainbow.

"When I was courting Johnny Rainbow my parents thought he was a pop singer or something!"

I was back on the line of the A9 road and also back to lower altitudes: 800 feet, the lowest since Blair Atholl. Loch Insh took quite a lot of film, the reflected trees and the old church again being such a contrast. I meant to go to church but had the wrong times. I collected a food parcel from Mr Fleming, the forester, neighbour on the other side of Milehouse. He kept exotic pheasants, which explained some of the odd noises I had heard. I washed lots of clothes and hung them out. My kilt was waiting too, for it is a grand walking garb. Alas, even at the last buckle, it could not find anywhere to hang above my ankles. So I parcelled it for home, wrote a dozen letters, did some logistics, wrote up the log, cooked and ate a huge meal and went to bed and read till all hours. Life is not long enough.

> Hold sun, for just another hour of day!
> We know pale dusk's when all ships weigh
> And sail off; and the last sunset
> May be best of all—but not just yet.
> I have a thousand miles to travel, friend;
> Then sail me under, make a glorious end.

Monday 20 May   THE MILEHOUSE WORM

Bookworm that is. Milehouse has a splendid bookcase. It rained most of the day so I was happy to read by the fire, lost to the world of the Walk and reality. In the evening I went to telephone David and Marina, as the next morning was my deadline for Kincraig. At 7.15 the line was engaged. I watched the speugs nesting behind the board proclaiming "Smith's Stores". It was "closed" when I had bought some provisions earlier. At 9.15 the line was still engaged despite trying to get through every few minutes. I was not very good-humoured by then. The exchange could not help. In the end I phoned Mary Gordon, two doors along from David, and asked her please to report my safe arrival —and see if they had been on the telephone for two hours and more. Of course they had not; just more gremlins in the system.

Spring had slipped into the comfier clothes of summer. I could have lingered quite happily in that rich green landscape. It was still full of bird sounds: snipe drumming, the wuthering of the peesies, the babel of the *stuirteag* out in the marshes and, loveliest of all summer calls, the sandpiper.

I lingered long before my fire at night, loath to break the idyll. Milehouse is a great wee place. I filled up the form to send off to the custodian, Ann Winning, wrote her a letter and left unwanted things in a cupboard. A last brew. A last dram of "Jura". Bed. An hour of C. S. Lewis. And then only the honking of the fancy pheasants next door and the quiet, soothing sound of the wind in the larch trees.

VII

LOCHABER AND BACK

"Life is an alternating current, illumination coming from the contrasts."

F. FRASER DARLING

Tuesday 21 May WEST OF THE A9

The evil reputation of the A9 road was thoroughly manifest today: no freewheeling, a persistent headwind and thus a bottom-gear grind all the way, and three times I was ditched by big brutes of lorries, twice just blatantly "breenging" past as if I did not exist. As "an aid to pedestrianism" the cycle was a dead loss.

My only pause was to look at Ruthven Barracks, a roofless, stark ruin with a vivid, typical history. At one time it was the home of the Wolf of Badenoch. In 1451 it was demolished by the Earl of Ross, in 1546 Locheil and Keppoch were held fast there by Huntly before being beheaded, in 1582 the young teenage James VI and I was decoyed there and captured by Gowrie and Mar, in 1594 Argyll laid siege to it, in 1647 General Leslie captured it, in 1654 Cromwell's general, Monck, was there, in 1689 Dundee burnt it. That is a selective coverage. It was thirty years after the last event that the present barracks was constructed. A sergeant won fame and promotion for a gallant defence against the Jacobites in 1746. Two days after Culloden, Lord George Murray and others re-grouped there, hopeful of renewing the fight. The Prince, however, had despaired and exile and death was their end. No wonder there is an air of sadness about the gables. It looks over great marshes and the low skyline of the rainy Monadh Liath.

The sausage, eggs and chips I had at the transport cafe at Dalwhinnie were better than any I'd ever had at hotels. I collected a food parcel and went on past the Wade bridge, through endless road works, past Balsporran, to pitch the tent just over the watershed where a roadside sign gave "Drumochter Pass, 1,506 feet". A peewit was nesting fifteen yards off.

This really is a Wade road, completed in 1729, when the soldier-navvies celebrated with four oxen roasted whole and four kegs of brandy. It links with the Corrieyairack road to Fort Augustus. Wade was "Commander of the Forces in North Britain" till 1740, but is chiefly remembered as a road builder. It was ironical that the rebels of 1745 were the first to use his roads. He built about forty bridges, many of which are still in use today. And all at £70 per mile. To appreciate the pass, climb Meall na Leitreich above Loch Garry—a remarkable series of moraines makes it as choppy-looking as sea.

I returned to Balsporran and set off for the hills to the west. A made path goes up Coire Fhar and let me reach the top of Geal Charn in an hour and a half. From the road several "stone men" give a human likeness from a moving car and many misjudge the ascent by taking the scale from them. Some are ten feet tall. The group gives easy going but the map does its best to hide the summits in vague contouring and misleading heights. There are two cairns on Geal Charn which scrapes into the list by all of five feet. It gives a long view down Loch Ericht, which, in five visits, I've seen for about two minutes in all. Today the landscape on the other side was a glitter of a thousand sequinned lochans.

The col to A'Mharconaich was teeming with deer as it always seems to be. It is a swelling slope of grass. The map shows a spot, 3,174 (small cairn) but the real summit, 3,185 feet, lies a good half mile to the north-east, at the end of the ridge. I had just escaped from this flat summit area when an inky storm came spluttering up Loch Ericht and it began to snow "upwards". There was a feel of thunder so I was undecided whether to go on, wait, skirt, or whatever. I ended doing all these things which did not make for good progress to the *top* of the hill.

"He tae Cupar mun tae Cupar." I made a cowardly race to the top of Beinn Udlamain, the *hill of the shaking*. It loomed out of the mist like an irascible porcupine, for the cairn was sprouting old fence-posts in all directions. My run down the other side scattered dotterel which went off in pantomime runs—fascinating birds.

The col for Sgairneach Mhor is very boggy, riven into peat hags. On the sweep up and round above it I found I was heading off for the wrong bump, so corrected course. It seems such an easy hill, but, again, it is easy to go astray on it. The summit is an erect and proper "stone man" on the edge of Coire Creagach, 3,210 feet, not the 3,160 spot shown on the map. Descending the rim of this corrie the rain came on for the rest of the descent. I drew into my waterproofs like a tortoise into its shell.

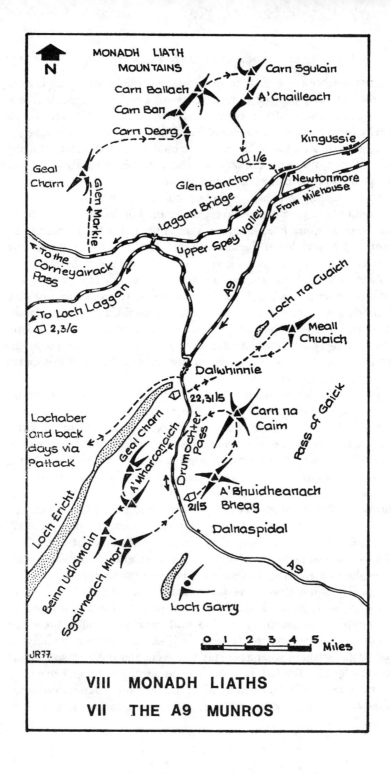

VIII   MONADH LIATHS

VII   THE A9 MUNROS

The lower slopes are always squelchy. The burn was low and easily crossed to gain the scruffy track which now runs right up Coire Dhomhain, which is really a valley hidden within the sweep of the last three of today's peaks.

I was in the tent again at 7.30 for a night of rain and traffic noises.

Wednesday 22 May EAST OF THE A9

I began the day by going up the burn by which I was camped. In the space of half a mile I found in it the corpses of a stag, a crow and a sheep. I also found a good antler which I shoved in my rucksack.

Well up on the heathery reaches of the hill I could still smell the rotten pong of decomposition and knew the worst. The antler had leaked a repulsive slime all over the rucksack—fortunately not on food, camera or logbook. There was no handy water, and in the throes of dealing with this the rain came on. Be warned, all who dream, reality often has prickles!

A'Bhuidheanach Bheag is dismissed by most as a dull plateau, but the eastern side has a great corrie, well seen from the top of An Dun in the Gaick Pass. Bheag means small, yet it is the highest summit hereabouts. There is a trig point marking the top, also a fence. (A cairn at a quartz outcrop a hundred yards to the north can mislead in mist.)

The Aonachs, Mor and Beag, next to Ben Nevis, are also the wrong way round, Beag being higher than Mor—but this is rather how they looked from below when people were naming them (it is only in the recent past that silly people started wandering about on top of the hills. Because these people were local they used the same descriptive words: More (big), Geal Charn (white cairn), Dearg (red), Ghobhar (goat) and so on.

Today's hills are in a vast area of moss and bog, but in certain lights, with piling clouds, the view can give a spaciousness unknown in lumpy Perthshire or crowded Lakeland. It is dotterel country. All day long today the golden plovers were weeping their complaint to the grey, sad skies, a sound of utter heartbreak. Squeezed in under the clouds I could just make out the Gaick Pass to the east and beyond it the even more desolate "moine" of the Ring of Tarff. The old drovers' way, the Minigaig, has to climb to 2,750 feet in crossing from Atholl to Speyside, the Gaick slices through the hills in a deep trough.

"The Loss of Gaick", an incident enshrined in folklore, tells of an avalanche disaster in this latter pass which happened on the first of

January 1800. A notorious recruiting officer and four friends were overwhelmed in a shooting bothy. A stone with a Gaelic inscription marks the spot. There is another tale, of a poor, starving family which was actually saved by an avalanche sweeping off the steep slopes to leave a huge snowball beside their cottage. When it was broken open it produced three brace of ptarmigan, six hares, four brace of grouse, a blackcock, a pheasant, three geese and two fat stags.

Today's walking gave the less attractive tops rather than the logical passes. The boundary fence can be followed usefully but I was happy to cut corners as much as possible. The fence shies off before the second Munro, Carn na Caim. It is seldom a good thing to rely on hill fences for navigation; they seldom go just where you want; nor can tracks be trusted, even on narrow ridges. Frequently their initial markings was the work of deer or sheep, and these have more intelligence than to seek out summital exactitude.

Chuaich is often done from here but the going is bad, and as I had to shift back to Dalwhinnie again from my Drumochter Pass site, I went down to the A9 direct. The shoulder below had been torn up to extract the quartz rock and the bulldozed track up to the workings is an ugly scar as seen from the A9. One more example of the need for landscape control.

Collecting the tent I pedalled down to Dalwhinnie, dry, with the wind behind, and ignored by mad motorists. The Portnastorm Cafe was visited for another dose of sausage, egg and chips, and at three o'clock I set off along the track beside the aqueduct for Chuaich, a Munro which is a useful "quickie" for the motorised walker. Meall Chuaich is a pudding-shaped lump, the most individualistic of these shapeless hills and a good viewpoint. It can be romped in an hour from the loch at its foot. I followed a new Land-Rover track for a bit and then sneaked up a slot of burn with the reward of being able to lie and watch deer grazing about twenty yards off.

I trotted down the north-west corrie, steep but not rocky, to see the water intake. There was a hut where instruments recorded the flow. A plaque said "Cuaich-Seillich tunnel, 22310 feet, completed 1940". This tunnel captures water from the Gaick Pass and feeds it to Loch Ericht at Dalwhinnie. Loch Ericht has a dam at both ends, and from its south-west end drains to Loch Rannoch which in turn flows on to the Tummel-Pitlochry series of dams and power stations—a unique multiple use of water.

A notice proclaimed Loch Cuaich was stocked with rainbow trout, and the limit of three fish must be checked with the head keeper—with a 50p per fish fine for any cheating. As I cycled back along by the aqueduct I met the keeper and chatted awhile. He was wild at the ravages of the new A9 for which the moor was being torn up beside us. "My wee birds! My wee birds! Could they not wait till they'd done nesting?"

I went to see Mr Oswald, the keeper for the Ericht hills, but he had won a prize holiday and was off in Majorca. He had thoughtfully left my parcel with his mother. After a chat I went off to pack. Food parcels! If only we could eat grass. Or heather. I phoned Dollar and also Gerry Peet, the custodian of the C.I.C. Hut on Nevis, to arrange a key for next weekend. A good round lay ahead. While in the phone box a redpoll sat on the bike. There was wind enough to blow away the cuckoo that infested the wood where I camped.

The sounds of tree-surf, of trains and traffic all merged pleasantly in sleep.

Thursday 23 May NO POLTERGEISTS

The wind died, the rain came lashing down and the blasted cuckoo began at 4 a.m. It went off at eight (the rain that is: the cuckoo went off on the hour, half-hour, quarters and much in between), and depression turned to a sort of desperation. I hung the tent to dry as I was leaving it. Originally I thought it could be left standing, but a stone's-throw from the A9 was a bit risky. The kind ladies in the shop stored it for me. It was bliss to go off on the bike down the empty miles of Loch Ericht, the grey loch trimmed with the verges of golden broom. I sat out a shower at the lodge. Above it some thirty stags stood to watch me go by, while several white garrons came cantering along beside me. Over the rise the bulk of Ben Alder appeared, bright and mottled, reaching up into the clean, shiny clouds. The freshness was a delight, the loneliness a tonic. I hid the cycle and strode on.

Loch Pattack was a fine reflecting pool. More white ponies were grazing on the alluvial greens which fight it out with the peat hags. A bridge of wobbly slats allows the pedestrian to cross, the track just uses the shoreline, sometimes in and sometimes out the water. Beyond the loch is a junction of tracks where I once had an alarming experience.

I had come through from Moy on Lagganside, heading for Culra (as once did Prince Charlie). The thick cloud, with me all the way, was stirring and about to clear. Suddenly there was a loud bang. I *felt* the blast of it, and dropped quickly to the ground cursing folk who fire guns in a fog. The clouds almost instantly rolled away leaving the brown reaches of Pattack clear. Not even an early midge stirred. There was not a soul to be seen. I suppose there is an explanation but nobody has given me a likely one yet.

I reached the bothy at Culra just before a heavy shower, so sat in it for a brew, looking out the doorway as the trailing curtains swept through the Bealach Dubh between Ben Alder and the Lancet Edge— a view instantly recognisable, the very epitome of a pass. When I set out again I found a dead deer just up the burn. It was the fourth dead deer I had seen that day.

The bothy book went back to 1966 and in it I found an entry by Brian and Alan Ripley. They too came in from Dalwhinnie and had two nights here doing in turn the groups south and north of the Bealach Dubh, before heading through it for the Ossian hills. There is a useful line of bothies linking the A9 with Fort William. At Loch Ossian is a fine, old-fashioned hostel, too, which can only be reached on foot, or by train, or by cycle. Knowledge of these havens was allowing me to yo-yo to Lochaber and back without a tent.

Slides are an abiding reminder of the day's towering cumulus clouds. I wended up towards the pass, then jumped the silvery burn to take the stalkers' path over the moors. This leads up to a pass, the Bealach Beithe, which divides Alder in two: the vast plateau of the Ben itself, the largest area outside the Cairngorms and Nevis to top 3,500 feet, and the splinter summit of Beinn Bheoil which used to have the magical height of 3,333 feet and be Munro number 111. Ben Alder's plateau shape is seen from all over Perthshire and the Cairngorms. It is as far from roads as can be, south of the Great Glen. It has good winter climbing and some summer potential—largely untapped.

My path led up to the loch in the pass, vanished, and then re-appeared beyond, only to die again at the top of the pass. Some supernatural power seems to stop all tracks to Ben Alder bothy, down the other side, for the track in from Rannoch stops, like a chopped worm, a mile short, and the lochside track from Dalwhinnie has been destroyed in many places by the raising of the water level. The good weather had gone by the time I reached the col: a grey ceiling as far as the eye could see. I returned down to the loch and up the Garbh Choire which was saturated and clammy with mist but at least provided a lee out of the storm. I took the line of a burn, then worked up ribs and gullies to the rim of old cornice. It was snowing hard on the plateau when I broke through, so I left a tiny cairn to mark my exit and tramped over the old snowbeds, head down, till I met the trig point and cairn. Ben Alder means *mountain of rock and water*, which is probably what it is made of. Bheoil is the *hill in front*—of Alder presumably.

I back-tracked without delay and by the time I was at the loch again my feet were soaking and the corrie was noisy with the sound of many waters. It cleared as I cut up and along for Beinn Bheoil, the *mountain in front*, a knobbly ridge, high above Loch Ericht, which is a great viewpoint. Schiehallion's cone was set in a halo of rainbow. The incomparable Neil Munro, in *The New Road*, could have been describing my view: "the moor stretched flat and naked as a Sound . . . all untracked and desert-melancholy . . . cotton sedge strewn like flakes of snow . . . grey like ashes, blackened here and there with holes of peat. The end of it was lost in mist from which jutted, like a skerry of the sea, Schiehallion."

From the pass I dropped down to the bothy. Sunset came in vivid yellow light and towering black clouds. The bothy stands by a lonely bay, with a solitary guardian tree, a place of character and charm.

The B.F.M.C. had had a Meet here a month before but the only food that had survived was several tins of baked beans. I had them for supper, breakfast and lunch—and was not fit to live with! My treat today was thick, *fresh* onion soup; its preparation brought tears to my eyes. I drew the rickety bed close to the fire to dry clothes. Tetley coffee bags made endless brews. The night was noisy with storm and life in the wainscot. No poltergeist activity, however.

This is no joke. I know sensible, rational, couthy, even dull folk who would on no account stay there. If you want to read of the sort of things that go bump in the night here, borrow W. H. Murray's classic *Undiscovered Scotland* (Dent 1951). To be fair it must be added that the last owner did not hang himself on the back of a door as even Murray retells. The S.M.C. Journal for 1951 had a note from A. E. Robertson: "McCook died in his bed at Newtonmore, honoured and respected . . . a very fine type of Highland stalker, level-headed and sensible." So the disturbances have nothing to do with him. I have never noticed anything in the years I've gone there, often alone, in auspicious circumstances. This is not negative evidence, however. Some people

F

just do not experience these sort of things. The bothy is there if you want
to conduct personal experiments.

Friday 24 May   STAOINEAG IN SUMMERTIME

Ben Alder's most distinguished visitor was the eighteenth-century
gangrel Charles Edward Stuart, not that he really intended such a close
contact with the wilder parts of Britain. For a week in August 1746 he
was in hiding up on the hill behind the bothy (nobody knows where
exactly though the map gives a confident guess) along with Cluny
Macpherson, Cameron of Locheil and Dr Cameron, all wanted men.
Word was brought of French ships off the Arisaig coast, and he set off
from his hiding-place to leave Scotland for ever. Cluny Macpherson hid
hereabouts for seven years. Stevenson in *Kidnapped* leads Davie Balfour
and Alan Breck to Cluny's Cage.

The topping and tailing of the day gave that vivid colouring that is
associated with wetness but it was a grey, dull day on the whole. I simply
followed up the Allt Tom a' Chogaidh to the loch, a dry meander among
an extravagance of peat. I brewed at the loch, but it would not clear,
so I scrambled up on to Sgor Gaibhre, down to the Mam Ban and on
to Carn Dearg, all without pause—and with no view. The north-east
wind was bitter, so I trotted down to the old Corrour path. There were
motor cycle tracks to remind that the Six Day Trials roar through here
once a year, a sight so out of place as to be amusing.

Craig, Glen Affric and Loch Ossian Youth Hostels are in a remote
and superior class, each in a superb setting. I would not swop one of
them for a score of the misconceived Grade One palaces. At Ossian we
once enjoyed meeting Hari Dang, an Indian Everest climber, who was
recuperating from frostbite while acting as warden. His stories kept
the kids happy and I enjoyed reading several of his sensitive, poetic
writings.

A mile on from the hostel is Corrour Station and not far from it a
sign gives "Corrour Summit, 1,350 feet", one of the highest parts of the
West Highland line. Today's hills, and even the addition of Beinn na
Lap on the other side of Loch Ossian, can be done in a day's romp
between trains. My favourite hill lies above the station with a view
over the Moor: Leum Uilleim, a name which sounds like the name of a
hero from a legend. It is *William's leap*.

On the pretty track down to Loch Treig I met the shepherd walking
up with measured stride, dog at heel. The Grey Corries, and even Ben

Nevis, cleared, showing a dusting of snow on their tops. I skipped along
—in this withdrawn Walk the barometer seems to be the register of
feelings, my spirits going up and down as it did.

Loch Treig was exceptionally low and even had a waterfall dashing
down a little gorge that would normally all have been under water.
This is part of another great water-system. The upper reaches of the
Spey and Pattack are caught and led to the Moy reservoir, which in turn
feeds Loch Treig, and from here a tunnel runs round under the hills to
descend from out of Ben Nevis to the British Aluminium works by
Fort William.

Creaguaineach Lodge and the bright valley beyond were alive with
birds: raven, stonechat, tits, dipper, sandpiper, merganser, peewits,
pipits, all were proclaiming that life was not bad at all. The valley was
brilliantly green and lush after the spell in the browns of the
Cairngorms. The dainty butterworts were out. The river glowed as if
molten. Staoineag bothy beside it had recently been done up by the
M.B.A. and Ian Mitchell seemed to have taken personal care of it. We
were to meet later. Idiot vandals had ripped off much of the old wooden
panelling. After a search I found pencilled names above the fireplace:
"Gus Cameron, Jock Stenhouse, James Hunter, Andrew Hamilton,
Alex Lindsay, James Marshall, Bill Drysdale, 13.3.63" and "Sandy
Drysdale, Ian Routledge, Frankie Spence, John Carroll, Pete Adamson
10.10.64". It seemed impossible that ten years had passed since those
visits—when we had crossed Rannoch Moor in midwinter and traversed
all the Mamores in autumn. And now I was there in the fairest of
summertime.

Saturday 25 May   THE MAMORES
Blissful silence; no wind, no cuckoo. Even the bare boards were unable
to spoil sleep. I had read till all hours and yawned my way through
breakfast. It was a magnificently fine morning, one that lay lazily as a
cat. Sandpipers and greenshank were calling, the Ben reflected in the
river. I threw away my French vocabulary and went singing westwards
up the strath. A peculiar double day it proved to be.

My first pause was by the lochan under Sgurr Eilde Mor where a
diver carried on a noisy courtship not thirty yards away even though I
was sitting in full view. In that empty setting it was as if the wilderness
itself was crying out. Marvellous sound.

The Mamores in a day is a good hefty hike but it was put in the shade by Philip Tranter who did it and then went on to add the Grey Corries, Aonachs and Ben Nevis—within 24 hours. As if that were not enough, a woman in her fifties repeated the feat.

The nature of the ground can be gauged from the names: they are all *Stobs* and *Sgurrs*—no gentle *Bens* or *Mealls* or *Srons*—though the last peak is, rightly, a *Mullach*. A popular range, giving good ridge walking, with scalloped corries, airy crests, and ten Munros. In winter they can be superb: the Devil's Ridge, the An Gearanach tops, Binnein Mor are all narrow. The group is best done east–west, so one walks into the sunset. It is also logistically easier that way.

Sgurr Eilde Mor and Binnean Beag are both out on a limb in the extreme east, so it is good to have them out of the way at the start. There is a path linking the cols that demarcate these two end hills, a continuation of the one shown coming up from Kinlochleven. Binnein Mor, 3,700 feet, is the highest in the forest and dominates the east end, a summit thrust up by narrow ridges with sheer flanks. I lingered on it, enjoying the sunshine. It was too good to hurry and I was quite content to be what my granny often called me—a great slitter.

Na Gruagaichean, the *maiden*, has a top split into two paps with a gap of perhaps two-hundred feet between, which the one-inch map does not show. An Gearanach and An Garbhanach are both given 3,200 feet and translate as *short* and *rough* ridge. They require a bit of scrambling and in winter can be alpine in character. I was not sure which was the Munro but could not resist the fun of going along the crest and back. On Stob Coire a' Chairn I was enveloped in cloud, a change as swift as curtains dropping in a theatre, and a shock to realise it was 4 p.m. With five Munros ahead I would have to hurry. I did, and the tops were peeled off in about four hours, in thick cloud, viewless and dull. Am Bodach and Sgor an Iubhair took me west.

Sgurr a' Mhaim, the *peak of the pass*, is the hill dominating Glen Nevis. As Munro number 50 it is always a convenient yardstick. Its quartz capping can look like snow and tourists by the thousands must have slides of it at home labelled "Ben Nevis". The "bad step" on the ridge out to it is perhaps exaggerated—it can be jumped across. If you missed, of course, a couple of bounces would land you down in the corries. Back under Iubhair, which deserves to be a Munro, I took the zig-zag path down to the lochan below, a path long known to us as Jacob's Ladder. On our school traverse we had a swim in the loch and a lazy brew. Today I simply crammed in the rest of my available food

1 The Long Tradition – Sir Hugh Munro (right) and friends "on the hill" in the early days of the game.

2 3 (*above left*) Rev. A.E. Robertson – the first man to complete the Munros in 1901. (*above right*) Brian Ripley, leader of the 1967 attempt on all the Munros.

4 (*right*) Blackrock Cottage, the L.S.C.C. climbing hut with Buachaille Etive Mor behind.

5 John Hinde, who led several R.A.F. long-distance Munro treks in the 1960s.

6 7 (*above left*) Sandy Cousins at Cape Wrath at the start of his 1971 trek. (*above right*) "Kitchie" – Hamish's dog which climbed all the 3,000ft peaks in the British Isles.

8 (*left*) The lowest ebb of the trip was experienced in this pass between Knoydart and Glen Dessarry.

9 (*right*) A mug of tea outside the tent at Loch Hourn.

10 (*lower right*) Ben Sgriol from the prehistoric hill fort of Torr Beag.

11 (*below*) One of Knoydart's rugged peaks – Garbh Chioch Mhor.

12   The Long Tradition – Sir Hugh Munro (beard and bonnet in back row) and other Scottish Mountaineering Club members at an early Meet of the Club.

13   Maol Chean-dearg from Beinn Damh with Bidean a' Choire Sheasgaich.

14 (*above*) The pinnacles of Sgurr nan Gillean from Garbh-bheinn over the bump of Ruadh Stac.

15 (*right*) Braehead School's last Munro – on Lurg Mhor, east of Achnashellach.

16 (*above*) Seana Bhraigh – one of the really remote Munros in the north.

17 (*inset*) The end – Ben Hope summit after 112 days.

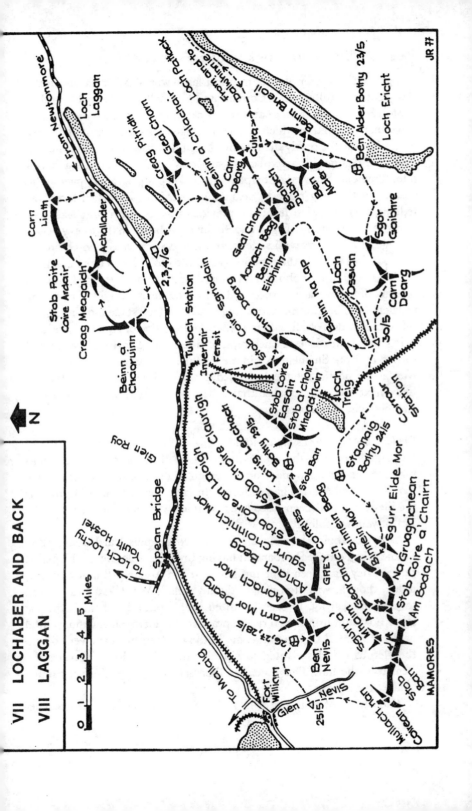

and groped on up for Stob Ban. A lost lamb was bleating its woe in the misty corrie. Mullach nan Coirean and "home" still seemed far off.

Stob Ban is *white* from quartz stones capping it. At 2,950 on its north ridge there is a bump which is often mistaken for the summit. The way to the Mullach is partly defined by cliffs, but I used the compass a bit. The rock changes to a red colour suddenly, and the cairn is a rufous pile. Previous knowledge helped me to keep up a good pace. The descent of the long ridge to near Dun Deardail (a vitrified fort) was tedious, an impression from the previous traverse with Braehead, too. However, it led home. If you choose the right break in the trees you can indulge in a long grass glissade, of the seated variety, a good ending to a 10,000-foot day. By the time I reached the hostel I had done 21 miles.

The hostel was mobbed and noisy. As soon as I stepped into its steamy din, my face turned red with the heat. David Gunn, the warden, had food for me and George Luke had left some too—and gone off to camp. Best of all, I found Alan Boulton, one of Ann's pupils, and being well-trained he at once produced a brew. Charles Knowles had turned up from Sheffield to join me for the next day or two. Everything was far too hectic, the meal gobbled down, and bed as per regulations. Only next day did I realise that I had now passed the half way—on Am Bodach, *the old man.*

Sunday 26 May HALF-WAY PICNIC

I was glad to leave the promiscuous bustle of the international hitch-hiking brigade and wander off in search of the campers. I rang home too. David and Marina had collected the canoe, which was all right, but the life-jacket had been discovered by mice who had turned it into "a sort of yellow confetti".

As it was about ten o'clock I found George, plus Val Hadden, Bob Binnie and Tommy Dunbar still having breakfast. Charles and I joined them. They had been over the Ben and the Aonachs the day before; today, though, was "too nice to do anything". We talked and brewed the morning away. George admitted that I outdid him in both: the latter no doubt from much recent practice, the former from almost total neglect. The C.I.C. key had come in the mail, so two cars went off up the glen as Charles wanted to have his there in order to traverse the Ben from the hut. This done, we then set off up the hill, very much against the stream.

The variety of clothing, or lack of it, was amazing. I once saw someone going up the tourist path wearing fisherman's waders which I thought a bit extreme; today, the extreme was the other way: flip-flops and hot-pants. Verily, they have their reward. The quirk, however, was that it was we who received the odd looks—madmen obviously heading uphill when everyone else was going down.

We were into cloud when we turned off, through by Loch Meall an t-Suidhe. The going was unusually dry. We rounded under the Nevis cliffs to the hut. The C.I.C. (Charles Inglis Clark Memorial Hut) had been painted and modernised. Many mourn the bad old days of the coal fire when the cast-iron stove would glow red hot and climbers sat about near-naked in midwinter watching the butter melt. It had a grubby atmosphere all of its own. Now a clean, pathetic gas fire blubbered away in its place. Outside the hut I could smell fumes from the pulp mill, the distillery and some nearer sheep. City-dwelling Charles could smell nothing.

We ate to a stand-still and sat browsing through the big ledger of a hut book. It was brought up in 1971 by "D. Lang *assisted* by N. Quinn". In April of that year a gang noted their ascent of Point Five Gully as 18 hours. Two days later John Cunningham and Bill Marsh took 2¾ hours—the application of the new techniques which have so changed winter climbing. A well-meaning hand had kindly amended their time by adding a figure one in front of the 2¾. It takes a while to adjust! Sandy Cousins had stayed during his Cape Wrath–Glasgow trip. In December 1971 two climbers had peeled on Gardyloo, from the top pitch, and got off unhurt; they then fell again, this time being killed. John Hinde reported finding three men and a dog dead under the Douglas Boulder in 1972. Last year a Dundee University gang had to bivy in poly-bags outside because everyone thought someone else had the hut key. One hopeful offers a half bottle (of what?) to the finder of a lost Chouinard axe. Does he not know that McInnes combs the foot of the cliffs each year, with his dogs which are trained to find metal objects?

The C.I.C. is a great howff, even though the litter round it gives the lie to the conceit of climbers who tend only to blame others for this sin.

The hut was opened in 1929, a memorial to the son of a member killed during the Great War. The date was April the First. The Rev. A. E. Robertson pronounced the blessing and prayed that it might be a refuge in time of danger. Two climbers obligingly fell down Observatory Gully and staggered in while these proceedings were still in progress.

Monday 27 May c.i.c.

The day was a wash-out. We revelled in the comfort. Our only visitor was an Australian-German who had slept on the Ben the previous night and went off "up the creek" to cross the arête. He vanished in the storm but though Charles monitored the newspapers we heard no more. . . .

Charles is essentially a ski-mountaineer; he has probably been up more hills this way than most "climbers" on foot. We both were members of the Eagle Ski Club and had been together in Austria, Switzerland, Pyrenees, Morocco, and just before this trip, in the Polish Tatras, along with Donald Mill of the S.M.C. Recently he had slipped into the Munro habit, ticking them off in the Tables.

At the end of the last century there was an Observatory on top of Ben Nevis. During the period 1883–1904 the records produced an average of 261 gales a year (i.e., winds of over 50 m.p.h.; gusts of three times that velocity were noted). The average rainfall was 157 inches and the mean monthly temperature just below freezing. If the Ben were a few hundred feet higher Britain could have her very own glacier.

Each September there is a race run from Fort William to the top and back. The record, set in 1976 by David Cannon, is 1 hour 26 minutes 55 seconds, a time most people take just to walk *down* to the glen from the C.I.C. It is comforting to know there are others even crazier than oneself on the hills.

The day went well enough, though it was a "waste", I suppose. It was right to have one day off in seven, that is a scheme which has both human and divine authority; another day like this would hint more at divine retribution.

> I dreamed of a great mountain
> To be climbed next day
> But the rains came down in torrents
> And washed it all away.

Tuesday 28 May still c.i.c.

The storm went on; so did Charles who had to motor back to Sheffield. His car now lay, unhandily, at the head of Glen Nevis, so he too vanished off to cross the Carn Mor Dearg Arête.

I read the only book in the place, then cleaned the hut in self-defence. Outside I buried 26 buckets of rubbish. The noise of water had increased. A brief clearance showed the Douglas Boulder: wet and black; a later clearance showed it snowy white.

The C.I.C. is a genuine alpine hut, built of the local stone, walls six feet thick, it fits into the landscape now as if it had always been there. It fits in to the landscape so well, indeed, that one of the games climbers play is "Finding the C.I.C. Hut". You are always reaching it, with massive packs, in wind, rain, snow or darkness, or any combination of these. Luckily the prevailing wind is up the glen.

It is surprising what you can find in a hut where no food is supposed to be left. I fed well despite the extra day. The meal was disturbed by a mouse which I caught in a bucket and despatched. Its brothers and sisters came and clouted about all night with their boots on to get their own back.

A last trip outside showed it was still snowing.

'Hail, snow an' ice that praise the Lord; I've met them at their work,
An' wished we had anither route or they anither kirk."

KIPLING

Wednesday 29 May   EASTINGS AT LAST

In the mousey hours I had lain working at the logistics to see how I could make up for the lost time. I reckoned it would need a bit of doubling-up, and leaving Beinn a' Chlachair to be done from the north, later, rather than on this run eastwards back to Dalwhinnie.

It was obviously going to be a day of snow showers but not bad enough to delay any further. I locked the C.I.C. at 6.30 and set off in the statutory direction of the Arête. Boulder-hopping was a slithery game and the easy line up from Coire Leis by the abseil posts was barred by sheets of ice. The steeper rocks to the left were better, giving a scramble. Cold work on the fingers, though, as snow had to be brushed off each hold. Another 900 feet of boulder-hopping led up to the highest midden in Britain, the summit of Ben Nevis.

The derivation of the name is disputed but I think *hill with its head in the clouds* is more likely than *mountain of heaven*. The Ben took its rightful place as Britain's highest peak only in the early nineteenth century and therefore has less history than many lower summits. There used to be a plaque on top (long before the present scruffy rash) which proclaimed: "Ben Nevis, 4,406 feet", then, in modest, smaller print, "Erected by the Scottish Mountaineering Club". The new maps have given it 4,418 feet and no doubt it has been metricated.

I did not wait for the weather to clear. I thought of Charles back in his Sheffield Insurance Office and went smugly off for the Arête to Carn Mor Dearg, racing along in an effort to beat the next storm. The wind was not bad. I snuggled in to the cairn and watched the trailing curtain of snow sweep across the Nevis cliffs.

An old S.M.C. member was once explaining to a novice how on very narrow ridges like the Arête the only way you could save somebody falling off down one side was to jump off the other so the rope could balance across the ridge and thus save both. Having scaled the Ben by the Arête, with his mentor, the novice said he had remembered the instruction: had the leader fallen, he would have jumped off the other side. The elder shook his head. "Och laddie, yon is a technique that is best kept for when we are using a rope."

I gave up waiting and went down the East Ridge in a swirl of spindrift. In winter this can be a ridge of great beauty, the snow building up, not into a cornice, but a thin, wavering crest. Down at the col it was dry again. One winter, while sitting at this col, we watched a gentleman pass by, umbrella up, wearing a plastic mac, grunting away at a tune . . .

The flank of the Aonachs was steep and slobbery in the conditions— far more alarming than if it had involved real climbing. The plateau was windy. I left the sack and hurried to reach Aonach Mor and be back before the next blatter, for footprints are not always a reliable navigation aid. There is an almost Cairngorm-like gravelly quality to the top here, and the Aonach corries seem to be holding the snow even longer than the eastern hills these days. The next shower caught me on the col to Aonach Beag (the higher)—a shower of that evilly wet snow which makes dry, colder snow seem positively benign.

Aonach Beag is a hill I have come to respect (it has still to be thoroughly explored for its winter climbing potential). On several occasions its bald skull of summit has given trouble. There is only a tiny cairn and this can vanish in winter. On one trip its position was guessed by some orange peel which showed through the snow. I had peered into the near white-out to see my companion, Mike Smith, about to step over a faint crack line. I yelled at him to stop. It was the cornice beginning to break off. We were right on the edge. Today the summit was giving a repeat presentation of another problem.

The whole dome was icy. The angle was by no means steep but with

neither axe nor crampons that was no consolation. It was not possible
to contour lower, for both flanks fall in cliffs. I found a likely chunk of
stone to act as an ice-axe and chipped away at the unavoidable bits.
There are times when it is best to be alone.

To revert to Mike Smith, at that time a pupil of mine at Braehead.
I very nearly gave in my notice after the incident, but stayed for another
ten years during which time we had no genuine hill accident. The
pupils were given a freedom and responsibility far greater than most.
But any accident would have been my fault—I would have had to live
with it. I give it as a warning to romantic youngsters who dream of
becoming an instructor, leader, teacher, whatever the title. The P.E.
man can allow errors on the soccer pitch where mistakes may lose goals,
on the hill they lose life. You are playing for keeps.

Since the Cairngorm disaster of course the tendency has swung to the
other extreme. Everything must be safe—which is not mountaineering.
If we decide to take another's youngster on the hill we cannot salve
our conscience by trying to kid ourselves, or the parents, that it is safe.
The mountain is an illiterate thug who has not read the books and
plays to no rules.

For once the cliff edge of Aonach Beag was useful for navigation.
There is a north-east ridge which has suffered neglect. An old account
declares, "The narrow part in the middle . . . is the most sensational of
any of the great ridges outside Skye". Unlike the Aonach Eagach, you
cannot park your car at the foot of it. There is a big winter route to be
done up the face under Stob Coire Bhealach, the corner bump at the
end of the circling cliffs.

Prior knowledge helped me to wiggle down through the cliffs, south
a bit from there, to reach the col before the start of the Grey Corries
ridge. It is not a good area to wander about in if there is thick cloud, not
unless you have a parachute. Sgurr a' Bhuic is an odd peak of upended
strata, full of holes, as you sometimes find in schisty rock. It is worth
climbing for the view: being out from the main range it has the finer
panorama.

The Grey Corries is an old apt name for a long switchback ridge of
quartzy rock. It has been likened to a row of pit bings, but this is a
slander. The corries in the north have some grandeur, the westmost
being as rough as any in Knoydart. You will walk more on naked rock
to collect its four Munros than anywhere else outside Skye. I recommend
their traverse right through from Glen Nevis to Tulloch.

On Sgurr Choinnich Mor I met an English lad who had been camping below at Tom an Eite on the old drove road, part of the Road to the Isles. The ridge down has some slots in the strata which act as crevasses when snow-covered—I have twice seen people fall into them. I slid down old snow to the col and the best of the ridge beyond, scrambling where I could find rock, up to Stob Coire an Easain. I met another solitary figure there. On Stob Coire an Laoigh I met a family I had seen on the Nevis path. Our greetings were cut short by a vicious snow shower. I passed yet another solitary Englishman, who explained it was the Whit Week invasion. Footprints in the snow led east but I never saw the party; I thought it interesting that only one party out of all these had the gumption to travel *with* the weather, rather than suffer its periodic lashings.

The sole of my right boot was beginning to pull away. I promptly found an old bit of lace and tied it up. Just in time: ten minutes later it gave way completely. I tied a protective hanky round my face for the ascent of Stob Coire Claurigh, 3,858 feet, the highest of the range, while the storm produced what looked like ragged hail. It was quite evil while it lasted. A glimpse to the hills of June, a glimpse to the hills of April relieved the present struggle. Stob Ban is a sort of coda to the Grey Corries Symphony.

From it I dropped down to the Lairig Leachach, another old drove road from Loch Treig to Glen Spean and the west. There is a poor bothy in it, which we knew in its finer days in the past. To us it was "Payne's bothy" as he showed it to us when staying at Inverlair. He was the keeper then. He had lost an arm in the Korean War. Now, there was no flooring left and it was grubby. The book had complaints from the shepherd about folk using his "stabs"—and comments from Sassenachs asking what these were! (fence posts) A surprising number of schools had been there—Melville, Watson's, Kingswood, Aberdeen Grammar, Rannoch—apart from fellow gangrels such as Nancy Smith and Richard Wood, or instructor types like Blyth Wright or Klaus Schwartz. It suddenly felt crowded. I spent an hour retrieving bits of wire and string and tied up my boot in a glorified cat's cradle. It was another noisy mouse night.

Thursday 30 May   TRIG POINTS ROUND LOCH TREIG
Easain and Mheadhoin were the local Inverlair hills for many Braehead kids, known always as *This Yin* and *That Yin*, names transferred to a pair

of Wullie Dugs back home. The "Stob Corries" are a fine pair of hills, bounded by Loch Treig to the east and Coire Lair to the west. Their main joy is the setting, for as hills they just fail to enthuse, all the features seem just short of being good. My log dismissed them in six lines but revelled in the descent to Coire Lair with its pastoral scene of cows browsing on the bright green of grass among the brighter green of new birch growth. After the sterile days past it was as refreshing as a dram. Stob Coire Easain and Stob a' Choire Mheadhoin sound like malts.

I looked for, and saw, cloudberry, chickweed wintergreen (summer star) and dwarf cornel—a trio of exceptionally beautiful alpines. This was a bit of country we had combed with the kids, for the lodge of Inverlair was given to us by British Aluminium and we wanted to have it as a centre. It could have been a great scheme but it was strangled with red tape. Instead, we had the freedom of Scotland, which we used to the full; not that I could see it ever having developed into a placid sausage-machine, timetabling stereotyped courses, boring the staff, disenchanting pupils and soiling the very landscape which should delight —which is the end result of far too many outdoor education schemes.

We were self-contained groups, doing the sort of thing ordinary people did on the hills. Each term a programme would be produced for the next term. All pupils received this, and then applied for what they liked. They were never "sent". You might juggle a bit to make balanced parties; but then you knew the boys and girls already. They were not impersonal statistics to be suffered for a week. The trips were real too. We might be dropped, say, in Glen Strathfarrar and collected ten days later at Loch Duich—and until then we were on our own, self-contained, self-reliant, not playing at things, nor conning the kids with simulated adventure. They revelled in it and it has made me cynical about the way the Educational Establishment has developed. At Inverlair, for instance, we were banned from living in the building while working on it. Too dangerous—but we could camp on top of the Ben in midwinter. We camped outside and worked on until that was stopped —it was not right that kids should take work away from tradesmen. (So back to the simulated in the school workshop.) The teaching profession I think deserves much of the trouble it gets.

Not being based on one spot the kids came to know Scotland as a whole. They could rile adult Munro-baggers with accounts of visits to the most out-of-the-way summits. I recall one perky visitor to Inverlair asking a fourteen-year-old for his tally of Munros, he having all of fifty. The lad, embarrassed, confessed that he stood at 101. Quite a few of them have gone on to climb in the Alps and Norway and Morocco, but reward enough could be the conversation the other day when I received a telephone call from someone I had not heard of for seven years. "Hello Hamish. Do you mind yon hotel we went into when we got washed oot o' Moidart? I'm gettin' marrit next month an' I thocht it wid be a great place fir wir honeymoon."

The school has closed, but a host of memories remain. There was not a Munro they had not been on, so how could I forget?

> Doon the road we gang oor gate,
> Past the gorge, the bridge, the brae;
> Backward spy ower Speanside
> A' that bides—'tis we that gae.

So an Inverlair Song went.

The eighteenth-century house had been used as a prison for Hitler's deputy Rudolph Hess after his parachute landing in Scotland during the war. The cell still exists with its bolts and bars.

The Spean has some fine gorges and falls under the bridge on the road leading to Inverlair, but up above these today I just hopped across on the exposed pink boulders and walked along to Tulloch Station. Behind it is the old coach house which had been turned into a small outdoor centre and factory for producing tents, cagoules and so on. (It was later sold to the Army.) It was from here that my tent had come, although I had left it at Dalwhinnie I was able to give Dave Challis, its designer, an enthusiastic report. We chatted over tea, dealt with food parcel and mail; it was tempting to stay, but the sun shone and it was still a far cry to Ben Hope.

I took the forest path up to Fasgadh, wondering if Nancy Smith or Davie Glen might be there. Nancy runs a highly individualistic "hostel" there for gangrels, climbers and folk from all over the world. Today it seemed deserted. I wandered on through Fersit and up the Allt Chaorach Beag which had cows surprisingly high on it. There was also one big black bull. The observant may notice the map shows a stream here splitting into two; this is not an error, but one of the very few examples of this oddity. There was a heron by Lochan Coire an Lochain, 2,500 feet up. The corrie arms here are both Munros: Sgriodain on the west overlooks Loch Treig, while Chno Dearg lies to the east, and translates as the *red nut*, a description I thought more appropriate to myself. Between Stob Coire Sgriodain and the loch is the Fort William railway: here squeezed in by the steep slope and giving a succession of cuttings and tunnels. The railway allows good days hereabouts as you can return or start using it from a base at Nancy's. Sgriodain is the *hill of the scree corrie*.

Instead of circling back to Fersit, I went south to add Beinn na Lap. There were several cast antlers on the hill today. I dropped down to hit the head of the long trough that cuts off Lap. Lochan Ruigh Phuil on the watershed had dried out. The meandering rivers are just too wide to jump. Once across I brewed and finished off all the food I could allow that day. Beinn na Lap is the *boggy mountain*, which is true on this side, but the Loch Ossian flanks, which I went down to the Youth Hostel, are usually dry. It is a very easy Munro. It looks right into the throat of the Nevis glen, westwards, while in the opposite direction Ben Alder's bulk once again looms large. I sang into the rising wind and trundled down to the hut.

The hostel was not officially open till Saturday but the warden, Tom Rigg, made all welcome. My face "blew-up" with the heat of the room. Kettles steamed on the old range. You fetched water by the bucket from the loch. It was all a youth hostel should be. Tom had been warden there before, and told us of his days helping with the stalking and the real regret with which he left at the back end. A Watson's quartet were camped outside on a Duke of Edinburgh "Gold" Expedition while their assessor lorded it within. The wind was doing its best to blow tents and hostel into the loch. The bothy last night felt a million miles away, already. I'd had two good days of between seven and eight thousand feet, with thirty miles from the C.I.C., which felt even longer ago. The consciousness of what lay ahead seemed always to sweep the past into immediate oblivion.

Friday 31 May NEW BOOTS, PLEASE!
Dave Challis had promised to phone Dollar and pass on my plea for new boots. It was one thing he did not manufacture. I remember once throwing a brand-new pair into Loch Ossian, in despair, after they had badly blistered my feet. The next day I fished them out and they soon moulded comfortably. Drastic remedy! For the Long Walk I had broken in three pairs beforehand.

On one previous walk along Loch Ossian, in winter, the ice had been broken by a storm, and the broken wafers were piling up with a loud, continuous hissing which was most unusual. Today the heronry produced its particular noise.

A path leads past from the lodge at the end of Loch Ossian, crossing the Uisge Labhair by a bridge; but later it peters out leaving you to pick a way on for the Bealach Dubh, 2,300 feet, the pass through to Culra. Running parallel to this pass, to the north, is a line of four Munros. The hills have well-bitten northern corries and bulky slopes to the south and swoop along in pleasing fashion. Most of the tops are over 3,600 feet, and I've often watched the deer in summer come up to lie on the lingering snow patches. Today it was cold enough to wear a cagoule. I saw an eagle, a bird that had been surprisingly scarce, but then I had been much in sheep country, where there is still lawless slaughter. The first Munro, Beinn Eibhinn, means the *beautiful hill*, but it is simply a great lump. Aonach Beag is next, the highest of the group. Geal Charn (another, unnamed by the O.S.) has a wide plateau and a Top, Sgor Iutharn, *Hell's Peak*, which is the spike of Lancet Edge, the framing edge of the Bealach Dubh as seen from Culra.

A bit of care is needed to hit off the descent from the plateau to continue to Dearg. The col has corrie lochs on both sides, the one to the north with the name of Loch Coire Cheap. Carn Dearg is a rockier, scree-covered hill, with quite a brutal descent to Culra bothy. A dotterel went dashing off on a blur of legs over the red scree. Two dead deer lay in the stream which served as the bothy water supply.

I crossed the moor back to the road and retrieved the old bike. "Stowaway" was an appropriate trade name for it. Belting down to the lodge was hard on the wrists and the rough track needed all eyes; deer were smelt rather than seen in passing.

Near Dalwhinnie Station I called in at the schoolhouse and collected a parcel from the Parkins. He was a member of the local Mountain Rescue Team but was about to move south. We had a chat and I think I gave away my real ploy. I collected the tent next and was soon back at the Cuckoo Wood waiting for Lorna Marsh and Bob Binnie. I had expected them about 7.30 so had a brew made then. I drank it and several others, wrote until dusk at ten, then lay listening to the wind in the firs.

Another section was over. Twenty beyond half-way. They certainly piled up. Now I could head west, if a bit circuitously; then the Great

Glen, the crossing of which was bound to be a spur. I felt fine physically, I had had no foot problems, and was receiving plenty of mental stimulus from people, books and incidents. I ate well, slept well, and when Bob and Lorna finally turned up, I even found I had new boots, thank you. The old ones had taken me to 237,850 feet, over 802 miles for 159 Munros.

VIII

LAGGAN

There is not good or bad in the hills; just life, just death. There is
only a calendar of seasons and the tick-tock of day and night. Sit
relaxed and still, and the life of the hills will creep up to you
unafraid, rest, and the very air will whisper wonderful things in your
ear. Even the bleached skeleton in the grass will give a message of
comfort, in the Word's old sense of strengthening. The strength of
hills is His.

Saturday 1 June THE DULLEST HILLS IN SCOTLAND
I must admit my log book entry for the day was headed "Monaidh
Liath Puddings". They are not the most dramatic hills we have.
However, one thing they can offer is navigational exercise in a thick
mist, particularly west of the actual Munros. I've had my share of
criss-crossing them, and think they are maligned: they have a quality of
remoteness and silence which their bigger counterpart, the Cairngorms,
cannot offer.

I used the bike; wind and hill were both in my favour over the brae
to Laggan Bridge. One lay-by had a notice saying "Beware of the
adders", a good anti-parking gambit. I bought goodies from the shop
and scoffed them at Crathie. I had to fix a cotter pin, and thought I had
a sheep to rescue under the bridge, but it was dead: a crow was busy
picking out its eyes. *Whisky Galore* helped walking up the track.

West from where I'd left the bike, you can go by Garva Bridge and
Melgarve to the Corrieyairack, the famous pass over which Wade
built a road (1731) to connect Aberfeldy and Fort Augustus. It goes up
to 2,543 feet but is a desolate crossing. One of the first people to profit
by it (a twist of fate) was Prince Charlie. Montrose came over somewhere in this region on his great winter march to Inverlochy. They say
it's haunted by a lone piper . . .

Today's Geal Charn was small and unpretentious: with only one
feature, a fine craggy corrie on the east, above which is a sneck or
window (the Uinneag a' Choire Lochain) which separates Geal Charn
from its south top. I left Glen Markie at a sheepfold and hopped across

the river boulders, again let off gently, then wended up Beinn Sgiath and along to Geal Charn, which has a large cairn for such a plain summit. The ascent was a bit dull and I was still half asleep after my late night. Today, however, I was, at last, doing something I'd long wanted to do—all the Monaidh Liath Munros in one sweep.

The Monaidh Liath are aptly the *grey moors*. They fall into two very distinct areas: the five scattered above Glen Banchor, which joins the Spey at Newtonmore, and this odd, solitary Geal Charn, away towards Laggan, six miles across the grey emptiness.

The cloud had lifted so I felt happy to stay high, but it would probably have been no less tiring to have cut down to the Markie again and used it as a highway. But I had my six miles of moor: empty but for monotonous plovers crying, a few deer, a few dotterel. It gave every variety of bog and brae without being difficult like the Mount Keen day. Above the final col was a solitary gate, standing like a lost sculpture by some facetious modern artist.

There is another such solitary, fence-less gate in the Ochils; sheep tracks converge for miles on it, go through the ever-open portal, and then spread out again across the slopes.

The first of my group, another *red hill*, Carn Dearg, 3,093 feet, is the highest. It is also the only one with a bit of shape: a spur juts out and forms a double-wave of ridge. Below it, and worth taking in on the ascent by its path, is Coire Lochain Dubh, a deep hole of a corrie, the crags backing its lochan, probably giving the only climbing in the whole range if someone would go and try them.

The Monaidh Liaths also have distracting fences. The next hill, not another Geal Charn, but equally meaning *white hill*, is Carn Ban which is shown with the fence passing the top; it does not. A mile further along, Carn Ballach, *cairn of the pass*, has a veritable collection of cairns to choose from.

Carn Sgulain, "a mere stony eminence on the ridge", is perhaps appropriately the *cairn of the basket*. I arrived on it with a ptarmigan brood scattering and their mother flapping about. Driving clouds and rain finally arrived, too.

A bite in the lee of the cairn and then the way led off into the storm— angling down over wet slopes to the wet col for A' Chailleach, *the old wife*, a long whaleback from which I was glad just to take a bearing and try and reduce altitude quickly.

Once off the very steep top slopes, the group became gentle and hag-ridden. I came out of the cloud—and for minutes just could not place anything, for features below meant nothing and above was hidden. "The compass is always right," I muttered, and followed it, endlessly it seemed, over bog and brae until finally I was looking down on a wee wooden bothy, just a shed—but expected—and giving some shelter. I peeled off dripping waterproofs and read for an hour till the worst of the rain drew off.

I found some old names scribbled on the wall. There was Joe and me in November 1962. *That* was a day, marvellously cold and a rosy, beautiful dawn from Carn Dearg. In May 1968, I was with Ann Winning, Tom Izatt, David McNab, John Parker, Ian Flaws, a day when snow-melt on still frozen ground made for saturation of feet. March 1971 with Andrew Patterson, Tommy Cameron, Willie Harrison and Jim Morrison. Jim had also done the Monaidh Liaths before, with Ann I think, for, with four out of five Munros done, it suddenly struck him that there was something familiar about the hills. From which you can draw the moral: keep records, or you may end doing the Monaidh Liath twice!

I made a quick descent. My feet could not be wetter, even after a slithery river-crossing. I came down to the end of the public road in Glen Banchor where I'd arranged to meet Lorna and Bob. There was no sign of them: no car, no tents. Just a friendly cuckoo calling.

Some day I will do the Monaidh Liath again (the summits, that is), but it will be on *langlauf* ski, and some day I want to follow Glen Markie and the old drove road through to Fort Augustus. You cannot exhaust the potential of even the dullest hills in Scotland.

Having finished off *Whisky Galore* (alas, the book), and near frozen by two hours' reading, I began to walk to Newtonmore. If they had broken down or something, I could sit waiting a long time. Main's Hotel would be cosy.

Half a mile down the road, I turned back again due to some sixth sense, and from the road-end went down to the river itself—and found them! I knew it was a great camping spot, but had not thought it possible to get a car down to it. They had, of course, so there was no car up on the expected bit of road. While I'd frozen for two hours, they had been lying snug in a tent less then 200 yards away.

We made up for lost time: instant coffee, tent up and a gargantuan meal of fresh everything. Next day they told me it had been a night of gales and rain.

Sunday 2 June   PEDALS WEST

Perhaps it should have been "paddles west", though at four o'clock I took photos of the dazzle of sun on the birch-held river. A roe deer was grunting away across the stream when I woke Lorna and Bob with coffee. They had collected the bike yesterday, so once again I went off on it.

The wind was fresh and I was travelling dead against it. At Laggan Bridge they tooted past and I found them ensconced in the Laggan Hotel drinking more coffee. Dave Challis had left a new waterproof for me with the Camerons, who also had a parcel. A heavy shower passed.

The other pair went bombing off to the hills they had abandoned in yesterday's deluge. I had a grim struggle along Loch Laggan, which rather spoilt the enjoyment of a favourite loch. West of Moy Lodge, the length of Loch Laggan battered behind at last, I pitched the tent between road and river-cutting. Scrub birch sheltered it completely. It would be unpleasantly wild on top so I was quite content to call it a day.

Lorna's van was only fifty yards away, so I squatted in the back sorting out parcels and preparing for the next few days. I also cleared off mail that needed a reply. Some vicious squalls caused the van to rock about as if riding at anchor. Along the road, a stand of trees echoed like surf, and the sound of rushing water grew to impressive volume.

Yet it was splendid in its wildness. Who would have their mountains always tame (any more than a wife)? Wordsworth's lines always come to my mind when storms are galloping free over the land:

> "The sounding cataract
> Haunted me like a passion: the tall rock,
> The mountain, and the deep and gloomy wood,
> Their colours and their forms, were then to me
> An appetite; a feeling and a love . . ."

It was a day fought out by sun and rain, and victory was given to the rain.

Lorna and Bob came in a bit battered, scoffed some more coffee, and rushed off. One Munro had been their weekend haul. Civilisation seems in such a rush! Perhaps, at the finish of the Walk, I should just turn round and go on for ever; yet the Walk blatantly used civilisation—escapism soon comes down to earth-reality. Fresh food, company, news and mail, and the bliss of a new book in the wet: civilisation is very nice, thank you!

It was a night of gales and rain, quite worthy of Wordsworth.

Monday 3 June   THE MALT HILLS

After ten hours' sleep the storms had settled into the "showers and bright periods" beloved of the forecasters. I set off for Beinn a' Chlachair (a name which has a gurgly, single malt flavour), enjoying a chat with the Luiblea shepherd, then followed round a sweeping bend in the river which was bright with broom. The Bealach Dubh hills lined themselves up beyond a waterfall, a brief scene of delight before I plunged off across bogs white with hare's tails drying in the wind. All the ground from the Moy Reservoir to the hills, and through to the gates of Loch Ossian, is now planted.

Across the moor, I joined an old, established track which does a rising sweep round to Lochan na h-Earba. On the flank of Pitridh, a fresh scar of rockfall showed clear. The path had been surfaced with rounded river-stones and I collected a pocketful of them to tumble and polish. A stalkers' path leads through to Loch Pattack and Culra. I used it for a while and then cut across to go up the stream that led right into the wide-smiling corrie mouth of Beinn a' Chlachair.

Hopes of a typical corrie lochan are disappointed—there is none. You would hope for good cliffs, judging by the distant view—there are none. Poor Beinn a' Chlachair just fails to deliver the goods. The best route is a narrow, winter ridge on the south side.

The corrie gave shelter from the wind until I met the full brunt of it on the plateau. One bright period actually gave me a summit view and what with the peak's own plateau, Geal Charn's next and then Ben Alder's, it looked strangely as if you could just walk straight over to the cairn on Ben Alder.

Beinn a' Chlachair means *mason's hill* and much of it is bouldery. I flanked down, keeping above the level of a line of seepage. The dry spell called for lunch; then when the clouds rolled in again, I "felt" my way up Geal Charn. It is also called Mulloch Coire an Iubhair, *hill of the corrie of the yew trees*, if you do not want another Geal Charn.

The map does not show the ground well, but the summit is unmistakable, as beyond the bouldery dome you see a cairn like a Tibetan "chorten" beside the trig point. In mist it can be hard to find. The wind was fluting tunefully on the holes in the trig point.

Back-tracking through the saturated clouds, I bore off down very wet slopes to swing up to Creag Pitridh, *crag of the hollows*. This little hill has a shape all of its own which makes it prominent from both ends of the Laggan strath. The note left on it has never been returned.

I descended by the west ridge for variety and to have a look at the rock-fall I'd noticed from below. There was more debris than expected, and some spiky overhangs and hollows such as you sometimes get in schisty rock. Wending down the rakes, I kept putting up small numbers of deer and, below, a really big herd traversed under the crags.

I collected another pocketful of pebbles as I wended back to the tent. An enjoyable, if unremarkable, day. There was time to read until the warblers in the scrub sang the evening away; then it was a fresh apple and into bed. Such a gentle ending to the day was no preparation for the foul night. My log next day simply said, "awful night, suspect the onions"—which is enough.

Tuesday 4 June COME WIND, COME WEATHER

It had rained most of the night, and I breakfasted in a mood of near despair as it went on and on. The rain could well have drowned the Matterhorn as deep as a Mendip mine—and this *was* June, the blessed month of dryness.

In an unpleasant frame of mind, I dressed and stomped off into the wet to call its bluff. From Moy, I followed a swollen torrent uphill, crossed the deer fence, and then had to go much further upstream, on beyond burn junctions, until the river reached safe proportions to make a crossing possible. I followed a tributary to Lochan na Cailliche, the bog myrtle scent rising under my feet. Slowly I began to enjoy the walk. It is never quite so bad once you are committed.

Keeping above another water-seepage level, I traversed across to the Allt na h-Uamha, *river of the cave*, which demarcates Beinn a' Chaoruinn's craggy east face and cuts it off from the Creag Meagaidh hills. I have never been able to find a cave, but the river is full of superlative swimming pools.

One sweltering day, a party of us were descending, longing for a dip, when we heard voices coming from a likely pool downstream. When we topped a rise, we looked down on a gang of middle-aged women (to be kind) disporting themselves like Rubenesque goddesses in the river. I dare not say which club I think they were. Such a quantity of pear-shaped nudity took us momentarily aback; then we diplomatically withdrew, unobserved. As we detoured off, one of my young charges grinned at me and commented, "Aw, Hamish, it's enough tae gie ye a complex fur life!"

Strangely, the river gave no problem today, though very swollen. The lee of a boulder was used to snack under when a wicked storm rattled by. The butterworts were no doubt relishing the wet: they seemed to be crawling all over the place like refugee starfish in search of the sea. Starry saxifrage was also in flower.

The ridge in the middle of the east face gave a nice dander up—as far as the wide main ridge where the storm was waiting in ambush. Beinn a' Chaoruinn, *hill of the rowan*, has an undulating summit-ridge with three tops; the centre, once a deleted Top, has suddenly become the Munro in the recent revisions.

I was glad of a new waterproof; the rain poured down as I followed the cliff edge over and down to the col, the Bealach a' Bharnish (2,686), which marks the start of the long grassy haul up Creag Meagaidh—which, like its derivation, was obscure. At 3,700 feet, it is a big brute, a veritable mastiff of a massif, with a sizeable plateau and cliffs with winter-climbing on a par with that on the Ben, Glencoe and Lochnagar.

It was a relief to see the cairn appear when and where expected. Further on is "mad Meg's cairn". Various stories are told of this huge pile of stones, marking no summit or spot of known interest. It is ten feet high, contains few really big boulders, and, as the ground is hollowed round about, some of it could simply have been dug out and heaped up. On the east side, traces of stairs mount to the top. It resembles an Inca sacrificial mound or some such monument, and might even be worth opening up to see if there is anything inside.

I let the wind blow me over to the 1,500-foot cliffs of Coire Ardair, and then followed their diminishing height to "The Window", a conspicuous gap leading through from the corrie. This particular window is famous as being the pass used by Prince Charlie on his journey from Cameron country en route for Culra and Ben Alder. It is at about 3,200 feet. The loch in the corrie is at over 2,000 feet, and from it a good stalkers' path leads down to Aberarder.

This easy option downwards made me think sourly of Steinbeck's comment—"we can do strange things when we want to . . . and nearly nothing without pressure". I went on. A brief clearance gave a glimpse of the cliffs.

The climbing in summer is scruffy, but in winter Creag Meagaidh's cliffs and "Posts" (gullies) come into their own. It is interesting to see that Raeburn (the Scottish Mummery) was early in this field—and J. H. B. Bell, during the pre-war period, with his penchant for vegetated verticalities.

Charlie Gorrie tells of climbing there with Jimmy Bell on an attempt on one of the Posts. They had been swimming in the loch and the approach was light-hearted. The redoubtable Dr Bell led off and Charlie followed, sufficiently gripped to ask if Jimmy had a good belay. "Of course I've got a good —— —— belay!" Charlie climbed on and arrived to find Jimmy Bell busy struggling into his trousers, the rope meanwhile held in his teeth!

The last person to stamp his mark here was Bell's modern counterpart: Tom Patey. His winter girdle traverse, solo, has gone down into climbing folklore as well as history.

On my first visit in winter, Mike Lindsay and I saw the second largest avalanche I've ever seen in Scotland. The largest was a vast slab avalanche off the north slope of White Whisp in the modest Ochils; not even in the Highlands.

Miles of undulating crest led eastwards; along it are strung seven Tops, two being elevated to the Munro peerage, including the first, Stob Poite Coire Ardair. The fence should not be taken as a good guide. The wind was shrieking on its posts, and the rain was belting down as I had not previously had it on the Walk—at least, not at above 3,000 feet—not the best of conditions for navigating. Fence and cliff edge are both apt to lead astray. I plodded along, munching soggy peanuts and more than ever convinced all mountaineers are daft. The rain was bouncing off the surface like ball-bearings, but at least the storm had been from behind.

At Carn Liath I left a note (not returned) and then turned to fight my way off its stony dome, a punitive experience. I ran and slithered downhill, fast, and soon popped out from under the black clouds. The Allt Coire Ardair twisted like a live snake, and I trundled down and took the path to the farm. A good amble along Loch Laggan gained the tent at ten to eight—three *Irish Short Stories*' distance. There I hung the book up to dry and devoured a large meal.

Before the meal was over, I became conscious of something odd. It took a while to dawn on me that the wind had gone; for the first time in days the land lay completely quiet. My relief was short-lived. There were midges! The first few thousand all came crowding about the tent: the original Scots mist. The site had been great for protection from the wind. It could hardly have been worse for a muggy calm and the little devils. I sealed myself in for the night. After three nights there, I knew every bump intimately.

My spirits stayed content, though, for now I had achieved all the Munros south of the Great Glen. It was a landmark, a pleasing one. Things were on schedule without too much effort. I did not like the thought of midges henceforth, but they just had to be tholed.

I had experienced hard days—like today—and had taken it all without too much complaint from body or soul. It had to go now, for so much had been done (252,000 feet, 922 miles and 68 days, to be precise). I dreaded the thought of anything that might interrupt the walk: a broken leg, say. Even after a week, it would lose genuine continuity, would become failure. And the thought of having to go back to the beginning—was unthinkable!

I lay back and watched the beads of condensation forming on the fabric above my head.

Wednesday 5 June THE GREAT GLEN AT LAST

The morrow being made of the past todays, I woke to rain—a gentle, midgy hiss of it on the streaming tent.

It was very pleasant in bed, drinking tea and bird-listening: skylarks, wagtails, sandpipers and warblers were all going full blast; blessed insect-eaters, while overhead a snipe was "drumming". I could just hear a distant rush of water. The rest was silence.

When the rain eased, I packed up and, before setting off, had a crack with the shepherd again. He was telling me of his prowess as a weather forecaster. "Ach, I aye say 'it will come tae rain'—and I've never been wrang yet."

I was tempted to call in at Tulloch or Fersit, but the dry was obviously only given while the west was calling up reinforcements. It was no time for being sociable. My single stop was for a brief look at the relief model of the British Aluminium complex of dams and catchments, which is sited by the roadside overlooking the west end of Loch Moy. This man-made loch alters in level drastically with the rainfall effects and British Aluminium's usage. Spouts on the dam can be opened one by one till, in conditions of peculiar deluge, all six may be sending jets into the gorge and the spray upwards like smoke. I've seen it once or twice and very impressive it is. Today a mere two spouts were operating.

It is from here, and back beyond the Loch Laggan cutting (where I'd been camping), that water is led to Loch Treig and then by the Nevis pipeline to the Fort William power station. It actually skirts round the foot of the Ben, maintenance being carried out by a small railway system, now, alas, defunct.

I cycled on to Roy Bridge to shop. North up the glen lie the odd "parallel roads" which I would have seen if footing it. The main road was longer, but a change. Tinkers were parked alongside the road, something I can remember here since my early wandering in the Highlands, which was done by cycle. But as I grew older, and the roads more busy and dangerous, the hills came to dominate. Perhaps the pressures of civilisation are becoming too much even for the tinkers: you see fewer on the road now. Many a brew I enjoyed in their camps as a kid on those cycle tours.

At Spean Bridge I had reached the Great Glen, the long-awaited landmark. I shopped again, and bought a light but warm Shetland pullover at the Mill. I would not feel such a tramp going into hotels in future.

Given the choice of the hills beyond the Great Glen or those south of it, I would choose the former, even though I would lose the Ben, and Glencoe, and the Cairngorms and much else: personally, I feel that the best of our wild hills lie from Ben More in Mull up to Cape Wrath. Ascents often start from sea-level, so even sub-Munros may mean far more footage than for Grampian summits. Who would swop Suilven for Geal Charn—any of them or all of them?

I ground up the brae in bottom gear to the "Commando Memorial": a dramatic bronze of three Commandos who gaze over the wide landscape to the south. This was the country where they trained, and Scott Sutherland's monument (1952) does the subject and the setting full justice. In an earlier time, it was at High Bridge, visible in the valley below, that the first shots of the "Forty-five" rang out—and the story of Scotland swept on to its sad days for the Highlands.

In any highland village the war memorial tells grimly how laird or pony-boy left the glens never to return. The trend is still away, but to the towns. The locals find it hard to obtain a foothold in competition with the affluent who want holiday homes.

> They would not let me buy
> The four grey walls and the roof of sky.

The deluge resumed, so, by the mouth of Glen Gloy, I was glad to patronise the Coach House Coffee Shop. An hour of reading saw little change and I went on by Letterfinlay above Loch Lochy. Across the water, my next bit of the Walk was hidden in the clouds, two Munros which on one occasion we reached by *canoeing* across the loch.

At the schoolhouse at Laggan, Mr Robertson had a parcel. The field-mice had been at it, and I left a trail of Millac along the road to the youth hostel. Fortunately, only that and a packet of Vitawheat had been touched.

I hung the tent up to dry in the cycle shed, washed my undies and myself, and hung the former to dry and the latter by the fire, mug in hand. The Frasers keep an immaculate and friendly hostel (he works for the forestry commission, she is the warden). A New Zealand couple on a motorbike (grand conditions for that), a solitary camera-laden Japanese and two Swiss made up the company.

I twice went up the road to try to ring Mike Keates. After the second "no reply", I went on to see the "Well of Heads" by Loch Oich (the Caledonian Canal's highest point). This is an odd monument that few motorists even notice. A base inscribed with the tale in Gaelic, French, Latin and English, is surmounted by a column at the top of which a stone hand, holding a *skian dubh*, dangles seven severed heads by their hair. The headless corpses were recently discovered in a mound by Inverlair: "The heads of the seven murderers were presented at the feet of the noble chief in Glengarry Castle" (not very politely) "after having been washed in this spring, known since as the Well of the Heads, Tobar nan Ceann." If you drop down the bank, an arched passage leads to the old well—now under the modern main road.

The "improvements" to our highland main roads are a boon to those of us who use them to reach a place where we then go on foot, but the car-bound tourist finds them merely an irresistible call to speed up again and so goes whizzing through the very scenery he had presumably come to observe. The "Road to the Isles" is now a real race track: lovely Loch Garry, the pass of Glen Shiel, the waters of Loch Duich, all flash by, so the motorists can then crowd into Kyle and squabble over parking places. . . .

I had to nip along next morning at eight a.m. (in the rain) to ring Mike Keates to tell him that the bike would be at the youth hostel. He was now my "base man" in place of the Dollar Broons.

Thursday 6 June WINDOW-SHOPPING

Fort William owes its name to William of Orange. Earlier defences were at Inverlochy Castle where the Comyns acquired the lordship of Badenoch and Lochaber in the thirteenth century. The present ruin is a four-square turreted bastion beside the River Nevis.

Inverlochy was the spot where Montrose thrashed Argyll in 1645, a battle gleefully recalled by that half of the Highlands who love not the Clan Campbell; but far more, it is a memorial to one of Scotland's truly great figures, a hero coming at the end of centuries sadly lacking one.

Montrose had taken fire and sword down into Argyll to sack Inveraray and was returning up the Great Glen when the pursuing Argyll set up camp at Inverlochy. With armies sealing both ends of the Great Glen, Montrose decided to attack Argyll. He had less than 2,000 men. They turned off into the hills eastwards—an area of featureless Monaidh Liath bog and brae—desperate in January snowfall and darkness, came down Glen Roy and, skirting the Grey Corries and Ben Nevis, fell on Inverlochy by surprise. In consternation, Argyll rowed off to his galley while his army was slaughtered.

Five years later, Argyll was to watch (from behind a curtained window) in Edinburgh, as Montrose was led to the scaffold, a man betrayed in far Assynt for money, unthanked by the king for whom he had virtually gained Scotland, perhaps one of the greatest military generals of all time. . . .

Cromwell's General Monck came to deal with Lochaber and he built a new fort not far from Inverlochy Castle—whose name he transferred. Today a Victorian mansion (now an hotel) of the same name, a few miles to the north, adds to the confusion.

The town that grew up round the fort became the present Fort William. After various vicissitudes and more recent attempts by local landowners to stamp their names on it—Gordonsburgh, Duncansburgh, for instance—officialdom finally gave in to the *vox populi*. Fort William it is, or, often simply "The Fort", as Ben Nevis is often simply "The Ben".

The town must be one of the most blatant examples of poor planning. From Loch Eil's massive pulp mill to the hideous white boxes high on the braes, from British Aluminium's pipelines down the flanks of Ben Nevis to the sprawling ribbon development down Loch Linnhe, it is a mixed-up mess of the industrial and the residential.

Compared to most continental countries, our Highland towns are desolate places in which to pass a wet day. I took the bus into the town to relish the ludicrous contrast to my walking life—and regretted it. The interesting West Highland Museum was unfortunately shut.

There is a swimming pool, so I went there.

Swimming trunks were not on hire, and I got an odd look when I replied, "Och well, can I just have a towel then, please." (With most of my clothes drying at the hostel, I was wearing my trunks.) I had a long, long hot shower (the last had been at Nevis Youth Hostel) and was agreeably surprised not to have washed off all my colour—some sunburn remained after all. A pool is a bit dull to oneself and after hearing the record of "Elvira Madigan" for the twentieth time non-stop, I'd had enough.

I called in at "Nevisport", who had supplied some of my gear, and emerged with a pile of old magazines; for the rest, it was window-shopping only. I took an early bus back to Loch Lochy. Still it rained. There had only been two really good days since I had set off from Glen Nevis nearly a fortnight before. I turned in early.

The dormitory, filled with its quota of humanity, grew intolerably stuffy, so I crept over and opened the door to create some draught. The lad in the next bed had a filthy cold, the Germans snored, the air was smelly with humanity. I longed to be back in the tent along with the rain and the midges, beyond the Great Glen.

IX

WEST TO KNOYDART

Silence of wind and of sea and of sun,
The silence that is life when life is run;
Give me silence that is the best of joys
And its questing the very best of ploys.

Friday 7 June SEVEN GAZ CYLINDERS HID BEHIND A WALL

I had a cup of tea with Mr Fraser and was off at 7.30. The loch beyond
Laggan Locks was showing quiet reflections of hills, trees and gorse
bushes. I was suspicious. Too bright too soon, will rain by noon. It
rained at 11.30, to be precise.

The walk down past Kilfinnan was pleasant. The flora of wet and
wilderness was thriving: lousewort, butterwort, bog cotton and myrtle.
The forest is mature and felling has started. In the muggy conditions I
was soon a-drip with sweat. I left the rucksack at the ruin of Glas-
dhoire, and took the old stalking path for the Cam Bhealach.

The air was fresher once out of the trees and into the cleft of the pass,
which was green and full of sheep. Two fishing boats crossed the visible
slice of loch leaving a herring bone pattern from their wakes. From the
top of the pass I angled up and round to gain Meall na Teanga (*hill of
the tongue*), the last pull up on to the ridge being slippery and steep. There
was a small cairn and then a bigger one fifty yards further south.
Meall Coire Lochain, 2,971, is the only height shown on the one-inch
map—the new 1 : 50,000 does not bother to show any.

In early days I climbed the Sron, it being the highest of the hills
seen across Loch Lochy, and because the map gave 2,971 feet over
this side of the pass, I had no idea there was another 3,000-footer. I had
faith in the O.S. in those days! The hills are pleasing, anyway, and so is
2,957-foot Ben Tee just to the north, a mini Schiehallion which
dominates the gentle eastern end of Loch Garry. For a long time my
lads had held it against me, for they went off to climb it by themselves
while I was laid low with 'flu. Conversations would begin, "When
you've climbed Tee instead of just drinking it . . ."

An obvious zig-zag of stalking path leads on to the *nose of the rough*

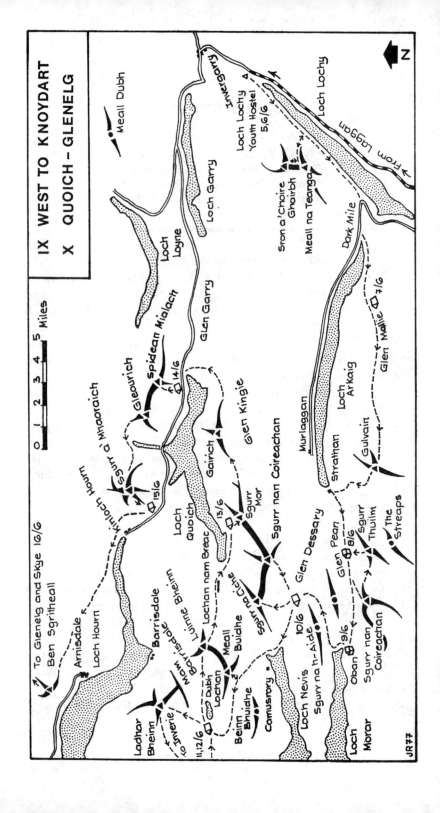

IX WEST TO KNOYDART
X QUOICH - GLENELG

corrie, Sron a'Choire Ghairbh. I arrived in mist and rain. Its *rough corrie* lies on the other side encircled by the arms of this rather tame hill. A questionnaire left today was returned ten days later. Back in the forest at my sack I heated a tin of soup and had pieces, but no sooner set off to walk on south, out to Clunes and Achnacarry, than the rain belted down, a real helm o' weet again. The book went away, "skins" went on, the sun came out, the skins came off. The forest smoked and I sweated. I read along the red-surfaced track: a Nigel Tranter historical novel.

The Chattingtons, at the forestry houses, were not at home so I sat under the trees by the Dark Mile, among the heavy-scented hyacinths, and read for an hour. Then I met Mrs Chattington, so soon had my parcel. With a bit to go an offer of tea was actually refused!

My rucksack suddenly felt very heavy, for it was a hefty parcel and even allowing for a good meal from tins there would still be a lot of weight to carry during the days ahead.

The Dark Mile is a fine avenue, hemmed in by towering hillside plantations, the branches drooping over the road draped with moss. D. K. Broster uses "The Dark Mile" as a title in her trilogy of romantic novels set in this area after Culloden. They are still popular enough to be found in paperback. The *Mile Dorcha* leads to the east end of Loch Arkaig where a river pours down from Gleann Cia-aig (pronounced "Kaig") with a fall into a deep black pool overlooked by the bridge. A path up the glen is a good approach to the Loch Lochy hills.

In August 1746, towards the end of his wanderings, Prince Charlie spent two weeks in hiding in this area, "in sundry fast places", including a cave now lost in the forestry plantings. I found a fast place among the big trees and went through my parcel. No wonder it was heavy, there were far too many Gaz cylinders. I ate a huge meal from tins, buried some food in the forest, and hid the surplus Gaz behind a dyke where it could be found easily by the next weekenders. I continued past Achnacarry for the south side of Loch Arkaig, still able to read on a rough road.

Achnacarry House is the home of Cameron of Lochiel. The Duke of Cumberland laid the place to ruin in 1746 and the Commandos, during wartime training, accidentally tried to burn it down again. Restored, it is still the home of the present Cameron clan chief. Here is mature parkland and wild wood, forestry plantings and birch, set among

G

flowing rivers and loch scenery: a few miles along, when I'd left the last struggling Scots pines, the heather and bare corries were wild and empty. The transformation from Great Glen westward by any route is startling.

People were fishing in Loch Arkaig. Children in a "Wendy House" among the trees peered curiously at me as I peered curiously at the strange wee house. Where the River Mallie flows into the loch I was met and escorted by a great mob of curious cows, a sight which obviously amused the occupants of a passing Land-Rover. With my noisy escort bashing about in the bog and myrtle I turned up the glen, leaving the long loch, for it is trackless.

The south shore forest of Loch Arkaig was burnt during the war and the scars still stand in gaunt, dead trees. It is now being replanted—the workers commuting daily across the loch by boat from the switchback road. I found a quiet corner of the river and hoped another herd of cows, just up the glen, would not find the tent. The remnants of old Scots pines (some 300 years old) and new plantings made it a delightful spot as a pale evening sun shone down the glen.

I demolished another meal and worked out the needs ahead, for it was possible, with the petrol crisis, that Ian Mitchell might not arrive from Fife at the weekend. The wind died down after supper. The midges came out. I went in.

It had been a good day again, over 20 miles. The "human animal was happy" as Rebuffat puts it, and was I not into the land beyond the Great Glen at last, westing in starless summer to the sea and all that was best?

Saturday 8 June   WEST, WHERE ALL DREAMS LIE

Six-footed rather than four-footed beasties were about in the morning. It was bright and fresh, with eiderdown clouds and brief slips of blue. Wouldn't a dry day be nice for a change! I off-loaded two pounds' weight by leaving a jar of honey and a pot of jam perched on a boulder by the track. I would like to have seen the reactions of the finder.

The old pines died out and the glen became, slowly, more barren, of poor grass and sedges, of bracken, and at the end of the track a semi-derelict cottage which would make a fine bothy. The upper reaches of Glen Mallie are much wetter, the river narrower and fringed with alders to the last. The going, as I slowly sauntered upwards, was so easy that I just carried on reading. I was still aware, though, of the lengthening corridor of view back down the glen—and of the fresh, yellow light of returning summer. It was as if the hills and glens had had a thorough washing and were now hung out to dry. They smelt fresh. They looked clean. Ah, that wonderful additive, the sun!

An odd wall ran up over the col to the Allt Screamhaich, whose corrie, from above, was a rock-rusted cauldron, flecked with tiny pools. Each pool had a little lawn and each lawn made a bed for a few deer. Even though I zig-zagged up, outlined against the sun, they failed to move.

A steep bouldery slope brought me to the summit of Gulvain (or Gaor Bheinn), where I went round and round the cairn gaping at the view and clicking away till I'm sure I had photographed a 360° panorama, all good.

The West was a jumble of spiky summits and deep-cleaving valleys—there was nothing soft or rounded. To the south east Ben Nevis stood out as a bold shape, shrinking the Mamores with its height. Bidean, Starav, and things beyond Etive were all blue and edged with sun. South lay the massed array of hills forming quiet Moidart and Ardgour —perhaps the largest tract of rough mountain country without a Munro. The length of Loch Shiel quivered below its guardian hills. Up this loch Prince Charlie sailed from Moidart to raise his standard. A monument to the event stands beside the road. The Streaps (2,988 and 2,916)—again not Munros—were etched starkly; they are among the very steepest of all hills in Scotland; bare Thuilm lay behind. The Cuillin were there, saw-toothed, beyond the piled blocks of Knoydart and Ciche, beyond the one touch of softness—Glen Dessary. Sgurr Mor took its high, double-topped, stance beyond Glen Kingie, in front of the Saddle and the Glen Shiel ridges, in turn before the Affric ranges.

Yesterday's hills seemed almost tame compared to this western mob.

My tent was draped over the cairn to dry off, while I prowled round it and round again to look and look at the panorama. One fault with nylon is that it retains overnight moisture until really aired like this. If it goes up unaired, the interior is damp, a problem yet to be resolved by manufacturers.

I left a questionnaire behind. Patrick Simms, the Secretary of the Ross-shire M.C. found it, but added he was off back to "native Ireland after five years' Munro bagging". He discovered the note only a few hours after I'd left it, having come up Gleann Fionnlighe from Loch Eil and traversed the South Top—the normal route for most, but my descent route to Glen Pean can be used in reverse: a crafty, back-door approach. The name means *back-shaped hill*.

I went down the very steep flank to a col where I kept a bit to the north so had many ins-and-outs over the gashes cut by streams—hard on the ankles. There was a wee loch near the watershed and once down the glen I had a picnic, and a paddle in exquisitely cold water. The glen is dominated by the Streaps, hills you would have to bargain quite a few Munros to equal.

A 500-foot pull took me slanting up easy slopes to cross the ridge and drop down the rake into Gleann a' Chaoruinn, which must be one of the oldest through routes in a district where north–south communication is singularly difficult. It leads to a fine pass (1,586 feet) hemmed in by the steepness of Thuilm and the Streaps.

Strathan at the end of Loch Arkaig could once see a score of shepherds gathered for the shearing. Now sheep do not pay. Lochiel has sold off glens here, and private forestry is the new thing for Pean and Dessary.

There were figures at the bridge across the Pean (just east of where the Allt a' Chaoruinn joins it) but I had the glen to myself. I collected the odd bit of bog wood for the bothy. A new forestry track was coming in along the slope above, which I found saddening, as this is probably the finest pass in the west and its obliteration by trees would be an act of vandalism. Let us hope the owner, Mrs Jean Balfour (Chairman of the Countryside Commission and a keen conservationist), has these dangers in mind.

The finely-sited bothy shows well the sort of work the Mountain Bothies Association is doing. It had been pointed, re-roofed and good windows inserted, so is now weather-proof. The upper rooms are still panelled and cosy for sleeping, and downstairs (stripped in the past by vandals), though barn-like and bare, has a fireplace. The work done partly with funds raised as a memorial to Wilf Tauber.

There were two sleeping bags. Ian Mitchell I'd expected, but with him was John Lawton whom I had last seen at the Spittal of Glen Muick. Ian was then the M.B.A. membership secretary and a great bothy fan. They, unfortunately for me, had been on the hills I had on my list for tomorrow, so even with friends around, I would not have hill company. Fresh food was much enjoyed. We sat by the bothy fire and I enlightened John (from Australia) and Ian (from England originally) about the doings of my ghost—Prince Charlie.

It was at the house of Donald Cameron of Glen Pean that Prince

Charlie began his foot-slogging in the months after Culloden. That mismanaged February affair lasted only 30 minutes (the barbarous killing that followed it went on for months, earning Cumberland his nickname, "Butcher"). The Prince fled, by horseback, to Loch Oich that same day, to Glengarry's castle, the "Rock of the Raven", then on the second day by the Dark Mile and Loch Arkaig arrived here. He went on foot through to Morar and sailed to the Isles. It's a story walkers should follow on the map, once they know the Highlands. It was an impressive journey. Later, returning from the Isles he was to come over the shoulder of Thuilm, possibly even over its summit, for his party skulked on top watching Glen Pean and Glen Dessary being "beaten" by the redcoats all day before they sneaked down in the dark, traversed Carn Mor's long ridge which rises to 2,718 feet, crossed Upper Glen Dessary and lay up again somewhere on the Ciche side the next day. The next night they descended Coire nan Gall to a "fast place" at the head of Loch Quoich—where we'll take up their route again.

Sunday 9 June THE FINEST PASS IN SCOTLAND

The forecast had been of sunny periods and showers but reality was giving a deal too much of the latter. John and Ian were cutting over the ridge of Carn Mor to visit A'Chuil bothy in Glen Dessary before walking out to Strathan for the long drive back to Fife. We all took photos of each other and set off—up opposing hillsides.

Before beginning my uphill stint I wandered up Glen Pean as far as Lochan Leum an t' Sagairt and managed to cross with a running leap. (All the rivers in Knoydart can be desperate in wet weather.) The reeds were bending to the breeze and the pattern of reflections was very pretty. Crags and trees crowded down to the water's edge and the pass beyond was a deep "kloof". With the ochreous grass colour you could almost have filmed a western there.

It was a no-messing-ascent of Sgurr nan Coireachan, aptly the *peak of the corries*, for this slope enfolds many a secret, deer-filled corrie. It is craggy and wild, with tumbling burns dodging down its flanks. The bothy shrank in size as I rose and Loch Arkaig, every now and then, had its silver light shut off by the grey damask of curtaining showers. On the summit these were giving a touch of snow. Cow-wheat, thyme and bedstraw were all in flower.

Turning east I lost the best of the view (the east–west traverse is better), but had the showers pushing me along the many ups and downs leading to Sgurr Thuilm, or Sgor Choilean, *peak of the holm*. Keep to the crest between the Munros: contours do not pay. (You may find unusually large *books* of mica.) These hills are bulky big brutes but present no real problems.

The big curve of the railway viaduct at the foot of Glenfinnan and the monument to the '45 were both quite visible—and the bewildering pile of mountains beyond. The viaduct is historically interesting as being one of the first to be made of concrete, by Robert McAlpine, who pioneered the Fort William–Mallaig line. Now we take it so for granted, then it was a new-fangled material (though known back to Roman times). This railway is a vital line for hill-goers, for both south and north of it lie great mountain tracts which can be circled without having perpetually to return to a car. A boat from Mallaig into Knoydart is another good starting method, walking out eventually to train back to the start.

I went straight down off Thuilm: steep and a bit slippery underfoot. The sun came out again. I staggered into the bothy with both rucksack and arms full of bog wood, and found a Professor of Logic and Metaphysics installed. He had come from St Andrews to see the bothy: Wilf Tauber had once been a pupil.

I procrastinated over a "sort of" meal. I was not wanting to leave at all—a not uncommon experience this trip. Perhaps the schedule was a necessary discipline; but there was a subtle thrall in the very things I was seeking to flee: telephones and motor cars—the perpetual safety factor.

I left odds and ends of food by two new rucksacks lying in a corner, perhaps they were the figures I'd glimpsed on Thuilm. I noted my doings in the bothy book. An entry there from a Canadian explained his great-great-great-grandfather had left Glen Pean in 1794 for Ontario.

Not being an enthusiastic reader of guide-books I did not know that the better side for passing the loch in the pass lay to the south. "The loch *can* be passed by a laborious ascent on its north side" which I proved: climbing first above cliffs that dropped directly into the lochan, and then descending down shattered crags and trees, rather in the manner of a Tarzan with rucksack. A dead goat lying below was discouraging.

That fun over, I was intrigued to find the pass wending on for well over a mile: corner after corner with a central twisty stream and steep, rocky slopes, hemming it in. The season was progressing. Pipits' nests now held young instead of eggs. Hot, raggedy sheep stood to watch me pass.

I came on an area (like the entrance to the Lost Valley in Glencoe) where a cliff had fallen and filled the glen with boulders. Wending through them I suddenly came on a lost lochan: a small, jet, reflecting pool, delicately set among vivid birch and boulders, wine-coloured in the sun. Above towered a bold edge of cliff. This whole miniature landscape was a complete surprise.

The big pass just to the north is a bleak place in comparison, even on the sunniest of passages. This may only be 400 feet of pass—but it has no superior anywhere. Beyond it lay the watershed and a glimpse of Loch Morar. A crazy gate marked the start of a good stalkers' path and a singing descent through wild scenery led to a tame valley-bottom where there was the usual ruin marking old prosperity and another lochan—an unwinking yellow reptile eye of colour. Round a corner was Loch Morar. I was puzzled by a view of hills far to the west. They looked *very* familiar, but I could not place them for some time: the Rhum Cuillin.

Loch Morar is separated rom the sea by a river, only three hundred yards long, leading to a sea bay of brilliant white sand which continues, bay after bay, by Traigh to Back of Keppoch. The loch is over a thousand feet deep, the deepest fresh water to be found in Europe, and you would have to move west beyond the Outer Hebrides, and off the continental shelf, to find a comparable depth in the sea itself. Like Loch Ness (over 700 feet deep), Loch Morar has a reputation for harbouring a beastie of some kind, by name of Morag.

This is country associated above all others with Charles Edward Stewart, for in South Morar he landed and escaped in 1745 and 1746. I think part of the reason his story has been so romanticised is that it was the last flash of a way of life which the rest of the country was already rejecting: Stewart finery and Hanoverian plainness, religious bigotry and the new liberalism. Perhaps by being rid of the Stewarts, we were saved a French Revolution later. What remains sad was the harsh way the social changes came about, and the way the land and its people were forsaken, broken, and cleared, right up to this present century.

Anyone expeditioning in this wild west must be camel-like in self-sufficiency. Since Achnacarry I had not passed an occupied house, and to escape from here would entail a hard day south or west, northwards I would simply run into the Rough Bounds of Knoydart, a landscape even more isolated and empty.

I followed the path among the grassy knolls to the edge of the loch, picking up the odd bit of wood for a fire. The amount of plastic was surprising, even here. I was also keeping a look out for bigger finds. Back in 1746 a treasure of 35,000 louis d'or was brought up the loch and carried through to Glen Pean into the safety of Cameron country (money for the rising, typically arriving *after* Culloden). It was thought to have been buried by Loch Arkaig, perhaps at Murlaggan, if it reached that far. Anyway, it was made so safe that it has not been seen since. Two possible reasons could account for that!

I passed an old, disintegrated landing stage, and there, tucked into the hill with a lawn of wild grass running down to the loch, was a cottage.

Oban had a forsaken look about it. Great steel shutters and plastic gutters and piping obviously showed a determined and recent occupation —yet it stood empty, the wind already having stolen a few sections of roof. Kinlochmorar, the house on the opposite side of the loch, had dark windows, empty like blind eyes, another deserted spot. Both buildings had solitary rowans not far from their doors. Rowans were grown for luck in times past, but luck has long since deserted the glens. Only the odd gangrel stravaigs this way, or the odd boat plouters up the loch. It is as desolate—or peaceful—a spot as you could desire.

"The chip-chip-chipping of a snipe and the mocking call of a loon flying west; these were the sounds of evening." So I wrote in my log and added, prosaically, but sucking encouragement from bare mathematics: "A hundred Munros to go."

Monday 10 June THE LOWEST EBB

> "And when he was up, he was up,
> And when he was down, he was down."

It was too warm a night for good sleep. I spent much of it *on* rather than in the sleeping bag. Mice were scrabbling about in the panelling of my bare room in the empty house.

The loch was calm when I rose at seven, but the dull sheen of gun-metal grey had an ominous look about it. I set off wearing just a Damart vest and nylon shorts to try to reduce the volume of sweat expected. While I was busy dealing with a craggy headland opposite the cottage, the loch crumpled into ripples and a drizzle began.

Campers by Kinlochmorar had their belongings scattered in the ruin and, trustingly, a bottle of malt lying! This once large two-storeyed house was falling down—odd furnishings, even a double bed, were still *in situ*, but by a year later vandalism had reduced the interior as if an I.R.A. bomb had been thrown into it. Oak, sycamore and rowan protected the building and a straggle of narcissi told of past affection.

I was faced with another dramatic pass now: Gleann an Lochain Eanaiche. Above it lay Sgurr na h-Aide, a narrow ridge, which seen, end on, from Glen Dessary, or along Loch Arkaig, is often mistaken for Sgurr na Ciche. The slopes of this flank rise at a continuous forty-five degrees for over 2,000 feet. Carn Mor, the other side of the glen, is steep as well, but lacks such crags and slabs on its long eastern shanks.

There was an excellent path up the glen which gave easy gradients. The river plunges at times through some good gorges, tumbling wildly down in successive falls, and carving out holes in the rock, then at other stages meanders gently along. Lochain Eanaiche was a lonely spot.

A bit further on the path degenerated into a foot-track and eventually just traces of beast-track. The ground rose only another hundred feet in over a mile up to the watershed (*c.* 750 feet), a narrow gut (like a small fault) which makes it different from any other pass I know. It ended with the burn twisting down from the left in a splashy fall; then there was quite a dip to link with a meandering burn which flowed to join the River Dessary.

By the top of the pass the rain had come on hard. I was dripping with sweat inside my waterproof top and bottom, though still clad in my minimum. The atmosphere grew colder, but the physical effort of breaking round to the Mam na Cloich 'Airde path kept me warm. Not for the first time I now put a foot in a bog and drew it out black to the knee. I could not be wetter below knee level, anyway, so a walk in the next burn cleaned it.

The rough going slowed me down and I began, suddenly, to feel ridiculously cold. A brief clearance showed the hills ahead (which I was hoping to climb) plastered with snow well below the 2,000-foot level. The rout was complete. Their ascent would have been madness in the conditions, and my state had suddenly become serious: I had become very cold indeed. It was time to camp.

Finding a dryish bump on that blasted weather-scoured col was not easy. Most of the ground was inches deep in water, at just the time I was in a hurry. I eventually chose a knoll where the underlying rock wasn't too close below the thin skin of moss and lichen. Then I found I'd left the tent pegs back at Oban.

"What sort of crazy game was this? It was ridiculous. Time to pack in. It was just not worthwhile. I must be donnert. Daft." Such were my feelings as I grovelled about collecting piles of stones for holding the tent. At least I had the poles. My hands and legs were numb with the icy wetness by the time I got the tent up. Thank goodness it was simple to erect.

At the back of noon I stripped off everything and crawled into the sleeping bag to thaw out. It took half an hour and a couple of brews before I stopped shivering. I was too near ending up as one of Ben Humble's statistics to be amused—even in retrospect.

I ate the last of my bread. My two tea bags were stewed to death, and raisins were counted out one by one. I did have an evening meal spare, though, plus emergency chocolate etc. I could survive a delay, and a cache lay at the foot of the pass. It was loss on the schedule that worried me. I had a tryst at Loch Quoich dam for the weekend.

Perhaps I should make for Inverie and phone, make a meeting at A'Chuil or Kinbreak, then catch up beyond. If these conditions went on, Knoydart would be impossible. I worried myself into the deepest "low" of the trip, needlessly too, for I was only a few miles from friends who could have looked after me for days, and Inverie had a shop.

It was the numbing cold, I suppose, that depressed. It is no fun recognising in oneself the symptoms of an exposure case. I quote the outpouring in my log fully, partly because it is the only such to be found there, and for the sake of truth.

"Storms blast through periodically. Tent a bit drafty and noisy of course. Very wearying. Toughest area of all with difficult lines of supply and communication—and this November weather at its worst. (Still cold in sleeping bag yet last night sweating.) Heights barred by blizzards and valley driving rain and flooded wildly. Oh, it would be nice to pack in—but can't. Must hang on or even retreat and come again. It is so good when good, or even reasonable, but apart from the last three days it's been pretty awful for weeks. It is June, damn it. My shoulder tells the weather: the wet cold sets it gnawing away like a beast. Read a bit and early to kip. Morale low."

Tuesday 11 June ROUGH BOUNDS

"He who would make a journey must first make peace", says the old Chinese proverb.

The next morning seemed bright very early and the atmosphere had reverted to the stuffy warmth of Oban. A good sleep had worked wonders. I was away at 7 a.m. (I thought) and only ended at 9 p.m. (I thought), so had a long day, which closed as wet as the previous one but with morale high again. The setback had acted like a sharpener on the edge of determination.

Sgurr na Ciche, the *pap-shaped peak*, is the highest of the Knoydart summits. It has a special place in my affections because it was my last Munro, the first innocent time. That was nearly ten years ago and done just days before going off for my first winter in the High Atlas. I had come west by train to Glenfinnan and tramped through between Streap and Thuilm (mostly in the dark) to bivy in a filthy ruin by Loch Arkaig. The next day, via Glen Dessary, I had traversed to Ciche, in tiring snow conditions and then walked out to Glenfinnan again the same way, into darkness again, just in time to catch the evening train to Glasgow.

Now, I skirted up via Coire na Ciche to the bouldery gully descending from the col between Sgurr na Ciche and Garbh Chioch Mhor. This is as good a line as any from the Glen Dessary side if doing Ciche first or on its own. The approaches from the north have been barred by Loch Quoich; direct from Loch Nevis the ridge is very long.

There is probably no mainland ridge as complex as that beginning on Ben Aden, taking in Ciche, Coireachan and along to Sgurr Mor. The going is rough in the extreme: bare mountain rock: ribs and ridges, walls, slabs, gaps with the navigation tricky due to all the tormented twists and turns.

Perhaps it is as well that so much of the best does lie far west and north, and often far from civilisation; people tend to have served some apprenticeship before they wander into these regions. Loch Nevis, to me a place of sunny peacefulness (or "gey weet" peacefulness) has *frightened* people not used to the isolation or grandeur.

From the col at the head of my gully, the Feadan na Ciche (Ciche's whistle or chanter) the route proved surprisingly easy. Not altogether trusting the compass I left tiny "stone men" along my route: skirting up left on steep grass, gaining the crest, then left again—all fairly natural lines between the steep walls which looked huge in the mist. Pockets of snow still lay inches deep but on the whole it had been stripped off almost as quickly as it was plastered on.

The Ordnance Survey deserve a reprimand for the mess they have made of this summit. There are now *three* trig points, in various stages of disintegration! I wended back, tumbling my wee markers as I went, and had soon reached the Feadan. Some day Ciche will give me a view.

A long hogsback ridge—a hedgehog ridge—lies between here and the next Munro, giving two summits: the Garbh Chioch Mhor and Garbh Chioch Bheag—the large and small rough paps. You will not get over them without using your hands and if you try you can use your hands a fair bit. I found quite a good rake along the south flank and on it put up an eagle, who gave me one cool look before dropping into the clouds.

A ptarmigan family broke and scattered at my feet, one of the chicks rolling head over heels down a slab. How the mother bird finds them all later is a marvel—or perhaps she doesn't. You often see a dozen tiny bundles of fluff, but in July there are usually just three or four in the exploding flight. The mother beat her wings against my legs. I took a picture of her against the lichenous rock which showed her marvellous camouflage. Sitting birds just do not move sometimes, and you may only notice them because they blink an eye.

Navigation on the Garbh Chioch is made easy by the presence of a wall. To the north is Coire nan Gall which is precociously slabby without giving real climbing. Prince Charlie came up from Glen Dessary and descended into it in the dark. From the Bealach nan Gall the west ridge up Sgurr nan Coireachan proved easier than expected. I simply did an up and down it, and then turned south west from the col: a slanting line which eventually led more or less back to the tent site.

The descent gave quite a bit of slab and rock, and many a hanging-garden gully. Marsh mallows, globeflower, roseroot and saxifrages loved their wet recesses while eyebright and thrift kept to drier parts. Thrift is Virgin Mary's Pillow, *Cluasag Mhuire* in Gaelic. Deer went off constantly, usefully showing where to break through the odd difficulties.

Glen Dessary was all dollops of sunshine and shadow. It once had a Wade track (not a road), and Cumberland established a camp there. Miss Jenny Cameron of Glen Dessary had led her men to Glenfinnan on a white horse, no doubt by the pass under the Streaps. The three cairns at the head of this pass marked the meeting of Lovat, Glengarry

and Locheil lands. The latter alone is left and he recently sold
Glen Dessary to the woodmen.

I collected the tent and began the diverse delights of the descent
from the Mam na Cloich 'Airde, the *pass of the high rock*. Even in this
bleak spot I found a ruined shieling. A fenceless gate marks the watershed. I crossed a river, pulled up—and then the plunge down to Loch
Nevis truly began—as dramatically as opening a door.

The path is built up in tight angles or curls down in fine sweeps.
There is one rushing stream crossing it, about which I was concerned,
for one wild November, when I was escaping from Knoydart, I very
nearly drowned in that spot. It was surprisingly easy today though
requiring a certain amount of "leaping from rock to rock".

I crossed to have a look at Finiskaig: the roof had fallen in from
neglect and as the M.B.A. had offered to do it up at their expense, such
neglect is sad. As a bothy it had been the only place for miles where
emergency shelter could be found—a possible life-saver. A geologist
was camping by the ruin.

The tide was well out and still ebbing I was glad to see. The map is
correct in showing the path running between the tide lines as it rounds
the head of the loch. Great areas of sand are bared at low tide and this
is an area loved by wading birds.

In the 1920's an S.M.C. Journal account describes a round trip from
Glasgow: train to Fort William, sail in to Inverie, and then via Sourlies
east to Spean Bridge, train back to Glasgow. Quite a weekend. The
cost was thirty-five shillings. (Sourlies is now fully restored as a bothy
which makes a very useful haven.)

The Carnoch river flows into the head of the loch beside a large area
of green patchwork pieces cut by little channels. If you *have* to pass at
high tide you may have some scrambling to do: the crags, like the head
of Loch Morar, fall steeply to the shore, or sea.

Coming in by steamer, passengers are ferried ashore by rowing boat
to Camusrory. Crossing the Carnach can then be a problem. I remember once, on the boat, telling tales of this fearsome river. Another
passenger was all ears, too, and chancing to land with the first boatload,
set off over the brae before we had all assembled.

When we topped the rise and could see the Carnach I was relieved to
see it was not in spate, and by going a little way on we crossed without
even taking boots off (the only time, ever, to date). Coming downstream
again we met the other passenger pulling on his breeks and still in bare

feet. We received a somewhat dirty look! Like every river between
Loch Quoich and Glenfinnan the Carnach can be desperate or impossible, something visitors normally never consider elsewhere, but vital
in the wet west. The bridge shown here on the map does not exist.

I waded across the Carnach mouth easily enough, but felt my feet
were very soft with so much wet and sweaty walking. Ben Aden, up
Glen Carnach, had a foreground of Camusrory ponies.

Tony Montgomery moved here and had established one of the best
little outdoor centres, first for Barnardo's, and then as "The Travellers
Trust". However, lacking the big backing of education authorities,
services or the like, it cannot compete and the centre is doomed in its
present form.

Here people "travelled", experiencing something of the reality and
riches of adventure. They might go off on ponies right through to the
Cairngorms—or sail off to Rhum or the Cuillins—or trek through the
Rough Bounds. A wonderfully dedicated staff has, over the years,
ensured that participants gained the maximum from their experiences:
experiences far more valid than in most centres in dull areas where the
same old stuff is churned out year after year.

Tony was away on his honeymoon when I called. Nicola Pilkington,
a well-trained lassie, produced tea before David Smith turned up.
David had long been a fixture here, and one of the pleasures of passing
Camusrory was to look in to see him or Tony.

My food parcel was there all right (52p postage); and, if I had to
lose tent pegs, the neighbourhood of an adventure centre was probably
the place in which to do so. I refused further tempting offers of
hospitality and, with the black cats seeing me across the lawn where the
lupins were still wrapped with seaweed from a January gale, I turned
to the highway again. A blessing on all such kindly folk.

I wandered up to the old ruins of Carnoch—once a keeper's house,
now a shell. Charles Inglis Clark, his father, Walker and Jeffrey stayed
there in 1913, having walked in from Glenfinnan. Their doings are
worth reading up in the old S.M.C. Journal (Vol. XII, p. 297) for the
similarities and differences to today's adventures. Some of their photographs are interesting: Kinlochquoich Lodge having since been
drowned under a Hydro scheme.

The excuse of removing some weight from the rucksack had me
pausing to demolish strawberries and cream. *That* was quite a morale-
booster too. However, to balance the renewed zest for living, came the

realisation as to why the Clunes parcel had had so many Gaz refills; this parcel, being posted, had none. I had one left and the next supply lay by Loch Quoich dam! It might have to be the old wood fire again: at least there were trees in Knoydart. But that would be a problem for the next day. I still had a pass to cross and a peak to climb, and the next dose of wet stuff was coming up the loch.

The path goes up in well-made zig-zags (not as per map) and the whole area here is craggy and wild (which the map does not indicate either). I had to don skins so was soon sweating away. The smir turned to steady rain and then to equally steady heavy rain. I plodded on up with the wet running off me in sploshy streams. Cuffs and feet were soon wet.

The Mam Meadail was a gruey spot, utterly bleak and completely saturated. I dithered. Having toiled up, Meall Buidhe was immediately above. If I did not do it now it would mean a further day, and a sea-level start. I sheltered my tent and things among a large group of boulders and set off upwards. It was *only* wet, the warmth removed the dangers of the day before.

It is an interesting peak to do in poor visibility; this side especially bears little resemblance to the old map contours. After breaking up through a lot of crags, I ended on a long narrow ridge which did not exist on the map. However up is up, and none of the dips were large enough to go astray on. At the east top I was on familiar ground and edged round the rim of cliffs, Creag Dhearg, which the map shows well down the corrie. The summit is a spacious green one, but I lingered only long enough to stuff a macaroon bar into my mouth.

Meall Buidhe, and its western friend Beinn Buidhe across the Mam, are both fine viewpoints, the latter probably the better with its broader seascape and a view perhaps of Sgurr na Ciche, at its sharpest, mirrored in one of the many lochans. One of the best of hill rounds is the combination of Meall Buidhe and Luinne Bheinn.

Coming down in my cloudy wetness I overshot the turning-off point on the non-existent ridge. Suddenly it "felt" wrong. I had run out of remembered features and markers. Back-tracking failed to help so I began to slant down and just as suddenly it "felt" right again—and sure enough on a boulder I found two perched pebbles left on the ascent.

Up and down from the col took two hours and another two passed before I was done for the day. The descent of Gleann Meadail is another piece of Scotland I have yet to see despite several visits. The saturation continued all the way down the path. Trees "moved" among the smoky valley mists and a rickety bridge took me over to the memorial on the road. Rushes stood silvered with the wet and the scent of the wild hyacinths was strong. On up the glen the myrtle gave a sharper, spiced scent—reminding of food!

It was already gloomy with dusk, and most of the light went as I tramped the road miles to the Dubh Lochain where there is an old cottage used by the estate as a boathouse. It was smelly with recent fibreglass work and the floor was largely wet, but in the black wet night I took the option and just spread the tent on a dry patch and slept on it instead of in it. Every stitch of clothing came off to drape the walls. I heated mince, sweet corn and spinach and had a couple of brews. It was bed I wanted.

My watch had stopped the previous night and I'd wound it at breakfast without noticing: hence, all through the day, I was running two hours out. Which was just as well; for it gave me Meall Buidhe. I was back on par.

Wednesday 12 June   ZIP

Concrete floor or not I slept well. The first glimpse of day was not encouraging: the weather seemed to be carrying on as it was, last thing. My island of dry in the middle of the floor had shrunk.

I was not wanting to be discovered; one may take being thought naughty but not silly. I pitched the tent in the lee of the ruin alongside. I doubled Alpen and halved tea to save precious Gaz. I guessed it to be eight-thirty, set my watch at that, and went off up the slope directly behind the bothy: a route to Ladhar Bheinn used more than once before.

It is quite a straightforward line from the Dubh Lochain side, though at first sight it appears barred by Sgurr Coire Choineachain. But the alternative, to go round that summit, is six or seven miles longer. Choineachain is a fine viewpoint; it is the hill you see immediately above Inverie when you sail in from Mallaig—and the Mam Suidheig, the dip behind, is a natural line.

I was soon soaked below knee level: "Euch" was my log comment. A wren came and made noisy comments too, and the usual cuckoo flitted past until a gang of pipits chased it—going, as you might say, hell for feather.

A large, but still dappled, calf went yelping off and a disapproving grunt came from the hind up the hill. Another was mooing like a cow. I had obviously hit a favoured calving spot. The calves are beautifully camouflaged and the hind will leave them for most of the day. Perhaps this is why her milk is six times as nourishing as a cow's.

Mam Suidheig is rather cut by peat bogs, but deer tracks allowed a gentle slant to be made down into Coire Torr an Asgaill. Not too much height is lost before crossing to the skirts of Ladhar Bheinn.

A fox leapt from a jumble of rocks and trotted across the hillside. As I was carrying no gun he seemed to cock a snoot at me. His presence I reported later, so word could be passed on to the keeper. I still giggle at the face of the keeper in Glen Lyon when I told him I had bumped into two foxes that day, and the relief when he found that neither had been on *his* ground.

I dropped to just under the cloud level, but had it again, like an irritating blanket on a hot night, all the way up the long slopes of Ladhar Bheinn, *the forked mountain.*

Ever so slowly the cloud began to move, a welcome change from the static wet of the last twenty-four hours. I plodded on. The trig point appeared and I was soon on top. There was no view—on a hill with a view as fine as any.

Ladhar Bheinn (the most westerly mainland Munro) is an impressive hill from any side—even the grassy southern slopes will impress, if not depress, with their length and steepness. Walkers not used to really wild country would be well advised to keep to this southern side for an ascent: either my ascent or descent route can be taken. They both drop 2,000 feet in half a mile.

The "obvious" ridge line from the top of Mam Barrisdale is complex and gives scrambling, and in winter can be a proper climb. The north-east corrie (Coire Dhorrcail) is one of the most splendid corries outside Skye. A path leads up into it and you can gain the ridge above. The summit ridge is all of two miles, a narrow crest in places. It is worth saving for a good day, both to see the very fine view and to ensure you find the summit. (The trig point is not at the highest point.) Tom Patey did some winter climbs in the corries.

The hills hem in Loch Hourn as dramatically as any fiord in Norway. I once canoed across from Arnisdale in November to climb the peak from the north. It was a raw, sunless spot, even on the good evening I landed. The next day, after camping overnight, I climbed up the fine northern ridge—thick mist all the way but of course this was no worry ascending, the top was known and had to come in due course. It did. Descending, however, I wanted to swing off on a curling ridge westwards to add a lesser summit beyond the Mam Li. At the appropriate place, estimated from several factors, I did so, and worked very carefully by compass. I became puzzled, for the lie of the land bore no resemblance to the expected, though, as little could be seen in such knobbly rough ground, I could have been anywhere. Eventually I gave up and just took a bearing due north for Loch Hourn. I came down below the cloud about two miles from, and at right angles to, where expected.

This was very bad for morale. It was quite incomprehensible, what's more. Chewing it over later I came to doubt the compass, but on other hills subsequently it worked all right—I was still using it on the Walk. Subsequently I learnt that there is magnetic variation on Ladhar Bheinn's north flank.

The bothy at Barrisdale is equipped and run by local people. Most week-days a boat plies to and from Arnisdale taking mail, and children to school. The next best approach is by walking-in along Loch Hourn from the head of the loch: a path without equal in Scotland. At times it is built up on naked rock above the sea like something in a Himalayan gorge.

I flanked down in tight zig-zags for over 2,000 feet so was glad to stop and take a quick photo of another deer calf lying motionless on the grass at my feet, neck outstretched, big eyes moist under their lashes. In the river, a dipper family was splashing about like a gang of Braehead kids. Stonechats were about again. At Camusrory yesterday I had noticed a stonechat on the bird table. Two other calves broke from cover to go screaming across the slope. A slope to avoid in June it seems!

Folach was another ruin, but of a comparatively modern building. Where fenced off the grass was green and bright. It was hard to imagine Knoydart well populated. It was Macdonell land, and the clan suffered as a result of the '45 like everyone else. Many emigrated to Canada. Glengarry was the seat of the chief, and it was to maintain a position in Edinburgh and London that so much of the land was bled. Raeburn's portrait of Macdonell of Glengarry in the National Gallery in Edinburgh appropriately forms the cover of John Prebble's *The Clearances*.

In 1840 the then chief sold out, except for Knoydart, and emigrated to Australia. In 1846 there was still a population of 600, but potato blight and the failure of the annual herring migration caused famine, and further poverty drove away many of the survivors. The chief returned to die at Inverie in 1852, but his widow has earned a special place in the hall of infamy for her brutal clearing of the estate the next year to make way for sheep. It would fetch a better price, cleared, when sold to a southerner. Four hundred people were driven from the little hamlets, their homes broken down or burnt under her personal direction, and then they were shipped like cattle to a waiting transporter, the *Sillery*, generously supplied by the government to take them off to America.

A few lingered on, living in constructions of sacking and turf, eating shell fish—and dying in the winter. That was the Clearances.

Today, an Ardrishaig firm were busy with yellow monsters chewing up a "road" which at present was all squelchy black mud. The Allt a' Mhuilinn led steeply down to Inverie through woods and rhoddies smelling of honey. The boat was chugging its friendly course into the bay and the usual group of people had gathered at the pier for its arrival—a scene as much part of Western life as fish, midges and wellington boots.

Sailing from Mallaig is possibly the finest way of reaching Knoydart. *The Clansman* once gave me an unscheduled landing on a remote shore simply by edging in so that I could leap from the bows on to the rocky shore.

The Ripleys when they landed at Inverie met a very unfriendly reception: the third week in September not being a diplomatic visiting period! They did my yesterday in reverse to end at A'Chuil in Glen Dessary, sleeping on corrugated iron sheets to keep themselves off the sheep droppings. Fortunately, the M.B.A. have saved that vital haven.

The shop had a fine selection of wine and I loaded up with all manner of fresh goodies: cheese, milk, tomatoes, bananas, rolls, butter and cakes. They had no meths, no paraffin, no Gaz, and no ideas—but my eye lit on packets of Zip firelighters. I bought two, and some tins of food for quickness—and "because they were there". (Who eats dehydrated when there are alternatives?)

I lacked a book for the tramp home and it seemed a long road in the stuffy heat and with a load of tins. The white houses strung along the bay always look attractive and the big house in its green setting has none of the misplaced flamboyancy of so many mansions. Inverie is lush with big trees and green farmlands, again giving the sense of contrast which was such a part of the Walk.

On the knoll near where the Mam Meadail path branches off, there is a monument which, in Knoydart, gives the Clearances story a modern appendix. The monument is to the late Lord Brocket's father. That Lord Brocket was the landowner at the time of the post-war land-grab; his name lives on, in the lines of a popular, not very complimentary ballad, if nowhere else. He had sacked people at will and generally made life intolerable for the local folk, some who had worked there for generations. An approach by locals for land was rejected and when "The Seven Men of Knoydart" tried to grab land for crofts, they were interdicted. A few years later Lord Brocket sold the estate anyway. Perhaps it is time for this feudal system to end. We have to cull the deer, but there could be a better system.

It was only a mile or two from the monument back to the loch and the tent. The estate road finishes there and the path on to the Mam Barrisdale is an old, excellent pony track. Patches of blue appeared in the grey clouds like lost pieces of a jigsaw.

All the tracks in Knoydart exist as shown on the one-inch map. Where they are shown as ending they usually do, and the reason is that to continue is probably impracticable. Many buildings shown fell into disrepair during the war. You go in to Knoydart prepared to be self-contained. They might not have Zip firelighters next time! This is not beautiful country but it is highly dramatic, very rough and blessed with the silence of remoteness. Saint-Exupéry defined silence as God's cloak spread out upon man's restlessness.

I'd never met anyone all day till I came on the road works, nor was I to meet anyone again, on subsequent days, till the weekenders arrived at Loch Quoich. With soap and soap powder from the cache, I washed undies (and myself) vigorously. Had I known the characteristics of Zip firelighters I would hardly have bothered. Cooking on them left dixies, hands, face and tent liberally covered in soot. A huge meal, extravagant and enjoyable, ended with oozing butter and jam pieces and fresh milk. A meal makes amends for many things. A touch of sun shimmered through the leaves of the tree growing out of the ruin—a change from yesterday's grey hours groping into black night. It was great not to be pushed for once. There was time to write home, to cut nails, to catch up on the log (the 1,000 miles up today)—and indulge in the old Knoydart game of chasing ticks, for which being alone had certain disadvantages, no offers of "you do me and I'll do you". The wind dropped and the midges swarmed out, so it was into the tent early. Mountains bring forth a peculiar joy which makes us willingly pay the coin of sacrifice and suffering to obtain it. Knoydart had proved a "high" even if the day before had been the lowest ebb. The walk would go, surely: the hills might trip me up, break me, kill me—but otherwise, now, they would not beat me.

Thursday 13 June SUN ALL THE WAY
One titbit from the past cannot be omitted: this was the famous S.M.C. "Yachting Meet" of Easter 1897. The ship was intended as a base for the Cuillin, but the weather drove her from there to Rhum and then to Knoydart.

The Meet report is exciting stuff—such as ascending Ciche, from Inverie, against the tide clock and the ship sailing. Raeburn was on his first Meet, and besides Sir Hugh (with his flute) were Bell, Boyd, Brown, Brunskill, Douglas, Gordon, Howie, Maylard, Ramsay, Rennie, Gibson, Robertson and Ling. Quite a talented gathering. Imagine if the ship had sunk!

Meets have deteriorated since those days. The original account ends, "And now being safely off the hills and steaming for the open sea, the mirth prevailed—the pipes were brought on deck, and the President (Munro), in all the splendour of Highland garb, footed it deftly through the Highland Fling—and reels were danced—a fitting termination to the Meet."

A heat-wave switched on at sun-up. Camp was soon cleared. Despite eating to a state of tightness, various items were surplus, so these, plus unwanted Zip firelighters, were parcelled up and left, with a note giving them to the finder, on top of the boat in the bothy. My last act was to gulp down milk kept as a treat. I found the last mouthfuls lumpy and a check showed some big black slugs.

The Dubh Lochain was like a mirror and Knoydart lay in unbelievable peace, yet I was walking through the wettest region of the country. Knoydart weather does sometimes prove bloody marvellous instead of just bloody. In six miles I shot off a complete 36 exposures, a spool of slides I've never equalled for variety: the reflections in the loch, footsteps on the sand, striped slopes of rushes, bobbing clumps of bog cotton, hands of "bloody fingers" under the trees, a birch in a golden

blaze of back light, Luinne Bheinn lifting all too high, and Choire
Odhair deep set, the roughest corrie in all the rough bounds. . . .

Knoydart seems a remarkable place for its beetles. Yesterday and
today gave a bigger variety than I've ever seen before. A cast from some
bird of prey was made entirely of beetles' cases. There were a lot of
frogs too. And there are the ticks. Before dressing I'd removed several
more of these unwelcome creatures.

Mam Barrisdale is 1,450 feet and I reached it feeling puggled.
However, with a breeze of sorts, the next miles were merely hard work,
not an intolerable sweat bath. On this sort of trip you "mun dree yir
weird" as it comes.

Luinne Bheinn to Braehead kids inevitably ended as "loony-bin".
Perceptive lads. To be fair, they had once suffered a Knoydart heat-
wave too. We toiled up from the Dubh Lochain and then from the
pass set off for Ladhar Bheinn—which explains my route of yesterday:
there is more to Ladhar Bheinn that the O.S. cares to admit. We
reached the top in a state of collapse and, as I wrote in an account of
the trip for a certain well-known magazine, "there we drank our bars
of chocolate". It was stolidly altered to "ate our bars of chocolate".
(The same editorial pencil once substituted "bottom slide" for "bum
slide"—which took years to live down!) That Braehead trip had been
our finest ever, for it was part of the "Killin-to-Skye Trek". We dropped
down to Loch Hourn from this pass and had to go miles up the loch
before we found water to drink: every stream had dried up.

I brewed on top of Mam Barrisdale. The dominating peak beyond
was Sgurr na Sgine, next to and more dramatic than the Saddle.
Strange, for it also plays this trick when viewed down Glen Shiel.

It was possible to skirt the first bump before the real hog's back oι
ridge. There were rocky bits enough for scrambling but I was too laden
and too hot to be very enthusiastic. Two eagles in succession passed
just twenty yards off, soaring along like birds of fire in the dazzle of sun.
On another visit I very nearly landed on top of one when careering
down the ridge.

I forgot to leave an intended questionnaire note on the summit and
was far too happy on the east top to go back. An oozing "jelly piece"
seemed much more important. My good intentions of adding Sgurr a'
Choire-bheithe had melted in the sun. A swim in Lochan nam Breac
sounded better. A big herd of deer going through the Bealach Unndalain
thundered by fifty yards below me.

A path wiggled down and by cunning use of rakes and ledges led to Lochan nam Breac. Here I had a sandy bay to swim in, to soap and clean self and clothes, to brew while things dried again. Noon was wrapped over with blue and tied with sunshine. Luinne Bheinn was framed between the rocky bulks of Ben Aden and Druim a' Chosaidh, looking unreal and remote already. Such afternoons are made for minimal effort, and that aquatic.

Lochan nam Breac is a collectors' piece: dramatically wild and lonely. My route had carefully been planned to include it. Eastwards, through a gap, the sight of the spike of Sgurr Mor, reminded that there was another day to come, and eventually I pushed on rather than camp there by the loch. Tomorrow might be worse, even hotter.

There are two streams flowing into the loch at the east end which start as one burn. Only in two other places do I know of burns which split and flow off on independent courses; but this is the weirdest, for the Allt Coire na Cruaiche here splits like a T-junction, one arm flowing quickly into the loch and the other setting off in the opposite direction, taking four times the distance to join the same loch.

The remoteness of this spot is emphasised because Loch Quoich (pronounced: Koo-ich), when dammed, flooded all the old approaches from the east. The water level is higher than the watershed, so there are small dams at this end above Lochan nam Breac. This had left the spot untouched but drowned a whole group of shooting lodge and tenant housing further east. You can try and guess the site from the paths that once converged on it, and now plunge into the loch.

Royalty once stalked here, and at drowned Glenquoich Lodge under Gleouraich but that glory has departed. So have trees; the road to Kinloch Hourn passes dead remnants and midge-loved splatters of rhododendron (which signify dead mansion houses as surely as nettles point to ruined cottages and rowans to vanished shielings). It is nice to meet the herd of Highland cattle by the loch, and there are sheep and stags which hopefully eye every car in winter for a hand-out. I practically had to push one out of the way to hide a cache back in February. Speculatively I eyed across the silver water. Food lay over yonder. Double caches and folk coming up tomorrow.

The Great Glen with its massive forests of pine seemed years distant —yet still lay just a day's walk away. Scotland's glory is this eternal contrast. The varied climate, underlying rock, geographic site and so on give an endless fashion parade of form, colour and vegetation. If

tonight I was to lie in poor shoddy, tatty with bogs, then in two days'
time I would as likely be camping under a monkey-puzzle by a glen of
leafy livery.

Loch Quoich was very low and several islands had popped up. It took
a hectic bog-hopping diversion to cross the mouth of Coire nan Gall,
that slabby bay where I met Prince Charlie's route again; perhaps the
most incredible part of his 22 weeks of wandering—longer than this
trek of mine and with man as well as mountain set against him. The
kilted charmer of the romantic tale came out of Coire nan Gall as a
wretched fugitive: thin and hungry, in tatters, and weather-worn and
probably as demoralised by midges as any man ever.

He and his company had come down here in the dark, what is more,
to a "fast place" at the head of Loch Quoich. That evening they climbed
Meall an Spardain to watch the troops below in Gleann Cosaidh. They
skulked across and up the Leac na Fearna ridge on the other side—
still within the cordon. Descending Coire Beithe in the dark they at last
made it through the enemy line somewhere near Loch Coire Shubh
and escaped up Coire Sgoir-adail after a day spent hidden right above
Loch Hourn where they could see the Redcoats all day. Another night's
work took them over the Bealach Dubh Leac to Glen Shiel and eased
the pressure.

Later I would use that bealach to gain the Cluanie Ridge from Glen
Shiel, and two nights hence I was to camp by Loch Coire Shubh.

One of the outcomes of the 1745 was the mapping of the Highlands.
Neither Prince Charlie nor the Redcoats had maps, which is hard to
envisage today with our superabundance; hence the Prince's constant
search for and use of "guides". In 1747 an infantry detachment arrived
at Fort Augustus and spent the next eight years surveying. Roy's map
was the result, one with which he himself was not altogether satisfied.
He had not had the best of instruments and was limited to too tight a
budget. It sounds familiar today. He was a youthful twenty-one when
this work began, and it was a year after he died, in 1790, that the
Ordnance Survey was founded. They of course began at the other end
of Britain: the first O.S. one-inch map was of Kent, in 1801. Now they
are in the throes of metrication and a huge re-surveying programme
with air photography, helicopters and other modern aids. British maps
have always been, basically, among the best and are likely to remain
so: which is why we love to find them erring!

Shaking loose of the bogs, I slowly contoured up and round to enter the next glen below Sgurr Mor. A grassy knoll on top of a boulder above the burn was an idyllic camp site, only spoilt, briefly, now and then, by jet planes diving through all sorts of unlikely passes and taking one by surprise.

The meal was made on the sooty horror of firelighters again—a simple meat, veg. and macaroni—a culinary task not particularly enjoyed. There would just be enough left to make a brew in the morning. The first peak was right above—deceptively close until a line of deer crossed its upper slopes and gave the true scale.

There was time to splash in a small pool under a fall—and to read, snug inside the sleeping bag. Oddly, lying in the tent I was actually missing the sweep of Grampian scenery—perhaps because I read Karen Blixen the other day, and now *A Story Like the Wind*, by Laurens van der Post with its evocative picture of the spacious African scene. That was where I first consciously realised that mountains and landscape played a vital part in my dreams and reality. I'd have been about seven at the time, a refugee from the Japanese sweep through Malaya and the battering of Singapore, so even then was aware of the dichotomy of man's evil doings and the marvels of the wild, open hills. *Jock of the Bushveldt* and the tales of the Great Trek were heady stuff, though it was then too that Gino Watkins and Shackleton were placed on their respective polar pedestals. All of which remains.

The Africa in my blood is very disturbing. (Am I not blood-brother to a Zulu chief with the scar on my wrist to this day?) It desires the veldt sweep of ochreous miles: the Grampians. Here I missed it, yet in the Grampians the other voice called. The blood of the Celt is strong, too, and where wild crests fall into the lochs of the west and the sun sets like blood in the sea, there I would most long to be. It works too on the larger scale: in Scotland I plot and ploy for the next trip abroad— but no sooner away than all the dreams are of home hills again.

The murmur of the stream and the occasional grunt of a hind, the flaring gold of a sunset, the glow of a body hot with sun: the day had been well filled with the small things of immeasurable joy. Like the Psalmist I was inclined to "live while the sun endures".

X

QUOICH—GLENELG

"If you have dwelt in the secret heart of the mountains, beholding
the full glory of their revelation, as they unfold their signs and
wonders from the going down of the sun to its uprising, nothing can
efface the memory of such nights."

—JULIUS KUGY *Alpine Pilgrimage*

Friday 14 June SOUTH SIDE

The first morning sound was the blatter of rain—a surprise after such
sunshine. One assumes the good days will go on for ever.

I followed the burn. The path shown up Sgurr Beag continues right
along to Sgurr an Fhuarain, though it has deteriorated. On the east
ridge of Sgurr Beag it actually breaks into a stone staircase, a relic
deserving preservation by the N.T.S. as an example of a feudal sub-craft
of the stalking hey-day.

Sgurr Mor is a great hulk of mountain and one not easily reached
from a road-end for the normal Munro-bagger. It seemed a good place
to leave a questionnaire. Ron Hardie (from Crail) and two others of the
Fife Mountaineering Club picked it up two weeks later. Ron was at
269, and not long after he succeeded in finishing his Munros. There was
something rather eerie about leaving a note in such a place and it being
found, as happened several times, by someone I knew.

Leaving the summit of Sgurr Mor the cloud rolled in, and all day it
rose and fell just above walking level. A dozen sheep, wild and un-
tended, went down the ridge before me. It was for these brutes the
humans were cleared from the glens—and now they in turn are a
financial liability, often neglected and running wild, unless, as in
Knoydart, simply cleared in their turn.

Down below I could see the bothy at Kinbreack, a restored stable.
Fifty yards along from it the "lodge" slowly rots and falls—a roof gone
here, floors gone there, the whole a mass of sheep droppings, even up the
crumbling stairs and in the rooms where once the wealthy patrons slept
in the stalking season.

Glen Kingie, which moats all this day's mountains to the south, is a desolate spot. From the bothy door down there, these hills form a wall as far as eye can see, east and west, yet there is no feeling of being shut in. It is a wide strath of ochreous grass and wild sheep. You can sit by the bothy door with the tang of wood fire in your nostrils, blue smoke clinging to the ground, snipe drumming in the sky and waders calling mysteriously from the river verge, enjoying the held-breath of a summer's night, utterly at peace.

But first you would have to reach it. No road goes to the door and the easiest path is a rather imaginative O.S. gesture. If the river is in spate the Kingie can be an impossible barrier and Loch Arkaig is a long way from anywhere. Man seems to have given up the glen. Perhaps here, as in few other places, you will find solitude. Months may pass without an entry in the visitors' book.

Kinbreack bothy, like many, has been done up by the Mountain Bothies Association: a small corps of hardened individualists who love the wild and lonely places. They don't go in for much publicity— solitude is one of the benisons of bothy life—but quietly, with land-owners' permission, the M.B.A. has saved many an old building, sometimes with incredible physical labour.

Bothies give a roomy shelter, instead of the confinement of a tent— and without a tent you can carry its weight in food, giving more days in the wilds without having to re-stock.

Sgurr an Fhuarain (2,957 feet) is a Corbett, its ascent a long grassy slope. The great crag markings on its east face are exaggerated—there is nothing different there from scores of nearby hills which get no markings at all, Sgurr Mor for instance. I left the east ridge by a path and then cut across to another which zig-zagged on to the steep end of Gairich, which, after that, was a gentle walk among endless deer and bleeping plovers. Gairich means the *mountain of yelling* which no doubt I did one December morning with Eck Rollo and Ian Moreland, when it gave the last Munro of the second time round.

Gairich has fine corries and a big south gully, but they are all too seldom in winter condition. The east ridge has one narrow bit. Over the moors I took a path down to new plantings and then joined the old right-of-way from Lochan to near the Quoich dam. The path eventually goes into the loch, the Hydro being no respecter of paths.

I searched about for sites by the dam and then pitched on a breezy knoll above it, quite invisible from the road yet covering it in best Commando fashion. The cache I'd hidden up a burn told its tale from afar: a confetti of plastic and paper betrayed its ravished state. The tins were safe enough, though breakfast misfired due to the labels having come off: spinach and Nestlé's cream made an odd combination!

I was very glad to see Gaz cylinders, and was soon tucking into stew and carrots, strawberries and rice—all tins of course. Before supper I walked up the road and made the dreamy occupant of a Dormobile jump when I asked the correct time. A morning rendezvous depended on it, and for days I had been on guesswork.

Clouds poured over Gairich all evening—a strange effect which no other hill was sharing. I sat in the evening sun and read. It was not perfection though: my buttocks were covered in red ant bites. Somewhere, I hoped, Bob Binnie was on the road. I finished the log and turned in. The next entry would have to wait until Monday. Life for the next few days would be busy.

Saturday 15 June THE QUOICH HILLS

I slept the sleep of the happy ones. There was breeze enough on rising to keep the midges away and by nine I was at the dam to meet Lorna and Bob: an appointment which once seemed so unlikely to be kept.

The next two hours were hectic. I used the car wing mirror to slice off some of the facial jungle. We also took some black and white pictures of the tent and doing various things—like digging up the cache by the Alltbeithe bridge and dealing with mail at the car. I hate publicity yet, perforce, need it.

There are times when one is happily cut down to size. Some of my girls once gleefully reported a conversation they'd overheard in an Aviemore supermarket where two men had ultimately decided it could not possibly be me after all as "surely he could afford decent breeches."

"We'll buy you a needle and thread, sur, for a treat," they offered. Another time, rock-climbing at Aberdour someone came up and said I must be Hamish. After I admitted it, he added, "I thought so. I recognised the dog."

After sorting out food, films and maps and replacing odd garments and making a parcel for Dollar, we returned to the dam to pick up the Long Walk. I set off towards Loch Fearna, while Lorna and Bob drove several miles west, first, as they had to circle back to the car. We met at the loch where I was busy answering letters.

There were loons laughing away on Loch Quoich, and I wondered if one of them had watched me bury the parcel down by the bridge. It had been found by mice but only the chocolate had gone. It seems as irresistible to mice as to children. I was worried, however, about the cache in Glen Strathfarrar. That one would be vital. Obviously I'd have to assume chocolate and all non-tinned items had been destroyed and carry replacements.

Cloud came and went but it remained dry which is enough to ask of Quoich. Bob went bouncing off while Lorna and I followed at a rational speed. We lunched late on top of Spidean Mialach, the *pinnacle of wild animals*. A note left here, decorated with rhododendron blossom, has not come back.

We wandered down to the col as cloud rolled in and were glad to find a zig-zag of path up beyond. We also found a coupit sheep and gladly left ex-farmer Bob the smelly job of righting it. We also enjoyed Bob's disbelief on the south-east top for he had assumed it was the summit— which now appeared half a mile off—magnified by mist to twice the distance and height. Gleouraich has *uproar* as its translation.

We separated here: Lorna going down to Loch Quoich by the south-west ridge and we two, bent on the third Munro, off for Alltbeithe to the north-west. Lorna's way off was down another quite remarkable made path: perhaps my favourite among them all. On it, "King Edward's Butt", tells of departed glories.

We had a path down too—once we found it. We had a bite before crossing the river to Alltbeithe and then cut over to the River Quoich direct, rightly judging it to be low enough not to cause trouble.

We took the path up Coir a' Chaoruinn, but it is certainly not kept up, and the good one zig-zagging up to the Am Bathaich ridge is much better. Having done the circling ridges, though, I wanted a new way. A great rockfall had strewn boulders down the slope and even across the burn. We wended up the steep slopes beside them, enjoying the rough craggy scenery, to arrive almost at the cairn of Sgurr a' Mhaoraich, *peak of the shell fish*. We also ran up into cloud again, so the dramatic view down Loch Hourn was missed. Munro regarded it as the most beautiful of all highland lochs, but I find it too shut in. Dramatic, remote, wild are perhaps better words than beautiful.

As we were not going to receive view or sustenance on top we angled off with the compass. Romping through the mist we set off more deer. One went for a mighty *skite* and left a long scar where it had slipped. Deer often seem infallible but under many a crag you will find the remains of a past accident. Eagles have been known to start them over cliffs.

We crossed the Allt Ban high up, and from the lip beyond could see down to the road and the lochs. Lorna's bright orange tent stood out vividly, mine was invisible. It was a steep drop down but seemed to go fast and at 8.45 we were in—a good romp behind—and a midgey purgatory ahead.

We piled in for tea, protected by a smoking Moon Tiger and lay gossiping for ages before facing the beasts again. My tent was free of them, but at the price of having a sweat bath as soon as I lit the stove. Through the thin fabric it was possible to see the seething millions crawling over everything.

Unhelpful bumps and the heat made it a weary night. Midges can bite through a sheet liner, I found. Later I crawled into the bag when it cooled. There was a drumming of rain.

Sunday 16 June HEAVENLY HELL

Climbers are long-suffering beings, but they have their rewards now and then. There are individual days which are all joy. They often come unexpectedly and unplanned, and for them we will endure much, for, when we have them, we are kings awhile.

They are usually inexplicable, for wonder is secretive and personal. We may mumble over a pint in a pub, "Aye, a great day", leaving it both said and not said. Thank goodness something defies analysis. Wonder? Beauty? Revelation? Poor atheist with no God to praise!

The neb of the morning passed me by and it was a quarter to eight before I set off. I woke the others and left some food. It was a drumlie sort of day with little promise beyond much walking.

Loch Coire Shubh lay like a grey puddle among the dark hills. Knoydart country this: bulging bellies of rock showing through the rotting skin of grass. Oddly, on each side of the loch stood a monkey-puzzle tree.

I contoured round on the path while the road and river both fell madly down to the flats of Kinloch Hourn: a strange touch of green farmland at the head of the loch.

Here in the past a population lived by farming, fishing, timber, smelting, boat-building and even a little mining near Glenelg for silver, lead and copper. In the eighteenth century herring fishing was flourishing: boats crowded in the inner loch here so you could cross their decks from shore to shore. 30,000 barrels a year were produced, then the herring vanished, deserting old, established routes and impoverishing much of the western seaboard. Arnisdale decayed, and now most of its string of cottages belong to the white settlers—absentee holiday-homers. In 1836 the population was 600. It is a grim tale, the misery completed with potato blights, typhoid and vicious Clearances—as in Knoydart.

On that Braehead "Killin-to-Skye" trip we came through Knoydart to round Loch Hourn and go on to Glenelg by part of today's route. Camping at Loch Hourn we woke in the morning to find the farmer had unexpectedly left eggs and milk at the tents. We did many treks, and the tougher the kids had it the more they seemed to enjoy it. There was no "simulated" adventure; if you broke a leg in Knoydart you were in for a rough ride. They knew it—and did not break legs in Knoydart. Youngsters are fitter, better co-ordinated, and safer than adults realise.

Adults set out brainwashing their own children from the earliest age *not* to be adventurous. "Don't do that, darling, you may fall and hurt yourself!" Children naturally climb trees, the tragedy is that adults do not. Much of the adult world considers all mountain activity a form of adolescent irresponsibility—to be curbed and controlled if not banned.

Kinloch Hourn today lay silent and grey. I leapt the Allt Coire Sgoir-adail quite easily. It is real river, quietly draining the vast soggy cirque—up which Charles Edward Stewart floundered heading for Glen Shiel—and then plunging down to Kinloch Hourn in a series of rough slides and falls. A path led through a gap to the woods of the estate house. It dipped, then rose again, to twist up behind another bump and then split, with branches taking separate bealachs to Gleann Beag and Glen More, great walking routes both.

By the time I'd reached the river which drains the Saddle to the south, the sun broke through. I brewed, finished off my book and dried the tent. It would have been an idyllic site to stay but my route continued on up a side stream to the Bealach Aoidhdailean (1,550 feet) with only a tracing of path. The view back gave a series of V-gaps, all in line, one inside each other, right to the start seven miles away.

A few miles down the other side led to Gleann Beag, but first there was Beinn Sgritheall (Sgriol) and between it and me lay two Corbetts with their distinctive drops all round.

I believed these could be skirted. North of the first was the Druim nam Bo, the *ridge of the cows*, which surely implied grass, for cows don't climb rough stuff, and the flank of the second was only half a mile wide, and though steep, memory recalled clear deer/sheep tracks across it.

So it worked out. I was soon on the col below Sgriol. The slopes seemed to be full of deer calves: some cowered and some fled bleating for their maws. Sgriol was a peak we always associated with school trips to Sandaig (Gavin Maxwell's Camusfearna, where his ashes are scattered on the grass of broken dreams) and though a long approach from that western side, it was our usual one. But the least-penal route from Arnisdale is to come up to the Bealach and along the crest, as I did today. It is a bit rough up on to the east top but after that there is a green ridge of pure delight.

Loch Hourn widened into the Sound of Sleat below, the isles of Rhum and Eigg were surfacing from a haze into the sun and in every direction one saw an extravagance of mountain scenery. Beinn Sgritheall is king of the little hills and not only my opinion. "The view remains in my mind as perhaps the most beautiful I have seen in Scotland . . . every stroke of the oars of a boat on Loch Hourn could be plainly heard, and the note of a dozen cuckoos shouting in all directions." That is Sir Hugh again.

I found a pure white thrift on the way up, a new mountain flower to me in its colourless form. Milkwort, lousewort, more campion, these are not uncommon in white form—caused by chemical deficiencies in the soil I'm told.

An English lad was already on the summit. He seemed to know his view. And what a view! Every aspect pleased:

Rhum, Mull, Jura, all the "country" of Knoydart, Moidart, Ardgour, Creag Meaghaidh, the Grey Corries, Nevis, Bidean, the hills of yesterday, the Glen Shiel ridges, Affric, the Lapaichs, Sheasgaich, Fuar Tholl, Torridons, Slioch and beyond, Applecross, the Cuillin of Skye and the Outer Isles. If I named off a hundred peaks on Beinn Dorain, I think I beat that here. I would not have swopped it for any mountain view in the world. It was also a formidable array. Had I done well till now, the view of summits northwards, all still to be climbed, was enough to sober anyone.

The English lad set off down to his car on the Loch Hourn road and I suddenly felt smug and superior again: my day progressed in a great sweeping tramp westwards, his had been a circle from and back to a car, as had been Lorna's yesterday.

I remembered to leave a questionnaire at the cairn; it was found four days later by John Hartley from Birmingham who also wrote a long letter. He was aware of the Munro disease, and wrote: "I look on the Munros as a lifetime's ambition, but not one to achieve as soon as possible, at the cost of pleasant days, which is what we go for. I like to think there is enough in Scotland to last me a lifetime. . . . Nobody visited Sgriol on the summer days between our visits: south of the border I have counted over 150 on the summit of Helvellyn during a Friday in April.

"It's fascinating to write and know the recipient only as a name. You, sir, might be a schoolboy having just tasted your first Munro, or you might be at the height of your career. I met Lord Hailsham on top of Macdhui in 1972."

I was loath to leave the summit, but with ten miles still to go, the day's darg was hardly done. A small vee of wake followed a buzzing boat up the loch. Loch Hourn and Loch Nevis have been, rather imaginatively, translated as the *Loch of Hell* and the *Loch of Heaven*. Physically and meteorologically that is usually apt.

Just how indented the west coast is, can be seen in the fact that between Ardnamurchan and Loch Carron it twists for 350 miles while the comparable distance up the Great Glen's fault line is 80 miles.

It was only later that I heard of another mountain event on this day. It was the 150th Anniversary of the Edinburgh Academy, and the school climbed 150 Munros as part of the celebrations. Sgriol, being a solitary, distant Munro, was not done, but parties were busy on the Glen Shiel switchbacks, and Colin Turner and party were opposite on the Cuillin.

Rather than simply retrace along over the east Top again, I cut down into Coire Min where a clear lochan was surrounded by paint-spotted sheep. The stream from it, the Allt Mhic a' Phearsain, becomes the Allt Srath a' Chomair before ending as the Amhain a' Ghlinne Bhig. Sgriol rose in a mixture of shadow and silver, bold prows out of dark shadow and flanks glittering with sun.

I cut the dog-leg only to find myself on crags above Gleann Beag, but even that was fun, teasing a way down by half-secret animal tracks and paddling joyfully over the river. A brew was very welcome. I covered six miles down Gleann Beag to Glenelg in an hour and ten minutes which was a fairly pleasing end to a twelve-hour day. It was a glen I knew well, milestoned by old *duns* and Pictish *brochs*, shaded by hazel

H

scrub and bright with yellow seggs. I walked with past company down to Eilanreach (lovely name), and along to Glenelg—which the kids would always ask you to spell backwards. I walked into the doup of the day with heart glowing as well as face. On days like this it was good to be Scot free.

Glenelg was as quiet as ever—watched over by the bronze angels of its ornate war memorial. The church is hidden among the trees (the first one here was founded by a hunch-back monk from Beauly) and the main street has a grassy, timeless untidy air. At the far end lived Dr Catherine MacInnes. A note for me was pinned on the door, but she was in and we were soon chatting away over coffee. The offer of a bath and a bed was not refused, the rain and midges having joined forces again as dusk fell.

I opened stacks of tins and shoved away plenty calories. Catherine leads the local rescue team (consisting mainly of forestry lads) and Ladhar Bheinn was one of their stamping grounds. I was delighted to hear that they had several experiences of navigation going astray on the magnetic northern flanks of that peak. The doctor obviously enjoyed a good crack with someone who was not a local patient!

She told a story of Jack Thomson at Glenmore Lodge out with a gang from Glasgow on the hill. One girl, rollers in her hair and all, girned about being tired, to which Jack replied: "Och well, lassie, I'll just stand you on your head and wheel you along."

It was after midnight when I collapsed into bed—stockings and vest washed, self bathed and the room strewn with gear and the contents of food parcels.

The rough wooing of Knoydart was behind. Skye lay across the water. I could even see it, though whether glad or not I don't know. They say here, "if you can see Skye it is going to rain. If you cannot see Skye, it is raining already."

XI

SKYE

"All the winds that blow on that far and happy isle may bring rain,
and most make a habit of it."

JOHN BUCHAN

First Skyeman, at bar, in October: "Aye, Donald, it's been raining
since June."
Second Skyeman, after deep thought: "Just so. Just so. *Which*
June?"

Monday 17 June DELUGE DAY

There was regret at leaving comforts but Skye was a lure as few sections
could be. I went over to the shop, packed, pieced the bike together
(Mike had dropped it off) then had coffee with Catherine; a procrastinating start. Behind lay 188 Munros—1,059 miles and 297,500 feet.

I walked past the Bernera Barracks which are identical in layout to
the Ruthven Barracks at Kincraig. *That* felt decades ago! A garrison
was kept here for fully thirty years after the Forty-Five.

The Kyle Rhea ferry plies this swift passage. On both sides are
identical old buildings which were once Inns. The redoubtable Dr
Johnson stayed there in 1773. In the cattle-driving days Skye beasts
were forced to swim the channel. Daniel Defoe wrote of this trade in
1726 while on his "tour". My interest crossing today was a school of
porpoise. The ferry swept across quickly but the rain caught it halfway.

I sheltered a while but it was obviously no passing shower so I walked
on, pushing up the brae. The Bealach Udal rises to 870 feet, in a
couple of miles, a brutal slog at any time. Now I know why it is called
a *push* bike. I sweated and battled in the deluge until ready to despair, a
yelling misery. Glen Arroch beyond had me pedalling *down* it.

I passed one of Scotland's scenic refuse dumps—there are quite a few
carefully laid out so that every tourist can get a view and a sniff. About
200 gulls were arrayed round this one. By Breakish I was peckish and
by Broadford I'd had quite enough. It had rained without stop all the
way and the gale had been entirely contrary. I was a day in hand,
anyway, if I needed to justify stopping.

An efficient young girl signed me in to the Hilton (guest house) for bed and breakfast. I went along to the Hotel for afternoon tea—and stayed for dinner. It gave me a chance to catch up on the log book, back to Loch Quoich days. A couple came in who had motored all the way from Killin in the deluge.

Skye weather is apt to be unreliable. It suffers from a sort of emotional instability: one day all sunshine and sweetness, warmth and kindness —the next throwing a tantrum and viciously attacking anyone daft enough to go near.

I recall just one episode from Braehead days. The wind had blown a booming, dry gale for half the night and then produced a Nilotic flood. At four we were conceding victory to the elements. The girls were perched on top of saturated sleeping-bags calmly frying eggs with the water lapping half-way up the primus tank. "All mod. cons. Running water in every tent," somebody yelled as they shoved a brew in my hand. The trouble was it was not running. Sewn-in groundsheets were merely creating paddling pools. We took our essentials and fled. Sligachan Hotel gave us a garage to live in, while we fetched the bus (which limped along on a borrowed motorbike spark plug) and we then retreated first to the bakery in Portree, and then to Broadford Youth Hostel. At Portree, however, I was called to the Police Station and told my father had died suddenly—and began a bitter journey home by bus, train and hitching. My brother from Hong Kong reached home before me!

My log was not encouraging; the incessant rain and Broadford's complete lack of facilities for the visitor rather depressed. Everyone was expecting me to finish and so few knew anything of the pressures. Who, these soft days, puts up with rain and roughing it for weeks and months? Water can wear away stone. I wrote: "Keep it cool; sit it out and battle on. It is such a battle, not physical, but is sheer mental effort." I had no option but to be flexible. The tree that cannot bend before the storm just breaks. I expected that there would be ups and downs. It is just another—acceptable—face of adventure. My remedy was at hand: a good dinner.

The meal was one of the best of the trip. I recall it all clearly: Iced melon cubes; Fillet of haddock, Mornay; Roast leg of pork and apple sauce, boiled and croquette potatoes, green beans, cauliflower, cress, gravy; Sherry-trifle and cream; Coffee—and *Faisca* to drink.

Broadford Hotel will long be remembered for its hospitality that wet

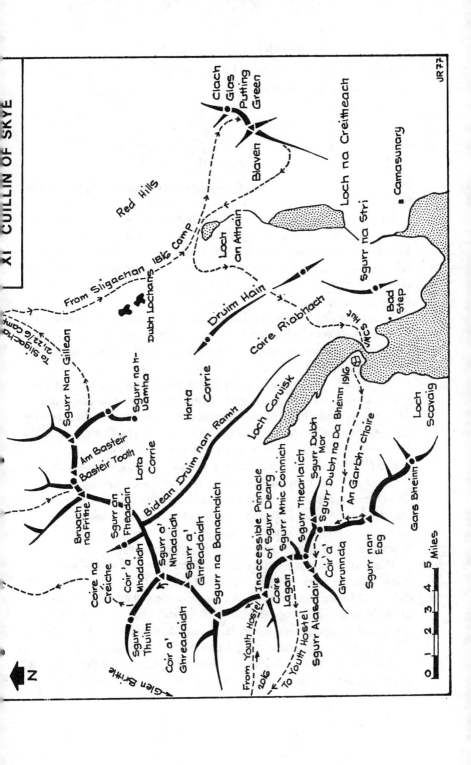

XI CUILLIN OF SKYE

N

Glen Brittle

Sgurr Thuilm
Coire na Creiche
Coir' a' Ghreadaidh
Coir' a' Mhadaidh
Sgurr a' Mhadaidh
Sgurr a' Ghreadaidh
Sgurr na Banachdich
Bruach na Frithe
Sgurr an Fheadain
Bidean Druim nan Ramh
Am Basteir
Basteir Tooth
Sgurr Nan Gillean
Sgurr na h-Uamha
Lota Corrie
Harta Corrie

Inaccessible Pinnacle of Sgurr Dearg
From Youth Hostel
2016
To Youth Hostel
Coire Lagan
Sgurr Mhic Coinnich
Sgurr Alasdair
Coir' a' Ghrunnda
Sgurr Thearlaich
Sgurr Dubh Mor
Sgurr Dubh na Da Bheinn 1916
An Garbh-choire
Sgurr nan Eag
Gars Bheinn
Loch Scavaig
Loch Coruisk

To Sligachan 21, 22½, 6 Camp
From Sligachan 18½ Camp
Red Hills
Dubh Lochans
Loch an Athain
Druim Hain
Coire Riabhach
JMCS Hut
Bad Step
Sgurr na Stri
Loch na Stri
Clach Glas
Putting Green
Blaven
Loch na Creitheach
Camasunary

0 1 2 3 4 5 Miles

JR 77

night, then back to the rather stilted atmosphere of the guest house. It was a wild night of storm.

Tuesday 18 June SLIGACHAN

> Like a pale King of Tarshish bringing his gift
> The sun came slowly to the courts of Day.

It had rained itself dry. The day eventually became bright, breezy and midge free.

The coastal road wends in and out of several lochs and over many braes but was not bad going. At Luib someone had painted "Vote Labour" on the rocks—with *blue* paint. Scalpay and Raasay in turn lay off-shore, the latter island unmistakable from any angle with the sliced-off top of Dun Caan, its highest point. Boswell danced a reel on its flat, grassy summit.

At last I came round under Glamaig—and there were the Cuillin: the warrior peaks standing quietly waiting, ready to ambush one with new experiences. They are a great sight. Nestling below them is Sligachan, itself a great sight.

The historic whitewashed hotel beside the old pack bridge, the few trees and rainbow dashes of water; these give a perfect foreground to the Red and Black Hills. Generations of climbers have been based on the hotel or camped across the road. The hotel had the Coruisk Hut key and other bits of mail. I was reading it when Peter found me.

Peter Miller was sixteen and one of Ann Winning's keen lads from Breadalbane Academy in Aberfeldy. We had fixed this meeting at the Lawers camp site. He brought more mail, via Ann, and by the time we had pitched tents up from the bridge, played a few games of darts and gone round finding lost tent pegs (you can aye tell a Fifer) it was happily too late to do anything except eat and sleep.

There are times when the old Sligachan pack bridge fills to its cap-stone with the rush of water. (When it does that you use your return tickets.) I hoped we were not in for a drubbing. The Ripleys had had quite an epic while doing the Ridge in the day: bad visibility, rain and greasy rock, trouble on Ghreadaidh and Mhadaidh and coming off Gillean on the wrong side to add a three-mile walk out.

Had I been alone it might have been tempting to do the ridge, but Peter was new to Skye—and I was playing a tortoise game.

Wednesday 19 June BLAVEN AND CORUISK

> Much at ease with space all round,
> Peace in heaven, in flesh, in ground.

The overnight promise was not fulfilled and we set out only at 8.30. The hills were cloudy but we had to gamble on the weather. I 'phoned the police to explain empty tents, a precaution against trigger-happy mountain rescuers.

Glen Sligachan never palls. Peter almost went off up the wrong side of Marsco as everyone seems to do first time. Redshanks were calling and golden plovers. Bog asphodel, the flower of August, was in bloom already. We passed "Eric's Pool", so I told Peter of a heat-wave carry-in when we'd stopped for a dip. Eric alone did not go in. He came running up to push someone else in, but was heard and dodged just in time. Like a caricature in an old movie he went rushing on, back pedalling in mid air, and plopped into the pool—fully clothed!

Loch an Athain was where we had always camped. The expected summer-piper (sandpiper) was flitting round the edge of the loch. We hid most of our gear in the heather, and "burned-up" towards Blaven. The rain came on. The deep heather soon saturated our legs. Heather is *not* common in the west (outside the fanciful song-writers). The air was revoltingly hot and stuffy.

On the col between Blaven and Clach Glas is a small area of mossy green known as the "Putting Green". On a previous trip one of our lads, David McNab, had reached it first and excitedly yelled down to me to hurry. Expecting an accident or something urgent I gasped up the screes to join him. With a proprietary sweep of the hand Nabby said, "Is it not great?" So much for those who would declare the kids have no aesthetic reasoning. We looked down to Loch Slapin where the white Torrin marble under the shallow waters had made a brilliant turquoise pattern. No view today, though it was still an impressive perch.

The traverse of Blaven–Clach Glas is one of the finest bits of Cuillin traversing: pure Alpine rock-climbing. Beyond Clach Glas and some minor tops the "Black" Cuillin suddenly abut on to the crumbly pink granite of the "Red Cuillin". One takes liberties on gabbro that would be undreamt of elsewhere.

Blaven is the odd Munro off the main ridge, a portentous postscript to the gabbro galaxy. (It is occasionally tacked on to the traverse of the main ridge and called "The Greater Traverse" but it is in no way a true continuation and seems a pointless and artificial addition.) Walkers are best to keep to the long ridge from Camusunary or the Loch Slapin side.

The route on from the Putting Green is complex, wriggling in and out of avoidable problems and climbing one or two steps. The first small one of these gave me the jitters after so long off rock—greasy trap is demoralising at the best of times, so Peter tiptoed up further right and I crawled after. We had a lead each up the next step and were soon on the path to the trig point. Blaven is the best place to see the whole range of the main Black Cuillin. Sgurr na Stri above Loch Scavaig is also an exceptional viewpoint.

Blaven is a Norse-Gaelic name: Bla Bheinn, the *blue mountain*. It was first ascended by the poet Swinburne and Professor Nicol of Glasgow in 1857—perhaps the third Cuillin peak to be climbed. Rather than descend the way we had come, we went along over the south summit and down the ridge a fair way before taking pot-luck on the notorious west flank. This is complex and riven, full of scree gullies, and areas of slab, pinnacles and undercut edges, just the place to throw Peter in at the deep end: a bit different from nice, clean, safe, roped climbing at Craig-y-Barns! I wondered if Peter knew Mary Stewart's story *Wildfire at Midnight* for its thrilling climax is set on Blaven on the very place we had come down.

We must, briefly, recall the "Coruisk Affair", perhaps as a warning, for the whole character of a place can be so easily altered when, as here, the army built bridges and roads and threatened to blow up the "Bad Step" with dynamite. It was all dreamed up in the name of safety and facilitating rescue operations when seas were too rough for boats, but at no time was the Mountain Rescue Committee of Scotland consulted. The scheme only came to light when the Army made a request to use the hut.

Tom Weir made the percipient comment at the time that the hut itself was an intrusion which altered the quality of remoteness. The planners went ahead despite vigorous protests from all who knew the area: two suspension bridges were slung across, at Camusunary and Scavaig, and a perfectly adequate path from Straithaird was turned into a horrible Land-Rover track. After the opening ceremony the

V.I.P. party preferred to *walk* the track. A trooper watching one vehicle, was heard to comment, "Any injured climber in that would be dead by now." An officer defended the road with, "It's only a good weather track."

As far as I know no casualty has been taken out by the track yet, and the Scavaig bridge was swept away the following winter. We noticed a few traces as we crossed by the boulders, reaching the hut at 6.30, a ten-hour day which had taken the total of feet ascended, so far, to 300,000.

After supper I sat up till all hours, for I discovered a copy of Eric Shipton's *Upon That Mountain*, a book which has influenced so many of us. I lay awake a long time thinking of this great explorer, his simplicity and his vision, and I'm sure went on the better for it, refreshed and with resolve hardened.

Thursday 20 June   TOPS TO GLEN BRITTLE
Over breakfast we watched a rapidly-advancing frontal system, and lingered in the cosy hut until 9.45.

We crossed the Mad Burn. It was high but not in spate. It can be an effective barrier to the hut. You can imagine climbers' feelings on seeing the hut only two hundred yards away—and beyond reach. We followed it upwards and then took the gap to the Garbh-Choire, so very aptly, the *rough corrie*.

The sky at dawn had been as frail-looking as tissue paper but had soon dissolved into sodden tatters—now the shreds were thrown in our faces! We lowered ourselves through holes among the boulders and crawled into a completely dry haven. Through a small skylight we could see the rain sweeping past: horizontal and vicious.

The black walls hemming in the corrie would appear, stark and streaming, in brief clearances, then vanish into the grasping clouds. We enjoyed it while in the safety of our howff but feared for the future as we scrambled on up the corrie in extravagant "boulder-hopping"— the boulders were sometimes the size of double-decker buses. Eventually the pale, ultra-rough, rock of "The Castle" towered above us. On one side a fallen block makes a hole through which you scramble to cross the col itself. Easy enough scrambling along the ridge took us up Sgurr Dubh na Da Bheinn, from which the Munro, Sgurr Dubh Mor, lies off to the east with a good gap between. It is usually skipped doing the Main Ridge, unless also taking in all the Munros.

Skye is walking country for the more expert: for those who are prepared to scramble a bit and not be intimidated by exposure and complex route-findings (the compass, remember, is useless on the tops). Skye is Valhalla, Mecca, the Ultimate. . . . As even rock-climbers will admit, Skye wandering can be fun on an off-day.

Sgurr Dubh Mor ("Scooby Doo" to my irrepressible pupils) is not easily reached from Da Bheinn. A left-flanking rake leads off down, but you must scramble up again for the col. Take the right flank from there, and, on the final tower, zig-zag up right, then back, to ascend the prow itself. The ridge up from Coruisk gives 3,000 feet of rock climbing of a slabby sort almost from sea-level to the summit. "Doing the Dubhs" is a classic not to be missed by the Climber.

We popped through the hole back under An Caisteal and traversed it for the long ridge out to Sgurr nan Eag. The few problems can be by-passed on the west. Several bumps have false cairns.

The way up Eag from Coir a' Ghrunda has few difficulties though the beaten-way seems to lead straight into a booby trap slot on which I've seen quite a few victims struggle. Nearly everywhere in Skye you can get round most problems, a lesson Kitchy was to teach us as, time and time again, we would look for the dog to give him a lift up a step, only to find him gone, and then grinning down at us. Even Kitchy had a special delight in Skye scrambling, his only problem being that his pads wore through after a week on rough gabbro.

We returned along crest and flank, skirted An Caisteal again to collect our sacks, and dropped down the bouldery flank to lunch by Loch Coir a' Ghrunda. The scene was of varying shades of rain which stopped for our brewing, and the clouds began to break up. As it cleared we began to add potential peaks to our day's plan. Gulls came swooping in to join us—eerie flights in the mist, piercing calls, and splashes in the steel-smooth surface. Oatcakes and cheese, jam pieces, K.P. nuts, raisins, biscuits, Bournville—we did well enough not to grudge the odd crumb to our birds of fair omen. After all we could see Alasdair with its grey scree skirts and shawl of mohair mistiness.

Sgurr Alasdair is the highest Skye summit, named after Sheriff Alexander Nicholson who made its first ascent in 1873. He was a Skye man, a journalist, barrister, and Gaelic scholar. His first route was the descent of the West Ridge of Gillean (Nicholson's Chimney) when he was thirty-eight.

When doing the Main Ridge a quick diversion is traditionally made to include Alasdair. The gentle walker is faced with the famous "Stone Shoot", which is the longest scree run in Britain and purgatorial in ascent. Alasdair deserves better and a reasonable way can be made from Loch Coir a' Ghrunda to the col linking Alasdair and Sgumain. Alasdair looks downright impossible from the col, barred by a small cliff, a famous *mauvais pas*, strictly for climbers with long reaches and good Policies. The rest must make along right, to the first rather obvious and worn chimney, and climb it. The steep, gravelly looseness above is probably much more dangerous. The top is a fine viewpoint: both of the other hills, and also of the blazing seascape. The feeling of being perched above the sea makes this end of the Cuillin an extra joy. The ridge between Da Bheinn and Alasdair was the last bit to be explored. It includes the Thearlaich–Dubh Gap and is to be avoided by the walker.

We had a clear, soft view from the top of Alasdair. The polluting brightness of waterproofs pin-pointed figures all over the place, all rushing up things now the day was improving. It is difficult to start early in Skye, I don't know why, but in June it hardly gets dark, anyway.

With no wind the midges will chase you to the top of Alasdair. Rock-climbing under those circumstances is apt to drive one to the verge of insanity. Midges are no joke: I have seen fine streaking performed by innocent swimmers who knew not what they did; I have seen pedestrians cross the road to avoid a blotchy, bitten friend (muttering something the while about the infectious diseases hospital); I have seen strong men weep, and children cry.

Sgurr Alasdair was the dog Kitchy's last 3,000-foot summit in the British Isles. He was a Shetland Collie, the colour of autumn birch leaves, and had spent much of his life on the hill. He was very much the mascot of Braehead School and it was apt that his last Munro was achieved on Braehead's penultimate expedition.

Peter and I found Thearlaich a greasy rooftop. Peter did not like the loose rock on the descent to the Gap under the seemingly vertical prow of Sgurr Mhic Choinnich, *Mackenzie's Peak*. Climbers will tackle the prow by King's Chimney but the scrambler need not feel cheated; Collie's Ledge is laid on for him—possibly the most sensational situation the British walker could happily get himself into. Apart from the initial step to gain the ledge even the dog can do it unaided so it is *not* difficult at all.

Collie's Ledge leads back on to the ridge proper but by-passes Mhic Choinnich's summit, so we had to wend along up slabby rooftops to reach it. Peter and I had taken two hours from Alasdair and were surprised to see it was 7.30 p.m. Skye days go like that. We would have to hurry if the youth hostel was going to be our home that night. It lies well up Glen Brittle.

We reached it at 9.30—a weary Peter was having quite an introduction to Skye—having bombed down and out past Loch Coire Lagain hardly pausing to look at the wall of Sron na Ciche—the best of all climbing cliffs in Britain. The Cioch was throwing its elongated shadow across the face and the colourful dots of climbers could still be seen on several routes. One of my unfulfilled dreams is to bivy on the Cioch!

Peter and I cut across the grassy lower slopes by the Eas Mor, the *big waterfall*. The grass off-loaded its share of ticks on to our legs, so we had a body search before turning in. We bought stacks of tins and had a stupefying meal, feeling flushed with the romp down and the heat of a building. It had been a twelve-hour day. How different its ending from the start, beginning in rain and despair, ending in sun and delight.

Friday 21 June   THE CENTRAL, HEATED, COOLIN
John Buchan, writing in *Blackwood's Magazine* (June 1906), describes the magic change. "You awake one morning to a clear rain-washed earth, a pale-blue sky, a thin chilly wind from the north, and an amphitheatre of gaunt black hills. Thereafter for a week or a month the weather is flawless, and you spend days in an enchanted world of essential colours, infinite distances, and an air as pure as leagues of hill and ocean can make it." He knew Skye well of course—and the realisation of its unique character: "the essence of Skye climbing is the extraordinary feeling of space, of endless waters, and illimitable fields of air, and man himself set on a small rock looking out at immensity . . ."

The heat of the renewing sun could be felt in bed. Skye was playing extremes again. We bade farewell to Mrs Taplin, the warden, at 8.30, soon wished we had been off hours earlier. It was a day of "grillade".

Tramping up Coire na Banachdich had us wringing with sweat. We were glad to stop for drinks, and we filled all the available bottles. Even my log seems to have become dehydrated: "whaleback rocks, scree and rubbish lead up Dearg." Sgurr Dearg is the Munro which has brought many dreams to grief, for its summit is not just the expected top of the ridge but a long, stuck-on fin of rock which overtops it a bit. It is still called the Inaccessible Pinnacle—or just the Inn. Pinn.—and for some walkers it is all too aptly named. Sir Hugh Munro himself never managed to scale the Inn. Pinn. and one wonders how many hillmen have followed him in having done all the Munros bar this one and possibly a personally-chosen final one?

We dumped most of our gear on the ridge and skirted down along under the sheer west wall of the flake: it is vertical for over 100 feet from the screes to the top, then steep ground, screes and crag tumble in confusion down to Coire Lagain. The east flank falls precipitously down to the Coruisk side. Just the wafer of rock remains: 60 feet high on the short prow facing the ridge-top of Dearg, bulging out in a slight overhang, and perhaps twice that length up the back ridge—the easy way, with which we were content today.

The odd hold wobbles a bit as you tip-toe up; the crux requires a right big toe on a very small hold, and that digit of mine occasionally fails embarrassingly—ever since I broke it bird-watching in Morocco. We led through in small "pitches" to gain the maximum fun out of it.

We sat about on top for a while, then rigged an abseil off the steep side: our doubled line only just reached the foot.

During a typical Braehead circus here we once had fun with the dog. Everyone had been climbing up and abseiling off in various directions. The last enthusiast was abseiling off when voices were heard coming from that west wall. Eventually a hand appeared and a head peeped over—to find a dog sitting there watching him. The head vanished.

Animated discussion below was followed by a brief look once more by the leader, and a clearly audible "There is so a ——— dog on top!" followed his second withdrawal. The last two of us quickly abseiled off and boys, ropes, dog, all vanished. The top was still empty when we left. I would have given a lot to have heard the conversation when both climbers reached the top!

From some angles the Pinnacle looks like a squat clown balancing a banana on his nose, for a few oddly-shaped boulders are perched on the chunky summit, and are useful for abseils.

We were watched as we abseiled off: early as it was the mobs were arriving. We ran a free information service for a while. Some lads from the hostel were a bit surprised; nascent Munro-baggers, they had not realised "things like that were involved".

We skeltered down the rubbishy flank of Dearg and on for Sgurr na Banachdich. The numbers operating along the ridge have now caused a plethora of paths, useful or otherwise, all over the Cuillin. In thick mist some of these can be quite misleading for even the false trails have had so many on them that they look like useful routes. Banachdich has paths now which outflank many of the ups and downs. But don't be tempted to outflank all the fun!

The very easy "tourist route" comes up via Coir' an Eich. The derivation of Banachdich is *smallpox peak*—possibly from the pock-marked state of some of the rock. It is also called Sgurr na Banachaig which is the *milkmaid's peak*. Off Banachdich, the paths leading down scree and scrag on the west are correct. (A misleading track goes east, if you want to go west, so to speak.)

There is another distracting path, which goes horizontally across left, where straight up is best, on Sgurr Thormaid. This is named after Professor Collie: *Norman's Peak*, a rather modest sub-summit for the greatest of the early explorers. Beyond here the interminable central ridge beckons: Ghreadaidh and Mhadaidh, the Munros, like two jagged hedgehogs meeting nose to nose—all spikes and bristles for we poor fleas to make our way along.

I can never recall the details of this central part of the Cuillin. Their remoteness tends to draw climbers much less often, and every Munro seems to have several tops to it—complex, endless bumps to try to recall after twelve hours of sun or twelve hours of wet groping. It merged, today at least, into a sunny, tip-toe memory. Peter had now adjusted to the peculiar Skye situation of romping about unroped above big drops and the dry rock was greeted with zest.

There was a roof-top down beyond Sgurr a' Ghreadaidh (pronounced Greeta), the *peak of the thrashing* [*winds*], double-topped and good non-stop scrambling. In the heat and "merely Munro-bagging" we were not loath to do our share of flanking. Off Ghreadaidh we were soon faced with an odd rock hunk which is turned on the left. We then crept down and in under a disintegrated dyke which would have been a fine bivy site with its view down Coruisk. Its cool shade was bliss. We even had all we needed to make a brew.

We scrambled back up round and headed quickly up Sgurr a' Mhadaidh (pronounced Vatee), 3,012 feet, the *foxes' peak*. ". . . among the rocks we went, and still look'd up upon the sun . . ." From Mhadaidh we flanked down towards the Thuilm saddle but at the right level (where the rocks run into scree) we swung back into Coire na Dorus—for a known water supply. It was warm but we gulped down pints of it and filled the bottles again.

We went down the screes a bit and then took a traverse line across to the col. The cliffs of Mhadaidh from here are arranged in superb long buttresses—corrie scenery as fine as any in Skye. It deserves better of the rock climber.

Traversing Sgurr Thuilm is a good route off. It is an easy descent by Coire na Dorus. From the Thuilm bealach we dropped down a bit on the Coir a' Mhadaidh side, then doubled back under the cliffs and by a succession of rakes and screes and slabs reached the corrie floor. An easy way—if you can find it—and with skyscraper ridges soaring overhead. It is one of my favourite spots in the Cuillin.

We went on round under Sgurr an Fheadain with its famous cleft of Waterpipe Gully, one of the great gullies from the early days of climbing. Green Coire na Creiche betrayed its cattle-gathering past. Creiche almost looks like crèche. It means the bovine equivalent. Tradition has it that Macdonalds and Macleods once clashed here on a raid and virtually wiped each other out.

Beyond it, a rising path took us to the Bealach a' Mhaim. The vivid, cropped, grass slopes were lively with rabbits. The col itself is wide and bold, with a little pool. It is on the old highway from Sligachan to Glen Brittle, and if you have not yet been to Glen Brittle try to reach it on foot by this historic path for your first visit. It is comparable to reaching Zermatt over the hills rather than up the railway.

The descent to Sligachan was all joy. The Allt Dearg soon becomes a bubbling stream with endless turquoise pools.

It seemed years instead of days since we had left Sligachan to start culling our Cuillin Munros. Several other tents had surrounded our pair in the interval. We drank and ate prodigiously till it grew dark. The midges had a session when the wind dropped. My last memory was of a cuckoo. This one, to be different, had a three-note call.

Saturday 22 June THE PEAK OF THE YOUNG MEN
Yesterday we had been a bit overwhelmed with the sun, so today we set off early—a quarter to six—while the sun was still handling the world gently.

We went back up the Allt Dearg path. This morning the sun was shining straight into its churning tubs and falls. A river of champagne,

but we had no time to drink. A gentle wander took us up the long
Fionn Choire, probably so called from the great areas of light-coloured
gravels.

Bruach na Frithe, the *brae of the forest*, is one of the easiest of Skye
Munros, and the only one besides Blaven which has a trig point.
The O.S. obviously have limits as to where they will hump cement.

We had gone up tightly under Sgurr a' Fionn Choire to leave our
sacks. Two people were just setting off from their bivy by the corrie's
high water patch—worth knowing, for it is almost the only reliable
water to be found near the Main Ridge.

There is a section of ridge between the Bruach and Mhadaidh which
does not have Munros and is probably the least frequented of all.
Bidean Druim nan Ramh has a complex triple summit where the ridge
does a twist, easily lost in mist, and before the Bruach there is one of the
lowest cols (2,494). It is the make or break section of the traverse.
Suddenly, on Bruach, you see all the last peaks, you know there is
water, and faith springs again.

For Peter and me the day's summits were black shapes set against the
sun; but a pushy east wind held off something of its temper. It is quite
a view: the Bhasteir Tooth, like something hammered out of molten
metal in some Iron Age of creation; Gillean, rising like a totem pole
from the giddy, dancing ridges that swirl out from it, and Uamha, the
last, least, and loved end to it all. There is nothing quite like Skye.

By the time we had dawdled along to the Bhasteir Tooth the two from
the bivouac were starting up Naismith's Route. As we had only a line
(we were not supposed to be climbing, we had to keep remembering)
we dropped down on the Lota Corrie side to take the "easy" diversion
—an obvious break upwards, and then rakes and dykes back to the
Tooth.

Naismith's is the straight climber's route and only *Difficult*—but you
begin with a traverse across the wall before going up the vertical face
above, so it is beautifully exposed.

W. W. Naismith is a famous name from the past. What M.L.C.
victim has not heard of his "Rule"? It was Naismith who really moved
things leading to the founding of the Scottish Mountaineering Club in
1889. He was a man of deep Christian faith who had been climbing
since he was fourteen (Ben Lomond), but it was within the S.M.C. he
produced his notable leads: the traverse of the Cobbler, Spearhead
Arête, the eastern traverse on Tower Ridge, and this face route on the

Tooth. He refused to be elected President of the club but will never be forgotten as its "father figure".

The Tooth is a quite incredible "Top": a slanting roof set above vertical walls, as unique a perch as the Cioch, a sphinx among the pyramids. Sometimes the loose stones on the roof-top slide down and block a hole which is the exit flue of a remarkable route—King's Cave Chimney. This route begins on the Sligachan side of the Tooth in a slot which soon becomes a real chimney, so you actually wiggle about inside the mountain—like a barium meal—till you pop out right on the summit roof.

Not being a Munro made it doubly appreciated. Am Bhasteir, the *executioner*, is the Munro. The tooth simply leans out from it like some decaying denture. There is no direct route between them—yet! A by-pass is made on the right with an awkward undercut little chimney the only problem. Peter was romping it all now, another willing victim to the lure of Skye.

The long easy ridge off Am Bhasteir is slabby and gravelly, so security is not at its best, wet or dry. The crest is better even with one awkward step. Not an easy walker's hill.

It was with a certain sadness we traversed along the well-worn trail for Gillean's West Ridge; this was the last of the Twelve Apostles. Our Skye days began so dubiously and had given such lingering pleasure. I led the chimney up to the ridge and Peter the traverse of the Pinnacle. We then coiled the line.

An Inverness quartet bombed past, having romped along the ridge —a casual weekend ploy. What a difference to someone at the camp site last night who had only done Alasdair, by its Stone Shoot, and on the strength of that planned to do the ridge. "Do I need a rope?" he had asked. . . . This is the beauty of Skye: to some it is the ultimate of ambition, simply to gain the vital summits; to others, the whole Main Ridge can be a romp of a day. All find it good.

The West Ridge is fascinating. It ends by threading the eye of a needle, the ridge merely the thickness of one block of gabbro. To the left the Pinnacle Ridge raises its four tops up towards the summit. Bright figures, like spiders, seemed to be spinning thin webs as they tangled ropes along the final peak almost directly below us. Sgurr nan Gillean is the *peak of the young men*.

It is the last Munro but, like Sgurr nan Eag at the other end, there is a lesser bonus top to mark the true end of the ridge—better in this case for, while it is a walk to Gars-bheinn, Sgurr na h-Uamha, the *peak of the cave*, has a last wee surprise up its sleeve.

The quartet got us to photograph them on top; and then asked which was the way off! The Tourist Route is notorious—for this conjures up the gentlest of ascents normally. But not here. The way is long and hard and not a few have found it a very full day on its own. My log simply catalogued the descent, "Ridge, rubbish, moor and bog." The bogs were dried and cracking again. A pool of yellow spearwort acted as a reflecting pool for Marsco. It was all heat haze and shimmer. The early start had been rewarded.

I took a bath in the river. The white hotel among the whispering trees, the old pack bridge, the familiar Gillean-Bhasteir crest, it is a scene which can hardly have altered since Collie's day.

It was to Sligachan that Collie retired—and there he died—in the grim days of the Second World War.

In 1886 he had come to Skye to fish, but became hooked on the Cuillin which were to become a passion. In the next two seasons he climbed every summit, often with John Mackenzie of Sgurr Mhic Choinnich fame: a sort of Young-Knubel combination.

As Skye was a war-time restricted area, Sligachan must have been a quiet spot. The last glimpse we have of Collie is from the pen of a young man, Richard Hillary, in his book *The Last Enemy*. Hillary, a young pilot, was there convalescing, and not long after writing this classic story was killed in action. He and a friend, Noel, were at once attracted by the austere beauty of the setting.

"We were alone in the Inn save for one old man who had returned there to die. His hair was white but his face and bearing were still those of a mountaineer, though he must have been a great age. He never spoke, but appeared regularly at meals to take his place at a table tight-pressed against the window, alone with his wine and his memories. We thought him rather fine."

The two young pilots went off and had an epic on Bruach na Frithe in the mist, thoroughly enjoying it. On the way down they even fell into a pool in a gorge where they had gone astray. To their after-dinner tale the landlord's sole comment was "Humph"—"but the old man at the window turned and smiled. I think he approved."

I am sure Collie did.

Peter packed to go off on the evening bus. The hotel was full, so instead of a dinner I had to dream up a meal of left-overs; soup and

apple flakes mainly. The sun left the site all too soon; the red colours
ran up the Red Hills, the last slanting rays came streaming through
under the bridge. I lay writing this and watching the little incidents of
camp life. There was a very definite "end of holiday" feel to it. Skye is
so uniquely different that these last few days seemed quite divorced
from the rest of the Walk. Tomorrow it would be back to the office, so
to speak.

Sunday 23 June   THOU SHALT NOT CYCLE ON SUNDAY
Wind-direction averages never favour the cyclist: in a land of westerlies
I set off into a strong east wind. The landscape was devoid of people,
Broadford a ghost town, Kyle deserted. Breakfast had been apple
flakes and twice-brewed tea bags, at which my stomach was complaining, but at Balmacara, the Kyle Stores provided welcome fresh
food and drink. I struggled on to Dornie, effort rather subduing enjoyment, for the colours were vivid and the whole landscape decked in the
sort of green one associates with bad taste in clothes. I sprawled between
road and water where I could see Eilean Donan Castle on one side and
the view out of Loch Duich on the other.

Eilean Donan must be the most photographed building in the
Highlands, though few people now enjoy the view down on to it,
possibly the best angle, for the new road speeds them along the lochside.
It's an ironic twist of fate that this bit of fine road was engineered by
hillman extraordinary, Philip Tranter, the first man to have done the
Munros twice. He died in a car crash on the way home from climbing in
Turkey. Had he lived, who knows, he might well have been writing
this book! An all-round mountaineer, based on the West here, he was
the driving force of the Corriemulzie Club with its famous "feich trips"
and pioneering climbs in the remoter regions.

The history of the castle can be found in many books including Seton
Gordon's *Highways and Byways in the West Highlands*. This great writer
has given us about forty books over the last fifty years and few have such
a love for the hills and wildlife. Like Collie, he had retired to Skye.

I was away in my day-dreams when I became aware that Peter was
talking to me. His parents' caravan was parked a hundred yards off.
I had a job to persuade them I really did not need a full three-
course lunch. The morning of fasting had become a day of indulgence,
and it was a bloated climber who wobbled off. From the bridge I could
see a glimpse of the wild hills beyond Loch Long. The bridge was built

in 1939 so that "puffers" (coastal steamers) could get through into the loch. A hundred years ago 200-ton schooners were built here and the local "parliament" met down on the slipway.

The Five Sisters had drawn a veil about their heads but the scenery was still jewel-like. At last I pushed into the National Trust camp-site at Morvich at the head of Loch Duich. Donny McLean had three parcels for me: a cache left by Mike Keates, a weekend box from Ann Winning (she had been unable to wait) and left-overs which I thought I had off-loaded on Catherine McInnes. I was not going to starve.

XII

THE BIG GLENS: SHIEL, AFFRIC, FARRAR

"In the Highlands it is mountain after mountain, mountain after
mountain, for ever and ever."

THOMAS WILKINSON

Monday 24 June SADDLE SORE

After Skye, this was intended as a rest day but the goals and the gods
sent me off instead. Rest could come with the next deluge; if the Shiel
ridges could be done dry it would be a great help.

The wise were up, for, as on so many summer mornings, the touch
of glory had soon gone, replaced by a middling green opulence. Even
the loch was green with the forest reflections—while in the eye of the
view lay the mote of a red fishing boat. It seemed a long way up to the
quarry which sits as such an eyesore right across the road through a
glen so important to tourists.

A little after ten I took a useful stalking path upwards. I'd bought a
paper and read of Scotland out of the World Cup with no lost games, of
the Lions walloping the Springboks, of Wimbledon and of the F.T.
Index at a new record low. On average I thought I was well out of
things.

It was a day for pants-only again. I was muzzy with a cold and on
several occasions sent sheep skelping off across the hillside with my
sneezes. Like an Eskimo, my contacts with civilisation had given me a
bug. The path ended on the ridge which hides the Saddle from the foot
of Glen Shiel—however fine the peak appears from up the Glen.
Beyond lay Coire Caol and the rocky ramparts of the Saddle with its
famous Forcan Ridge which gives some scrambling.

I cut across the corrie today, to keep out of the sun. It was dark and
cool. A hind, lying by the burn, had died while calving, a sad sight.
Rocks gave some scrambling and I went up the steep north ridge where
the ground was shiny with black mica. The other side of the ridge has an
even finer corrie; Loch a' Choir' Uaine was low from the dry weeks of
April. An eagle was working round the headwall in easy flight and
passed fifty feet below.

The ridge ends in a definite "top" which is the summit. Along another thinly curved ridge lies a trig point, which is slightly lower. Today I did both to avoid any possible ambiguity.

The Saddle is only 3,317 feet but dominates the south side of Glen Shiel with its configuration of five crests and several deep corries. It has its place in a Top Twenty. Just below the trig point, on the south side, you may find a pool for a deliciously cold dip. Very few summits provide this service where it is most wanted—at the top. I wrung out my sweaty pants, washed them, and by the time I'd eaten my pieces sitting on the lawn, they had dried. The pool was still rimmed with snow so a brief paddle was enough for today.

The view was very clear: one of the best of the trip. Ladhar Bheinn dominated but much else fused from propinquity. Rhum, Eigg and Skye were all lined like a fleet in the Minch. Loch Hourn had not a ripple on its placid depths. Sgurr Mor was big, Sgurr na Ciche, for once, poor. It was possibly the view of the Walk's "crux": entering Knoydart had been the most depressing day, the Rough Bounds had restored, Sgriol gave the finest of all views and the Cuillin had been a holiday delight. As I sprawled in the sun on the Saddle I began to feel really confident: only a disaster could stop me now. I was beyond reach of depression or despair—which was perhaps as well, as it proved.

A south flank down, a wet traverse of the col, another rising traverse and Sgurr na Sgine, *peak of the knife*, was soon added. There are two tops, the eastmost being slightly higher.

Faochag, the *whelk*, is a Top, sited nearly two miles back round the corrie rim to the north. It is easily recognised from Glen Shiel: the brutally dominant and simple cone next to the more complexly-designed Saddle. Sgine is tucked away out of sight, except for the walker coming over the Mam Barrisdale in Knoydart.

Sgine's north ridge I have come to call "Concorde Ridge". Alan Moreland and I were descending it one winter: a steep, narrow ridge but not technically demanding. Fortunately we had roped-up for with no warning there was an indescribable sudden double-bang. Alan virtually let go with the shock and slipped off his holds briefly. My heart nearly stopped a second time as I heard the fearful sound of a wet snow avalanche. Being on a narrow ridge no avalanche could have hit us even if the conditions could have produced one; but reflexes work quicker than rational thought. This second shock revealed itself in a vast flock of terrified ptarmigan. The sound had been the noise of their wings.

I don't think the Saddle–Sgine day has ever let me down, summer or winter, it has always blessed us with sun, a tradition I was glad to see maintained. I dandered down again. On Sgine I'd seen *white* moss campion. Years before I knew of white forms, I had found a white milkwort on the Saddle and cursed all my ineffectual flower books which gave no picture of it.

It was roasting in the tent. Odd conditions for Christmas Pudding. French voices from next door added a touch of unreality; imagination was happily working an Alpine camp-site out of it. Good coffee, fresh fruit, and other luxuries were consciously relished knowing the lean days to come. Jimmy Watt, from Edinburgh, an old gangrel and C.T.C. man, had walked up the road with me in the morning; now we sat chatting in the golden evening. We had similar wedge-shaped tents; dwarfed among the tourists' frilly "cottages".

My day of sun had taken its toll and I went to bed glowing and hot: Saddle sore all over!

Tuesday 25 June SOUTH SHIEL SWITCHBACK

The trouble with writing about a big switchback of ridge is that memory tends to blur the detail. I still cannot recite the names of these peaks, never mind remember the details, despite several traverses. It was another sun-smitten day—almost too sunny.

There were midges on waking. Just dashing out and away from the tent left my legs with a score of bites, and that was at seven o'clock. The Bealach Duibh Leac, the *pass of the black slab*, is 2,400 feet and just one bump along from where I'd been on Sgurr na Sgine yesterday. It is an old right-of-way over to the head of Loch Hourn. Prince Charlie slipped over it after breaking through the Knoydart cordon. He then headed up the glen for a well-earned respite beyond Conbhairean. Of that later. The Glen Shiel road was built by Caulfield, Wade's lesser-known successor.

The Scottish hills are criss-crossed with rights-of-way. I always feel the Scottish Rights of Way Society and the Mountain Bothies Association are two bodies all of us who use the hills ought to join—they both do so much for us that a small subscription is only a right return. A. E. Robertson, the first "Munroist" and founder member of the Scottish Rights of Way Society, has never been equalled in knowledge of the subject; but if he saw the need for such a society all those years ago, how much more is it required today.

I had a path to follow so immersed myself in *Ring of Bright Water* and only looked up when the mew of a buzzard or the tumble-song of a lark caught my ear. The streams were tepid and too low for any swim. The path became sketchy but eventually landed me on the Bealach whence I followed the wall up and down and along to Creag nan Damh, the *rock of the stag*, a summit of many false summits.

Sgurr Beag, the next bump, not being a Munro, was traversed on the

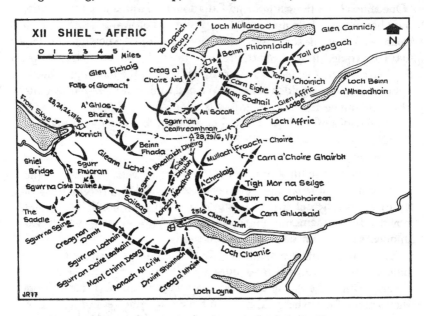

south, from col to col, laziness rewarded with finding a stream—welcome water, though warm. Sgurr an Lochain is higher and the view expands to the fullness one always thinks of in this district of great ridges. Ben Nevis was in view again. I began to feel I would never break away from its familiar shape. On Sgurr an Doire Leathain, *peak of the broad thicket*, I left my book by mistake. I'd been reading on the move again—and lazing at cairns over the book. I dropped in search of water but warm peat pools were all I found, as I skirted along to sit in the shade of a crag and demolish some tinned raspberries and Chicken Supreme. Scissors made a messy substitute for a forgotten tin opener. Beyond Sgurr Coire na Feinne, *peak of the Corrie of the warriors*,

skirting on the grassy south flanks I found a welcome trickle of water
again.

These slopes lead down like massive limbs to the man-made arm of
Loch Quoich. The bridge on the Loch Hourn road was clearly seen—
black against the silver shine—while figures passed westwards on the
crest above. I wonder if they found my book? Having lost one paperback (which I'd read often, anyway) I fished out tomorrow's and
started it, another sailing story, *Dove*, by Robert Lee Graham who set
off *when sixteen* to sail round the world. I was soon jotting down quotes:
"One learns from the sea how little one needs, not how much" . . . "I'd
want him [son] to love nature. I'd want him to love animals, mountains,
clean water, sea life."

It was an easy pull up the next Munro, Maol Chinn-dearg, the *bald red
top*. I envied the deer in the deep shadowy corries; there was no shade
on the crest. The poor beasts were puzzled by the noise of my passing,
looking nervously all round—but not up. Aonach air Chrith, the *shaking
height*, was reached by a narrower ridge with rocky steps. Two very
pink bodies were lying asleep by the cairn but woke when my cold
shadow fell on them. They *said* they were traversing the ridge. Below
the next col, for the third time in the day, I found welcome water to the
south: quite a large stream—even shown on the map. It oozed out of
the earth as warm as if held in the mouth for minutes. It was liquid
though. I flanked a bit and was soon on the curl up to Druim
Shionnach. A dark hare, with white front feet, went dashing past—set
off by a couple with two small children who came whooping up from
the north ridge on to the *ridge of the foxes*.

The continuing ridge (roughly south-east) is a narrow, broken crest
which gives a surprise to visitors. Once, ski traversing, I recall swivelling
round on it with tips and heels both sticking out over space. The map
does not really show that sort of narrowness. The sweep down and up
beyond is gentle, and suddenly, it is over, the Cluanie Ridge, the south
Shiel switchback. Creag a' Mhaim is a rather adolescent swelling to
end such a day, the *peak of the pass*.

Deer shot out of all the shadowy corners as I flanked down. The
rough going by Loch a' Mhaoil Dhisnich (my sneezy state could say
that fine) led to a good stalking path and I was soon walking with the
whirling, crying peewits across the bridge to the Cluanie Inn. This old
charge house on the road to the west is where Dr Johnson decided to
keep his famous journal. He went down Glen Shiel and over to Glenelg.

(Descending the other side of Mam Ratagan he rode two horses turn-about!) He had lots of things to say about the Glen Shiel hills—none of them polite. The Inn snuggles into the sweep of landscape as old buildings do.

My purchase of seven Cokes took their entire supply. I drank two, had one with an excellent, plain dinner, and the rest were saved for the morrow's likely sun-beating. I enjoyed a wallow in a bath with musical plumbing, and read there, and in bed.

Some thought to statistics gave me 36 Munros from here to Achnashellach and 34 beyond. So this indeed was a big section. Oh, if it could progress like these last two days! The sun had made my thighs tender: "rare" I think is how a chef would have described them. I'd carefully kept a shirt on to protect my burden-bearing shoulders.

The seven-mile Cluanie Ridge gives a haul of seven Munros. It never falls below 2,500 feet in six miles, and perhaps only on tomorrow's side of the glen, or on the ridges of Affric and the Lapaichs beyond, can there be its equal for length and height. It was a 6,850 feet and 20 miles day. The S.M.C. guide book, I see, says the traverse is "best done with two cars"—which must be rough on the suspension!

Wednesday 26 June   THE BROTHERS AND SISTERS RIDGE
A real bed was a luxury but nevertheless I was off at 8.30 after a good breakfast—surely a record for an hotel. I took the east bank of the Allt a' Chaoruinn Bhig, a pleasant, tumbling stream, gouged out of rock in places with here and there silvery waterfalls. For a while there were swarms of long-legged flies.

The A' Chralaig group to the east was holding back a great ocean of cloud, but now and then waves of this brilliant white mass would break down the slopes towards me. It distracted the eye all the way up little Ciste Dhubh, the *black chest*. A black bog-pool was full of floating, tattered bodies of moths—like confetti in a dirty street puddle.

Down in the glen to the north is Cam Ban bothy which was done up as a memorial to Philip Tranter. An entry in its book read, "Did the Five Sisters of Kintail today"; another hand had added, "Bloody sex maniac". The name "Five Sisters" is often used loosely for the whole north Shiel ridge but it really belongs to the western summits which appear as regular paps when seen across Loch Duich. We have long given the eastern tops the name of the Five Brothers of Glen Shiel. Brothers and Sisters combine to give another great day.

I finished *Dove* as I wended up the next Munro—and realised time was pushing on if I was not. Ciste Dhubh curls away north from the main ridge and is more often than not excluded by those traversing the ridge. Sgurr an Fhuarail is named on the map, but the Munro is not: Aonach Meadhoin which lies a bit further on. The ridge off it was narrow and nice. Sgurr a' Bhealaich Dheirg is the highest of these brothers. Its summit is a big cone of a cairn stuck out on the narrow north ridge—with an odd 100-yard wall leading to it. The map rather implies a plateau.

Looking west, Saileag, the *little heel*, is hardly noticed, though its southern slope must be one of the steepest and most even gradients in Scotland. A traveller in 1803 passing down Glen Shiel wrote of the slopes as being "an inclined wall, of such inaccessible height that no living creature would venture to scale it". Yet no doubt locals had. The Bealach Lapain implies an old pass. I left a note and it was found the next day by Michael Scott from Ayrshire who gave his "reason for starting" as "too old for anything else".

Sgurr na Spainteach is the *Spaniards' peak*, a name recalling a Jacobite sideshow on its slopes in 1719 not far up from the now by-passed Telford Bridge. This minor rising, which included a contingent of about 300 Spanish soldiers, ended before it really began, in a long and disorderly skirmish on just such a June day as today. One feels a bit sorry for the poor Spanish yokels. We are told that Rob Roy was involved too—far from his usual range.

It was near where I left the road yesterday that Prince Charlie (as fugitive) had lain hidden behind a boulder for all of a long, grilling, summer's day. Be warned, this is not normal Kintail weather. "The Cluanie Curtain" is the local name for the grey sweeping rain more often met with as one nears the region. Today it seemed in reverse: the east still dammed back like a great white wave.

Sgurr na Ciste Duibhe, another *black chest*, is quite a rugged peak and takes one on to the Sisters. Sgurr na Carnach is rough and not being a vital Munro I flanked it a bit which led to complications. I *smelt* goats without actually seeing any. The day was both hot and clear. I could see both Ben Nevis and the Cuillin. Jets flew through Glen Shiel; like tiny models. The hills at this end start on sea level and rise with brutal steepness, one reason why most prefer to travel east–west.

Sgurr Fhuaran, 3,505 feet, is the highest on the ridge. It is a superb viewpoint, lording over much else in the vicinity. I sat on top and drank the last of my life-saving Cokes, enjoying that great peace which only the restless know. This is the central and grandest of the Sisters: beyond again lie Sgurr nan Saighead, 3,050 feet, newly promoted to a Top, *peak of the arrows,* and Sgurr na Moraich, 2,980 feet, *peak of the shellfish*: scalloped corries and ridges not to be missed.

Today, however, I explored a direct route down to Glen Shiel: 3,500 feet in a mile and a half. I returned to the col and then traversed up a bit to hit a shoulder south of Carnach where I knew there was a steep rake. This led down all right, the careful study of yesterday paying off with an easy line of descent which took an hour. The river merely required boulder-hopping.

It was too late for the shop, but a vast meal was soon demolished back at Morvich. Sleep was painful: burnt thighs and a cold. And my boots were disintegrating again.

Thursday 27 June   DOING LOCH DUICH

I had reorganised the original Walk plan to enable the big Shiel ridges to be done unladen, now I was having an off-day: all this a conscious gathering of strength for the long trek to Achnashellach. There would be no helpers, the heaviest rucksack, and only one reliable parcel on the way. I was not unduly worried, willing to take what the hills gave. I felt I had already been pushed to the limit. Anyway the mountains were and are my environment. I was going neither with eyes shut nor starry eyed.

Fraser Darling wrote *Island Years* while recovering from a broken leg, the result of an accident while going down a field to milk a cow; yet he had climbed and canoed and caved among Hebridean islands for years. As he warns, "danger may be in the illusion of safety". More *walkers* die accidentally than *climbers*. More die on the casual afternoon descent than when fighting uphill. The commonest cause is the simple slip. In all the Walk I had only the odd slip—fewer I reckon than in any week at home, that most lethal environment of all.

A bad cold seldom makes for good judgement so I relied on the homework already done and after a long lie set off in holiday mood to "do" Loch Duich.

Task one was dealing with food. I could hardly squeeze into the tent for assorted boxes. Soon one was packed with what would go with me, another with tonight's meal and a couple with what would be left, along with the bike, for Mike Keates to pick up some time. I paid for the camp-site, to ensure an early start on the morrow, then wandered along to the shop. It was coping with busloads of animated tourists. I fled down to the Kintail Lodge Hotel for coffee, stayed on for lunch and then coffee again: there was lots of mail to clear off. The day was warm again: green, grassy summer now. A red fishing boat bobbed on the tourist-blue loch beyond a row of white foxgloves. The tide was high and the thrift heads were bobbing like corks in the foamy water. Pied pipers were rushing about like busy waiters and a heron stalked the burn, every now and then stabbing into the water with his great beak.

Back at Morvich I prepared another vast meal. The Ripleys, coming out of the north, had shopped gleefully and eaten to a similar state of "bloatation". After the feed I began my next book, *The Man in the Iron Mask*. At ten to eleven I remembered I had not phoned Mike or David/Marina. I dashed down to the phone box and eventually contacted them. Mike would meet me at Achnashellach and would bring replacement boots. I had bled a finger, broken a pair of scissors and somehow wired my soles on to the uppers last night. They would have to do till then.

A crowd of us, walkers, pot-holers and such like, gathered for a late brew. In June it is very hard to turn in before the last kissing colours leave the slopes. We sat looking at Fhada and A'Ghlas-bheinn—my gateway into Affric on the morrow. As so often, I turned in feeling a great content. I recalled and repeated the grace spoken at our first Braes o' Fife dinner:

> For wir bonny bit peak and a guid climb too,
> For a dram o' the malt and a brew or two,
> For friend, and ficht, and a' the blaws that wind may blaw,
> And a' the saws that evening gangrels saw,
> The guid—and bad—and the just so-so
> Hill days and holidays. . . .
> > Dear God,
> Forget not the earth where aince you trod
> And tak the thanks o' men and mountaineers.
> > > Amen.

Friday 28 June THE GATES OF AFFRIC
The great glens running east–west, north of busy Glen Shiel, have a very different atmosphere from that well-known, well-used area. They

have the emptiness of being far from the beaten ways of man, shut off into a huge area, strath and ridges in bewildering quantity, the highest summits north of Ben Nevis, far from the sweep of sea. Again, it is so different from anywhere else in the Highlands. This changing from one area to another had the same quality of refreshment that one enjoys meeting old friends. I set off for this new and vital section in good spirits. The Odyssey has a line that set the mood: "Past the gates of the sun and the home of dreams they went".

The Gates of Affric for me are the peaks of Beinn Fhada (Attow) and A' Ghlas-bheinn—or at least the pass between them, the Bealach an Sgairne. I would climb the peaks and go through the pass into Affric. A rapid-fire cuckoo began at three in the morning to make sure I was wide awake and away in time.

Both these peaks appear from Loch Duich: Fhada as a massive, notched, wall and A' Ghlas-bheinn seamed with long gullies. Affric can be reached up Gleann Lichd under that south flank of Fhada, but Fhada has superb corries facing the other way. A little lochan at 2,000 feet on Fhada's southern slopes must be one of the oddest sites for a camp (in deep frozen winter) I have ever had. The extreme left, looking up, shows Fhada's crest as deeply dented. It is. There is one *mauvais pas* which can bar walkers, but it gives good scrambling, and ridge-walking at its best.

A mile from Morvich I left the tarred road—for probably the longest mileage during the Walk. I was also carrying the heaviest rucksack: it must have weighed at least 35 lb. I read my way up Gleann Choinnea-chain, the gentle path, for once, not doubling as a burn. Above the zig-zags I perched on a knoll for a break, then left the load, to take to A' Ghlas-bheinn, which is pronounced something like "Glashven", and usually dismissed with little good said of it. All of 3,006 feet, I suspect it suffers from grudging Munro-baggers, simply thrown in with Fhada or done on an off day, so dismissed or forgotten.

This is a pity for it is a complex little hill and has a splendid view. I have a Christmas picture of a party sunbathing on it. I do not have pictures of another Christmas when we battled in a blizzard up the long ridge from the pass. I had warned of many false summits (someone claimed there were sixteen), and going up we had one side plastered, coming down, the other, so we ended in an icy armour. Kitchy spent most of that day in my rucksack and I was just glad he was a Sheltie and not a St Bernard. On two different trips we have been glad to splash, like speugs, in the pool a mere stone's throw from the summit. No, I will have nothing said against A' Ghlas-bheinn!

North of this peak are the Falls of Glomach, reached from either Loch Duich or Glen Elchaig, east lies Loch a' Bhealach and the boggy strath of upper Affric, all dominated by the Kangchenjunga of Scotland: Sgurr nan Ceathreamhnan. South is the spectacular side of Fhada, west the glitter of Loch Duich and a hint of far Cuillins. Who could ask more?

Knowing the long ridge of A' Ghlas-bheinn I decided to flank first, then head upwards. At once I became snarled up among crags, then barred by a slot of gully. It was not even an easy mountain it seemed. While messing about like this I was attracted by the angry calling of hoodie crows and then saw an eagle flying with one in its talons. It dropped the dead bird over the pass so that it fell like a black rag, and the eagle then swept casually up over Fhada, the rabble of hoodies yelling after but unable to match its pace.

I scrambled up a burn to Loch a' Chleiridh. Even at 2,600 feet the water was warm. It was no wee summit pool but one of Olympic dimensions. I had a swim, of course, then followed the natural lay of the land up to the ridge and along to the summit. The Torridons suddenly looked near, but, like the Ben, they would do a fair bit of advancing and receding before they were actually reached.

I had a picnic back at the rucksack; eating till I felt as bloated as a full moon. A side path, not on the map, breaks off to skirt round into the Fhada corrie, going on through green bays and ending on the low saddle of Meall a' Bhealach—a spot where I had a welcome pause. In autumn I have perched there in the rut with every hillside covered with deer, the stags roaring mightily. It was as if they were all crowding in, knowing it to be N.T.S. property and their hides safe. The view looks straight down Gleann Gniomhaidh into Affric. I wandered on peacefully to Fhada's beacon of a trig point.

The Sisters of Kintail faced me over the depths of Gleann Lichd: sunny crests and black, shadowed glen. They used to be known as the *big hill*, Beinn Mhor, which balances Beinn Fhada, the *long hill*. Tiny dots of colour were coming over the Plaide Mor as the plateau is called: lucky people who would have the great westward view clear today.

I romped off down, peeling off layers of clothes, as a cook might strip an onion, regretting that Attow did not have a high lochan too. I collected the heavy rucker and went through the pass, quite a defile, to find myself in Affric. The pass is at about 1,800 feet and part of an old route. St Duthac used it in the eleventh century and there is a well named after him just down the east slope a bit. Loch Duich is Duthac's Loch. The path dropped down to Loch a' Bhealach which is very nearly on the watershed for it does not flow to Affric as expected, but north, then round to the west to help feed the Falls of Glomach.

These are frequently praised as being our highest and best, which they are not. I am often amazed that visitors go into superlatives at places pin-pointed in their guidebooks—and then miss their equal or better simply because there is no sign saying, "Marvel here!" Perhaps it is as well. One of the problems facing climbers who write about the hills (as I am doing now) is to balance enthusiasm with giving away what one would prefer to keep secret. Fortunately I am covering the Munros, a well-established treadmill, though even here I take care *not* to mention some things about some areas. Elitist! No, jealously conservationist. Bodies like the Scottish Countryside Commission would "promote" a "wilderness experience", which is a very contradiction in terms. Experiences are not promoted. You cannot teach an appreciation of beauty. Glomach is fine, and let us leave it at that.

I walked right down the upper reaches of Glen Affric dryshod, which was a novel experience. Various ways-in converge: mine through the Gates of Affric, the Gleann Lichd path up by the Cam Ban bothy, and the pass from Loch Cluanie, perhaps the most direct. On the slopes of the Mulloch where the last-named drops down there is the wreck of an aircraft. A propeller has been built into a bridge near the hostel. I strolled over the meadows to this haven accompanied by a puffing herd of cows. The hostel is an old "iron" lodge: green-painted corrugated iron, with fine wood-panelling in its rooms, the door a bright red and the usual guardian rowan nearby. It was one hostel you could be sure not to meet the plastic-soled, international bums who swamp the roads in summer. It is a far cry from the bob-a-night atmosphere. You have to go to the bothies to find that these days. We are told that today's youth expects higher standards, that we must conform to international ideas; but I wonder who says so. Youth? I suspect hot water is more attractive to the middle-aged committee men who run such things.

I dropped my armful of bogwood at the door. A lark was nesting less than ten yards away. The warden welcomed me with a cup of tea—

perhaps there is hope for the old association yet! Bill Lockyer was a student at Strathclyde University. His bednights that spring had ranged from zero to twenty-two. There was nobody else just now. The Ripleys had been there and been told the hills were "out of bounds" (during the stalking season) but they, perforce, went—so had their cards confiscated.

Alltbeithe was an old lodge, and many early accounts by the S.M.C. founders mention staying there. They were gentlemen climbers given the hospitality of gentlemen owners. It was a very closed-shop world. In volume one of the S.M.C. Journal, Munro, himself a landed gentleman, tells how best to bypass the bothy on Mam Sodhail where watchers lived all summer for the sole purpose of warding off sheep, both four- and two-footed. He carefully spells out all the rights-of-way. It sounds very modern. There is a paper in a later volume which takes the S.M.C. humorously to task for thinking this area "unexplored": the writer, a professor of geology, had been over all the summits years before—carrying a fifteen-pound hammer, what's more. He too stayed at Alltbeithe, now the youth hostel.

Munro thought that in Affric as "nowhere else are rock and heather, lochs and islands, natural forests and falls blended in such beauty". He also gives a description of traversing the area with "sentries" popping up every few miles to query his being there. "Of course I was on a right-of-way, and need not have answered, but had I not a passport?" He diverted to take in Mam Sodhail and the Falls of Glomach and ended at Loch Duich—some walk. He nearly wept on arrival to find that the inn was out of beer. (The next day he traversed Sgurr Fhuaran, the next traversed Sgriol via the Mam Ratagan, and then went south by the *Clansman* to Glasgow, to dine the next night in London. Try that today!)

Bill and I sat before the peat fire recalling these giants of yesteryears. We had steaming mugs of tea in the gloaming, for it hardly became dark at nights now, then went out to brush our teeth at the burn, once we had shoved a lurking cow out of the way. The only books were several Bibles which allowed an hour of reading (I carried only a tiny New Testament). I found a suitable text, which has since been pinned up in my Dormobile, a sort of glorified mobile bothy: "Stand ye in the ways and see, and ask for the old paths, where is the good way, and walk therein, and ye shall find rest for your souls."

I

Saturday 29 June   CONBHAIREAN CIRCLE

I was up at seven, and not long after that the warden from Cannich Y.H. arrived, having *run* up with mail for Bill. Runners have my admiration if not emulation. I sometimes think that I walk only because it is too wet, or cold, or hot, or midgy to lie around doing nothing—which is what would have been nice today. It began with a throw of mixed colours, the sun dappling the long east ridge of Attow, but it ended "gey dreich" when a book by the peat fire would have been saner pleasure.

The Mulloch was never climbed by procrastination. Its vast slopes I put out of mind by reading my way upwards. I walked into a sheep at one stage—I don't know who received the greater surprise. The deer stood and let me pass very close. It was sweltery hot for such a brutal hill, one with no easy line up, unless it be the link to A'Chralaig, but that was my way off. Slowly I pushed the cluster of buildings into dinky proportions, then lost them as I rimmed round the corrie that gives the hill its name of Mulloch Fraoch-choire, the *top of the heathery corrie*. A party of four ravens was flying along noisily: father with his deep croak, the rest with adolescent voices cracking, all the while wheeling and diving and performing marvellous tricks.

There was a nasty opaque quality to the light as I left the Mulloch. The crest is broken into pinnacles but in summer a path now wends through these. In winter it can be quite a place. We were once turned back in May by double cornices. The grand highway led on to the south, to A'Chralaig, another massive brute of unrelenting approaches. A south wind was again proving piercingly cold so I scuttled on round and down to the Bealach Coir'a Chait to rest there. The day was rapidly closing in.

> "Shaken mists a space unsettle, then
> Round the half-glimpsèd turrets slowly wash again."

A'Chralaig had been the last Munro of the third time round the Munros, a winter day with Bob Aitken, Alan Moreland and Andy Patterson.

I outflanked Conbhairean to reach the outlier of Carn Ghluasaid, a plateau-like summit which may have a path all the way up from Lundie on Loch Cluanie, yet still entail a search if it is misty. This group is worth two visits: perhaps a summer day for the eastern Ceannacroc

Forest circle of hills and a winter day for the big two. The Prince Charlie's Cave marked on the map does exist.

Lorna Marsh, John Lawton, Mike Keates and Peter Miller (all at odd times involved in the Walk) formed our gang which once had a bivy at the cave. The Prince hid there for nearly a week, perhaps using two separate howffs. He had just managed to escape the cordon of Redcoats and probably arrived over Conbhairean, so was no doubt thankful to rest a bit, being well guarded by the Seven Men of Glenmoriston. From here he went down into Affric and Cannich, originally planning to go well north, to take ship at Poolewe, but hearing the ship had gone, he turned south by Glenmoriston and Tomdoun to Locheil country at Loch Arkaig. After two weeks he went to Ben Alder and finally west again to ultimate escape. He must have been a hardy hillman by the end.

I crossed Sgurr nan Conbnaireah, 3,634 feet, the *peak of the dog men*, quickly for there was that sniff-at-the-heels awareness of electricity in the air. My cagoule went on for warmth. The ridge is a far and desolate one, with a long valley on one side and the bites of corries on the other: the first with a Cairngorm-like Lochan Uaine, the second with the Shelter Stone the Prince used, then lesser hollows leading round east—a fine circle to complete. On the col to Tigh Mor na Seilge, *big house of the hunting*, there is a strange slot and the second summit (3,276 feet) is a wilderness of quartz veins. Little Loch a' Choinich had dried out into a black smudge.

Not having been struck by lightning I went on to bag a wanted Corbett, Carn a' Choire Ghairb, which presumably must be a good viewpoint down wooded Glen Affric. I struggled up to the big cairn on the lip of its plateau in driving rain, then dashed over to the real summit and on, following down the westward lie of the land. The glen below was all planted so, after taking a soft, green gully down, I had to deal with fences and furrows to gain a road, by which time I was thoroughly saturated by rain from above and wet from below. Movement produced heat enough and it was enjoyable. I saw an eagle. On top a ptarmigan had attacked my legs, on the Corbett I saw the first grouse for a long time. Alpine bistort flowered both on the Mulloch and in the wood here, and there were lots of orchids and cow wheat. There is *always* something. . . .

The forestry road leads down to Athnamulloch where there was a skirmish in 1721 when the government rent-collectors of forfeited estates were opposed by the locals. I cut the corner, so to speak, and got away with it as all the black bogs lay dry and cracked. Even the River Affric was just a few splashy steps.

I hit the great east–west track just as the rain came on again, and this time it really meant business. The hills remained clear, and there were some odd effects as the sun just failed to shatter the glassy world of wetness during my hour's tramp "home" to the hostel.

Dozens of despondent young soldiers were going the other way. They seemed to have a knack of stepping on the hems of their voluminous capes and sprawling in the mud. "Transport and hot char at the public road," seemed to be the sole vital thought; that they assumed this lay at the Lodge was something I had not the heart to correct—the public road lies an hour to the east. My cheery "Hi!" received looks which clearly said, "Bloody nut case! What's he got to be so cheerful about?" It was all very character-building no doubt. Thirty-seven unhappy figures on I reached the hostel, and char, and a fire—that's what I had to be cheerful about.

A lad from Kent and three of a family made the place seem positively crowded. I hung my clothes, and my map, to dry; then got down to some serious cooking. We thought of the poor lads tramping east, for the wind had gone and the big battalions had arrived: the midges. In the warmth of "the room" I nearly fell asleep writing up the log. Today had been about eighteen miles and 6,000 feet. I was finishing a fifth log-book and guessed I would need one more; so six logs of 40 pages of 220 words made up 53,000 words—so much for "not having written anything"!

Conversation was good. It touched on the reasons for doing this sort of hill game, all very high and lofty were the motivations mentioned; but after a pause we came down to earth. Why do you climb? One of the company answered: "I take to the hills to escape a wife who plays bridge, a son who plays the bagpipes and three daughters fighting over one telephone."

Sunday 30 June CEATHREAMHNAN
Queen Victoria said of the Gaelic, "It is a very difficult language, for it is pronounced in a totally different way from that in which it is written." Either way hardly helps with the above indiscriminate abuse of the alphabet—or what of Mam Sodhail, Carn Eige or Beinn Fhionnlaidh?

These Affric hills are massive rather than beautiful, grand and wild in a Waverley Novels sort of way. Ceathreamhnan is an exception: a tent-ridge summit set above great sweeping flanks and long ridges. It looks fine from all *quarters* and it is good on the ground.

There were logistical problems. The main ridge has some outlying Munros to the north, then Loch Mullardoch blocks off the Lapaichs which would therefore have to be traversed with full pack, especially as the parcel at the other end could well have been consumed by mice, though the keeper at Affric Lodge also had a parcel. The longer I stayed at the hostel the less food I would have to carry—but the more miles to walk. Some compromise was needed and I worked out a tactical plan accordingly; all part of the fun of a trip like this. After so many visits to Morocco I was quick to add *Insh'Allah* (which translates as God, weather and midges permitting)!

The English lad was packing *tins* to carry out, which presumably he had carried in. The Aberdeen trio were away for the same hills and I followed them on the Allt na Faing path, which runs up by a ravine where a hoodie nests blatantly in a tree. The cows had drifted up to over 2,000 feet and speckled the slopes. Given a dog or two it would have been tempting to take them over the pass just to imagine the consternation there would be on finding Glen Affric empty!

The path actually peters out before the col. I left the sack there to add An Socath, a poor wee nameless Munro on the O.S. map. Having swallowed Sgurr nan Ceathreamhnan and others, the O.S. seems to have stuck at Gaelic names too, so just stops naming things hereabouts —though missing the two An Socath Munros seems rather personal. It is interesting that the Munro Tables have been available for all these years, but neither their information, nor other research, has appeared on the new O.S. maps. This area is as blank as ever—at twice the price.

The Aberdonians were coming down as I went up. The pools had evaporated, and skirting Coire nan Dearcag I found the lochan much overgrown with reeds. A golden plover was nesting. I almost stood on the eggs. I had cut the corner again to reach the col north of the big hill. There I hid in a known slot in the rock while big dollops of rain came in. Without the sack Ceathreamhnan gave a happy ascent. It is pronounced something like "Kerranan". It has a double top, linked by a curving ridge which can be good in winter, when I have seen fine cornices on it. The other party had also cut across but gone for far away Aird first so as to home back to the hostel over the big one. I was not coming back, so after a look round I set off after them.

I had a bite at the sack first. Deer below were puzzled. One beast gave a great bellow. The Sithidh river ran like a silver thread in the shadowed tweed of the glen. It looked a long valley—and it was matched by the long ridge above that led to Creag a' Choir'Aird. It looks merely undulating but the reality is all rough and broken, with endless bumps, which the map cannot show. It is as well to keep to the crest. There is a definite col before the Munro, which is bitten into on the east by a corrie of little lochans; then grassy slopes lead to the summit.

I crossed paths with the others; their position had shown up in tiny dots of colour. As this hill is about as "far ben" as you can find anywhere, it was unusual to have people on it. Ken Andrew, writing in the *Scots Magazine*, suggested, "When I die I think I'll give my friends some exercise and ask them to scatter my ashes over the end of Creag a' Choir'Aird."

I left the Munro to bale off down the east corrie, a very steep slope. The flanks lower down were alive with deer: hinds "talking", calves yelping, the odd roar. There were a hundred more across the burn. Gleann a' Choilich, to which I had descended, has the remnants of a path but with the damming of Loch Mullardoch making a great barrier there is little south–north movement apart from walkers. Bogwood fills big peat patches. I followed the path down towards the loch, then cut up when it went down, to find a breezy knoll on which to pitch the tent. I could see a boat on the loch but had to retreat into the tent as the wind dropped.

The tent seemed to attract scores of spidery insects, which covered it, fortunately on the outside. Just a few determined beetles came in, to go scratch-scratching over the nylon. I lay day-dreaming, out of books, out of company. I filled in my log with mixed feelings: "Leave here: tent, stove, pots, sleeping bag, etc. Quite a bit of tea, milk, oatcakes, soup, cheese, etc., so even if Farrar cache eaten, should make Gerry's. The last 30 after that—and with support. Just get this bit over. 'Push!' and 'Tomorrow may be worse' still the goads."

Monday 1 July　NEAR PANIC

Gerard Manley Hopkins pleaded, "And I have asked to be Where no storms come". Obviously he was not a climber. You cannot argue with the wind. If "push" you need, then "push" you must, and if "tomorrow may be worse", then it need not surprise when it is. But it does!

The rain came on at midnight and battered away hard. I kept "giving it an hour" but eventually I set off into it, perhaps more angry than despairing. It was a real soaker, the cloud right down, an atmosphere as stuffy as a hospital. Wild beauty, like a green apple, can have a bitter bite to it.

Aird, for awkwardness, is matched by Beinn Fhionnlaidh up which I climbed straight from the tent. Benula Lodge and the easy approaches are all under water now, so it is a long way from anywhere—another arm jutting out with a Munroists' Munro. I was only sorry to miss the view down Loch Mullardoch, a long reach of water, seen at its best from here. Tom Weir had stayed at Benula Lodge years ago. My favourite book of his is the early, autobiographical *Highland Days*. It has the freshness of youth, and it is quite a shock to see how much things have altered since he wrote it. Many of the families he stayed with have gone now; Hydro schemes, new roads, plantings, pylons, have all changed the landscape.

The story I always recall, though, is one in an old Cairngorm Club Journal. The Rev. D. C. Mackay recounts a winter cycle journey from Loch Duich to Cannich via Benula in 1910. "I came face to face with a pedestrian . . . his astonishment seemed to be greater than mine when he beheld the apparition of a cyclist calmly emerging, as it must have appeared, from the depths of a lonely mountain loch in the midst of a winter storm. In order to reassure him, I remarked it was a fine day, but instead of an answer in the affirmative, or even in the negative, he merely stood and gazed after me. I reflected that probably the poor man was a bit eccentric."

I left a note in the cairn of Fhionnlaidh. It has never come back. Perhaps no one has been there since.

It was compass work again, down and over a bump, and then flanking along under Carn Eige, *cairn of the notch*, which was taking on a certain wildness. This flank once produced life-saving water on a scorching summer trip. Today it was all water—and so was I. It ran down my face, driven by the wind. The effect was mesmeric and I was very glad to come on the ruin of the old deer-watchers' bothy. I had overshot Mam Sodhail, *the barn*. The couple of hundred yards back and up to the top were "more boisterous than pleasant". I "cooried doon" in the hollow cairn and watched the storm fly past above me. It was like being on the *Captain Scott* in a gale in the Minch! The water seemed to be hitting the cairn like breaking waves, quite impressive. Reaching the shelter had left me gasping.

Pierre Mazeaud, in his chatty autobiography, tells of storm "reducing complexities to simplicity", but here it was doing the opposite. True, I was rather finding myself "restored to the stone age" (and I liked my broch), "up against the facts of nature . . ." but I was faced with a situation any general would dread: my lines fully extended and under heavy attack. By Loch Mullardoch, to the north, I had a tent (I hoped); at Affric Lodge, miles to the east, I had an essential food parcel; while at the hostel, to the south, lay the rest of my gear. All I now needed was to break a leg!

I climbed out like some poor Jock ordered "over the top" and set off for Carn Eige, the twin of Mam Sodhail, as Ben More is of Stobinian. At least I could try for it before having to flee downwards. My hand holding the compass froze (and gave agony warming up later) while it was virtually impossible to see ahead. I stumbled down to the col which was like a wind tunnel. Crossing it I was knocked down a couple of times. I battled up to the trig point, at 3,880 feet the highest thing between Ben Nevis and the North Pole. I put my back to the trig point and pondered.

Descent to the tent would be direct into the storm and so was out. Back over Mam Sodhail for the hostel would be easier, but a cheerless prospect of a roof with little food. East it would have to be, and a walk up the glen, then an additional day for the two Munros still further east on this ridge. Of course, going down to the Lodge, the weather *might* clear and I would then be in a position to nip up for the two tops.

I set off, grimly counting steps to be really accurate. I knew the ridge was by no means straightforward: a mile of this easy ground led to a corner bump, Creag na h-Eige, then swung round Coire Domhain in a series of pinnacles. I fought to the corner top. As I paused on it, willing back a picture of the ridge seen years before, the inner picture changed to reality—just like that. It cleared, as quickly as I can say so: one moment a blind, rushing world of wetness, the next, the clouds tore to shreds and before me the rock teeth were against blue sky. Gerard Manley Hopkins had a phrase for that too. I looked down one jewelled corrie after another to Loch Mullardoch and yelled, "Glory be to God for dappled things!"

The transformation was fantastic. I went rushing off in case it changed its mind. As the wind was still yowling on the ragged ridge I traversed upper Coire Domhain. Its lochan lay without a wind ruffle, yet I could hear the blow just a few hundred feet higher on the ridge. I tracked the snow patches of this beautiful bowl, feet saturated, the wet no longer mattering, and regained the ridge for the prow of point 3,705, which I am sure has a name, if only the O.S. would care to tell us. In places the now decaying stalkers' path is actually built as a stair as it comes up the prow. It is not shown on the map.

I kept in the lee for much of the way and reached the combed dome of Tom a' Choinich at 2 p.m. Definitely time to eat. Not long after, two muffled figures arrived from the east. The voices sounded familiar but it took a while to place each other. They were the Crams from Edinburgh. They were Top-bagging for the missus, he having done the Munros in 1939, the eighth and oldest-surviving Munroist. He had retired recently from being a Judge in Africa. There can be few Rolls-Royces to which climbing teams return to dig out the primus for a brew. At present, though, they were roughing it in a caravan. We had a gossip about Africa and Scotland. I had encouraged them to visit Morocco where they ran into the worst weather for forty years—I was surprised they even talked to me. I was given a tomato to eat and had a job convincing them I was not really starving or in need. Not now.

We went our opposite ways. I know the meeting cheered me up. I ran down the east ridge with its criss-crossing path and over the wide reaches to Toll Creagach, where, last year, I had found a cuckoo sitting on the cairn. The views were sharp as they can be after rain, the vivid blue and white of the sky had the brightness of a newly-cleaned painting. I kept chortling away in contentment. I had the two after all, and there lay the Lapaichs, there lay the Farrar Four. "Going to climb you! Going to climb you!" I sang, echoing an old Paul Robeson record. The other way, Conbhairean was at its best, I could see the Cuillin, and Ben Nevis even. And they had all been done! It was to the north I looked again.

I trotted down to join the Toll-Tom path for Gleann nam Fiadh, which was a different world: in the sun and out the wind. I eased off boots to bathe my feet if nothing else. When I took one boot off I found the gooey mess of a squashed black slug between my toes. Obviously I would never make a real explorer. Fancy forgetting to knock out one's boots in the morning! The glen was full of song, but a shorter route direct to the Lodge took me over a ridge instead of down the valley and round. On the moor the baby plovers went scuttling about my feet and dunlin slipped off among the peat hags.

The setting of Affric Lodge is superb: white, well-proportioned house, almost moated by reflecting waters, giving a crazy bonus of pines and birches, while the vivid greens of the lawns and early bracken contrasted to the moors and stony hills. I was there at the back of five but could find nobody about, so sat down to wait, quite content just to look at the magical view—or the busy tits, redpoll and twite. The locked-up dogs gave tongue, hearing the vehicles before I did, and soon the place was a milling confusion of men and dogs back from a day with the sheep.

The Head Keeper produced my parcel. He also had some words to say about a well-known gear-seller whose "advertisoment" he had read and from whom he had bought a jacket which had not been over waterproof. "They do not know what rain is down there." I was inclined to agree.

Sadly I refused Duncan MacLennan's hospitality and set off for the two-hour hike back to the hostel at Alltbeithe. Almost where it had started to rain two days before it did so again—hard. I thought of our Cyprus aunt who was due home soon, for the "summer". Her comments on the weather were usually brief. Of winter she declared once: "The weather's just the same, but in winter they may give you a fire." Bill had a fire on when I got in, first of July though it was.

The tatty Bibles again produced a suitable text, rightly in Job: ". . . No covering in the cold. They are wet with the showers of the mountains and embrace the rock for want of shelter." Even as I copied it out by candle-light a big brown drip fell on to the page from my stockings, hanging before the bogwood fire.

Tuesday 2 July THE LONGEST DAY

Many memories of this day were washed away in its ending, but its many little delights made it a "great day". I was away before seven. A cloudy sky refused to divulge its plans, but I took the cows being lower as a bad sign. I went up the path again and right down Gleann a' Choilich to be at the tent by ten. It was repitched that night at 9.30 after 7,000 feet of rucksack carrying, quite the longest day in hours out.

The Cluanie Curtain seemed drawn across the south and the Lapaichs received a deluge while I was brewing. It was nice not to be singled out for treatment for once. Everything in the tent was dry. I had a plate of porridge while packing up. The tent flaps had been well weighted with stones. These I carefully removed from the grass—there is no sadder sight than a once bright patch of grass given a smallpox rash by campers leaving stones on it. There was another tent where the river ran into the loch: an obtrusive orange one, a cheery sight, but on the whole I prefer tents to be unseen . . .

Past the eroded peat laid bare at the head of the loch I paddled over to the lower slopes of An Socath. There were quite a few ruins, and an old path heads west down to Iron Lodge: wild country all, but with several bothies and long through routes. This west end of water was once Loch Lungard; today it looked as if it were two lochs still for the narrows a few miles to the east were narrower than usual with the low water level. I took myself well up the hillside, on to Meall Shuas, before sitting to look at it. With the sun shining now, and big cumulus cloud-shadows bowling along the bulky hills, it was a scene both cheery yet empty. Larks were singing in breathless flight overhead.

Beyond the rim of Coire Lungard and before the pull up An Socath's cone, I found a bubbly spring of water. Icy refreshment. The view was better than from the summit a thousand feet higher. Bidean–Lurg Mhor formed its centre: two splendid peaks, claimants for the "remotest" title. Maol-bhuidhe Bothy below them is one we have first-footed on several trips, a bothy defended from most directions by deep rivers. If you visit it in winter, be prepared to join the brass monkey club.

Patt Lodge, five miles along the watery glen from the bothy, sits a few feet above the raised level of Loch Monar, which drowned Strathmore Lodge on the other side. It is still lived in, and must be about the remotest habitation in the country. It is served by boat up the loch, but even the loch is reached up one of the longest and emptiest glens in Scotland. Its nearest town, I suppose, is Beauly.

There is a story of the gaugers arriving from Beauly one day at the end of last century and spending a hot and fruitless day searching the glen. Ready to leave finally, they begged a glass of milk at a croft house. This was given—but laced with some of the local distillation. The officer commented it was "the finest milk I ever tasted" and tactfully withdrew. Another local had told the minister that he would always speak the truth regardless, and this was soon put to the test by the excise arriving to search houses. He was a bit nonplussed but then stammered out, "Awa' in, man. You'll find a barrel o' the best under the bed." With a withering comment, the gaugers passed on elsewhere.

An old crone always used the ruse of feigning idiocy whenever a search was on: sticking her tongue out, rolling her eyes and making awful noises—all the time sitting perched on what they were after.

A. E. Robertson, a great collector of local lore, tells of one Jamie MacRae who was such a notorious smuggler that the landowner could no longer ignore his doings and fixed a pact that ended his trade. He dismantled everything and buried his still. Later at Beauly Market he contacted the excisemen and let it be known that he might be able to help them discover a still, if the stated £5 reward was forthcoming. He then led the party back to Patt and discovered his own still for which he was duly rewarded. A. E. Robertson actually knew Jamie, so the event took place not so long ago. It has always struck me as an iniquity and an infringement of personal liberty that one is not free to distil, as one may brew, one's own stuff. However, if it staves off national insolvency, I suppose we have to put up with it.

I had my drink of cold water and wended on upwards. The Cuillins took their place along the skyline. Sgriol was a big feature as well. Since adding the tent to my load, my shoulder, till then crying out with rheumatism, had been all right again. There is a narrower summit crest to An Socath than you would gather from the map, which is true of all these ridges, which are often craggy too. Names are hardly given to peaks or rivers or anything. The white trig point was oddly balanced on the next bump east by a white sheep. As it was recently shorn it must have made a fast ascent. Filthy Munro-bagger! I saw campion and cyphel in flower on the crest before the steep drop down to the col.

An Riabhachan is also steep from the col, the ridge is well-defined, rooftop narrow in one place and full of the ups and downs of crazy strata; the craggy flanks offer no short cuts. It is a strange hill with a summit ridge running for about two miles at over 3,500 feet. With the distinctive paps of An Socath and Lapaich at either end, it is instantly recognisable from a long way off.

It seemed a long ridge today. From the summit I began to contour down and round but the map's slight portrayal of corries proved to be steep-edged, "scrag" (that unhappy cross between crag and scree) and hard old snow. By the time I was down to the next col I was quite weary. My boots, which I had wired together at Morvich, were now splitting up the back as the stitching went.

I stopped at the burn beyond to brew and paddle, which was refreshing, and I went fast up to the col from Lapaich to Sgurr nan

Clachan Geala, a fine top to its south. This *peak of the white stones* is well named, there is a big white scar on its south flank.

The combing effect was awkward going up Lapaich: it was like marching up irregular stairs. I saw a figure descending to the col, an Edinburgh lad, I later discovered, who was wandering through to Affric—one of the very few real gangrels seen on the trip. At the summit, 3,773 feet, Sgurr na Lapaich, *peak of the miry moss*, is seen for the

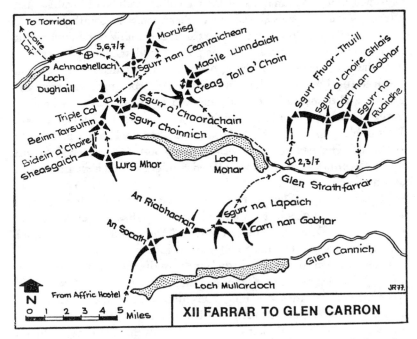

fine hill it is, the spike having a quite misleading name, being the culmination of big ridges and deep, loch-hiding corries. It shows well from the east, where it is used to give the local weather forecast.

I went down the south-east ridge which is very steep and broken, all boulders and slab and steep gullies sloping off, great stuff in winter and a welcome spur today. I overhauled two figures and hurried on to leave the sack at the col and collect Carn nan Gobhar, for the west had turned a black shade of grey that boded ill. Carn nan Gobhar has two cairns to confuse people: one large and old and wrong; the other, smaller, newer, and 200 yards to the north-west is correct—about forty feet higher though it does not always look it. The two figures caught up:

Suilven Strachan and Marion Niven of the L.S.C.C. Their "Dougie" made me long for my "Kitchy". They were camped down below. I wonder how often Sgurr na Lapaich has three parties visiting its cairn?

Most people do these hills from the Loch Mullardoch dam (the water is taken by tunnel to Loch Benevian). Glen Cannich was once Clan Chisholme country. Chisholme's Stone just along from the dam is mute testimony to the Clearances. It is extraordinary that in 1832 evicted clansmen living in Canada sent their chief an address of loyalty—just after they had all been kicked out of their homes in Strathglass.

Garbh-choire should always be treated as a warning, for frequently it means its name, *rough corrie*. This one proved mild, the long gentle slopes just what the weary lad, running before the storm, needed. I was soon down to the forest level, fine old remnants of Scots pine, but awkward ground and desperately hot and muggy. I forded the Uisge Misgeach, to the delight of the midges, then found a bridge not far below the spot. I scrambled up to the Hydro road and then took the old track to Inchvuilt. The race, though, was suddenly lost. Desperately I fought into waterproofs as the heavens opened. I might as well have been in an automatic car-wash.

Boots and all, I splashed through the River Farrar near where the Uisge Misgeach joins it, then bullied myself up to where my cache lay buried. There was a flat spot for the tent, I knew, and it was soon up. I dug up the parcel. The mice had been at it.

I took it down to the river and cleaned up the mess. It was only then I found that just one of four inner parcels had been destroyed but it had to be the one with the loose things like oatmeal, milk powder, sugar and so on. There were lots of tins, to eat here, and enough light stuff to see me through to Gerry's hostel at Achnashellach. Somehow I found myself with seven Gaz refills again.

I stuffed everything into the tent, did a quick peel-off and followed suit. Apart from my feet I was dry enough. The girls would be having a right time on the hill, though. I drank six cups of tea in a row and felt much better. By eleven I had eaten to a disgusting state and lay back with a last coffee listening to the drum of rain just six inches above my ears. A herd of noisy kylos came and stood looking at the tent, mooing mightily. Even a cuckoo added its monotonous call—the last I was to hear for the summer, though I did not know it then of course. There is a certain romance to rain when one is safely out of it.

The Ripleys probably thought otherwise while here. Their tent-pole snapped in a storm during breakfast and they had to seek shelter at Broulin Lodge. Two days later, at Loch Mullardoch, they were flooded out. Who says history does not repeat itself?

It was too dark to write up the log. It had been a close-run day, all the way from Glen Affric with the Lapaichs thrown in. But I was through, well-stocked, and surely could make Gerry's now. I drifted off to sleep to the swish and roar and patter of water. Chesterton once wrote, "The roaring of the rains of God none but the lonely love." I would not have swopped my little tent in the rain for a palace in the sun.

Wednesday 3 July   THE FARRAR FOUR

Over breakfast I wrote up yesterday's log, and there was quite a bit of tidying up, so it was nearly nine before I set off into a world glistening, but dry. Shiel, Affric, Lapaichs, Farrar had given transverse ridges after ridges which I had been stitching together steadily. The Farrar Four were the last of these before the crossing of Strathcarron, a glen which was coming to have the lure that the Great Glen once had had, weeks ago.

A path led up, from near the tent to the west end of the ridge, by the splashy, noisy stream of Loch Toll a' Mhuic, a corrie lochan set round with crags. It then became vague and ended with a rising line under Fearstaig to gain the main ridge. Fearstaig, a Top, means *sea pink* or *thrift* but there was none in evidence. I was soon blown up Sgurr Fhuar-thuill, *cold hole*, the first of the Munros. These four are an easy group, as if nature had expended all her efforts on Shiel, Affric and Lapaich. I like them. There is a grand highway feeling and they are not cluttered round with other hills. North lay the Strath Conon hills, no Munros, so seldom visited—great hills, often admired from Achnasheen over Strath Bran, but seldom climbed. I had been exploring Telford churches when they first showed themselves. The view south and west is of the big ranges. Lapaich is at its best. It is told that one of the Frasers of Strathfarrar, who was to fall with Wolfe at Quebec, slipped out of his barracks at Inverness the night before they were to embark and took his homesick way to the glen just to look west to Sgurr na Lapaich once more.

I could see clearly as far as the Loch Treig hills to the south. North I could see Klibreck, the penultimate peak, in Sutherland. Quite encouraging. Another Top was skipped to gain Sgurr a' Choire Ghlais, the dominant Munro of the four (3,354 feet). You can take your pick of two cairns and a trig point in between. The descent beyond was slippery as the mossy surface was apt to slide off. Number three was another Carn nan Gobhar. In the lee of the cairn I piled on my Damart clothing. The sky was turning grey again—a repeat of yesterday?

I left a note in the cairn and wondered if Suilven and Marion would find it, but they came down by the tent in the evening and said they had not observed it. The paper had been picked up about half an hour after I had hidden it. Harrold Thomson from Glasgow answered the question, "Are you a Munro-bagger? (be honest)" with "Of course!" With 210 clocked up he could hardly be anything else. It was interesting to see how these remoter, beyond the Great Glen ones, were being done by people with big tallies—the Lord High Executioners of the game. I was to meet Harrold in the autumn when showing slides to the Glasgow Glenmore Club. I wonder if he has managed to finish his round yet? The nearer the end, the harder they become.

A quartzy crest drops for the pull to Sgurr na Ruaidhe. The rain came on and it poured all the way up and much of the way down till I was nearly out of the Allt a' Mhuillin glen. I came on a Stevenson Frame with rain gauge and anemometer and recalled once catching my lads "birling" the latter round, quite innocent of what they might be doing to the weather records.

Strathfarrar is a sad, cleared glen, with many ruins pointing to a considerable population once. A mention in 1848 tells of burning twelve miles of pine, oak and birch to "improve" the sheep pasture. Now there are cows back—but not people. Young birds seemed to be everywhere too. I saw young wheatear, stonechat and cuckoo.

Remembering to wind my watch was always an effort. It had stopped again today but the girls were able to tell me the hour. I am sure life was not intended to be lived by the clock anyway. Cycling up here just after the war I once asked a local the time and was told it was "near enough Thursday". In a Bed and Breakfast I asked the date, being confused in my log, and the man of the house searched for a newspaper, then declared, "She is saying the twentieth of July, whenever that was."

I had started steaming a Christmas pudding as soon as I reached the tent so, not for the first time, had my meal in reverse: the pudding with cream; chicken fillets with carrots and cabbage; leek soup. I stayed in the tent for warmth; though dry it was piercingly cold, no doubt snowing on the Lapaich. The landscape had a bruised yellow and black look to it.

The Farrar Four are usually done from the south like this. The glen is barred by a locked gate but a key can be obtained at Struy for day visitors—or you can cycle, an example set by Munro himself, who took a day off stalking in Glen Cannich to bag these hills. He mentions that there was a crofter's cottage where the Allt a' Mhuillin comes down to the Strath. It has now gone. The locals pronounced it Moily, though it is on the map as Mulie, and the Bartholomew map gives Millie. It could simply derive from Mhuillin which is a *mill*. Complications with the transliteration of Gaelic names are not new. It was to an island on Loch a' Mhuilinn that Lovat fled after the 1745 while Cannich was the Prince's furthest north.

I could hear a hunting kestrel from the tent. Wildlife was a vital part of the Walk's enjoyment but being on the side of the birds, I have only made casual mention of commoner things: the haunts of snow bunting, dotterel, greenshank, osprey, divers for instance I would not mention. Gone are the days, I hope, of "There was an osprey nesting in Glen Letmeslay, and I've got the eggs to prove it." Another great pleasure was seeing the grand sweep of seasons: I had gone from purple saxifrage to purple Carlin heather on the botanical scale, from the north-flying geese to the falling-silent of the cuckoo on the ornithological calendar; winter, spring, summer had come with a sweep that was Wagnerian instead of the normal weekend *Eine Kleine Nachtmusik*. There was wonder in it all; on the grand scale and on the small.

The mouse came into the tent with its nose quivering. Did it already know of human goodies, I wondered, one of the despoilers of my parcel? Or was it just hiding from the wind-hovering kestrel? Like as not it happened to live here and I had come along and pitched on top of its High Street. Years ago I recall sitting in a wood when a squirrel came racing along, to trip, head over heels, across my legs—obviously an unexpected blockage on its street. Anyway, the mouse soon began to rummage about. I was lying on my tummy with a bit of Vita Wheat in my hand and it tickled its way across my knuckles and happily started eating it. A piece broke off, so it picked this up and sat back, on my hand still, and nibbled away at it, shoving it in with both hands. At home or in a hut I would no doubt have had another reaction to such daylight robbery; but as we were both living close to the soil, what was a bit of cardboard between friends? Why it should have been so unconcerned I do not know. Perhaps I had been out so long now, that I just smelt part of the landscape.

Thursday 4 July   TRIPLE PEAKS TO TRIPLE COL

Four Gaz cartridges, a jar of honey, a midge spray and some tins were reburied; weeks later Mike Keates collected them when in the glen. It was grey and cloudy when I set off up to the dam. Noisy gulls were calling on the islands with their drowned skeletons of trees. Monar Lodge was noisy with dogs of all kinds. One terrier was all for joining me and several miles on had to be driven off by mock severity and pretended stone-throwing. When Lapaich cleared I heaved a sigh of relief. The day would be all right.

The Lodge slipway only just reached the water, it was so low. Boats lay like stranded fish. Later a buzzing from the west materialised as the shepherd from Patt making a trip out, no doubt glad of a dry day. New stalking paths run along the shore with well-made bridges—a nice change from the usual ill-made Land-Rover tracks gouged out by bulldozers. Being careful I omitted a wanted Corbett, An Sithean, the *fairy hill*, and later in the year received a real drubbing on it for my canniness now. Various routes were possible but I took the most direct approach to today's peak—if peak can be used of such a hill, the flattest of bulks. It is generally known as Maoile Lunndaidh though the Tables gave Creag Toll a' Choin as the highest summit—the new Tables and maps have now reversed this just as they have swopped Creise and Clachlet above Rannoch Moor.

New paths seemed to be everywhere, I followed several in turn, from burn to burn, gaining height almost effortlessly to the lip of the Toll a' Choin, *dog's corrie*, the rim of which I climbed up to the cairn. I went out to the other one and back to make sure of the Munro! Willie Milne of Forfar found the questionnaire I left—several weeks later. To my "Are you a Munro-bagger (be honest)?" he replied, "At times". Humph! With 230 and on that remote spot. He did add, "Today, yes", to hedge his bet.

My log waxed quite ecstatic over the view—which I placed with Dorain and Sgriol as supreme this trip. It ended: "But it was the opening of the north that made the day. Apart from some Deargs, Assynt and Sutherland, all the hills to go were suddenly in view: this whole area, the Coire Lair hills, the Torridon giants, Slioch, the Whitbread Wilderness, the Fannichs, Wyvis . . . Wow!"

Spurred on by this revelation of an ending I wended round the rim of strange Fuar Tholl Mor, crossed the plateau and dropped to the col. The sole was coming off my left boot, now, but I hoped it would last up to Loch Gaineamhach where I wanted to picnic. Just two strides off the loch it flapped off completely. I sat and brewed by the outflow, fixed the sole and then went on round the corrie rim for Sgurr a' Chaorachain of the ringing name. Bidean an Eoin Deirg is just a Top, but a bold, fine peak too: the whole flank above the loch is good in winter as is the traverse from Chaorachain to its twin Munro, Sgurr Choinnich, a peak the O.S. seemed to have given up, for it is no plateau as they suggest, but sometimes knife-edged and builds up big cornices. There is a toplet where the Conbhaire ridge joins, then the summit cairn perched on the precipice, then a lumpy, airy ridge to a grassy bump and the descent to the triple col of Bhearnais.

The view west from this ridge set me into glee again—the dazzle of sea and sun with Rhum, Skye, Sgriol, Knoydart all there. I could even see a tiny Ben Nevis, while the near hills were great, and north lay An Teallach and Coigach—vanishing into a haze of apple redness. Even Moruisg, across the Pollan Buidhe, sprawled like a contented lion, soaking up the sun. "It should purr," I wrote. It is as well we cannot see the future. Moruisg was to growl. This was the last day of fine weather I was to have.

I pitched the tent on the triple col, its door to Lurg Mhor, its back to Feartaig. I sprawled on the dry turf very happily doing nothing, except when frogs would insist on trying to burrow under me. The solitary life was no hardship. I was never lonely. At a lecture after the trip I was taken to task by one gentleman who said in forty years on the hill he had never yet gone alone. I felt sorry for him. Did not Munro, in the very first volume of the S.M.C. Journal, write of the joys of being alone, especially when it was hard. Until one can relish going alone experience is incomplete, or at least, less complete. Solitude, tonight, was like a benediction.

Friday 5 July DIRTY TRICKS

Between the Bealach Bhearnais camp and the Bidean–Lurg Mhor Munros is another Beinn Tharsuinn. I have tried every way to sneak past it and warn the reader, the easiest is just to go over it. It is a good hill which drops steeply to the Bealach an Sgoltaidh beyond which lies the intimidating "end" of Bidean a' Choire Sheasgaich, a cliff deserving some attention from climbers. Walkers go round. If you enjoy a bit of scrambling, a steep gully breaks upwards through the black cliffs to end just beside a tiny pool.

From there, several rock steps lead on along the shoulder. There is another loch, shown on the map, which is deep enough to give a swim. Not today though, the rain had started and it was in a gloomy mist I teetered along to the summit of Bidean a' Choire Sheasgaich. Thanks to Philip Tranter there is now a peak in the Hindu Kush called Koh-i-Sisgeikh. (There is also a Koh-i-Morusg.) *Small peak of the reedy corrie* is the translation of Sheasgaich; Lurg Mhor, its brother, is just *long shank*, which is what it is.

I reached it after a dedicated plod through the rain and left a note there, which was to have quite an eventful life. With the Bernais bothy being worked on by the Mountain Bothies Association at that time, I did not expect it to last long on such a handy Munro. Nor did it. It was found two days later by Bob Aitken, an old Alpine partner and companion on scores of Munros. He and Penny were not at the bothy either, but they wrote to me. Oddly, I had not long ago written to them.

Aberdeen 9th July

Dear Hamish,

I was intrigued to have your letter. I'd begun to suspect something was afoot when I tried to imagine what "big trek" could interest you! Speculation was cut short on Sunday when Penny and I were your "first comers" on Lurg Mhor, two days after you had been.

We went over to the West thinking about Skye but we caught the heavy showers and blasts of gale at Achnashellach so drove over the Bealach na Ba (spectacular in that weather) and—tell it not in Gath—took Bed and Breakfast in Applecross. It was grim, with waves breaking over the road, so we don't envy you your day on Lurg Mhor!

On Saturday we trekked up to the Bealach Bhearnais, camped there, and went up Feartaig to watch a watery sunset. On Sunday we did Sheasgaich–Lurg Mhor. I certainly had not thought to tread so close on your heels. Like Dow or whoever it was said about the four beards over every top before him. . . . Anyway since it was us, we left the questionnaire for the next comers—might be interesting to see how long it is. The M.B.A. however seem out in force. We could see their tents at Bernais from afar. I hope the weather cheers up for you and the midges are not too bad. A night in Glen Etive last weekend warned us.

Look forward to hearing more. Yours,

Bob.

The questionnaire did not turn up. However, in October at Carlisle, at the M.B.A.'s A.G.M. the bothy, ben and bike tandem of Bernard and Betty Heath confessed to having found it. At a ceilidh at Bernais it was filled in so facetiously that they decided it could not be sent! This couple, now living in Thurso, are probably the most famous of all bothy folk. They became engaged while working at one; the only surprise is that they wed in a church. Just think what they missed: an archway of saws and trowels, spotted dick (a sort of Polyfilla) instead of wedding cake, bare boards to sleep on. . . . Bernais was being done up as a memorial to Eric Beard, a friend of mine, a friend of all, who had been killed on the M6. "Beardie" and his honey butties will long be remembered, like Ian Clough, Tom Patey and Jim MacArtney, not just for his feats, but for the marvellous person he was. Those four dying within a year gave Scottish climbing a set-back it took time to get over. Beardie was most famous for his record runs, some never equalled yet: things like the Cuillin Ridge in four hours, or the Cairngorms big four from Glenmore in the same time. He had *run* Nevis—Scafell Pike—Snowdon.

At Gerry's the next day I read about Beardie in *Mountain*, and also of John Merrill setting off on a 1,300-mile walk along the Irish west coast; "the longest ever in the U.K." (I hoped the Republic liked being called U.K.) He expected to carry 40 pounds and wear out a pair of boots. After today I stood at 1,367 miles—and hardly coastal walking. I trembled a bit at the thought that even then someone might just be completing a walk over all the Munros. Though any idea of a race is one I would hate, I did not fool myself about the priority: I wanted to be first.

Anyway, Lurg Mhor was far from anywhere; all would be revealed in a few weeks more. Lurg Mhor was a sentimental journey in that it was Braehead School's last Munro. Coming off it Alan Moreland was adopted by a two-day-old deer calf to his embarrassment. We had done the round from Gerry's. Gerry had been worried that an old couple, the Bells, had set off for these hills and not come back, but I told him Jimmy and Pat Bell were no doubt snug somewhere. They were too.

At over seventy he had found it tough going, so they found a howff for the night. "Och, I had a bar of chocolate to eat and my wife to keep me warm." David McNab, one of the lads, who had climbed on the Ben (and since in the Alps and Norway), was amazed to meet this figure from the past. "He's really *the* J. H. B. Bell who did routes in 1929? But Hamish, he's history!"

I had a brew back on the Bealach Bhearnais while the tent rattled in the rising storm, then followed the flooding path down to the valley, There is a bridge over the Pollan Buidhe down a bit, but with soaked feet I just walked through the river. It was tempting to abort for the day and do Moruisg tomorrow from Gerry's but that would add quite a bit of walking, so being lazy, I did it today—or it did me rather. The eternal optimist I put the tent up "to dry off". In the teeming rain I walked up the road to Glenuaig Lodge. In this game you have to take the bad with the good. "If ye flee wi' the craws ye mun hoot wi' the owls." Moruisg deserves better than it receives from most visitors. Most Munro-baggers nip up and down it from a high spot on the Glen Carron road and get poor reward. Both north and south of Moruisg and on Sgurr nan Ceannaichean in particular are fine corries and winter routes on faces and gullies. The summit is a succession of slight swellings, each cairned, so being sure in mist is problematical unless you have seen it clear previously. I went up by an old stalkers' path behind the Lodge. This led to rainswept bogs. My poor compass hand froze again. I intended to traverse along to Ceannaichean and down to the tent from a path off it, but on reaching its slopes the fight directly into the horizontal rain had become dangerously prolonged and I cut down. Several times I would start to step forward—and end several steps backwards. It was a fight to make any progress *downhill*. Munro, under such conditions, occupied his mind debating whether such activity was classified as "a hobby or a crime". I was concerned for my tent, left lightly pegged in a glen which had become a wild wind tunnel.

The tent still stood. I had left some food soaking, so cooked and ate it and had a brew. Periodically big gusts set everything racketing wildly. One blow was unlike anything I have ever known: for five minutes it just poured through, then casually switched off. I had been hugging the poles. It was high time to remove. About two years later the Corbett Sgurr nan Ceannaichean was promoted to a new Munro. This I think was a mean trick!

I went quickly down the road to Gerry's, for the time was already after seven. There were deer as usual on the strath before the drop into the big forest of Strathcarron. The river was running dirty and high. The hostel was very welcome: known faces, hot bath, a drying room, music. I intended making the most of it.

The iron door to the North was now open at last. I had had eight days in a row since Morvich and they gave high averages of 17 miles and 5,600 feet per day. Mike Keates arrived having come round via Morvich to pick up the bike and parcels—and he brought spare boots.

Saturday 6 July GERRY'S

Mike went off for An Ruadh Stac, one of the area's best hills, though not a Munro. I had a "rest day", which meant telephone calls, clothes' washing, log writing, rubberising the tent seams, dealing with mail, cooking and entertaining visitors.

Bob Wilson and family looked in from a holiday up north in the morning and in the evening Ann Winning and Pam Cain called, *en route* for Bernais bothy. Richard Longford, the resident geologist, gave a lecture on the planets, Liz was typing away in her caravan, Andy Cronshaw was playing his flute upstairs all day. Gerry alone seemed to be taking his ease, enjoying his recent retirement from the railway.

"Hostel" perhaps brings to mind the wrong image; Gerry's, like Nancy Smith's at Fersit, is the very antithesis of the usual youth hostel. One is assumed to be reasonably sane, sanitary and sober for a start. Rules and hours there are none. Those mountain types who have discovered its comforts (beds, baths, drying room, store, music . . .) are in the habit of returning. I am sure I had seen everyone there before. Gerry converted a row of railway cottages into this haven.

Trains pass close to the front fence—the scenic and fascinating Kyle line which probably survives only as a commercial sacrifice to the Mammon of Kishorn. The original line went to Strome (1870), the Kyle addition coming in 1897. Now Strome is the loading place for the platform site. The railway was foretold in the early seventeenth century by the Brahan Seer, who lived near Dingwall. He had prophesied, "Every stream will have its bridge, balls of fire will pass rapidly up and down Strath Peffer and carriages without horses shall leave Dingwall to cross the country from sea to sea."

Achnashellach is a quiet spot where the glen levels out into strath, rather deep-set among the forested hills, rather wet, and very much a haven. It has been the place for several years now to which I have come with Christmas "courses". Christmas dinner there has become a tradition. Gerry makes a fine stuffing to go with the duck—plus all the usual trimmings. It is a crazy contrast to come trekking through the winter hills and then sit down to such *haute cuisine*. One Christmas Day it was so wet the hills were just not possible, so we went down to the Carron for some river-crossing practice, an aspect of training which is apt to be skipped, but several present on that occasion were glad of the knowledge when it had to be applied in reality in arctic Norway. The Carron, 100 feet wide and waist deep, was an impressive sight. In it, my new waterproof trousers filled with water—and then "exploded", the pressure splitting all the seams wide open.

Achnashellach Hostel is sited in a glen without other accommodation and is a key link in through routes: from the east as I'd come, or west to Torridon (Youth Hostel or Ling Hut). The whole area has fine rights-of-way—such as the Coulin Pass just above the hostel, the Torridon end of which A. E. Robertson regarded as one of the most beautiful spots in Scotland. Achnashellach is the *field of the willows*.

James Hogg, the Ettrick Shepherd, explored here in 1803 and letters of his tour, written to Sir Walter Scott, were later published. He walked to Strathcarron from Lochaber. At Craig, Achnashellach, he had hoped for a bed but could only find whisky and Gaelic-speakers so was forced over the pass to Kinlochewe, where he arrived "somewhat fatigued". I knew just the feeling—but I also knew of Gerry's.

Sunday 7 July THE BEGINNING OF THE END
I had originally planned to do a series of regular articles during the walk, but decided this would be a form of slavery and rather impractical as well. Also, I would hate to be beaten and the whole world know it. Now, however, I felt I could let the cat leak out of the bag! It would be an added incentive. So I sent off an article to Lesley Munn at the *Glasgow Herald*, with pictures which had been taken earlier on the trip.

Mike went off to swim up Fuar Tholl. The rain swept along the tops of the forest. I would begin tomorrow with the crossing to Torridon, and beyond lay just on thirty Munros, often in good groupings of five or six a day. I could therefore look on this happy respite as the beginning of the end.

XIII

TORRIDONS

"An explorer says, I am not going to let life trample upon me. I am going to trample on myself. What is more, I am going to do it for fun."

FREYA STARK

Monday 8 July   THE REDS AND THE GREY

The forecast was unhappily correct and I finally left the lost world of Achnashellach Station at 8.30, fully waterproofed for the silvery heather path and the wetness of the forest.

The Station is a lonely spot. In 1892 the engine of the Dingwall–Kyle train was detached in the glen here to do some shunting and the brake van failed to do its job. The engine-less train bore the passengers off down the incline until a rise brought it to a halt. It then began to run back the way it had come. In true Hoffnung fashion it met the engine coming to look for it. Achnashellach was originally a "private" station for Viscount Hill's country residence, but the glory has long since departed.

I splashed away up the path through the great pines. Fuar Tholl, that dominating, heartless bulk of mountain, was hidden in mist. Coire Lair, while as fine as any, was a mess of dirty cloud. I wandered along in a dream, familiar landmarks passing as blindly as features on a foggy trip from office to suburbia, and had to shake myself consciously back to the task in hand. The red Torridonian sandstone then gave good scrambling; up on to the grey Cambrian quartzite, rough and slippery; up to the muffled summit of Beinn Liath Mhor, which was very much a *big grey hill.*

It is the only Munro which needed a third attempt to climb it at all. On the first Joe Matyssek, Mike Smith and I had turned from the Coulin Pass to add it. It chased us off with a wicked summer hailstorm. We ran down the vile flanking screes like mad things just to warm up again. The old hostel at Achnashellach was very welcome that night. The hill also gave a Christmas camp recently when a big dry wind rattled the tents all night. We had no flysheets—optimistically being above freezing level—so it was as well it stayed dry. Candles were blown out *through* the canvas walls. Wild dawn had us looking across to the mighty miles of Liathach: shattered walls leering out of prehistory—a startling reminder of our brief snowy span of years. Red and black and white were the colours of reveille that Christmas day.

Alas, no view today to the Torridon array. It was just, out with the compass, turn about and bundle down to the track, then follow it up

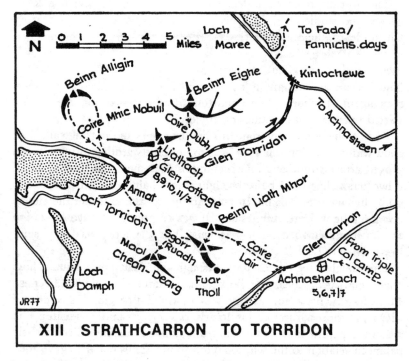

XIII   STRATHCARRON   TO   TORRIDON

into the throat of the pass. A circle of stones by the shivering lochan gave scant shelter for a snack and once again previous knowledge came in handy—I skirted crags happily through the mist to gain the ridge up Sgorr Ruadh, *red peak*, the highest of these hills twixt Carron and Torridon. I retraced my steps to the pass without a pause.

Coire Lair is lined on one side by the two-mile flank of Beinn Liath Mhor, on the other by Sgorr Ruadh and Fuar Tholl; this latter is the better side, having some savage rock climbing (and good winter climbing) which has attracted climbers such as Patey, Marshall, MacInnes, Boysen—which should be hint enough.

The pass could never be dull, and under the beating of storm gained stature today. Once through it, the path swings west for the Bealach Ban and the Coulags Glen which runs down to Strath Carron again. (All the paths on the map are fine stalkers' paths.) Half way up the Coulags Glen is Clach nan Con Fionn, the *stone of Fionn's hounds,* yet another where this legendary hero is supposed to have tethered his hunting dogs.

The mist cleared on the Bealach Ban, so I had some sardine sandwiches and studied the third peak of the day across the Glen: Maol Chean-dearg, the *bald red hill.* My path cut across the head of the Glen to the Bealach na Lice (pronounced: leek), the *pass of the slabs,* which then descended to Loch Torridon—my obvious way out. Above lay a bald, red buttress, so after a bit of heather bashing I was soon on sound rock again. The best of the buttress proved too wet, so had to be skirted but there was scrambling enough.

I was soon on top—and soon off! Some winters ago we had come up a good winter gully on the north cliff, so curiosity led down it today. It proved a disintegrating rubbish chute in "summer" conditions. Below it lay tiers of lochans, about which deer were milling, having been put up by five walkers. The deer were a strange mixture of pale and rufous colours. The walkers only realised they were being followed later. On one loch a whooper swan was calling and later passed overhead flying down to Loch Torridon with a regular swish of great cloud wings. The path, following the tilted strata of the sandstone, curved round and down to Annat; sea-level again, the last time being way back at Morvich.

One of the oddities of this trip was how seldom the sea-line was followed; a pity as so much of the charm of our hills lies in their balanced relation to the sea, too often it was

> A far-off fringe of sea,
> Half-glimpsed, like eternity.

I wandered along to the cafe at the Beinn Damph Hotel and buntered down a large afternoon tea. Mike had planned to leave the cycle here to cut the road plod up to Glen Cottage, but there was no sign of it, so I set off to walk, speculating imaginatively. . . .

At the Fasag junction someone had daintily painted over a "sheep" road sign to turn it into one showing a mammoth. It rapidly had become a minor tourist attraction, the N.T.S. Tourist Office not infrequently receiving quite serious queries as to where the elephants could be seen. Alas, bureaucracy being what it is, the appropriate road works department was not amused. In the autumn I noticed it was back to a sheep again.

Mike, mercifully, had not gone astray, but had left the bike at another path we had been discussing. As I had the cycle padlock by mistake he had used his, a combination one, to chain it to a fence. A note cryptically told me the combination: "Your house number + 78 × 100 + 2." Who but a mathematics lecturer could have dreamt that up? He was soon dishing out game soup, cod and white sauce with delicious fresh vegetables; fruit and cream.

Glen Cottage remains, for many of us, filled with memories of Dave and Liz Goulder who had run it as another independent hostel. Because of their musical talents it came to stand for something as sweet as the song of the pines that gave it shelter. It did not quite suit the tweedy N.T.S. image however; so Dave and Liz went out, and on their separate ways—only Liathach of the red tiers of rock and the grey tears of tumbling waters, only Liathach remained, inscrutable as the Sphinx.

> Stronger than all who sang or wrote,
> Mountain of seasons; it never spoke.

Now the cottage was a temporary Youth Hostel, run by Irene Reilley, while husband Neil was one of the squad working on the palatial new hostel down at Fasag. The Reilleys are kindly folk and the evening passed quickly with chat and song. Neil got out a Jew's harp. An Edinburgh school party made it homely.

The S.M.C. have a hut just up the road by Lochan an Iasgaich—so even when the Glen Cottage closes there is still cheaper, non-institutional accommodation available for climbers.

It had turned stormy again by the time we lay in the bunk house. The pines strummed and danced before the black, blank skerry wall of Liathach. I slept poorly. Too well fed? Or the powerful cups of coffee? Or the cows bellowing the night long?

Tuesday 9 July TRIPTYCH: ALLIGIN

Alligin, gashed and gabled like some semi-ruined fortress, is the furthest west of the great three. Worth a good day for its view of sea and peaks, for us it was still dreich and any idea of all three big Torridon peaks in the day rather went the way of the sun. Mike and I set off up Coire Mhic Nobuil at 9.30, dedicated rather than delighted.

At the first wee fall we crossed the bridge and angled up into Coire a' Mhadaidh. There I enjoyed crossing the huge boulderfield, scrambling in and out of subterranean regions in search of odd plants and just oddities in general. Mike had differing thoughts of what was enjoyable, but having been beguiled into the middle of this geological maelstrom going on was the quickest way out. The Great Cleft of Alligin was the source of this massive stonefall. It must have been impressive to see a few million tons of rock trundle at once!

The boulders wasted a happy hour but the procrastination failed to improve the weather. As we bore up right the falls coming down the cliff were simply being blasted back up again. We zig-zagged up the slopes of Toll a' Mhadaidh Beag to land right by the cairn. It gave a wild picnic spot. The "Horns", the bumpy pinnacles of the eastern arm, briefly showed, with a cloud-churning Liathach beyond. It was as well we had not chosen the full round of Alligin. The going was a bit better away from the cone of Sgurr Mhor, as the highest point is called. Beinn Alligin is the *jewelled mountain*.

Under the cone of the Sgurr, the Great Cleft was "woofing" as the gale drove up its narrow throat. You could step in and out of the flow of wind. The rim round to Tom na Gruagaich gave no real difficulties, but from its top we took a bearing to ensure we descended Coire nan Laoigh. Being the normal ascent route its worn track soon made the compass superfluous.

We met a dog dashing about and lower down the owner peching up, an older lad. I'd taken a photograph of the corrie depths, with Loch Torridon white-lined below. It was raining hard for the heathery, myrtle slopes above the road. Bog asphodel was in flower, no doubt it relished the conditions.

From the cross-roads, we drove on an off-route visit to the Beinn Damph for tea. There deluge followed deluge. Back at the cross-roads I reverted to self-propulsion. I stopped to photograph the road sign of the mammoth. I could not find my precious Rollei camera. Somewhere descending it must have fallen out—it was a very despondent gangrel who returned to the Glen Cottage. I phoned the N.T.S. centre, I left a message for Donny at the shop, I tried to telephone the local police at Loch Carron, but it was his night off. I sulked off to bed to dream of mammoths and prehistoric things trampling cameras on Alligin.

Wednesday 10 July   TRIPTYCH: LIATHACH

> Too much wind is wearing
> But too much rain is sad;
> Better Ardnamurchan
> Than Torridonian slab.

An early start paid off. Forecast and estimations pointed to a reasonable morning before the return of the monsoon. Liathach dry would be a treat.

Mike and I went straight up from behind the cottage: a brutal ascent but Liathach hardly gives any gentle approach. We scrambled up the rocks of the burn itself to avoid the deep heather. It was an impatient stream, babbling a childish persuasion and hurrying off down to the wood, and the meandering Torridon River. From above the view is strangely like a contour relief model, for the rock strata runs horizontally in regular steps. It's a landscape where the hard bones of creation lie just below the surface.

In a *Climber & Rambler* survey I once did, Liathach and An Teallach were chosen way ahead of all else as the two most magnificent peaks in Scotland. Liathach is the more demanding. You could climb An Teallach with your hands in your pockets—but not Liathach. Its long length gives no gentle route; few places outside Skye give situations all day where a slip holds the possibility of testing immortality.

The Torridon hills are N.T.S. property and the Trust, sadly, have signposted paths and encouraged visitors. Bodies, I suppose, always feel they must justify themselves and be seen to be actively developing— but surely that is the last thing good for mountain regions. Any parks system for Scotland has in it these destructive seeds. Kurt Diemberger writes: "It is not only the beautiful which we seek; the tremendous draws us irresistibly." He could have had this barrier of spears in mind.

We climbed our happiness hour by hour up to the crest and perched on the quartzite cone like the lords of creation. Description would be prosaic.

From below the way often looks barred by sandstone steps but these above the cottage can be turned easily enough. (On descent only the heathery ledges are visible and the drops are hidden.) Above half height the last steps are passed and only long grassy slopes remain up to the ridge. From there you look dizzily down to the north corrie lochan—Loch Coire na Caime—and realise just what a crest it is.

Westward lies the Am Fasarinen pinnacles, once dutifully climbed, now, like the Cuillin ridge, often scored with easier by-passing paths. Even the contouring paths are spectacular, however. Originally they were deer or sheep tracks which wended in and out of improbable gullies and crags on the glen side. The cliffs are sheer to the north. Ringing Coire na Caime to the west are the famous Northern Pinnacles. Mullach an Rathain is the fine west-end big peak beyond which lie reasonable routes up or down. Eastward lies the quartz cream-topping to the sandstone cake: Spidean a' Choire Liath, the *peak of the grey corrie*, the highest of all Liathach's spires, once the memory-aiding height of 3,456 feet, now merely 1,054 metres.

It is quite a situation, but all too often it is shrouded in mist and drizzle, if nothing worse; after a score of ascents I cannot recall having had much weather-luck on it. Reputedly you can see from Ben Nevis to Ben Hope; but on a clear night you can see the moon!

The "tourist route" is now a worn groove up Coire Liath, a classic example of concentrated use encouraged by cairning. It swings right at the top to gain the crest a long way from the summit. The high slopes of bare grass can be very slippery—both in snow or when really dry. It is a fine ridge-walk once up.

Today, as on most visits, Mike and I descended what I regard as "my" route—which is all I am going to say about it. It takes you down sneakily yet directly. The deep heather just before the road was active with thousands of mottled butterflies. The coos were causing havoc to the tourist traffic by wandering up the tarmac—and not using passing places to allow overtaking. I came on someone I knew, John Cheesmond, who was about to set off up Liathach, so enjoyed a bit of a gossip. Many hours later he came in to the cottage for a brew—very wet and bedraggled. Liathach was back to normal.

As Mike and I were down by 1.30 we went off in his car, first to the Beinn Damph for tea and pancakes then, in the returning deluge, to search the slopes of Alligin for my Rollei. This being the smallest of cameras able to take slides it was precious. We did not find it. I telephoned the police, left word at the N.T.S. centre and with the Reilleys. We continued our trippery doings by running up to Kinlochewe to collect a parcel from the MacBriartys at the hotel.

By the time we were back at Glen Cottage the weather was atrocious.

It blew in mobs of stray French and German lads who stood dripping in the crowded kitchen. Talk of innocents abroad! Names on maps had been taken for villages (back in France) and they had the scantiest of gear to face a Torridon storm. We found one huddle of youngsters under a small canvas square tied between some trees, desperately trying to light a bonfire. The village hall I think took them after desperate phonings by Mrs Reilley, and Jim Hall ferrying them in the Liberton bus. Like fieldfare, the last stragglers seemed to take days to clear the area. We later heard tales all down this coast of their wanderings . . .

The weather was very similar to yesterday's—both as to type and to timings—as if even it could not think up anything original for once. We sat in the noisy, steamed-up common room: walkers and hillmen all. One of the Edinburgh gang was a good guitar player and they all were quietly efficient. It reminded me very much of Braehead. We had a wild dash through the gale to the bunk house, crazy house-lights flooding out among the dancing trees and the rods of rain glittering as they fell on the scurrying figures.

The Torridons were certainly playing it rough. The Ripleys had done all three in the one day—a contrast to this desperate hen-pecking of mine. A Cairngorm Club Journal of 1908 had a nice description of Liathach, now both gladly and sadly done.

"Liagush, rising sheer
From river-bed up to the sky,
Grey courses of masonry, tier on tier,
And pinnacles splintered on high.

"Splintered, contorted, and riven
As though from the topmost crown
Some giant plougher his share had driven
In a hundred furrows sheer down."

Thursday 11 July   TRIPTYCH: EIGHE
"A wicked day: six lashings while out over five and a half hours. Still it was the 250-up and into the twenties to go.

"We used the Coire Dubh path a bit and then crossed the river to plod up to the ridge, keeping to vegetation east of the scree flanks. One pause. Steep but easy going though it landed us on the stony, cloudy ridge further along than expected and there seemed dozens of ups and downs before Coinneach Mhor. Occasionally the mist tore apart to give grim views of Coire Ruadh-Staca. The stream falling from the lochan in its black heart waved about at the wind's will. We hurried out to the Munro." Such was the brief log account of a hard-enough ascent, albeit the easiest way to the Munro, Ruadh-stac Mor.

Beinn Eighe (pronounced "A" as in "aid") could roughly be compared to a curvaceous letter F lying on its back so that in the west there is a deeply enclosed north corrie with a long leg running east. The highest point, the vital Munro, of course, is out at the end of one side of the corrie, so it poses problems. My own favourite "bagging" day would be to sweep round the Coire Dubh path to enjoy that walk between Liathach and Eighe, then round to gain Coire Mhic Fhear-chair (a claimant for the title of the most dramatic in all Scotland). From there scrambling can lead one to the top of Sail Mhor, the "top" on the western prong of the F. There is a rock step before you can swing east on to the long main ridge. This can cause fun or despair depending on visibility and capability. Once past it you may spot the odd piece of aircraft wreckage. Some of it is strewn right down the cliffs. You can actually belay to wedged wreckage climbing on the routes—some of the finest in the land. I have seen deer chewing away at it.

At Coinneach Mhor, if you want the Munro, you drop down to a col (where we cringed to eat) and out along that prong of the F. You then retrace back to Coinneach and end along the main ridge: peak after peak built into a grey wall between Glen Torridon on the right and a prehistoric landscape to the left—an area of bare rock, bogs and a thousand lochans, bleak in the extreme. This way of doing all the minutiae of Bheinn Eighe ensures the thirsty traveller ends at the Kinlochewe end, where there is an hotel.

Today we were denied any view of the great corrie, its dramatic tiers of crags (routes of classic vintage, routes of frightening severity and routes as yet only dotted lines to the eyes of faith or fancy), its deep-set loch, its view out into that spacious, silver-stippled wilderness with a windy Hebridean sky rimming the furthest beyond. Our heads were bowed as dedicatedly as any mendicant—or bingo-playing house-wife. Every now and then the rain squalls knocked us about. We thankfully scrabbled up the final off-white cone of scree, then did a smart about-turn.

From the "picnic" col we traversed fairly easily to the main ridge and baled off down the flank—a midden of scree and scrag but fast.

K

We scattered deer: one fine royal and a switch among them. We chuntered down the Coire Dubh path to the road. Across the lochan we could see the S.M.C. Ling Hut, below its banks of moraine paps. Behind it is Sgurr Dubh, the peak dominating the Glen—one with a host of peculiar lochans on its flanks. Being only a Corbett, it is seldom "done", though a fine wee hill. It was plodding over to the Ling for one Christmas that a plaintive voice commented, as we topped the brae, "Well, at least the path flows downhill now".

Torrents and the Torridons are commonly connected, alas. The Ling Hut had entries enough on this theme. I liked one cynical note:

1.1.62   Beinn Eighe, thawing.
2.1.62   Still raining.
3.1.62   Still raining.
4.1.62   Still raining.
5.1.62   Still raining—probably—went home yesterday.

Ling regards the climber from a picture on the hut wall. He and Glover stand there, two old cronies, figures from forgotten times. Ling was born in 1873 and inherited something of Raeburn's position—they were a formidable partnership—Norway, Alps, Caucasus; but it is perhaps appropriate his hut is here in the North West for he was the great explorer of the remote faces: Fionn Loch, An Teallach, Torridon, Suilven, Sutherland all saw first ascents in the early decades of the century. He died only in 1953—on the way to a climbing meet.

We were into Glen Cottage at the back of one. Mrs Reilley was there alone so we luxuriated in front of the fire, chatting over mugs of tea. Mike made supper while I teased away at the logistical skein. Days went so quickly!

I packed in hope for the next day. The dream of the triptych had somehow fizzled out like a camp fire in the rain. I took a book to bed and read while the wind swayed the Doire Vulich trees in swishing rhythms. The cows bellowed their misery. The sunset was as sad as a withering flower.

XIV

FADA—FANNICH

What are two drops of turbid rain?
LONGFELLOW

Friday 12 July BY SLIOCH TO SHENAVALL

It was not raining in the morning. A peculiar and puzzling "glow"
filled the sky to the east. We said farewell to the Reilleys and Glen
Cottage. I reached Loch Clair before Mike passed in the car. I was
sad to be leaving Glen Torridon, even though it had detained us day
by day, Munro by Munro; but, "Ane by ane maks ane an' a'" as
George Macdonald wrote.

Torridon is a glen of brutal beauty: Liathach like some giant's
castle to which one had to keep turning eyes—in case it planned some
mischief to the poor cyclist, then the flanking miles of Beinn Eighe with
its consciousness of strength, straddling the landscape like a colossus
and secretly, greedily clasping Coire Mhic Fhearchair to its hidden
heart. These are peaks such as men dream about and children paint.

A pair of peregrine exploding from the heather verge gave an exciting
moment just after Mike passed. He was at Kinlochewe waiting. I
phoned Marina, David and Kenneth to say cheerio as they were
setting off that evening for Brittany. I had walked right through
Dollar's summer term. The walk owed a great deal to their patient
management at base.

Brian Ripley, talking to Tom Waghorn, recalled the Kinlochewe
midges "in their teeming millions forming something that appeared like
a thick fog in Manchester". They were absent today, thank goodness,
and not because it was too vile and windy. It was a day with a sun to
draw peace from the soul like water from a moss. Bliss! Midges do not
like bright sun, nor wind. (The latter ensuring I had them as a fairly
infrequent pest this trip!)

Mike and I separated by the end of Loch Maree: he went on to
Dundonnell and lugged in a hefty pack to Shenavall, while I was going
there via Slioch: the fourth day of but a single Munro, but a glorious

change from the last three. The end of Loch Maree may be a short-cut but it entails the crossing of several rivers and lagoons. At the first main river I managed to soak my undies and the next drove me well upstream and demanded a real crossing, waist-deep, with a stick for support and boots on. Struggling in this spate I just about fell over when a jet zoomed across at low altitude.

Loch Maree, with its remnants of old Scots pines, and the background of Slioch, is a loch of outstanding beauty. It is only thirty feet above sea level and the river between loch and sea (Loch Ewe) is less than two miles long. "Kinlochewe" is thus rather misplaced. It is a loch full of legend and equally unlikely history. The Loch Maree Hotel, a famous fishing establishment, had a six-day visit from Queen Victoria in 1877. Her authority was put to the test when the local postie refused to carry her mail *on the Sabbath*: a refusal she both understood and accepted. She visited Isle Maree that day and dutifully read a sermon to the accompanying ghillies. She then added her coins to the lucky wishing-tree!

This island is named after St Maelrubha who came from Ireland in 671 to Applecross where he founded a monastery which became a famous sanctuary. St Maelrubha is second only to St Columba among early Scottish saints. At least four places claim he is buried there. Isle Maree had a curative well, and cures for insanity were long sought here. It dried up after a shepherd tried to heal his dog in it. The island had Druidical connections and a bull was sacrificed as late as the seventeenth century. Strongholds and refuges abounded among the twenty-seven islands and the wild shores. It has known warring Viking galleys and the chugging Victorian steamer "Mabel"—all equally gone. The road has been rebuilt alongside the south-western shore, replacing the original "destitution" road, and ensuring motorists can pass at twice the speed of seeing anything. The Nature Conservancy Council have a visitor centre, forest trail and picnic spots. They own extensive tracts of precious old landscape. In the lay-bys you might even be lucky and see a pine martin or two coming to rummage among the litter bins.

It is only remnants we see of the old forest of Caledon which extended from here right to the Lowlands. Letterewe, along the north-east shore, at one time had ironworks. Ore came by sea and loch from Cumberland and the local oaks were felled for the charcoal. One furnace consumed 120 acres of wood per year. There were seven furnaces at one stage. Many of the workers were Fifers. There is a story told of the first minister to try and convert the folk at Letterewe who so incensed them that they stripped him naked and tied him to a tree to be eaten by the midges. An old crone released him eventually. He was half crazy, as can be imagined. He cursed the place so that no godly people would ever inhabit Letterewe.

An old right-of-way runs down the loch to Poolewe on this north side. Mail was carried originally by runners along it. The road is only nineteenth century. Communications were much more dependent on the western seaboard before that.

I followed the path along to where Gleann Bianasdail comes down from under Slioch and turned up that dramatic gash which separates the peak from a plateau land of tiny lochans. The right-of-way goes round by the Heights of Kinlochewe up to Lochan Fada. This was more direct for Slioch.

A couple were camped in the glen and jumped when I greeted them as they had not heard my approach. There is a fine path and the scenery is spectacular: the deep-set gorge with its inky pools and brown falls, a glimpse of blue Maree and the hulk of Eighe beyond, dazzling in the early sun. They had chosen a delectable site.

I took the path up to its highest point and had a brew before following off up the raking sandstone strata. This led to the east corrie of Sgurr an Tuill Bhain, which is well-defined, a green spot among black and russet crags. I met the campers again, who had come straight up. The mist effects and vivid colouring made it a trigger-happy camera hill. (I was using a spare camera now: an older, heavier one than the Rollei.) We followed the narrow crest round the hollow heart of Slioch to its twin summits. The southern has a trig point from which Loch Maree and the west lies spread like a map; the northern, of almost identical height, looks north from its eyrie situation into the heart of our largest and best tract of unspoilt landscape, to A'Mhaighdean (the remotest Munro) and the sweep of Mulloch Coire Mhic Fhearchair.

I left a note on top of the trig point where it would be obvious. It was noticed two days later by an S.M.C. member, Leslie Kaczynski from Glasgow who, with a tally of 200 Munros, had the neck to say "No" to the question, "Are you a collector of Munros?" Quite possibly he is not, of course. Basically I'm not—and consciously becoming less so. There are too many playing that game now, and certainly at weekends the solitude is often missing.

On the way down I spent some time stalking goats which are often seen along Slioch's flanks. Slioch is *spear head* and presents its western cliffs to the traveller across Loch Maree in what must be one of the finest of hill portraits. The easy approaches are all from the Bianasdail side. Back at the rucksack I brewed again and followed the path down to its end where the river leaves remote Lochan Fada. The view up the loch is one of strange loneliness. Along it a heavy black squall was racing, and it was skins on, up the boggy brae beyond to the Bealach na Croise. Careful navigation was needed as the actual gap on this old drovers' route was hidden by nearer bumps.

Through the pass I found an old distintegrated path which led down to near Loch an Nid. The south-east ridge of the Mulloch above looked like a displaced part of the Cuillin ridge: ragged and flanked by a gleaming wet slab. Along above Loch an Nid great acres of turf have peeled off like a carpet to lay bare the grey quartzite flanks of Sgurr Ban. Above Loch Nid I found the tiny stone shelter where we had brewed a year before—so naturally used it again. I do not regret one moment of the many brew spots on this trip. There was a blessing in lying back with a brew in such scenery. It still, equally, gave its benefit when cowering in lee of a boulder in the storm.

The bealach had been the watershed, and from *loch of the nest* it was just a case of a five-mile tramp down the river Nid to Shenavall bothy— racing the rain and, for once, just winning. At the corner, where the glen swings west to become Strath na Sealga, the Dundonnell track came in. Pennant in 1772 traversed from Dundonnell to Kinlochewe by this route. Back, I could spy the Eas Ban, a favourite waterfall on Creag Rainich, ahead lay the glitter of Loch na Sealga, the *loch of the hunts*, and the red slopes of An Teallach. Deer went prancing across the river, dancing through the silver spray they splashed up.

Mike was already at the bothy so we were soon eating: dehydrated foods, yet willingly so, happy to be on the road again, no longer a "centrist" (even in Torridon).

The Torridon cows were here replaced by noisy sheep. I spread my sleeping bag on a scented bed of rushes. Deer browsed the grass outside the door. It was very much "home".

We sat by the fire, Mike and I, with a couple who had just had a week on Rhum. It was difficult writing up the log. We gossiped. Or read through the bothy book. One entry was apposite: "If you light a fire please put it under the chimney so the smoke will go away."

Another by David Doff, perhaps, should have been a warning: "It

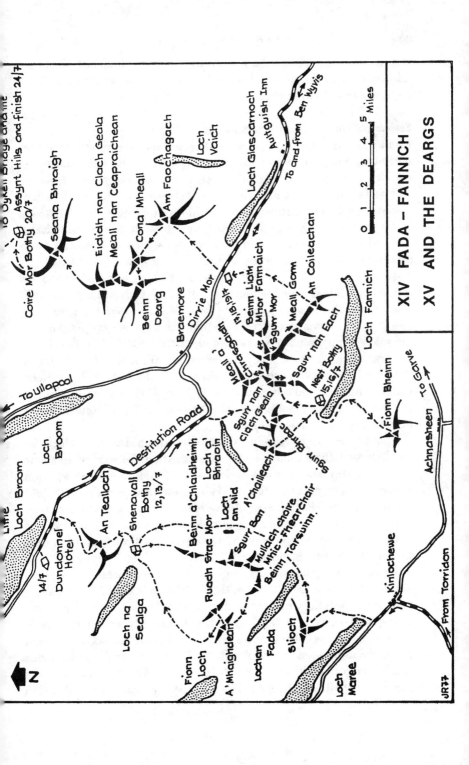

XIV FADA – FANNICH

XV AND THE DEARGS

rained and it rained and the streams rose higher and higher; then the
rain ceased and the streams became smaller, the sun appeared and at
night we looked at the stars."

Saturday 13 July   THE WHITBREAD WILDERNESS

I had gone out once in the night, setting off the startled deer from the
sheep-cropped grass round the bothy. A greenshank cried down by
the loch. A rusty moon was half covered with the damp rays of cloud.
Not promising. Dawn came very much as if afraid to face the day, like
a schoolboy sniffing outside the Head Master's study.

We were not keen to go. I'd shifted my bed as the roof began to leak,
the drops tinkling merrily into assorted pots and pans. Willy-nilly, we
set off into the saturated world at the back of eight.

The course of the river from Loch an Nid, as it swings round to
Strath na Sealga, forms a moat for Beinn a' Chlaidheimh, the *hill
of the sword*, which rises opposite the bothy. On the map its top appears
as a plateau, under 3,000 feet, its flanks steep but not craggy. In fact
the summit ridge is narrow as a roof top, over 3,000 feet, and its flanks
are craggy and broken. Not long before the Walk, Jim Donaldson of
Braemar had dropped me a note telling that the O.S. had produced
two new Munros and other changes. Beinn a' Chlaidheimh was one of
the two additions, Ruadh Stac Mor the other. The historic 277 had
become 279. (It is now 280.)

About three miles on from this peak lies Beinn Tarsuinn which Sir
Hugh missed (like Chlaidheimh) because the O.S. showed it below
3,000 feet. It, earlier on, was added to the Tables as number 277 and
given a height of 3,080 feet. Tarsuinn was accepted in 1927, but
Chlaidheimh and Ruadh Stac Mor were not, though it was mooted then
that they broke above the magic altitude.

Fortunately they both lay on the sweep of this already planned day,
so, for the Walk, made no real difference. New Munros—what a
nasty moral obligation to face in one's happy retirement!

It was a pity that this foray into the Whitbread Wilderness was having
to be made with the weather "contrarious". It is perhaps the finest area
of unspoilt landscape in Britain and owes this largely to the redoubtable
Colonel Whitbread who does his best to discourage visitors on his land,
yet at the same time has fought off Hydro and mineral developments
and has not ruined it with Land-Rover tracks. My fear is that when he
dies all this will be changed. His may be the name the proletarian

gangrels love to hate; but, as with many matters, there are two sides to the question.

South of Shenavall, to the shores of Loch Maree, and west to the coast, lies a landscape which could well be the wildest we have. Areas of it contained more water than land, the land is often bog, yet rising out of this are some of the most magnificent cliffs in the country, plus a whole muddle of Munros, which even the O.S. failed to delineate until 1974. The compass is not always reliable and the map not always accurate. Elitist that I am, I do not intend to describe it further. Today I was just thankful I already knew it well and could steer blind through all the many "interesting parts". Mike, I don't think, had done six Munros in a go before, nor had such a determined mentor. He certainly found it an experience. I hope he has gone back to *see it* since!

We wended up the glen a bit before crossing the river. Taking boots off was wasted effort as the deep, wet heather soon had us soaking from the thighs down. By the end of the day my feet had taken on a horrible purple hue from dye and glue. I'd plastered for possible tendon bruising, but had no trouble beyond one tiny blister on a toe.

Beinn a' Chlaidheimh 3,000 + (pronounced Ben-A-Clay) presents a rugged bluff to Shenavall and wending up this without diversions was one reward of a good memory. You felt and sensed crags and slopes rather than saw them. The smir of rain never eased. The south ridge took us down to cliff-rimmed Loch a' Bhrisidh. We brewed there, and froze waiting for the tea. Never mind, the best view of the day was the billy actually boiling. It was only the driving force of something like the Walk made a continuation at all rational.

We swung round to the grassy flank of otherwise stony Sgurr Ban: a great mound of greasy quartzite. It stayed wet for the pull up Mulloch Coire Mhic Fhearchair, the highest point of the day. The summit was merely wetter and bleaker. Fhearchair is *Farquhar*, another man's name.

We romped down the south ridge and then cut the corner bump to the watery col east of Beinn Tarsuinn, the old number 277. It is a worthy Munro, though today the bars of red sandstone were running with water for the pull up to the main top. Beyond this, after a dip, is "the Table", a flat hunk, then a pinnacled ridge with some wee scrambles offered, including one Adam and Eve step. The drop to the north is sheer and dramatic.

The col west of Tarsuinn is about 1,700 feet and riven by black peat bogs. They never seemed to come into view as we sloshed down wetly through the cloud. We kept south a bit to miss the worst of the bogs, and set a herd of deer careering off. A watery glimpse of Lochan Fada reminded us of the other world below the clouds. We found the burn which ensured we were on the right peak, but in the swirling world of cloud with every stream burbling and rushing, we were glad enough of a glimpse of the deep-set Gorm Loch Mor, as an additional feature. Endless green slopes led to the top of A' Mhaighdean, *the maiden*, (pronounced: Vyejun) perhaps my favourite viewpoint of all Munros. Today the view extended no further than a hundred yards.

The delineation of this peak on the map is as casual as others hereabout and it is one where the compass may be unreliable (something still to verify, as we only realised it might be erratic on this visit, and a clear day is wanted). The peak had great cliffs on its south-west flank and also on its north-east flank, the ridge between, running north-west, being narrow and barred with sandstone walls and stacks. This ridge can be reached from Fuar Loch Mor easily enough. The eastern slopes alone are easy.

The view, normally, is extensive: An Teallach and Beinn Dearg Mhor array finely to the north (with a glimpse of the far north beyond), westward is the splatter of lochans and the glitter of sea, Cuillins and Hebrides, a landscape of water essentially, while south, the miles of Beinn Lair's cliffs are spread like some battlement with armed Slioch and the Torridons peering over.

A' Mhaighdean is probably the least easily reached Munro: defended by long, hard miles, lack of accommodation, and weather of an unpredictable nature; so to sit on its crest and watch a summer sunset is apt to stay a dream for most. Its approach in winter, when the hours of darkness exceed those of sad daylight, is even more chancy; yet I have been blessed by both. The latter was an unusual occasion in that it was made possible by Lochan Fada being frozen into a grand highway, easy going, instead of a snow flounder along its shores of dessicated bog. I had a lift to the Heights of Kinlochewe but walked out to the Ling Hut: a long day, ending under an icy extravagance of stars. Ah, those were the years—when we had genuine winters in Scotland!

Sir Hugh Munro visited it in 1900 along with Ling and Lawson on a day like ours—"the worst of a very wet week". All three carried aneroids and verified the peak was indeed above the magic plimsoll line.

We felt our way down to the col and then zoomed up Ruadh Stac

Mor the other *new* Munro. It presents a dripping, disintegrating face to the col, but it is easy enough to wriggle up and then skirt the worst of the sandstone screes above. The summit has a new trig point, built neatly of the local stone instead of concrete.

We unwound down to the col again and in a mini Shelter Stone had a last brew-up and the only real rest of the day. It was the first dry spot we'd had. I've slept there overnight while a great snowfall blanketed the hills—and slept on to wake, dry and cosy still, to this magical metamorphosis. This whole area is uninhabited. Kinlochewe on Loch Maree to the south, and Dundonnell to the north, are the nearest habitations, besides the western seaboard strip.

Tom Weir, in *Highland Days*, recalls visiting Carnmore by the Fionn Loch (west of A' Mhaighdean) when it was still occupied. He had had his tent and belongings blown away and found a haven indeed with the MacRaes. They rowed in their food supplies twice a year. It must have been one of the remotest family homes in Britain, yet Tom wrote of their content. "Laughter was never very far from them." Shenavall too used to be lived in. A sixteen-year-old teacher travelled round these remote dwellings in turn. It was not uncommon to be cut off from Christmas to Easter.

We picked up the path from the col and skirted down past a bleak Fuar Loch Mor. An eagle soared through the mist and deer danced off out of sight, phantom shapes in the murk. We joined the "main road", the fine right-of-way that comes from Poolewe to Dundonnell over this pass, and set off for the five-mile tramp home. The path does a cork-screw down into Gleann na Muice Beag. The waterslide was thundering in spate after our day of rain. A group of red deer calves stood on a knoll as we passed. Our only pause was to look up Gleann na Muice itself, but instead of its ring of big summits we looked into a swirling wall of cloud.

Larachantivore is maintained and used in the autumn by the estate. Again, whatever people feel, it has no Land-Rover track blasting through to it. The Colonel walks. (The "Whitbread" and malt goes in by pony no doubt.) The wire bridge, with wooden slats, across the river here is periodically damaged by spates and so is dismantled each winter. Cutting the corner today presented no problems: as our boots were full to overflowing we just sploshed through the soupy moss. The Sealga can be a problem.

Many a debate has taken place over its fording. In very dry periods you can leap one spot and boulder hop another, but normally it holds a paddle at the least for those who would head into the wilderness. Long may it stay that way.

We simply splashed through and up to Shenavall. Welcome haven. We had been away over twelve hours with hardly a pause as it was very seldom not raining. There was a smug satisfaction as we sipped our brew by the bothy fire. Every stitch of clothing hung before its smoky bogwood blaze. We agreed it had even been an enjoyable day. I produce a suitable text from the Song of Solomon:

> "Many waters cannot quench love,
> neither can the floods drown it."

Lively conversation round the fire passed the evening hours quickly enough. A lot of it centred on the stalking season, and various problems arising from that. The hills are a fine common denominator and I count many keepers, shepherds and landowners amongst my friends. We all love the same things after all.

It need not be irksome to keep off stalking ground. The largest areas of popular rock-climbing are not stalked over and the largest untouched areas of rock, the sea cliffs, are free of nesting birds then. Even the Munro-bagger can plan his wanderings to utilise N.T.S. and other areas: Glencoe, Glen Shiel and Glen Torridon are three such bases for a start and there are others where stalking does not occur or the week-ends are left free. Almost *anywhere* could be visited if diplomatic enquiries are made locally. The great passes and other rights-of-way are expeditions for this season: the big passes in the Cairngorms, the Gaick, Corrieyairack and scores of others. Or perhaps this is the time to visit "Furth of Scotland", for its comparable delights.

On a recent visit to Dundonnell I heard from two English couples of walking through these hills and four times being accosted (in manners ranging from polite to extremely rude) by parties. One redoubtable owner explained that their scent could shift deer. On it being suggested that his no doubt was doing the same he replied the deer were his to do as he liked with. As they were on a right-of-way that argument cuts both ways.

The surest way to trouble is to apply different standards to suit one's own selfish convenience. If it came to the crunch the landowners can only lose. The soft answer still is the easiest way of avoiding wrath.

Deer are as much a "crop" as wheat or cows, so why should walkers stravaig to the detriment of one more than the others? Jobs are hard enough to come by in the Highlands; keepers and the like are the salt of the earth—whatever some may think of those who inherit and trade the land once filched from the people.

Mountaineering and deerstalking are both important recreational activities, and also an important part of the Highland economy. They need not clash as long as each gives the other consideration and courtesy. Stalking is not just an extravagant sport. Deer numbers, carefully worked out, have to be culled each year to maintain a healthy stock and to prevent beasts starving or raiding agricultural land. (They were originally forest animals and their present way of life is one of forced artificiality; for better or worse, man has to look after the deer.) The stags are at their best from mid-August to mid-October, so stalking takes place then.

Outwith that period few restrictions are imposed by estates on hill walkers and other visitors—who after all are only too glad to use paths, bridges and other facilities made available to stalking interests and money. It is usually not too difficult to find out what is going on—from the nearest pub, youth hostel, hotel or the estate keeper, factor or shepherd—and then fix up a mutually beneficial day for the morrow.

The sort of discourtesy shown to the English couples mentioned above can only cause resentment. They knew nothing at all about stalking, had they done so they might well have kept away, even though there was a right-of-way through the glen. Notices, or confrontation designed to intimidate, can only lead to quick loss of goodwill. Information should be more obviously available. (A note pinned to a tree five miles up a side road is *not* helpful.) Quite apart from economics, social ideas, or politics—with which we may disagree—we should have the respect of one sport for another, especially as we have to share the same "pitch"— along with skiers, botanists, geologists, rock-climbers, photographers, canoeists, bird-watchers, fishermen and others.

Shooting and hunting deer must be as old as man: a flint arrowhead has been discovered by remote Loch Etchachan in the Cairngorms. Anyone with an interest in deer should obtain the books of Lea McNally. He was a keeper and marvellous observer and photographer of red deer. He now works in Torridon for the N.T.S.

I almost regretted not walking on until the autumn, for what regular hillman does not thrill at the first sound of the rutting season? To lie in a lonely tent and hear the first roar fill a frost-misted glen is exciting, an annual shock. The sound has unutterable wildness in it, a deep calling to deep, stirring the ancient depths of urban man who has forgotten the smell of the earth. At the sound of this challenge we all become cave men once more; yet it is also a sad sound, marking a definite season, another year slipping towards its end. The sound reminds of swift-passing time—and shouts out to us to use what is left. Our life's walk is so short.

Sunday 14 July "YOU CANNA' FORGE YON"
An early sortie showed "No a starn in a' the carry" as Tannahill described one murky night. I went back to bed with poor hopes for An Teallach.

We woke at seven and as it looked as bad as ever we went back to sleep again. An hour later Mike got up and began "hyraxing"; rummaging and rustling among our gear like those beasts do. I received breakfast in bed and sat reading the bothy book. We were procrastinating.

The book was full of well-known friends' names and was as chatty as most. The weather was theme number one. "Whoever left Tolkein's *Lord of the Rings* is my hero. Dark days' reading."

"I left a candle in the window to guide the wanderers home."

"A thirty-one hour rain shower recorded."

"Pinned down here by storm, midges and inertia."

Dutch visitors were astounded at the isolation and scenery. Drinking water from streams was to them a sure route to the undertaker. A Danish lad quaintly wrote: "Here is all that which are micing in the Danks natur; it make me happy to see it. I wished I can right better Inglish so I can experes what I want to say." The wooden spoon goes to the Munro-bagger who recorded "breasting The Maiden."

It was heading for noon before we set off in a smir of rain and the tops buried in cloud as ever. We wended up the Shenavall burn and across the spongey moor towards the Dundonnell track. Mike, rather thankfully I suspect, left me to the mercies of An Teallach and headed for his car.

I cut through by the lochan (where sandstone and quartz fuse) to reach Toll an Lochain, one of the top two or three corries in the land. Well is it "toll", or *hole* for the small hollow is completely filled with the loch and girded round by mighty slopes and cliffs which at the far end drop sheer into the water. The skyline, when there is one, is of jagged peaks and pinnacles—an array unequalled outside Skye.

From the end of the loch I just wended back and forth up to the arm of ridge enclosing the loch on that side. I managed to keep on grass all the way till on the ridge which was followed over various sandstone towers to the summit, Bidean a' Ghlas Thuill, the *little peak of the grey hollow*, an odd name for splendid Munro 69, which is girded with red sandstone. I could just see the next peak along, Sgurr Fiona; beyond it lies the leaning summit of Lord Berkeley's Seat, Corrag Bhuidhe, and Sail Liath—all jagged peaks giving the finest of sweeping traverses. From the summit they curve away like a petrified breaker as it topples on some god-forsaken strand.

MacCulloch in his *Highlands and Western Isles* must have recorded one of the first traverses: "I continued along the giddy ridge, in the hope of seeing its termination; but all continued vacant, desolate, silent, dazzling and boundless ... its apparent altitude greater than of any single mountain in Scotland, excepting perhaps Ben Nevis."

Contrast that to Pennant in his "tour" of 1772: "West, a view where the awful, or rather the horrible, predominates—peaks with sides dark, deep and precipitous; with snowy glaciers lodged in the shaded apertures ... here Aeolus may be said to make his residence—fabricating blasts, squalls, and hurricanes."

Actually his description is not so inapt. We once battled our way over the mountain, roughly on today's line, with a Braehead party. Ann Winning had to take the lighter girls down; the heavier boys were roped for the towers as the gusts between threatened to blow them away. We *crawled* up the final slope. We all gathered again in the Dundonnell Hotel—of which more anon.

Today lacked the ferocity but gave no better visibility. It was too chilly to linger. No sweeping view of the Lewis coast or the Summer Isles, no distant Macdhui. Again it was navigation from memory; down and along the various pebbly domes to pick up the path which twists its way down to Dundonnell. It comes out just by the Smiddy, a hut belonging to the Edinburgh J.M.C.S. and converted tastefully as a memorial to Jim Clarkson who was killed near the C.I.C. Hut. It looked busy this summer weekend.

I reached the hotel reasonably dry. (The showers had dampened and the wind had dried in balanced combination.) A vast quantity of tea was consumed and the comforts of the hotel enjoyed. It has a snack-bar and various other facilities to pamper the inner man. It also provided a dinner which was one of the two best of the trip: leek soup; silverside; fresh strawberries and cream; Chianti and excellent coffee. It is always a treat, after a self-catering stay at the Smiddy, to dine there. After our wet bothy days it was even more of a treat and we ended the day with a midgey camp at Camusnagaul.

To revert to our Braehead battering on An Teallach. We reached the hotel soaked to the skin and while the girls ordered a spread of tea we, one by one, changed in the toilet. We had a small, cosy, inner room. On the table was placed tea and a great stand of sandwiches, scones and cakes—the sort of thing one sees all too rarely now.

I reached out to pour the tea and my wrist touched the hot water jug. I jerked back, giving the tray a good jolt, Tom grabbed to save the cake stand but instead simply knocked it straight into Kay's lap. She leapt up. The tray toppled. A cat had been hiding in a corner as Kitchy, our dog, was in with us. It bolted. The dog chased. Ann fell over the dog.

All this and more happened simultaneously; within seconds we had reduced the room to a shambles and ourselves to a state reminiscent of a custard fight from the days of silent films. We had a hectic clearing up, and a rather puzzled waitress brought a replacement. "You do have healthy appetites" was how she politely put it. We were nibbling our sandwiches, still in a state of shock, when the door opened and a dainty old lady looked in. She spoke to someone behind her. "I think we should come in here, dear, it's very cosy and peaceful."

An Teallach is perhaps the finest of all British peaks. Tom, after our disastrous Dundonnell tea, had been told that An Teallach (pronounced An Cheallach) meant *the forge*. His reply was, "You canna forge yon. That's the real thing."

Monday 15 July   TO THE NEST OF FANNICH

Across from the camp-site rose Beinn Ghobhlach which though a mere 2,082 feet is a splendid viewpoint, commanding a wide seascape as well as the hills.

Like so many hills here it is built of tiered sandstone. The North West, of course, sets the geologist going with some of the oldest rocks in the world, yet the sandstone (said to be 800 million years old) is only half as old as the gneiss which runs up the coast and gives Sutherland in particular such a scoured, barren and lifeless air—and its peculiar spaciousness and clean brightness, the wide sweeping beauty of "desert". Further in, the hills become more rounded, their contours gentle, their cols fiendishly boggy. These are good old schisty hills, which have edged up westwards over the sandstone and gneiss in "the Moine thrust" the edge of which runs conspicuously to the north of Ullapool.

Mike was going home for a couple of days while I headed off for the Fannichs. Having the bike, it was pressed into service. The run through Dundonnell was pleasant but the brae beyond goes up to 1,100 feet— and, for the first time in weeks, there was an east wind, a perversity well known to cyclists.

This sweep of road up the Dundonnell River, first a gorge full of waterfalls, and then a sweep of yellow moors, is known as Destitution Road, so named because it was constructed as a charity project during the 1851 potato famine by Mackenzie of Gairloch. Many people are surprised how recent such roads are—some of the roads in the west were not surfaced until after the war. We used to go off touring, the whole family on cycles, in the mid forties, when rationing entailed posting parcels ahead. "B and B" signs had not been invented. Ben Nevis, Ben Lomond and other of my earliest Munros were done then. Spare spokes and tyres were never forgotten. As the tourist industry has flourished so the cycling fraternity has dwindled, the remnant being found in the most unlikely spots. It's no surprise that many of the Rough-Stuff gang are also bothy fanatics.

It was tough enough peching across the moor. I paused at Fain, once the boozer for the road builders, and now rapidly falling down. A photograph of it, with An Teallach beyond, showed three ruins in all. Sunny though it was, the scene was truly one of desolation. I pushed on with the Fannichs arrayed ahead. Where the road sweeps down and round for the view of Loch Broom and the deep cleft of the dramatic Corrieshalloch Gorge, a track wends off down to Loch a' Bhraoin, a curl of water overlooked by the spurs of the day's hills.

Cairns by the loch here mark the burial place of raiding Lochaber caterans: far from base, for it was not diplomatic to beggar your neighbour. Raids were sometimes made with dates of cattle marts in mind to save even the bother of driving the beasts home!

Loch a' Bhraoin means *loch of the showers*. Today it was happily failing to live up to its name. Shenavall's rainfall is about 100 inches, Ullapool's less than half of that. A tip for tourists based in the West when the weather forecast becomes "showers of a continuous nature" is to head *even further west*, out on the peninsulas if possible, where you can often enjoy sun and dryness while the backcloth of hills is curtained off, wet and grey.

There is a footbridge at the outflow from Loch a' Bhraoin leading to the Cuileig Glen and once into that quiet glen I brewed, as it looked as if the weather was deteriorating. I kept on the west side of the glen, slowly gaining height, breaking through crags with an enjoyable burn scramble. This landed me in a wide corrie full of deer. I saw another eagle too.

Druim Reidh rises to a bump, unnamed (Toman Coinich) shown as *c.* 2,750 feet but almost certainly over 3,000 feet; a missing Top. I left my sack under an overhang where I sheltered from a brief shower and then wandered up Sgurr Breac. It has a cairn on its grassy dome but a rib of rock to the east seems fractionally higher. Traversing over Toman Coinich I ran into Bill Myles from Edinburgh, along with his dog "Mungie". He was staying at the Smiddy. We chatted for a while but it was a snell spot. Later I received an eight-page letter continuing the conversation. We were talking of access, and of the growing pressures about which we have had so little to worry in the past. They come upon us now, though.

Bill went off for Breac and was coming back for A' Chailleach but I did not see him again. He was not wearing polluting orange after all. Bill saw the questionnaire on Breac and left it; it was found five days later by an "unashamed" collector of Munros from Cumbria, Martin Hudson, who added to his total the ones he "hoped to do" the rest of that week. This was surely chancing fate! (He wrote later to say it rained every day they were in Scotland.)

A' Chailleach *the old woman* is an odd peak of hollows and levels, carpeted in cyphel, and due to its situation a fine viewpoint, even today when the clouds had lopped the summits off the bigger hills. A fence runs from col to summit and I back-tracked to retrieve my rucksack left hanging on a post before "baling-off" down into the Nest of Fannich: a green bowl of glen, teeming with deer. From every rise I looked down on sprawling herds. There were many calves about and they were surprisingly vocal: the young almost mewing and the parents giving gruff barks once they spotted the intruder.

The walk down to Loch Fannich and the Nest bothy was pleasant. Deer gave way to a group of nosey white garrons and then beefy cows. The end of the loch was laid bare in acres of bright sand and contrasting bands of peat where the stream flowed in. It was blowing wickedly cold from the east, waving the trees by the door. After the inevitable brew I simply sat by the window—in a bit of dwam—and soaked in the atmosphere. I wrote:

"This bothy [now not often available] is one of the most peaceful places I know. It weaves a magic that leaves one under a spell. It is hard to describe; it is not outstandingly remote or scenically splendid, but it combines such a galaxy of the almost-best that the result is a delicately-balanced beauty.

"Outside the window shimmering willows dance in the breeze. A redstart rasps away and a baby wagtail noisily pursues its mother, begging for food. Curlews are calling as they arc down to the edge of the loch. A pair of divers go splashing into its glitter. Their call, all wildness and freedom, takes me dashing out, to squint into the sun to follow their flight.

"Through the gap, beyond where old Cozae Lodge used to be, beyond the big boulder with its grass tammy, is the unlikely shape of Slioch, blue with distance. Straggling up behind the bothy are scattered groups of trees. They remind me of people stravaiging home after church: friendly and unhurried, free from the pressures of life. Bog cotton nods on the vivid green banks and along the path is a mini garden; tormentil, milkwort, lousewort, bedstraw, eyebright and hawkbits—again, nothing rare, but adding their collective charm."

Martins were playing tig round the chimney pots and peewit, redshank, and summer piper had all added their cacophony of sound as I'd wandered along path and shore collecting the white ribs of bogwood for a scented fire. Being alone was an added pleasure though I could not shake off a feeling of expectancy. Someone was going to arrive I was sure.

> I waited in this lonely place
> For a step upon the yard,
> But no man came to break the peace—
> Nor was the waiting hard.

I thought of the first time walking into the Nest. A twist of the path suddenly revealed the house: gables and windows painted blue, stonework clean and pointed, the slate roof surmounted by a variety of tall chimney pieces, a green corrugated porch added to the entrance. There were even blue and white checked curtains at the windows.

Surely it was occupied; and I had no tent. Perhaps the occupier would allow me to use one of the out-houses. . . .

On the door was the familiar M.B.A. plaque. The porch was stacked with bog wood and resinous pinewood. It was a bothy all right. I settled into the room on the right.

As my days of this long wandering were now consciously ending I felt an almost selfish possessiveness for this marvellous country. I knew it well but the journey had still been a revelation, a renewal of faith.

Tuesday 16 July PIPELINES AND PIPEDREAMS

I set off at 9.30 in full waterproofing convinced I was going to have another drubbing. The night had been all storm with just one pause as the wind changed from east to west.

Fionn Bheinn is a solitary bump above Achnasheen, miles from any other group of Munros. It had been quite a logistical game to decide just how to fit it in. As I had normally used it on courses as a training peak, or ski school, or even climbed it between trains, always from the south, doing it from Loch Fannich, the north, was the most pleasing possibility.

With the burns in spate and the ground waterlogged it was necessary to go well up the Nest of Fannich to cross its river. Rarely can you usefully cut corners: one of the spectator sports at this bothy is watching new arrivals rounding the end of the loch and running into dead-ends. There is no bridge at the Cabuie Lodge site and the Chadh Bhuidhe river can be a formidable proposition. Iron girders in it told of a past bridge. The Lodge is a heap of brick and mortar, destroyed no doubt by the raised water level. It took me an hour from bothy to south shore of Loch Fannich—about half a mile as the fly crows.

The low level of the loch made it possible to walk along on the exposed gravels, an easier proposition than the cut-up, boggy hillside. Bridges and traces of drowned track were exposed. Two miles along the loch there is the end of a pipeline (and Hydro track) which wends off at a gentle angle along the northern flanks of Fionn Bheinn, capturing much of the water which would have flowed out west.

One Hogmanay the snow was so deep that in the end we found it simplest just to walk along the top of the pipe itself. Tiptoe-ing round the open intakes gave moments of caution. Kitchy was with us on this winter escapade. It was to be his last Munro, for he died a few weeks later.

Today I wended along to intake number 35A, then took to the hill, crossing the burns which drain Toll Mor, the fine northern corrie. I skirted the rim of this on the west, watching stabs of sun darting from the clouds to light up the grey world now and then. The summit trig point (no cairn) was cold and exposed. I continued round the corrie rim and back to the pipeline. The end of the loch gave much less trouble thanks to the six-hour difference in water level: last night's rain had by now drained into the loch. Later a fishing boat drifted up. Three children and several dogs were put ashore to romp on the sands and wander upstream.

I was in at four so was quite pleased with the day. Simple values and simple desires make for content. The challenge of wild nature merely excites: worries are mainly concerned with the things of civilisation, so called. Surely the quality of life is what counts? Living is more precious than longevity.

Picture the Nest at Hogmanay. Five of us went there to be away from it all, but I think there were thirty-seven residents as the Old Year gave way to the New. Many of them were members of the old Corriemulzie Club, rising phoenix-like, at the place of its founding. It was not surprising a memory was drunk to Philip Tranter, for few people crowded their lives with good hill days as he did. Huge in frame and temperament, his enthusiasm led to many adventures in the remotest corners. I remember once sitting next to him at a club dinner and we played a game of just mentioning Scottish place names in turn; each name followed by a minute's silence. We made each other sick with the cup of remembering. One name he mentioned was "Nest of Fannich".

The bogwood fire flickered and smoked, helping the odd candles stuck in empty whisky bottles round the room to give a weird half-light. In the centre of the room an eightsome reel was being danced. Two pipers in the old pantry took turns with providing the music. The rest of us crammed round the walls, three deep, glasses in hand, bottles circulating. Outside, the snow fell steadily, adding to the foot of powder already piled over the landscape. We bedded in the wee sma' 'oors and we rose before daybreak to first foot the white hills of the Fannichs.

I had actually enjoyed a brief pipe-dream out in the sun when, at seven o'clock, Lorna Marsh arrived with some friends—over my hills of yesterday. A real surprise—but she had met Bill Myles at the Smiddy so knew I would be there still. Another odd coincidence was seeing the name Dave Norgate in the bothy book. He shared a flat with Mike who was now helping me over these last days. The book has several entries from cyclists: one who gave the date as the 30th of February. Ann and an L.S.C.C. gang had been there a year previously. The R.A.F. 1970 North-South Traverse team had used the Nest. The Ripleys too had been there, enjoying sizzling hot days in the Fannichs and having their first clash with stalkers. One August entry read: "Sorry to contravene 'close' season—plain lack of knowledge on my English part." There was even an entry from a honeymoon couple!

Wednesday 17 July   ROLLING UP THE FANNICHS

The mice were rummaging about in the fireplace all night, making an incredible amount of noise. I left the Nest at 7.10, with no sign of life from the others, and wandered up the path to the col between the western pair and the rest of the Fannichs: which I then began to collar in steady succession. The sharp edges of the ridges were shown up by cloud welling up against their crags. It was clear for Sgurr nan Each with the Choire Mhoir glen below a glitter of silver, but Sgurr nan Clach Geala, one of the two giants of Fannich, stayed cloudy. A dozen piles of orange peel indicated some recent litter-louts. The eastern cliffs make navigation easy. This was a typical Tranter crag: ignored by the O.S., it yielded a 700-foot grade V ice climb ("Gamma Gully", done with Ian Rowe in 1965).

The col beyond has a part time loch on it and a bit to the west lies a large split boulder—both good aids to memory navigation. The dip to Meall a' Chrasgaidh is one of the wettest cols in Scotland. I have never known it dry. Beyond Chrasgaidh are paths which give splendid approaches to the Fannichs. It is a range with more paths than the map indicates. This west end has an openness to it which delights. The Fannichs rather fall over each other, but here the Deargs and An Teallach are seen across miles of clear air.

I splashed back from this outlier, and regained the main ridge for Sgurr Mor, 3,637 feet, a cone of greasy rubble which is unmistakable when seen from distange ranges. I admired the Geala cliffs before climbing up into cloud again. Both these hills had lingering snow patches. Just beyond I once innocently caught a leveret which then proceeded to scream like mad, to my consternation. I also have a picture of Kitchy sitting, like a professor of botany, gazing raptly at a patch of white moss campion on this highest summit of the Fannichs.

Sgurr Mor has cliffs running out to a northern spur with a Munro on it: Beinn Liath Mhor Fannich. A tiny shelter en route allowed me to leave the rucksack. I raced out and back just in time to use the shelter and sit out a nasty sleet and hail shower. I'd brought water up from the col returning (a permanent source) and made quite a good meal. The roof leaked and the sheep had got in to soil the floor, but it was out of the lash of the wind.

The easting after that became pleasant. A back wind for once. The sun shone again. "Truly the light is sweet and a pleasant thing it is for the eyes to behold the sun" (Ecclesiastes 11:7). Meall Gorm was next and just beyond its stone howff I ran into Lorna and company, who were after the lot, east to west, a day comparable to the Mamores. I wished them luck as it was already 2.30. They had come up from the lodge on Loch Fannich to An Coileachan, *the cockerel*.

The rucker was left on the last col and An Coileachan done speedily to race another blatter. It whipped past trailing white curtains of hail. I left a questionnaire. The note lay for about ten days and knowing the finders its return backs the assumption that only Munro-baggers seek the most eastern Fannichs. It came in months afterwards from that inveterate gangrel, Nancy Smith of Fersit, along with her gannet mark II, son, Ewan (14). He did his first Munro at 4 because "he had no other alternative". But ten years later he has—and still goes. They were based on the Nest and apart from the *Captain Scott* watch, the only people returning questionnaires who were not car-based.

I had arranged a meeting with Mike on the Dirrie More for 5 p.m. so had a spur to drive me down the long five miles north to the road. Across my map I had already written "Bog, Bog, Bog" down the route of the River Li. It was a steep drop initially to Loch Gorm. The slopes were covered with athletic frogs which bounced and crashed down the brae. It was quite an enjoyable bog trot, making the meeting spot with two minutes in hand.

After some tea I was busy messing about in the stream like a child, when Mike arrived. He had been held up at Aultguish Inn while they searched for my parcel.

The Dirrie More is the highest reach of this great through route from coast to coast. An Teallach and Wyvis guard its opposing ends. It is seldom without some breeze, so a good spot to camp in midgey summer. The good road was built in the 1800's by the Fishery Society when Ullapool was a busy fishing port. Tom Patey had been Ullapool's doctor. Not far off lived another Doctor Tom—Longstaff, the great Himalayan pioneer.

Mike produced supper while I sat and dealt with a stack of mail, prepared for Wyvis, and studied the days to go. From one of the many boxes in the car I pulled out the twenty-second—and last—map of the Walk. The 1,500 miles had been clocked up today.

A rainbow arched over the view eastwards to Wyvis, north, the Deargs were *liath*; portents had I known it. We would end with a bang not a Whymper, as I think Dougal Haston put it.

Thursday 18 July   THE SCENT OF HONEY

At 3.30 there were midges just to disprove the efficacy of the site, but the west wind was soon blowing again. Mike went off determinedly for An Faochagach and I cycled off for Wyvis. Mike thinks of himself as a gentle soul but I maintained anyone who has collected Munros with half his dedication has quite a share of aggression. He finished his round not long after this trip.

It was good to cycle both with the wind and slightly downhill— though the return journey would have both in opposition. The Glascarnoch Reservoir was grey and choppy. Hidden under the dam at its eastern end is Aultguish Inn, a hospitable place with an air of loneliness akin to the Kingshouse on Rannoch Moor. Its walls are decorated with pictures taken during a period of deep snow when it resembled the Arctic. The half-engulfed vehicles date the scene. Munro had been based there venturing forth on to Fannichs and Deargs, using a cycle —or pony trap.

At Black Bridge Strath Vaich joins the main valley, a favourite glen of mine; at Inchbae, Strath Rannoch joins in, while north and east of it lies some of the most desolate of all moors, leading eventually to Glencalvie and Strathcarron, names sinister in the annals of the Clearances. At Croick Church you can still see names and pathetic messages scratched on the glass, the abiding witness of the evicted crofters who sheltered in the churchyard there in 1845.

Ben Wyvis now has its western aspect planted, a verdant waistcoat, which is not altogether welcomed by walkers. Setting off from Garbat, where I chained my bike to the wreck of a car, I made large alterations to my map. Probably the easiest approach is up to the Bealach Mor and over An Cabar, returning off Carn Gorm to a track west of Meallan Donn. This gives a fine, high, traverse, and Wyvis has a fine view being solitary, all as it should be for the *big, noble mountain*.

My own route used roads and firebreaks to reach the main river which

I then followed up. It grew steadily colder as the wind strengthened. The spongy nature of the ridge's mossy covering made it hard to hurry. One walker-cum-golfer celebrated his Munro completion by saving Wyvis for the last and "playing himself in" along what could well be a golf course. The last hole is Glas Leathad Mor.

I swung up on the lee side: the scalloped eastern corries there being so different from the even western flank, and donned skins simply to combat the piercing wind. Over the summit and from the first dip beyond I trotted down at once. A high square of trees, burnt by the searing winds, gave shelter for a bite, then it was back to the game of linking rakes and tracks down to Garbat.

It had taken forty minutes cycling east; returning took more than twice as long. Mike was back just before me. After supper we went along to the Inn for a drink.

The Ripleys had Wyvis early on their route, of course. After it they had a rest day at Killin Farm near Garve. Their log had a familiar ring to it, apart from the medical statistics: "Festered, picked wild raspberries, sunbathed, ate great amounts of rich food, and pampered feet. Sores and blisters: Brian, 17: Alan, 3; David, 3."

There were 10 Munros ahead for me now; in a rash moment we ordered a half bottle of champagne to be used on Ben Hope.

The day's best memory, though, was nearing Inchbae Lodge and suddenly having a strong scent of honey blow from a field of clover. It had been a long time since I had seen a clover field and the clean, sharpened senses revelled in its richness.

Friday 19 July DIRRIE MORE

Today would have given a repeat of the wet day from Shenavall so we stayed where we were, snug as walnuts in their shells. The long sleep was welcome and I had old Braehead logs for reading. These produced quite a crop of howlers, some of which I noted down:

"We climbed Devil's Point and Cairn Towel . . . walked round the Bend to the C.I.C. Hut . . . shining formica in the rock . . . an eigg for our tea . . . two dukes flying across the water . . . we rumped down the snowslope . . . an insect-invested glen . . . golden plumbers were calling on the moor. . . ."

The tent tended to collect earwigs (golachs or gallachers in the older tongue) so in the afternoon we flitted to Aultguish again. "The muddle of mountains" to the north was still black with cloud. Aultguish is

burn of the pine, though a singularly treeless spot. Over tea I wrote
a review of Desmond Nethersole-Thomson and Adam Watson's *The
Cairngorms*, which had been delightful reading for several days.

We collected our small bottle of champagne. I'm not very enthusiastic about it as a drink, but out of respect for Sir Hugh, what else would
do? Nor obviously am I very superstitious, buying it in advance.
Perhaps I should have been!

We returned to the tents to eat. The weather would have to be very,
very bad to deter us on the morrow.

XV

THE DEARGS AND THE NORTH

"Will there be a few folk left in the world when Progress is choked at last by its own too much? Yes there will be, a few folk will return by stealth to the wind and the mist and the silences. . . ."

GEORGE MACKAY BROWN: *Hawkfall*

Saturday 20 July THE EMPTY QUARTER

The overnight "Hunting Winds" had moved on as I set off into the last fighting group, then caught me on Dearg, a hill I have always distrusted. The Dirrie More bogs led to Loch a' Gharbhrain, the largest of five lochs that are strung like irregular beads on the thread of the Allt Lair which runs right up into the heart of the group. Skirting round to the west I came on old ruins and bright green grass, the abiding testimony to past habitation.

It became a great bird hour: a snipe went ricocheting off from the moss, an eagle swung lazily over the line of lochans, up in the corrie the mountain blackbirds were chacking busily among the berries and on the long, bare shoulders of Am Faochagach golden plovers were telling the world of their woe. They certainly eased bog-hopping, river-teetering, and brae-bashing. Am Faochagach is a bit of a mouthful—and one which seems to have been spat out by the rest of the group. It lies in Coventry to the east, the culmination of successive adjectival bumps. The questionnaire left here was not found till August 9; a long wait. It's obviously not an appealing summit! Arnold Hardman, who found it, introduced Munros to his two sons that day—a long way from home in Hampshire.

This hill once gave a gang of us a midsummer bivouac when we simply spread sleeping bags and slept under a glowing sky. Today the call was to hurry. Beinn Dearg had been smoking like a volcano and the "smoke" was streaming eastwards. So I trundled off over Meallan Ban, which has a bigger cairn than the summit, and began to skirt down too soon. Like much "rough pasture" on the maps of the North West this was crags and gullies, so I had to scramble up again before finally descending to the fourth loch: Loch Prille.

Loch Prille ends on the lip of a 500-foot slide of water. Today the slide, working in partnership with the wind, was doing its best to fly back up into the loch again so that the odd stepping stones on the lip were constantly swept by flying sheets of water. You chose a lull—and ran. Yet fifty yards beyond was a nook so calm that I settled for a brew. A circle drawn with this spot as centre and with a radius of two miles, takes in some truly dramatic country—which is enough said. This enormous area north of the Dirrie More, right up to Oykell Bridge, is a great "Empty Quarter". It has some superb through routes, there are a few lonely bothies, the atmosphere is closer to the ice age than the twentieth century, but woe-betide the incompetent or unfit who strays into its fastness. I set off up the *enchanted hill*.

Loch Prille to the top of Cona Mheall was ribbed with rock and steep and clean enough to give scrambling. The wind added an element of the unexpected. Near the top the ridge became a jumble of blocks. The summit was reached in an hour. Yelling Dvořák themes I followed a drunken course over the boulders. An orange dot in the lee of the wall leading to Beinn Dearg became two figures. Luckily for them the wind was blowing my song in the other direction. Nevertheless they set off up ahead of me. I hid the rucksack under a nook of rock and had a piece. The rain came on. I scuttled up in the lee of the wall, passing the English couple, and then duly received the brunt of the wicked storm on the last exposed slopes. Last time it was an electrical storm. Verily Dearg is an evil mountain. I kicked the cairn and ran.

Beinn Dearg can be a fine summit when clear. It looks to Loch Broom, Coigach, Am Teallach and the Fannichs. Great country, Beinn Eniglair (2,915 feet), two miles over, is the best viewpoint of all and worth including in the group. There are fine paths up from Inverlael. You need them—the going is rough everywhere.

I procrastinated through another snack, but it seemed set foul for the duration. Mike was motoring round to Oykell Bridge and up Corriemulzie to the bothy in Coire Mor—many miles to the north as the crow might just manage to fly. He had all the food and gear. There was nothing left at the Dirrie More. I would have to try to go on. Like the ant called Pythagoras I'd have a few unhappy compass bearings to battle along before writing Q.E.D. to the day.

So I crossed the wall and struggled through the murk to the lochans. The other two appeared briefly and I wondered what they thought of things. The gusts tore great curtains of water off the lochans and smashed them over the boulderfields—once or twice they made attempts at blowing me into the water. I staggered round into the lee and squelched up the sodden slopes of Meall nan Ceapraichean.

The next Munro lay across one of the three east–west through-routes that radiate out from the head of Gleann Beag. My descent followed a threefold pattern, first down sandstone boulders, then wee quartzy crags, then a conveniently angled rake of exposed strata. At stage two the clouds tore apart, the rain stopped, and Dvořàk started again.

The stalkers' path at the col is clear but it comes up only as far as the watershed. The descent to Gleann Beag is a do-it-yourself job. From the col it is a mere 500-foot scramble up to the top of Eididh nan Clach Geala where you can amuse yourself trying to decide which of the cairns, 100 yards apart, is the real summit. All I could see in the wild scene was Stac Polly, small enough to cringe below the heavy roof of cloud. I could hardly stand on top of the *summit of white stone*.

After crossing the right-of-way from Gleann Beag to Inverlael the ground becomes even more broken: the contour lines on the map are no indication; it is a relief always to find the rim of the glen of the wending Douchary River, as it is demarcated by crags. On this day the rim was white-lacy with all the water flying up and back in the gale. Verily, it could have been after wandering in the Deargs that the Psalmist penned:

"I sink in deep mire, where there is no foothold;
I have come into deep waters and the flood sweeps over me."

When sure of the col I had a brew—before running the aquatic gauntlet of the flying spray. It was five o'clock by the time I reached Seana Bhraigh, the *old high slopes*, at last. Despair on Dearg, delight on Seana Braigh. Below lay the night's haven. The reefs could be shaken out, an evening spinnaker set.

The Ripleys on Seana Bhraigh recorded: "best day yet—could actually see something!" The Luchd Choire below fell away steeply in big crags: a winter playground first opened up by the Corriemulzie Club, but even in summer presenting ribs and prows and shadowy depths, a landscape on which ancient cartographers could well have scripted "Here be dragons".

I skirted down round the west rim, pausing at a wee lochan embedded in the navel of a gap and then stopping short just beyond when half a dozen deer came careering along straight at me. A branched forest of antlers charging down at one is a bit unnerving but their intent proved non-aggressive. Twenty yards short they suddenly caught sight of me and came to a hilarious motorway pile-up halt before untangling and dashing off down the slope on the port beam. Not far on, a hare almost repeated the performance. Several wheatears flitted up the slope.

Only man could account for such universal panic and sure enough I soon came on Mike contouring up to the ridge.

The west end of Loch a' Choire Mhor was shallow enough simply to paddle across dryshod—a nice change. I collected wood along the shore until the bothy was reached. It was a small bothy rescued from a long line of empty ruins. Dave Simpson and I were back there for the next freezing, moon-blowing Hogmanay. Only three or four parties had visited in between. Mr Stevenson the shepherd from Corriemulzie knew many of the old bothy lads. Only the real gangrel penetrates this remote corrie with its shivering waters and black Sgurr. John Hinde's name was in the book, recording their Hope to Lomond trek. (Ben Lomond was his Munro 277.)

Sandy Cousins on his Walk "enjoyed the evening sitting at the door of the bothy sipping Drambuie, listening to an opera and watching the deer playing like children in the shallow lochan. My pipe smoke drifted out on the calm air . . . I turned in on a warm straw bed." No doubt the same straw that we enjoyed now, three years later.

The Ripleys had not been so lucky. On Ben More Assynt they wrote, "Feet sore and very tired on the path. Very heavy rain. All rivers flooded." Next day they were thrown out of a howff at Oykell Bridge: a "depressing day". On the next they nearly set fire to the bothy here and, leaving it, fell into a river.

The year after the Walk, Hogmanay at Coire Mor was to be the quietest possible. Dave and I both fell asleep early. I actually woke at eleven but the fire had gone out, so I snuggled down in the sleeping bag once more, listened briefly to the call of a wild whooper and the judder of the wind in the roof, and slept the year out.

Now, Mike had bought a newspaper. It told of Makarios being chased from Cyprus, Franco handing over in Spain. There must have been many gaps in my knowledge of current affairs. The paper kindled the fire nicely. Widow night swept the daylight wetly away and, once our candles burnt out, raged wildly all through the empty hours of blackness. Never did bothy feel cosier.

Sunday 21 July AIRBORNE IN ASSYNT

We went out down Strath Mulzie, a lonely glen leading up into the Deargs from the north. There seemed to be a large collection of mechanical debris: old cars and tractors—a hard landscape for steel never mind tender tendons.

Just before the lodge Mike had left the bike after motoring up the lower glen to an impasse. To speed things up we took turns on it and then he went off for his car. The track, as climber Raeburn once put it, "was laid, corduroy fashion". We regrouped at the Oykell Bridge Hotel, quite a contrast, sitting in a carpeted lounge drinking coffee out of Persian Flower china cups along with the tourists and fishermen.

Lord Louden and President Forbes fled this way to Ullapool and Skye in 1746 after the Rout of Moy. Little did they know Culloden would follow so soon after. They could almost have met the Pretender fleeing as well: that would have been an odd quirk of history!

Montrose escaped this way, too, after his last bid for the exiled Charles II. He had his horse shot under him at a skirmish by Loch Shin. Injured and starving he sought shelter at Ardvreck Castle on Loch Assynt only to be betrayed and "sold" by MacLeod of Assynt. Montrose was led, bound, to Edinburgh and execution. MacLeod received £20,000 and a quantity of stale oatmeal from the government. MacKenzie of Seaforth, whose lack of commitment directly led to Montrose's defeat in the north, devastated Assynt. Ardvreck Castle stands a black ruin against the silver loch to this day, not far beyond Inchnadamph Hotel.

The wind was still blowing strongly, shaking the trees by the hotel. It was a dry gale so we decided to push on. With hindsight, we should have known better: every great blow of wind I can remember eventually broke into a wild deluge. However, the mottos also banged away: "Push! Push!" and "Tomorrow may be worse". It had been ten miles from the bothy, now followed ten more, cycling uphill into the wind, a push to sort out the calf muscles.

There was a great deal of new tree planting, which will alter the landscape considerably. Beyond Loch Craggie, nearing the watershed, I became aware of something away ahead. It could only be Suilven. Even as I pushed on to the top, the familiar pap-shape finally cleared of cloud. I had it in me to be jealous, for Suilven is no Munro; nor is Cul Mor nor Stac Polly, nor any of the jumble of improbable Coigach peaks.

Altitude in the North West means little. The peaks rise in startling shapes from watery moors of scarred sandstone in Coigach; and even bleaker gneiss in Sutherland—Quinag, Foinaven, Arkle . . .

Only Ben More and Conival top the magic line and, fine as they are, they do not rouse the connoisseur as some of the lesser heights: single malts, all of them!

In midwinter I remember gazing at them in wonder across the Minch from the *Captain Scott* as she sped, all sails set, in rosy dawn from Stornoway. We anchored that night in the lee of Isle Martin under the flushed sunset walls of Ben More Coigach. Between, all day long, we could look at jagged, arctic summits, seemingly rearing from the sea. Standing aloft among the billowing canvas, it was a scene as romantic as Conrad or Jack London could have pictured. There is nothing in Britain to better the North West.

Sutherland is just *south land*, the South Land of the Vikings, won by them before William the Conqueror landed in England and only lost by them to William the Lion, King of Scots, in 1196. Assynt is probably a Norse name as "Ass" means *rocky* in that tongue. The landscape would fit quite unobtrusively into their homeland.

Limestone in unusual quantity gives a green lushness to vegetation and is responsible for the vanishing rivers, caves and potholes on the western flanks of Ben More near Inchnadamph. The O.S. are not responsible for map rivers vanishing—they do it in reality. Peach and Horne excavated a cave in 1917 and found bones of lynx, arctic fox, bear, reindeer—and man (*c.* 6000 B.C.).

I'd had enough of pedalling by the time I caught up on Mike. He had a brew ready at the Ben More Lodge road end. Unfortunately he used potato powder instead of milk powder in it. It was 2 p.m. before we set off for another good day's hill-bashing; no reason why not with long evening light. Mike planned to circle back over the Assynt pair while I would push on and we'd meet at the north end of Loch Shin. The theory was sound. Had not such an old hand as W. W. Naismith set off at 5 p.m. without map, compass or even decent boots?

These two Munros are most often climbed from Inchnadamph to the west. I recommend adding the sweep of Breabag: as sterile and crazy a hill as you will ever find. Weird formations and utter loneliness mark all this region.

About a dozen years ago a young shepherd from near Inchnadamph was found drowned in a pool near the foot of Ben More. The strange thing was that a few nights previously he had been sitting morosely in the hotel kitchen. When teased by one of the maids he told of a nightmare in which he saw his bones lying out on the flank of Ben More. The area is full of lore and legend, frightening to some people.

The population from the Assynt hills was cleared off in 1812. The landscape is therefore empty. However, a Land-Rover track led off up the Oykell, and was followed by a stalkers' path which vanished for a mile or two for no obvious reason. It was good going: shirts off, company for once, a view of sun and shadowed ridges, and Conival and Ben More Assynt bold at the glen head. Conival has a black pinnacled ridge which faced us and promised fun, while the summits are linked by a ragged sweep of ridge.

We pulled up the path to the Dubh Loch Mor and had a picnic—no brew, though, the wind was too bothersome. We lingered only for a chilly ten minutes and put on more clothing. It took just that much time for the sky to become overcast. A blatter was obviously coming (small streams were already blowing back on themselves) but, we thought, it would be brief, a passing shower. I suppose it did pass, too, but not before toying with us as casually as a boy kicking a ball about a back yard.

The lower slopes of the dark ridge were already sufficiently exposed for the wind to knock us about. We eventually crabbed into the lee. Mike decided to go down, and set off muttering about climbing for pleasure and needing to take out further insurance before joining any more mad Broon escapades.

I could not retreat. I was on par, so to speak, for the estimated finish: just these two Munros and two others away; three days all going well.

Men are sometimes given to dream of white ships sailing everlasting oceans so that an ending is inconceivable: there can be no final port, nor destroying storm, just a dancing bowsprit above the far-eyed figure on the bows, a wild perpetual motion. Now, thinking was put by, not out of fear but because I was sailing out of sight of reason, crashing into the violence of nature with great joy. This element of testing is an inescapable facet of mountain adventuring. Without it the hills would be as antiseptic and puerile as a modern swimming pool.

So I cringed on the lee slope watching Mike stagger off like Charlie Chaplin. He soon vanished into the cloud and horizontal rain. I filled pockets with sweets and chocolate, zipped up completely and crawled back into the fight. It was interesting. The Garbh Choire, on the right,

L

was wonderfully *rough* with the wind roaring as I don't think I have ever heard it before, and the waterfalls smashed and sprayed upwards in utter confusion. I thought of Naismith who had lost himself on this hill. And of Hillaby who had done likewise.

The crest of the ridge became the route, of necessity, for the lee side was craggy, and scrambling on it too dangerous in the gusts, while on the other side, receiving the full blast of the wind, any movement was impossible. It was quite amusing to find the easiest of climbing reduced to such a pantomime. In one rock chimney I suddenly found I was completely airborne above the holds I'd had—static in a bridging position momentarily, but for long enough to realise the sensation, and savour it.

There were indeed times when progress was impossible, when it was a case of holding on, averting face from the wind, and waiting for a lull. The rain beat like rods on the bare bones of the landscape; a magnificent malignancy. I found a pathetic frightened sheep hiding in a niche. A ptarmigan's nest lay deserted, the eggs cold.

The last part of the ridge was easier. Conival's trig point was not exactly cosy. I shoved soggy chocolate into my mouth and groped off by compass for the sweep of ridge to Ben More, invisible in the shredded sky. The world was reduced to elemental noise and motion, intimidating but unavoidable. In glee I yelled Joshua's cry of "give me this mountain!"

Speed was now essential yet caution imperative. There was a long way to go and a rising river to cross. If it became impossible to wade, then I was up the spout—and adventure could topple into disaster all too easily.

It was great, just great! A sheer parody of a progression: wind-dictated quadrilles and waltzes with every now and then a change of channel to a boxing bout with myself on the losing side. I remember at one knock-down just lying there giggling at the situation. How could you explain this madness to the layman?

The slippery ridge eventually rose to a selection of summits for Ben More (Britain's highest *gneiss*) and after dashing from one to another, like a dog in a park, I set off again by compass for the north-east ridge.

The way down felt interminable but was reasonably defined; the compass was not needed. Saturation was complete, the rain sloshing in on the flank. A shivering skin of water covered the grey stones but eventually the rocks gave way to spongy moss and grass equally water-laden and slippery. Steeper slopes led down to rough bog and moor, alive with surprised-looking deer, and the Allt an Aonghais led on to the main Cassley River. It was quite tiring having to hurry, and hurry so carefully.

The Cassley had already risen, and my first effort at crossing, watched by sardonic stags, ended up to my waist in a hole. A second attempt found the river too deep and swift; the third was successful—just. It was not at all cold, fortunately, but the antics of dressing again in the rain were a bit damping.

Difficulties over, the tension of the traverse eased and I splashed happily down the path to some Hydro works where I discovered the remainder of my way out to Loch Shin was tarred road. Anti-climax. I ate most of my remaining food. The exit up over Maovally was effortless with the funnelled force of the wind behind at last. Pipits, rising from the verges, went slicing off—backwards!

It was a trundle down to Loch Shin, cutting corners and skiting on the slimy surface when off the road. A great spout at the end of a pipeline was spraying into the loch. I had a fit, briefly, for there is another loch beyond Loch Shin and I could not see the split and imagined all the extra miles that would be needed. The Hydro had the last laugh for the raised level ran away back into a side valley making a great detour. Here, at Corriekinloch, the full funnelled blast met me again.

So did Mike, and we shot off for friendly Overscaig Hotel, arriving three hours after I'd left the top of Ben More, on which I had, unbeknown, completed my fourth round of the Munros.

Being 9.30, meal time was passed, but, ensconced in our room, we were brought a vast pot of tea, and my sodden garments were carried off to the kitchen for drying. Surreptitiously, out of the wardrobe, we produced and consumed a succession of tinned goodies, not in any standard order, but immensely welcome nevertheless.

Clean sheets, a bath—things which had not even been imagined earlier—made a good end to the miles and feet.

The rain still battered at the window as I tumbled into bed. Like Naismith I would not have missed the day's experience.

Monday 22 July ON AT ANY PRICE

Yesterday's crossing was typical of Assynt's empty landscape; even though the Hydro road and structures protruded a human element seldom found among the bens and glens here. Prebble writing of Sutherland well pictured it: "Lonely, brooding mountains that seemed to be awaiting the resumption of creation." The Clearances have a great deal to answer for; but not quite so much as many people today seem to think. The changes had already started. The end result is Sutherland's present population of only 7 persons per square mile.

The weather was still vile; dry clothes were donned with a certain despair. I had originally planned to walk across to Crask, but with the continuing deluge there could well have been problems with rivers and also with new plantings. I opted to cycle round. Loch Shin gave midgey stillness, but the rain came down hard for the ten-mile drag beyond to Crask. We met there for a good bar-lunch, then abandoned "Long Walk" activities for the day.

We went down to Altnaharra, another fishing hotel, and read the day away. The car-park was lined with Rovers and Volvos—and Mike's wee Simca. One plush shooting brake had, on its bonnet, a model of a dog holding a pheasant. The company at dinner was decidedly "tweedy" too and the talk all boasting or excusing the result of the day's fishing. From the windows we could see the rain-stippled reaches of Loch Naver, reminding again of the Clearances.

I was amazed once when English friends, one a history teacher, declared they had never heard of the Clearances. *The Highland Clearances* by John Prebble tells the story and is now readily available in paperback.

Basically, sheep were found to be more profitable than people—so the people were removed—evicted and scattered to the corners of the earth, beaten by laws they did not understand often delivered in a language they did not speak; they were coerced by a ministry (arrayed on the side of the owners) who told them it was God's will they move; they were betrayed by centuries of faith in their chiefs and leaders, who now were either absent or the instigators of their betrayal; they were, if need be, physically compelled: their houses burnt over their heads, their goods destroyed, their persons beaten and abused.

It is not a pretty story, though it is an enigmatic one. As one writer points out, by 1837 Skye had produced 21 Lt. and Maj. Generals, 48 Lt. Colonels, 600 other officers, 120 pipers and 10,000 N.C.O.s and men. Napoleon discovered their martial prowess to his cost. Sutherland soldiers had followed Gustavus Adolphus and gained a European reputation. The Highlanders had been used again and again as soon as the 1745 furore had passed away. Culloden itself was no Anglo-Scottish battle. The Clearances, likewise, cannot be simply put down to Gael-Sassenach antipathy.

On the whole, the work of Clearances went smoothly. Between 1831 and 1832, 120,000 people left the Highlands, with no major rising or resistance. The old system that finally collapsed after 1745 had been very much a military world: the chief needed his people. After 1745 he was more likely to need a lawyer and a factor. The army gave work for his surplus clansmen. But older even than Culloden, was the growth of population: Thomas Pennant had reported large-scale food shortages in the north; there was appalling poverty; potato blight periodically caused famine. Often the men went off to the army to avoid starving.

Strathnaver, which runs down from Loch Naver, opposite Altnaharra, was part of the Sutherland domain. In 1812 there were 2,000 people living in the glen. They were driven to the coast and told to become fishermen. At Rossall, Patrick Sellar evicted 88 people with great brutality. For fifty years a native of Strathnaver, Donald MacLeod, who settled in Canada, waged a war of words against the Sutherland atrocities. His "Gloomy Memories" are included in Alexander Mackenzie's *Highland Clearances*, probably the most important old book on the subject. At Kildonan only three families (out of a population of 2,000) were not burnt out of their homes. The emigration ships were often little better than slavers; the cholera and misery were indescribable.

The outcome is the deserted Highlands of today, brought home to me again and again when enjoying the hills of Ireland. You can stand on top of Galtee More and both see, and smell, the turf (peat) reek. The hills rise from a patchwork quilt of fields and cottages. It is a living landscape. The view down Strathnaver was no doubt similar once.

"A great shining thing is gone forever from the glens," was how George Mackay Brown put it. *Cha till, cha till, cha till mi tuilleadh.* I will return no more.

Tuesday 23 July PENULTIMATE

If everything begins it must likewise come to an end. I was certainly not keen to take up civilisation again, "a round of demands, provocations and doubts", as Bonatti pictured it. I had rediscovered the provocative call to the next horizon. It had been salutary. Depressions, whether meteorological or personal, eventually fill. Life is usually sunny periods, with showers. For long periods of rain one simply dons oilskins and wellies—and plods on. To full measure I had enjoyed Clemenceau's definition of liberty: "the right to discipline ourselves in order not to be disciplined by others".

I had no complaints. I have always believed that good adventures are given to those who are already walking in the right direction. People have since said to me about the Walk, again and again, "Oh, I'd love to do something like that, but . . ." This walk was essentially a rebellion against the *but*.

Breakfast was rather dull and I was glad to be whisked up Strath Vagastie and back to Crask to resume business. The greens and yellows of the strath were lit by sunshine, while from Crask the view westwards over the moors was to rainbow-split blackness.

A fine path led east up Strath a' Chraisg. I picked up dozens of big hairy caterpillars, which eventually uncoiled and began crawling. Hands and arms were covered in them eventually but the game palled when one adventured down my neck.

I turned off up the Allt Domhain which soon became a nice secretive stream. Up one deep slot which I was following I had a unique ornithological experience: a dipper had been flitting ahead and on this occasion splashed just out of sight into a pool on a bend; *instantly* it came shooting back past me, only reduced to diminutive size. My initial wonder turned to laughter—the dipper had landed beside, and frightened off, a wren, and their identical shapes did the rest.

I reached the ridge near Carn an Fheidh, when a look at the stormy west set me scurrying along the miles of Ben Klibreck, the *mountain of the fish*. I was rather peeved to see no real problems between Loch Shin and Crask; yesterday I'd missed a good walk for a hard cycle. By Loch Bad an Loch, a tent gave the only vivid colour. The final cone, Meall nan Con, was trailing clouds, and snug inside the circle round the trig point I ate and waited for Mike. An orchestration of wind was playing through the stones. I recalled a previous visit when we'd arrived to find the summit shattered, the boulders scarred and scattered. A lightning hit we presumed.

The Vagastie slopes have some crags. Rock-climbing up one buttress we once scrambled into an eagle's eyrie. It had incorporated a number of fence posts with which the ridge is littered. But those cliffs will forever be associated in my mind with a winter escapade which could have been a serious affair.

Lack of snow low down lured us upwards without ice-axes, and the gully began as an easy route—simple step kicking. It steepened. We continued. It became harder. Eventually we stood on disintegrating ice masking the vertical fall which threatened to topple everything down. With a considerable drop we had little inclination to climb and even less to descend. Luckily in David McNab I had a companion who was steady, even if still at school. After a spell of cutting ice with a penknife, it was obvious any traverse out was hopeless. We must go up. A bulge of ice blocked the view. We had the dog, Kitchy, and he was "sacrificed" to the reconnaissance. I heaved him over the bulge. A few minutes later his "come on" bark came from some distance away, so on his advice we forced the pitch and escaped. A silly escapade, but the person without any such tales is the loser. I don't try to justify climbing, or danger; but I defend the right of man to choose to look higher, to try harder. Life should be like a kaleidoscope; no matter what turns it takes, it falls into a many-coloured pattern. Contrast is one of the great pleasures of the mountains: dry must follow wet, laughter must know tears, ease come of toil, joy after fear, mountain and valley, rock and ice, bird and flower, land and sea, man and God, life and death.

George Meredith rather overstates it: "every step is a debate between what you are and what you might become." My own personal fear is one summed up by Chris Bonington: "The real danger to a climber isn't on things like the Eiger in winter but just in doing a lot of climbing over a long period". And during the last few months alone I had enjoyed a lifetime of mountains. I live on borrowed time!

I had nearly fallen asleep when Mike arrived to rouse me. He had returned the car to Altnaharra, and come up from the north-west. We went off along the ridge and were rewarded with a clearance. Loch Choire below was an area of bog and lochan and great loneliness. Morven was the only big hill beyond. Northwards our eyes were irresistibly drawn to Ben Hope and Ben Loyal, those Tolkein twins at the end of the walkers' world. Assynt remained wrapped in its black habit.

We strode along with the wind and then off the col to hit the Klibreck Burn for its last mile to Loch Naver. The strath seemed luxurious after the windy tops. The farm had crow-stepped gables and harling to remind me of Fife.

An hour in the Altnaharra Hotel with tea and scones prepared for the last pull. I would use the bike and we could camp below Ben Hope; then climb it tomorrow.

The River Mudale was being fished by one of the serious gents from the hotel. His wife gave me a queenly wave from their Rover as I pedalled past. There was a very heavy shower on the Meadie brae but I dried out again quickly. All the way from Altnaharra to Loch Meadie has been forested. West lay Ben Hee, dramatic in the storm clouds of the next attack. The poor lilies in Loch Meadie were in flower, but underwater as the level of the loch had risen above their elastic stalks. A dead adder lay by the roadside, a victim of a passing car.

I raced down Strathmore as hard as I could, but the shower caught me a quarter of a mile short of the camp Mike had set up. I dived into the car and we sat for ten minutes while the rain hammered noisily.

Just up the road was Dun Dornadilla, a fairly-well preserved Pictish broch. Ling, the explorer of so many hills in the north, thought it "a suitable name for a fly". The last brochs I'd seen had been in Glen Beag before Glenelg: aeons of experience ago.

While Mike produced supper I (not presumptuously I hoped) worked out the final figures. Tomorrow would be a busy enough day, all going well. Before turning in I also finished the Gospel of John: saved as the titbit for my traverse of the New Testament during the Walk.

It was nice to end from a camp even if the rain, midges and wind took turns at pestering. It is when two of those three combine that life becomes unbearable.

I had no feeling of being poised on the brink of a "success"; the last night in the tent was, as so many others, self-contained and contended despite the fact that tomorrow I would return to the traffic of life—and you know, perhaps, what Monsieur Hulot makes of that.

My thoughts were mainly forward. Music-starved for many months I could have a glut of all the favourites. I actually wrote down my thoughts there and then: Beethoven's Ninth first, then the March from Aida (these were utterly linked to the hills back in Braehead days), then Fauré's Requiem, Greig's Piano Concerto, *Butterfly*, the wide spaces of Sibelius and the shock of the Russians, Andes folk music, some of our own songs from Liz and Dave, James Fisher and The Corries, *The New World* ... I forced myself away from the game. It was too much to contemplate.

Financially I decided I could not manage the Alps and they somehow seemed too cosmopolitan and brash after these solitary weeks. Skye first then, for the B.F.M.C. Meet and to help Mike along some of the bits that rather discourage walkers. Then home, above all else; to sink down into that bliss. The future could wait, though I realised it could never be the same after these months of freedom.

It had been a disciplined, slow progression—which was very good for me no doubt being of somewhat choleric disposition. Its solitary nature had rather worried me in prospect. I was introverted enough! But the result had been all good, I had become a calmer individual and learnt more of content and peace. Few are lucky enough to escape the ties of life and ascend their happiness; and, having done so, I found a veritable ladder leading up to Heaven. It was also a very humbling experience.

There have often been periods when I have known the hills alone. Many of my early doings were solitary simply because I never knew others with like interests. Eventually one made one's own converts, a small gang who roamed the Ochils locally. Over the previous score of years I'd climbed over 1,500 Munros (even the poor dog had done 700). Yet of the 279 only about 60 had ever been done alone. I'd now rectified that with a vengeance. By the end of 1974, with two more visits to Skye, all the Munros had been covered, solo. With so much of the time during the hill years synonymous with responsibility, being alone had been a tonic.

One of the delights had been the length of it. The idea of stopping just seemed unbelievable, and unwelcome. There was a marvellous rhythm in this simple life. One of its joys had been to see, from within, as it were, the sweep of the seasons: frost and snow to summer monsoon; bird migrants arriving, eggs, young and fledglings—first cuckoo heard, last cuckoo heard; deer endlessly (speckled fawns through to stags in velvet), divers and eagles (120 birds listed), foxes, otters. . . .

So now it's all but over.

More than ever I love my own land—its sweeping and often bewildering changes and challenges, its joys and delights, its incomparable peace and beauty.

Wednesday 24 July   TO LIVE IN HOPE

We moved about in bare feet over the soft, wet-clean turf. Breakfast did not take long. The midges saw to that.

We donned boots and waterproofs, then just plodded off at 8.30, up the saturated grass, and broke through the scarps on to the upper slopes. I suppose there was reasonable motivation for being out on such

M

a dreich day. The hill simply looked like a dead sheep: bare ribs sticking out through a tatty fleece of cloud.

We played about on little rock problems. A raven croaked in the mist but the weather steadily became wetter and piercing cold. After eighteen days of varying degrees of wet and cold it was only moderately unpleasant.

The scruffy cairn and trig point came at last. I patted the cairn with a heartfelt "Thanks be to God", then we scuttled like crabs into its lee for shelter, had a snack, and opened the hoarded bottle of champagne with numb fingers; very unobstreperous rejoicing. Was champagne ever drunk in such miserable setting? Our argument whether it was supposed to be served chilled or at room temperature was resolved; here they were the same thing.

Ben Hope, 3,040 feet (Norse word *hob* meaning a bay), deserves a bit of praise—it is a great wee hill. Had we not kept it for last after all? It lies east of and above the loch of the same name in a great tiered cliff, riven with gullies and ribs, explored by J. H. B. Bell to be sure. David McNab and I spent part of one Christmas poking around on the cliffs in gales and horrible snow before going off for our daft day on Klibreck. The eastern side is gentler but gives long approaches. Most people simply ascend from the sheep buildings a mile down from the broch of Dun Dornadilla—as we were forced to do on this unsmiling day.

I deposited my very battered woodpecker feathers on the cairn. This was a bird extinct in Scotland after about 1850 but recently it has been steadily moving north. Ben Lomond to Ben Hope is a big jump however . . . We chuntered down in an hour deciding champagne had much to recommend it after all. It was a warmer, cheerier descent though the weather had not altered.

The last two verses of "Jude", a great doxology and a ringing tune, kept repeating themselves in my head. How often they had rung out after fine hill days—what more appropriate here? God, it was good.

Wet layers were soon peeled off and then we both jumped into Mike's car and drove off. I think that brought it home. It was over, dared and done: the 1,639 miles of padding and pedalling, the 112 days, the 449,000 feet of ascent. I picked up my Dormobile from Bonar Bridge where it had been left by David at a garage. Mike and I met again for dinner in the Station Hotel at Inverness. Posh clothes again. And a bed eventually. And a bath. And for the first time, simply no necessary compulsion for the morrow. No set course. We could go out all night. Celebrate.

In fact it was merely sad, as are so many endings. The success was, ultimately, unimportant—the quality of the living alone really mattered.

> "Yet the mountaineer who sidles on
> And on to the very bending,
> Discovers, if heart and brain be proof,
> No necessity ending."
>
> BROWNING

Tomorrow we would head for Skye and Cuillin verticality—a nice holiday for "Hamish the Hill". We would join a club Meet there and that for certain would bring back joyful normality. It had been a good trip but it would be good to be home.

Oddly, the first thing I found once home was something I scribbled many, many years ago. I was looking for another reference at the time but nothing could be more appropriate than the "Ten Commandments of Mountaineering".

I hope I have kept the faith.

1. Thou shalt prepare thoroughly before starting.
2. Thou shalt set out early.
3. Thou shalt set out properly equipped.
4. Thou shalt choose thy company with care.
5. Thou shalt not destroy anything that is thy neighbour's.
6. Thou shalt often keep silence to hear the mountain speak.
7. Thou shalt leave no sign of thy passing.
8. Thou shalt remember others in their strength or weakness.
9. Thou shalt bend to the weather and be strong.
10. Thou shalt be humble—and praise God.

AFTERMATH—OR REASONS WHY

As soon as the Walk was over Mike and I rushed off to Skye where we had a highly successful week's climbing. Had I in fact been mentally or physically run down; or stressed or suffering deficiencies (all gloomily forecast), a week such as we had would have been impossible. I have never felt so relaxed as I did towards the end of the Walk, I was fit and co-ordinated, and crafty enough to reap Skye where other Braes o' Fife members were cursing the place and fleeing its brand of weather-made frustration. I returned home for my fortieth birthday.

I'm not so naïve as to underestimate the strength of my assault. I loaded the dice as far as I could but, looking back, I also had my ration of luck. If April and July weather had been reversed there could well have been no story to tell. But if you plan with the worst in mind the outcome must seem not so bad after all: the optimist is often a fool heading for disappointment whereas the pessimist finds life full of pleasant surprises. Besides, I trusted in God—and kept my porridge dry.

Reasons for mountaineering are as varied as the participants and largely subjective. Analysis is of doubtful validity, I fear. Basically we do it for fun, or no doubt a Frenchman would express it better: it's a passion, a love-affair—and who would ask to justify love? To the unhooked it is just damn silly—but so is stamp collecting, sailing, or any activity done for pleasure. But the layman wants some understanding of what he regards as a dangerous activity, though I doubt if he can find it, any more than he can understand why a runner strains to achieve a four-minute mile.

There is a whole mixture of coloured pills: the lure of challenge and testing, the delight of achievement, the contact with our ancestral simplicity, the escape from a normal petty existence, the finding of values, of beauty, of vision. These are worth living for—and possibly dying for.

Walter Bonatti in the preface to his autobiography said the following which gave my teenage situation exactly: "As a child I always found it much easier to deal with nature than with men. I have always found in her a sort of loyalty which made possible a silent and affectionate communion, whereas I found myself floundering, bewildered and unprepared amid the often underhand methods used by man. This contrast between the world of nature and the social world was in my eyes the essential contrast between happiness and unhappiness. So I fled to the mountains with a feverish eagerness."

As a child, chased about the East by war, as a refugee in racial South Africa, as an omnivorous reader . . . I was all too aware of the "greatness and misery of man". If man could be so beastly, how could there be God?

Yet living in the country, with hills ranged around (whether Valley of the Thousand Hills in Natal or couthy Ochils at Dollar), I was also intensely aware of the marvellous and beautiful in nature. When things were intolerable (and I also, no doubt, intolerable) I used to flee quite consciously to the hills for balm. The dichotomy between man, sin, evil and creation, harmony, beauty was a despair. There had to be God? But how reconcile the opposites?

The answer came in the Mull of Kintyre at a "Highlands and Border Camp" where among regular Bible readings I attended, I heard a marvellous exposition of Paul's letter to the Romans, which gave me an experience of God's grace that lifted the clouds, so to speak.

During the Walk I read right through the New Testament again; if not quite in one go, in fairly large hunks—a delight. Such treats, too, are crowded out so easily in the rat-race of so-called civilisation. Life's pressures are very seldom a problem except at home—and are often the result of an inability to solve basic problems.

My Walk represented a long pilgrimage, a time of quiet renewal. God is best found among the hills—there are few pagan shepherds. But the hills are no idyll: the countryman knows most of birth and death, dawn and dusk, sun and star sweep—and finds God real. God is sure and steadfast; it is man who breaks himself against life. At the deepest level I suspect this is why I climb.

I suspect, also, that in some circles despair rather than hope is the driving force: climb the great peak or route and at least there will be some earthly immortality! Is this too cynical? With today's lack of reverence for life I don't think so. For some "at the top" it is a very important element. Some struggle to remain there, others having made their rude gesture climb no more. A psychiatrist would enjoy the company of those Tom Patey called "Apes and Ballerinas".

The silent majority, the millions who may climb for a lifetime and never write a word or do anything to catch the eye of fellow mountain-eers or the wider public, have, I suspect, the steadfast rewards. Truth is seldom found in extremes. The average all too often keeps silent. This Walk in some ways was also a gesture—the average stepping out of line and singing his song of faith in a world which has lost faith, of finding hope, at the last—and a certain, secret, vindictive delight. This is mine and nothing can undo it, no legislation cancel out a mile of it, no man tax it, or destroy it. In some ways it's a gesture bordering on the blasphemous, only my heart-cry on coming to that misty trig point was, in all humility, "Thanks be to God".

For so many things. Above all else for the fun and enjoyment—which has never been put better than in the good book itself: "For ye shall go out with joy, and be led forth with peace: the mountains and the hills shall break forth before you into singing, and all the trees of the field shall clap their hands." ISAIAH 55: 12.

APPENDICES

BIBLIOGRAPHY

INDEX

APPENDIX I

EQUIPMENT

This appendix will no doubt come in for its share of criticism as well as providing hopeful ideas—after all, magazine articles, price lists (inflation has done away with catalogues it seems), manuals and whole books are given to discussing gear *minutiae*. I have no magic formula.

My gear was good. Some of it was new for this trip and chosen from years of bitter testing in the Highlands and Islands but I'll wager the old ex-W.D. gear with which I began, so archaically regarded by today's youngsters, was little worse or heavier. The substitution of man-made materials for natural has been no improvement. The efficiency of gear seems to be related in inverse ratio to its price.

Some items were chosen simply because of availability: I could not afford to renew with possibly better, lighter items. Being diverse, even perverse creatures, no two of us would pack the same gear, choose the same route, wear the same clothes, eat the same food. . . . *Chacun à son goût*—which a pupil of mine once suggested meant "chuck in what's good".

I don't cut the handle off my toothbrush. These little objects, even in total, are not where weight accumulates. The biggest weight accumulators are things like waterproof trousers and jacket, bivy bag, tent, rucksack, stove and sleeping bag.

Kugy, in his great book *Alpine Pilgrimage*, was a bivy adept in the rugged Julians. "We travelled light. . . . And strange to say all went much more easily than today, when heavy rucksacks convey for me all the marvels of the modern age of climbing." Cynicism is not new it appears!

But to take the items one by one.

Tent: I had one of Dave Challis' *Tulloch Mountaincraft* tents. It weighed a bit over 3 lb. The groundsheet was tray-shaped (to float above all wetness) but instead of being sewn-in, which ensures that condensation drains inboard, it was held in place by elastic tabs to the tent proper, which was simple single skin nylon one, high at the front and streamlined to the feet end. Condensation thus ran into the ground harmlessly. No inner needed. Door extensions were made of cotton and zipped in various ways. It had valances. In a hurry 8 pegs saw it erected.

Stove and Cooking Items: Most of the time I used a 120 *Camping Gaz* stove, a compromise choice, preferring its clean, non-spill, easy-to-work running to the more efficient *Primus*, which gave difficulties for carrying and storing paraffin safely. In early days and for the Lochaber trip I used a *Meta* stove, ultra-light but fiddly to work. The new-type stand is ludicrously fragile for hill use.

For cooking I had the smallest (2 pint) dixi from a set: the pot did for cooking, the lid for brews and an extra wafer-thin disc of aluminium served as an extra lid so what was on the stove could always be covered, thereby saving time and fuel. A squashy 1 gallon watercarrier proved excellent— when folded my nylon mesh string-bag of food fitted into its odd shape well. (String-bag is strong and contents are visible.) A quarter of a *Golden Fleece* scourer likewise was worth its ounce of weight. My spoon was edged sharp enough to cut so I had no knife/fork or other bits and pieces. Three plastic or aluminium containers of differing sizes served (1) as milk-maker/container at camp and waterbottle on hill, (2) for holding jam/honey etc., (3) for salt. All other foods went into poly bags—as many as necessary for safety.

Sleeping Bag: A Black's *Norseland* (4 lb) gave reasonable weight/quality ratio. It was my heaviest single item. A light sheet liner was always used.

Bivy Bag: Usual bright orange thing.

Rucksack: Packframes I dislike on the hill and after many years of using a "Tiso Special" in many lands, that was my choice. It has an armpit-length pull out so could serve as extra bedding, either under me or with me inside it. No exterior pockets either. Simplicity often equals efficiency.

No insulation, padding, matting or what have you was used. Except on snow these are just bulky extras. The rucksack, tent-bag, waterproofs and any spare clothes did just as well.

Clothing: I wore a long-sleeved *Damart* vest which doubled as pullover, plus a good shirt with sleeves long enough to cover hands in place of gloves. If still cold, the cagoule jacket went on. Non-nylon underpants and ordinary flannels did the nether regions (breeches are a big con for hill walking). When hot the trousers rolled up, otherwise they tucked into good, soft wool stockings. The Damart vest also proved better than a shirt in the heat. Spare clothes were a Shetland pullover; a sun/rain hat; long-johns to start, then nylon swimming shorts; and a pair of thin nylon socks—the last purely for decency in hotels when stockings were probably hanging out the window drying!

Boots: In the year of preparation I bought three pairs of *Sportiva* boots which were cheap enough, light, fairly soft, and also fitted my wide flipper-feet. A large plaster sometimes seen on my left heel was to stop bruising the tendon. (One foot is half a size different.) I take sizes 9½ (left) and 10 (right) so anyone with the same problem, but in reverse, please get in contact! Three pairs allowed reserves and they were all broken in thoroughly in advance. Blisters were never a problem. Anklets kept dirt out.

The price of the boots went up a considerable percentage in the year of planning—so even as an investment this did no harm. Three pairs were used, but because one right and one left disintegrated, in reality, I only irrevocably lost one pair—which I think good going.

Waterproofs: I started with my ordinary set till I realised how heavy they were, so soon swopped to lightweight ones. The jacket was replaced by a *Tulloch* one and it did till the end.

A sponge-cloth, rolled up, fitted my back to mop up sweat and keep the rucker off a bit.

Camera: I carried a tiny Rollei 35S which took many hundreds of transparencies (Kodachrome 25) until I lost it on Alligin. For black and white a Yashica sometimes came up at weekends.

Odd Box: A waterproof plastic box contained the following:

Toilet paper	Youth Hostel membership card
Jiffy tin opener	Emergency Procedure Form
Compass (*Silva*)	Money and cheques
Whistle	Odd change—for phoning
Matches	Thread, wool and 2 needles
Spare film(s)	Repair strip (for cloth, nylon or canoe)
Comb	Lens cloth and brush for camera
Mini-scissors	Vitamin pills (never used)
Stamps, stationery	Two wound dressings
Savlon (½ tube)	Elastic bandage
Safety pins, 2	Some swabs
Cycle chain link	Dressing strip and various plasters
Piece of scourer	a few Panadol tablets
Biro, pencil stub	Toothbrush (no paste)

Soap and soap powder were in cache boxes now and then. A piece of candle was carried at the start and later midge cream and a gut fishing line were added. A watch and a hanky lived in a pocket, odd bits of string usually ended there too.

Tools, spare tube, etc., for the cycle lived with the brute so were not carried.

At any time I usually had a paperback to read, one of the six log-books I filled, one of the 22 maps required, the small loose-leaf Route book (brother had the duplicate)—and a slim 2 oz. New Testament.

It seems a fantastic amount when written down but it was all used, or might in certain emergencies, and it is a slimmer list than most would produce. The test was in the carrying. As Tilman says: "It is rather a problem deciding what you must take and what you can leave behind, but it is amazingly simplified when you know that you have to carry it all yourself."

The rucksack weighed about 23 lb and only twice ever exceeded 30 lb.

Accumulating and sorting went on for a year in advance; spares had to be in appropriate caches or in the Dormobile. No lack ever continued beyond the next weekender's visit.

APPENDIX II

FOOD

"A well-balanced diet costs little more than an ill-balanced diet, and it is only a question of care."

ERIC SHIPTON

Many years ago I went through the phase of learning all about vitamins and calories and so on, but being fond of my food I soon came to the conclusion that eating reasonably gave all the calorific intake required for my modest mountaineering.

Walking off into the blue struck me as being a poor reason to forgo the pleasures of eating ("God hath given us all things richly to enjoy") so I ate well; which was, besides, much easier than trying to relearn all that alphabetical mathematics concerning food.

Food I divide into three kinds, in descending order of preference—and probably nutritious value—fresh, then tinned, then dehydrated.

Fresh: This was fixed through my family in Dollar who had a weekly standing order: (1) for mail and newspapers, film, toilet paper, and requests given by phone; (2) for food: 4 slices bacon, 6 eggs (boxed), fresh meat and vegetables for 2 meals, 3 bits of fresh fruit, 2 tomatoes, ½ lb. cheese, poke salt, smallest brown loaf, odd home baking, 2 pints milk, ½ lb. butter, spices.

This was brought up by the weekend support teams and ensured I ate very well for at least two days a week. Only between Glen Shiel and Strathcarron did I have a weekend without it. I was too difficult to find at that stage.

Tinned: Every cache contained at least one meal of tinned items: meats, vegetables, fruit and so on (see list below) which were a great morale booster. (The strawberries and cream after the Knoydart depression will never be forgotten!) Their food value was obviously good.

Dehydrated: The rest of my weekly cycle. Improvements in variety and flavour have been made recently by manufacturers, and I usually mixed fresh or tinned food with it. Vegetables I tended to soak at the mid-day brew so they reconstituted as I walked.

The following were always regular items: tea bags, Tetley coffee bags, sugar, milk powder (Millac), bread-substitute (Vita Wheat, Macvita, Tuc, Water or Cracker biscuits), oatmeal, muesli (Alpen), biscuits, sweets, packet soups (quick-cooking ones, but not "instant" horrors), Knorr cubes, one of potato powder/rice/spaghetti/macaroni, one of jam/honey/syrup/marmalade, K.P. peanuts, raisins, chocolate, cheese and West's sardines.

I normally kept to tinned meat as much as possible even if this gave some extra weight. (I'd challenge that the weight of fuel to reconstitute non-tinned meat is probably as great!) These were bought in bulk, established favourites that never palled, even once a week for months on end: Shippam's Chicken Supreme, Chesswood's Curry with Beef and Mushrooms, Plum-rose's Bacon Grill and Beef Olives, Grant's Haggis. I also enjoyed Scotbeef Mince, Goblin Hamburgers, Heinz Beefburgers, Fray Bentos Steak and Kidney Pudding, Meat Balls, and various curries and cold meats, ham, tongue, chicken, etc.

Tinned mixed vegetables (Smedley's) and Indian corn (Green Giant) were regulars, spinach a treat (Lin-can).

Heinz Steam Puddings, Christmas puddings, Bird's Instant Whips and Angel Delights, tins of all kinds of fruit, Ambrosia Creamed Rice and Semolina, Nestlé's Cream, condensed milk, these rang the changes for a sweet—along with the basic Bachelor's or Swell dried apple flakes.

Bachelors have long been my regular provider of dehydrated vegetables: peas, beans, carrots, cabbage and onions being the choice.

At times I had Drinking Chocolate, Ovaltine and Horlicks to drink (the last dangerously like potato powder in texture and colour).

Biscuits were a personal choice: various Simmers' ones, gingernuts, wheaten, oat crunchie and Jacob's Club. As ever I consumed many Lees Macaroon and other bars, Bournville, Duncan's Wholenut, Red Bounty, were the regular chocolate choices. (The R.A.F. lads, going N–S, once rose to an input of 12 bars a day—each.) I managed 2 at the most but relished sweet treats now and then like Fry's Turkish Delight, condensed milk or tins of fruit. Robertson's bramble, Nelson's marmalade and various Scott jams went on pieces. Sometimes I had peanut butter. Sardines and Kraft Cheese Slices were regular lunch fillings. Crawford's shortbread became a great favourite.

I liked my regular items and never knew what a cache would contain so I was never disappointed, and often cheered, by dealings with food.

THE QUESTIONNAIRES

I intended covering many more of the remoter summits with my question-naire but became very lax about this. All too often I left them in the tent or rucksack only to remember on the summit. However, some patterns did emerge.

I left 29 and 23 came back. 2 were found the same day as left, 3 the next day and only 6 lay for more than 10 days. (18, 19, 15, 19, 15 and 20 days—generally on dull and remote tops.)

During April and on to mid-June 75 per cent were picked up by week-enders, from mid-June to the end of July 100 per cent were picked up by those on holiday—BUT, these were by then beyond the Great Glen where this would be a natural tendency. The weekenders were still no doubt busy further south. Six of the returns were from residents south of the border.

Ages: 2 in teens, 11 in 20's, 4 in 30's, 6 in 40's and 1 in 60's. (You have your fling, tail off, and come back it seems.) The younger tended to be weekenders, the older used holidays—but again the survey shifted north into the holiday period. Ages at which they began "collecting": 1 at 4, 8 in teens, 11 in 20's, 2 in 30's, 1 in 40's.

The lowest "bag" was 20, 9 were in the 100's and 7 over 200 (including one who said he did not collect Munros).

Of the 23 only 3 were with the dreaded official parties (of 14, 8 and 13 people).

Nineteen of the replies admitted using private transport (cars) whether at weekends or during holidays, 1 pair was hitching (aged 49 and 14), 1 party was camping in the Cairngorms but did not say how they reached them and 1 gang arrived by sailing ship (the *Captain Scott*).

The pressures on other land users is very slight on the whole. Apart from mid-June onwards they hardly exist: keepers, shepherds are tending to have weekends off, these days—and that's the only time the hills are busy. Later, the holidays start and people will be encountered every day doubtless; but the lambing is past, the birds are hatched and the stalking is to come. There can hardly be complaint at usage at this period. I should imagine a clash of interest only comes from mid-August into September (a period I make sure of being abroad!) and then it is clearly up to climbers to co-operate their pleasure into other's profit.

Generally the remoter landscape has not suffered from wear-and-tear or litter. The areas of pressure are blatant: places like Glencoe, Cairngorms, Torridons. These are dramatic and romantic and the tourist bodies, N.T.S., etc. all cry "Come!" Thank goodness it's a far cry to Seana Bhraigh.

STATISTICS

This is the only time I have ever worked out careful statistics. One interesting figure which comes out is that, on average, you take 1,500 feet and four miles per Munro. All the long trips (Ripley, Hinde, Cousins) give the same result—so you can work out your life tally. It is not advisable to try and work out the average cost per Munro. Inflation makes this difficult as well as discouraging. Make what you can then of the following facts and figures from the Long Walk.

Mileage: 1,639 (estimate was 1,254)
Footage: 449,000 (estimate was 360,000)
Time: 112 days (estimate was 112 days)
Daily average: 4,000 feet + and 14½ miles.

There were 279 Munros at the time (now there are 280) and 5 were climbed a second time. Five Corbetts were also done, so 289 peaks of note were involved. Tops and other bumps were not particularly noted; they are on the whole artificial and less interesting.

Of these summits 213 were clear on top, 76 obscured. People were encountered on 44 peaks. Six friend(s) accompanied me on 12 hill days over 29 summits (12 in Skye). I was alone for 100 days over 260 summits. April had a run of 23 dry days; July had 2. Snow fell on 10, rain on 69.

Accommodation. Nights were spent: 62 camping in 47 sites, 19 in 10 different Youth Hostels, 7 in 4 huts, 10 in 8 hotels, homes, a private hostel and 13 nights in 10 different bothies.

14 days gave no Munros, 12 being compulsory "rest days" and 2 stormbound at the C.I.C. Hut. On 10 I travelled but collected no summits. 19 days gave 1 Munro, 17 gave 2, 15 gave 3, 17 gave 4, 7 gave 5, 8 gave 6, 2 gave 7, 2 gave 8, 1 gave 10.

April, 27 days, gave 58 Munros, 1 repeated, 3 Corbetts = 62 peaks.
May, 31 days, gave 100 Munros, 4 repeated, 1 Corbett = 105 peaks.
June, 30 days, gave 66 Munros, 0 repeats, 1 Corbett = 67 peaks.
July, 24 days, gave 55 Munros, 0 repeats, 0 Corbetts = 55 peaks.

1974 gave a tally altogether of 344 Munros while only 9 times have I ever struggled to an annual haul of 100 plus.

21 days gave less than 1,000 feet of ascent.
3 days gave 1,000 feet + of ascent.
3 „   „   2,000 „   „   „
9 „   „   3,000 „   „   „
8 „   „   3,500 „   „   „

19 days gave	4,000 feet	+ of ascent.
10 ,, ,,	4,500 ,,	,, ,,
10 ,, ,,	5,000 ,,	,, ,,
7 ,, ,,	5,500 ,,	,, ,,
7 ,, ,,	6,000 ,,	,, ,,
6 ,, ,,	6,500 ,,	,, ,,
5 ,, ,,	7,000 ,,	,, ,,
3 ,, ,,	7,500 ,,	,, ,,
1 day ,,	10,000 ,,	,, ,,

12 camps were over	500 feet.
20 ,, ,, ,,	1,000 ,,
3 ,, ,, ,,	1,500 ,,
4 ,, ,, ,,	2,000 ,,
3 ,, ,, ,,	2,500 ,,
1 camp was over	3,000 feet.

APPENDIX V

MOUNTAINEERING GAELIC

This is not the list of a Gaelic expert; it is largely gleaned from my own experience of mountain names and therefore is likely to be of use to others who have faced similar confusions. Maps and guide books will often give different spellings, many corrupt, never mind the shades of meaning that allows the *white hill* for instance to be spelt six different ways.

The very word HILL has a multitude of descriptive variations. A *ben, beinn* or *bheinn* may be any shape but *stob* implies pointedness and a *sgor* or *sgurr* will be dramatically so; pinnacle is often *stac*. A *stuc* will be big and rough while a *meall, mheall* will be a dull lump and a *druim* a long back or ridge. Bold peaks may also be *bidean, bidein, binnean*. *Carn* or *cairn* may imply a stony, rounded summit as well as the pile of stones. *Cruach* will be a bold hill shape, *maol* a bare top, *mam* used for a gentle-sloped hill and *monadh* often covers a plateau of old pasture or gentle summits. *Aonach* sometimes means a ridge and a *sron* or *sroine* is one running down into the valley, *druim*, ditto, or merely a spur. A hillock can be variously *tulaich, torr, tom, cnap, cnoc* or *sithean* (pro: shee-an, often a fairy hill). *Ord* is a solitary out-lier. *Creag* or *craig* is a crag or craggy summit. *Fiacaill* is a toothed ridge.

Corrie (the Welsh *cwm*) can be spelt *coire, choire, coir'*, etc. *Beag, beg* (small) and *mor, mhor* (big) are very common adjectives. Many of these names are a reflection on the importance of cattle in the highland way of life at one time. A hill stream is usually *allt*, sometimes *easan* or *eas* (also means straight waterfall) or *uisge* (i.e. water). Burn is a lowland Scots word. *Glen, gleann, ghlinne* is a narrow valley and a *strath* a large, open one. A pass in the sense of a col is usually *bealach* (pronounced: balloch), *lairig* is a through valley, and *mam* may be used of one with gentle sloping approaches. Lake is *loch*; *lochan, lochain* the diminutive—and you might even meet wee lochans! *Abhainn* (*avon*) is river.

Pronunciations; some basic sounds: *Bh* or *Mh* at the start of a word is aspirated "V" (e.g. Meall a' Bhuiridh = Mell a' Vooree). This shows what happens with final *idh* too. An initial *Fh* is silent, *Ph* sounds f, *Sh* or *Th* sounds h. *Ch* is always pronounced guttural and *g* hard.

Many names are corrupted, which adds difficulties. Achintee, for instance, should be Ach'an t-Suidhe, meaning Field of the Seat. For fuller lists of mountain names consult the lists in W. H. Murray's *The Scottish Highlands* or the other district guides of the S.M.C. The following list is kept brief, mainly using commoner descriptive words which will help to piece names together. Names can help in many ways—see my June 16 day for one such use.

a'/an	the (definite article)	cailleach/ chailleach	old woman
aber/abhair	confluence	caisteal	castle
achadh	field, plain	camas	bay, bend
airgiod	silver	caochan	small stream
airidh, airigh	shieling	caora (ch)	sheep
ard/aird	promontory, height	caol, chaolais	kyle, strait, thin
		cam	crooked
ath	ford	cas	steep
auch/ach	field	cat/chait	cat
bad	clump of trees	cean/ceann/ken/ kin	head (pro: ken)
ban/bhan	white, fair, pale		
beith	birch	chaorachain	torrent
b(h)eoil/beul	mouth	chaoruinn	rowan
bo/ba	cow/cattle	choinneach	boggy or mossy place
brae/braigh	upper part, height	cioch/ciche	pap
breabag	little upland	ciste	chest, coffin
breac	speckled	clach	stone, stony
brochan	porridge	clunie/cluanie	meadow place
bruach	bank, steep place	coille	wood (pro: coo-lee)
buachaille	shepherd		
buidhe	yellow (pro: boo-ee)	con/choin	dog
		creachan	rock
cabar	antler	cuaich/quoich	deep hollow, cup
cadha	narrow pass, ravine		

cul	back
cumhann	narrow, strait
dal/dail	field, flood plain
damh/diamh	stag
darach	oak (wood)
dearcag	berry
dearg/dheirg	red (pro: jerrag)
deas	south
diollaid	saddle
diridh	divide, water-shed
doire	small wood, thicket
domhain	deep
donich/donn	brown
drochaid	bridge
dubh/duibhe/dubha	black/dark
dun/dhuin	castle, fort
each/eich	horse
eadar	between
eag/eagach	rocky gap, notch
ear	east
eas(a)	waterfall
eighe	file
eilean	island
elrig	deer pass or trap
etchachan	juniper
eun/eoin	bird(s)
fada/fhada	long (pro: Attow)
fearn	alder
feithe	bog (pro: fey)
fiadh/fheidh	deer
fionn	white, light-coloured
fraoch	heather
fuar	cold
fuaran/fhuarain	well, spring, sward
gabhar/gobhar, etc.	goat
gall	lowlander/stranger
gaoth/gaoith	wind(s)

garbh/ghairbh/garve	rough or thick
geal(a)	white, bright
gearr	short
giubhas	fir(s)
glac	narrow valley, defile
glas/ghlais	grey/green
glomach	chasm
ghobhlach	forked
gorm	blue/green
iar	west
inbhir/inver	river mouth
inch/innis	island, river meadow
iolaire	eagle
iubhair	yew
ladhar	hoof/fork
lag/laggan	hollow/small hollow
lair(e)	mare
laoigh	calf
larach	site of ruin
leac/licc	slab, stony slope
leacach	stony place
leathad	slope
leitir/leitreach	hillside, slope
lcum	leap
liath/leith	grey
linn(e)	pool (below falls often)
luib/lub	bend
mairg	rusty-coloured
mara/mhara	sea
meirleach	thieves, robbers
mhaim	breast/pass
mhadaidh	foxes
mheadhoin	middle (pro: vey'n)
mhaighdean	maiden
mhuilinn	mill
min/mine	smooth
moin(e)	peat bog/moss
nid/nead	nest
odhar	browny-coloured (pro: ower)

oidhche	night (pro: Oech-a)	tionail	gathering, assembly
or	gold	tobar/tiobair	well
poite	pot	toll/tuill/thuill	hole, deep corrie
poll/phuill	pool/mud	torc/tuirc	boar
raineach/rainich	fern/bracken	traigh	beach (pro: try)
reidh(e)	smooth, plain	tuath	north
riabhach	brindled/greyish	tullach/tulaich/ tulloch	knoll/hillocks
riach	speckled/greyish buff	uaine	green (pro: oo-an)
righ(e)	king (ban-righ = queen)	uamh (a)	cave (pro: oo-a)
ruadh	red (bright)	uisg(e)	water
rubha/rhu	point/cape	ulaidh	treasure
ruigh/ruidhe	shieling/cattle run		

sabhail (toul)	barn	baile/bal	township
sagairt	priest	bar	top/point
saighdeir	soldier	bodach	old man
sail	heel	bran	raven
sean(a)/sin	old	braon/braoin	shower(s)
seilge/sealg	hunt(ing)	caim	twist
seileach/seilich	willow	caora(ich)	sheep
sgairaich	screes	capull	horse
sgiath	wing	chroin	cloven
slochd/sloc	deep, hollow	chrois	cross
sluggan	gorge, gullet	cill/kil	cell/church
sneachd(a)	snow	cir/chir	comb
socath/succoth	snout/between streams	clachan	hamlet
		croit	croft
spidal/spittal/ spideal	hospice	dris/driesh	bramble spot
		eilde	hind(s)
spreidh(e)	cattle	fas	level place
sput(an)	(small) fall, spout	frith(e)	deer forest
		ghluasaid	moving
subh	berry	glais	burn
suidhe	seat	glomach	cleft/chasm
tarbh/tarf	bull	greigh	cheek
tarmachan	ptarmigan	labhar	loud/resounding
tarbet/tairbeart, etc.	isthmus	leis	lee(ward)
		muc/muic	pig
tarsuinn/ tharsuinn	across, transverse	ob	bay (dim: Oban)
		puist	post
tcallach	forge, hearth	socath	snout
teanga	tongue	steall	waterfall
tigh(e)	house	uig	bay

This is only a brief list. You *could* find 50 words for HILL alone, so I have not tried to be systematic. The *reds* and *blacks* and *whites* are too easy, yet so many names are now so corrupted or puzzling as to be meaningless: Aosda, Claurigh, Chrasgaidh, Creise, Faochagach, Fhuaran, Ghaordie, Heasgarnich, Keen, Mayar, Mharconaich, Narnain, Sgriol—for a start. Others like Bynack or Macdhui or Nevis have several conflicting derivations suggested. This is why you will certainly find differences between the old and the new O.S. maps, my text, Jim's maps in this book, and Munro's Tables. There is no hill with the Gaelic for *sheep*, for they came later—when Gaelic itself was being evicted. The innumerable *goats* might just have a bearing on our recreational activity!

BIBLIOGRAPHY

Baker, E. A.: *The Highlands with Rope and Rucksack.* 1923

Barnett, Ratcliffe: *The Road to Rannoch and the Summer Isles.* 1946

Bell, J. H. B.: *A Progress in Mountaineering.* Oliver and Boyd 1950

Borthwick, A.: *Always a Little Further* Jn. Smith or Faber. (Highly amusing)

Broster, D. K.: *The Flight of the Heron; The Dark Mile; The Gleam in the North.* (Jacobite romantic fiction, in paperback)

Brown, P. and Waterson, G.: *The Return of the Osprey.* 1962

Buchan, John: *John Macnab* (poachers' tale); *Montrose.* (Historical)

Campbell, M.: *Argyll, The Enduring Heartland.* Turnstone 1977

Clark, R. W. and Pyatt, E. C.: *Mountaineering in Britain.* Phoenix 1957

Darling, F. F. and Boyd, J. M.: *The Highlands and Islands.* Collins/Fontana

Firsoff, V. A.: *In the Hills of Breadalbane.* Hale 1954

Fraser, D.: *Highland Perthshire.* Standard Press, Montrose 1971

Frere, R. B.: *Thoughts of a Mountaineer.* Oliver and Boyd 1952

Gordon, Seton: Any books of his are worth finding. Start with: *Highways and Byeways in the West Highlands* (1935), and *Central Highlands* (1949), both Macmillan, and *The Cairngorm Hills of Scotland.* Cassell 1925

Gilbert, R.: *Memorable Munros* (distributed by Cordee, Leicester), 1976

Grant, I. F.: *Highland Folkways.* Routledge 1961

Haldane, A. R. B.: *The Drove Roads of Scotland; New Ways Through the Glens.* Both Nelson. (Authoritative and readable)

Heinzel, Fitter, Parslow: *The Birds of Britain and Europe.* Collins

Holden, A. E.: *Plant Life in the Scottish Highlands.* Oliver and Boyd 1952

Holmes, W. K.: *Tramping Scottish Hills.* E. Mackay 1946

Humble, B. H.: *The Cuillin of Skye.* Hale 1952

Johnson, Samuel: *Journey to the Western Isles of Scotland.* 1775

Lindsay, M.: *The Discovery of Scotland; The Eye is Delighted.* Hale

Linklater, E.: *The Prince in the Heather.* Hodder 1966

Macrow, B.: *Torridon Highlands.* Hale 1969

MacCulloch, D. B.: *Romantic Lochaber, Arisaig and Morvar*. Chambers 1971
MacInnes, H.: *Call Out*. Hodder 1973
Mackenzie, Osgood: *A Hundred Years in the Highlands*. Bles 1949. (A classic)
MacLeann, C. I.: *The Highlands*. Batsford 1959. Paperback 1975
MacNally, L.: *Highland Year*; Highland Deer Forest; *Wild Highlands*; *Year of the Red Deer* (all Dent). (Expert naturalist/photographer)
Matthews, H.: *British Mammals*. Collins N. N. 1952
Moir, D. G.: *Scottish Hill Tracks*. Bartholomew 1975 (2 vols.)
Munro, Neil: *The New Road*; *John Splendid*, etc. Blackwood. (Novels)
Murray, W. H.: *The Scottish Highlands*. S.M.T. 1977. (Wide in scope, a must) *Mountaineering in Scotland*; *Undiscovered Scotland*. Dent. 1947, 1951; the former in paperback. (Most famous of Scottish climbing books.) The West Highlands of Scotland. Collins Companion Guide 1968. (Thorough)
Nethersole-Thompson, D.: *Highland Birds*. H.I.D.B. 1971
Nethersole-Thompson, D. and Watson, A.: *The Cairngorms: Their Natural History and Scenery*. Collins 1974. (Superb)
Nicolaisen, W. F. H.: *Scottish Place Names*. Batsford 1976
O'Dell, A. C. and Walton, K.: *The Highlands and Islands of Scotland*. Nelson 1962. (Geography)
Patey, Tom: *One Man's Mountains*. Gollancz 1971. (Collected writings, songs)
Plumb, C.: *Walking in the Grampians*. Maclehose 1935
Poucher, W. A.: *The Magic of Skye*. Chapman and Hall 1949
Prebble, J.: *The Massacre of Glencoe*; *The Highland Clearances*. Secker
Price, R. J.: *Highland Landforms*. H.I.D.B.
Raven, J. and Walter, M.: *Mountain Flowers*. Collins N.N. 1956
Scott, Walter: *Rob Roy*; *Waverley*. (For starters)
Scottish Mountaineering Club Journal. Published each June, the authoritative journal on all things Scottish. Older copies are fascinating.
Scottish Mountaineering Trust. The S.M.C. publications have no rivals.
Simpson, W. D.: *Portrait of the Highlands*; *Scottish Castles*. Hale
Sissons, J. B.: *The Evolution of Scotland's Scenery*. Oliver and Boyd 1967
Slesser, C. G. M.: *Scottish Mountains on Ski*. 1970
Smith, Janet Adam: *Mountain Holidays*. Dent 1948
Stephen, D.: *Highland Animals*. H.I.D.B. 1974
Steven, Campbell: *The Story of Scotland's Hills*. Hale 1975. *Glens and Straths of Scotland*. Hale 1970
Stevenson, R. L.: *Kidnapped*; *Catriona*, etc.
Stewart, Mary: *Wildfire at Midnight*. Hodder, paperback. (Murder set on Blaven)
Taylor, W.: *The Military Roads in Scotland*. David & Charles 1976
Tranter, Nigel: prolific novelist, try his trilogy on Robert the Bruce
Wainwright, A.: Scottish Mountain Drawings. *Westmorland Gazette*
Walsh, M.: *The Key Above the Door*. (A romance)
Weir, Tom: *Highland Days*. Cassell 1949. (Youthful wanderings.) *The Western Highlands*. Batsford 1973. *The Scottish Lochs*, 2 vols. Constable
Wood, Wendy: *Moidart and Morar*. Moray Press 1950

INDEX OF
THE MUNROS

CLIMBING THE CORBETTS

CLIMBING THE CORBETTS

Scotland's 2,500 ft Summits

by

HAMISH M. BROWN

ABBREVIATIONS

BFMC	Braes o' Fife Mountaineering Club
c.	*circa* (around, approx.)
CIC	Charles Inglis Clark
MBA	Mountain Bothy Association
NCC	Nature Conservancy Council
NTS	National Trust for Scotland
ON	Old Norse
OS	Ordnance Survey
SMC	Scottish Mountaineering Club
UC	Ultimate Challenge

SOME USEFUL ADDRESSES

Atholl Estates, Blair Atholl, Perthshire, telephone 079681–211/230

Gerry Howkins, Achnashellach Hostel, Craig, Achnashellach, Strathcarron, Wester Ross, telephone 052–06232

The Mountain Bothies Association, General Secretary, 2 North Gardner Street, Glasgow G11

Nancy Smith, Fasgadh, Fersit, Roy Bridge, Perthshire (no telephone)

Rhum: The Chief Warden, White House, Rhum by Mallaig, telephone 0687–2026

CONTENTS

PHOTOS IN THE TEXT

between pages 148 and 149

LIFE AFTER THE MUNROS

WITH MORE AND more hill-walkers actively climbing all the Munros and scores now completing their list each year, one begins to wonder what happens after the Munros are done. Do all these walkers quietly fade away, ice axes hung on the wall and the old boots mouldering in the loft, or is there some drug, some Royal Jelly, to lift their eyes once more to the hills?

You'd think there would be something about Munroists that would show, some visible mark of the miles and footage they've put in. This would be useful for Munroist-spotting but, alas, they come fat and thin, old and young, blonde and brunette, hairy and bald. You can usually tell Siamese cat owners by their haunted, persecuted look; but Munroists, against all expectation, appear just an ordinary cross-section of society. What do they do when they have finished ticking off the list?

I've a good friend, Charles from Sheffield, who was a dedicated Munro-bagger in a way I could never be. I could not take all that motoring for a start. Most of his Munros were done at weekends, from Sheffield, because holidays were saved for climbing, ski-touring and trekking in the far corners of the globe. It was the dedication I found staggering, his single-minded application to scaling those hills. I don't know how he puts up with me, for I am easily deflected by historic sites, wildlife and a natural laziness which has saved me from many a meteorological hammering. Another mutual friend based in London was also heading towards completing the Munros and the two of them slogged it out in hectic rivalry. Donald just got there first but Charles had been doing the "Tops" — the hundreds of subsidiary summits — as well as the separate mountains that are the Munros. Donald was tragically drowned in Knoydart but Charles went on to complete the 3,000-ers of England, Wales and Ireland and the 2,000-ers of England and Wales. He was running out of lists!

Quite a few people cheerfully start all over again and repeat the Munros. I've done this myself because, if you are wandering the Scottish hills, you willy-nilly accumulate Munros, and when you reach over halfway, well, you can't resist tidying them. I may be lazy but I am tidy!

Munro's *Tables* also contain two other eponymous lists: the Donalds which list all the Scottish hills *in the Lowlands* which exceed 2,000 feet (Galloway, the Borders, Ochils and such delights), and the Corbetts which list all the 2,500-foot summits. Life after the Munros, for walkers in Scotland, often means doing the Corbetts, and Charles, having cleared off all the other possibilities, had a resurrection into Scottish activity by joining the Corbett-baggers. I suspect there are quite a few of his breed flitting about but, being more solitary and nesting away from the busy hills, the status of the species is hard to estimate. They are not listed, as are the successful Munroists.

The Corbetts have a separation of 500 feet (the Munros are not so defined) which gives them an individuality frequently missing in the Munros. There are fewer "dull" Corbetts than there are "dull" Munros, though dull is a word I would use of no hill (it is usually a comment on the person rather than the setting). The views from Corbetts frequently surpass the views from Munros and there are plenty of them which are magnificent hills in their own right: The Cobbler, Ben Loyal, Clisham, Goat Fell, The Merrick or Garbh Bheinn of Ardgour are each worth a score of Geal Charns of over 3,000 feet. I advocate doing the Corbetts *simultaneously* with the Munros, but often this advice falls on unbelieving ears.

However, one weekend Charles admitted I'd been right, there was an English Bank Holiday and a fair proportion from that country migrated northwards. The Munros were crawling with Sassenachs yet, over the long weekend, Charles, the dog and I never met one person on our Corbetts. Charles climbed many more than I did — having done the Corbetts years ago (and having topped up with all the new ones from the map revisions) I could enjoy *not* having to try and match Charles's *blitzkreig.*

I drove up to Glen Shee on the Friday afternoon and had a pleasant evening of reading, writing and music. Being in bed before midnight was a treat. At 1.30 a.m. Charles found me and bedded-down alongside my Dormobile. At 7 a.m. I took him a mug of tea. We planned for the days ahead over breakfast and then drove over the Cairnwell to pitch a camp in Glen Clunie. Braemar camp-site was full, and dozens of tents were pitched in the glen as well. At every spot where people park for Munros there were cars. In Braemar we nearly ran over Jim Donaldson, editor of the *Tables*, which would have been rough injustice.

We cycled up to Derry Lodge (wickedly being allowed to decay, like so much property on upper Deeside) and on up the Luibeg till too rough for comfort. Sgor Mor was our objective: the Corbett above the Dee/Geldie junction. It gave a walk over gentle moorland, the heather full of dwarf birch, to a granite knobbliness of summit — and a mighty view. It was so typical a Corbett view, all the better for its isolation and facing the sweep of Cairngorms rather than being jostled in their crowdedness. We were back at the car by lunchtime and I knew what would come next. "I may as well do Morrone," Charles suggested. So we drove up to its path starting above Braemar, and after Charles set off I drove round to meet him off the Clunie side. I managed three hours of work before he arrived. A hard frost whitened the camp that night but the snell weather was great for walking. Charles shifted into top gear next day.

Carn na Drochaide above the Quoich was our initial summit, and the dog and I then explored the Quoich and had a pleasant low-level day before going down to meet Charles at the old Bridge of Dee (1752) at Invercauld. This old military bridge, in its wooded setting, with Lochnagar behind, forms a classic view. Photographers in droves were taking pictures of it, a dangerous game with the holiday traffic. Charles came back with the two Culardoch scalps and a sun-wind-burnt bald bit on his head.

Monday I had to do other things in the morning so Charles climbed the Corbett above Glen Clunie and we met at coffee-time on the Cairnwell Pass before dropping down to Glen Shee for Ben Gulabin, the peak that so dominates that green oasis. We went up a burn to the col behind it and then pigged ourselves on blaeberries for the 500 feet to the summit. I'd forgotten just how fine a viewpoint it was. This is the refrain you will hear from all Corbetters: the view! the view!

I was home for teatime but Charles set off for upper Glen Isla, bent on adding Monamenach; three Corbetts in a day again. In case you think this normal, it is not. Only because Braemar itself is 1,000 feet up, can you romp over several like this. Two in a day usually entails quite enough work and often driving between. Three or more is very seldom possible. But Charles is dedicated, and he completed his Munros on 30 December 1987.

It only seems right, then, to dedicate this book of Corbett days to him, in gratitude for many good shared ploys at home and abroad. Slainté! Tearlaich. What will you do now with the Corbetts completed?

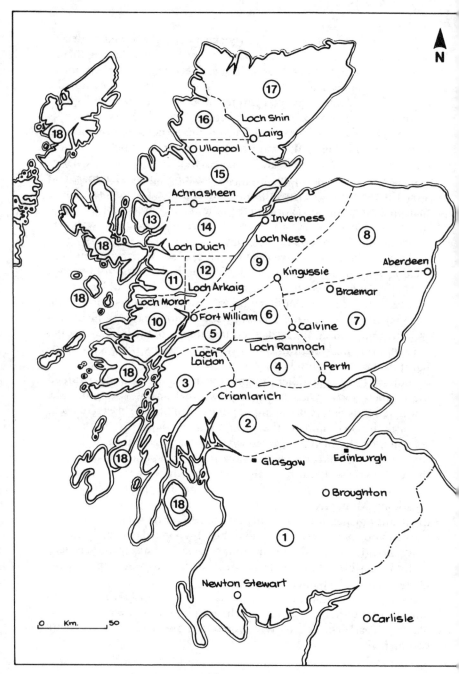

CORBETT SECTIONS

INTRODUCTION

IN HAPPY DAYS of youthful ignorance I climbed and walked wherever fancy led — which was over most of Scotland. Munro's *Tables* (with their threefold listings) were not yet known to me. When I discovered this slim but seductive volume it was all too easy to tick off many hundreds of names in all three tables, which is really not a thing to do if one wants to retain a sane and casual freedom.

Like so many before me (61 to be precise) completing the Munros became a most desirable objective and, fulfilled, repeated (six times over), while the Corbetts and Donalds followed. Now, I am not basically a Munro-bagger, as they are called, for proportionately the time I give to Munros is probably far lower than that of most walkers, especially those avowedly seeking these hills. Months, in any year, may be spent abroad; I canoe, ski, botanise, bird-watch, sail, take photographs and sketch, and I have other hobbies, other interests. I don't think mountains alone, listed or unlisted, any more than climbs, should be a person's *only* interest. That they can be a vast blessing and provide contentment is just one of life's rich bonuses. By all means tick off the Munros, the Corbetts and the Donalds. No one has any call, beyond sour grapes, to criticise you for seeking pleasure in so doing.

The Munros have obviously dominated the lists, but there are only a few walkers, I'm sure, who are so ensnared by them that they do not also happily charge off to the odd Corbett, Donald or unlisted nothing at all when fancy or chance takes them. You cannot just skip Suilven or Stac Polly or plenty of others. Beauty of form and the joy of being there is not restricted to any particular height. Munros are climbed because they contain a spark of magic and that magic remains even when the last 3,000-er is sclimmed. The good news is that there is life after the Munros: the Corbetts.

At once let me plead with active Munroists to be equally busy with the Corbetts, *simultaneously*. Whenever a Munro is on the schedule, check if it has a Corbett possible on the same walk. (Ben Aden can be linked with Sgurr na Ciche, Auchnafree Hill with Ben Chonzie and so on.) Doing Munros and Corbetts together is more practical in the long run (the economics of hill going is a subject in search of a thesis) and also more satisfying, even if it means the Munros may take another year or two to complete. It is not a race! There is a false idea that climbing Corbetts is, somehow, a poorer game. This is nonsense. The Corbetts are every bit as satisfying as the Munros — for reasons I hope you can find for yourself. By definition the Corbetts are much more solitary and individualistic. You will not find seven of them lined up on any easy ridge. As well as being more independent in character and setting (and partly because of it) they frequently command finer views than the majority of Munros. They are at the height from which mountain views are at their best. Corbetts are more widely scattered geographically than the Munros so they ensure a widening of the exploratory factor. Galloway and the islands would alone sell me the Corbetts, and some of my best-loved areas are not covered by any of the lists. However, all the lists give a spur, an incentive, to visit new territory. Walking, for walking's sake, for mere exercise, for "training", hardly appeals to someone as lazy as myself; I need the spur of something like a set of tables to bully me on to my hind legs. The *Tables* both lead and drive like a good schoolmaster.

Information on the Corbetts is often difficult to obtain, and while this, to me, is no liability as I seldom swot an area before a first visit, for those with short holidays and a brief ration of weekends it can be annoying. Nobody, after all, is forced to read a guidebook, so those who object to such are hardly being logical, or fair to others, when they voice displeasure. *Chacun à son goût*. . . . This is not a guidebook, then; at least not in the accepted sense. It is one man yarning about his Corbetts and therefore there is no standard presentation; of some hills I write extensively, of others briefly; it is a very subjective game after all. The practical information is there but it has to be discovered. Instead of a bold guide statement like "Do not try to cross the Allt a' Tobrect in its lower reaches in wet weather. It can flood for several miles from its entry to Loch Numor", you will find the story of the mess we made of crossing at that notorious spot — and can draw your own conclusions!

While giving largely first-hand accounts of expeditions over the Corbetts I have woven into the text most of the practical information needed for these hills. Going to the hills (Munros, Corbetts or any other) should be fun, and part of that fun is in the dreaming and planning as well as in the execution. So you will not find statistics of miles and hours laid down for you. That is something you should be working out yourself, anyway, and *on the map*, not just at second hand.

I originally planned to write this book chronologically, but details of many of my earliest ascents are forgotten while more recent escapades are fresh in mind as well as recorded in carefully kept log-books. If it is to be of practical help I feel the day-to-day story should also have a solid core of useful information and its lay-out would be more helpful if following that of the present *Tables* — they are due for revision within the next few years. Most people will want to dip into this book for specific hills rather than read a continuous narrative. We don't "do" the Munros or Corbetts very logically or efficiently anyway.

I would recommend the practice of keeping a hill log-book. Memory is fickle, and often it is the small details that make a day; these are so easily forgotten unless written down at the time. One friend of mine, who keeps complaining he is so "useless at names", would find them easier to recall if he had regularly noted them down. I started this habit only in 1960, using notebooks with a small, close-lined format, but am now on notebook number 178. In these I stick postcards, illustrations, even stamps — any related material — as well as contact prints of all black and white pictures and some colour prints from slides. They are a treasure-chest for degenerating brain cells!

J. Rooke Corbett is number four in the Munro list (1930) but his own list of the 2,500-foot summits, which he had also climbed, was published only posthumously. With a re-ascent of 500 feet on all sides the hills were listed with a cold logic lacking in Munros — not that that has stopped the alterations and amendments and revisions due to Ordnance Survey re-mapping and a certain editorial whim. The present sections are far too large, and using the list is often difficult. Having completed the Corbetts long before the re-mapping/metrification landmark there was some topping-up to be done and a sad farewell to be given to others, demoted to obscurity, or promoted to the notoriety of Munro status. Being naturally iconoclastic there is something satisfying in seeing the logical clarity of the Corbett list suffering the effects of man's natural talent for chaos. For better or for worse this book closely follows the list as set forth in the last, 1984, edition of Munro's *Tables*.

As most walking is done using the 1:50,000 OS maps the appropriate sheet is given for each hill and ideally this should be dug out and *studied in conjunction with the text*. Each heading gives the Corbett section number, followed by the number of the peak within the section, the peak name, its height in metres, the 1:50,000 sheet number(s), its six-figure reference and the translation of the Gaelic name. Where heights do not agree with the 1:50,000 sheets they will be from the 1:25,000 sheets or more recent OS information.

Many of the Gaelic names of geographical features are now only preserved on the map, for local keepers and shepherds (nearly all English-speaking now) have long replaced most of them with their own practical "convenience-namings" — which is the whole point of names. Names are a lively, changing subject and it is only we slaves of the map, rather than any residents, who use the early Victorian fossilisation of the centuries of Gaelic namings. So many names have stories behind them which are now quite lost. Why is it "stone of weeping"? Who is William and why did he leap?

The pronunciation of Gaelic names is often difficult and I've given a few helps where possible. Translations are not always obvious, as many original names have been simplified or Anglicised out of recognition. There is a useful Gaelic guide in the 1984 Munro's *Tables* — which are worth buying for this alone. For a score of the more difficult derivations I must thank Iseabail Macleod and Ian Fraser for their researches. Topographical Gaelic, with a bit of study, soon becomes fascinating rather than frightening. I'd also like to thank Don Green and Brenda Macrow for permission to use extracts from their accounts of some days. My thanks too must go to Sheila Gallimore who has had to cope with typing this work; Gaelic names I'm sure were not made easier by my handwriting.

As most people are now car-owners or approach their hills by car this is kept in mind when describing approaches. Some private estate roads may be available, but with complicated negotiations I find it easier to be completely independent and either walk or use a push bike which, in Scotland, is "an aid to pedestrianism", not a vehicle. Many remote glens can be reached by post buses from the nearest town, often a railhead, and there are other train, bus or boat services which can be useful. The annual *Getting Around the Highlands and Islands* is a valuable publication.

Cutting free from a car is a blessing rather than a disaster, and it is not for nothing that the annual Ultimate Challenge coast-to-coast event has its "high-level" route pinned to doing twelve Munros and/or Corbetts. My previous *Mountain Walk* and *Groats End Walk* books tell of the extremes of being car-free. This is a much more prosaic collection of odd days and holidays, such as we all take, and can therefore associate with. "The sun always shines on the days you describe", is a criticism I hear now and then. But weren't summers always sunnier in the days of youth? Plodding through the rain makes for soggy prose as well as sodden feet and memory recalls more clearly the very good days — or the diabolically bad ones — so if I've been on a Corbett several times, as I have many, a good day is quite likely to be described. I make no apology for this. I've gone out on far too many miserable days when I should have known better.

About 150 different people have been with me on Corbett days — I must have been persuasive over the years — and I hope I can convince you that this is one of the better games to play in the Scottish hills. Be warned, though, once you start ticking the list it will soon have you in thrall. The dedicatory piece before this Introduction appeared in the *Glasgow Herald*, and several other days have been described in this, Scotland's oldest national newspaper; I thank the *Glasgow Herald* for permission to reprint them here. I would also like to thank all the people who have been with me on the Corbetts. One of the pleasures of hill days is the people involved. I just wished I'd been able to meet the man responsible for this game.

J. Rooke Corbett was a District Valuer, based on Bristol, but several times a year he would be in Scotland, exploring its hills, often with Scottish Mountaineering Club friends. He joined the SMC in 1923, attended nearly all its meets, served on the committee and was a joint editor of the *Northern Highlands* general guidebook. He was the second person to complete the Munros and Tops, in 1930, one of a small gang of eight pre-war Munroists, of whom four also did the Tops, a proportion not maintained in these slack times. He also made the ascent of every 2,000-foot hill in Scotland, still a very rare feat. He accomplished this just before a heart attack in 1943 which curtailed his activities somewhat, and presumably his tables of the 2,500-foot summits, which now bear his name, were compiled from this experience. They were not published during his lifetime. Corbett was a quiet, retiring man of cheerful inner strength. He walked again after his heart attack and few knew of a growing paralytic affliction. He died, aged 72, a few years after the war.

There are only two full-scale articles of his in the *SMC Journal*: one on the Paps of Jura (one Corbett!) and the other on "Aneroids and Munros", which reflects his interest in things scientific, and accounts for many short notes on topographical observations — they were finding new Munros even in the 1930s. Corbett had a distinguished education at Cambridge but even then he was a powerful long-distance walker. He once walked home from Cambridge to Manchester. Later he was an original member of the Rucksack Club and took delight in such ploys as all-night expeditions.

The list of Corbetts was passed by his sister to the SMC and soon incorporated into Munro's *Tables*. With a few minor amendments it is as he left it, Corbetts being more clearly defined than the Munros. Corbett never stated that there had to be a 500-foot re-ascent, but it is implied and employed, distance and difficulty being ignored. Subsidiary "Tops" were not listed. Just how much alteration there has been to the mapping of the landscape came out in the new metrical era. Jim Donaldson checked the maps, and the result was 17 new Corbetts and 11 Corbetts removed, leaving 223 Corbetts. There was a thunderous silence following this event, but Corbetteers are probably older and wiser than mere Munroists and have learnt to live with the vagaries of the OS and SMC during their Munro apprenticeships. Various comments on status changes, Corbett names and other odd features are made in my text but the summary at the start of the 1984 tables gave 19 new Corbetts and 13 deletions, still a total of 223.

That however was not the end of the story. Since then Beinn Teallach has been promoted to Munro status and Cook's Cairn has been eliminated, so the tally is really 19 promoted, 15 removed, making 221 Corbetts. Those who possess only the 1981 edition of the tables should be careful. Charles, with only a score to go, was given a jolt when I told him of two unobtrusive extra Corbetts in the 1984 list, Beinn Each 2:14 and Sron a' Choire Chnapanich 4:9. It is worth comparing Sron a' Choire Chnapanich as it appears on the First and Second Series maps (Sheet 51). You will see why I emphasise the importance of the latter. Since starting on this book I am glad to say nearly all Corbetts (except those on Sheet 37) are now on Second Series sheets.

There are anomalies in the heights of Corbetts which I have given up trying to fathom. One day the *Tables* may be definitive but not until the OS has sorted out some problems. Hopefully the SMC will tidy up the sections, too, but this book follows what we have at present, imperfect though it be.

No list of Corbett-completers has been kept, though a few names appear in the notes in the *SMC Journal*. Maybe this is a good thing. In 1985 (one of the wettest years ever) Craig Caldwell from Milngavie did a continuous bike and hike trip over all the Munros *and* Corbetts, an astonishingly gritty feat. Not long before finishing this book Craig looked in and we had a grand chat. Just looking at his map with the route shown on it could have kept us talking all night. There were not many bits of Scotland left untouched, and that, in the end, is the richest reward of doing Munros and Corbetts and Donalds and uncle Tom Cobbleys and all: you come to know the land in a quite unique way, a knowledge which cannot but be transformed into a lifelong love affair. This book is a tale of 221 flirtations — and one rockfast marriage.

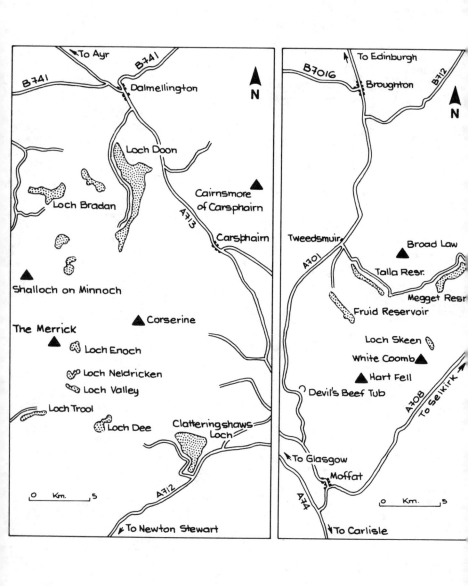

SOUTHERN SCOTLAND

Section 1: 1. SHALLOCH ON MINNOCH   768 m   OS 77   405907
The heel of the Minnoch ridge

Section 1: 2. THE MERRICK   814 m   OS 77   428855
The branched finger

BACK IN THE days when we had counties The Merrick was the highest point in Kirkcudbrightshire, at 2,764 feet. Of Scotland's 33 counties all had highest points over 1,000 feet, and 25 of them had highest points over 2,000 feet. We tend to forget how hilly Scotland is *over all*. The division into Highlands and Lowlands is misleading; we have Highlands and Notsohighlands! The Merrick Hills, or The Awful Hand as they are also called, tend to be neglected partly because of this misconception. On a Bank Holiday, Glen Coe will be swarming with visitors (half of whom drove up the A74, a squirt east of Dumfries), yet you could walk for days over the Galloway Hills and meet no one else, which is daft seeing they have the wildest scenery and the roughest landscape south of Rannoch.

Kirriereoch Hill a mile north of The Merrick has been removed as a Corbett, but as Shalloch on Minnoch is north again you will still traverse it in linking the two Corbetts. The Awful Hand has a split-level system: a high-level highway linking the Corbetts and a lower-level clearway to the east (Mullwharchar, Dungeon Hill and Craignaw). They are about all that is clear. The rest of the area seems to have been drowned in a flood of forestry. Only the highest summits rise, *nunatak*-like, from this clammy choke of conifers. Now and then the trees can actually enhance the scenery, and the prime example is Glen Trool, with its remnant of natural forest, which is also the customary starting-off point for The Merrick.

Glen Trool is a bit like Wasdale: "round the back" of all the hills, a bit remote. The comparison ends there; for Trossachs-like Glen Trool, in the words of Ken Andrew, one of the South West's champions, is "a superb little glen . . . a scene of astonishing variety with its woodlands and broken slopes. Meadows on the valley floor merge with the coarser grasses, heather and bracken, natural woodlands merge with planted, larch with pine, pine with spruce . . . sheep, cattle and even goats dot the rugged landscape which maintains a wide variety of birds and other small creatures." Driving up one early morning in colourful mid-October I had to dodge a roe buck, a red deer hind and a gambol of goats, all in the time it took to pass the length of Loch Trool to the car park by the Bruce's Stone, a monument to a clash in 1307 when Bruce was starting his bid for the Scottish throne. Some of the goats have learnt to scrounge food off the tourists. The adders are much more wary; I've never seen one despite many visits to the area. The Rev. Thomas Grierson in his *Autumnal Rambles among the Scottish Mountains* (in the 1840–1850s decade) has this warning on adders: "As serpents are common, long worsted stockings should be worn and no person should attempt roughing it without a pair of Horrell's best double-soled shoes." He thought Glen Trool "perhaps the most romantic spot in the south of Scotland".

The path for The Merrick is clearly signposted and heads north up by the Buchan Burn past Culsharg (a shepherd's house in Grierson's day) to the slopes of Benyellary, *the hill of the eagle*. It is all thoroughly planted now, so there is a feeling of relief on gaining the breezy open slopes of the hill. A dyke leads all the way up to the top of Benyellary, and when I reached it the subtle, early morning colours had turned the many lochs to the east into burnished silver.

The swell of The Merrick fills the north (over a dip, the Neive of the Spit), and gives an easy, grassy walk up to the highest point, after Goat Fell, in all Scotland south of Ben Lomond. The dyke hits the corrie of Black Gairy half a mile west of the summit, and its rim can be followed up to the trig point. The OS First Series crag symbols are vastly exaggerated, often being little more than broken ground. The dog and I traversed over to the springs of Gloon Burn for a drink and cut straight up to the summit with its cairn, scattered erratics and trig point.

A good ridge leads down to the col (with Loch Twachtan to the east) and then pulls up to Kirriereoch Hill, which gives the best view of The Merrick. Then it drops steeply to the broad saddle of Carmaddie Brae with its collections of lochans, rises and falls over Tarfessock to the Nick of Carlach before the grassy cone of Shalloch on Minnoch is reached. These summits are the knuckles of the colourful Hand, with fingers pointing west, and Benyellary the cocked thumb. Some of the summits and braes are stony but the walking is exhilarating — and worth saving for a good day. The peaks of Cumbria, Northern Ireland, Jura and Arran are all visible, as is Ailsa Craig (Paddy's Milestone) in the Firth of Clyde while, below and to the east, lies a remarkably wild landscape which can give an excellent return to base.

This return I describe is long and rough so should only be tackled by experienced hillgoers. It is not advisable in really wet weather. Most walkers will be happy to descend westwards off Shalloch on Minnoch to the car park at Laglanny or north west to the Straiton road at

Pilnyark Burn. This needs some arranging of transport or, as I did on one occasion, the use of a cycle which I'd left there in readiness. On this autumn occasion I took another option and, returning to the Nick of Carclach, I dropped down east to Tunskeen, which is half a building that was turned into a primitive bothy in 1965, the very first such building to be saved by the nascent Mountain Bothies Association.

From there you can name-drop back to Glen Trool: Castle on Oyne, Rigg of Millmore, Eglin Lane, Mullwharchar, Dungeon Hill, Craignaw, Loch Neldricken, Loch Valley and the Gairland Burn. The "Murder Hole" shown on Loch Neldricken has been transposed from its real site elsewhere by the novelist S. R. Crockett in his most famous book *The Raiders*, which captures this wild area very effectively. I think he could not resist the names. Who could, with places like Craigmawhannal and Craigmasheenie, Lump of the Eglin, The Wolf Slock, Clatteringshaws Loch and Curley Wee? There isn't room here to describe this wilderness of granite, bog, heather and water, the real heart of these hills, but they are well covered in the SMC's *Southern Uplands* and in several older books. *Classic Walks* and *The Big Walks* (both by Ken Wilson and Richard Gilbert) also cover the area, though The Merrick is the only hill appearing in both these lavish publications which perhaps indicates its challenging qualities.

Section 1: 3. CORSERINE 814 m OS 77 497871
    The crossing of the ridges

Corserine is the second highest summit in Galloway and is just one of many summits topping a long, continuous north-south ridge which is separated from the Merrick range by a long valley running from Clatteringshaws Loch to Loch Doon (the Doon of Burns's "Bonnie Doon"). This valley, from the Dungeon lochs to Loch Dee, is known as the Silver Flowe and is a notorious bog only to be crossed in drought conditions or when frozen solid.

The Big Walks gives the outline of a route from Glen Trool over Benyellary, The Merrick, then across Gala Lane to Corserine and the Rhinns of Kells ridge and back by Loch Dee but this is rather charging about for the sake of charging about and misses too many interesting points. Corserine is quite awkward enough to reach by itself, at least if one is going to make a good expedition rather than a mere Corbett raid. The usual problem is of transport when traversing a long ridge, but here, for once, there is a useful bus service along the A713 east of the Kells range (Ayr–Castle Douglas service) which allows long days on the hills. There is a Youth Hostel just off the A713 (Kenloon 616883) which can make a jumping-off point for several days of hill and bothy wandering. An example, which gave me a perfect trip, began at Polmaddie Bridge. I walked up to Shiel of Castlemaddy for the night, traversed the Rhinns of Kells to White Laggan (Loch Dee), traversed the Dungeon Hills to Tunskeen, topped The Merrick on the way to Back Hill of Bush and went out to Dalry over Meikle Millyea — Donald/Corbett-bagging at its very best.

To keep to the autumn visit above (1:1, 2) I'll describe the simpler attack on Corserine. It was all new country to me then. I motored a couple of miles along the side of Clatteringshaws Loch to the locked gate where the forestry road branches off, then used a cycle. The dog was sometimes carried, and sometimes ran behind. There were so many new plantings and forestry roads to add to the map that I was constantly stopping. (Make sure you have a Second Series map.)

Back Hill of Bush was a fairly luxurious bothy. It even had an armchair which, on another occasion, I hauled outside the door to enjoy a dram in the evening sun; I was sitting half asleep when there was a crash on the window behind my head and a stunned wren fell on to my lap. Someone in the bothy book had warned of meeting a brontosaurus in the Silver Flowe bogs. I *think* he was joking.

The old path over the ridge behind the bothy had largely gone, so perforce I used the wiggly forestry road to gain height. There was not even a stile on the top deer fence. It had rained hard overnight and my legs were soon saturated from the grass; on the lazy ascent to Corserine the fuggy dankness left the hairs on my cheeks silvered with water droplets. The dog looked like a drowned rat. Corserine is a rounded, grassy dome with five ridges criss-crossing the main north-south line (hence the name). The easiest route from the east is to drive up to the bridge before Forest Lodge then walk on by Fore Bush, Loch Harrow and the North Gairy ridge. When staying at Shiel of Castlemaddy I followed the forest road to Goat Craigs and on over Carlin's Cairn. An entry in the Shiel bothy book was amusing. A lad had made a bivvy in a firebeater shelter, not knowing of the bothy. "I lay all night with a fence post to hand, scared stiff and expecting to be attacked at any time by pumas or something which prowled around making their grunting calls. At first light I fled and was glad to find this safe place." (Roe deer *do* sound a bit like large felines.)

Living in Carlin Craig I naturally had to go on to Carlin's Cairn, a mile north of the Corbett and not much lower. It is topped by a big *chorten*-like cairn which, legend has it, was built by a miller's wife who was granted land by the Polmaddy, a reward for aiding the fugitive Robert the Bruce. The cairn gave shelter for a snack and we then headed south for the shaly tops of Millfire, Milldown and Meikle Millyea, the last a bald flat summit with its highest point to the south west, not at the trig point to the north east. On the Hawse Burn is a memorial to a 17-year-old shepherd who died of exposure there in 1954. Another blizzard, on the main ridge above, once caught a funeral party carrying the wife of a shepherd and they had to abandon the coffin for several days. An old dyke joins the ridge before Milldown and runs all the way to Little Millyea. Millyea is murdered Gaelic: Meall Liath or grey hill. Gaelic, lost long ago in Galloway, has led to a real corruption of place names.

We skirted Milldown to gain the Downie's Burn corrie and so back to Back Hill, soaked to the thighs by then and glad to put on the kettle. A forestry vehicle dropped some firewood off for the bothy but I dried out while cycling the nine miles back to the car at Clatteringshaws Loch.

The road on to Newton Stewart is full of interest. Another Bruce's Stone by the loch, just after we'd joined the A712, celebrates the Battle of Raploch Moss in 1307. Half a mile on is the Galloway Deer Museum, and near Murray's Monument there is a particularly attractive bit of country with good walks, waterfalls, viewpoints etc., an area where the feral goats are allowed to roam free, but out of the forest. Murray, of the monument, was a local shepherd lad who ended up as Professor of Oriental Languages at Edinburgh University, where he died in 1813 still only thirty-seven. He had learnt 28 languages by then. He once had to translate a letter addressed to George III by the King of Ethiopia. He was the only person in the country capable of doing so.

Section 1: 4. CAIRNSMORE OF CARSPHAIRN 797 m OS 77
594980

> "There's Cairnsmore of Fleet,
> And Cairnsmore of Dee;
> But Cairnsmore of Carsphairn
> Is the highest of the three."

— so a Corbett which will take the hill-wanderer into a pleasant part of the South West which he might otherwise miss. On my first visit I thought the ochrous domes a bit like the Ochils. Having abandoned a planned day on the Kells range the weather improved so I simply parked by the Water of Ken and headed up the Craigengillan Burn to reach Cairnsmore over Beninner. That rather casual walk would need some re-routing now as vast areas up the Water of Ken have been drowned with conifers. The farm road from Craigengillan Bridge up to Moorbrock is now the obvious line of access.

The most popular route starts from outside the village of Carsphairn at the Green Well of Scotland. Follow the track on the east bank of the Deugh to the Benloch Burn, a hollow locally called Midge Ha', skirt Willieanna, then simply head up Dunool and on to the Black Shoulder from which an easy walk leads to the summit. From Knochgray (east of the village) a path to Moorbrock and the Ken can be followed and Cairnsmore reached over or round Beninner. The two combine for a pleasant day's walk. From the top you realise just how vast is the extent of the Galloway hills.

What I saw on my first visit made me plan a proper visit to these hills. There was a bothy locally which would be fun for a night out, and besides its Corbett, Carsphairn has a cluster of "Donalds", those Lowland 2,000-foot hills of the third list in the *Tables* which I'd been pecking away at while motoring to and from the south. The next visit came while driving back from a trip to Morocco and Corsica; I quote from my account written at the time (1978):

. . . from friendly Dumfries I motored up to Thornhill and Penpont and then by the wee road up Scaur Water where we lunched and packed under some big trees. The bird life was varied: bullfinch, sandpiper, warbler, blackbird, kestrel, cuckoo. A shepherd with two dogs stopped for an hour's blether then I continued along the twisty upper glen. The trees finish and a grassy sweep of hills was about me when I parked at the road end. During the rest of the day only one other car came up, turned and went off without stopping — so they missed hearing the curlews, thrushes, pipits, redshanks, snipe, and hoasty sheep. It rained most of the time but I was able to keep the sliding door open and drink in the sounds and scents of "my ain countrie". A contrast to Peakirk and the Fens two days ago and even more so to the Atlas or jagged Corsica. The glen is almost a mirror of our geographical history: ruined castles, holiday homes, forestry plantings, hills of sheep and the grey sadness of rain.

Thursday 22 June: a good day and delighting to be on home hills once more. I was stiff by the day's end. Departure was at 8 a.m., up Polskeoch Rig. All day I was stopping to add new features on the map. Forestry workers drove up and set off to work on Fortypenny Hill opposite. I skirted by Ryegrain Rig to reach outliers Blacklorg Hill and Blackcraig which lie above the Afton Water, "sweet Afton" of Burns' song. Donalds of course. Curlews down below and skylarks up above made the day's *continuo*. There was a spacious feel to the tawny hills with little sign of cultivation, other than the invasion of forestry and fences everywhere. Back at my rucker I had tea and while fetching water found a meteorological balloon. Going up Meikledodd Hill a loud bang made me jump and, looking back, I saw a pillar of smoke rise out of the Kello Water glen. (A good route not to be on!) Between Alwhat and Alhang I passed the source of the Afton. The Holm Burn, leading south to the Ken, had an amazing array of little bumps like moraines, but are more likely to be old mining tips, and beyond the Ken, and beyond ken, were ugly blanketing trees again.

A col led to the second block of hills, higher and rougher than where we'd been. Windy Standard had a stark trig-point. The vast Carsphairn Forest rolled away beyond. The outlier Trostan Hill had such spongy grass that it was tiring to walk on, like soft snow. Dugland was the last Donald addition and then it was brutally down to Clennoch, an old shepherd's house now saved as a primitive bothy. It was only 2.30 but the rest of the day went with a book while rain on top of rain rattled on the flat roof. I actually took to the bedshelf at 8.30 and woke thinking I was in a *bergerie* back in Corsica. . . .

Friday 23 June: An early start (6.15) to use the grey but dry morning, a wise move as the afternoon broke down again and was "gey weet". We wandered up the Bow Burn, and some rocks on the watershed made a recognisable spot to leave the rucksack. We set off up into the saturated mist, and a fence did likewise but then sloped off southwards. The ground steepened but we were almost disappointed to find the huge cliffs marked were simply small crags and scree. We went straight up and landed just 20 m from the summit trig-point of Cairnsmore. The granite-strewn summit is reminiscent of the Cairngorms.

The summit was left on a bearing for 600 paces and at that precise spot there was a big cairn. My second bearing led me down, and up on to Beninner. (I wasn't sure if I'd come over it on the previous occasion.) The back bearing took me down to the col and from there a fence dutifully led me down to my rucksack.

In thicker cloud I went up the other side to find Moorbrock Hill and carefully, with map, compass, altimeter and dead-reckoning made my way over its NW Top, a col, another Alwhat and Keoch Rigg, the last of the dotty Donalds. I'd worked back to be almost above Clennoch again and planned to exit by the path that crossed the hills from it down to the Holm–Ken valley. I paced off what the distance should have been and began to go uphill. No path. So we followed the compass down the Bawnhead ridge and never saw a path anywhere. [It has gone from the Second Series map.]

Nether Holm of Dalquhairn was still lived in and had sheep and cows pastured round it. The Water of Ken was a bit grubby so a clear side stream provided the brew water. The tarmac was reduced to two strips, the grass between making a kind surface for feet, then it became just a footpath — until cut by new forestry work. Forestry activities up the Polvaddoch Burn were responsible for the muddy Ken. The gentlest of watersheds led us back to Polskeoch and the Dormobile. An hour of tidying up and we drove off, singing with content, back to Thornhill and on for the Dalveen Pass and Moffat where John Cairney did his "Robert Burns" presentation. He is a good look-alike. The show was nicely done, sad in a way, but not sentimental and the poetry was treated as it deserves. What a grand "welcome home" day.

Section 1:   5. HART FELL   808 m   OS 78   114136

Section 1:   6. WHITE COOMB   822 m   OS 79   163151

Section 1:   7. BROAD LAW   840 m   OS 72   146235

I am glad the Border Hills have a scattering of Corbetts for there is a suspicion that they would be less-visited without these specific lures. My conscience is clear, for all my motoring life I have purposely taken time off to explore the Borders when travelling to and from England or the continent. It may be a grabbed hour for one historic site or it may be a week trekking across the wilds of Galloway, but persistence paid off. It was one area I did not need to raid when completing the Corbetts became an obsession (doing the Donalds is another story), and I have long sung the praises of a hill landscape, still peopled and proud, a contrast to the desert that laps so much north of the Highland Line. Like Orkney, the Borders can feel like another country. Even the hills are different and, after crossing Rotten Bottom between White Coomb and Hart Fell, there may be a temptation to give thanks for that.

In February 1891 the young and lusty Scottish Mountaineering Club held its first official meet at the Crook Inn, Tweedsmuir, and Broad Law was climbed by all and sundry. There had been informal meets before then, of course, and it was only three months later, on the Queen's birthday, that a party traversed White Coomb and Hart Fell. To show how little has changed I summarise the note in the journal about their day on the Moffat hills.

The party left Moffat about 9.30 a.m., driving up Moffatdale to below the Grey Mare's Tail. A cold wind was blowing down the valley and they were not sorry to leave the trap "and set legs in motion". Starting at 11.10 they climbed quickly up the roughish ground by the fall, crossed the burn, and continued till in view of Loch Skeen, a loch created by the natural dam of moraine debris. Lochcraig Head, with its screes falling to the margin of the loch, was their objective and this was reached by a right-flanker up steep grass, arriving at 12.40. The biting wind had them scurrying round the crags that circle Loch Skeen, a "lovely little loch, lying in a veritable cradle of bare stony slopes topped by precipitous crags". It brought them to White Coomb, "the highest point in Dumfriesshire". From there they made for the long flat ridge of Hart Fell, keeping to the watershed between the Moffat–Annan drainage and the Tweed.

Oddly enough the Tweed is to the west, but runs to the east coast while the Moffat waters enter the western Solway — and the upper reaches of the Clyde are not so distant. Burns wrote of

> "Yon wild mossy mountains, sae lofty and wide,
> That immerse in their bosom the youth o' the Clyde."

Hart Fell gives a good view over to Queensberry and the Lowther Hills, perhaps my favourites outwith Galloway, because they are not so wild and mossy. This gang pointed out the aptness of the name Rotten Bottom on the map, and there still are some quality peat hags. Hart Fell was reached at 3.20, the clouds broke up and they took a longer break to admire the view.

Keeping along the ridge towards Swattlefell (Swatte Fell to us) they admired the steep, scraggy trench of the Blackhope Burn before striking down the Birnock Water to reach Moffat at 5.40. "A most enjoyable tramp" was the verdict on the day.

Some things have changed of course. The Grey Mare's Tail has become such a popular tourist attraction that careful work has had to be done to counter the track erosion that had developed. The NTS however have tried to keep the car park and approaches as natural as possible. The fall is still a fine sight, and its waters, frozen, have become popular as a climbing route. What would the 1891 party have thought of that? I don't think they would approve of the conifer plantings up Moffatdale.

From the head of Loch Skeen it is quite easy to climb up to the col between Lochcraig Head and Firthybrig Head, or White Coomb can be approached more directly up the Midlaw Burn. There is no way of avoiding Rotten Bottom between the Corbetts. Hart Fell offers several ways down to Moffat or elsewhere, and Moffat itself is a delightful wee town to finish in. There is a famous statue of a ram in the square (the sculptor forgot to give it ears) which points to the importance of that creature in Border economics. Moffat was something of a spa back in Victorian times, as Moffat Well on the Birnock descent indicates.

If you descend off Hart Fell to the south west over Arthur's Seat, you come to Hartfell Spa, a chalybeate well, not sulphur like Moffat Well. Higher up the Annan valley is the deep hollow of the Devil's Beef Tub and the road from the top of the pass, and on to Tweedsmuir is another good starting or finishing point for a traverse of these hills.

The grandest scenery is not on the tops but rather in the glens which bite back into the grassy plateau above Moffat Water: the Blackhope, Carrifran and Loch Skeen glens. It was a bleak February day that first took me up by Loch Skeen and down by the Blackhope Burn. I'd forgotten my ice axe, had a white out on White Coomb and never a car came to offer a lift back up the A701. I'd still offer this as a worthwhile alternative. They are impressive glens and add considerably to the character of the range. The old county boundary is marked by a wall which was most useful for navigation that day. Doing the Donalds has meant further visits to the prows between the glens.

From Firthybrig Head an easy walk leads north to Moll's Cleuch Dod and down to the Megget Stone (452 m) at the top of the pass between Talla Reservoir and Megget Reservoir, which offers another alternative traverse: Megget to Moffat. As Broad Law, the highest of the Manor Hills, lies north of this pass all three Corbetts could be linked easily enough if one could arrange to be dropped off at the Megget Stone. Ah, for the days of simply hiring a trap. Heading south I once drove up from Talla Reservoir (a 1-in-5 hill) to enjoy a windy walk up Broad Law over Porridge Cairn. The first wheatears were probably wishing they were back in Africa. The wind screamed through the fences and washed over the grass, plovers were pleading and the blue-brown landscape seemed to move with the gale. A wig of white cloud fell down the nape of Broad Law, covering Cramalt Craig, a Corbett now deleted. That night I camped in Langdale.

There is now a radio beacon on top of Broad Law which would no doubt surprise the members of that first SMC Meet were they to be whisked back today. Forests, dams, tracks, fences have really changed the hills quite a bit — but the fun of the game remains. Being based at the Crook Inn they took the natural line up the Hearthstane (Heystane) Burn and on by Glenheurie Rig, rather dull now as it is the line of the radio station's maintenance road (but then, all the Tweed spurs and glens are planted and/or tracked). Broad Law has a broad view: of hills beyond the Highland Line, of the English Lakeland fells, of the Cheviot. The SMC had absolutely no view as there was thick mist on top.

They descended (unintentionally) to Meggethead and had to return over by Talla (no reservoir then) to Tweedsmuir, quite a long round; but the next day saw new arrivals, Douglas, Munro and Stott, intentionally repeat the misty crossing to Meggethead, then they ascended the Winterhope Burn to the hag country leading over to Loch Skeen and the Grey Mare's Tail, from where, in wind and rain, they tramped along to Moffat in their big hobnailers. Border Corbetts can be as demanding as any others.

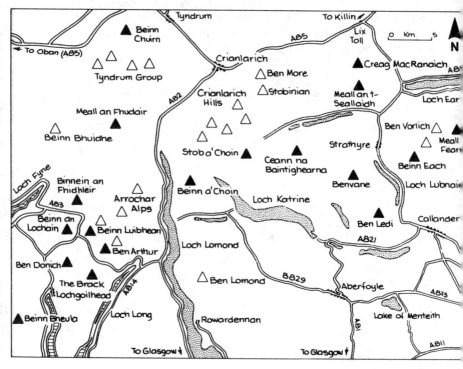

NOTE: Black triangles indicate Corbetts, White triangles Munros.

LOCH FYNE, STRATHYRE & LOCH EARN

Section 2:   1. BEINN BHEULA   779 m   OS 56   155983
   Hill of the Ford

THE NAME BEINN BHEULA always struck me as sounding like something out of *Pilgrim's Progress*. It became a Promised Land to me as a boy in wartime, staying at Carrick Castle on Loch Goil. Boats, woods and hills were a magnificent playground — and quite a contrast to being bombed out of Singapore or staying as a refugee in South Africa. Not that Carrick was entirely safe. When Greenock was heavily bombed the friendly hills were dark against a sky of flames. A wee steamer, the *Comet*, would take us to and from Carrick (or you rowed to Portincaple for a train) but now there is just a bus which makes the long haul round over the Rest and Be Thankful. Between Lochgoilhead and Carrick it runs under the "home" hills: Cruach nam Miseag and its big brother Beinn Bheula.

The Cruach (606 m) was the first hill I ever climbed in Scotland, tacking along behind my big brother Ian and an older girl who knew the area well. Racing down, Margaret turned to warn us of some "deep irony pools" and promptly ran right into one, landing up to her waist. We boys thought this very funny.

Beinn Bheula, two miles west of the Cruach, had to wait some years, but it never lost its special place in the imagination. Much later still Fife opened Ardroy, its outdoor centre, at Lochgoilhead and, as County Adviser, I managed to stay there occasionally and renewed my love of this corner of Scotland. Ah, if only we could have west coast mountains with east coast weather!

After a morning rock climbing, a companion, Ian, and I had leave for the afternoon so we slipped off to go up Beinn Bheula. From Lettermay a forest road runs up the glen for a mile, then we broke out of the plantations (a silvicultural despond) to scramble up the burn coming down from Curra Lochain, a charming lochan in an old pass through to Strachur on Loch Fyne. The stream cascades down in a series of falls so we played Mr Bold and Mr Old on its greasy rocks. After inspecting the remains of a crashed aircraft we set our faces to the rough NE Ridge and the several schisty bumps that led to the summit. There we took a brief ease to look over the Delectable Mountains, till Ian pointed out that supper was being served in an hour's time. So we set ourselves for a sprint. We could see the sailing boats heading in to the centre, stowing sail and everyone rowing ashore. We just made supper.

Beinn Bheula is a good hill to have above an outdoor centre. It is a varied hill with plenty of complex ground, interesting corners, a rich flora and, as the highest peak in Cowal, a grand view over the woods and waters of the west. It has corries to east, south and west and clear-cut ridges. There are some caves on its NW spur, Carnoch Mor. Next time, however, I want to link it to Cruach nam Miseag, for old time's sake, descending to Coromonachan or Cuillimuich and on to Carrick Castle. There's so much I want to do before passing on, permanently, to Bheula land.

Section 2:   2. BEN DONICH   847 m   OS 56   218043

Section 2:   3. THE BRACK   884 m   OS 56   245031

Ben Donich and The Brack are hills I've climbed several times in several combinations and, as I can't decide which is best, I'll briefly summarise the route options. Few Corbetts are quite so accessible, for there is a northerly arc of road round them from Lochgoilhead to Coilessan on Loch Long and these places are linked by a footpath cutting across just south of the Corbetts.

The forestry have a road (not open to vehicles) all the way down Loch Long but it is only the branch up the Coilessan Glen which concerns the Corbetts. The southern end of the Ardgoil wedge between Loch Long and Loch Goil is known as Argyll's Bowling Green, a humorous touch which is quite accidental, for it is simply the murder of the Gaelic *Buaile na Greine* (sunny cattle fold) which originally applied to one place on the south east of the peninsula.

Ben Donich is in the rough form of a cross and the north, east and south ridges are all reasonable routes. It is a grassier hill than The Brack but there are some crags. Perhaps the North Ridge is the most satisfying in ascent (it is the shortest). I went up it the day after Beinn Bheula for this reason. The dog was not well and had to be left in the car and I wanted him to be at the vet's that afternoon. I found a convenient firebreak up on to the North Ridge from near the top of the Rest and Be Thankful, which also gave a 300-m start. It is pleasant to descend the South Ridge to Lochgoilhead because you are looking on to the sea and the village. Last time I counted over 100 boats on the loch.

My old friend W. K. Holmes, of *Tramping Scottish Hills*, once combined Beinn an Lochain and Ben Donich one sweltering summer day, and on the descent began having fantasies about being offered tea by a party he could see picnicking down in Glen Croe. The bright red and white frocks of the girls could even be seen but, alas, as he descended, the picnic party turned into a roadworkers' dump and the colourful frocks were only painted barrels!

The Brack, though lower and more compact, is rugged and has some real cliffs on its north flank and the hill is really very hemmed in by trees. One way to avoid them is to take the route up Coilessan Glen to gain the SW Ridge. If ascending on the Glen Croe side it is worth studying the breaks from the A83 before setting off. This is perhaps the most interesting route as you can see the cliffs on the way. Follow the forest road on the south bank of the Croe past Creagdhu and up the hill until, beyond a double bend, you can follow up the east bank of the burn descending from The Brack. The path from Lochgoilhead up by the Donich Water and on for Coilessan also allows access to the SW Ridge. Some of these routes have been signposted or marked by the Forestry Commission.

The two hills can be combined from either Lochgoilhead or Ardgartan. At the latter there is a camp site and a modern youth hostel right on the shore of Loch Long. The hostel has panoramic windows looking out to the loch, with The Cobbler seemingly peering over its roof. An early start makes for a pleasant walk up Glen Croe, on the forest roads, and then the old motor road which is still occasionally used for rallies. Look out for the Rest and Be Thankful stone on the pass. This also allows the peaks to be traversed in a "homeward" direction. An anti-clockwise circuit from Lochgoilhead is the easiest combination, descending Ben Donich's South Ridge and then making for the bridge over the River Goil. The peaks are nowhere difficult. All crags can easily be bypassed; but it is still typical Arrochar Alps country of lumps and bumps and false summits, which can be very confusing in mist. And if you want something different, you can always have a night out in "Cobbler View", a howff (shelter) under one of the big boulders which have crashed down from the precipice on The Brack (250036). The big gully in the cliffs is "Elephant Gully" which is "likely to appeal more to the botanist than the climber". Much of it is subterranean and the climber finally emerges through a hole on to the hillside, "the hole in the elephant's bottom" so to speak.

Section 2:   4. THE COBBLER (BEN ARTHUR)   884 m   OS 56
    259058

The Cobbler was the first Corbett I ever climbed. It was one of the first hills of any sort I ever climbed. The peak has a stature and an allure far beyond mere lists. I had been up it many times before I knew what

"Munro" or "Corbett" meant. For a couple of years, as a young man, I lived in Paisley and having just acquired my first climbing rope — a new-fangled (fankled) nylon rope — it was hardly surprising that the Arrochar Alps in general and The Cobbler in particular became familiar and friendly ground. My introduction to The Cobbler was not so friendly.

Having cycled across Scotland to the old Ardgartan youth hostel (during schooldays) the sight of The Cobbler was too much for one reared on the couthy humps of the Ochils. (John Leyden said The Cobbler had "the appearance of a ruptured volcano", and Dorothy Wordsworth wrote, "the singular rocks on the summit were like ruins — castles or watch towers".) The bike was abandoned next day when I wandered along Glen Croe then angled up in a direct line for that weird jumble of crags. Above the trees I was on to soggy snow, which became something of an effort. An old photograph, sharper than my memory, shows a boy in short trousers leaning on a shepherd's crook, school scarf blowing in the wind.

The South Summit is a great hunk of crag and my route brought me face to face with it. Without much hesitation I began to wend up the crag but there was soon a new feel of nothing much below my feet and ever-steepening rock ahead. I did not like the thought of going on, but going back down was even more discouraging. It is a situation we all find ourselves in periodically — at least I hope so — the core of climbing lies in the balance of fear and frolic. My course of action was soon enough settled. I saw a brass plaque fixed to the rock and when I scrabbled over to it I read something about someone having fallen or died on that spot. "RIP".

The meaning of Rip eluded the young tyre, but I took the hint and slithered down and flanked up past the South Summit. It was separated by a distinct col and looked anything but easy. My eye traced hopeful lines, marked in snow, but I realised that descending it, unsighted, would have been a different matter. "Experience", as the French saying goes, "is the sum of near misses".

The shocks of the day were not over, for The Cobbler has a sting in its tail. Like the Inaccessible Pinnacle in Skye, though on a much reduced scale, the mountain top has a rocky (15-foot) protuberance which actually rears higher than the expected summit. In Pin and Cobbler require *climbing* to stand on their real tops. I looked at the frost-hoary, split hunk of schist with some surprise but had scrambled enough on rock to study it with practical hope. There was this great split in the top rock and by scrambling into that one could surely wriggle up and out on to the summit. The feasibility of this route depends on the body circumference of the assailant. It was no problem to a young lad but, ooh, it was cold on fingers and knees. My yell of glee was probably heard in Glasgow. My moans as I thawed out frozen fingers I kept to myself.

The easiest way up the final rock is to go right through the split and out the other side where an easy ledge curls up to give access to the top. The scramble is quite exposed and, like the Inaccessible Pinnacle, can frighten off the walker who has avoided all scrambling. In those cases a rope can be a most reassuring article of equipment. Later on it was roped climbs that brought us back again and again to that triptych of crags that can be seen so temptingly from Arrochar.

The name of the hill goes back some hundreds of years and supposedly derives from a fanciful picturing of the North Peak being the cobbler leaning over his last, the Central Peak, while his wife Jean, the South Peak, looks on. I've never heard it referred to as Ben Arthur. Being so close to Glasgow it became hallowed ground to those pioneers of the depression days who escaped to the hills. Jock Nimlin, John Cunningham and others were hero-names to me when I came to know it. Alistair Borthwick's classic book *Always a Little Further* has a chapter called "The Cave" which gives the feel of those days. The Arrochar Alps are riddled with caves. One I discovered by falling into it when what I thought was firm ground proved to be a hole covered with heather. Some of these places have been swallowed up by forest plantations but the popular route of access to The Cobbler up the Buttermilk Burn was diplomatically left clear and, if overgrown a bit, it is now a well trodden path.

The convex slope keeps The Cobbler hidden for a long time and its sudden appearance is a grand bit of mountain swank. The Narnain Boulders ("Shelter Stone" on the map) have seen generations of climbers sleeping under them and practising on them. Narnain is the Munro on the opposite side of the Buttermilk Burn to The Cobbler, and it, too, has plenty of climbing and scrambling interest. You can actually enter a rift in it and climb right through and out the other side of the hill. The Arrochar Alps were lure enough that, even when teaching in Fife, our school gangs would often be wending up the Allt a' Bhalachain towards The Cobbler.

If the South Summit is the hardest to climb, the North Summit is the most spectacular to be *on* for the top juts out in an overhanging prow of rock. The Cobbler has a good view to Ben Lomond and the waters of the Clyde. It is altogether a very fine mountain. What a lucky chance led a young boy to within sight of its dramatic profile.

Section 2: 5. Beinn Luibhean 858 m OS 56 243079
  Hill of the little plant

Keeping some form of personal record is advisable for those busy ticking off lists. One forgets otherwise. Some years ago I parked at the Butterbridge end of the Rest and Be Thankful pass and traversed Ben Ime to Narnain at the behest of my Munro-bagging dog Storm. I then put in a claim for The Cobbler which doesn't have to be anything to beguile visitors. It was crawling with people, being July, so we soon headed off for the Bealach a' Mhaim. I then did a bit of checking and realised Beinn Luibhean was a Corbett, so we diverted to take it in as well. This is actually a satisfying round of four interesting peaks and one I'd recommend. It was only later, checking my record, that I discovered I'd already been up Beinn Luibhean a decade earlier. Memory can be a fickle thing, for the previous visit had obviously been as good, as I could tell from reading the log book of the period. Hence my advocacy of keeping some form of report *at the time*.

Nearly half of this Corbett's height has gone by the time one drives up to the Rest and Be Thankful so it could be done in the same day as Binnean an Fhidhleir (2:7) or Beinn an Lochain (2:6) or, if still Munro-bagging, in the round mentioned above. That first visit saw us lingering in Glasgow on the Saturday morning after a wild night of storms but the thought of *seeing* The Cobbler in new snow took us off up the familiar Loch Lomond road to Arrochar and, being that distance, well, we might as well go up something. Beinn Ime is a good old standby. We set off up the burn that edges the wood on the NW flank of Luibhean (a path is now worn up it) with the new snow rather heavy until we rose above the freezing level.

The four lads with me would benefit from a bit of responsibility so I decided they could do Beinn Ime alone while I'd wander up Beinn Luibhean (unaware of its Corbett status) from where I could keep an eye on their progress. We parted after a snowball fight across the burn. I went as directly up as I could, rather than by the Corbett's col with Beinn Ime, so as to watch the others and also to use the NE facing rocks for some sport. In those days one cut steps in snow and I raised a good sweat hacking up a gully. There are only minor, avoidable, crags on the Corbett. Some showers and spindrift came and went but it was quite pleasant and I made a lazy descent down the North Ridge. The tiny dots on Beinn Ime eventually made the top — and vanished. (Thoughts of Mallory and Irvine!) The snow fell more solidly as I went down by the wood, back to the

Dormobile. Half an hour later the lads swam in, "wet below the waist line" as one of them misquoted T. S. Eliot, and looking like snowmen, and in high glee at their winter climb of the biggest of the Arrochar Alps.

Our camp that night was rocked by storms and at some black hour we had to crawl out and tighten guy lines.

> "At two o'clock in the morning, if you open
>   your window and listen,
> You will hear the feet of the wind that is
>   going to call the sun."
>   Kipling

Section 2:   6. BEINN AN LOCHAIN   901 m   OS 56   218079
            The hill of the lake

As a deleted Munro, Beinn an Lochain has gone into eclipse but it always occupied something of a maverick position. I grew up with it being 2,992 feet on the One Inch map but 3,021 feet in Munro's *Tables*. The map's spot height was not the summit, and Munro & Co. enjoyed working it out with their aneroids and filling Notes pages of the *SMC Journal*. The 901 m given on the metric map *and* in the latest *Tables* is the real height, the OS assures me. It was a pleasant hill as a Munro, and remains such, despite the bureaucratic messing-about with altitudinal mathematics.

Having early connection with Carrick Castle has meant a lifetime of travelling over the Rest and Be Thankful: Beinn an Lochain has been climbed summer and winter, alone or with friends, and several times with school parties. It has character enough to be a proud part of the Arrochar Alps. The slightly concave east face above Loch Restil is what everyone sees and this, being craggy and broken, can give some good sport in winter when the greasy schist and wet gullies are all safely frozen. Walkers are advised to reach the summit by the ridges that bound this face, up the NE Ridge and down the South Ridge being the best combination. There is plenty of room to park at the head of the pass.

The NE Ridge is fairly broken by steps and crags and becomes narrower above the northern corrie (with its debris of a stupendous rockfall) then a succession of false summits leads eventually to the real one. There is a bird's eye view down Glen Croe with its twin roads and geometrical plantings, The Cobbler above and Ben Lomond beyond. Arran, Jura and the western seascape is of special interest, for the seaboard is arrayed more than usual. Any hill view has an extra satisfaction for "old hands"; one looks to *known* peaks and glens and islands where one has wandered the golden years away.

There are few problems descending southwards and once the cliff edge disappears there is just the big, steep skirt of grass to angle down back to the Rest and Be Thankful. If the day has hours left then there is always Beinn Luibhean across the road or Ben Donich across the other road.

Southey, on tour in 1819, gives a description remarkably straightforward for the period. "Leaving the inn at Cairndow (Loch Fine) the road almost immediately begins to ascend Glenkenlas, a long, long ascent between green mountains sloping gradually from the stream which fills the bottom. On the right is a remarkable streak, or ridge, of large stones, appearing as if forced out like a torrent from a large hole in the hill above [the rockfall?]. The road turns to the right; the mountains green to the summit of the pass, and to their own summits also; and large loose crags are lying about in numbers, and in all directions. On the summit is a seat looking down Glencroe bearing the inscription 'Rest and Be Thankful'."

Section 2:   7. BINNEIN AN FHIDHLEIR   817 m   OS 56/50   230109
          The fiddler's peak

This name is given to the peak that forms the central tower (811 m) of the battlement of hillside north of Glen Kinglas while the Corbett is nameless and 1½ km further east, above Butterbridge. Personally I feel this hijacking of any convenient neighbouring name should be avoided.

Glen Kinglas is a classic "glaciated trough" of a valley with both sides presenting continuously steep, wet, scraggy slopes which give little variety on any ascent. The views are restricted going up. I should imagine the summits give good views to Beinn Bhuidhe and the Lui group but on my single ascent it rained all the way up and the cloud was down on the tops. I bagged the Corbett only because I was there, wandering home after some good days on Islay and Jura. You can't win them all.

I just went up from Butterbridge to the Corbett and down again. Had the day been clear it might have been pleasant to walk along the ridge to the trig point on the lower summit, Binnein an Fhidhleir, or to wander in the other direction to the 597 top from which the complex of hydro roads and catchments for the Loch Sloy dam can be studied. Walking back down the upper Kinglas Water you pass Abyssinia. This slightly disappointing hill could be combined with

Beinn Luibhean and/or Beinn an Lochain to make a clean sweep of the Rest and Be Thankful Corbetts.

Years ago when acting as student courier to a bus-load of American sailors we stopped in Glen Kinglas to let the visitors see some Highland cows on the slopes of Binnein an Fhidhleir. Being assured they were safe, several lads walked up the hillside for photographs. Highlanders are docile, but nosey: they began to amble forward out of curiosity. The sailors stopped. The cows came on. The sailors retreated, the cows came on the faster. A minute later the rout was complete with the sailors splashing down in full flight with some excited cows lumbering after. I received no tips that day.

Section 2:   8. Meall an Fhudair   764 m   OS 50   271192
          Gunpowder hill

Meall an Fhudair was a return to normality, the first week home after a ski holiday under the array of the Eiger and Jungfrau when we had days of the deepest powder snow I've ever tried to drown myself in. The very day of returning I was off to Fife's outdoor centre at Lochgoilhead instructing potential leaders, some of whom were old friends anyway. Seven of us had a day on Meall an Fhudair as part of the training. Surprise, surprise, it was a Corbett I had not been up before. Perhaps because it was such a contrast, my memories of the day are very clear.

If the Alps impressed with their bigness and grandeur, the home delights lay in a host of little things: the daffodils in flower at Inverarnan, or the brace of mallard which kept complaining up the burn ahead of us, or the pheasant that exploded from our feet in a shower of feathers (feathers with the most jewel-like markings), or the tang of spring gale, or the view across Glen Falloch to the Ben Glas Falls — a whisper at that distance and so white against the tawny slopes of winter-colouring. We followed the Allt Arnan, a cheery, tumbling burn with one worthy waterfall and a score of splendid pools. As the water level was low we scrambled up on the rocks wherever possible, always good training for several skills.

Over a lip we joined a hydro road which ended at a small dam half a mile further up the Allt Arnan. The dam was simply an intake — presumably the water is piped west over the watershed to the reservoir that has drowned most of the Allt na Lairige Glen. This name *stream of the pass* indicates an ancient regular route and it is in fact the easiest line from the north end of Loch Lomond through to Glen Fyne and the sea. The slopes of Troisgeach have peculiar rocky, lumpy ribs, but rather than go up straight away we followed our burn to its source in a round lochan just below the spongy watershed. After a snack we headed up for Meall an Fhudair, scrambling on such rock as lay in our path. We spent forty minutes on top hoping for a view but the clouds would not roll away. The grandstand view of the Arrochar Alps, Lui and Beinn Bhuidhe is actually recommended in the *SMC Guide*. While the rest headed down for Glen Fyne, one lad and I, perforce, returned to Inverarnan for the minibus.

East of Meall an Fhudair is a col with an odd proliferation of tiny pools and lochans. There must have been several dozen, far more than can be shown on the 1:50,000 map. We explored them in the passing and grudgingly angled down off the hill. There is a sudden delightful change of view when the lip of the Loch Lomond trench is reached; eyes are suddenly held by the downward richness, a vivid contrast to the sterile heights. There was plenty of expected fauna on the descent: ptarmigan, deer, hares, a mountain blackbird, grouse and the first wagtail of the season. After a brew we drove over the Rest and Be Thankful and met the others at the foot of Glen Fyne. They arrived just as the kettle began to sing.

Section 2:   9. BEINN A' CHOIN   770 m   OS 56/50   354130
            Hill of the dogs (or hounds)

Beinn a' Choin is the peak that dominates the Rob Roy country. It is now well moated by Loch Lomond, Loch Arklet and Loch Katrine, but the last two have been much enlarged by dams (Glasgow's water supply) so the scenery has altered considerably since Rob Roy's day. It was a much wilder landscape then, with more trees and deeper heather, and many more people. About 150 people lived between Loch Katrine and Loch Lomond, for example. The landscape, which we take so much for granted, has a long and continuing history of change. Sadly much of it has been exploited, and the Highlands are now a dying waste of wet desert. Man, supposedly the most intelligent being of all creation, is the only one that cannot live at peace in his niche. Poor world, when we have gobbled it up entirely . . .

These were some of my cheerless thoughts as I left the Dormobile at six in the morning to follow the Snaid Burn up from Garrison of Inversnaid. "Garrison" points to the days of a military presence trying to tame the unruly MacGregors. Rob Roy married his Mary at Corriearklet and had houses in Glen Gyle as well as in the glens to the north. Glen Gyle was quite an important through-route for cattle (legally or otherwise), from Glen Falloch and further west, leading to Strathyre and Crieff.

A heavy shower had me sheltering in the tree-clad gorge of the Snaid but the midges poured out to make a meal of me so I carried on, up the burn by Stob an Fhainne (peak of the Fianna, those mythical Celtic warriors of both Irish and Scottish folklore). The going was soft. The rain was hard. It was disgustingly hot and in the end I stripped to my Y-fronts and just got wet. The rain was quite enjoyable.

A fence runs from Stob an Fhainne to Beinn a' Choin, which was useful as the final cone was in cloud. "Moundy, rough hills", Rennie McOwan calls them. I was less polite. Dog or hound occurs in the name of quite a few hills. This often harks back to the Fianna, who were great hunters, but it can also imply a place where hounds were kennelled for hunting either deer or men — MacGregors as like as not. Either could apply here, I feel.

Across Glen Gyle is a pass with the cheery name Bealach nan Corp, *the pass of the dead*. This was the route taken by MacGregors on their last journeys. (Everyone wanted to be buried on home territory.) The outlawed clan were called "the children of mist". In this wild country with its maze of passes they were never easy to control.

At the summit I ate the one marmalade sandwich which had not become soggy and threw the rest away. Within a minute gulls had appeared through the cloud and were squabbling over their booty. How did they know it was there? They followed me down the hill, grabbing and dropping my apple core in turn before squawking off in disgust.

Given a better day I might have circled to Maol Mor above Loch Katrine which is an even better viewpoint than the Corbett, itself "a magnificent viewpoint" (McOwan). The Arrochar Alps, the Ben Lui group, the Crianlarich hills, Ben Lomond, an inner ring of Corbetts and the various lochs certainly give the view character, but I wrote that evening, "It's the jumbled, shut-in, lumpy, grassy, scabby sort of country that lies across Scotland's midriff — not a patch on the country out in 'the golden remote wild west'." It does not seem to have been the cheeriest of ascents. Was it the rain? Was it me? Was it the background of those old unhappy doings of long ago?

Beinn a' Choin is rather remote, even with a vehicle. The motor approach is by Aberfoyle (not by Loch Katrine) and the road is narrow and slow-going. You can also walk over from Inverarnan in Glen Falloch, up by the Ben Glas Burn and then south by spiky Ben Ducteach and several more "moundy rough hills". Another way would be to take the passenger ferry across Loch Lomond to

Inversnaid. This is signposted and you may have to signal to the other
side of the loch for the wee boat to come and fetch you. Many early
travellers came this way: James Hogg in 1803, Robert Southey in
1819, the Wordsworths and Coleridge in 1803. With a poor road
system, boats and ferries plied everywhere.

James Hogg, as a shepherd, came through these glens several times
and in a letter to Sir Walter Scott in 1803 gave some reminiscences of
his herding days. A fog once caught them and they spent the night on
the hill (probably Maol Mor rather than Beinn a' Choin) waking to a
stunning fresh, clear morning. "Loch Katrine with its surrounding
scenery stretching from one hand, Loch Lomond on the other. The
outline of Ben Lomond appeared to particular advantage, as did the
cluster of monstrous pyramids [the Arrochar Alps] on the other side.
One hill, in Strathfillan, called Ben Leo [Laoigh] was belted with
snow, with a particularly sharp, peaked appearance of a prodigious
height.

"Besides all this I had drunk some whisky the preceding evening
and had a very indistinct recollection of our approach to that place, and
it was actually a good while ere I was persuaded that everything I saw
was real. I sat about an hour contemplating the scenes with the greatest
pleasure before I awakened my comrade."

The Ettrick Shepherd slept on the same spot twelve years later, "to
experience the same delightful feelings", but woke instead to hideous
yellings and, throwing off his plaid, found four eagles circling over
him. "Go away! I'm not dead yet!" was his reaction.

Section 2:   10. STOB A' CHOIN   865   OS 56   416161
              Dog peak

Section 2:   11. CEANN NA BAINTIGHEARNA   771   OS 57   474163
              Her ladyship's head

There is a fine mountainous area between the Trossachs and the Loch
Voil valley which offers good cross-country routes and hill wanderings. Stob a' Choin would be a notable peak were it not so hidden
away, and Baintighearna lies in pleasant surroundings. Baintighearna
is a convenience name; it really applies to the rocky bluff overlooking
Loch Doine and not to the Corbett which, like so many hills, is left
nameless by the Ordnance Survey. (Pleas to the OS to name all
Munros, etc., fall on deaf ears, but presumably local shepherds have
names if the OS cared to enquire.)

With Storm keen to do Corbetts I set out to link these two, a combination which had once before given me a solitary tramp; but the traverse is one where a friendly driver is an advantage. I drove up to the car park before Inverlochlarig intending to leave the push bike, then return eastwards and up to Ballimore in Glen Buckie to start the traverse. However, I realised there was a stiff pull up to Ballimore, and the lochside road was a bit of a switchback: too much "push" for the bike at the day's end. It was also a "bright and beautiful" summer morning which would probably cloud over all too soon. We set off for Stob a' Choin there and then.

The hill thrusts up boldly in a surge of green, with plenty of crags to give it some detail, a knobbliness so typical of the area. The crags are all very obvious and can be avoided and the rocky summit is perfectly easy. More care is needed in descent; the Stob is very much a hill for a day of clear visibility, not only as an aid to safe navigation but to relish the summit panorama. "It is a hill with splendid views", says Rennie McOwan in his *Walks in the Trossachs and Rob Roy Country*, a book covering much of Section 2 and giving interesting historical notes as well as routes of all grades.

There has been a great deal of bulldozing of roads in the area so the Second Series map is useful. There is a road right along (through the middle of the plantations) on the south side of Loch Voil and Loch Doine, and from the bridge over the main river near the car park/picnic place tracks radiate up and round under Stob Breac to the Invernenty glen and westwards towards Stob a' Choin. From Inverlochlarig a track runs up the main valley westwards for four miles. The bridge over the main river, a mile from the farm, is worth remembering but normally the river can be crossed anywhere.

We crossed the bridge near the car park and, from Blaircreach with its clumps of conifers, puffed our way up the lower part of the bold NE Ridge of the Corbett. This, strictly speaking, leads to an eastern top, itself knobbly and with a deal of ups and downs leading to the summit. We cut round into the hollow north side of the mountain: Coire an Laoigh, *the corrie of the calves*, presumably once a favourite deer-calving ground for the area, is now heavily under sheep. We came out at the bealach below the final cone of the Corbett. What an unrelenting ascent — and what a rewarding view, with a gathering of Clan Munro to west and north!

The whole area reeks of real clan history. In the popular imagination it is Rob Roy Country. He was born at Glengyle, lived at Inverlochlarig amongst other places and is buried at Balquhidder. The valleys are full of ruins pointing to a heavy population not so long ago. Glen Gyle to the south was an historic droving route, which also meant reiving and military use as well. Loch Katrine is now the jealous property of Glasgow Corporation who apply a no-go policy to its shores — while they ply a tourist boat on the super-hygienic waters. However one can cycle (or walk) along from the Trossachs public road end, and Stob a' Choin and Ceann na Baintighearna could easily be done from the south.

The Bealach nan Corp (that is known as the *pass of the corpses*) further west was the funeral route into the Lochlarig Glen. The Allt a' Choin, lower in height, leads up to a boggy pass. The Invernenty Glen was used, however, and the Glen Buckie–Glen Finglas link was an important one. Scott, with his *Lady of the Lake* and *Rob Roy*, virtually set the Scottish tourist industry in motion and the Trossachs still buzz in summer. The hills, however, are strangely empty. Back at the car park (now full of cars) there were three parties setting off. Yes, they all agreed, Stob a' Choin was the finest peak in view, but they all streamed off for the Munros to the north — so well seen *from* the Corbett.

We had descended by Coire an Laoigh and boulder-hopped across to the road down to Inverlochlarig. A curlew patrolled overhead, wailing, and young wheatears flitted among the stones. Storm walked through a flock of sheep on the road without paying them any attention, which rather silenced a potential salvo from a shepherd. We had a "crack" instead. They are, perhaps justly, a bit anti-dog for so many visitors bring untrained beasts and let them run uncontrolled. Litter and vandalism were other complaints. I find it surprising (and sad) that the yobbo element is found even among hillgoers. Surely we go to the hills to escape the frustrating urban world, not to bring its attributes and attitudes with us. A quick coffee and we drove back along the lochs to Balquhidder, branched off across the charming old bridge over the loch's outflow and so up Glen Buckie to Ballimore where the Calair Burn runs under another stone span. Just across the bridge is a sign pointing out the right-of-way to Brig o' Turk and the Trossachs.

Glen Buckie is a pleasing corner. The glen is well wooded lower down, has tree-girt pastures round the farms of Ballimore and Immeroin (the only lived-in centres now) and wide sheep-ranges running to its head. Beinn an t-Sidhein (*fairy hill*) and Ben Vane enclose the valley but the major drainage, the Calair Burn, breaks in from the west at Ballimore, its waters fed by the two burns which clasp the eastern aspects of our second Corbett, Ceann na Baintighearna. The view, as one follows the damp path, is to the big ridge descending from the Corbett and separating the Fathan Glen and Gleann Dubh. The extreme northern end of Ben Vane's ridge is a succession of bumps, and Bealach a' Chonnaidh across the lowest gap suggests that the old route cut over there rather than up the wetter valley. The Brig o' Turk path rounds this spur of Ben Vane and runs up to an easy col under Ben Vane itself. The turning was a superb viewpoint, looking over a wide basin, full of free-ranging cattle and a fold of bleating sheep, with Stobinian's characteristic lopped-off summit cone through the gap beyond. The day had clouded over but the afternoon, instead of rain, gave periodic breaks, so sun, showers, clouds, wind and midges came along in a random succession. At times the weather changed quicker than I could unpack a camera to photograph some effect.

Having chased the view round the end of the hill there seemed so little distance to the col that we went up to view the other side (a bulldozed track and a sprawl of reservoir has rather changed the descent route) and from there Ben Vane looked so near that we went up it too. A Corbett at hand is worth two in the book.

The haul up grassy Ben Vane coincided with a sunny spell and was quite a toil. We met a couple of people on top. "Corbett? What's that?" showed they were just normal (sane) visitors. The Stuc a' Chroin–Beinn Each ridge across Loch Lubnaig, and the ridge from Ben Vane to Ben Ledi, looked equally jagged and rough — both excellent traverses. Back at the pass we contoured as much as possible (some bog, some heather) to gain Gleann Dubh which we circled between steep upper flanks and the heathery glen bottom. Dubh is *black*, or *dark*, and in the general green-ness of these hills the heather of the glen does appear dark. ("Glen Dubh" on the map can often be a warning of rough going due to bog and/or heather.)

The Corbett has a trig point even if it does not have a name. A spell of clouds on the *dubh* side of safety (drum rolls of thunder) had us scurrying off fast, dog panting and unhappy. He dislikes thunder and I only enjoy it from safer — lower — altitudes. We descended the big East Ridge but then cut over to pick up the Brig o' Turk path at the viewing corner. It cleared again for the photographs I wanted. Rather than return down the valley we went up to the Bealach a' Chonnaidh. A kestrel perched on a crag decorated with natural *bonsai*. We followed a sheep path along to look down on Glen Buckie. North of Calair Burn the fields were dotted with red deer. They are "farmed" along with the usual sheep and cows.

An alternative recommended route for this Corbett is to start at Balquhidder, cross the bridge and go along past Stronvar (once a youth hostel) and Muirlaggan, then take a path or rake up to the Bealach Driseach to reach the Corbett from the upper Fathan Glen, returning down Gleann Dubh and Glen Buckie. On a winter traverse of the pair I started and finished at Inverlochlarig (no car park then), descending west off Baintighearna down a burn of spring cascades to the Invernenty Burn. That was a very windy trip and my original high camp on Stob a' Choin had to be abandoned and a sheltered nook found at the head of Glen Sgionie. South of Stob a' Choin is the country described in John Barrington's *Red Sky at Night* (Pan Books), an idealistic description of the life of a shepherd.

Section 2:   12. BENVANE   821 m   OS 57   535137
             White hill

Section 2:   13. BEN LEDI   879 m   OS 57   562098
             Hill of the gentle slope or *God's Hill*

"Ben Ledi is prominent from Stirling and imposing from Callander", someone wrote at the turn of the century. One wonders what the pioneers would have thought of the view of Ben Ledi from Callander introducing a long-running telly soap opera as it did for *Doctor Finlay's Casebook*? The comment is still true, however, and every time I drive over the hill road from Stirling to Doune I experience a lifting of the heart as Ben Ledi rears ahead, first of the hills beyond the Highland line.

Benvane is a much more retiring hill but, as Rennie McOwan declares, "it therefore has views far more striking than many a higher hill". I find Benvane the more friendly with its green and open northern aspects rising above cheery Glen Buckie while Ben Ledi has been strangled with dank forestry plantings (through which glutinous paths have been gouged) and dotted with grim names like "loch of the corpse", and Stank Glen and the like. I've been up them both by various routes but a traverse of the pair gave me the best day and is the outing I'd recommend for the walker.

Ben Ledi used to be most often climbed from the south but farming on the lower slopes has switched the popular lines to the east flanks: paths go up from the Bridge over the Leny and via Stank Glen. These have had a great deal of use and are in a sorry state. Commission policy chops and changes and waymarking has recently been removed to try and ease the pressure. I think, now, I'd start at Brig o' Turk and wander up to the Glen Finglas reservoir and tackle Ben Ledi from the west. However, on my traverse I went up the Stank Glen (the name comes from the Gaelic *stang*, meaning pool) and had quite an obstacle course as a storm a few years before had flattened many trees. Since then new roads have appeared and the forest has been cleared. The route lies up the south bank of the burn. There are some falls worth seeing but my main memory was of the "Seven Boulders" which lie about the slopes above the treeline. These have some historic howffs and offer sport for the rock climber. I spent half an hour scrambling on the first of them but then realised time was going all too fast so I pushed on for the ragged skyline. The boulders are up left when you escape the trees and a burn leads on to a high, secretive corrie which is another fine feature: a real cauldron of snow on my March day.

It was barely freezing and too hazy for extensive views. One of the tentative derivations of the hill's name is *mountain of God* which perhaps harks back to pagan ceremonies once held on the summit. All round this region the hearth fires were allowed to go out before midnight at the end of April and, on the first day of May, the Celtic New Year, they were renewed with flames kindled in the Beltane fires on top of Ben Ledi. There was feasting, with weird rites and ceremonies, and despite Christian overlayers something of this lingers in the bonfires and May Day ascents of hills even now. Dominating several passes into the Highlands, Ben Ledi is also a natural site for forts — as Dunmore and Bochastle show, the former perhaps Pictish, the latter a Roman outpost.

Lochan nan Corp, by the low point on the switchback traverse to Benvane, commemorates a drowning tragedy at a funeral party. There were some quite dramatic "coffin roads" in the old days: the route to St Bride's Chapel at the south end of Loch Lubnaig was probably their destination, this being the Mackinlay burial ground (one of that scattered clan became president of the USA). Having toiled up Gleann Casaig the bearers laid their burden on the ice of the lochan — which promptly broke under them, with considerable loss of life. I made sure of seeing the lochan but it was black water and only fringed with a wreath of ice.

Loch Lubnaig means the *crooked loch* in the sense of *loch with a kink in it* and Ardnandave Hill makes the bold thrust that creates this feature. The hill dominates the loch much more than the terminal big hills, and grumpy Maccullough, loquacious Sir Walter, the willing Words-worths and plenty of others have all (rightly) commended the view. Having walked *north* to this fulcrum top I turned almost *west* for the continuation to Benvane. It too had a small hidden snow bowl of a corrie near the summit. Ben More and Stobinian were boldly white against a blackening sky. Night and storm were probably on a collision course. I turned down eastwards to the watershed between Glen Buckie and Loch Lubnaig.

You could not do so now; new trees wash well up below Benvane's north east slopes. But you can descend to Creag a' Mhadaidh (*the fox's crag*) and then down the grassy slopes to the old shielings at the head of Glen Buckie, or simply keep to the ridge as far as fancy leads. There are grand views down Glen Buckie. A car can get up to the big farm of Ballimore (*the big township*) which, with Immeroin across the glen, is a survivor of the several "farm-touns" or hamlets in Glen Buckie. So far they have not been swallowed by trees. Brig o' Turk to Ballimore I reckon is now the most attractive traverse.

Above Glen Buckie on the other side is Beinn an t-Sidhein which dominates Strathyre. A path straggles up through the trees to cross its southern shoulders and on down to Immeroin. On one ferociously wet meet of the Scottish Mountaineering Club a party of us crossed this col and back by Balquhidder with evergreen Tom Weir, the then President, setting a cracking pace.

I mentioned Maccullough earlier. He found Ben Ledi rather lacking in charm, writing, "I thought that I had known Highland rain in all its forms and mixtures and varieties in Skye, Mull, Shetland, Fort William, Lawers, Glencoe, but nothing like the rain on Ben Ledi did I ever behold, before or since." His tomes of travel were addressed to Sir Walter Scott and he did not hesitate to take the poet to task, wishing he had laid the "venue" of his "Lady of the Lake" in St Kilda or the wilds of Ross-shire because of the clanjamfray of tourists the work had let loose about the place. What would he make of today's clanjamfray?

My traverse had been made at the end of another SMC Meet. Before dining the previous night in the New Inn at Strathyre I'd taken my push-bike high up a forest road to leave it near the watershed under Benvane, whence we made our way after dealing with one electric fence, and one barbed-wire fence which was decorated with the stinking head of a long-dead fox (Creag a' Mhadaidh was not far above!). The dog went into my rucksack and we whizzed down to loch level. Caulfeild, Wade's successor, had built his military road west of Loch Lubnaig, a line which was also taken by the railway. Axed in the Beeching days, it has reverted to being a road, which was a joy to cycle, in quietness, dodging the frozen dubs, while across the loch came the mosquito drone of holiday traffic.

Callander was busy as a hive but I called in to the chip shop and bore off a supper to eat on the hill road where I could sit and look at that vast panorama of the Highlands, with Ben Ledi boldest of all. The dark colours of the hill reached up into darker clouds, shot through with angry reds, which flared, like a fire, and stuttered out, like dying coals, into night. If Ben Ledi was "prominent from Stirling and imposing from Callander", from half way between the view that evening had a brush with perfection.

Section 2: 14. BEINN EACH   813 m   OS 57   602158
            Horse hill

Section 2: 15. MEALL NA FEARNA   809 m   OS 57   651186
            Alder hill

Beinn Each is a recent entry to Corbett's list and, though still 811 m on the map, the OS assures me it is 813 m in reality. I describe it together with Meall na Fearna because by linking them over the intervening Munros you can have "a splendid day's sport", which means a long, hard but satisfying day's tramp. It was only a few months ago I did this myself, up till then these hills had been visited in various other combinations.

A quarter of a century ago Sam and I, on 27 January, had a frost-touched, river-steaming camp at Strathyre and traversed Beinn Each and Stuc a' Chroin in very icy conditions. A year later, on 27 January, Sam and I with several other friends traversed right on to Ben Vorlich. The next winter the Stuc became my first Munro on skis — and my third *day* on skis. In all I've been on these hills with a score of different friends so there were memories at many places during the recent solitary traverse, made from the head of Glen Artney.

Beinn Each is no great distance from Loch Lubnaig at Ardchullarie More from where a right-of-way goes over and down Glen Ample, but Glen Ample has been given over to massed conifers and thereby loses a great deal. (It was at Ardchullarie that the great explorer James Bruce wrote the story of his travels, having been branded a mountebank by a sceptical press. "Cutting steaks from live cows — ridiculous!" Yet this had occurred in the Highlands not so long before never mind in Ethiopia.) Trees also swarm over the ridge above Loch Lubnaig to fill the Allt Breac-nic corrie south of the Corbett therefore, if heading for the Keltnie, descend the long SE Ridge, a ridge, incidentally quite devoid of anything calling for the crag symbols so generously given on the First Series map. Cars can be driven up from Callander to the end of the tarmac near Braeleny, a useful gain in height, and another alternative approach. The oddly artificial-looking Bracklinn Falls are worth a diversion en route. This rough road goes on to sheep sheds at Arivurichardich (what a resonant name!) from where another rougher road contours round under Tom Odhar to link with the Glen Artney estate road.

Meall na Fearna is basically reached either by Glen Vorlich or by Glen Artney, the latter providing the better combination with the other hills. On driving out of Comrie follow the Braco, then the Cultybraggan Camp signs to gain the road up Glen Artney. A parking place has been left below the small, plain, attractive church up on its knoll, but the tarred road goes on up to the bridge over the Ruchil Water. In summer the glen has a green lushness, a contrast to the heathery northern flanks. The underlying schisty rock creates this richness. It is very much sheep country with free-ranging cows, too, and deer up in the wilder fastnesses. Sir Walter Scott's picture of Glen Artney is highly romantic.

As one follows the estate road up Monadh Odhar the Lodge looks very attractive. What a view it has, down the glen especially! The long ridge running from Meall na Fearna to Glenartney Lodge effectively shuts out all views of the Munros/Corbetts till the Monadh Odhar is passed. (The crest of this ridge is all peat hags, not crags.) Several white garrons came cantering over to Storm and me on top of the rise. The summits were cloud-covered but the whole visible landscape was bright with summer green.

The road twists down, upstream rather than as shown in the First Series map (where a shelter belt of trees has been planted across the river), crosses a sturdy bridge and wends on towards Arivurichardich. We followed track then path up Gleann an Dubh Choirein. The *black corrie* of the name is the one between the Munros, dark with peat hags and crumbling crags, but the path leaves the ruined sheilings at the junction to go on up to the Bealach Dearg (*the red pass*) between Vorlich and Fearna. The pass is reputedly haunted by a ghostly piper and the way the wind was shrilling through it for us one could well imagine weird music not of this world.

Storm and I followed a side stream which led up to the summit of Meall na Fearna with the minimum of bogs. We even managed to stalk some hinds and young calves to about twenty yards but one climbed up on a hag and would soon see us so I stood up and fired, hopefully in that brief moment when they froze in surprise, before galloping off. For once I had the right lens on. I've so many pictures of distant, bobbing caudal patches!

We were below the rip of cloud with the "big top" crest of Ben Vorlich invisible. The flank below the cloud level looked quite formidable, face on. It is steep, too, but by cutting across a bit below the Bealach Dearg and traversing I was able to cut up on to the SE Ridge fairly easily. Blasting rain made for an uncongenial summit. We fled the stark trig point. The welcome snack had to wait till down on the col. Rocky steps led up to what appears a difficult buttress on the Stuc but a path is now well marked up it. For interest I went left and after botanising in a tumble of boulders climbed straight up. The Stuc *is* craggy but Vorlich by no means deserves the crag symbols given to it on the map.

The weather kept hinting at clearances (it was probably quite a pleasant day at valley level) and slowly eased as we followed the many contortions of the zigzag ridge to Beinn Each. There is a connecting fence (ruinous) to help in misty conditions. We tried various outflankings but these seldom paid off (knobbly ridges usually prove easiest along a crest and the final bold thrust leaves only the one option of up). The cloud cleared to give partial views. With the white racing overhead and the dark shadows sprinting over the hill slopes there was the odd sensation that it was Beinn Each that was moving, that Ben Ledi and Benvane, Baintighearna, Ben More and Stobinian were charging at us on some Valkyrian steeplechase.

From the col beyond we descended into Coire nan Saighead (*corrie of the arrows*) but turned out of it to pick up the lie of the land down into the valley. We crossed the burn, as the far side looked less marshy, and to obtain photos back up to the Corbett. Somehow we drifted up the hillside so just went on to cross the old pass of Meall na h-Iolaire (*the bump of the eagles*), part of the Callander–Glen Vorlich–Loch Earn route. We cringed in the lee of one of the decayed peat hags but were rewarded in the end with views both to Each and to Fearna. The eastern slope of the pass spills down in an extraordinary scattering of bog bergs. We rimmed the bumps of the col and angled down to another new sturdy bridge a mile up from the foot of the glen. The legs just began to feel the last miles of tarmac but roadside raspberries, a *white* scabious and grass of Parnassus gave excuses to stop. It had been quite a long day after all.

When Sam and I had tackled Beinn Each we had gone over the ridge to reach Glen Ample (pre-plantation days), a route that had been followed by Naismith and Thomson on New Year's Day 1894. They came off the morning train, then traversed Vorlich, the Stuc and Beinn Each to descend the Keltnie road to Callander where they reached the station with five minutes in hand for the evening train. Plumb (*Walking in the Grampians*) mentioned staying at Ardvorlich House and drove from there to Callander. When the party was ready to leave again they found their collie had vanished, but by the time they drove the sixteen miles round the dog was home before them — via the Keltnie, over the Eagles col and through the Bealach Dearg. Beinn Each was to prove Charles's last Corbett, achieved on a flying visit from Sheffield via Dunoon.

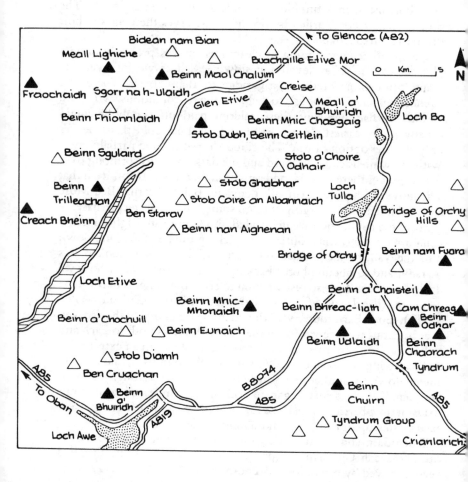

LOCH ETIVE, GLEN ORCHY & AUCH

Section 3:   1. BEINN A' BHUIRIDH   897 m   OS 50   094283
Hill of the (stags') roaring (voo-ree)

BEINN A' BHUIRIDH is on the natural circuit of the grand Cruachan ridge traverse though I must admit to having missed it out on several occasions and when eventually I climbed the hill I was really engaged on other business. But "because it was there", at the end of a sweltering summer's day the summit was a good place to put the day to bed.

The story of that day is fully told in *Hamish's Mountain Walk*: the second of the 112 days spent walking over all the Munros. The day began on the far side of Mull but it ended with a camp high on this Corbett, which made it rather special. Beinn a' Bhuiridh is quite a distinctive hill in its own right, however overshadowed by the Cruachan Munros, and sticks up boldly in the view from the Strath of Orchy and Dalmally. I'd perforce walked up the Hydro road to the shapely dam as my bike was left at a house by St Conan's Church near where the road starts. St Conan's, a church I always find fascinating, had to be revisited. The heat was intolerable and every trickle of water gave the chance of a drink. I took several rests to gaze down Loch Awe. Loch Ness and Loch Lomond may be bigger but Loch Awe is the longest loch in Scotland. The view was clear right down to New York.

A stream comes down from the Larig (*sic*) Torran which separates the Corbett from the Munros and was welcome for its glorious shade. I splashed in it with the gusto of a dipper, then followed up beside the burn to pitch the tent just below the col. "Lairig" usually points to historical use as a pass and Wallace reputedly used this pass to outflank the men of Lorn holding the Pass of Brander. Cattle crossed it to graze in the basin now filled by the Cruachan Reservoir. My side of the pass was comparatively gentle; the eastern side, Coire Ghlais, is much wilder, with bands of cliff on which the early stalwarts of the SMC found the exercise they wanted. I wonder if much climbing is done on these cliffs in winter now?

After setting up the tent and downing several mugs of tea I wended up to the top of Beinn a' Bhuiridh. The summit was all lumps and bumps and scattered melt-water pools. Sunset strode in and the burnished loch soon turned to lead-grey, leaving the world raw and chill. A lone *feadag* (plover) was calling.

The most satisfying route up Beinn a' Bhuiridh is over Monadh Driseig, starting from opposite Kilchurn Castle. Loch Awe is always in view, the Laoigh group shows well and one looks up Glen Strae's trench. Coire Ghlais is also an interesting approach and, if heading towards it, one can utilise a track (once a mineral line) which contours round to the abandoned lead-workings from where a path of sorts leads to the Allt Coire Ghlais–Allt Coire Chaorainn confluence. If a full round of the Cruachan ridges is undertaken the starting and finishing point will probably be the Falls of Cruachan car park. There is a path up the west bank of the burn to the dam. A trip to the underground power station is an unusual extra for a visit to these hills. There is an interesting Hydro display in the visitor centre.

Section 3: 2. BEINN CHUIRN 880 m OS 50 281292
            Cairn hill

With Ben Lui so near I thought there would be something in old *SMC Journals* about Beinn Chuirn (it is not infrequently taken for Ben Lui by people motoring west along Strath Fillan), but the volumes were silent on Lui's little look-alike. Beinn Chuirn gave me a good return to the hills of home after a summer in Norway.

I'd driven up and found a quiet spot for the van on the old road to Cononish, a site which was a favourite until plantings and locked gates and new tracks changed everything. There was a semi-permanent caravan nearby and its old, bearded owner spent his days panning for gold. He showed me the month's haul. Four poachers arrived in the moonlight and spread their blankets by a wood fire. The cold night led to a breathless, sharp, clear dawn, making an early start a joy in itself.

The hour up to Cononish always seems long and my old dog Kitchy was very slow. I put this down to lack of exercise but later discovered he was not very well — for which a traverse of Beinn Chiurn and Ben Lui was hardly a rest cure. We took the burn that comes down by the farm and followed it, then cut the corner, to reach the steep wee corrie on the east face. A slot of a gully to the left and a top rim of cliffs looked as if they could offer some winter sport. The corrie offered ripe blaeberries which I ate while the midges ate me. The summit has quite a big flat area and when we popped out on to it the dog gave tongue as if to say "Thank goodness that's over". I gave a yelp, too, for in a sudden revelation there was a tone-poem view of Cruachan in the west, rising from a sea of cloud.

I'd chosen my route upwards to explore that eastern corrie but most walkers would find it pleasanter to ascend by the gorge of the Eas Anie, which yields a succession of waterfalls, one of them big and impressive. A path to the old mines and on up the SE Ridge makes for quite easy going. This mine was opened in 1739 — the story of mining at Tyndrum is worth reading. At the time of the Forty-Five an English contractor, Sir Robert Clifton, had leased the mineral rights and had done quite well. He, strangely, was a Jacobite and the Argyll militia took the opportunity to sabotage his works. The Mine Adventurers of England carried on till 1760, then, after various changes (take-overs are nothing new), the Scots Mining Company acquired it and built smelting works near Tyndrum rather than sailing the ore down Loch Lomond to the Clyde. By the end of the century the prosperity had gone. The second Marquis of Breadalbane made a costly gamble rather than any fortune. The last lead extracted was in 1923. V. A. Firsoff's invaluable book *In the Hills of Breadalbane* has several pages about the Tyndrum mines.

In the autumn of 1987 an exploration company (which had already spent £250,000) was making hopeful noises about the findings of their two drills operating on Beinn Chuirn. Who knows, we may yet have a Corbett with a productive gold mine on its slopes.

Kitchy and I wandered over to the 773-m bump, and the casual nature of the day went when we saw how deep a drop led to the Allt an Rudd and how much of Lui there was beyond to be climbed. Black cherry jam pieces on Lui's summit rewarded the hot toil up. It was another six years before I was on top of Lui again and on that visit I also had black cherry jam sandwiches, a coincidence only discovered on referring back to the log account of the day. You can gather I like black cherry jam — and keep a note of trivial pursuits!

Storm did Beinn Chuirn by the shortest reasonable route on a day of dashing winter storms: starting at the vital bridge at Glenlochy crossing (six miles west of Tyndrum) and angling round to go up the Garbh Choirean, which was less rough than the weather — another enjoyable raid.

Section 3:   3. BEINN MHIC-MHONAIDH   792 m   OS 50   209350
         Hill of the son of the moor

In *Hamish's Groats End Walk* (p. 71) I describe a walk through from Loch Tulla to Loch Awe by Gleann Fuar and Glen Strae, and either of these glens would be a good approach route to Mhic-Mhonaidh. There is some new planting defending Gleann Fuar, and the path shown ends past the ruins of Druimliart, birthplace of the bard Duncan Ban Macintyre. Further up the *cold glen* there are some fine stands of old Scots pines. There is only a little loss of height by Coire Bhiocar to gain the sweeping ridge of the Corbett.

Looking up Glen Strae the SW Ridge appears as a distinctive cone.

In very wet conditions it might be worth avoiding the Corbett altogether from this side, as the River Strae can become unfordable. In normal conditions you just use the road up the glen, paddle the river and work up to follow the An Sgriodain ridge to the summit levels. The view to Cruachan and Loch Awe will give good excuses for resting.

I've now made two ascents of the Corbett from Glen Orchy, a better choice than the map might suggest with the huge takeover of forestry. From the bridge over the ragged Eas Urchaidh a forestry road swings up by the Allt Broighleachan to end on a little "meadow". When Storm and I went up one autumn we came upon two foresters busy loading a stag on to their vehicle. We met several deer inside the forest over the day — where they are not very welcome. On the meadow great tits, gold crests and a wren all fussed their way down the burnside trees. A go-anywhere vehicle was parked in the clearing and a track, beaten by it, crossed the burn and forked. We took the left fork which wended on, a bit wet in places, to the edge of the trees near the watershed. (On the previous occasion there was just the preparatory ploughing which gave purgatorial progress.) We had a snack by the Arigh Chailleach shieling ruins, where one rowan flamed red among the orange autumn slopes. The day echoed to the roar of stags and the corrie above had several dozen deer grazing across it. By keeping in the slot of the burn we managed to stalk up among them unseen. The wind was blowing down on us. On the uppermost slopes we almost walked into a fine stag which stared in disbelief before giving a croak and prancing off over the snow. We landed right by the cairn which is so large and precisely circular (like a breast) that it might be prehistoric. In its centre stands a nipple of modern cairn.

Most of the big hills were cloudy but Cruachan was displayed in ermine splendour. The Starav–Stob Ghabhar peaks to the north, and the Lui group to the south, are well seen from here — the Corbett superiority of view once again. Conditions were too cold for lingering and we scampered along to the lochan which is surprisingly deep and would make a welcome summer summit swimming-pool. The grain of the strata gives a succession of steps to descend and we circuited round, above all the gullies, to make a direct descent through the trees back to the meadow. There was no problem with the trees as there were plenty of breaks but the grass had grown rank and tussocky so it was hard going. We would have been better off regaining the outward track.

Out of curiosity I looked up the index to early *SMC Journals* and found three entries for Beinn Mhic-Mhonaidh. Several early meets at Dalmally account for them. The latest note was of Hogmanay 1920 when a party was made up for Beinn Mhic-Mhonaidh and reported enthusiastically of its qualities, both as a climb and as a fine viewpoint. The earliest mention was a short article in 1894: ". . . although under 3,000 feet and therefore unclassed as a 'Ben' (i.e. Munro) it is worth a visit from Dalmally for those who have exhausted the 3,000-foot hills in its neighbourhood." Munro-bagging obviously began very early.

The writer, Francis Dewar, was quite wrong in his thoughts on the "apartness" of the Corbett: "I distinguish it by the peculiarity of its standing entirely apart, an unusual circumstance, I think, in hills of its altitude" — where this apartness is, in fact, a hallmark of the sterling quality of Corbetts. He hit the other feature of most Corbetts. "The view from it is a particularly fine one, at least 35 first-class Bens, from Lomond to Bidean and Cruachan to Beinn a' Ghlo. Lochearn's Ben Vorlich is striking and Ben Lui presents a unique appearance." Dewar crossed the Orchy and ascended as we did, "a beautiful walk" on which he saw hares, deer, ptarmigan and an eagle which "caused some disquietude by circling over me in what I considered a too inquisitive spirit".

At the end of the Dalmally New Year Meet in 1901 Maylard, the president, and Sang were alone on the last day and decided to "ring the brow of Beinn Mhic-Mhonaidh with an SMC halo". Sylvan Glen Strae led to a foaming torrent (the Allt nan Guibhas) and an easy victory, but "the glory of this virgin peak was greatly enhanced by half-veiled glimpses of the surrounding mammoths. Only 2,602 feet but it was cold as the North Pole. The hill teemed with stags." Typical Corbett commenting.

The descent was to give some jolly good sport: "The OS sheet showed a bridge over the Orchy close to Larig farm [Lairig Hill is the only name on the map now] but put not thy faith in OS sheets! The farm is a ruin and the bridge is not . . . the road looked so inviting on the other side but the tangle impeded progress and the failing light made hardship harder and the future bleaker still. The River Orchy is deep and wide . . . it was a stormy breast-high crossing and a secret to be kept from insurance agents . . . a mile and a half further down a bridge appeared from nowhere, mockingly spanning the torrent. . . . That night in the Dalmally Hotel we were grieved that the rotameter gave only 21 miles for the day's work." Our round trip from Glen Orchy was a mere eight miles.

Section 3:   4. BEINN UDLAIDH   840 m   OS 50   280333
             Dark (gloomy) hill

Section 3:   5. BEINN BHREAC-LIATH   803 m   OS 50   304339
             Speckled grey hill

A sub-zero March morning saw me parking at Arinabea in Glen Lochy 2½ miles west of Tyndrum and heading off up the course of a burn in order to avoid the solid plantings of trees. The trees are now considerably bigger and nearly all Glen Lochy has been afforested but this is still the quickest route for these hills, even if it is not the best.

I had some fun getting the dog over the top deer fence. We ended on the col between the speckled grey hill and the wee hill (Beinn Bheag). The Corbett was a big bald bump and we wandered round its rim to see the view. There was a fine symmetry looking over to Auch Gleann with its torque of railway line. Ben Lui and Ben Oss shone like armour in the sun. Cruachan was hidden by Beinn Udlaidh whose eastern flank above deep Coire Ghamhnain looked as if it might produce climbing but just doesn't. Trundling down to the col we set off six stags. They galloped away over the saddle, dark shapes against a lemon brightness of winter sun.

Hard snow all the way up on to Beinn Udlaidh was useful. The second Corbett was an even better viewpoint, for the toothy tops of Cruachan were added to the panorama. It is also a big dome, or plateau, but is crag-rimmed on many flanking slopes while Coire Daimh is perhaps more famous for its winter climbs when the liberal summer leaks freeze into welcome ice. Some of us were once discussing how funny it would be to write a spurious, but very serious, article on some new climbing ground. This would have to be accessible enough to tempt climbers (a lazy breed) but also quite unknown. I suggested Coire Daimh. A few weeks later we were reading about a flurry of new routes in a recently-discovered corrie: Coire Daimh.

The main feature of Coire Daimh (*the corrie of the stags*) is a line of quartzite crags and a top rim of schisty rock. Perhaps the clash of rock causes the copious wetness which can, occasionally, yield good ice conditions. The quartzite crosses the north ridge of the hill as a prominent straight dyke which can be spotted from the Blackmount road. It is continuous enough to be shown on the map.

Last autumn, Sandy, Stan and I left my car a mile south of Bridge of Orchy and drove in Sandy's car up to the big bend near the top of the road to Tyndrum. By following the edge of the wood above Coire

Chailein we had a very easy ascent up Beinn Bhreac-liath but one which gave an ever-widening panorama in quite special fashion. It was a day of magical, crisp clarity. We arrived simultaneously with Andrew, from Inverness, who'd come up from Arinabea and we all went on together up Beinn Udlaidh to picnic by the slabby cairn. Andrew went south, we descended down the North Ridge and then followed the odd quartz dyke down to the Allt Ghamhnain to hit the Glen Orchy road a mile before it joins the A82. With just one car a full circuit from the north would be as good and preferable to the Glen Lochy line. New plantings now stretch two miles down Glen Orchy from the Allt Ghamhnain, so Coire Daimh has become rather isolated. Glen Orchy is a quiet backwater compared to Glen Lochy, and this alone would make the northern approach more satisfying. Glen Lochy's most flattering aspect is the view *down to it* from the col between the Corbetts: a gunbarrel view over Lochan na Bi away to the jumbled hills of Crianlarich.

Section 3:	6. BEINN ODHAR	900 m	OS 50	338338	
	Dun-coloured hill				
Section 3:	7. BEINN CHAORACH	818 m	OS 50	359328	
	Sheep hill				
Section 3:	8. CAM CHREAG	885 m	OS 50	375346	
	Crooked crags				
Section 3:	9. BEINN A' CHAISTEIL	885 m	OS 50	348364	
	Hill of the castle				
Section 3:	10. BEINN NAM FUARAN	807 m	OS 50	361382	
	Hill of the well				

This is probably the only day among the Corbetts which can naturally produce a tally of five ticks for the list. As the day entails nearly 2,000 m of ascent (*c.* 6,500 feet) it will test the fittest muscles, especially as the slopes of this crowd of Corbetts are invariably steep. I've never been over them all on a single expedition but my excuse is that Cam Chreag had not been invented before 1981. I'd already been up some of the others individually before a May romp round the then four Auch Corbetts.

The now five Auch Corbetts have contorted and fascinating watersheds. Cam Chreag is really one of the Glen Lochay peaks, the Forest of Mamlorn, while Beinn Odhar and Beinn Chaorach are Tyndrum hills, much of their drainage running to Strath Fillan and eventually to the east coast by the Tay, and the Auch Gleann and Gleann Coillean both drain to the Orchy, Loch Awe and the western seaboard. All being Corbetts gives them a special entity.

Beinn Odhar appears as a fine cone to the south, a look-alike for Beinn Dorain for which it is sometimes taken. This peak stands boldly above the pass from Tyndrum to Bridge of Orchy and is a good start to the day over these Corbetts. Even the SMC district guide so far forgets itself as to write enthusiastically about Beinn Odhar. "The view encompasses almost all the high mountains of Perthshire and Argyll. Ben Lui stands up grandly to the south west, and to the west Ben Cruachan dominates the horizon . . . the Blackmount peaks make a fine array while, closer at hand, Beinn Dorain, Beinn a' Chreachain, Creag Mhor and Heasgarnich show their bulk. Eastwards there is a glimpse of Ben Lawers and the Tarmachans, and to the south east the familiar outline of the Crianlarich mountains. Ben Lomond and the Arrochar Alps appear in the distant south. Altogether it is a wonderful panorama"; and, one suspects, known because of the hill's tempting shape and easy ascent. Beinn Udlaidh, westward, has a fine view, but whoever has praised it?

My most memorable ascent of Ben Odhar was a winter one. Ernst, Iain, George, Storm the dog and I went up it on a January day that saw some wild and wet weather move on and a cold clarity blow in. As a quick rescue of the day it proved a winner. We went up the normal SSW Ridge route, which gave a portal-view to Loch Tulla and to dramatic sun-cloud effects to the south. On top the wind-chill factor was unpleasantly emphasised. Hands had to be warmed after every photograph taken. George had been coming along slowly and we had to start down before he arrived as it was too cold to linger. George was George Roger, an ever-smiling friendly enthusiast who had had a lifetime of wandering the world's mountains. An ex-president of the SMC he was slowing with increasing years but the tenacity was still there. A year later (again from Bridge of Orchy) he was out in appalling conditions and both he and his dog were hit and killed by a train on crossing the Auch viaduct, grim news that met Charles, Ernst, Belinda and me when we turned up at the Meet from our own pasting on Sgorr na Diollaid (14:6) while staying at Cozac Lodge.

I had a windy ascent at the start of the long day, but Argyll had been singled out for good weather in the forecast. The first two (now three) Corbetts are on the Argyll–Perthshire boundary. On the level shoulder of the SSW Ridge of Odhar, just before the final rise to the summit, there is a tiny lochan which would make an eyrie-like camp spot. Beinn Odhar was my 100th Corbett and old Kitchy's 50th.

On the way off I also looked at the other tarn, drained by the Allt

Choire Dhuibh. The SSE Ridge rather curves off to the south, Coire Thoin to the right being, to translate euphemistically "backside corrie". I left my rucksack at the col before going up and down the steeper flank of Beinn Chaorach, a hill which perhaps deserves its name. Have you noticed how few sheep hills there are in the *Tables*? Goat hills there are in plenty. The dominance of sheep came centuries after hills received their names. (The multiplicity of similar names, often queried, is simply due to local people naming their own hills. They were not aware that, in umpteen other areas, other people were also producing Ben Mores and Sgurr Dubhs.) The sole feature of Beinn Chaorach is its trig point, the only one of the day.

From there to Cam Chreag is the easiest part of the full day. By its recent inclusion we can gather there is only just over 500 feet of re-ascent. Beinn Chaorach does not merit a mention in the SMC district guide, which might be to its credit for Cam Chreag is dismissed as "an undistinguished hill with a flat, mile-long summit ridge, which is rarely climbed for itself but may be included in a traverse from Creag Mhor to Ben Challum". I first climbed it on a traverse from Beinn Chaorach to Ben Challum, the Auchertyre horseshoe. This gave a good view of Ben Challum's north face which, too broken for rock climbing, gave Charles and me some sport one winter when we came up Gleann Choillean from Auch to reach the peak, which peers over the Chaorach–Cam Chreag col as one drives south from Bridge of Orchy. Gleann Choillean is an alternative start for this day's walk; it depends where you want to return to at the end of the day and there is little really to choose between the Auch road end and the top of the pass.

From Cam Chreag there is a long easy ridge down to the Abhainn Ghlas; and the Allt a' Mhaim, which joins it, is the natural continuation up for Beinn nam Fuaran. On my long day I returned west off Beinn Chaorach and then had some miles of glen walking by the Allt Cumhang and the level upper Abhainn Ghlas which, lower, is swallowed by the artificial waters of Loch Lyon. Centuries ago plenty of traffic went through to upper Glen Lyon but now it is trackless and difficult. Even the shepherds use boats.

Beinn nam Fuaran is rather lost in a welter of hills and the pull-up is the longest since the initial ascent of Beinn Odhar, but the view along Loch Lyon is the reward. The biggest col of the day, and the only real saddle, has some peat bogs and leads to a rather heartbreakingly, evenly-angled ascent of Beinn a' Chaisteil. The peak's name is entirely due to its appearance from Auch, for it thrusts westwards as a bold prow, split by a big gully (climbed in 1899) and with curtain-wall flanks running back above Auch Gleann and Gleann Choillean. Beinn

Dorain, quite the wrong shape, still bulks large and high across Auch Gleann.

The 883 height is a spot height and not really the summit. The cairn, too, is 100 m north west of the highest point — all very confusing. The way off is clear: to the south east, along and above Creagan Liath until it is safe to cut down into Gleann Choillean. I've come up more directly but don't recommend that as a descent route. After a day largely on easy grass it is odd to have to escape from a rocky, cliff-guarded keep of a mountain.

My day actually took in Beinn a' Chaisteil before Beinn nam Fuaran (leaving the rucker on the col) and I angled down steeply to As-an t-Sithein in the upper Auch Gleann, to camp inside the old sheep fank and go on over Mhanach–Chreachain–Achallader the next day. I'd only just pitched tent when the first big raindrops introduced an evening and night of heavy rain. The batter on the roof and the plaintive crying of lambs and curlews gave the site a feeling of extreme solitude. Duncan Ban Macintyre, the poet, lived up here at one stage.

Section 3:   11. CREACH BHEINN   810 m   OS 50   024422
              Mountain of spoil

"To discover the peace that dwells upon hill tops you need go no further than our Homeland hills. On them, among their rocks and heather, you will be given something that not even the lords of the Himalayas are able to give."

So wrote Frank Smythe in *The Kangchenjunga Adventure* and so Creach Bheinn was to me one restorative weekend when respite from pressure was badly needed. On the way up I had an interesting day with Tom Weir and a TV crew doing a piece about my Munros trip, then I joined a local club meet at Black Rock. While some of them were keen to do the Munro, Beinn Sgulaird, I was left to myself for its neighbour, Corbett Creach Bheinn. Having spent so many days and years not only with others, but in charge of others, a solitary day was always a glad release, a quiet restfulness in which to relish the peace that only the hills can give. A day of fresh spring welcomed me to Loch Creran.

Just along from Druimavuic a useful forestry road led up the Allt Buidhe. The landscape had the lushness of the west. Nearing the end of April the primroses and anemones were in flower and wheatears were setting up homes on the heights. In the car I'd come close to running into a cuckoo, the first of the year. A sparrow-hawk was beating along the upper fringe of forest.

I followed the Allt Buidhe, but the crags to the south were nothing like as dramatic as the map suggested so I cut up to gain height quickly and to escape from the scratchy vegetation lower down. For interest I kept to a burn. The purple saxifrage was just starting to drape the dank banks. There was quite a distinctive NE Top (803 m) and a gentle walk along to the summit of Creach Bheinn. The view is like that from Beinn Sgulaird, with the addition of granity Sgulaird; it is of the west, western, sea-circled hills and oceans of sky.

Creach Bheinn can easily be added to Beinn Sgulaird if it is thought of in time. Curiously some years after this day I was back with Charles and we came up the Allt Buidhe again, then he ascended the Corbett and I went up the Munro for the sake of the dog Storm. Charles had to drive back to Sheffield afterwards. There wasn't time for both of us to do both hills.

Creach Bheinn looks west, down Gleann Dubh to outer Loch Creran, to Eriska and Lismore and the wild Corbett country beyond Loch Linnhe but, sadly, the *black glen* has been swamped with a sprawl of spruce. The corrie can be circled, and a long ridge gives a good high-level walk (on to sheet 49) before one descends fire breaks to South Creagan near the old railway bridge. (Foot/cycle crossings were always permitted and it used to amuse my school gangs to cross the bridge and then watch motorists' expressions as they came on the same group again.) This ridge can be reached by descending slightly north of west to pass above the Eas Garbh (*rough falls*) gorge and its pleasing waterfalls. If a car has been left at the road by the Allt Buidhe it is easier just to contour round and over the ridge to reach the *yellow stream* by a descending traverse that keeps one safely out of the jaws of the forestry.

Creach Bheinn's derivation leaves one speculating. A *creach* was a raid, usually with the pillaging of cattle as its prime objective, so does this name commemorate such a despoiling? Who raided whom? And who gave the name to the silent witness? There is a great deal of social history hidden under the names on our maps. Perhaps some of it is best forgotten. The desert of the past can be the peace of the present. Raiding Corbetts certainly does less harm!

When Charles and I drove off on our visit we had to go round by the drive of Druimavuic House as the main road was under water; high tide, a westerly gale and high streams combining to flood it. Even when you pass under normal circumstances there is often a tangle of seaweed festooning the roadside fences.

Section 3:   12. BEINN TRILLEACHAN   *c.*840 m   OS 50   086439
   Hill of the sandpipers

A friend once suggested Beinn Trilleachan should be *hill of the sandpaper* but then he was a climber and had been gripped up on the popular Etive Slabs. The granite is indeed rough as sandpaper. The first time I climbed this Corbett I was also to become thoroughly gripped — but on a winter escapade.

I woke thinking it was snowing but it was just my down sleeping-bag that had split open to fill the Dormobile with feathers. I was on a crowded local club meet at Inbhirfhaolain but nobody would condescend to go for a mere Corbett: climbing, skiing and Munro-ing had the priority. Those who set out for Bidean or Starav failed to reach their summits. Big is often bloody in foulest February. Even the frenetic climbers were not contemplating routes on the Etive Slabs, that palette of mighty climbs that looks down on Loch Etive. I sat in the Dormobile by the pier sipping a coffee and trying to become enthusiastic about going up a hill on a dribbly morning. It slowly cleared and I set off to traverse under the slabs, which were running with water. At the foot of the white waste of rocks I found a karabiner.

My route led up and across, avoiding the great face, but I still grabbed some fun, scrambling on granite walls and slabs and gullies. Too soon I was on slobbery snow and my new ice-axe (this was a dozen years ago) was tested for the novelty of being able to bang the pick in and pull on it. With old axes a pull usually meant the axe flew out, and one of the few falls I've had climbing was caused by just that. Fortunately I merely dropped for 30 feet through the air and landed in deep snow, injured only in my dignity.

Somewhere, high up, above Ard Trilleachan, after having several tussles with "problems" I managed to become stuck in a corner. The rock was pushing me out of balance and to move in any direction was hazardous. There was a great deal of nothing below my trembling legs and a snow boss overhead. It was a situation where to do anything was dangerous but to do nothing would soon prove disastrous. The newly-tested axe was swung hard into the frozen turf over the snow eave and I scrabbled and pulled, up and over the bulge, with everything committed to the ice-axe holding. It held, or I wouldn't be writing this. Great stuff, adrenalin.

After some twisting up I hit the summit ridge and the summit storm hit me. Sleet turned to snow, wildly driven by a gale. Fortunately it was blowing from behind so I scampered off along the crest. There are a couple of miles of knobbly granite ridge, with a 767-m top above the slabs, but even the pull up on to this was easier than it looked. There are no escape routes and it is a long way to Meall nan Gobhar. I was all too aware of the great drop on my right. The loch, when it appeared through gaps in the storm, seemed to be directly below. When it was safe to turn down I sat and slid much of the way. Still 1,000 feet up I came on a ship's bucket which presumably had been blown there from the tide line. There are traces of an old path from the head of Loch Etive over to Glen Ure but there is no chance of straying as the massed afforestation drives one down to the sea. Last century a missionary preacher regularly crossed by this path to hold services in Glen Etive. Before the advent of the road across Rannoch Moor, Glen Etive was a very remote spot, generally reached by boat. My weather lower down was just wild and wet but, not for the first time, a Corbett had given good sport while bigger hills were beyond reach.

Trilleachan is best done on a more reasonable day, for the summit is well guarded by cliffs and distance. The country between it and Beinn Sgulaird is boggy and foul enough to discourage any link from there and its southern approaches are beyond the back of beyond. The head of Loch Etive is a grand spot. Another ploy is to walk down through the hazel woods by the loch (path), well past Ard Trilleachan, and then wind up, a circuit always being more rewarding than there-and-back by the same route. The hill is aptly named and the lochside rings to the *willy-needy willy-needy* calls of that bird of summer-welcoming, the uncommon sandpiper.

Section 3:   13. STOB DUBH   883 m   OS 41/50   166488
             The black peak

Inbhirfhaolain, the cosy hut in Glen Etive, is dominated by Stob Dubh. "You'd think it would be climbed more often being so near the hut," someone once suggested.

"Have you seen it from the hut?"

"No."

"Well, those who have can usually find excuses for not climbing it."

The black peak dominates very successfully. It fills the view as one drives up from Loch Etive, a bold prow, cleft by a gorge on its southern flank.

That gorge, or the ridge straight up from Glenceitlein, are perhaps the best routes up Stob Dubh but it is well worth continuing, to make a traverse over Beinn Ceitlein (*the hill of concealment*) to descend to the Allt a' Chaorainn. The last tower of this east ridge is An Grianan (*the bower*) and is one of the many Glen Etive spots associated with the legend of Deirdre of the Sorrows. The Allt a' Chaorainn is a big river of fine granite pools but, in spate, may only be passable a mile upstream. Those who don't mind a yo-yo sort of day can go on and traverse 5:4 Beinn Mhic Chasgaig, the neighbouring Corbett, which is climbed even less often than Stob Dubh.

I must confess to having gone up Stob Dubh only once though I've used its flanking glens on several occasions. During my tramp over all the Munros, the Starav–Meall nan Eun group had given me a desperately hot day and when I was on the col behind Stob Dubh all I wanted was water. Swimming in the Allt a' Chaorainn won easily over any ascent. All too often Stob Dubh is a dark, soaking hulk, as it was on the nasty November day I climbed it, crossing the River Etive at Dalness and going up the north ridge — which is as brutal as the west ridge already mentioned. "A quartzy shambles plastered in snow" was my untechnical description. The SMC district guide tells us the hill is "a complex of mica schist, quartzite, rhyolite and dykes of porphyry almost surrounded by granite".

The best of that day was finding a dead stag, a Royal, and eventually I bore the head off as a trophy. Unfortunately it had died in its prime so the antlers were firmly attached to the — smelly — skull. Even pounding with a hunk of granite could not snap them off, yet, had the beast lived, they would eventually have just fallen off. Had he lived he could have become an Imperial, one of the lords of the mountain. (Deer are judged by the number of points or tines which each antler has: brow points, bay, tray and the threes on top making six a side, the twelve points of a Royal. Fourteen is an Imperial.)

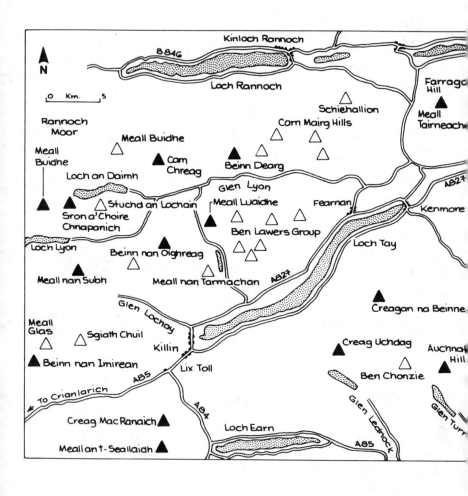

BREADALBANE, GLEN LYON, GLEN ALMOND

Section 4:   1. BEINN NAN IMIREAN   844 m   OS 51   419309
        Hill of the ridge

FREQUENT MUNRO-BAGGING combinations round the head of Glen Lochay have ensured several visits to "lowly" Beinn nan Imirean, as Firsoff calls this Corbett: "The last of the Glen Dochart Hills which have disintegrated into formless moorland." Poor Beinn nan Imirean. Strangely it was one of the first Corbetts I ever did, back in 1962, admittedly when miles and feet were treated rather cavalierly.

A lift south had dropped me at Crianlarich and a mile eastwards I pitched my tent in a sheltered hollow by a burn, a site we often used until road improvements simply bulldozed it out of existence — and also removed a nasty hump-backed bridge which had yielded entertainment as speeding motorists took off from it and crashed down beyond in showers of sparks.

A friend and I had traversed Sgiath Chuil the year before, from Glen Lochay to Glen Dochart; this April day gave me a chance to add Meall Glas and Ben Challum and, of course, Beinn nan Imirean stands (in)conveniently between them. No sooner had I climbed up on to the road than a car offered me a lift to Glen Coe so I took the chance of a run along to the Auchtertyre road-end and made the conventional traverse of Ben Challum. The superb snow conditions of the day before had gone and with the temperature away above freezing, plus odd showers of rain, there was a penetrating wetness to the walking. The clouds sank lower and lower and I faced a day of dedicated effort rather than any carefree rapture.

A long sitting slide (glissade is too grand a term) down Stob a' Bhiora took me rather far down into Glen Lochay. The slide was no doubt quicker than walking, but the subsequent peat-rough ascent round Beinn nan Imirean to reach Meall Glas was exasperating and exhausting. Meall Glas rewarded with the cloud girdle slipping just enough to look over the top of the white, out of which rose all the giants from Ben Lui to Ben More to Ben Lawers. I dumped my sack to add the East Top (it was Munros *and* Tops that first time round) and then headed for home. Beinn nan Imirean was rather in the way and "as there was plenty of time" I traversed over rather than round the Corbett. I then baled off into the valley cloud rather casually (compass in pocket) so ended up hitting Loch Essan rather than Loch Maragain as planned. I felt as if *I* was disintegrating as much as the formless moorland. An exhausting flounder led to the frustration of being right opposite my tent but with the unfordable River Fillan between. It took another hour to go round by the Crianlarich viaduct and I stumbled into the hotel to order a vast pot of tea.

"What a wretched end to the day. I spent an hour drying off and doubtless letting lifts go by. Went along to camp and threw out my soup and struck the tent in a downpour. Still, I'd only walked up past the station when a Black's van stopped and took me at a spanking pace to Erskine Ferry where a quick change to a bus allowed me — just — to reach the youth hostel in time. It was far too much for a day. Ben Challum is worth a return visit but the Imirean–Sgiath Chuil country I never want to see again."

My youthful judgment has long been rescinded, for that area has given plenty of good days. On one Ultimate Challenge Tony and I traversed from Crianlarich to Killin, a sort of postgraduate course in bog studies, and on Imirean put up one of the biggest herds of deer I've ever seen. Part of the difficulty of these hills comes from their odd lay-out: on both north and south there is a lower skirt of gentle-angled moorland which, by its very gentleness, has held water and decayed into peat bogs, dubh lochans and wending streams. Auchessan Farm is the easiest approach to the Corbett and the Fillan–Dochart is not a defence to tackle other than by a bridge. If nothing else Beinn nan Imirean is a useful educational Corbett.

Section 4:   2. Meall an t-Seallaidh   852 m   OS 51   542234
             Hill of the sight

Section 4:   3. Creag MacRanaich   809 m   OS 51   546256
             MacRanaich's crag

Tantalising glimpses of these hills can be had when motoring up the A84 between Strathyre and Lochearnhead though the major feature is the huge, uniform slopes of Auctoomore Hill — the Braes of Balquhidder. These have been planted, which does not help with access to the Corbetts.

Glen Kendrum, Kirkton Glen and Monachyle Glen are all passes used in olden times but Kirkton Glen is the only one with a good track all the way from Balquhidder through to Glen Dochart. Edinchip is the home of the MacGregor chiefs and close to Rob Roy's grave at Balquhidder. I decided to start my Corbetting there and finish at the head of Glen Ogle where my newly-acquired folding cycle was securely chained to a tree to await my arrival and whizz me down, and round to Balquhidder again.

The present Balquhidder church dates to 1855, the ruined one from 1631, but is on the site of an older one still. St Angus, the local patron saint, had an oratory nearby. In 1589 the MacGregors had cut off the head of a royal keeper in Glen Artney and they brought the grisly trophy back and laid it on the altar of the church here for a macabre oath-taking. Rob Roy, who lived in several houses hereabouts, his wife Mary and some of his family are all buried in the churchyard. The grave is clearly indicated. There are several historic relics in the church but it was shut at seven in the morning.

Kirkton Glen was a bit claustrophobic on a steamy-warm day in May. I found a firebreak and then a stream course which led me up out of the trees quickly, if sweatily. A crow flew over with something in its claws; I clapped my hands and the startled bird dropped its prize. I had to dodge a big bone.

The summit of Meall an t-Seallaidh was in cloud. Bits of fence were ignored (they lead astray as often as they may help) but I found the cairn easily enough, and the trig point over a bit. The name, it is suggested, celebrates the view, especially of the four lochs: Loch Tay, Loch Earn, Loch Lubnaig and Loch Voil. This is typical schisty country complete with folds, hollows and knobbles. The tiny lochan by the Cam Chreag came as expected. We descended by a gap to the *beallach* and had a second breakfast in lee of a tilted slab of rock. Purple saxifrage was still hanging down in carpets on the crags.

As eating did not bring a clearance I set off up the crags opposite. It was like tackling Bidean a' Choire Sheasgaich from Beinn Tharsuinn, only Creag MacRanaich had to be searched for among the ups and downs. There was a big cairn on one top but I was not convinced it was necessarily the summit. Other tops had other cairns. The hill is apparently named after a "famous" robber — though nothing is known about him now.

I wandered off northwards and then took a rough bearing to the north east. Glen Ogle was a big enough target to hit after all. Half way down, flogging through the heather, I came out the cloud and I also suddenly realised that I'd left the vital wing nut for holding the cycle together back in the car at Balquhidder.

Sunday lunchtime is not the best time for walking down Glen Ogle. I thumbed in self-defence and a car stopped when I was half way down the glen. The driver was going to Lochearnhead but kindly ran me on to Kingshouse, from where I walked along under the Braes by Auchtoo. By the time I'd driven up to collect the bike (still unused!) the rain was falling heavily; so at least acting on the forecast and going early had been the right decision.

Section 4:   4. CREAG UCHDAG   879 m   OS 51   708323
             Bart, Uigeach: *crag of the hollows*

Section 4:   5. CREAGAN NA BEINNE   887 m   OS 51 (52 for Glen
             Almond)   744369
             The hill of the rocks/crags

The resemblance of this area to the northern Pennines recommends it
enough as good walking country. Many books describe it as heathery,
which is misleading, and the ascents of these Corbetts can be made on
easy grass slopes. Western flanks seem to be grassy. There certainly is
plenty of heather; there are peat hags on cols and plateaux, and a lot of
rock breaking through. Some pleasant glens cut deep into these hills
south of the Tay, and a web of old drove roads are still rights-of-way
of character.

   As a teenager most of my holidays were spent in the Highlands,
staying in howffs and hostels (who could find or afford a tent?) and
exploring "by bike and by hike". Quite often the bike and hike were
simultaneous as a clear dotted line on a pre-war map (cost 1/6d)
proved to be a long-forgotten path. Now and then new reservoirs
(with Loch Mullardoch the extreme case) would ambush a route, or
another mountain had been secretly drowned in friendless conifers.
Glen Lednock was just caught in time. Now its dotted line is under
water.

   Most of the nearer roads had been cycled, so part of the fun then was
to find new ways through and over the hills. If I drew the line at
cycling through the Lairig Ghru, Glen Lednock from Comrie to Loch
Tay seemed an obvious line. Loch Lednock dam was going up and the
track over the pass brought home why it is called a push bike. I pushed
it a long way that day.

   Visits to the Munro Ben Chonzie or the area's Corbetts or to Sput
Rolla or the Deil's Cauldron had taken me back to Glen Lednock at
irregular intervals and, each time, rekindled the desire to walk
through to Loch Tay.

   Glen Lednock supports a dwindling number of sheep and an ever-
increasing amount of bracken. Rearguard farming. Despite a long dry
spell Sput Rolla was still attractive: a wide brocade of a fall draped
down gashes cutting across the glen. We drove up to the dam. The
water level was low and the loch was surrounded by a glaring band of
exposed rock, sand and gravel. The water itself was being churned up
by half a gale and the sky was an all-grey composition of rectilinear
shapes. I just hoped we could win through dry.

On a recent autumn day, Storm and I took a rough farm-track along to a small wood, below which a fank was perched on a shelf of spoil into which the waves were biting. The burn of the wood came down a deep cleft with a bridge of sleepers leading to the fank. It was a rumbling bridge. The walls of the cleft were hung with lady's mantle cushions, and heaths, and bluebells and a colour-explosion of rowan berries.

The creation of reservoirs has frequently made the alternative walking very unpleasant. I would have thought the flooding of an old right-of-way would have entailed some moral if not legal obligation to make a substitute but the Hydro obviously don't. The flanks of Loch Lednock are, however, well trodden by sheep and a good enough path has evolved through bestial necessity. We battered along into the wind.

Nearing the top end there was an area of broken schisty rocks where a burn came down, which formed a secretive shelter where we sat out of the wind. A tent-sized flat of grass just asked to be used. Apart from the scars of Hydro it was an idyllic spot and the blaeberry clumps in the rock were a blaze of red autumn tints.

The north west corner of the loch had dried out. The new map shows paths rounding the head of the loch but a walk along the north shore is quicker and easier. Our path heaves out of the loch and over the pass with more cartographical confidence than reality.

I thought I spied a rising path, not far beyond the round dyke of a sheep shelter, that led up a grassy ridge and crossed a bigger burn at a cairn. The burn came down from a band of crag beyond which lay the final bulk of Creag Uchdag. This would be the obvious way up, but I wanted my pass as well, so carried on. There was no obvious path sloping up but a clear one contouring and, as the map one climbed only to have to descend to the pass, it seemed a likely alternative. I took it.

All went well and after a perch with a last view down the loch we entered the narrowing upper glen. It had the real feel of a wild pass (many just don't) and after one bit where my track vanished (as sheep tracks do) we were confronted with a rocky hollow which cut deeply back into our slope as a rotten crag. This effective barrier probably explains why the old path climbs high up. The sheep track went boldly up the heather to round the obstacle. Iron-orange seepage spilled into it and the crags were flame-bright with tinted willow herb, that dedicated coloniser which an old flora of mine describes as "a woodland flower of the Alps which has established a few colonies in the south of England".

Two streams and an old boundary fence come down off the grassy flank of Creag Uchdag to demarcate the watershed. It is a pass of lumps and bumps and sloping down to a gate-gap in the fence-of-no-wires was the green sweep of the old track. At one time it must have been a well-made, well-kept route. Going down on the Tay side it was easy to follow.

First we left the pack and set off up the hill, making a left-flanking move to gain a broad easy ridge and to enjoy having the wind right behind to push me up Uchdag.

Back at the col my first thoughts were of a brew but it was too windy. Where the path crossed the Finglen Burn we seemed more sheltered and on went the tea. Storm brushed past and set his fur on fire! When I was eventually sitting back, cup in hand, to enjoy the break, the wind dropped and the last midges of the season descended on us.

Another great gash of a burn came down the eastern slopes and it was interesting to see, in that sheep-shorn landscape, how this inaccessible gorge was bursting with trees and vegetation. It was quite impassable and sheep tracks went uphill on both sides as well as across the foot. Wise walkers use the wily ways of sheep and deer rather than fighting the landscape.

New boots were rubbing one heel so we stopped on a breezy knoll with a fine view up the Finglen. The first-aid bag had only a long strip of plaster and I had no knife: stone-age tools cut off the strip needed and we chuntered down to the cultivated lands of the Tay. The loch stayed hidden till the last slope.

We managed to lose the line of the path in the pattern of fields but came out to the road where a Scottish Right-of-Way sign pointed to Comrie. Ardeonaig lay 300 yards on.

Ardeonaig is now little more than a popular fishing hotel, but it was once the inn for a trans-Tay ferry. St Adamnan (Eonan) is supposed to have had a cell here. One winter night in the sixteenth century a gang of MacNabb thugs, twelve sons of the chief, landed here with a boat and carried it over the hills I'd just crossed. They used the more westerly glen up, and went down Glen Beich to Loch Earn where they sailed out to surprise their MacNeish enemies on their "safe" island castle. Heads and boat were carried up to the watershed but the boat was then left. It finally rotted away last century. I think I'll stick to hike and bike.

Strong walkers could do Creag Uchdag and Creagan na Beinne in a day from Invergeldie in Glen Lednock. This would still give three uphill sections but the going is much easier than one would expect in that rough landscape. After ascending Creag Uchdag along Loch Lednock descend to Dunan (a derelict house) and climb Creagan na

Beinne up and down by its south ridge then regain Invergeldie by the elusive track west of Dundornie. If you drive up to the dam you then have 600 feet up the road at the end of the day. Creagan na Beinne lies above the Ardtalnaig–Glen Almond right-of-way (well visible) or the Ardtalnaig–Dunan–Invergeldie track could be taken in *en passant* while making a through route. This was more or less what we did, except we cut a corner or two rather than tramp miles of tarmac eastwards.

My first visit was a windy traverse one November, and a good round too: I parked at Ardtalnaig Lodge and went up skirting Beinn Bhreac, traversed Creagan na Beinne to Dunan, "burned-up" Creag Uchdag and returned along Tullich Hill with a pink and grey sunset behind Ben More and Stobinian: a grand day. Coming off Uchdag that day I saw remains of mining which are described in V. A. Firsoff's *In the Hills of Breadalbane*. Welsh miners dug for gold in them there Corbetts!

The wind had died down by the time Storm and I left Ardeonaig and the weather was obviously deteriorating: a worrying prospect with the car on the other side of the mountains. Where the road eastwards began to pull up we took an old green track up a field which soon gave us a big but stormy view along Loch Tay. Huge ash trees lined the track so it must have been very old. There was a ruined village in the top fields and the hillside beyond bore traces of old walls, ditches, tracks and more ruins. If the people have gone it was encouraging to see plenty of free-ranging cattle.

My steady, rising traverse led in to the Allt a' Mheim at the junction of streams just above the wooded level and we tucked in out the wind for a breather. It was a burn of clinging willows and tinted ferns. We crossed and followed the side stream to the col joining Tullich Hill with the Uchdag bulk. It was a satisfying col, looking down into a long valley with the walls of the pass at its head vanishing into the clouds. This "tunnel" was our route. We made a long descending traverse to the col, putting up several parcels of deer. The pass had half a mile with only one contour line and I was glad it was in an unusually dry state. Storm found a bog, though, falling through a covering of heather so only his hind legs and tail were visible. He came out with his face plastered black, looking most indignant.

Dunan lay in a pleasant hollow, backed with a scattering of unusual moraine bumps. In the valley they were symmetrical cones but up on Creagan na Beinne they had been spread and flattened across the hillside. Gleann a' Chilleine, the old drove road to Ardtalnaig, is overlooked by very steep flanks, the Corbett side blushed red with the season's colouring, lit by a momentary stutter of sun. We had a brew at the derelict cottage (it had molehills in the floor) and left the sack there, to wander up Creagan na Beinne. We followed a burn for a while and just ambled on up the easy grass slopes to the peaty dome. In the swirling cloud I was certain the hills to the east were higher. I just hope the summit doesn't move one day!

A blackness swept through (no doubt giving Lawers a drenching) while we scuttled down to eat and drink some ounces off the rucksack weight. Our third uphill lay ahead. I was keen to try and find/use the old route to Invergeldie. It is so sure on the map but I did not find it low down before we broke off on our preferred alternative. If we crossed the col and went down to Invergeldie we would face a 600-foot road-haul back up to the dam, but if we cut over and down more directly, we'd only have half that footage upwards.

We dodged from one stream to another, using their grassy borders or the odd animal track to avoid thrashing up the heather (it was a north-east facing slope). Hares bounded away in all directions. One came haring round a hag and ran right into Storm. If a dog could glare Storm glared. The col was an expanse of decayed peatbog, easy walking, but beyond it was very cut up and only the dryness made it easy as we could walk down the drainage cuttings. The lochan (at 740308) does not exist any more. The peat and heather gave way to grass again and then we hit an estate track which led us down parallel to the Allt Mor. Grey curtains of rain were moving along the loch and we were only two minutes home to the Dormobile when the rain reached us. You can't cut it much finer than that.

Section 4: 6. MEALL LUAIDHE 780 m OS 51 586436
  Dome of lead

Section 4: 7. BEINN NAN OIGHREAG 909 m OS 51 543414
  Cloudberry hill

Note: 4:6 is more correctly MEALL NAM MAIGHEACH, *Hill of the hare*

The frustrations of an office job demanded an escape to the hills for the weekend. Thanks to flexitime I was off reasonably early and arrived at the pass over to Glen Lyon with an hour left of November's grudging daylight. I had a quick snack and we set off there and then for Meall Luaidhe.

There was a layby beside the watershed cairn shown north of Lochan na Lairig and we went from there to Meal nan Eun and along to the Corbett. It is not a good route, however logical, for it is very peaty for most of the way. Dusk and a single star made it feel a lonely summit and then, suddenly, it became magical. The winter cold came down like a tangible thing. Or perhaps a musical one — a ringing triangle, perhaps, as the ground grew a frost and a million stars came out. Warm inside my duvet, Kitchy and I snuggled into the cairn for an hour before I could bear to break the spell. Lawers and her satellites were dark shapes against the stars.

Recently Storm and I went up Meall Luaidhe again and managed to avoid nearly all the peat bogs. We started at the tin shed on the crook of the road where it joins the Allt Bail a' Mhuillin (583416) and did a sweep across the shallow corrie to ascend finally west of the wall that runs up the hill. In descent we followed the wall right down to the road — easiest of all, even if there is more uphill than from the top of the pass. It had been a miserable early morning but cleared on the hill so we had splendid dappled sunlight effects on the Tarmachans up lonely Coire Riadhailt.

Meall Luaidhe would be more interesting if climbed from Glen Lyon. A track goes up the Allt Gleann Da-Eig. (Why is it *the glen of the two eggs*?) It is worth returning via the viewpoint of Creag nan Eildeag which so dominates views up Glen Lyon. Its north flank is a mix of cliff and scrub, so descend southwards into Gleann Da-Eig again. Lead was once mined on the hill, which explains its name. There is another Meall Luaidhe across Glen Lyon in the Carn Mairg hills, and the pass west of Oighreag has this name too. From the shed mentioned above, one spill tip can be seen in lower Coire Riadhailt.

On that night expedition we took a more direct route back to the pass but still floundered in bogs. The torchbeam glittered off the frost and mica particles. My only stumble was falling into the ditch by the roadside. We spent the night in the pass, a cold one in the tin box of Dormobile, but being cold was an aid to rising early. There was an Eastern SMC Meet that morning on the lairig — and I wanted to claim Beinn nan Oighreag first.

I drove to the shed at the crook of the road (see above) and, by torchlight again, slowly traversed up and along to round Meall Buidhe to the Lairig Breisleich. This was a bit of a flounder. The bogs, as on Luaidhe, can be largely avoided by setting off up one of the small streams to gain the higher grassy level and traversing on the green rather than the brown, but this alternative could not be observed in the dark. A stag let out a bellow from very near. The hairs stood up on the back of my neck! Later, in the lairig, Kitchy set up a grouse to give us another fright. Munro and Stott came to the Lairig Breisleich by this route one winter and the latter described it as a "villainous frozen bog, all peat haggs and heathery hummocks". (They were *en route* to Meall Ghaordie.)

The squint of day came as we tramped up the white slopes on to the north ridge of the Corbett. There was one star that put in a deal of overtime before packing in the night shift. The summit fails by only 22 feet in its attempt to become a Munro. In the 1930s there was a brief period when its promotion looked likely and the hill received several visits to try to verify its height; since when it has returned to its slumber. J. Gall Inglis, in 1932, described a peculiar wind when climbing the final slopes. The wind was strong enough to have the party leaning on it at such an angle that on one occasion Inglis fell on his back when it suddenly dropped — which it did frequently, and instantly, then slowly built up to full strength again. The "new" road over the Lochan na Lairig pass was so narrow and without passing places that they preferred to drive right down Glen Lyon rather than risk meeting another vehicle.

There was not much opportunity for me to linger but I kept the 9 a.m. meeting in the Lairig na Lochain and, by placing vehicles at both ends, we had a grand day over the Lawers range. Another car parked beside our collection was not claimed till long after dark — just when I was at coffee and dram stage and wondering if a rescue lay ahead. Out of sheer relief I gave the lads a dram, and kept my fears to myself. They'd been enjoying themselves and who was I to comment on tramps home in the dark? That week had seen me giving thought to what I called "The Long Walk", the non-stop tramp over all the Munros, and it was this weekend, as much as anything else, that dragged the idea from the realm of dreams to become a practical proposition. I'd had enough of the office. The stars and the sun called. The wind on the hill was free.

The next day I added Cam Chreag to the Corbett tally, a day described in 4:11, but I'd also decided that I'd return one day, with more time, to Beinn nan Oighreag and the Lairig Breisleich. The pass lost its one-time importance with the construction of the Lawers road over to Glen Lyon. The Lairig an Luaidhe, west of Oighreag (nothing to do with the Corbett) is another historic link from Glen Lochay to upper Glen Lyon.

It was a decade later, with Charles on the Corbett trail, before the return to Oighreag. My Dormobile was left in Glen Lochay and we drove up the Lochan na Lairig road in Charles's car. It was early March and we had to bash through some drifts on the way up, then, just before the loch, there was one giant drift which stopped Charles driving any further. So we set off on foot and took the same sort of line as I'd done before. Drifts *and* bogs this time. The fence led to the first bump and then to the top of the Corbett, quite helpful in the cloud. It was cold on top, with the thin tunes of winter winds playing on the frosty cairn. We soon headed off southwards down the ridge to reach the Glen Lochay road at Duncroisk. A buzzard flew up from its picnic on a squashed rabbit. The weather had turned mild enough to sit outside over tea, then I drove home to Fife and Charles headed for Sheffield.

Section 4:   8. MEALL NAN SUBH   804 m   OS 51   461397
      Hill of the soo (raspberry)

"West of Meall Ghaordie there is a rather uninteresting group of hills stretching towards the Learg nan Lunn. They can all be climbed easily from the south, but they have no features of interest."

That is all I've noted in the authoritative sources I've looked at, a check I sometimes make, perhaps to balance my own maverick opinions! This time I may seem to be in agreement for my log book of the day girned that it was "a frustrating series of knolls, bogs and detours". I'd started the day camped at Cashlie in Glen Lyon and had been up Meall Ghaordie (a much finer Munro if climbed from the north) and was to go on over Beinn Heasgarnich and Creag Mhor to camp below Ben Challum. As this high-level backpacking expedition was described in *Hamish's Mountain Walk*, I'll give only a brief note on this Corbett.

That day, heavily laden, I took in a majority of the Glen Lochay peaks, so what about someone having a go from Killin to Tarmachan and on over the complete Glen Lochay skyline back to Killin? It would be a notable round. After several weeks of non-stop walking, I wrote that the miles from Meall Ghaordie to Beinn Heasgarnich gave the hardest going up to that time. They are tough enough for "rather uninteresting" to be rather untrue. I found specific interests that wasted over an hour of the morning's floundering.

The going was heavy certainly. "Long miles of very rough and peat-boggy schist with deep heather", was my inelegant log-book summary. Hares and ptarmigan were forever exploding at my tortoise feet. At one stage I sat for a long time watching deer browsing in the Lairig Liaran just below me. Even in mid April there were grunts and groans and a variety of sounds from these supposedly silent animals. I then spent half an hour by a pool which seemed to be only 10 per cent water and 90 per cent frog spawn, and was heaving with frogs who vanished at my tread, but after I'd sat for a while eyes would pop out and after twenty minutes the scene was an entertaining one. Two, gripped together, swam off with immaculately synchronised strokes while another could not co-ordinate his limbs at all and another spent ten minutes battering at a wall of spawn as it tried and failed to fight through. Strange, isn't it, how some areas teem with frogs while others, which look much the same, never seem to have them?

That was all happy procrastination. I was glad to have the chaotic acres above clear of mist for you could never be sure of the exact summit of Meall nan Subh otherwise. It even looks a "frustrating series of knolls, bogs and detours" on the map.

The ascent of Meall nan Subh can be made very easy by motoring up Glen Lochay, a quiet glen of many charms and some good waterfalls, and then up the Hydro road from Kenknock. A locked gate may bar the Learg nan Lunn road over to Loch Lyon at the top of the pass, which seems a bit of cheek considering public monies built the road. This hill could equally well be done from the Glen Lyon side in combination with Meall Buidhe and Sron a' Choire Chnapanich — but perhaps you'd prefer the watershed walk round Loch an Daimh to take in those Corbetts which do not even gain the put-down of "uninteresting". No hill is uninteresting. You canny subh your granny aff the bus!

Section 4:   9. SRON A' CHOIRE CHNAPANICH   837 m   OS 51
              456452 *The nose of the lumpy corrie*

Section 4:   10. MEALL BUIDHE   907 m   OS 51   427449
              The yellow dome (boo-ee)

The *SMC Journal* for 1984 broke the news of "a new Corbett", discovered by Jim Duguid. This was Sron a' Choire Chnapanich, the name being obtained from the 1:25,000 map as was the startling height of 837 m rather than the 686-m contour on the 1:50,000 First Series map.

Only when I started writing up the Corbetts for this book did the oddity of the hill become apparent. The First Series 1:50,000 shows it separated from the Stui hills by a mere four contour lines — 200 feet in old measurements — so how could it be a Corbett? Even accepting the 1:25,000's 837 m, what was the separation? It all became so frustrating that I took the easy answer and went and measured it myself, a good excuse for a day on the hills above Glen Lyon. We set off for Meall Buidhe first, a big Corbett, both in bulk and height.

We parked under the dam, whose outflow explodes upwards like a fountain. The loch's level was low and we initially hopped along the exposed boulders on the north shore to admire the patterns and textures of the well-cleaned rocks, then we angled up steeply to pass under the crags (hanging garden of flowers as they are out of reach of sheep or deer) and on north-westwards across gentler, very featureless grassy moorland slopes to end at a cairn perched above the upper Feith Thalain. This area could be very confusing in cloud. The cloud was coming and going for us, but on the whole we could see what we wanted, topographically if not photographically. The scene was all Whistler tints of grey.

We dipped to the col and then plodded up the ridge, which has the posts of an old fence, to circuit round and up Meall Buidhe, which is not far off being a Munro, though it is probably one of the least-climbed hills in Scotland because of its 8 m shortfall. During the Munro-in-one expedition I could not resist making a high-level traverse from Meall Buidhe to Meall Buidhe — the range north of Loch an Daimh which, when I first knew it, was two lochs, Loch an Daimh and Loch Giorra. In the dry summer of 1984 they became two lochs again, the local keeper told me. The level of the new reservoir joining them was low enough today that they had almost reverted. Our morning reverie was interrupted by the noise of a train and, sure enough, down on the edge of Rannoch Moor, a caterpillar train was eating its way across the wasteland, just as had happened on the Munro trip.

A fresh south-east wind was blowing, allowing us to walk into a herd of deer which was crossing the col east of the Corbett. The deer that saw Storm and me ran, but there were more behind who still cantered up unaware of why the leaders had shot off. They just kept on coming, scores of hinds, with youngsters at heel.

From the Buidhe col I dropped past a peat patch to traverse along the flank of the glen quite easily, ending on the col below the problem Corbett, a real jungle of peat hags and runnels. I had a bite to eat which gave my two altimeters time to settle, then I noted the heights carefully.

The ascent to the Corbett is over as kindly a surface as you will ever find on a hill. The heather or moss-sedge mix seems to have been woven like a carpet — with a deep pile. There is one area (quite clear when coming off Buidhe) where a band of bright green runs down the slope from the seepage of a horizontal fault. This was dotted with mountain violets, looking so delicate in that wild, upland world. Across on the *sron* of Meall Buidhe a long line of deer were clearly seen against the grey sky. A deer track led up at an angle to bypass the crags and obviously linked with the col I'd just crossed. The whole gentle slope of the Allt Phubuill valley is blanketed with peat hags — not a good way to the Corbett.

I was still on the old fence line but I tend not to mention fences as they can be more of a hindrance than a help in bad weather navigation. Perhaps if a fence was clearly following a county boundary, which is marked on the map, I'd give it prominence but not otherwise. I've been led astray too often by trusting fences instead of using map and compass. On these hills there are fences, old and new, all over the place. Cows, as well as sheep (and deer) range over these green domes. Glen Lyon's green is partly from the rich underlying rock but also from the evil-spreading bracken. It is the longest glen in Scotland and this walk is at its western extremity, the uppermost houses having gone under the waters when Loch Lyon was dammed after the war.

The summit of the Sron was a superb one, a real nose (*sron*) jutting out to the north. Our perch gave an eagle's eye view *down* to the slim version of Loch an Daimh and also *up* to the Stui (Stuchd an Lochan), still very dominant in the east. While the altimeters caught up, Storm and I wandered down the green prow a bit. The turf was starred with the flowers of dwarf cornel and cloudberry. How such a soft vegetation survives in such an exposed spot is a puzzle. The cairn is tiny as there is no stone close to hand on that tower of peat. A skylark was in full song overhead.

The *SMC Journal* note goes on a bit about the name of this Corbett, but a walk up the hill would have cleared any theoretical speculation. The summit is such a marked nose that, logically, *sron* has to be in its name. Nor is it the flat sausage shape of the 1:50,000 First Series delineation. The altimeters made the pull up from the col to be 735 feet.

As it was a draughty summit Storm and I ran most of the way down. Deer were grazing under the crags to the east and when I knocked a stone down they heard the clinking sound and fled along the hillside. At the south col we sat among the bobbing hare's tail, over a bit from a forlorn-looking gate, and did some more arithmetic. The difference on that side was 676 feet. My figures were a quick estimate from metric altimeters but the hill clearly had 500-foot clearance, definitely a Corbett.

With no hope of cancelling a Corbett we ambled on again, by Meall an Odhar, for the pull up Stuchd an Lochain (the Stui). The weather was going, however, the east having a cheerless, dark, late-Goya gloom to it as we headed down to Pubil fairly quickly. By the time we had changed sweaty garments, had tea and written up some flower notes the rain had started. For those to whom dates are vital, the car radio was full of Boris Becker being bumped out of his chance of a third Wimbledon title. It was that wet year. The keeper at the house under the dam said the road over to Glen Lochay was not locked. We made our exits over that pass, though we saw nothing.

Section 4:   11. CAM CHREAG   862 m   OS 51   536491
                   Crooked crag

A second *crooked crag* Corbett (near Tyndrum) came in with the
mapping revisions, but Cam Chreag to me is always the Glen Lyon
hill for, with Braehead School having a bothy in the Black Wood of
Rannoch, it was within our sphere of influence. The hills between
Schiehallion and Rannoch Moor we came to know well and, as
always, a lasting affection arose from the acquaintance.

If "we captured the rainbow and rode its shining path" on those
days at Rannoch there were still good days afterwards as well.
Following my November days on Meall Luaidhe (see 4:6) and Beinn
nan Oighreag early on the Saturday (4:7), I still kept a 9 a.m.
rendezvous with an Eastern SMC Meet for a day traversing the
Lawers group. Staying up high in the pass overnight was a wise move
as, on the Sunday, when I drove down into the shadowy depths of
Glen Lyon the ground was glittering from a hard frost. At seven
o'clock I set off for Cam Chreag from the bridge above Gallin.

That November weekend Kitchy and I wandered up the dark
heather with its scattering of old pines. The heather eased with height
gained and grey rocks occasionally broke through, very much the
desolate moorland of much of the area. Cloud was welling up from
the glens as the temperature changed and Meall Buidhe soon
disappeared — but the Corbett stayed clear, a not unusual state of
play. This hill's name presumably comes from the crags that stutter
along its eastern face. It is fairly featureless otherwise but gives good
views, to Lawers –Tarmachan in particular and to really wild country
to north and west.

As the day was young I decided to go on to the Munro Meall
Buidhe. The only snag was that my map (One Inch) ran out just west
of the Corbett. Where exactly was Buidhe? I sat and tried to recall all I
could from previous visits. In a col down the north ridge of Cam
Chreag lay Cul Lochan and on one occasion we'd come up the Dall
Burn and passed it to a vast wildness below Glas Choire, that
symmetrical hollow under the rim of Meall Buidhe. Glas Choire had
to be south west from the Cul Lochan and as Meall Buidhe curved
round the corrie the east top of the Munro (Meall a' Phuill) had to be
more or less directly west of my position. I set off, by compass and
memory, in search of the Munro.

The cloud actually cleared on Meall a' Phuill and a grand day evolved
so we added the Stui as well, the best of Glen Lyon's hills, before
returning to the Dormobile and Monday morning back at the office. I

had absolutely no worry at trying this "blind" navigation because, if I became hopelessly mislaid (not *lost*) then I only needed to steer due south and I'd have to come down into Glen Lyon or Glen Daimh.

This basic grasp of lay-out is something which is seldom mentioned in textbooks or classroom, yet I'd say it is one of the essentials of navigational skills. The Black Wood of Rannoch is a fearsome big place but my gangs of young teenagers would cheerfully go off into it for hours at a time, and often did become mislaid (you're only *lost* when you sit down and give up thinking) but could always win out because they knew every stream ran down to Loch Rannoch and its road, beside which the bothy was situated. They just went down to the road and turned right or, if they'd crossed the Dall Burn, turned left. Nothing complicated with map and compass but something better. The confidence engendered was remarkable. Map and compass came easily after that.

If you could arrange it (friend with car, post bus or whatever), Cam Chreag is a good excuse for a walk through from Loch Rannoch to Glen Lyon, rounding or going over the Cross Craigs to the Cul Lochan and on up the north ridge. Do add Meall Buidhe and descend to attractive Loch an Daimh with the Stui ranged as its backcloth.

If strictly Corbetting, the new bulldozed track approaching Cam Chreag up the glen from the east could be used to link on with Beinn Dearg (4:12). Off track, the country between the Corbetts is not recommended.

Section 4:   12. Beinn Dearg   830 m   OS 51   609497
Red hill (jerrak)

Just west of Beinn Dearg is the Kirk Road or Lairig Chalbhath (Lairig Ghallabhaich), an historic old drove route from the south to Loch Rannoch, which is still tracked and gives the easy route to the Corbett from the north. From our school bothy near Dall, traverses of the Carn Mairg range sometimes began by that route up to Beinn Dearg. So many Corbetts *can be* combined with Munros that this becomes one reason for doing them simultaneously rather than Munros first and Corbetts second.

The only time I went up Beinn Dearg from the south was on a day when crisp winter conditions were sliding into the more usual monsoon that passes for winter in Scotland. The temperature rose quicker than I could. We went up from Camusvrachan, one of those establishments sitting below a complex drainage system so typical of these hills. These bellyfolds of hidden glens above Innerwick,

Camusvrachan and Invervar, are rather attractive: green in their depths, heathery higher and with framed views over pretty Glen Lyon to the Lawers hills. There are some huge herds of deer, and throughout our school days at Rannoch we sometimes spotted a rare "white" stag. Such beasts are never shot and are still viewed with a certain superstitious reverence. On one estate I know, a tenant insisted on shooting a white stag — and was asked to leave the next day.

I followed up the Cul Lairig stream for shelter (this was pre-trees) and then caught the west wind up on to Beinn Dearg. As the west began to chuck down a mushy mix of rain, hail and sleet, I scurried on with the storm to the next col and then rushed down the Dubh Choirein. With only an hour of daylight left there was no time anyway for the logical continuation to Carn Gorm, perhaps the best of the range, to complete the round of the Camusvrachan watershed. All the Glen Lyon hills are under deer so should be avoided from midsummer till the end of October. Given a good day Creag Ard should be taken in. As Firsoff says of Creag Ard and Beinn Dearg they "stand handsomely above Glen Lyon and the system of little glens and corries which divides them from the sprawling massif of Carn Mairg". In 1892 Stott recounted a Glen Lyon trip with Munro and wrote something similar: "A bold bluff hill, well-named, from its red shingly shoulders guarding the west side, the steep green slopes of Carn Gorm on the other." The current SMC guide (with a Munro fixation) says nothing at all about Beinn Dearg.

Section 4:   13. AUCHNAFREE HILL   789 m   OS 52   809309
         Hill of the field of the deer forest

"The wind was loud, the rain was heavy and the whistling of the blast, the fall of the showers, the rush of cataracts, and the roar of the torrents made a noble chorus of the rough musick of nature than it had ever been my chance to hear before." So wrote the ponderous Doctor Johnson when confronted with a wild night in the Highlands. Dave and I had a November camp in those conditions up at the head of Glen Lednock above Comrie when the storm did its best to wipe away a full moon. Whooper swans called on the loch and Sput Rolla down the glen was a solid wall of water instead of its usual braided beauty.

We set off from Invergeldie at 7 a.m. in the first gloom of day, having risen early "in self-defence". Geese were struggling south-wards through the tattered clouds. The first hare went charging off up the icy path and then went head over heels on a frozen puddle. I once counted fifty hares in a look along the dark heather flanks of Ben

Chonzie. It was spring, the snow had gone, but the hares were still parading in their white coats. Most heathery eastern hills have hares, but Chonzie has a world take-over programme under way!

Dave and I followed the old right of way up the Invergeldie Glen and then cut across north of Chonzie to drop to the wide Moine Bheag col and up the other side to reach Auchnafree Hill, the Corbett. The wind bullied us along so it was just a case of reaching out a foot and seeing where it landed us — eventually at the big cairn, a bit south of the long fence running to the south east. Had it been Dave's car rather than mine back at Invergeldie I would have blown on for the fine high-level, but slowly-descending, seven or eight mile walk to Meall Dubh and then either down to Newton Bridge or by the Shaggie Burn to Crieff, to be met there with the vehicle. Ah well, you must always leave something for "next time".

We backtracked to the Moine Bheag and contoured under the crags overlooking Lochan Uaine to keep out of the wind as long as possible. In hard snow it would have been dangerously steep when eventually we climbed up for the summit of the Munro. Loch Turret was sending sheets of water over the dam at the south end. Dave cracked: "They'll think it's raining in Crieff." We were back at Invergeldie by lunchtime.

This is probably as easy a way as any to gain Auchnafree Hill, or traverse it on a walk from Crieff via Glen Turret Reservoir and on by Creagan na Beinne to Loch Tay. Auchnafree is a great barren dome but the flying buttresses holding it up on the Glen Almond side give it a certain architectural merit, which makes that the most aesthetic approach.

There is parking just along from Newton Bridge towards the Sma Glen (Glen Almond is closed to cars) and an hour's walk will see one on the slopes of the Corbett. I've used a folding bicycle to shorten the time if not the distance when I also wanted to see the stone circle further up the glen. If transport can be arranged I'd suggest going up the Corbett from Conichan, then descending to Larichfraskhan. Instead of returning down the glen, a walk up through the scraggy pass of Glen Lochan to the public road at Loch Freuchie is a delightful addition to the day.

From Conichan skirt the Eagle's Rock southwards to Coire Chultrain. You can then search for the Thief's Cave on the way up. This large refuge was once used by a sheep-stealer, Alister Bain, who was eventually apprehended in the cave while roasting part of his booty. He was duly hanged on the gallows at Perth. The upper corrie is steep and craggy but easy enough. The Kirk of the Grove (a natural pile of big rocks at 831311) is an old secret conventicle site where services were held, free of persecution, in covenanting times. You have a choice of sacred or profane routes. Mad cyclists could even take their bikes to within a mile of the summit, for the Second Series map shows new tracks everywhere, even to the 700-m level. Somewhere up here the last wolf in Scotland was supposedly slain but there are as many such claims as there are beds slept in by Mary Queen of Scots. Auchnafree Hill is ringed by an extraordinary number of big waterfalls: Sput Rolla, the Diel's Cauldron and the Falls of Turret, Barvick, Keltie and Monzie. Exploring these on a wet day is a pleasant occupation. The details can be found in Louis Stott's *Waterfalls of Scotland* (AUP 1987).

Section 4:   14. Meall Tairneachan   780 m   OS 52   807544
             Hill of Thunder

Section 4:   15. Farragon Hill   780 m   OS 52   840553
             Feargain's Hill

These were hills I always had to fight for in our bothy days in the Black Wood of Rannoch: Schiehallion was too near. Considering how visible the Farragons are from the Queen's View, or from the old military road over the hills south of Aberfeldy, they have remarkably little written about them. Detailed books on Pitlochry or Aberfeldy keep silent and even the SMC district guide simply omits this chunk of mountain country. Strange, for Farragon Hill seems a well-kent name.

The only book I've seen mentioning Farragon is *Fair Perthshire* by Hamish Miles, long a favourite of mine; but he only touches on Farragon while describing Grandtully Castle in Strathtay: "From the other [north] bank of the Tay here the ascent of Farragon Hill may easily be made. It is no great matter as climbing but the view from the top is remarkable — better than many far higher peaks reached with greater toil." He mentions MacGregor outlaws living in the recesses of Farragon — and recesses imply a complex country, which is certainly true. Few skylines are more ragged and a clear day is advisable for these peaks.

I had a day clear recently, doubly fortunately, for my day was an unexpectedly tasty filling in a sandwich of diabolical weather — that wildness from which Faldo won his golfing crown at Muirfield in 1987 and, while looking for a biro on the summit to mark in all the new bulldozed roads, plantings, the Foss Mine, etc., I discovered I'd brought the wrong jacket — and my compass was in the other, back in the car near Lick. Escape would never have been difficult: all drainage to my right would have been "home" but in that complexity a mist falling could have cost the Corbetts.

Somewhere east of Frenich Wood is the best place to start. Finding a bit of verge to leave the Loch Tummel road clear is not so easy. Storm and I followed up the first burn east of Lick, rising through a pleasantly wooded hillside. Birch predominated and the burn rushed down a flowery cleft. Over the day I must have spotted nearly every hill-flower that one will readily find in July. Perthshire hills are often rather dismissed for quality, but the schisty rocks produce a flora seldom equalled elsewhere.

The day before had been so wild that I left home only to go and see *Vivat! Vivat Regina!* at the Pitlochry theatre and then to spend the night in the Dormobile. No Holst of stars sang the planet asleep so the midge-calm Sunday morning came as a surprise; the rucker was quickly packed and we set off about ten o'clock.

As the woods thinned out there were some vivid patches of foxglove spires. A lamb with the trembles startled us as we walked through the smother of bracken. We passed by an abandoned sheep fank with the burn ahead held by a quiet corrie full of sheep and deer. Flies were a pest and, sweaty or not, I soon pushed on, taking the east fork in the burn and angling up to gain the ridge behind craggy Sron Mhor. Beinn Eagagach (Eagach usually) appeared ahead as a shapely cone and it was tempting to cut over to add this third of the range's summits.

Instead I circled the next bump on the west; as hoped, we kept coming on parcels of deer, most of the hinds with month-old calves at heel. We cut east of Creag an Lochain and saw the green knobble of Farragon Hill through the gap. Deer tracks in the heather were a great help in picking a route through all the bumps. Lochan a' Chait (*loch of the cat*) appeared, below, from the last col only just before the pull up to the Corbett. A sharp wind drove us into a nook in the summit crags to have some lunch. The flowers of mossy saxifrage lay like confetti on the blaeberry greenness that is such a feature of these ragged crests.

The view was indeed remarkable, even if all the bigger hills were cloud-covered. To Ben Vrackie and southwards I looked over varied tints of blue, shot through, here and there, by wandering bands of sunshine. Below me, the moors above Weem and Strathtay were a patchwork of new corduroy plantings with several roads coming up onto the patchwork. A new road (from Blackhill) comes up to pass Loch Derculich and zigzags up to the col between Farragon and Eagach before turning along the latter and Creag an Fhithich then down to Loch Tummel. This would make the ascent of Farragon from the south very easy, but less interesting than the wilder northern approaches.

St Fheargain was an early Christian missionary in the Pitlochry area and Farragon could well be a corruption of his name. We did not stay long on the summit of Farragon Hill. After a photo of Schiehallion towering over Meall Tairneachan we scurried down out the wind, circling the head of the big Frenich corrie of corries. Lochan Lairig Laoigh (*loch of the calves' pass*) points to an historic crossing point, but the *kylos* must have been athletic beasts in those days. A bulldozed track rounded the northern end of Creagan Loch and led across the top of the next corrie to the rather messy area being mined. A rare quartz rock is the reason for the mining activity though, being Sunday, all was quiet and still till three youngsters on trail bikes, with dogs following after, roared over the moors and off up the access road.

This road zigzagged steeply up from the mine to round a spur, then wended north of the Corbett and down through the solid plantations above Loch Kinardochy to the B846. You could practically drive to the summit. Schiehallion, which smoked like a volcano (a familiar feature), looked very big and bold from the top of Meall Tairneachan (Tarruin'chon on older maps), and the Carn Mairg range was flatteringly arrayed. I could also see Beinn a' Chuallaich above Kinloch Rannoch. Wade's road up from Tummel Bridge was an intrusive straight line in a world of curves. Great cumulus clouds and rags of blue gave a brightness to the scene. My first ascent of Tairneachan had been on skis, from the limekiln at Tomphubil, in a blasting of spindrift. That was pre-plantings. Now the easiest route for the Corbett is to walk up the mine road, not open to vehicles.

That day a poisoned toe was proving troublesome. I'd worn mini wellies for comfort and these were a boon on the descent. Doire Leathan, to the north, is the sharp cone which catches the eye so often hereabouts and along, under it, was a green rake (pointing to a leak-level between rock layers) which would make for soft, if wettish walking. I hobbled along the rake and, from the end of the ridge, had started to descend to the Frenich Burn when the heavens opened. It did not rain so much as just drop water wholesale. This thunderplump left everything saturated, just as we reached bracken level, and the pitted sheep paths became slippery in the extreme. The flies were back too. Well do they say, "Don't praise the day before the evening." In five minutes our dawdle was turned into a struggle, needing care and concentration.

The Frenich flows in a deep cutting which we followed, rather than the heather slopes above, crossing from bank to bank, slithering and being soaked from the thighs down. Eventually we were forced on to the east bank as the burn plunged into a gorge where the west bank is taken over by big forestry plantings. At the fields above Lick the bracken became head-high. We forced a way through it to a stand of big larch-trees which paraded beside an old made path down the side of the burn to a little wicket gate by the bridge on the Loch Tummel road. Frenich House has the burn flowing through its grounds, a bonus in an outstanding garden which I looked at from a seat on the bridge parapet. We'd been on the hill for six hours.

I drove over by the Braes of Foss, stopped briefly at the Foss Mine road-end, passed the Glengoulandie deer park, crossed Wade's Bridge to Aberfeldy and on to Grandtully Castle which was open under the Scottish Gardens Scheme. "Nothing like a circum-motoring of the Farragons to end their traverse," I thought as I sipped welcome tea at what Hamish Miles called "a handsome pile". Farragon, across Strathtay, was hidden by its own opulent lower slopes. The north is the grand side of these hills.

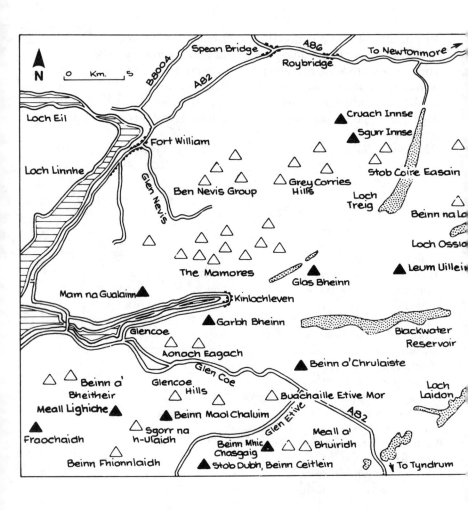

LOCH LINNHE TO GLEN ETIVE TO LOCH TREIG

Section 5: 1. FRAOCHAIDH 879 m OS 41 029517
Heathery hill (free'achy)

AT THE END of 5:3 I mention the fossilising effect our maps have had on Gaelic names. This *heathery hill* would almost certainly have had its name changed to *hill of trees* and probably prefixed by a rude adjective, even before walkers could render it in Anglo-Saxon. You just cannot climb Fraochaidh without having to tackle trees, which may be at any stage from recent planting to recent felling and every nastiness between.

I cycled up Glenduror to the bothy, not easy as there are changes to the forest roads as well, and crossed a bridge over the river (023536) to tackle Coille Dhubh direct. We were soon engulfed by blowing cloud, and the whole round trip is one I'd as soon forget.

From various criss-crossings of the valleys my recommendation, now, would be to start at Ballachulish and take the path up above the River Laroch, then the left fork that crosses over to Glen Creran to its highest point before a long, rather "up and down and in and out" traverse to the Corbett. At least this allows a tree-free ascent and the more aesthetic "walking west". Whatever its sins of forest, heather, bogs and braes (and probably midges) all is forgiven when one reaches the summit of Fraochaidh and looks out over the glitter of the west. It is not only the thought of the trees that makes one postpone the descent. Beinn a' Bheithir under snow has the curvaceous purity of a Marilyn Munroe.

The quickest, simplest descent is by the west ridge for a mile and then north to Glen Duror through plenty of trees. A better route is to descend the steep south ridge and go on a mile to Beinn Mhic na Ceisich (Sheet 50) where there are two options: south then east to reach Glen Creran without any afforestation to fight, or west then north to reach the forestry road on the Salachan Burn which gives a minimal amount of tree-bashing. The Salachan Glen gives a pleasant walk down to the road along Loch Linnhe (Sheet 49). Whatever route is chosen depends on having someone helping with a car. If you just want to go up and down the same route I'll leave you to choose your own arboreal alternative.

Down in the forest on the south side of the Corbett are some limestone caves, and where Glen Stockdale spills over into the Salachan Glen are some others, including Uamh na Duilean Briste, on the side of a gorge just off the road (982519). When it was "discovered" in modern times an old ladder was found half way along its 300-foot passage. Alan Jeffrey's *Scotland Underground* has notes on all the explorations hereabouts.

Section 5:   2. MEALL LIGHICHE   772 m   OS 41   094528
            The doctor's hill

At one time a third of my life was spent in Glen Coe, either climbing hills or climbing routes, so it is an area I rather tend to avoid now in overcrowded summer. My great joy is being in the wild and lonely places. Glen Coe is wild but it is seldom lonely and the very fabric of the mountains shows the wear of a million tramping boots. Meall Lighiche's late appearance as a Corbett made a visit imperative and, running into that novelty, a dry spell in Glen Coe, we revelled in returning to what is undoubtedly an area of outstanding natural beauty. Traverses of the wee Buachaille and the Aonach Eagach were made for the sake of the dog's Munros, and as Storm also required Bidean we set off for this Corbett over the highest point in Argyll — hardly the conventional route to Meall Lighiche.

The road up to Gleann-leac-na-muidhe is the normal approach and the road continues up to the junctions of the streams that embrace Meall Lighiche, or Creag Bhan rather, as its craggy northern arm is called. It is probably easier to ascend this bold rump of *white crags* than tackle it in descent, and this route gives an approach to the Corbett along a splendid high crest. That excellent but unjustly ignored hill, Sgorr na h-Ulaidh, fills the view southwards while Beinn a' Bheitheir shows her shapely curves in the west and the Ben bulks over all the jumble to the north. Bidean presents its least prepossessing aspect.

By setting off at 7 a.m. we ensured having Bidean to ourselves. Clouds boiled up out of the glens to dramatise the summit. We then descended the back side of Bidean to reach Beinn Maol Chaluim (5:3), traversed Sgorr na h-Ulaidh, and climbed up Meall Lighiche direct from the linking col. Three buzzards were mewing and spiralling above the col, and the slope up the Corbett was so virgin that I actually commented on this in my log. Dropping down to that col and descending by the Allt na Muidhe would be a good way to complete a visit to a Corbett which is an excellent addition to the list.

We met one person on our walk, though we could see tiny dots of figures on Bidean all day. The NTS Centre car park was packed, the favourite visitor pastime being reading the Sunday papers, an interesting spectator sport with periodic visitations from the midges when the breeze died away. Meall Lighiche could be linked with a traverse of Beinn Fhionnlaidh and Sgorr na h-Ulaidh from Glen Creran but the tree plantings would have to be taken into account. You won't find that an overpopulous approach — and Glen Creran is singularly beautiful.

Section 5:   3. Beinn Maol Chaluim   904 m   OS 41   135526
        Callum's bare hill (Bin-mel-halum)

Bidean nam Bian, the highest summit in Argyll, and the giant of Glen Coe, is one of the very best peaks in Scotland for everything one seeks on a mountain, whether easy walking, long ridge traverses or climbs of all grades. In winter it becomes a majestic Alpine peak — and should be treated with due respect. The gentle walker, merely after this Corbett, should make its acquisition a summer ambition.

Like all the hills hidden behind the bulk of Bidean, Beinn Maol Chaluim suffers an undeserved neglect for it is out of sight and out of mind from the centrist activity of Glen Coe. The Corbett is really a Glen Etive mountain and, like everything else above that glen, the slopes are steep, craggy, and full of character. It just happens to be attached to Bidean by a high pass, the pleasant Bealach Fhaolain, which is a lure to the spectacular traverse of Gleann Fhaolain rather than just a slog up the Corbett. Our first nibble at this area was a flight from midges.

With a gang of kids I was camping in Glen Etive where we endured a night of sheer hell from the piranhas of the insect world. Our morning porridge turned grey on the spoon between dixie and mouth. In despair we struck the tents and fled to Glen Coe Youth Hostel by the most direct route — over the Bealach Fhaolain and down the Fionn Ghleann. Neither Corbett nor Bidean deflected us from that journey! The Fionn Ghleann would be the normal route to the Corbett from Glen Coe. The Bealach Fhionnghoill is overlooked by big crags but these can be turned on the north and an easier descent made from the Bealach Fhaolain back to the Fionn Ghleann.

My most recent visit to Callum's Hill was incidental to climbing Meall Lighiche, a "new" Corbett (5:2). From Bidean one looks down on the Corbett, as on nearly everything else, but Beinn Maol Chaluim is as individual a peak as Stob Coire nan Lochain or Stob Coire Sgreamhach. The descent off Bidean was the dog's least enjoyable part of the day. It is steep and largely vile scree, and a right-flanker is essential to avoid the crags which ambush on the direct line to the col. In winter this slope can be icy and a slip would probably shoot one down into the Fionn Ghleann with fatal, Coire Leis-like efficiency.

From the col we had an easy walk along and up the Corbett. At one stage we were sitting quietly when a big dog fox traversed the hill just below us. Foxes are always proclaimed as nocturnal animals but the foxes of the Highlands are often encountered in the daytime, quietly going about their business. They are nocturnal in urban-rural settings, I suspect, purely as a matter of survival. A fox, like us, has no objection to lying in the sun.

Beinn Maol Chaluim is capped with quartzite, which lies on top of the schists that make up the hill. The quartz rocks are on top simply because of the colossal folding of the earth's crust in far off times; normally they are below the schists. The Torridon giants are the extreme example of this folding, and geologists originally gave all sorts of explanations, for even they could not conceive the reality that Liathach had been turned over as if the young world had been ploughed. The lower slopes of Chaluim owe their green brightness to the richer schists which also give a more lavish flora.

As mentioned above, the best route to Beinn Maol Chaluim is the circuit of Gleann Fhaolain. Start at Dalness from where unrelieved steep slopes lead up to the shapely summit of Stob Coire Sgreamhach. There are big views down Glen Etive and down the Lairig Eilde. Any awkward steps on the crest can be turned on the south flank. The ridge sweeps on with a dip to the head of the Lost Valley merges with the ridge coming in from Stob Coire nan Lochain, and reaches the top of Bidean, a viewpoint which for once loses nothing by its superior position. You could probably name off as many peaks from the top of Bidean as you could on any Scottish summit. The continuation to Beinn Maol Chaluim has already been described; the descent is down the long south ridge to the Glen Etive road, just off the map, but there is a wide gap in the trees which have so effectively cut off Gleann Fhaolain itself. (The Etive trees are a plague of almost midge proportion.)

The Corbett name is tautological, for both *beinn* and *maol* mean "hill". *Maol* is always used of a rounded, bald, dome sort of hill, emphasising its shape: Callum's bald dome. A baldy lad called Callum no doubt was the victim of his friends' wit in giving this name. Callum (Malcolm) is long forgotten. The name sticks, fossilised on the map for ever and ever. Keepers and shepherds rarely use map names, which are practical aids, after all. We named all sorts of places above Dollar in our boyhood Ochils — and some of these have been likewise fossilised — they have proved useful. Baldy Callum's grandchildren might well have called the hill something else from their own associations with it. Post Clearances it would have probably been in English too. Names were living things before the Ordnance Survey pinned them, like butterflies, in the map cabinet.

Section 5: 4. BEINN MHIC CHASGAIG 862 m OS 41 221502
(named after a person)

This is rather a forgotten hill, a mere appendage to Clachlet — a Clachlet appendix — which most people manage to live without. Corbett-baggers will eventually come round to it, of course, and gluttons for punishment could well traverse Stob Dubh (Ceitlein) as well in a single expedition (see 3:13), which is a more strenuous day than the circle of Chasgaig–Clachlet–Creise.

A gang of us once did so, but in reverse order, Sron na Creise being easier *in ascent* we'd decided. A box on wires allowed us to cross the River Etive dryshod but when last I looked, this novel "bridge" was all chained up. The River Etive is fordable only in good weather. As Creise's Munro moved south a mile with the major revision, you can still add two Munros easily enough to the Corbett. It would be a waste not to, really, for the huge, lumpy, glen-gouged hills on the Etive side of the Blackmount have an austere, almost Himalayan grandeur to them. Alltchaorunn is the starting point and a path leads up into the Ghiubhasan Ganga. There are fine granite pools in the first mile and a threefold choice of route thereafter: 1. straight up the West Ridge, turning a crag at 400 m; 2. by the burn which curves up on the south side of this ridge; 3. up the Allt Coire Ghiubhasan to mount to the col joining the Corbett to the rest of the Blackmount hills. If willing to paddle the Etive, this col, or its bordering ridge, can be followed from the other side. The amount ascended will still be the same. The summit is a strange saucer of a place and in bad weather it can be difficult to pinpoint.

The best of the Corbett lies in linking it with Clachlet (*Clach Leathad*) and a short diversion can add the Munro of Creise (238507) as well. Rannoch Moor, being 1,000 feet up, has a completely different character to the shadowy depths on the Etive side. The descent from Clachlet to the Bealach Fuar-chathaidh is demanding; the Bealach is the secret link from Glen Etive to Rannoch Moor at its innermost recess of Coireach a' Ba, and you may feel happy just to descend the Ghiubhasan rather than go up again in order to descend the Aonach Mor ridge. Ben Starav and Cruachan look well from this round.

Section 5: 5. BEINN A' CHRULAISTE 857 m OS 41 246567
Rocky hill (croo-las-tay)

This was a convenient outing for 1 January 1968 when a crowd of us were based at Lagangarbh. We'd had some fairly desperate climbs during the previous few days as snow fell on snow and thaw on thaw, and going anywhere on foot (or even by car) was eventually almost impossible. Seeing in the New Year had eaten up several hours of the day, we did not make an early start.

John was from Australia, David from Cambridge, Robbie from East Scotland and Bob from the West: a right mixed bag. Our ages spanned over fifty years. A further delivery of snow had been dropped off overnight and I took my skis for the ascent. An unusual absence of wind meant some fog on the moor, so the view was given suddenly after we'd climbed for half an hour: the Buachaille like a frosted citadel across a pantomime moat of mist. It was a weary flog up, even with skins, for the snow was heavy. Later the snow was powder or worse. The mist rose like smoke and we only had tantalising glimpses from the summit.

Our ascent, which was not difficult, took us up the west ridge from Altnafeidh over Stob Beinn a' Chrulaiste. The main rockiness lies on the south flanks of this approach. I was tempted to ski down the SE Ridge to the Kingshouse but time was a bit short. The Blackwater Reservoir was frozen over and I thought then that skates would be the way to explore it, for the shores are extremely bog-bound. How the drovers coped with the vast herds of cows that came south down the Ciaran and over the hills to Kingshouse is a mystery, even if the Blackwater was then a series of lochs, not the massive barrier it is now. I still want to skate it. There are two good Corbetts on the north side of the Blackwater (5:8; 5:9) which are a bit out of the way from this Rannoch Moor side.

Rannoch Moor is one of the places verbally abused by John Maccullough, who was perhaps the first real explorer of our mountains, and who could charm on one page and rain sarcasm on the next. According to him we looked down on an "interminable Serbonian bog, a desert of blackness and vacuity, solitude and death". He had hired a horse to cross the Moor, which was a mistake. He "might have remained in Glencoe. A ride this was not. I cannot even call it a walk, for half was traversed by jumping over bogs and holes. I may fairly say I jumped half the way from Glencoe to Rannoch."

Those of our gang on foot were glad enough to use their up-furrow on the way down. The skiing was not good. At the end the skis kept balling-up. It was snowing hard by the time we were back at the hut and an hour later, when we set off for the fleshpots, six inches of new snow lay on top of all the rest. Under the circumstances Beinn a' Chrulaiste was quite a successful first summit of the year.

More recently, when I tried to catch up on some friends who had gone off for Chrulaiste from Kingshouse, I set off from Jacksonville and went straight up. A big gully, left of the summit, was left on my left and

I followed a tongue of pink porphyritic rock which gave enjoyable scrambling. It is clearly seen from the road. The west bank of the deep gully would be the quickest and easiest line of all.

Section 5:   6. GARBH BHEINN   867 m   OS 41   169601
             Rough hill

Garbh Bheinn, which is well-enough named, is a secretive hill, for the Pap of Glencoe blocks the view to it from the west and the battlements of the Aonach Eagach loom over it to the south; even seen across Loch Leven it does not stand out. The Corbett is a good hill to stand *on*: it has the Mamores in full array to the north. Unlike many in the list, this is one to be climbed from sea level. The view is earned.

The easiest approach is by the maintenance road up from Kinlochleven to the town's water-supply reservoir on the Allt Coire Mhorair. Burn-addicts can follow the stream to its source on the slopes south of the summit, those in a hurry can take a direct line up on to the 734-m eastern top and reach Garbh Bheinn that way. Up the valley and down the ridge would be a good combination. The southern slopes are grassier and less hostile than the northern, which are steep and rough. I once went up from Caolasnacon and have an abiding memory of bracken, birch scrub, heather, greasy slate crags, clegs, midges and drizzle. On the summit there was blue sky overhead, but cloud lay all around and I saw nothing. A pile of beer cans and other garbage at the cairn soiled the experience much more than these natural perversities. It was on those northern slopes above the kyle that Stevenson, in *Kidnapped*, had David Balfour lying up in the heather while Alan Breac sought food from Caolasnacon (*the narrows of the dog*). I bet the clegs and midges were as bad then as now.

In a 1914 *SMC Journal* W. Inglis Clark enthusiastically advocates Kinlochleven as a mountaineering centre, comparing it to a Norwegian fiord. "How can one reach Kinlochleven?" he asks. "By train to Ballachulish and thence by small steamer. Leaving Edinburgh by early train we reach our destination about 11 a.m. and by returning at 2.30 p.m. it is possible to make the double journey in a single day" — in other words Garbh Bheinn was a day-outing by public transport from Edinburgh.

He also describes the footpath from Glencoe village to Kinlochleven along the south slopes of the loch and its annoying habit of going over crags rather than round them. The road was completed only in 1922, having been started with the labour of German prisoners of war. The narrows themselves were quite a formidable barrier on the sea approach, having bad tides and needing constant dredging. Kinloch-leven still has an air of unreality about it. One does not expect an industrial complex in such a corner. The houses are now colourfully painted to counteract the long weeks when the sun is blocked off from the town. You can blame Garbh Bheinn for that.

Section 5:   7. MAM NA GUALAINN   796 m   OS 41   115625
                 Pass of the shoulder

This is a Corbett for a Sunday morning, usefully allowing for a return to a Scottish home the same night. It was the last Corbett I climbed on my final weekend as a normal office worker. The next week I left my job, was laying caches for the Munros expedition and then went off to ski and climb in Poland to gain some fitness for "the Long Walk" as I thought of that 112-day Munro tramp. Because all my maps were packed I could find only one map that had some of this Corbett on it. The missing bit was sketchily drawn on the map margin while in the Kingshouse bar on the Saturday night. Sunday did not dawn so much as drown.

   After a late breakfast the weather brightened enough "to go and have a look", a phrase which often heralds an escapade (or justifies a disaster) but here was merely practical fact. I drove round the south side of Loch Leven so as to look across to Mam na Gualainn and pick out a reasonable line. I'm not sure now why I didn't just walk up the path from Callert over to Lairigmor. It crosses high on the Corbett's west shoulder with a branch stalkers' path wending up to 620 m. Eventually this was the way I took Storm up the Corbett. The path now starts a quarter of a mile east of Callert (signpost), with parking just round the corner, and wends up through oakwood to a knoll with fine views, then on up the hillside, avoiding the Callert farmlands. Two miles east of Gualainn lies Beinn na Caillich, 764 m, which dominates Kinlochleven's view. It has a path all the way to the top (very clear) and is a good ascent to start a traverse to the Mam.

   Perhaps I'd had enough of the Callert path on that first visit for its status as a right-of-way was disputed all through the decade I was a director of the Scottish Rights of Way Society (a body, incidentally, which I feel every regular hill-walker in Scotland should support with their membership, both out of gratitude for past defences and for the problems still to come). The right-of-way was established in the end, this being an old coffin route, and Callert being the ferry port on the north side of the loch to reach Eilean Munde burial ground. As a boy I was rowed out to the island by a local man of great age and when, in conversation, I mentioned the name Campbell, he glared at me and then turned to spit into the sea.

Maybe he influenced me to drive round by Kinlochleven to park at a cemetery on the north shore. I followed a track up past a sheepfold which contained some big rams. A sparrow-hawk was winging through the trees and buzzards called higher up the hill.

I followed up a hysterical stream, still high with overnight indulgence. The slippery ground at one stage had me going for a slide and when I grabbed the bank in reflex reaction the old bracken gave me a bloody cut.

I'd chosen the roughest line of ascent but everything was too sodden to allow safe scrambling. When I broke up on to the ridge, waterproofs went on to counteract the vicious wind and I funked out of the storm in the lee of the summit crags to study the Corbett, Garbh Bheinn, across Loch Leven. This hill was backed by the white crest of the Aonach Eagach, much whiter on this north side than that overlooking Glen Coe (the north-south differences can be quite important for winter route selection), while the Mamores (south side) were grey and white, a streaky-bacon effect. Between the Corbett and the Mamores is the Lairigmor, part of the old military road from the south to Fort William. I'll never forget a school trip when we walked through the pass during a heat wave. The bare, scree flanks of the lairig reflected the glare and heat, and twice, clothes and all, we flopped into streams only to dry again before long. We were walking from Killin to Skye along old drove roads, this being one of the historic parts of the road from the isles. Now it has a summer flow of West Highlandwaymen. When I last walked through, west-east, two score of them charged past me, then I had the glen all to myself again. The majority did not seem to be enjoying their day very much. "How far to Fort William?" I kept being asked. As they were festooned with maps and guidebooks it seemed an odd question. Every time I replied I added an hour to my estimate — but nobody seemed to notice.

From the summit of Mam na Gualainn the Pap and Beinn a' Bheither were luridly lit in a clash of sun and cloud, but the Ben wore a bunnet of black so my smugness at a dry ascent suddenly seemed misplaced. A desperate romp down failed to beat the next deluge. I was saturated below cagoule level but as the storm went on for the rest of the day I suppose I was lucky. My thoughts were gloomy enough. What if the weather was like that for the big trip? What had I let myself in for? You can read what in *Hamish's Mountain Walk*; however, there is simply no comparison between a big trip like that and merely pecking away at the lists over odd weekends.

The commitment is total. An hour off Mam na Gualainn I'd changed clothes, was dry, fed and enjoying the hospitality of a friend in Fort William.

Section 5: 8. GLAS BHEINN   789 m   OS 41   259641
       The green hill

Section 5: 9. LEUM UILLEIM   906 m   OS 41   331641
       William's leap

New boots in Fort William before the train to Corrour Station and a night at Loch Ossian Youth Hostel gave me Leum Uilleim. The boots hurt so much that they were dumped in the loch to soak overnight. They were then moulded by a pre-breakfast romp up this fine viewpoint. We caught the *morning* train out. That was a pure Corbetting raid, which has one justification: dissatisfaction will ensure a desire for a more leisurely visit. Every time I travel the railway this peak tempts. It is a shapely tent rising over the northern flanks of Rannoch Moor. Corrour is 400 m up but the Corbett still gives a big view of everything from Ben Nevis southwards and, eastwards, along Loch Ossian to the gunsite pass of the Bealach Dubh. Leum Uilleim can easily become a favourite hill, whether skied between trains or sleeping out on it on midsummer's eve. Best, as so often, is the memory of a journey . . .

The alarm failed to wake me and I had a rush to catch the morning train at Bridge of Orchy. The early January snowfall had thawed out to leave the hills with a mottled effect. Leaping off a train at Corrour Station is always exciting. Having a path from it to one's chosen hill is almost overdoing things. The path wanders over the boggy moor and crosses the mouth of Coire a' Bhric Beag to land one on the drier slopes of Tom an Eoin. The Glasgow train grumbled up from Loch Treig but a tongue of cloud reached out from Loch Ossian and hid the "low" ground, then flowed up and over the hill. One gain was almost walking into two unsuspecting stags.

Leum Uilleim is double-topped with Bhric corries to north and south. On the waist of saddle between the tops I dumped my heavy rucksack, quite sure of finding it again as firm footprints were left on the snow. The cloud cleared briefly as I went up the final cone and below, southwards, shone the sprawl of the Blackwater Reservoir, a huge longitudinal moat which, like Loch Quoich, has drowned several once-useful stalking paths. In a strange way it has isolated these Corbetts; access from Corrour or Kinlochleven is easy in theory —

but when did you start a hill day from Kinlochleven? The shores of the Blackwater were created by the devil to break Christian souls; and they are as rough as along the north side of Lochan Fada for A' Mhaighdean.

I sometimes wonder how others plan and approach their hills, be they Munros, Corbetts or whatever, so I was fascinated to read an account of Don Green's in the Grampian Club *Bulletin*. That cheery Dundee club has a large number of list-tickers, the inheritance of Eric Maxwell, perhaps, who once kept the records of those who had done them all. Don drove to Rannoch Station one June and joined the north-bound morning train, meeting a friend and his dog who had joined the train at Crianlarich. They descended at Corrour.

The moorland approach to Sron an Lagain Garbh was remarkably dry and in the frequent sunny intervals the ridges enclosing Coire a' Bhric Beag with its big snowfield presented an inviting prospect. Among the peat hags we flushed a meadow pipit from its nest, which contained four eggs.

The females drew ahead but Misty got a lot of mileage out of returning to check that Gordon and I were following. On the sron which soon became well defined, then rose in rocky steps, we disturbed several stags in velvet. The top of our ridge was marked by a small cairn from which the summit of William's Leap was half a mile to the south-west. Like so many Corbetts, Leum Uilleim is a grandstand for Munros: Schiehallion, Beinn Laoigh, the Black-mount summits, Glencoe, the Mamores, Grey Corries and the Ben Alder forest were spread around us.

Misty soon disposed of her packed lunch plus titbits from her companion's pieces. We watched a north-bound steam excursion train, looking like a Hornby toy, toot and pause at Corrour. With plenty of time before our south-bound train was due the whole party opted — especially Misty — to visit the summit of Beinn a' Bhric.

The intervening bealach was surprisingly dry and a short climb brought us to the cairn. From it there was a striking view across the wetlands of Rannoch to Lairig Gartain's U-shape, with the summits of both Buachailles in cloud. The descent of Tom an Eoin was a canny daunder with expanding views all round. Stob Coire Easain's south ridge, delicately etched in snow, rose temptingly above the end of Loch Treig. As we descended to warmer levels Loch Ossian became the foreground for the Bealach Dubh and the great colourful plateau of Ben Alder.

After the unhurried descent on a sunny afternoon we sat below the track enjoying the dappled view of our sky-line round as we quaffed the carry-out which Gordon had thoughtfully cached in the morning. The south-bound train pulled in just four minutes late and we were soon back at Rannoch. A modest but satisfying venture, it has sown the seeds for further excursions using the same approach.

It sounds familiar, doesn't it?

With my summit view gone I returned to my rucksack on the col and on over Beinn a' Bhric, the lesser western top (872 m). There was a brief glimpse north to Loch Treig from whence comes a path to skirt Loch Chiarain, between Leum Uilleim and Glas Bheinn, and then plunge into the Blackwater. Another path keeps west of Loch Chiarain then splits, one branch going to the Blackwater and then down to Kinlochleven, while the other traverses round Glas Bheinn before going down to the town. At the south end of Loch Chiarain stood the bothy which was my haven that night after I'd spludged down through the thawing snow off Leum Uilleim.

I arrived early enough to be grabbed by Leen to go down to a wood dump by the Blackwater for a big beam each. You had to have a companion: whoever sank through drifts could not rise again without help. Eight others had arrived by the time we returned and people kept drifting in, from Alltnafeidh at the entrance to Glen Coe, from Kinlochleven, even from Ben Alder cottage. The bothy was an upstairs room in the shell of the building and it soon built up its own inimical atmosphere. Officially an MBA committee meeting was being held, but this did not prevent interruptions for brewing punch. Hours, brews and drams later there was relative quiet again, just two rows of sleeping-bag mummies with big daddy Denis in the middle.

A rather manky morning followed and as I'd been up Glas Bheinn not so long before I went out with those heading, via the Blackwater dam, back to Alltnafeidh which also ensured a lift back to my car at Bridge of Orchy. Alltnafeidh had been my approach for Glas Bheinn, while staying at Lagangarbh. Memories of moonlight on Chrulaiste and the wandering beams of passing cars, the familiar black shapes of the Buachailles and the Lairig Gartain, reading Alastair Borthwick's *Always a Little Further* and listening to the last night of the Proms.

Dry weeks had left the normally wet walk through by Lochan na Feithe quite dry. I had been on the watershed for daybreak. The Crowberry Tower looked very spiky from there. I crossed under the dam and then wandered up the hillside for Meall na Cruaidhe (570 m) with its tiny tarn beside the path that angles up from Chiarain. There was little view but it was too raw to sit and wait for a change. A line off southwards to avoid the steep eastern flank led me to the path out from the bothy. It and the Feithe glen and the Lairig Gartain are all in a straight line (a geological fault?) which made for a view inside a view inside a view. The monument is to a London vicar, the Rev. Alexander Heriot Mackonochie, who died there in 1787. This time I crossed the top of the dam before going down to look at the score of graves — the price of building this dam. Dates were from 1905 to 1909, one was a *Mrs* Riley, one "Not Known", others showed what a mix the navies were: Gillies, Hughes, Wilson, J. Smith, McFadden, Johnstone, Dunlop, McKay, Murphy, Dow, Day, Darkey Cunningham, Derry, McKenzie, W. Smith, Wallace, Brady. Borthwick tells a bit about their tough life, but Patrick McGill's *Children of the Dead End* is a vivid novel based on the author's experiences during the construction work. It is still in print.

I took the dam road west for a bit and then cut up on to the old military road to the Devil's Staircase and so back to Lagangarbh. Several people have spoken enthusiastically of the high, level NNE Ridge of Glas Bheinn — that, I think, will be the next way to the top. It would be a good excuse for another cross-country trip starting at romantic Corrour Station.

Section 5:   10. SGURR INNSE   808 m   OS 41   290748
                   Peak of the meadow

Section 5:   11. CRUACH INNSE   857 m   OS 41   280763
                   Hill of the meadow

I've often wondered which "meadow" these hills are named after. Perhaps at one time the area round the Lairig Leacach was under cultivation, or perhaps it was Coire Laire which is so dominated by Sgurr Innse or maybe just the Spean valley itself. Considering how the Corbetts are surrounded by big Munros they, or at least Sgurr Innse, are remarkably prominent landmarks. I suspect they were named from the early users of the Lairig Leacach. The flat ground there would be a natural resting point for cattle on the move. In the great droving days the Lairig Leacach was an important part of "The Road to the Isles".

For several years our school struggled to try and establish Inverlair as a residential centre before the bureaucratic Fife authorities scuppered those hopes. In the end we were not allowed to sleep in the building (a one-time prison for Rudolph Hess), in case someone was hurt. Yes, we could camp outside, or camp on top of Ben Nevis, but not inside the building. . . . We were stopped doing any restoration work (surely the most genuine, educative practice the kids could have?) because this might take work away from proper joiners. Those Inverlair days, however, gave us a chance to wander and explore the surrounding countryside, to head off on multi-day treks, to botanise, to rock climb and sclim every Munro within a day's walk — Beinn a' Chlachair to Creag Mheagaidh to the Grey Corries was a pretty good classroom! The promotion of Beinn Teallach to a Munro was only inconvenient for my new dog Storm.

Much of our rock-climbing instruction was done on the rocks of the gorge below Inverlair though every now and then we would wander up Coire Laire to climb on Sgurr Innse or the Stob Corries. The two Corbetts are both craggy but our activities were confined to Sgurr Innse which is a much more dramatic wee peak. The easy way up it lies on the side facing Cruach Innse and, in descent, route finding can be tricky, with crag piled on crag and the transverse ledges not always easy to see. Sgurr Innse so dominates with its portly presence that it comes as something of a surprise to find Cruach Innse is the higher hill.

We came to know them from the Coire Laire side but occasionally the keeper (who had lost an arm in the Korean war) would drive up the Lairig Leacach by Land Rover and give us a lift to the bothy. To us it was always Payne's bothy, a good base for the hills and passes round about. The incorporation of these Corbetts with a walk through this fine pass is the day I'd particularly recommend for bagging the Innses.

Start at Corrour Station and take the path and estate track down to Loch Treig and Creaguaineach Lodge. The Easan Dubh is a fine fall in the gorge between the lairig's guardian hills. Follow the east bank up the Lairig Leacach. The Corbetts eventually dominate the pass. The rake up the Sgurr is clearly seen — and best used unless wanting some scrambling or climbing — but the Cruach is a more straightforward traverse. Rejoin the road before it is swallowed in the plantation. Below the trees there are traces of the old miniature railway which followed the British Aluminium pipeline from Loch Treig to the works in Fort William (the so-called tunnel under Ben Nevis). The line, even now, can look confusingly like one of the Parallel Roads. The last few miles to Spean Bridge are by the attractively wooded banks of the Spean, the well-named Grey Corries bold on the southern skyline.

This walk can be done between trains, in either direction, but the actual walk is easier going south-north, as Corrour Station stands at over 1,000 feet. An alternative is to descend Coire Laire after traversing the Innses. Tulloch Station can then be used — or a night may be spent at Nancy Smith's hostel at Fersit (see p. 7), an enjoyable experience in itself. My last two visits were both on through-treks, the last a May Ultimate Challenge, when Nancy's hostel was a welcome haven from the earliest midges I've ever met.

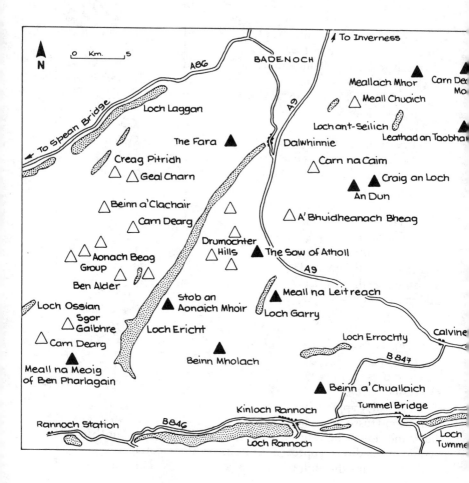

LOCH RANNOCH TO LOCH LAGGAN & BADENOCH

Section 6: 1. MEALL NA MEOIG (of BEN PHARLAGAIN) 868 m
OS 42 448642 *Hill of whey*, Pharlagain perhaps *grassy hollow*

MANY YEARS AGO I climbed Sgor Gaibhre and Carn Dearg in a circuit from Rannoch Station. I was not then aware these were Munros but I do recall going over Beinn Pharlagain (it sounded just like ptarmigan), such is the lure of a name. When Meall na Meoig of Beinn Pharlagain appeared as a Corbett I could not be sure of having ascended it. I set off to do so — from the CIC Hut.

This is not as crazy as it sounds. I'd just completed a *cycle* link of country summits: Carrauntoohil, Snowdon, Snaefell, Scafell Pike and Ben Nevis, the climax being a stunning sunset from the CIC Hut after traversing the Ben and Carn Mor Dearg. The idea of cycling home did not appeal (main roads in mid-summer) so I left the hut at six the next morning and called in at the Youth Hostel for a shower and my cycle. When I rolled out the bike I found there was a flat tyre; I blew it up and raced for the train.

Good intentions of repairing the puncture on the way failed due to chatting with the guard; I left the bike tethered at Rannoch Station and set off under the viaduct for a floundery crossing to the Allt Eigheach and the useful track all the way up into Coire Eigheach. It was a sticky, hot, hazy day as I followed the side burn up as long as it lasted, drank lengthily and dandered up the penultimate "new" Corbett. The area felt vaguely familiar, that knobbly world with the lochans. Only later did I see the intriguing feature of the lochan east of the Corbett having *two* outflows. Some day I'll have to go back and check if this is really the case.

That valley approach is recommended. Pharlagain is all lumps and bumps and tussock and bog, and the direct line is rather trying. Up the burn and down the ridge would be reasonable. Quite unreasonable would be a direct approach from Ben Alder cottage. The Cam Chriochan runs through unrelieved peat country, both difficult and dangerous.

I went on northwards to add Sgor Gaibhre and Carn Dearg but descended quickly into the corrie as I was desperate for water. I drank some, paddled in some more and then ended having a sort of bath. I was not very keen to descend. Syd Scroggie's words (on Loch Ossian) applied: "Summer seemed in love with idle days." The Mam Ban bogs were cracking in the drought and the views had the paleness of watercolours about them. After tea in the station café I caught a train back to Corrour, pumped the tyre, again, and just reached the Youth Hostel before it was flat once more. Tom Rigg welcomed me in but, though it was hot and the old "range" was blasting away, the windows were kept closed because of the vicious assaults of midges. They were as bad in the morning. I defy anyone to repair a puncture under those conditions. I pumped the tyre and raced for the station, sanity and home.

If travelling by train it is quite possible to break the journey and do these hills from Corrour to Rannoch stations (or vice versa). My doings were a bit complicated by having the cycle but the opportunity was not to be missed. Without puncture or midges I'd planned to cycle east from Rannoch Station to Pitlochry for a train home from there. One last warning. Going direct from the station to the Allt Eigheach track is a dry-weather short cut. Under normal conditions it is best to take the estate road from Loch Eigheach.

Rather sadly, Beinn a' Chumhainm has been deleted as a Corbett as not having a 500-foot re-ascent. It is a natural continuation of this Munro traverse and well worth a visit. Keep it on *your* list.

Section 6: 2. STOB AN AONAICH MHOIR   855 m   OS 42   537694
                       Spike of the big crest

Section 6: 3. BEINN MHOLACH   841 m   OS 42   587655
                       Shaggy mountain

"The road that leads to Rannoch is the gangrel's royal way."
(Ratcliff Barnett)

My last sortie to these hills led to a near fiasco. Storm just managed to add the shaggy mountain to his list but Aonaich Mhoir was left unvisited. I suspect that "unvisited" — and perhaps unloved — is the state this remote hill long occupies for most Corbetteers. "Speak as they please, what does the mountain care?" (Browning) A difficult cull is Aonaich Mhoir.

Dog and I were in the Rannoch area but, being the stalking season, were keeping off the hills until the weekend when I decided on a quick "raid". There is no stalking on Sundays. Late on Saturday we set off up the old right-of-way that goes from Rannoch to Dalwhinnie via Loch Garry. (The route comes down to Annat, not to Craiganour.) Once above the fields we came on an old village in the hollow of the burn, a stark reminder of departed life all over the Highlands — and on the way back we sat there for an hour of bliss, agreeing with the prophet, "Better is a handful of quietness than two hands full of toil." (Ecc. 4:6)

My plan was to follow the track so far, head up Beinn Mholach and on towards Aonaich Mhoir till too dark to see, sleep out, then, on the Sunday, add the second Corbett and tramp part way down the long Hydro road to Bridge of Ericht (the sane but stultifying "voie normale") — only I'd branch off for the hill track by Meall Garbh and the Killichonan Burn to hit the lochside road just west of Talladh Bheithe. Here I'd left my folding cycle to speed the return to the car at Annat. I had a good sleeping bag (being crisp autumn weather), a stove and food, and a bivvy bag "just in case".

Dandelion days are apt to blow away and as we crossed the rather squelchy moors to the final upheave of Beinn Mholach I knew we were in trouble. Clouds had come rushing over and a sleety rain started when there was about an hour of daylight left. To save weight I had no torch, so even a straight retreat down the road would not be welcome. We needed shelter. A vicious front going through would not be very pleasant on top of the hills while coffined for ten hours in an orange poly-bag.

Less than two miles off I knew of a hut (not on the map) — but it might be locked — while, in the opposite direction, lay a building (on the map) which I'd never seen and feared could just be a ruin. We chose the latter, however, and after struggling up to Mholach's big cairn descended with the rain now sheeting across the hills. (The forecast had said "scattered showers" or something equally innocuous.) "Even if there's a gable standing, at least that would shelter us from the worst of the punishment," I muttered. "It's all your fault anyway, dog, wanting to do the Corbetts!" The building remained invisible till the last moment. But it was a building. And it was open. A most welcome howff.

The rain lashed down all night and on into Sunday morning. There was a certain smugness in standing at the window watching a parcel of deer splashing across the flooded glen. When the rain eventually gave up, so, perforce, did we. A retreat was made back to Annat.

Aonaich Mhoir was shortly after earmarked for a canoeing trip to Benalder Cottage, and Beinn Bheoil set down as our Munro for the "Boots Across Scotland" charity attempt on scaling all the Munros simultaneously. Anything to avoid the long tarred road in from Bridge of Ericht.

Loch Ericht is a strange water and stories persist that there was once an inhabited valley where now we have the loch. The loch is dammed at both ends and when the engineers were working on the dam at the Dalwhinnie end they found evidence of an ancient outflow to the

Truim. Some catastrophe is supposed to have occurred and the ancient parish of Sgireadail was overwhelmed and the loch's outflow changed to the Rannoch end. Off Aonaich Mhoir a fisherman, pulling in his boat's anchor, hauled up a small gravestone inscribed, "Elspet Robertson. Died 1545."

In the summer of 1802 James Hogg, the Ettrick Shepherd, wrote to Sir Walter Scott, from Dalnacardoch, of a sortie through by Loch Garry to Rannoch and back by a peak to the south east of Loch Ericht. He could have climbed one or other or even both these Corbetts. He found a ptarmigan which "fled fluttering to wile us away from her young" so he must have been high. Ben Arlenich (Alder) with remnants of snow was much commented on. He could pick out the far Ochils and eastwards the view "was lost and bewildered amongst the vast ranges that surround the utmost limits of the Bruar and Dee . . . every time the fatigued eye wanders through them they remind one exactly of the billows of the ocean; such a prodigious extent of country is crowded with them, rising and swelling behind one another, and that which the eye fixeth on always appears the largest."

The choices have not changed much since Hogg's day — you enter this "prodigious extent of country" by Annat or Bridge of Ericht on the Rannoch side or through by Loch Garry from the A9. The eight miles of Hydro road from Bridge of Ericht is the one I'd recommend — to my enemies. Sixteen miles of hard road is not my idea of fun.

Section 6:   4. BEINN A' CHUALLAICH   892 m   OS 42   684618
              Hill of the herding

Beinn a' Chuallaich is the huge but unobtrusive sprawl of hill above Kinloch Rannoch, a spur of which, Creag Varr, so dominates the village. In bad weather the Allt Mor draining the huge western corrie of the hill can also be a dominant feature for, then, it roars down through the woods into the village. This corrie could well be responsible for the name of the hill. It is a huge, gentle hollow which would be the perfect place for summer grazing or for secreting cattle for safety.

Creag Varr was the nearest climbing crag to our school's Black Wood bothy but we never went on to the hill after a climb; I made an ascent some years later when Corbetts began to be a specific interest. I found Chuallaich to be a hill well worth exploring, even if my first visit, on a May afternoon, gave sleet, rain and clouds on top. I parked the car on the road from Kinloch to Trinafour and went straight up, certainly the quickest route as quite a height has been gained even before starting. A few words of warning, though.

There are additional plantings along the southern and eastern flanks so any starting point should utilise one of the paths shown. The most easterly path (over Meall na Moine) is just outside the planted area and is now the best start (706615). This path leads by a hidden hut to a gate in the deer fence. All the streams are captured by an aqueduct, which explains the horizontal line across the hillside. The water is being led along over to the Errochty scheme. By chance a traverse of Chuallaich was my last hill-birthday-outing, a summer tradition I've always tried to maintain. If you are only likely to climb the hill once, then our route is what I'd recommend.

I drove up to the high point and dumped my folding cycle in the bracken, then drove down to park in Kinloch Rannoch itself. We set off up the Allt Mor, up the fall in a literal sense. There was not much water coming down and plenty of slabby rock to scramble on. The rock was a bit too greasy, however, and when we reached the water supply intake we followed a path up the west bank. The zigzags on the map are now an estate road which wends on above the trees to turn east across the Allt Mor above a dyke which runs towards Craig Varr's northern end. There is a footbridge (rather rotten) across the river not far above the wood which could be useful if the burn was in spate. We merely followed the burn.

The woods with the falls (really a long waterslide) had been windless, giving sweaty progress so the breeze on the heathery moors of the Allt Mor corrie was welcomed. There was an extraordinary lack of wild life. Even the hill flowers were past, except for the heather which was just tinting into flower — still pastel tones rather than the garish acrylite to come. Clouds were break dancing out of the west and rolling along the Carn Mairg hills. The burn ran in a slabby slot, its banks providing the first blaeberry feast of the year. I never tire of following streams up into the hills. My first solitary explorations followed them in the Valley of the Thousand Hills in Natal and moving waters have never lost their allure for me. Three days before, I'd been in Edinburgh for the launch of the sumptuous book, *Waterfalls of Scotland*. It lists over 750 falls. Perhaps here is a new list for tickers, something for after the Munros and Corbetts and Donalds and Bridges and Walls and Wainwrights . . .

We eventually followed a side stream and gained the heights north of Creagan Breac. The mass of Beinn a' Chuallaich appeared ahead and then vanished under a tide of cloud. With the good path to Loch Errochty crossed, there was only one wee pull and suddenly, through the murk, loomed trig and cairn. The cairn is a colossal erection for the quartzy rock is perfect for building. Indeed every bump round the corrie coming up seemed to have a "stone man" on it. We sat out of the tearing wind and our patience was rewarded after half an hour when the cloud ripped off and the view was displayed.

"The view is particularly good owing to the long stretches of low country which surround it in most directions, the Cairngorms appearing to special advantage; while on the neck of the NE spur lies Loch a' Caillich where the deer love to wallow." So wrote Charles Plumb in *Walking in the Grampians*, 1935, a book which still retains the freshness of its descriptions and points to an amazingly different world from the one we know. Loch Errochty had not been raised by its dam, then, for instance.

Schiehallion can't have changed, though. It dominates Loch Rannoch and the Tummel valley in unique fashion. Ben Vrackie and the Farragons rose in stark, dark shapes such as D. Y. Cameron loved to paint. The Gaick Pass (with Loch an Duin held between its Corbetts) is one feature to capture the eye. Nearer lie some vast moors, tawny and brown, leading away to Rannoch Moor. With Tony, on one occasion, and Sandy and Claudia on another, I've twice crossed that empty quarter on Ultimate Challenges, on the former going from Loch Ericht to Loch Errochty to the Bruar, on the latter to Kinloch and Blair Atholl. Beinn a' Chuallaich diverted us, north and south in turn, with all the assurance of a super tanker running into a regatta of dinghy sailors. God bless Beinn a' Chuallaich and all who climb on her. It was a satisfying birthday summit.

The view westwards brought back the words of the song: "By Tummel and Loch Rannoch and Lochaber I will go . . . By Ailort and by Morar to the sea." At Braehead school this had inspired a class project on the Road to the Isles, and, as a climax, we trekked the route outlined in the song. The song's origins are local — Marjory Kennedy Fraser's folks came from Tummelside. The tune had been composed by a pipe major and carried various military names as it made its way in the world of piping. A Barra man, Calum Johnson, learnt it from an island tinker and in turn played it on his chanter at a gathering in the Frasers' house. Kenneth M'Leod was, there and then, urged to write words to this splendid tramping tune and so, by Tummel and Loch Rannoch, the generations have gone.

On my birthday visit our route off, due east, ran into more quartzy crags than the map indicates (best turned by first descending south for a quarter of a mile, then off down to the east). There is a lonely corrie hidden up in the sweep of ridge to Meall nan Eun. A crow was croaking above us and we disturbed a mountain blackbird (ring ouzel) and a family of young wheatears — which hints at the bouldery nature of parts of the descent. There was a pipit or two, and a curlew drifting by on its wailing song. I don't know why the ascent route had been so devoid of life. Best of all, when I was retrieving my bike out of hiding, I came on a slow-worm sunning itself on a bank: still and glossy as a sculpture cast in bronze.

A derelict wall was being worked over by the wheatears. Farragon's cone and triple-topped Meall Tairneachan changed colours and weathers in rapid succession. All the showers seemed to keep south of the Rannoch–Tummel valley. We had it dry. The Meall na Moine path angled down to a gate which we were glad to use — and so back to the road.

Minutes later we were whizzing down the brae on the bike, Storm smirking over my shoulder from the rucksack. He dives into the rucksack with the happy expectation of a town dog jumping into a car. Children's faces grinned out the back of the cars that overtook us and, as I dismounted in the village, I noticed the car behind had a ciné camera trained on us. With the bike on board I promptly drove back up to where we'd been and on round to the old Wade road up from Tummel bridge where I parked and waited a fruitless hour for a photograph of our hill. The hill was clear but flat and lifeless under grey skies. While waiting I filled a dixie with blaeberries. I may not have had a birthday cake but Mary's blaeberry pie, once home, was a far nicer end to the birthday hill.

Section 6: 5. MEALL NA LEITREACH 775 m OS 42 639703
          Hill of slopes

Section 6: 6. THE SOW OF ATHOLL 803 m OS 42 624741

In 1729 General Wade rode up in his carriage from a "hut" at Dalnacardoch to a site opposite Loch Garry where his 500 Highwaymen, as he called his road-building soldiers, had prepared a feast. "We dined in a tent pitched for that purpose; the Beef was excellent and we had plenty of Bumpers." They'd built 52 miles of road that year and the line of that route is still generally followed by the A9 through the Pass of Drumochter today. If you park near Dalnaspidal Lodge for these Corbetts, wander up the Allt Coire Mhic-sith a bit, you'll find the ruins of this bridge: "Oxbridge" as it was called.

Dalnaspidal is *the field of the hospice* and was obviously a long-established stop for drovers and travellers coming south from Speyside through by Loch Garry to Rannochside. In 1863 Telford's protégé, Mitchell (after years of bureaucratic fighting), saw his Perth–Inverness railway opened. On the Drumochter county march and watershed, at over 1,500 feet, it is the highest mainline railway in

Britain. The new dual carriageway now tends to speed travellers through at twice the speed of seeing anything, which is a pity. Drumochter is an impressive pass and perhaps the best view of it is from the slopes of Meall na Leitreach. Both it and the Sow of Atholl can be climbed conveniently from Dalnaspidal.

I had Leitreach on a crisp, windy March day, setting off from Dalnaspidal and following a very boggy track straight up the lower slopes, a track made by one of the then new go-anywhere tracked vehicles. I was soon above the freezing level and hard snow made an easy ascent; there is less than 400 m to climb. There were deer everywhere and a plover wailing on the summit with its fine view of shapely Schiehallion, rising darkly out of a world of shivery silver tones and blowing a long plume of spindrift across the sky.

Drumochter, from this ascent, is an impressive pass, its depths an incredible jumble of moraines like frozen waves on a torrent, thrown into sharp relief by slanting sun and drifted snow. The intrusive rail–road–pylon lines shrink into their real scale: small works of men. There were deer everywhere when I slid down a gully and walked along a trod above Loch Garry. A parcel of stags splashed across the loch's outflow and the valley echoed to the various calls of spring wading birds. The wind picked up dervishes of snow which danced ahead and suddenly vanished. Anne Murray in a poem has the phrase "where the wind skins Drumochter" and it can certainly blow with flencing ferocity. A friend once combined Leitreach with Mholach (6:3) but had an escapade crossing the stream moating Leitreach opposite — so be warned.

That March day I went on to climb the Boar of Badenoch rather than the Sow of Atholl, being more interested in a botanical rarity than anything else. The Sow is the only site in Scotland for a heather whose normal home is in Norway. I didn't find it on the Boar. Even turning the Sow into a Corbett has not helped with my search. Both Boar and Sow are old friends. The Sow can easily be added to a round of the four Munros west of Drumochter; starting at Dalnaspidal on the south slopes for the Sow and Sgairneach Mhor removes the problem of crossing the Allt Coire Dhomhain to the north.

Torc is the Gaelic for boar and Badenoch is the name of the country to the north. The Sow of Atholl is probably a more recent fanciful name, the pass's watershed being the march between Atholl and Badenoch. The Sow is really Meall an Dobhrachan, *watercress hill*. Both Boar and Sow have steep flanks to Drumochter and it is worth going to the edge to be able to gain the view into the pass. What history it must have seen: Montrose, Argyll, Cromwell, Clavers-house, Johnny Cope, Jacobites and Hanoverians, the clansmen of

Atholl, Speyside and the west, drovers and packmen, Queen Victoria (incognito), the navvies and Hydro workers, right up to the modern juggernauts, stagecoaches and weekenders wending up to Aviemore and Cairngorm.

Driving southwards from Dalnaspidal keep an eye open to the left for Wade's Stone, a monolith set back near the Allt na Stalcair. This has a date, 1729, on it and commemorates where the northward and southward gangs of soldier-navvies met when building the Drumochter road. It was moved during the latest road improvements. I'd rather like to have seen Drumochter before man came here at all; however, these Corbetts give the next best impression of Scotland's Khyber.

Section 6:   7. The Fara   911 m   OS 42   598844
Presumably *faradh*, ladder

The *SMC Journal*, all six foot of it on a shelf, is a mammoth source for all sorts of hill information but when I looked up its indices, to see what anyone said about The Fara, the name did not occur. This is quite extraordinary for The Fara is a big Corbett which is often climbed on its own merit and not just for ticking off on a list.

The Fara is a hill I've been up five times — on four occasions traversing it during coast-to-coast or other long tramps. Loch Ericht is a bit of a barrier to trans-Scotland routes and you are forced up to Dalwhinnie to reach the A9. After a few times walking the road by Loch Ericht *anything* is a welcome alternative — even traversing The Fara! Quite a few Ultimate Challengers have done just that and been pleasantly surprised by the hill. The Fara is nothing much to look at but the view from the summit is one of the very best in Scotland, while there is also the unusual feature of the Dirc Mhor.

The first time I just ambled up and back from Dalwhinnie having dropped off some friends to blitz Munros east of the A9, but even that easiest of lines is no longer practical thanks to a band of conifer planting which runs from Loch Erichtside to the top of the old Wade road to Laggan (the A889). The easiest route is now to walk down Loch Ericht for a mile and then up the edge of the old plantings which leads on straight to the summit. Even doing that I'd recommend making a circuit to take in the Dirc Mhor and return by the Allt an t-Sluic, forestry or no.

The Dirc Mhor is a boulder-filled slot, hemmed in by crags, silent and dry, a weird spot which I found while walking from Ardnamurchan to Buchan Ness, the widest crossing of Scotland. It was a low-level alternative but has been first choice since. On that grey day it was quite atmospheric and I remember a joyous meeting with the gush of water below the cut where we sat among the birches for a brew. *Dirc* is dirk, the highlander's big dagger, an apt name for this stab-wound of a feature. A good path leads from the River Pattack road up by the Allt Beinn Eilde to finish in a wide basin, west of The Fara, whence an easy wander up the hillside leads to the Dirc Mhor, and a longer, easy wander up leads to The Fara's summit. Whichever side one climbs The Fara there is always a second view suddenly revealed on reaching the summit crest.

The Fara is a long undulating crest, and on another coast-to-coast, which was also linking Banachdich to Mount Keen (west-most and east-most Munros) I took to the slopes above Loch Pattack, making for Meall Cruaidh the first summit, and then relishing the $2\frac{1}{2}$ mile crest to The Fara summit. On the way up I kept taking photos of the Ben Alder hills and it was curious to see them "shrink" as we walked the miles to The Fara. On top the view to the Spey and the Cairngorms was added.

There is a huge cairn on top of The Fara. A wall leaves it, dropping east, and the last time up there, on UC 86, Chris, Tony and I were glad of its shelter: though it was sunny, for the first time in a week, a bitter wind was blowing and snow showers were trailing across the sky. Chunks of ice were blown off the cairn as we sat in the lee with the inevitable brews. On the path up the Allt Beinn Eilde we had found a half-full two-litre bottle of a "well known soft drink", which had been a welcome refreshment too. We left it as it had been left for us. Heading to Culra from a winter traverse I once found a loaf of bread on the path, which was most welcome too, once it had defrosted from nature's deep freeze.

Dalwhinnie has become a bit of a backwater with the new A9 "passing by on the other side" but it is always a good stopping place on these long tramps. There is a shop, a transport café, a useful hotel and pleasant B & B. And there is The Fara, its very own mountain.

Section 6:   8. An Dun   827 m   OS 42   716802
                 The Fort

Section 6:   9. Craig an Loch   876 m   OS 42   735807
                 The cliff of the loch

The word Gaick comes from Gaig (Gaa-ik) meaning a cleft place, a good name for this deep gash that is an historical pass from Speyside to

Atholl. The steepest, wildest mile of the pass lies between these two Corbetts, with Loch an Duin filling the slit and leaving little room one feels for foot-passengers. So far the estate roads have funked this gap. The country boundary bisects peaks and loch and it is an eleven kilometre walk, mostly up an unsurfaced road, to reach the march — the easiest route to the Corbetts.

This is a private road, and one where a cycle could be used to great advantage, but the most pleasing ascent of these hills would be to take them in on a walk right through the Gaick Pass from Dalnacardoch to Tromie Bridge. (The Minigaig Pass shares the northern part of the Gaick, see 7:7.) Some friends and I started at opposite ends to walk the pass and we met at the memorial to the loss of Gaick for lunch and an exchange of car keys — one way of dealing with the car problem. My log at the time recorded the walk being a much more satisfying route than the more famous Corrieyairack which we'd done the day before; and with several visits to both since, I'd not change that opinion.

There is a plantation above Dalnacardoch (a government-built inn of 1774, on the site where Wade was based when building the road through Drumochter) but after that the going is rather bleak up the Edenoch Water to Stronphadruig Lodge, which stands in a rather battered plantation. In 1986 Tony and I were glad to use the shelter of an outhouse to make hot drinks and apple flakes after a gale-blown crossing from Dalwhinnie. An Dun was on our programme then, but, with miles to go and a big wetting due, we left An Dun and descended off Vinegar Hill.

From Stronphadruig, An Dun looks like a colossal, natural *dun*, or fort mound. Where the estate road is shown finishing below An Dun there is a dam on the river, and this captured water flows through the pass and then is tunnelled to Loch Cuaich and so on to Loch Ericht, Rannoch, Tummel and the rest — an amazing re-use of a liquid asset. We stupidly crossed there and so had to paddle over to the abandoned lodge. After our refreshments we traversed a boggier stretch up to the col due east of the lodge (the building up the slope is a water-supply shed) to reach the Glas Choire, but by turning north Craig an Loch is easily ascended. *The cliff of the loch* is followed to a distant bare plateau summit with two cairns. The name is really A' Chaoirnich. The best way off is to the north west, for the whole west flank is a mass of scree, reminiscent of the Pass of Brander.

Loch an Duin's outflow is usually a safe crossing place (a good swimming strand too) and the burn on the hillside gives eyes and feet a feature, which helps relieve the mind for the steep toil up on to An Dun. Its cairn is at the south end of the elongated flat summit area.

Due west is the least brutal way off but it is quicker to head due south. An Dun gives a steep descent in any direction, but on reasonable grass.

The Gaick path passes along the west of Loch an Duin then swaps over to become an estate road again by Loch Bhrodain. Unlike Lot's wife, indulge freely in looking back to the steep vee formed by the Corbetts. Gaick Lodge is situated on the flats before Loch an t-Seilich and just north of it is the monument to the "Black Officer" and his companions who were swept away in an avalanche in 1800. Captain John MacPherson was a hated recruiting officer, so local sentiment soon spun myths round the story. The steep contours of the slopes and the plateaux above create avalanche conditions very readily and there are several records of massive disasters. One huge avalanche poured down when the locals were near starvation point and deposited at their doors 6 stags, 6 brace of grouse, 3 brace of ptarmigan, 20 hares, 1 snipe and a white horse!

Section 6:   10. MEALLACH MHOR   769 m   OS 35/43   777909
             The big hump

Section 6:   11. CARN DEARG MOR   857 m   OS 35/43   824912

These two Corbetts are both on Sheet 35 but for practical purposes Sheet 43 is also needed and possibly the NE corner of Sheet 42. They stand in a pleasant bit of the country which is rather neglected as it lies so close to the bigger Cairngorms. This is to the Corbett-collector's benefit and I've often noted these hills smiling and sunny while, just a few miles to the east, the Glen Feshie Munros were having their faces washed.

The area is riddled with footpaths and bulldozed tracks, as it is prime sporting estate country. This is a disadvantage for some months of the year but a great gain for the rest of the time — deep heather is not the gentlest of walking surfaces. It also gives a huge variety of possible routes for the clutch of Corbetts in this dark corner of Scotland. Leathad an Taobhain (7:7) can be done easily enough on a round with these two; I managed the three together in mid-December, starting at first light and cycling from Tromie Bridge up the estate road to the path junction beyond Bhran Cottage.

I dumped the bike and walked along the left fork to the weir on the Allt Bhran then followed the path on the north bank of this river. The path swings steadily south (path and stream junctions are right on the edge of Sheets 42 and 43 so call for a bit of care) and finally flanks up the eastern slopes of Coire Bhran to the pass of The Minigaig. This is an old drovers' route and the featureless crossing is made at *c.* 830 m (see under 7:7). The Corbett lies less than two kilometres away to the north east and is the nameless, solitary trig point, 912, the list name being hijacked from the lower western top. Here is the sort of place to take people who do not believe Scotland has any "wide open spaces". The bowl of the upper Feshie is an extraordinary "Empty Quarter" and the eye is led away through by the Geldie to the Deeside hills.

A track runs northwards from the Corbett, and on the next bump, Meall an Uillt Chreagaich, it has been bulldozed into an estate road. A snow storm caught me there, and as I followed the road in and out the folds of hill my port side became white. The snow went off as I rounded into the deep "sneck" of the pass that holds Lochan an t-Sluic, a blue eye that reflected the great plateau country above Coire Garbhlach — and the ugly bulldozed track up to those heights. A left fork, rather than going down the pass, leads up and then along above a plantation (which is right across the old footpath) and a stalkers' path continues up on to the saddle between the Carn Deargs. I zigzagged up through blowing clouds, meeting a large posse of stags near the col. The wind was cold enough for the dog to curl up in the snow when I stopped at the presumed summit of Carn Dearg Mor. Kitchy helpfully sniffed along our track so, rather than take hands out of warm pockets to navigate over Carn Dearg, I let him lead me down the zigzags to the road — giving the stags another surprise. The dog was white with hoar, as were my beard and my woolly garments.

The track ran along above a second plantation and then swung down northwards through a pass, which was just below the freezing cloud level. A shot rang out away to the north, probably a keeper culling hinds. A grouse going off was much more startling. A straight western walk over a lower bump, Meall an Dubh-chadha, led to the bigger lump of Meallach Mhor, allowing navigation to be fairly casual. Going into the icy blast I was thankful not to need intricate navigation. We hardly broke step for the Corbett and then romped down the burnt patches in the heather out of the murk of cloud into the cloudier murk of dusk. As my cycle lamp died on me the run out was much more exciting than the walking.

Without always going up summits, I've criss-crossed most of the paths in this area and they are all clear and often very useful. One alternative, for this pair of Corbetts, would be to start at Achlean, the end of the public road up Glen Feshie, and walk up the glen, crossing to take the track up by Lochan an t-Sluic and returning to Glen Feshie by the Feith Mhor. And what about a big day, perhaps based up Glen Feshie, walking up past the Eidart to take in Carn Ealar, Beinn Bhreac, Leathad an Taobhain and Carn Dearg Mor? The Ring of Feshie.

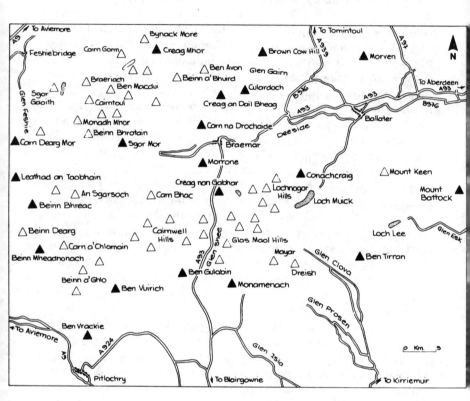

ATHOLL, GLEN FESHIE, GLEN SHEE, DEESIDE

Section 7: 1. BEN VRACKIE (BEN-Y-VRACKIE) 841 m OS
43/52 951632 *The speckled hill*

WE WERE A gang of young lads camping at Blair Castle when Ben
Vrackie, in 1956, became my second Corbett, not that I knew
anything of Munros or Corbetts in those days. One climbed, like any
young animal, for the uncontemplative freedom of fitness and
strength. Birds can spread wings; we earthbound creatures seek the
heights. The view is the same.

Ben Vrackie is very much Pitlochry's local hill, and one of the best
views of the hill is from Pitlochry's Festival Theatre with its sylvan
setting by the River Tummel. They are difficult to separate in my
memories and the one can be a pleasant sequel to the other. As a
teenage schoolboy I cycled from my home under the Ochils to make
some show, and the director showed me backstage and treated me to a
meal. I slept in a haystack that night and was home for church parade.
Later, as a teacher, a bus-load and a car-load of us went to see *Hamlet*
and slept out in the heather afterwards up on the slopes of Ben
Vrackie. You can sometimes twin your enthusiasms.

From any high point on the A924 road from Pitlochry to
Kirkmichael you can tramp across the heather moors to Vrackie,
rough going but with the odd sheep track to help. The view from the
summit is tremendous, especially westwards along the Tummel–
Rannoch trench to distant Rannoch Moor and its hills. Beinn a' Ghlo
looms large and, southwards, there is a good view of the Lowland
hills. There is a view indicator to help the visitor unravel the extensive
panorama, a memorial to the Leys School, Cambridge, which was
evacuated to the Atholl Palace Hotel during the war. The materials for
the indicator were carried up by donkey.

The knobbly, craggy, heathery world of the moors and tops is a
stark contrast to the wooded richness of the lower slopes, and to enjoy
Ben Vrackie fully it should be climbed from either Pitlochry or
Moulin or, at least, a descent made to the valley to complete a traverse
from any other starting point. From Pitlochry you can walk up Golf
Course Road to Moulin or you can drive up to this attractive and very
historic village where the path up Ben Vrackie is well signposted.
After a drive up a lane to a car park the walking starts through birch
and pine woods and heads by Loch a' Choire to the final rough
triangle of hill, the screes and crags being passed on the right. The

summit mass is an unusual lava issue in a world of schisty rocks. Ben Vuirich, the Corbett to the north east, just too distant to combine with Vrackie, is granite. Another route is to go or return via Craigower which overlooks the splendid woodland scenery of the Pass of Killiecrankie. You can also follow the burn up from Killiecrankie hamlet towards Loch a' Choire, skirting the crags to the left. This was the route taken by our gang of lads from Blair Atholl.

When I took Storm up recently by the "tourist route" we had a day of tearing wind and dancing snowflakes but the view south had a marvellous clarity. On the slope above the trees a bench gave a comfortable resting place to look down the Tay's gunbarrel view to the twin paps of the Lomonds in Fife. A plaque on the bench read "Terence Toole RAAF 1947–72" and curiosity had me ringing Hugh Campbell, an expert on Pitlochry lore, to find out more. He told me the Tooles came from Perth (Scotland) and often walked up Ben Vrackie; when their son, who had joined the Royal Australian Air Force, was killed in a road accident in Australia, they placed this bench here as a memorial. There was an odd sequel a few winters ago. An estate worker went up to feed the hill sheep and his tractor slipped on the ice. The tractor — and driver — were saved by the vehicle's slide being stopped by the bench.

Section 7: 2. BEN VUIRICH 903 m OS 43 997700
 The hill of roaring (stags?) (voor-ich)

Ben Vuirich is an unobtrusive Corbett and is probably one of the least-climbed hills of its size in Scotland but, as with some shy people, the hill improves with acquaintance. Those drawn by the Henry Moore shapes of Beinn a' Ghlo look over Vuirich from its Munros, when spying out the country to the south; motorists going from Pitlochry to Kirkmichael half-glimpse it when they look north from Glen Brerachan. Perhaps a Henry Moore sculpture on top would be a lure — it would be a worthy setting.

In the very first *SMC Journal* (1891) there is a brief note about Ben Vuirich by Sir Hugh Munro.

Thursday 22 January. Left Blair Atholl 9.10, a glorious day — hard frost, snow on the ground but a tearing wind, to avoid which followed Fender Burn until S and E of Carn Liath when, 10.40, left road and ascended the lee side to the summit, 12 noon. Sun but the wind raised the snow in spiral columns several hundred feet, penetrating everything, filling pockets, and drifting between my waistcoat and shirt, where it melted and then froze into a solid wedge of ice. I have never suffered so from cold. . . . The descent, like the ascent, was steep, and only practicable because of the soft snow. Crossed burn (Allt Coire Lagain) 1 p.m. and easy going to Loch Valican and Ben Vuroch, 2,961 feet, at 3.20, Glen Fernach at 5 p.m. and Dirnanean, two miles before Kirkmichael, at 6.30. Heavy walking all day in soft snow. At Dirnanean they had to scrape me down with a knife to get the frozen snow off me before I could enter the house.

Sir Hugh describes the good view from Vuirich: to the Cairnwell, Tulaichean and Beinn a' Ghlo ranges, but it is another character of those days, in the third volume of the *SMC Journal*, who writes about something some people never learn. Alex Inkson M'Connochie: "The summit of Ben Vuroch is flattish and bare . . . an hour spent there [July] but little to be seen. A happy thought struck us, and a slight descent was made, and then beautiful Glen Fearnach was visible for miles. An excellent view was also got of Beinn a' Ghlo and Loch Loch from a slender eight-foot cairn five minutes down in a northerly direction." On flat summits it is always worth a perambulation round the perimeter as well as freezing or broiling at the viewless summit cairn. It was the view, though, over Loch Loch that I recall from a visit many years ago. More recently, with Tony on UC 86, we had no view at all, when we climbed it more in desperation than delight.

That was the 1986 monsoon crossing, when we'd abandoned our plateau-route by the Tarf to the Cairnwell and Lochnagar, and had escaped south out of the hills east of Drumochter, enjoyed a coffee break at Bruar, a bar-lunch at Blair Atholl and taken the familiar road up to Loch Moraig (a black-headed gulls' Bedlam) and on under the near-perfect cone of Carn Liath. Being a Sunday we met a constant stream of walkers heading home from their punishment on the Beinn a' Ghlo Munros.

Vuirich could be added to the Ghlo Munros for a big but bearable day, which is what I'd once done, after cycling in up the Glen Fearnach estate road. Cars can be taken as far as Loch Moraig on the Blair Atholl side, and of course Ben Vuirich can be climbed from the south, but the moors north of Glen Brerachan are heathery-foul and the going is rough and craggy and altogether a toil. The Ghlo-side is the least *pénible*.

Rather than go all the way round by Shinagag, Tony and I cut the corner, paddled over the Allt Coire Lagain and followed the intermittent path to the bealach (585 m). An estate road is picked up just over the crest of the pass and this flanks along a knobbly spur before dropping down into Glen Loch. Here we left our packs and cut through towards Vuirich. We made a sweeping dip round and across the valley-head on to the flank of Vuirich. After ten days of rain it was a very wet slope but every now and then we found brilliant carpets of purple saxifrage. Tony found a grouse nest with ten eggs — and did the same on Monamenach the next day. The wind blew us up; on the descent we had to fight into it as well as sleety rain. We were rather tired at the end of an eleven hour day but with ten Munros done, Vuirich and Monamenach surely could be added, despite the daily deluge, to give us our twelve for a High Level crossing. So, perforce, Vuirich was done, a two-hour diversion at the supper-end of day.

The only glimpse of a view we had was of Loch Valigan, a grey touch on the dark moors. Had we been car-based at Loch Moraig the loch would have been visited either going to or coming from Vuirich. It would make a secretive camp in that crying emptiness. Ben Vuirich may be unobtrusive but it has the common magic of all mountains.

## Section 7:	3. BEN GULABIN	806 m	OS 43	101722
Hill of the curlew (or whimbrel) or Hill of the beak

This was the last of Charles's three days of liberty one holiday weekend and I can only raise my hat to his dedicated enthusiasm. I'd been quite happy to dander up one hill each day and then do a variety of other things (I've too many interests) but Charles knocked off two, three, and three Corbetts and drove back to Sheffield at the end of his day on Creag nan Gabhar, Ben Gulabin and Monamenach. Such dedication is either admirable or reprehensible — I'm not sure which. To be fair I did not hesitate to egg him on. Time and distance force such a dedication. I'd been through that mill myself. The benefit of having already done all the Corbetts was in relishing a real respite from pressure. I'd eaten my cake and was quietly having it again. Charles was just slaving in the bakehouse.

We had been camping on the Braemar side of the pass, so before driving south over the Cairnwell Charles had bagged Creag nan Gabhar. Though it was mid-August, the car windows were milky with frost. It had been a cold night in the tent with only a summer sleeping bag. We chose the easy way up Gulabin — which is the Glen Shee side.

Ben Gulabin looks its finest as one reaches the Spittal of Glen Shee from the south. It rises above a green corner, beyond the old hump-backed bridge and a cluster of buildings, in a series of steep steps, and that direct route up was one I made the first time. It was hard work. The easier approach is to go up the glen a bit and attack the hill from behind. There is a path shown slanting up from the road to the col behind Gulabin. This is an estate-type road and parking at its foot is neither safe nor welcome if someone wants to drive up. Half a mile further on there is a large layby with a stile to the slopes of the Corbett, the best starting spot — though road improvements may change the situation.

Charles and I angled across to join the burn, which we followed up beside or in this flow. It was banked with an extravagance of flowers. A dipper exploded from under a bank and thereby betrayed the presence of its nest. Storm suddenly jumped on to a tussock of grass and grabbed a field mouse. The burn led up to the track which we took, and then abandoned to go over and inspect the old ski hut. It was in the last stages of decay and a gale will soon blow it to bits, which will be the end of another odd howff. The forlorn posts of ski tows go up on both sides — all that is left of one of the original ski sites in Scotland.

We crossed the dip to continue up our burn: a grassy course through a hillside of clawing heather. The footage was hardly noticed for we *ate* our way up, guzzling handfuls of sweet blaeberries until the burn ended — or started rather — in a sphagnum pool not far from the dip between Gulabin and the Top that appears highest from the Spittal side.

The summit cairn lay in an extensive flatness and I walked its rim taking a series of pictures. The Corbett is a commanding viewpoint. The road could be seen sweeping up out of Glen Shee to the Cairnwell and Glas Maol and Creag Leacach lay beyond. Carn a' Gheoidh (Munro) was not nearly so outstanding as Carn Bhinnein (its Top). Glas Tulaichean lorded it in the west, the big corrie towards us. The Beinn a' Ghlo hills lay beyond the ridge across Glen Lochsie. The highest point of that ridge (Meall Uaine) used to be a Corbett, one of those to have been lost in the new mapping as failing to keep the 500-foot separation. The car radio had reported a Test Match abandoned and the south of England having force 10 gales and torrential rain, yet we lay by the cairn for a good half hour in shirt sleeves, enjoying the sun and shadow play as the great glowing clouds tumbled about the sky.

Coire Shith lay beyond the col joining our hill to the bigger country beyond. I don't think the name is referring to skiers, it is much older. Glen Shee is the Glen of the Fairies and a very old pass for us earthbound creatures. "Spittal" is hospital or hospice in olden times, a tradition carried on by the hotel. The Celtic story of Diarmid and the boar is set in the Glen Shee hills. The romance of Diarmid and Grainne is one of the most deep-rooted legends, and Diarmid's end and Finn MacCool's part in it is usually set on Ben Gulban (Ben Bulben) in the west of Ireland. The legends came with the Celtic invaders and now have Scottish settings.

It is worth wandering round the graveyard beside the old bridge, there are some well preserved eighteenth-century stones, one for a climber avalanched in the Alps. Behind the church there is a standing stone on a knoll, proving the site very ancient. Gulabin Lodge (Dundee Ski Club) has been a "hospice" to us on a couple of Ultimate Challenges. You can't help liking an area after accumulating memories.

We ambled down more or less as we'd come. Charles still had Monamenach to go, *en route* to Sheffield, and I had to return to Fife and then drive to Speyside. After a snack by the cars we went our ways.

Section 7:   4. MONAMENACH   807 m   OS 43   176707
          Middle hill

A bothy under Ben Vuirich is probably not the commonest starting point for Monamenach, but then Tony and I had our reasons. We were doing a high-level version of UC 86, and Ben Vuirich had left us with one Munro or Corbett to go. We had already been driven south by nine days of atrocious weather and were quite happy to forgo the Cairnwell–Lochnagar heights as long as we picked up one more peak. Monamenach was the tempting solution. After that we could spend the night at Kirkton of Glenisla and reach the coast in a day and a half.

Perforce we were away early and eleven o'clock found us enjoying coffee and toasted cheese sandwiches in the Spittal of Glenshee Hotel with several other Challenger friends. I phoned for a forecast and wished I hadn't — another vigorous depression was heading our way. We headed off fast. The first name on the map was hardly an encouragement: Tomb.

Monamenach is probably most often climbed by people driving to Auchavan at the head of Glenisla and then following the path up to the south of the final cone, a whole mile and a half and 1,300 feet of ascent. The hill deserves better and, if a tame driver can be organised, the walk from the Spittal has much to recommend it, even if it starts by Tomb.

Pleasant tracks lead along Glen Shee to the farm, Westerton of Runavey. In May the lambing was not long over and the fields were noisy with the new mutton intake, and a pair of piping oystercatchers were beating the bounds. We turned up a lane which ambled on over empty moors where grouse butts were the only sign of man. We

paused for a drink at a stream and, looking away up its course, could
see the scree-capped crest of Creag Leacach. Monamenach lay up a
valley ahead, Gleann Carnach, a big cone of almost symmetrical
contour lines. The track sidles across to pull up into the glen. To the
right lay Loch Beanie and a more direct pass down to Glenisla. Tony
and I had taken that route on a Challenge five years earlier. One of the
joys of that event is the endless variety of routes possible, not only in
outline but in detail. Having walked round every side of the hill and up
and down it by several routes I began to feel I know Monamenach a
bit. Perhaps the biggest insult a hill can have at the feet of a walker is a
single visit. Time alone I suppose excuses us. We can't repeat
everything however much we'd like to.

The previous time up Gleann Carnach had been with Sandy and
Claudia in 1984. We had found a gush of water in the upper glen, after
the track had ended, and had brewed there. I led Tony to the same
spot. We brewed and had a dish of apple flakes, then swung up to the
peat-gashed col. With the girls I'd rushed down the snow-edged burn
to Tulchan Lodge and on over Mayar and Dreish to Glen Doll; with
Tony, Monamenach would ensure our high-level route. We left our
rucksacks on the col and followed a derelict fence up to the summit.
You could have heard our yells of glee in Montrose.

Chuntering back to the col, we contoured round Monamenach on
mixed ground with plenty of peat to drop down to the burn draining
to Auchavan. Curlews and peewits were proclaiming spring and the
first lamb triplets of the crossing proclaimed the agricultural richness
of the east. We crossed to the east bank of the River Isla and the hour of
walking down its green roads to Little Forter were a lush contrast to
the barren summits. I'd suggest having one's tame driver waiting
there rather than at Auchavan, for those three miles of Glenisla are too
good to miss. The rest down to Kirkton I'd rather forget. Blistered
feet and nappy rash had me waddling like a duck. Kirkside House
made up for much, with a bath, dinner and a dram working wonders.
We'd managed to put in 22 miles doing Monamenach.

A more sensible round is to park at Dalvanie in Glenisla and go up
Glen Beanie and climb, in succession, Craigenloch Hill, Monamenach
and Creagan Caise, returning to Dalvanie; or park at Auchavan, climb
Monamenach from the south, drop to the col of our ascent and
descend to Tulchan Lodge, walking back down the Isla. Monamenach
is worth a clear day. It has a good view to the Caenlochan heights and
depths, and the view to the Lowlands is an unusual one.

Section 7: 5. BEINN MHEADHONACH 901 m OS 43 880758
Middle hill

The hill is wedged between two Munros and can conveniently be added to them on a long day's tramp from Glen Tilt. The road up Glen Tilt is private for vehicles, but permission is usually granted to drive up outwith the stalking season (contact the Factor, Atholl Estates, see p. 7). Beinn Bhreac (7:6) could be added to a walk to Mheadhonach but is described separately.

Ours was a dusty road when we drove up one May to camp near Marble Lodge. From there we climbed Carn a' Chlamain, then made the long bog-walk to Beinn Dearg (a massive pile of granite boulders) and took in Beinn Mheadhonach on the way "home", a harder day than map miles might indicate. On a winter attempt at these three, deep powder so slowed us that we had to escape down the Diridh Glen in the dark, missing Mheadhonach. Given really good snow cover this country offers some of the best ski-touring, and with that aid I've done all four Ring of Tarf Munros in a day easily enough. Weather and conditions decide so much in areas like this where there is a great deal of peat bog.

Dotterel and golden plover were calling among the hags as we wended over from Beinn Dearg. The Tarf country is a fair imitation of Arctic tundra. This aptly named Middle hill is a wedge of ridge bounded by Gleann Diridh (*glen of the wood*) to the west and Gleann Mhairc (*glen of the horse*) to the east, these streams then joining and dropping into the River Tilt. Both streams rise far north of the Corbett (Loch Mhairc is almost on the Tarf) which thrusts out south in what Dr Johnson would call "a considerable protuberance". The Diridh–Mhairc waters reach the Tilt half way between Gilberts Bridge and the bridge of Marble Lodge, and either can be used for access. On this occasion we angled down from the summit into the Allt Mhairc, which was full of deer, to exit round to our camp near Marble Lodge. The bridge shown on the Diridh–Mhairc river, just up from the Tilt, looks odd and isolated on the map as well as on the ground. There is no road.

> "There were mountains, of course, and a stream that leapt
> Rioting under the old stone bridge."
>
> (D. Fraser: Flamenco)

I find it a sad spot: the vivid green, the villages of tumbled stones, the shivering birch trees — and a sturdy bridge that has not seen wheels for a century. All this rich limestone area was cleared for "sport" in the bad old days. A great stir was caused in the 1840s when the Duke of Atholl lost a court case following his attempt to stop access to Glen Tilt, an obvious, historical right-of-way.

Queen Victoria rode through Glen Tilt to Deeside and wrote cheerfully in her journal about the "beautiful scenery", yet just seventy-five years earlier Thomas Pennant thought the pass "the most dangerous and the most horrible" he'd ever travelled. Between these two came the evolution of the general appreciation of scenery to which we are heirs.

Section 7: 6. BEINN BHREAC 912 m OS 43 868821
 Speckled hill (vrek)

This remote summit is one of the more inaccessible Corbetts, and the third highest. It is probably wise to include it with other Munros and/or Corbetts and not find it needing a special expedition later on. Beinn Bhreac is not a very distinguished shape and, being rather crowded by bigger hills, is not much of a viewpoint. There is some Beinn Dearg-like granite on top.

Any time I've visited this Corbett, I've been staying at the Tarf Bothy. Bhreac lies on a natural-enough route from Carn Ealar to Beinn Dearg if doing the Ring of Tarf but is not so convenient for a day expedition. Strong walkers could add it to the round mentioned under Beinn Mheadhonach (7:5) or just combine it with that Corbett, or add it to Beinn Dearg. One possibility would be to take in Leathad an Taobhain (7:7) and Beinn Bhreac (and Beinn Dearg) as a deviation from traversing the Minigaig Pass. There is no quick and easy route to the Speckled Hill.

The least strenuous would be to combine it simply with Beinn Mheadhonach. The flanking valleys of Mheadhonach, in their upper, near-level reaches, are a mass of peat hags; the going is therefore slow and "slaistery". Loch Mhairc nevertheless is a place of character. One could visualise the Tarf catching its waters in a few thousand years. I've seen foxes there on several occasions. I've walked across the loch when it was frozen solid. Late winter is quite a good option, for the frozen bogs then give easier walking than during the months of rain-enriched summer stew. A longer walk, but much on tracks, would be to reach Beinn Bhreac from the Glen Bruar side, over or round Beinn Dearg. The Feshie–Geldie approaches in the north are remote and give wet going, but could be shortened by using a push bike. Beinn Bhreac, one way or another, will demand quite a push.

Section 7:   7. LEATHAD AN TAOBHAIN   912 m   OS 43 (and possibly
              35/42   822858
              Slope of the rafters (Lay-at-an-Tayvin)

This Corbett lies less than a hundred metres above the summit of the
Minigaig Pass and can easily be included on a walk over that famous
old route from Speyside to Atholl. The pass is mentioned in the
sixteenth century and was, until into the nineteenth, a major drovers'
road. It pre-dates Wade's A9 line through Drumochter and was far
more important than the Gaick. Considering that the pass rises to
2,745 feet (*c.* 830 m) and must have been winter- or storm-bound for
months on end, one can only admire the hardiness of its users. From
Tromie Bridge (near Kingussie and Ruthven Barracks) to Blair Atholl
is 41 km (25 miles), a good day's tramp: a classic route. The Corbett is
a bonus.

An estate road runs up Glen Tromie and on to Gaick Lodge but we
take the branch turning left to a small weir on the Allt Bhran and then
on by the path on the north bank (adder country) which is the
Minigaig line. There is an unfortunate junction of rivers and paths
right on the join of map sheets 42 and 43 but, leaving 42 the path keeps
swinging southwards (the fork going northwards to the trees should
be ignored) by the stream and finally flanks up the eastern slopes of
Coire Bhran. In droving days the cattle were often gathered in this
corrie and driven over the pass in a huge herd. The summit of the pass
is just a dip in a rolling wasteland of peat rather than any definite
feature, and as it is just before the county boundary this line on the
map can be usefully copied into compass bearings to reach the Corbett
if the cloud is down, as it often is. Leathad an Taobhain is not strictly
the Corbett but the 902-m western top of two, the higher, 912,
nameless eastern one being the desired objective.

On my one visit to this watershed Corbett, after ascending by the
Minigaig, I headed back northwards to pick up the estate track on
Meall an Uillt. This leads on to Lochan an t-Sluic from whence I
traversed Carn Dearg Mor (6:11) and Meallach Mhor (6:10) back to
Tromie Bridge, a rare 3-Corbetts-in-a-day round, described under
those hills. The Minigaig undulates southwards (quartz cairns on the
upper slopes) to become an estate road again at the Bruar Water. This
is forsaken at Bruar Lodge for the original way on to the Allt
Schiecheachain bothy and then estate road again all the way to Old
Blair, the original hamlet behind Blair Castle. It is one of the great
classic trails and as such highly recommended as the excuse for the
Corbett, or *vice versa*. Adam Watson's *The Cairngorms* (SMC district

guide) has a good summary of this and other mounth passes, as has Robert Smith's book *Grampian Ways*.

Section 7:   8. SGOR MOR (Glen Dee)   813 m   OS 43   006914
          The big peak

Sgor Mor was one of several peaks "bagged" in a week of dashing about the wilds hiding food parcels for the journey on foot over all the Munros. I cycled up to White Bridge and then up the new estate road to the west of the Dee as far as the Allt Garbh, where the churned up granite boulders on the road verge made an excellent hiding place for a parcel of food, films, maps and so on. We then climbed Carn Cloich-mhuilinn, Beinn Bhrotain and Monadh Mhor and, as a bit of an afterthought, added Sgor Mor. This entailed two paddles across the River Dee and a hillside I described as "messy": not a way I'd really recommend, even for those in a Corbett of a hurry.

Charles, from Sheffield, had been teasing away at the Corbett list on every long weekend, so it was with some diffidence I agreed to join him for the August Bank Holiday on which he intended to do a demolition job on Section Seven. We made a rendezvous at a camping spot on the Cairnwell, and next morning set off on push bikes from the car park near the Linn of Dee, Sgor Mor the objective. The Linn was tame from dry weather but did not appeal as a swimming spot. Menlove Edwards once swam down it. The poet Byron very nearly fell into it, which would have lost the world the chance of Patey's parody on Byron's Black Lochnagar.

This time we pedalled up to Derry Lodge and, as many parts of the road had been newly spread with sand and gravel, this was hard work and not infrequently our wheels sank right in and we'd tumble off our mounts. Storm, on foot, had an easier passage. Derry Lodge is rapidly decaying and the famous bothy at Luibeg had recently burnt down (now rebuilt). Luibeg has never been the same since the late Bob Scott ruled there, a keeper of great character. We used the bikes as far as practical up Glen Luibeg and then dumped them in the heather. Without cycles it is perhaps easiest to start at the Linn of Dee and head uphill when clear of the forest, to reach Sgor Dubh: good walking once the lower levels of clawing heather are passed.

There was a constant stream of walkers on the path for the Lairig Ghru (and one suspects its bordering Munros). We boulder-hopped over the Luibeg Burn easily so did not need to divert upstream to the footbridge. A bit before the pass to the Lairig Ghru we slanted off to the Allt Preas nam Meirleach where we enjoyed a snack by its rush of clear water. Cairngorm water has a clarity and freshness that it is hard to equal. Golden saxifrage was colouring the edge of the stream and the slopes were purple hazed with the heather in bloom — another Deeside speciality.

As we wandered over the easy-angled moor I noticed there was an unusual quantity of dwarf birch among the heather, a pretty tree which grows only a few inches tall. We skirted the knoll of Creagan nan Gabhar and drifted up Sgor Mor's final rise with a keen north wind helping us along, a good approach for the sudden doubling of the view on arrival. We could look up the winding Geldie to Beinn a' Ghlo, and the western Cairngorms were well displayed. Being too chilly to linger we had a snack in lee of one of the rocky outcrops and chuntered down more directly, picking up and following the Allt a' Choire Dhuibh to the Luibeg Burn. The heather became deeper and rougher as we went. There were some big clumps of bluebells (harebells) on the river shingles.

To avoid some bog we shoved our cycles over the burn to Luibeg and picked up the road there. Storm was a bit weary and went in my rucksack for most of the run home; his head stuck out over my shoulder, grinning back at all the surprised looks we received from pedestrians. Charles shot off ahead — it was his turn for producing tea. He then drove off to Braemar and took in Morrone, alone, while I later went up Glen Clunie to meet him on the other side of his second Corbett. We dined and listened to Beethoven under a shock of stars and were snug in bed before the frost glittered the tent.

Section 7:   9. CREAG NAN GABHAR   834 m   OS 43   154841
           Goats crag (gower)

Creag nan Gabhar must be one of the easiest of Corbetts; it therefore tends to be done *en passant*, in a hurry, fleeing to or from Braemar, probably in bad weather. The hill deserves more considerate treatment than that (I have sinned myself) so when a recent "raid" was rewarded I felt I'd gained undeserved merit. I didn't think I was going to be given anything.

My Friday night run up the A93 came to a halt above Bridge of Cally. Weeks of gales and rain had Novembered their way across Scotland and December limped in on metaphorical (meteorological) crutches. When I found I was slithering and scrabbling on black ice under a sheen of stars, I gave in gracefully and spent the night in the next layby. I am much more afraid of driving and cars than I am of walking or climbing on the hills.

8   The Island of Rhum with its two Corbetts – Ainshval and Askival – seen from
Gallanaich on the island of Muck.

19   The summit rocks of the Cobbler with Ben Lomond in the distance.

20   A northern Corbett: Ben Loyal seen across Loch Hakel.

21 The ridge on the wilder side of Fuar Tholl, a bold peak above Achnashellach.

22 Meall a'Bhuachaille, a Speyside Corbett, a few miles east of Aviemore.

23 Talla reservoir, below the slopes of Broad Law.

24 Beinn a'Chaisteil above Auch, one of a group of five Corbetts.

25   Beinn na h-Eaglaise and Beinn Sgritheall.

26   The Farragons, viewed up Strathtay, Perthshire.

27 (*right*) Beinn Airidh Charr seen across the Fionn Loch, from the remote summit of A'Mhaighdean.

28 (*below*) Hamish and Storm at Invermallie with Bheinn Bhan behind.

29 (*left*) The Sgurr a' Mhuillin hills over Strath Bran, from near Achnasheen.

30 (*below*) Arkle, above Loch Stack, with the waters torn into the air by the wind.

31   Ben Gulabin above the Spittal of Glenshee.

32   Cul Mor, seen from the hamlet of Elphin.

I had a miserable night — my sleeping bag was inadequate for such cold. The water in the dixie, ready for tea in bed first thing, froze over. No gritter had gone past, or any other traffic. I had a late departure. During the short drive over the Cairnwell the weather changed four times: the sun shone, freezing mist rolled in, it rained and then snowed higher up.

I parked near the AA telephone box and headed east on the Bealach Buidhe path. There was a dusting of snow and the dog went wild with delight as he always does on the first winter walk: rolling about and racing in circles and finally hurling himself into my arms to give my freezing nose a lick. The main road vanished quickly and the friendly slopes embraced us familiarly. The path goes up a deep heathery gash into the hills with the burn flowing cheerily below. We found a well-chewed antler on the path and, on the flank of the Corbett, above the scree level, a herd of deer sped off, spraying the snow up from the heather.

After we'd crossed the burn we soon left the path (which is a bit overgrown anyway) and made directly up the hill, using the grassy runnels of burns or fire-cleared patches to avoid the deeper heather. The burns were a mass of ice, every dipping grass stem a shining sculpture, and the big bosses wobbling strangely as the water gurgled through below them. The clouds were down and it almost snowed.

Creag nan Gabhar has quite a collection of cairns on top. You can either claim one as the summit or build your own. After an inspection we cringed behind one for a "piece" and the finger-freezing task of inserting new batteries in the camera. The best of the view was across to Morrone. Wandering patches of sunshine in search of a climate were periodically lighting up the hill. The Cairngorms were glossy white but painted over with even whiter clouds. The knobbly hills beyond Glen Callater were much deeper in snow than the bigger hills south of us. These Cairnwell summits were all elephant-grey — a real pachydermatous herd of hills. The sun was glinting on something at Newbigging in Glen Clunie and there were odd colourful shapes which were a puzzle. I was too cold to change the telephoto lens for a spy but curiosity was suddenly satisfied — two hang gliders swung across the corrie below us. Corbett-bagging by hang glider, now that's an idea. The Sgor Mor across Glen Clunie used to be a Corbett, but the re-ascent is not 500 feet and it has been demoted.

We scampered back down more or less as we'd come, Storm taking great delight in discovering and sniffing along our up-track. At one stage he stopped abruptly and when I looked I saw dainty wild cat prints superimposed on my big boot marks. The beast had come on our trail, followed it for twenty yards, then carried on up the glen.

The wind had risen during our brief summit stay and went on rising even at valley level. I had a date in Braemar in the afternoon and I must admit it was pleasant to sit with a dram and look out on the deluge. The storm raged all night and the next day. Miles of upper Deeside flooded, and the Linn o' Dee was a fearsome spectacle of naked power. We had definitely had better than we deserved on our two-hour Corbett.

Section 7:   10. MORRONE   859 m   OS 43   132886
           The big nose (Mor-rone)

Morrone (I've never heard it called Morven) is very much Braemar's popular viewpoint, and with good reason: it commands a superlative view. From late August on into October is the best time for a visit which takes in an extravagant range of colours: of heather, green fields, dark woods, glinting rivers, fiery birch tints and the sweeping tint-on-tint of tumbling Cairngorm ridges and summits. I can't think of any other Corbett where you set out from a town, never mind one usefully sprawling at 1,000 feet. If you check the contours, though, you'll see the hill is a Corbett only by the odd foot or two.

Braemar is at a commanding meeting of routes which has ensured it a long and busy history. The first castle was built by Malcolm Canmore in 1059. The Earl of Mar raised the Jacobite standard for the Fifteen in Braemar. Stevenson wrote *Treasure Island* there while recovering from illness in 1881. The Braemar Gathering (first weekend in September) is world famous and always attended by the Royal Family who have their second home just down the road at Balmoral.

For Morrone, walk (or drive) up Chapel Brae to the car park shown on the map above Auchendryne. There is a pond beside it which acts as a reflecting pool — unless the ducks go paddling to wobble away the reflections in their wakes. Carry on along the road past Mountain Cottage, then swing left up through birch woods. Keep right of the fences and house. The road itself bears right (west) and at a fork take the left branch which goes up to the Deeside Field Club view indicator. Skirt the crags above this to the left and the path uphill thereafter is obvious. My favourite viewpoint is on the shoulder, once the angle of ascent has eased slightly, where there are several cairns lined up together. The view over "the waving outline of the distant hills" shows to best advantage from there. The angle continues to ease off up to the summit. The radio mast and buildings are part of an Aberdeen University research station, and the Braemar Mountain Rescue team has a relay station there as the reception is much better than down in Braemar at the Mountain Rescue Post. You can see why the reception is good: the view beams out to the huge panorama of the Cairngorms. The Corbetts north of Braemar can be examined with ulterior motives (Carn na Drochaide, Carn Liath, Culardoch) and with Sgor Mor and others edging the Ring of Tarf to the west and Creag nan Gobhar and Ben Gulabin to the south, Braemar is quite a useful centre for a profitable Corbett-blitz.

The descent can be made by the line of ascent or by going down the track south and then east. This track, built by the Mountain Rescuers, is fairly unobtrusive, unlike so many bulldozed tracks in the Cairngorms. A pleasant walk leads back along the road into Braemar, the main dangers of the day coming where the road passes through the middle of the golf course. Could hitting Corbetteers call for a penalty stroke?

Section 7:   11. CONACHCRAIG   865 m   OS 44   280865
            Jumble of rocks

This is another easy Corbett: most people start to walk at 400 m, at the Spittal of Glenmuick car park, which is reached by a pleasant drive up from Ballater. Conachcraig does not stand out, being a mere outlying spur of mighty Lochnagar but, looking as it does to that mountain on one side and out over Deeside to the other, it gives fair reward for minimal effort. My only regret is the eyesore of Lochnagar path and the bulldozed tracks that circle it, so obvious in a world of granite.

Conachcraig's summit bumps have plenty of granite boulders that probably account for the hill's name which, on the map, is given to the lowest, central bump, 850 m, while north is Caisteal na Caillich 862 m *the castle of the witch*. This northern top has the finest view, worth the little extra walk. Carn na Daimh, which catches the eye when motoring up Glen Muick, is *cairn of the stag*. There are usually some of these creatures living off tourist hand-outs round the Spittal.

Another route is to walk across to Allt na Giubhsaich and follow the big track to the col between the Corbett and the Meikle Pap of Lochnagar from which a very short ascent lands one on Conachcraig. There are alternatives, even if Lochnagar itself has already been done. One suggestion: walk round Loch Muick's south shore to reach the Glas-allt-Shiel (the lodge Queen Victoria built as a hideaway after Prince Albert's death) then go up the path by the Glas Allt waterfall to take the path that branches off right, rounding the Little Pap to gain the Meikle Pap–Conachcraig col. Conachcraig even looks good from this approach, and will reward a good walk rather than just a lack-lustre, list-ticking stroll. The northern approaches lie in the Balmoral estate and are best avoided in summer. Queen Victoria rode up Lochnagar more than once (as well as quite a few other big hills) and I've bumped into various members of the Royal Family up there, once being discovered playing with a wriggle of young adders.

Section 7: 12. BEN TIRRAN 896 m OS 44 373746
(Derivation unknown)

Ben Tirran is pronounced Ben Turran, which really goes better with Loch Wharral and some of the other guttural names hereabouts. The area is one that rings with splendid names: Burn of Slidderies, Wester Skuiley, Watery Knowe, Wolf Hill, Lair of Aldararie, The Witter, Many Wee, Potty Leadnar, Auld Darkney for starters, and that's on just one small bit of the map I've unfolded to look at Ben Tirran again. Strictly speaking Ben Tirran is the shoulder above Loch Wharral rather than the lonely 896-m trig point — which is the highest point on all this upland of bogs and braes north of Glen Clova.

I first went up Ben Tirran with a party of seven boys (on skis) and Kitchy the dog (who took a dim view of following skiers as they would not progress in straight lines). The hill is rock-free to the south, so a good one for novice skiers; but it was a tired party that finally descended to Rottal in the gloaming. The dog was tired too. A cheeky hare actually chased after him, cut across his bows, and sped ahead in mocking glee.

We were staying in the Carn Dearg Mountaineering Club's hut up at The Doll one March. That night six inches of snow fell and we had fun skiing down forestry tracks, at least till the tail-ender failed to take one corner, shot off the bend into the air and vanished down into the trees. There was a thud, and a tree promptly dropped its heavy burden of snow. The four-letter word that followed set the party hooting with delight. Even better was to come. Round the next bend a pine trunk lay across the road, invisible under the snow; teacher's skis went under it and the rest of me pitched over the top. Score: two bruised shins, one broken thumb, one staved thumb. Life without the use of thumbs is extraordinarily inconvenient. After a thaw, the weather banged off the big guns. We were snowed in with the ploughs taking several days to win through. Skis became a necessity: you couldn't manage on foot. We made the most of it and relished being late back, only the second time over twelve years of school trips.

My next visit to Ben Tirran was during an autumn coast-to-coast trip which took me from Loch Nevis to Montrose, and was one of the few times when I've been bodily heaved about by the wind. I've never experienced such a hurricane as I battled down to the Youth Hostel. A tree had probably fallen for the lights failed and we were issued with candles. The weather was still windy the next day when I was happy to climb up out of the glen to Carn Dearg and be blown along over Boustie Ley, the rim of Loch Brandy, Green Hill (far away?) to reach Ben Tirran's trig point. There are plenty of bogs but the walking is straightforward. Even in mist you can hardly fail to hit targets like the glacial corries of Loch Brandy and Loch Wharral. Coming from up the glen this would always be my choice of route — anything to avoid miles of tarmac.

That day I continued on by the Black Shank to the Shieling of Saughs (scribbled names on the ceiling go back to 1903) and out to Tarfside by Glen Effock. I stayed at the renowned Parsonage, being thoroughly spoiled by Gladys Guthrie who makes her home such a haven to walkers. I mention this because there are some superb backpacking tracks (old whisky-smuggling routes linking the glens) which run north-south rather than east-west and Tarfside is the only convenient B & B in Glen Esk. Several tracks head over to Deeside from Tarfside, and Mount Battock (7:13) is accessible, thus the walk could incorporate some Corbett-picking. Tirran and Battock are worth such a venture.

Ben Tirran was an UC 85 summit for Alison, Ian and myself, a bright and sunny morning to make three out of three good, if contrasting, days for this pleasant Corbett. We wandered up the path from the hotel to Loch Brandy, which was noisy with common gulls, and then traversed across to Loch Wharral. We hit the rim slightly too high so followed the Craigs round to Ben Tirran. With about seventeen others we luxuriated in The Parsonage that night before wandering on to the coast at St Cyrus.

The most recent visit, with Charles, gave good solid cloud on the tops which was a good test of navigation. We took the right-of-way up to pass right of Loch Brandy to Green Hill from where a long bearing led us, successfully, to the lochan just below the Corbett. Sheep loomed like elephants in the mist and vehicle tracks and cairned routes abounded, to mislead rather than help. The right-of-way is in fact cairned. From Green Hill it heads over point 857, White Hill, Muckle Cairn, etc., to descend to Loch Lee by the Shank of Inchgrundle — which is another tasty name.

The hotel at Clova welcomes walkers (there is a bunkhouse for the impecunious) and it is in many ways the best starting point if the best features, Loch Brandy and Loch Wharral, are to be seen. Lochnagar looks well from the summit and Mount Keen, for once, is more than a tiny cone on the Mounth plateau. All the tracks shown on the map exist on the ground. The one up from Weem has been bulldozed which rather spoils that line. The best buy is traversing from Clova to Tarfside.

Section 7:   13. MOUNT BATTOCK   778 m   OS 44/45   550844
              Possibly anglicised from *bad* (chump), *ag* (the diminu-
              tive) and Mount is from *monadh* (hill or moor)

Till recently I'd been up Mount Battock only once and that was with considerable haste as I wanted to visit a Stamp Fair in Dundee on the same day. I made up the Turret not long after six in the morning, near the back end of the year, on a clear but bitterly cold day. The fieldfare were working down as I went up and on the moors the many hares were already into "ermine", as were a belch of ptarmigan that flew past. My route used the bulldozed track up Hill of Turret and the Hill of Saughs but to escape the biting east wind I tumbled down by the White Burn. While brewing in the Dormobile a vicious storm left Mount Battock white, and in Glen Esk I had to shift a huge broken bough off the road. The early start, whatever its motives, had been a blessing.

I've just been up Battock again on a sparkling winter day when the mad March hares were blowing in drifts over the snow. With a night at The Parsonage beforehand, and a vast Indian meal at Forfar on the way back, Mary, Storm and I felt pleased with our 24 hours away from home.

There has been a proliferation of bulldozed tracks on a scale perhaps unequalled anywhere else and if the senses regret them the lazy body is only too glad to use them to dodge the area's peat bogs which are of a type that make Kinder a garden. In the first volume of the *Cairngorm Club Journal*, the January 1894 issue has an article on Mount Battock and Clachnaben which has this: "A fellow-member declares that the worst turn he could do his worst enemy would be to make him cross from Mount Battock to Clachnaben on a wet day." It is "really awful ground", of "abominable moss-haggs". The writer loved every minute of it; I'm sure he would be saddened to find Mount Battock and Clachnaben now largely linked by a bulldozed track. Some of the fun has gone. However, most tracks shy off Mount Battock itself; it still stands as an isolated dome that dominates the rump of the Mounth hills. The summit was one of the major stations used by the Ordnance Survey in mapping Scotland.

Mount Battock stands very much in the centre of radiating rivers which quickly cut deep valleys among the rounded heights. Some of these are short, the Turret and the Tennet flowing to Glen Esk, others are long, the Dye, the Aven, even the Feugh, which all head east and unite before entering the Dee at Banchory. Each of these valleys and each of the ridges between them is a potential route up Mount Battock.

The quickest and easiest ascent is the one I took, driving up to the Mill of Aucheen, then using the estate road up Hill of Turret. Coming back I'd swing south west and descend off Mount Een. Given more time and a tame driver I'd take that once fearsome stravaig eastwards to Clachnaben. It is not *stone of the hill* for nothing, the said "stone" being about 300 paces in girth and 30 m high. It is a famed landmark and a sort of Deeside totem. With no car to meet one, a round could be made from the B974 by going up Glen Dye and north or south of Cock Hill, reaching Mount Battock and returning via Clachnaben. The ruin of Spittal Cottage is the easiest start/finish.

One long, trackless tramp of character is to start at Tarfside (B & B at The Parsonage perhaps) and follow up Glen Tennet and down the Water of Aven to Feughside, with a diversion from the watershed to the Corbett which stands above the pass. Loch Tennet, illogically, is over the watershed and is the source of the Aven. The Aven is a long rocky ravine and the most impressive of all the "waters".

The Water of Feugh valley can be motored up to the Forest of Birse, a quiet forgotten glen with paths and roads going up every other hillside. These peter out on the boggy uplands but if you go on by one Cock Hill or another Cock Hill (and not the Cock Hill already mentioned) you will come to Mount Battock. You will have discovered something about peat country navigation. You will have a fresher appreciation of tracks and paths. Y'll hae clarty bits and be a wiser loon. And hae anither haund of unco names: Hill of Badymicks, Mudlee Bracks, Bonnyfleeces, Hen Hill, Lochnawean, Lamahip, Bogmore. . . .

Section 7:   14. CARN NA DROCHAIDE   818 m   OS 43   127938
Hill of the bridge (Droch-itsh)

The first visit to Carn na Drochaide came as a coda to an ascent of Beinn a' Bhuird and Ben Avon. We had climbed those two giants from the old camp site where the Lui joins the Dee and on the way back I left my gang of school kids to walk down the Quoich and prepare supper, while I "bagged" the Corbett, a game which was fairly new to me then. There was a winter later when Glen Quoich under some feet of snow was a magical place to camp in. Years and visits pass so quickly after each other but the quiet memories of beauty, peace and wholesomeness remain.

Quite the pleasantest day of a rather dreary August gave the most enjoyable ascent of Carn na Drochaide. It was the second day of Charles's August Bank Holiday blitz and we had kept this hill for the Sunday to avoid any clash with possible stalking or shooting activities. We took the familiar road out of Braemar for the Linn of Dee. Two miles on westwards there is the best distant view of the Corbett, nothing spectacular, a heather and scraggy uprising beyond the floodplains of Quoich and Dee, but very typical of the green and mauve bounds of Braemar. After the Linn of Dee the public road runs down the north side of the river and passes above the extravagant Victorian pile of Mar Lodge, hub of feudal upper Deeside, to finish at the Quoich Water. We parked in a quarried moraine where the martins had burrowed under the turf cornice and were swooping about devouring the early morning midges.

The Quoich Glen is made magnificent by a combination of water, trees and hills, and a good round walk is to go up it and through the peculiar Clais Fhearnaig gash (a continuation of the Glen Tilt fault) to Glen Lui where the river can be followed down to the Dee again. We set off up the east bank of the Quoich as the Corbett stands immediately above. The Linn of Quoich is a pretty narrowing of the river between cliffs and just beyond the footbridge above the gorge is the Punch Bowl (the "quoich" or "quaich"), a river-worn hole. Tradition has it that the Earl of Mar filled the bowl for the gathering of his followers at the start of the Fifteen. The river has now pierced a hole through the side of the bowl so its utility is lost.

There are some magnificent old Scots pines by the waterside, and ten minutes on from the Punch Bowl a path leads up and along the river-cut banks to give perhaps the best view of all: a glittering stretch of silver water and a fall, the whole held in the tree-green glen while above and beyond lie the brown and purple hills. We left the river and simply linked together useful deer paths through the heather, crossed the estate track and followed the curve of a shoulder up to Carn na Drochaide, leaving the corrie to our left. The heather grows progressively shorter with height gained and the final plateau is bouldery. Circuit on the edge of this flatness to gain the best of the view; at the cairn much of the view is cut off.

As there had been a snell north wind (a touch of frost even), the sun with that freshness had made the walk up a pleasure for August, a month so often cloudy and midgey and overfed with heat. Lochnagar lay in the eye of the sun but there was a big sweep of hills right round to Beinn a' Ghlo. Schiehallion's shape was a blue hulk beached on the horizon. Bhrotain—Cairn Toul—Derry Cairngorm—Beinn Bhreac — Beinn a' Bhuird — Ben Avon gave a fine sweep of Cairngorms while, forming an outer ring, all the Corbetts from far-west Leathad an Taobhain, to Sgor Mor, Morrone, Creag nan Gobhar, Carn Liath, Culardoch, right on to far-east Morven were visible. It was far too good a day to end there so Charles gathered his Corbett loins about him and set off for Carn Liath and Culardoch. I was delegated to drive round to Invercauld Bridge and have a brew and a beer awaiting his arrival.

Doing these three in a day is perfectly feasible. Invercauld is perhaps the best start/finish point if you have only one car, walking up the Slugain Glen, diverting for Drochaide, circuiting round on the path of Glen Gairn and over the identical heights of Carn Liath, up and down Culardoch, then out by the estate track to Invercauld. If doing Carn na Drochaide on its own, then the western flanks are the most kindly. Storm and I circuited back down them via Carn na Criche and then followed the stream of the western corrie. The breezy day so set the aspens quivering that they sounded like a waterfall. I pigged on the blaeberries growing on the aspen crag overhanging the burn. When we'd set off there had been one other car at the quarry. On our return there were thirty. An early start is an advantage on an August Bank Holiday.

Section 7:   15. Carn Liath (Creag an Dail Bheag or Creagan Dail Beag)   862 m   OS 43/36   158981
                Grey cairn (Wee crag of the pasture)

Section 7:   16. Culardoch   900 m   OS 43/36   193988
                Big back high place (Cul-aar-doch)

These two hills are defended by being remoter than the rest of the Deeside Corbetts but they amply repay any visit, for their remoteness compels one into a corner of sweeping vistas that is typical of the borders of the big Cairngorm mountains. Our local club approached them from the Gairn which allowed Ben Avon and Brown Cow Hill to be enjoyed as well, though enjoyment on Brown Cow was mostly retrospective.

I took everyone tea at 6 a.m. which is one sure way of ensuring people have to climb out of bed, and an hour and a bitty later we were off from the Luibeg camp site for the drive by Braemar, Invercauld, Crathie up to Glen Gairn, well to the east of the range. I had my bike to help with the long tramp in, but a stiff wind had me pushing up any rise. We still gained an hour. Kitchy found no difficulty in keeping up. Every now and then I went skidding on the frozen puddles. There must have been hundreds of crazy April hares jazzing about, some in scruffy cast-off winter garb, others handsome in summer "blue". There were deer and grouse, and the glen rang to the plaintive calling of golden plovers and other waders.

Corndavon Lodge was a ruin except for one big room in the west wing which was gaudily frescoed — it looked like a stage backcloth for *Brigadoon*. A hatstand stood in one corner. Trees and outhouses had all gone to ruin and there was a sad air about the place. A decade later I was to be glad enough of it, as you'll see in the Brown Cow days (7:17).

We were deep in the gleaming snowy mountains and had to deal with drifts on the road but we struggled on by the hidden lochans to Loch Builg. The loch was a brittle blue that soon broke under the wind to turn a surly grey. I pitched my tent in the lee of some ruins by the loch, and had an hour's respite before the foot-plodders arrived. We reached Ben Avon by Carn Dearg, with one heavy blatter of snow on the way and one more on the encrusted summit tor. Some of us had been blasted off Ben Avon back in February when camped up the Quoich; by comparison this was a satisfying success. It left me with just one Munro to go in winter conditions. The others arrived as I was leaving. They had full packs and camped that night at the Sneck, going out the next day to Deeside over Beinn a' Bhuird, while I added some Corbetts and picked them up on the way home.

The miles southwards were hard work and the descent to the upper Gairn a flounder in new snow. A cornice had fallen from the col. Deer in the glen foot were pawing up the vegetation. My log that day said we went "brutally up the slope as the easiest of choices: a thousand feet to the top of the double Corbett. Red outcrops, two cairns and a wall heading for Deeside. Lochnagar a magnificent winter spectacle. On each summit the other, in turn, looked higher. Cursed them both and dropped down the east ridge for a snack in the stable on the Bealach Dearg."

The Bealach Dearg (Red Pass) is the crux of an old right of way from Deeside to Tomintoul, and the easiest route to these Corbetts is up the southern track — which is described below. Now an estate road, it wends up on to the western shoulder of Culardoch (before twisting down to the River Gairn) leaving only the gleaming cone for a weary prod. The old dog curled up at every pause. What a pity I'd not tackled the Corbetts more seriously at an earlier date. He'd done two thirds of them but a heart attack a year later ended his life on the tops. We descended Culardoch's north ridge and at a vantage point stopped to eat the last morsels of food and photograph the silver-shine of Loch Builg below a sweep of curtaining snow. We descended to some old shielings (a superb camp site) and crossed a bridge to wander back to the lonely tent. It was 7.30 p.m. Curlews, a heron, grouse, black-headed gulls and drumming snipe were the last sounds I heard before taking an unbelayed tumble into sleep. For four hours I was unaware of anything, and then only too aware — but that is Brown Cow's story. It was a decade before I made the more usual ascent from the south.

Tony and I crossed south–north by the historic Bealach Dearg during UC 83 when we went from Braemar Youth Hostel by Loch Builg on to Cock Bridge and the Allergue Arms. This southern approach to these two hills is very pleasant. At Invercauld the old military bridge (1752) must be one of the most photographed in the country. Stabs of sunlight were flooding it. Lochnagar was very dark beyond. Pleasant parkland led behind Invercauld House of the Farquharson tribe, and was followed by a couple of miles of forest plantings west of Craig Leek and Meall Gorm where every clearing seemed to have a herd of spectator deer.

One story of the Farquharsons mentions the Bealach Dearg. The first chief attended kindly on the needs of a passing stranger and next day accompanied him a long distance on his way to show him the route over the pass. He later received a letter appointing him Royal Standard Bearer for Scotland, the reward of his visitor who had been the king. It proved a sad reward in the end for the recipient fell at the Battle of Pinkie.

Caulfeild considered the Bealach Dearg as a route north but thought it too difficult — so went round by the Lecht. In 1832 plans were again produced for a road but these too fell through.

We had another brew at the stable on the col after we'd climbed up Culardoch of the short-back-and-sides heather. The cloud chased us down and we sat listening to the grouse chuckling through the murk. A hare actually ran into the stable — but didn't stay for tea! By the time we reached the bridge on the Gairn the wind was raising sheets of spray off the river and by Loch Builg it began to snow hard. May can be like that. Isn't there an old saying "Cast nae cloot till May be oot"? Remember, this is the Arctic side of the Cairngorms: great country but to be treated with respect.

On UC 87 I traversed Beinn a' Bhuird and Ben Avon and descended to the Gairn for lunch before doing an anti-clockwise circuit over the Corbetts again. The north side is rather scarred with bulldozed tracks and paths (not all shown on the map) and the many ruins give the glen a touch of loneliness. One of the lochans by the Builg junction was a nesting site for black-headed gulls, *sturteig* in Gaelic, which is marvellously onomatopoeic. They were making a right sturteig. The three-day crossing took me from Aviemore to Ballater. The variations really are endless.

Section 7:   17. Brown Cow Hill   829 m   OS 36   221044

This links with what I've written on Culardoch, for Brown Cow was climbed from the same camp by Loch Builg after cycling in by the River Gairn track. Having been over Ben Avon, Carn Liath and Culardoch I slept the sleep of weary walkers — for four hours — and then woke up with a sense of unease to find there was a gale blowing, which was the end of peaceful sleep. Can they not invent a tent made of *silent* material?

At about 5 a.m. I started brewing but the cold, frosty night of stars was then swept away when it started snowing heavily. At the back of six I set off, anyway, with the dog in my rucksack and my belongings bundled on the bike's carrier inside a bivvy bag. The bike's gears were frozen solid — fortunately I'd left it in a low gear — and the wind bowled us along. At Corndavon we started up an estate road on foot but this was unpleasantly drifted so we just floundered over the heather in a direct line to the summit. Navigation had to be accurate: the hill is a vast dome with acres of flat ground on top. We hit it off all right and were rewarded with window-views to a dazzling Ben Avon and Lochnagar. Kitchy was complaining at the spindrift and cold which forced us to scamper down, on the same route but cutting corners and setting the hares charging off in all directions. The snow had stopped, the Gairn valley glittered and we bowled along with a tail wind. The only walk was the hill up from Daldownie to where the Dormobile had been left on the A939. Taking our luck we set off on the notorious Cock Bridge to Tomintoul road and added Carn Ealasaid (8:4) to the Corbett list before returning to Deeside to pick up the friends who had shared the camp at Loch Builg and then packed out over Ben Avon and Beinn a' Bhuird — Munro baggers all.

As a child I used to put up with one of those nasty chants kids inflict on each other. "How now Brown cow?" repeated endlessly could usually rouse me. I still don't know the source of this taunt but it gave me a feeling of affinity with the oddly named bump, a name which fascinated Queen Victoria on her treks through the valley surrounding it. Brown Cow Hill has invariably been generous to me.

Brown Cow Hill can equally well be climbed from the north, starting from Cock Bridge. There is a track south from Corgarff Castle which can be followed and the Corbett tackled from the east, or the River Don can be followed up and an approach made from the north. My recommended route for a day expedition would be Corgarff Castle, south to the col, traverse Brown Cow to the Gairn and return by Loch Builg, Inchrory on the Avon, and then east down the infant Don. The Avon at one time flowed eastwards on the course of the Don but another stream flowing northwards "captured" it, causing this peculiar right-angled bend and an empty pass eastwards. Charles Murray's "lythe Strathdon" thus lost most of its water through what is the country's finest example of river-capture.

Corgarff Castle is a stark tower surrounded by a star-shaped curtain wall — added in 1748 when Hanoverian troops were suppressing the last Jacobite hopes. Mar, Montrose and others used it on their campaigns. In 1571 the Gordons burnt it, and everyone inside (27 people) — a bloody history. The castle was garrisoned till 1831 but those last years were a check to whisky smuggling rather than potential rebellion.

Section 7: 18. Morven 871 m OS 37 377040
      The big hill

There are quite a few Morvens in Scotland — and they are all pleasing hills. Best of all perhaps is Morven in Caithness which does not even make Corbett altitude (but then neither do Suilven nor Stac Polly) while another Morven, which is more often seen than climbed, is this one set between the Dee and the Don. Wherever you climb, from the highest Cairngorms down to the eastern sea, Morven seems to be visible, an instantly recognisable cone, standing in bold isolation, on "the edge of cultivation", strangely aloof, strangely neglected, perhaps simply from always "being there", above the Howe o' Cromar.

Morven, my third Corbett, was done as an outing from a schoolboy camp at Ballater in 1957. I can recall the freshness of its windy miles but no topographical details. We found an adder, and when Tony and I traversed Morven on UC 81 we also saw an adder. Our camp site in Ballater was full of them. You could lie in the tent at night and hear them rustling in the hedgerow just outside. Beautiful creatures. Why they occupy some parts of the country and not others is a mystery.

Tony and I set off from the cheery Inn at Cock Bridge with the early sun picking out the newly painted walls of Corgarff Castle, dazzling white against the browns of heather. We took Caulfeild's military road south of the River Don, remembering the old youth hostel which was always so welcome after crossing the strenuous Lecht Road, and wended up to cross the modern road to Deeside at its steepest brae. A track led us to peat workings on Scaulac (741 m), then we walked east along the crest among a typical eastern exhibition of hares, to the huge jubilee cairn of Mona Gowan. Morven, three miles to the south east, was suddenly big and bulky. "Great, spacious walking" was how I described it. We dropped to the col and up to a minor western top where we left our ruckers to climb to the summit unencumbered. Three others arrived simultaneously from the east, the only people we encountered on the thirteen peaks we did on that May's coast-to-coast.

The eastern approach gives only 500 m of ascent from the A97 road which runs through the farmlands of the Howe o' Cromar, an oasis of chequered fields and woods surrounded by hills. The recumbent stone circle of Tomnaverie (488036) or the souterain at Culsh (505055) are two of my favourite viewpoints in the Howe: Morven at its best. Farm roads lead off the A97 and most have continuations up on to the hill, the easiest being by Roar Hill using the old track to the Gairn.

After retrieving our rucksacks we descended round and down Morven's southern slopes (grassy, with blaeberry and cloudberry in flower), crossed the Rashy Burn to pass by Roar Hill and angle down for the Howe. The lower slopes were rough and heathery; we were glad to use one of the farm tracks. I'd just said to Tony it was adder country when we came on a big fellow lying sunbathing at our feet. Morven is generally less heathery than other hills hereabouts but the grass can be tussocky though relieved by paths. A short length of tarred road was enough to make us glad to escape into the birch and water landscape of the Kinord NCC Reserve, passing north of Loch Kinord to see a Celtic cross before a delightful path led us into Dinnet for the night. Waders were noisy, "the scattering of curlew calls like raindrops from the source of spring", and kingcups shone golden in the sun.

Loch Kinord has a *crannog* (lake dwelling). The best feature of all I discovered only later or we certainly would have included it in our traverse of Morven–The Vat, as the OS translates it, an extraordinary rocky gorge carved by a long-diminished river, which drains off Culblean Hill into Loch Kinord. There is nothing else quite like it in the country.

Morven is easily reached by a variety of routes to the south, Ballater being a favourite tourist village. There are paths or estate tracks up the Rashy Burn or the Tullich Burn or by Craig of Prony — Peter's Hill — or from Larg in Glen Gairn up the Morven Burn — another old drovers' road, and also the route taken by Queen Victoria in 1859. She had a burnside picnic on the way, sketched and then continued on a pony which "being so fat, panted dreadfully". The queen knew her

Scotland and had ascended quite a few of the big hills: "such seas of mountains" as she called them. They walked down to the lunch stop, had tea at Morven Lodge and so home to Balmoral.

The Morven Burn valley is a huge basin with an eerie feeling of isolation. An estate road now goes up the Mona Gowan ridge behind the lodge to Glenfenzie and the A939. This is one of the few areas where we have only out-of-date First Series maps. Charles and I recently retraced the route Tony and I took. Charles had been up Brown Cow Hill and Storm had taken me up Earn Ealasaid when the rough miles in hot summer sun left us "gey drouthie". The only high water we found was the stream draining south east off Mona Gowan. An unusual *slochd* (gash) crossed that hill's eastern ridge. A fence runs all the way from Scraulac to the top of Morven. The unusual feature of that day was the silver-plated shine of Loch Muick set in the hills opposite.

The northern (Donside) approaches are less interesting and entail a bit too much forestry for my liking. The poet Byron wrote about "Morven of the snow" and described a temperature inversion on top. The snows will have to wait for next time — on skis perhaps. Mount Keen, Lochnagar, Ben Avon, far Beinn a' Ghlo, Bennachie, the east coast, Donside were all clear on my visits and in the far north, quite plain, was that other remarkable Morven, in Caithness.

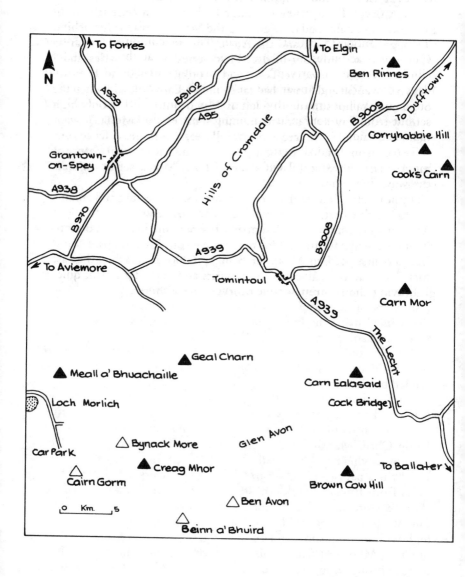

SPEYSIDE TO NORTH OF THE DON

Section 8:   1. CREAG MHOR   895 m   OS 36   057048
              The big crag

THIS IS A modest Corbett which can easily be combined with other Cairngorm activities — if one thinks about it at the time. I first climbed it when a party of us were making our exit from several days of wandering about the eastern hills, staying at the Shelter Stone and Faindouran bothy and climbing most hills between. We set out from Faindouran after a night of wind: gusts of 70 mph the radio had said.

Three of us headed west up the burn and were right on to the moors before the wind found us. We sat out one shower, watching the wavering white mass sweep away down the Caiplach towards Tomintoul, then had to batter into the blast to Dagrum. From there to the Corbett we walked with a marked list to starboard as we leant on the wind. The summit has typical granite outcrops with weatherworn potholes in them. Across the Lairig an Laoigh the Barns of Bynack can be seen, perhaps the oddest of all the granite tors.

Leaving the summit we were caught by a longer period of rain ("showers of a continuous nature" as I once heard the BBC say) that chilled us to the bone, and we were very glad to pick up the Lairig an Laoigh track and skirt Bynack More down to the stables where we could brew before walking out to Glenmore, by which time we'd been blown dry again. The Corbett can easily be ascended by those walking the classic Lairig an Laoigh.

On the ninth day of UC 81 Tony and I did a circuit of Creag Mhor and Bynack More before going on to Faindouran. We started from the Fords of Avon this time (reached from Kingussie via the Lairig Ghru, Macdhui and Loch Avon) so had only about 600 feet to climb, which is why I call Creag Mhor a modest Corbett. On UC 87 my partner managed to take *over four hours* for the easy five miles from Bynack Stables to the Fords of Avon — so I nipped up Bynack More and Creag Mhor and still had the tea ready before he caught up at the Fords. I'd also had a paddle in the chilly Avon, high with melting snow, for I had to take a boot off to remove a bit of Creag Mhor grit from inside a stocking. I don't like blisters. My partner brought up the topic of blisters and said whisky was supposed to be a good prevention — rubbed on the feet that is, rather than taken internally. One Challenger followed the advice: "I don't know if the whisky helped my blisters but it made my sleeping bag smell nice."

Section 8:   2. MEALL A' BHUACHAILLE   810 m   OS 36   991115
              The shepherd's hill (boo-a-chil)

The big northern corries of the Cairngorms steal the show when looking south from the Rothiemurchus–Glen More area but from anywhere *on* those giants the view to Loch Morlich and Speyside would be much poorer without the undulating sweep of heather-clad hills north of the Queen's forest. The highest, eastmost of these summits is Meall a' Bhuachaille above the Pass of Ryvoan (Rebhoan) — from which it is an easy walk.

Cars can be taken to just past Glenmore Lodge making the pass a quiet walk. Lochan Uaine (which can be all colours in the course of a day) lies in a hidden hollow in the steep vee of the pass among old Scots pines and juniper and blaeberries: Cairngorm scenery at its very best. A path runs up the hill from Ryvoan bothy (which is half a house). Ryvoan is the "Thieves' Pass", which recalls ancient raids by clansmen. Their route on by the Braes of Abernethy to Tomintoul is still a good walk.

I was once staying at Glenmore Lodge observing a rescue course. The day had started with a winter flight in a helicopter, through Ryvoan and up the Nethy to Loch Avon and west to return along the northern corries. (On a subsequent flight I was to be lowered, during a rescue, into an icy, floodlit Coire an Lochain, a magical experience.) Denis, the Youth Hostel warden, rang to say Lorna was staying at the hostel and would like a walk. Thus it was we set off through Ryvoan (still noisy with helicopter games) and went up Meall a' Bhuachaille from the bothy. Ben Rinnes to the north east looked a mirror-image of Schiehallion far to the south. This must be a view to one of the most tree-covered landscapes in Scotland. From the large cairn we dropped to the col westwards and turned down (a marked path) into the forest and out at the Reindeer House near the hostel.

Continuing west from the summit are Creagan Gorm (*blue little crag*) and Craiggowrie (*goat's crag*), which give a marvellous walk with views up and down the Spey and to the Cairngorms and Monadh Liath hills. They are cut off by the pass of An Slugan to the west and from this a forestry road can be taken out to the Coylum Bridge–Nethy Bridge road, or one can return to Glen More by taking the forest road through the Badaguish plantings. This crest traverse is one of the best walks in the area. My old dog did the traverse. Storm simply went up and down from Ryvoan — but that was a moonlight expedition to work off the effects of over-indulgence at the Ossian Hotel in Kincraig.

Section 8:   3. GEAL CHARN   821 m   OS 36   090127
            White hill (gyal chaarn)

As part of their Mountaineering Instructors' Certificate candidates being assessed at Glenmore Lodge had a day out on unknown hills where various skills could be quietly watched, navigation tested and, in casual conversation, attitudes and ideas drawn out by the examiner-cum-guinea-pig. Quite a few Corbetts within range of Glenmore Lodge are remote and rough, and were often issued as objectives to victims over the week. I'd name a peak the night before — this Geal Charn was nastily typical — and what we did, how, where and why, was up to the candidate. Geal Charn went to Joe, a lad from an Outdoor Centre in Northern Ireland, which had been bombed not long before.

Considering it was into October, the weather gave us such a grilling that the sweat running down my back was draining down my legs. We had a lift through the Ryvoan Pass to the fork in the road. The rest of the day was an endurance test over moor and bog with most of our energies going on searching for the next water-hole. In that bare, rounded landscape there was no escaping the sun. Deer, and there were scores, simply stood and let us pass rather than make any effort at flight. We went up the Lairig an Laoigh path from the Bynack Stable then angled over to An Lurg then Carn Tarsuinn and Bile Buidhe to reach Geal Charn. A trickle of water on its flank was a life saver. I don't suppose Joe could be held responsible for the conditions and he was new to the Cairngorms. We returned more or less as we'd come, cutting more directly down to Bynack Stable. The only other people we met were on the Lairig path. They were down to underpants and boots.

This route is not very interesting and gives a hard slog in any condition. The water of Caiplich, which moats the Corbett to the south, is notorious for leading people astray from the Lairig an Laoigh, and it is a long way downstream to the nearest touch of civilisation. An approach to Geal Charn from the Braes of Abernethy is preferable, starting either at Dorback Lodge (reached from Nethy Bridge) or even Bridge of Brown (the road to Tomintoul): either of these gives a pleasant walk.

From Dorback Lodge follow the estate road south eastwards to the watershed and then turn up for Geal Charn. Return westwards, skirting Bile Buidhe to pick up another estate road down by the Faesheallach Burn. Turn right at the T-junction and eventually abandon the road to strike through the craggy gap of the Eag Mhor (*big notch*) back down to the Braes of Abernethy. The day can be lengthened by walking over by the Burn of Brown and back by the Allt Iomadaidh. These northern outliers of the Cairngorms receive few visitors. The views north over Abernethy, the Hills of Cromdale and Ben Rinnes are open and the big Cairngorms loom to the south.

Section 8:   4. Carn Ealasaid   792 m   OS 36   228118
                 Elizabeth's hill

Carn Ealasaid is to Corbetts what the Cairnwell is to Munros: a hill rendered ridiculously easy by the presence of a high road — and also the unsightly presence of ski developments, not that there was much in the way of ski facilities on the Lecht when Sue and I visited Carn Ealasaid.

We had had a great overnight ski tour in the main Cairngorms and had driven west to Laggan hoping to ski up Creag Meagaidh but the weather was all wrong so we turned round and headed east. Of necessity we stopped at Landmark in Carr Bridge to buy maps of Lochnagar, our destination, but, determined to do something on skis, I suggested Carn Ealasaid, for we were taking the notorious Tomintoul–Cock Bridge road over the Lecht. As the top of the pass is 635 m there is not very much of Carn Ealasaid to climb.

A café and three rope tows marked the nascent ski centre. We skied off on skins up the slopes beside the tows, a bit doubtful as to finding the Corbett in the blowing cloud. We had no map beyond what I'd traced from a 20-year-old AA Road Book from the car. We were not too worried because, if we did end up at a loss, a course to the north east could only hit the A939.

A long rising traverse round the head of the glen of Camore Burn led to our hill. If the summer view (tones of brown and blue) had pleased before, the winter scene was as bright and sharp as a Brueghel painting. The skins came off and we made an even longer descending run round that valley. Having lost height we swapped again and skinned back up to the Dormobile. We had been away less than two hours. When Charles and I were Corbett-bagging in summer we camped on the Lecht's roadside verge in an attempt to catch a breeze and keep away the dreaded midges.

There is a pleasant high-level walk from Carn Ealasaid westwards to Craig Veann and the River Avon down to Tomintoul. A lift up to the Lecht to follow this route would be my recommended traverse of the Corbett. The north-south track that passes just west of Carn Ealasaid, from Blairnamarrow to upper Donside, is shown as a road on older maps. Between Blairnamarrow and the Well of the Lecht is a ruined cottage which hit the headlines in 1920, when it was used as a hiding place by Percy Toplis ("The Monocled Mutineer"). The wartime trickster was wanted in connection with a murder near Andover and took off northwards on his bike. When he lit a fire at Blairnamarrow someone saw the smoke and called the Tomintoul bobby. The two of them were shot at, when they approached, and Toplis escaped on his bicycle over the Lecht. (He was killed, some weeks later, in a shoot-out in the Lake District.)

Section 8: 5. CARN MOR   804 m   OS 37   265183
            The big cairn

Carn Mor is the rather self-effacing summit of the sprawling Ladder Hills. A mile and a half to the north east of the summit is the top of the Ladder Road, an old right of way from Glen Livet to Donside. The pass is still perhaps better known than the hills which, while dry and easy on the rolling summits, have a deal of peat bog on the cols and in the corries. A walk over the old road, with a diversion to Carn Mor, is highly recommended. The view down into Glen Livet is very attractive, being mixed farmland, still worked: flaunting greens and such a contrast to the brown waste-lands of most areas.

The Ladder path splits on the south side of the col with branches going down into Glen Nochty and Glen Buchat, both of which join the Don after a few miles. The former route passes the ruin of Duffdefiance just before the plantations begin. This odd name records a Glen Livet crofter who came over the Ladder and squatted here, in defiance of the proprietor, Duff. The Nochty joins the Don at Bellabeg where there is a striking *motte*, the Doune of Invernochty, which indicates the strategic importance of this junction over many centuries. Glen Buchat Castle guards the Buchat–Don confluence, a Gordon fortified tower of 1590.

Carn Mor can also be climbed very easily from the 638-m summit of the Lecht road, an expedition which is even better if made on skis. Though not giving such a starting-height, the Corbett can also be climbed from the car park at the Well of the Lecht. On the roadside a

tablet records that the Cock Bridge to Tomintoul road was built in
1754 by Lord Hay and the 33rd Regiment. (It is not a Wade road as is so
often stated.) Looking up the Conglass Burn a trim little building is in
view. This is all that is left of an ironstone mine opened by the York
Building Company who bought up estates after the Jacobite risings.
The ore was carried on pack ponies to Nethy Bridge, the nearest
plentiful wood supply, where it was smelted.

I once climbed Carn Mor by following the Conglass on beyond
the mine and then tackling the luxuriant heathery slopes up on to the
breezy tops, a day of constantly being startled by grouse and hares.
There were many black-headed gulls quartering the slopes, snowy
with cloudberry flowers, and the upper reaches rang with the
plaintive calls of erratic golden plovers. An early summer day of
sunshine made it a delightful dander and I wandered back to Carn
Liath before descending again. I collected ironstone samples before
returning to the car. Drinks were the first priority and I took my tea
to the burn and sat with my feet in the water while picking the
heather off my stockings.

The Conglass Glen is much easier in descent. Going up is a bit of a
heather flog. Charles and I, with two cars available, started on the
Lecht and followed the crest then backtracked a bit and charged down
into the glen. Several young deer calves went bouncing away as if on
springs, a much more efficient way of coping with the heather than
our stolid struggling or the dog's tired leaps.

Section 8:   6. COOK'S CAIRN   774 m   OS 37   299275

Section 8:   7. CORRYHABBIE HILL   781 m   OS 37   281289

These two hills gave me a smugly satisfying day. Thunderstorms at
Garve camp site led to all night rain. When it stopped at 10 a.m. I
departed down a congested A9 (bad old days) to Carr Bridge. A
cigarette thrown out a car window had set the moor alight and the
forest had burned for several days. Driving through the smoke was
like something from a war film. I went on by Granton, Cromdale,
Avon Bridge to Glen Livet. Basically I planned to cycle up by the River
Livet and tackle the Corbetts from the watershed. The time was 2.30
when I set off in a drizzle, but hoping the forecast of "brighter for early
evening" would be true. The drizzle soon ended.

After a stony brae up to Achdregnie farm the track descended again
and crossed to the south bank of the River Livet. I sat for a bit and
noted some unusual names on the map. What a gift for a novelist
they'd be: Shalg, Larryvarry, Urlar, Moniewhit, Crespet, Thunder-

slap, Ballintomb, Finnylost, Quirn. . . . The track was stony and grassy in turn and, past Suie, I took one "skite" in a gritty rut. The going became rougher and steeper so I dumped the cycle by the track and walked. From the watershed I followed the burn up (it disappeared occasionally) and arrived at the summit of Cook's Cairn just as the south wind blew away the last of the cloud. South of Cook's Cairn is the old right of way from Glen Livet to Cabrach, passing through Blackwater Forest and Dead Wife's Hillock.

I trundled down the line of some butts and up the other side of the pass for Corryhabbie Hill, preferring the cropped heather to the "road" which, low down, was deeply eroded and useless. The trig point was closely walled in, and there were nettles growing there. The weather looked black. I back-tracked at once. Before retrieving my cycle I found a cairn with a slab that had a crown and V.R. 1867 inscribed on it. Despite a loose cotter-pin the run back to the van was enjoyable. The kettle had just come to the boil when the heavens opened. But I was snug, with my mug, in the fug.

Hares were much in evidence all day. And silly sheep. I saw one fall into the river and another, startled by my approach, dashed off and ran into a hare, which shot off, too, and set a snipe careering up the glen. In all I saw a score of different birds.

These two hills could equally well be approached from the other side of the pass separating them: Glen Fiddich instead of Glen Livet, leaving the Dufftown–Rh nie A941 road at Bridgehaugh. A cycle would still be useful. There are about three miles to the sprawl of Glenfiddich Lodge where there is a choice: an estate road follows the Hill of Glenroads and then takes the long plateau-like NE Ridge up Corryhabbie Hill (this is "Morton's Way" on the map), or there is a footpath along the River Fiddich to the watershed. Up the road and down the burn would be my choice.

Map 36 is worth having for the Livet approaches while Map 28 is needed for the Fiddich route in. Corryhabbie Hill was an important survey station in the 1850 principal triangulation and was occupied for three months. Queen Victoria stayed a few days at Glenfiddich Lodge in 1867 (described in *More Leaves from the Journal of a Life in the Highlands*). She arrived in the early evening but her baggage did not arrive at all. She was not amused and at one o'clock made uncomfy alternative arrangements. One day she visited Auchindoun Castle and on another rode up the glen and over the watershed (hence the memorial). Auchindoun is a stark ruin. This was very unsettled country at one time. The Battle of Glenlivet (1594) and the Battle of Cromdale (1690) top and tail a brutal century.

Now Glen Livet and Glen Fiddich have friendlier associations. And the two Corbetts, not bad wee malts.

While working on this book I had a postcard from Jim Donaldson saying that Cook's Cairn had been "eliminated". The hill, I hasten to add, is still there. It is just no longer a Corbett, the dip to Cook's Cairn being under 500 feet.

Section 8:   8. BEN RINNES   840 m   OS 28   255355
              Headland hill (rinneis)

Ben Rinnes, being the most northerly of the North East's Corbetts, dominates the landscape for many miles around while its isolated position ensures a huge view north over the Laich o' Moray and across the Moray Firth to the hills of Caithness; south and west there is the wide arc of the Cairngorms, the Monadh Liath hills and the glens and bens beyond the Great Glen. Ben Nevis is visible on the western sea, as is Buchan Ness to the east. The River Spey wends below the hill. Dufftown lies only five miles to the north east and Rinnes is encompassed by motor roads yet it still manages to give a feeling of aloofness, rising as a bold cone above the patchwork fields of its lower slopes.

My only visit was a flying one, while travelling from Deeside to Speyside, and I spent longer in "Landmark" (Visitors' Centre) at Carr Bridge that evening than I did on Ben Rinnes. A minor road gains the maximum height possible at the end of the hill's east ridge (Glack Harness) and, with the intervening bump of Roy's Hill, the summit granite tor can be reached in an hour. The summit has the resounding name Scurran of Lochterlandoch and the name scurran (sgoran) is applied to two other tors. I ran most of the way back to the car but would recommend descending by the long, easy-angled NW Ridge to skirt the headstreams and then turn down by Baby's Hill to pick up a peat road to the distillery. Much of the hill peat has in fact been stripped off to fire the whisky stills.

In 1803, a Rev. James Hall bought a pony in Edinburgh and set off to explore Scotland. His account, all 622 pages of it, appeared in 1807. Hidden therein is note of an ascent of Ben Rinnes. He carried a barometer. On the way up he was cold, hungry and lost in the mist. Out of the cloud loomed fearsome beasts: a "phalanx of wedders . . . one in the middle having a pair of tremendous horns". When the mist cleared he recorded "a secret enjoyment, a calm satisfaction and religious fervour which no language can express".

And a good meal when safely down again. This is a very early account of a hill being climbed, for fun, and behind the ageing language there are obviously the same feelings and experiences we enjoy today.

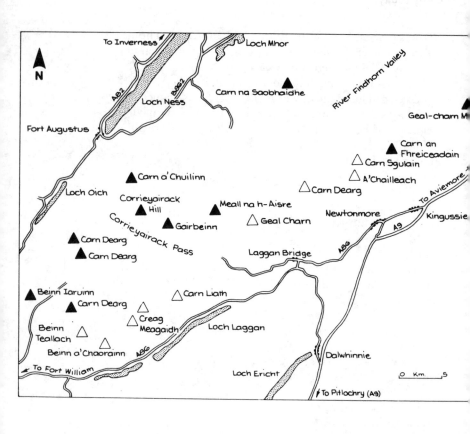

GLEN ROY & THE MONADH LIATH

Section 9: 1. BEINN IARUINN *c.*800 m OS 34 296900
Iron hill

ROBERT SOUTHEY, WHO toured Scotland with Thomas Telford in 1819, considered Glen Roy the best glen he had seen in the country. Happily it has Corbetts but no Munros.

The first time I went up Beinn Iaruinn it rained — after a beguiling blue sky had lured me upwards. But Kent was being battered by gales and floods. The second time I went up Beinn Iaruinn it hailed on me at regular half-hour intervals (ambushing bursts of fire out of the north) which was quite painful even with a cagoule hood up. Storm did not like the hail at all and tried to climb under me as I cringed wherever possible on a rather exposed mountain. "Mountain" is probably a rather flattering term for this unpronounceable Corbett.

Unlike green Carn Dearg on the other side of Glen Roy the slopes of Iaruinn are heathery and bouldery as well as steep. There is no reasonable easy way up so there is something to be said for following a short, sharp route rather than looking for extra miles and smiles. Coire nan Eun is my choice, inveterate burn-follower that I am. The easiest line keeps to the slopes on the north side of the corrie burn, just wandering up the heather and screes to the rough plateau and along to the summit — a bit tame and lacking any interest.

I'd parked where the burn crossed the road and set off up the burn itself. A birch-tree broke the force of the first hailstorm. A spider's web, spun between a clump of alpine lady's mantle and a fern, was shredded by the hammering.

One of the pleasures of scrambling up the course of a stream lies in its wealth of wild flowers. In such gullies lies the greatest concentration and variety of our mountain flora. Often the only trees in miles are the refugee remnants encamped in the gullies — safe from the devouring teeth of sheep and deer. The Highlands are a man-made desert, not a natural wilderness, and only in these secret corners can we gain a glimpse of the richer heritage we have destroyed. In the gullies, too, the bedrocks of the mountains are laid bare and our fingers can feel the rough strata of creation.

The Parallel Roads show up well, as the ledges are greener with grass while the slopes are deep heather-plum-coloured, but they are more fully described under the next Corbett, Carn Dearg. We had scrambled quite far up into the corrie, one carved by a very mathematically-minded glacier, when the next hail attack hit us.

Entertainment this time was a jet fighter thundering down the glen, below our level, and banking steeply to avoid the south side of Coire nan Eun which juts out in a jagged ridge. This ridge should be avoided in ascent or descent as it is cut right across with crags and foul ground. Having said this, Storm and I, faced with a curtain of scree to the right and a steep headwall, turned left on a rising traverse to escape the corrie on to this very ridge just below where it reached the plateau. We managed to avoid the worst of the loose stuff. Ben Tee, Sron a' Choire Ghairbh and Meall na Teanga at once caught the eye to the west. The view south was a wild mix of storm and sun searchlights. Cloud base was 3,000 feet — which is another advantage Corbetts have over Munros.

Hailstorm number three caught us on the rim to the summit. I just hoped there was no thunder and lightning mixed with the hail. Being close to nature has some limitations. Storm (the dog) was gazing down into the corrie and when I followed his stare it was to see an eagle slowly winging across the crags. Since Coire nan Eun is the *corrie of birds*, a name often given because of eagles or their eyries, this was a good place to see one. The hail did not seem to cause the big bird any concern.

We scampered over the summit and round into a bitter wind, and from the dip beyond turned down on that easiest line, keen to reach the glen before any more thrashings of hail. We just made it. We had one pause and sat with a fine view, both down and up Glen Roy, of the Parallel Roads. Achavady, two miles down, was the site where Montrose rested his army on its march to the Battle of Inverlochy in 1645. He is one of the few heroes to come out of that bloody century. The red Post van passed below and I watched its wanderings till it vanished behind the viewpoint car-park knoll. Three hours after setting off I was back at my Dormobile, enjoying the inevitable brew, while the hail battered on the roof to such an extent I could hardly hear the raucous tape of *Carmina Burana* that I'd put on. Music also has its place in the mountains, with or without the unscored percussion of a hailstorm. It was like trying to have afternoon tea inside a kettle drum!

Section 9:   2. CARN DEARG (South of Glen Roy)   834 m
             OS 34   345887
             The red cairn (Carn Jerrak)

In some ways you have to be ready to grab summits when you can. Carn Dearg was to be one such opportunist's ascent. We were working on the restoration of Brunachan, a cottage east of the river, below Coire Dubh; the Corbett was only a couple of miles away as the fly crows. After several hours of carrying gravel, sand and water for concrete mixing the old back needed a rest. And the sun shone. Whistling on Storm and with only a bar of chocolate in my pocket we set off up the burn.

"Burning up" a hill is a grand way of sneaking footage unnoticed. Gripped up with little technical problems on greasy schist, or hopping from boulder to boulder, so occupies the mind that height is gained almost magically. As I had a bag of cameras, some of the more hairy traverses above deep pools had to be skirted, but most of the ascent was made up the gully. There were good sheep tracks on the banks, too, and the slopes are green and grassy: steep but pleasant going and always, below, down the funnel of the gorge, was Brunachan and our cars parked beyond the river, a view which shrank steadily as we scrambled upwards. Brunachan used to have a quarry where quern stones (Lochaber Stones) were made. These have been found as far away as the Outer Hebrides.

Coire Dubh proper slowed us down as the scree edges were lush with blaeberries. We went up the gully clearly seen from below (quite straightforward), and soon tumbled out on to the edge of the sweeping grasslands above. The burn had vanished for a long time, buried below the slabby screes, but was flowing near the top and helped to quench our thirsts. We caught a chill north wind, too, and we quickly left the downward view for the more horizontal sweep of the grass-moor mile to the summit of Carn Dearg.

Carn Dearg is quite a high hill for this area — we could see over the western rim of Glen Roy to Ben Tee and the Loch Lochy Munros. North lay two other Corbetts named Beinn Dearg. Quite why there is this accumulation of "red hills" in upper Glen Roy I don't know, the area forms an entity and repetition is not really expected.

Carn Dearg's nearest hill-view is south-eastwards to Beinn Teallach (promoted from Corbett to Munro long after the rest which gave it a couple of years of unprecedented activity as all the Munroists had to come out of retirement and top up their collection) to Beinn a' Chaorainn (of the wandering summit) and to Creag Meagaidh's long sweep with the distinctive notch of The Window very clear. That eighteenth-century Munroist, Bonnie Prince Charlie, came through The Window on his long backpacking trip. Carn Dearg's best view is south-westwards to the silver waters of Loch Linnhe and the jagged bastion of Ben Nevis, the Aonachs, Grey Corries and Stob Corries. With the back-lighting of evening these looked fine indeed.

Having come up Coire Dubh we set off to descend Coire na Reinich, keeping well over towards its eastern and northern flanks before descending. The corrie is unusually steep all round but the south-westerly slopes are more broken-up with crags and are not a cheerful prospect approached from above. They are a mass of alpine flowers: the botanist would no doubt cheerfully risk his neck for a view of a vertical acre of *Dryas octopetela*. The northern flank of the glen is marginally easier in descent. We kept on the other and had a couple of deep-cut streams to cross. At the edge of the glen we gained a bonus.

Glen Roy is famous for its "Parallel Roads" and here I was able to photograph the top two in profile, very green in colour, against the browner lines across the hillside at the head of the glen. After centuries of speculation it is generally accepted that these odd level terraces that mark the hillsides of Glen Roy are the levels of ancient reservoirs which were dammed up by glaciers blocking off the mouths of the glens. (Southey and Telford speculated that they were man-made "for a display of barbarous magnificence in hunting".) There are three distinct levels, which can be followed for many miles, at 261 m, 325 m and 350 m. There is a large glacial terrace at the foot of Coire na Reinich and I could also see the bigger one beyond Brae Roy Lodge where Glen Turret and Glen Roy unite. I inspected the "Roads" on site and then followed a path down the River Roy back to Brunachan — arriving just in time to help unload more sacks of gravel from Jim's Land Rover. A concrete floor devours twice the material of any estimate. I then escaped across the river to supper in the Dormobile. By the time I'd reached coffee and the Emperor Concerto it was raining. The opportunist approach had paid off again!

The above route is how I'd suggest climbing Carn Dearg, but starting and finishing at the bridge a mile up from Brunachan. The river is not one that can be forded very often. From the bridge wander down the River Roy and then cut up into Coire Dubh. Make sure it is Coire Dubh. I nearly wandered off up the Allt Feith in my enthusiasm for scrambling up the dry-weather rocks of the burn. If really pushed for time, up and down Coire na Reinich is the way, but a traverse or a circuit is so much more satisfying. Beinn Iaruinn could be done in the same day but I'd advocate doing just Carn Dearg and exploring the upper glen a bit on a first day, doing the other Carn Deargs on the second, and Iaruinn on the day of leaving. Glen Roy is a rather special place after all.

Section 9:   3. BEINN TEALLACH   913 m   OS 41 or 34   361859
        Hill of the forge (*tya*-lach)

Beinn Teallach is not to be confused with An Teallach. The only thing they have in common is their building material of rock, water, bog and heather — and their pestering summer hordes of flies, ticks, clegs and midges. The builders made An Teallach into The Magnificent. Beinn Teallach was made from the leftovers. The Ordnance Survey, bless it, has raised the hill by two metres, elevating it to Munro status, but as it is still a Corbett in the current *Tables* I've included it here. With the masses going up it now, the Munro could well be worn down into a Corbett again.

Some people regard this elevation as a dirty trick but those Munroists suffering from advanced Corbettitis can afford to grin. It has merely done a quick change from Corbett 913 m to Munro 915 m. All the same scores of people who had sunk into quiet retirement after completing their Munros will now have to dig out the old leather boots, dust off their puttees and sally forth, alpenstock in hand, to add this thrusting newcomer to their bag. My smugness at having been up it several times was shattered by the dog pointing out that he had not.

I was staying at Nancy Smith's renowned hospice (a privately-run hostel) at Fersit, just north of Loch Treig (353783) (see p. 7), when a youth grabbed me and gleefully said he'd discovered a new Munro. As this tends to happen now and then my reaction was not encouraging, but Richard produced a 1:25,000 map bought at Nevisport that morning: Beinn Teallach was blatantly 915 m! (The height was later confirmed by the Ordnance Survey.) Ah well, it should put up Nancy's bednights.

Beinn Teallach is a coy hill that hides away, north of Glen Spean, with little to be seen from the A86 Fort William–Speyside road. Nancy's hostel is the handiest accommodation and Tulloch Station on the Fort William railway line is a convenient starting point, too.

The height is not the only thing to have changed. A vastly increased area has been ploughed and planted with conifers. First find your Beinn Teallach.

Roughburn on the A86 is the easiest starting point and there is plenty of off-road parking. A forestry road on the hillside is shown treeless, but with an extension of trees sweeping west for many miles. Fortunately this makes little difference to the approach. The dog found three young owls roosting in the grass by the track. They were able to fly and fluttered round silently like huge moths. Young trees produce new wildlife like this but the dark adult growth of a plantation is a desert. Oak, willow and other deciduous trees edge the road, and they will improve the scenery eventually — for a rather select type of spectator.

The track suddenly bends sharp right, up the hill (and goes on for miles across the southern flank of Beinn a' Chaorainn), but shortly after there is a branch leading left. Take this to its end and then the rough continuation down to the riverside where a couple of fields sit marooned in the tide of trees. There is a gate and the Allt a' Chaorainn is easily gained. Cross the river and reach the track shown coming over from the A86 at the Inverlair–Fersit road end. This river could be difficult in spate, when the east bank should be followed. The track is good and goes all the way up the glen and crosses the river more than once.

The glen is three miles long, with Beinn Teallach lying west of it and Beinn a' Chaorainn to the right — the latter a green slope of unbelievable uniformity. Both hills have their better aspects to the east, fine indeed on Beinn a' Chaorainn, fairly modest on Beinn Teallach, as can be seen during the walk up. For my first visit in a dozen years I found a white heather growing in the acres of *Calluna vulgaris*. I suspect the path is wet enough normally, but after the months of summer the many streams were welcome indeed, as were the early blaeberries. Only one drink came from a few yards below a long-dead sheep. The dog rolled on the corpse, of course, so was brutally washed — and seemed to enjoy that too. A breeze made the day perfection rather than purgatory.

The east face is named Coireachan Garbh, the *rough little corries*, and here some crag and scree break out to give a bit of character to the new Munro. Garbh, meaning rough, is a good map-Gaelic word to recognise and to heed. It usually describes the landscape well, and trackless routes up a "Coire Garbh" can be rough indeed.

The cairn on the lip of the col can be seen from well down the glen and makes a pleasant picnic spot. The col, or the Chaorainn slopes just above, give the most flattering view of Beinn Teallach. Beyond the col is some desolate country which is drained by the Burn of Agie to upper Glen Roy. Beinn Teallach could be climbed from that direction and is also easily combined with Beinn a' Chaorainn — which itself is easily combined with Creag Meagaidh. This path gives a good start to however many Munros are strung together eastwards. Beinn Teallach could also be combined with Carn Dearg (9:2) east of Glen Roy.

The path seems to amble along but the col tops 600 m and the view back is very much downwards. In the pulsing heat of our ascent the Loch Treig hills and the eastern Grey Corries were cardboard cut-outs, tinted in varying shades of blue. The NE Ridge of Beinn Teallach gives no problems and leads over a few swelling rises to the summit of broken grey stone. The best view is southwards and that is the route I'd suggest for the descent. You are soon off the stone grey and back on to the carpet green and purple of grass and heather. We eventually angled down to pick up the path again at the level of the fence which comes in above the trees and, in ruined state, wanders up the glen as well. (A gate on the col stands like some forlorn modern sculpture.) We reversed the moves through paddock and plantation, cursing the short ascent to the track for we were below breeze level and the heat and midges plagued us. Use the track, however. Short cuts don't pay.

Over the year after Beinn Teallach's promotion I seldom drove past at weekends without noticing a car or cars parked at Roughburn. Locals must have wondered what was going on. A fine winter's day tempted Storm and me back to the hill and we met eight different parties. Several threatened to lynch me for producing the new Munro. I said I'd have been far happier with it left as a Corbett and anyway Richard Webb "discovered" it — I just chose the wrong night to be staying at Nancy's. For the winter ascent we used the only real alternative from the A86, the old path shown on the map. As this is criss-crossed by new forest roads it is not at all easy to find and can be a bit of an obstacle course. On an Ultimate Challenge Tony and I crossed from Luib-chonnal bothy to Nancy's, taking in Beinn Teallach and Beinn a' Chaorainn in passing. We had snow on the tops, even though it was the middle of May.

Section 9:   4. CARN DEARG (South of Glen Eachach)   768 m   OS
        34   357948
        Red cairn

Section 9:   5. CARN DEARG (North of Glen Eachach)   815 m   OS
        34   349967
        Red cairn

The last time I was on these hills was quite a memorable day and one very much in keeping with the conditions of the rest of the UC 86. We had Corbetts both west and east of the Great Glen. The day from Cluanie Inn to Loch Oich is described later. We reached the Great Glen in the rain, which was still pouring down when we set off from Lundie View, just north of Loch Oich, with the objective of reaching Luib Chonnal over the Carn Deargs.

The track up into Glen Buck began right outside the back door, which is one way of testing the gears first thing. The path pulls up hard but normally rewards the toiler with a big view down the Great Glen to Ben Tee and her Munro partners west of Loch Lochy. The view is soon lost as the road twists into the hills but Glen Buck itself is pretty. The birches were in new leaf and the lambs were at the daft follow-my-leader stage. Our path was much less distinctive when we pulled up round into a side glen above the Allt a' Ghlinne, and we held our level till we met this stream at a small meeting of gorges where we crossed and followed the Allt na h-Eilrig, which ran in a deep cleft, woody and active, while all round were the barren moors. As we squelched our way up the bank we had one glimpse through a gap to the line of the Corrieyairack Pass and its indicative pylons. Before going into the cloud at a spot where four burns meet, we had a quick brew, one where the heat-loss waiting and the heat-gain from the tea were about equally balanced. Conditions were obviously going to be nasty.

We decided to outflank the hills ahead in order to leave our ruckers at a col south east of Carn Dearg 815 m before tackling its steep final cone. We followed one burn to its source and then carried on up onto a ridge where we took a bearing along the flank as we were now in driving rain and cloud. Perhaps we should have gone over the intervening bump for in the peaty bogs and runnels navigating was not easy; however, the bulk of Carn Dearg came when expected and we skirted round under its snowy skirts to find the gap with the rocky knoll to the south east. We were pretty certain of our navigation and cut up the snowy drifts towards the col, only we never did seem to arrive and eventually everything was very uncertain; if not lost we were temporarily mislaid. There was only one remedy: upwards. (All points converge on the highest point.) We reached the cairn carrying our rucksacks after all. The cairn could also give us a fixed point from which we set off with meticulous navigation rather than the casual that usually suffices. The cloud then shredded and for a couple of minutes we were able to check everything visually. The symmetrical hulk of Carn Dearg 768 m was straight ahead.

When we reached the Allt Dubh, the burn that rings Carn Dearg on the north, we decided to risk going up this second Corbett. We might manage before the weather really caused havoc. We did, just. First we had a brew again to warm our clammy, chilled bodies and, without sacks, were able to romp up despite the buffeting gale and periods of lashing rain. The hill is really a big convex cone, and I kept looking back across the valley at snowshapes through the clouds as an aid to navigation in descent. The wind made us reel about on the summit plateau: it was a case of "kick the cairn and down again", by compass over the viewless plateau, and then by the noted landmarks, trotting down the grassy steepnesses and odd bogs back to the ruckers by the Allt Dubh.

The rain was on for the day, obviously, and we didn't waste any time in setting off on the three Scots' miles of glen down to Luib Chonnal. Our supplies had previously been buried east of the river and the bothy is on the west bank. It is a big river. Our fears were that the water would soon rise to create an impassable spate. We criss-crossed the upper reaches which steadily became more and more difficult. The burn was sending down plenty of water. As sure as water is wetter than whisky there was an epic looming.

The problem was postponed by my off-loading my sleeping bag, cameras and some dry clothing on to Tony who thereafter would keep to the west bank and reach the bothy, dry and without too much bother, while I'd stay on the east bank and decide what to do once I'd found our food cache. I might have to ascend two or three miles up the burn again to where I could ford the flood, or maybe I could swim across below the Eas Ban junction where the spate eases in the flat valley bottom. There was one big side stream which gave some excitement going down, and there our Allt Dubh became the raging Allt Chonnal, quite unfordable. I picked up a made path and tramped down in a mix of gloom and worry, the likely swim setting the adrenalin to work in anticipation. Why do we do these things? The event was well called the Ultimate Challenge. I suppose Tony and I deserved our troubles for grabbing summits on our high-level route. Someone was to comment that their route was "neither high, nor low, but positively subterranean". The path turned down to the river and there stood a real, safe, solid, wonderful, magic footbridge! What I called the Ordnance Survey is unprintable. The bridge is by no means new but they do not bother to show it on the map.

An hour's work was needed to reach the cache (two parcels of food and two bottles of wine) and return to the bridge and follow Tony to the bothy. Kay, Jeannie, Helen and Martin of my local mountaineering club were already in, as were Ray and George, two old UC friends. As they had variously come via Knoydart and Glen Kingie, while Tony and I had come from Kintail, it was quite pleasing to have kept the rendezvous after such a week of floods and storm. We had a fairly merry night tucked in under the rafters, surrounded by rows of dripping waterproofs ("Berghaus is beautiful"), and the rain tattooing, like shoppers' high heels in a pedestrian precinct, on the old roof. Ours was a tempered conviviality, for relief and worry as well as the wet-heavy miles had taken their toll.

This is one route I'd recommend for the Carn Deargs (a two-day trip with the next day out to Tulloch/Laggan is even better) but to be tackled in settled conditions. Only the quickest and easiest way of gaining these two Corbetts has no danger from spates. For this you'd drive up to the head of Glen Roy (public road to Brae Roy Lodge only), cross Turret Bridge and follow the shepherd's track up Glen Turret to a sheep fank. From there you can puff up to the 350-metre parallel road and follow this round into Gleann Eachach. The Carn Deargs are sited north and south of the Allt Eachach's upper reaches. There are no problems.

If based in Glen Roy a better round is possible. Wander up Glen Roy to the Allt Chonnal, visiting waterfalls and other features, then go up the Allt Chonnal–Allt Dubh (our route in reverse) to the col and, after doing the Corbetts, descend by Glen Eachach and Glen Turret. These secretive glens and the peculiar parallel roads are the best of the day — the hills are unexceptional and the views lacking the sweep usually associated with Corbetts.

Section 9:   6. GAIRBEINN   896 m   OS 34   460985
              Rough hill

Section 9:   7. CORRIEYAIRACK HILL   896 m   OS 34   429998
              Hill of the rising glen

The Monadh Liath inevitably receive a bad press. At best they are described as featureless. This is a pity because comparisons are odious and to blame the Monadh Liath for not being Knoydart is daft. They are different, that is all. The quality of the walking is high. You can stretch your legs and really walk into or across these hills in a way you cannot do on the constant grinding ascents west of the Great Glen. Because they are a vast peaty desert, features become more important. A bothy can seem like an oasis. Because they are seldom visited the wild life is more obvious. There is plenty going for the Monadh Liaths, not least, having their southern bounds the line of the upper Spey and the historic Corrieyairack Pass. These two hills, and Meall na h-Aisre (9:9) are grouped together here for convenience and, with Geal Charn (the Munro), they form the bold edge of the plateau-landscape of the Monadh Liath.

Plenty has been written about the Corrieyairack Pass itself. With our modern road system its use as a main route seems strange and long ago. The use is certainly ancient. James I crossed the pass when making a foray against Alasdair of the Isles, but its great associations are with the eighteenth century when the route was made into a proper road by General Wade after the Fifteen Rising — in good time for Bonnie Prince Charlie and his army to use it in the Forty Five. They say the summit of the pass is haunted by a ghostly piper. As a walk the Corrieyairack is more interesting for its historical associations than for its natural beauty and one "improvement" to a crossing is to make the easy ascent of Corrieyairack Hill from the top of the pass.

The top of the pass had a meteorological building and pylons and fences and is a rather bleak spot. The summit expands the view. Spaciousness is a hallmark of the Monadh Liath landscape. From Laggan a car can be driven as far as Melgarve. Several Wade bridges line the route and Garva Bridge, which is crossed, is one of the General's most artistic creations, built, like many, to suit the site rather than as a symmetrical imposition. These hills would be done from the Great Glen side only if traversing the pass, because that side entails a longer walk and nearly a thousand feet more of ascent.

Since Corrieyairack Hill on the latest mapping is given the same height as Gairbeinn it has been raised to Corbett status as well. The only time I've linked them both was on an assessment outing from Glenmore Lodge when Cathy and Steve were being put through the mill for their Mountaineering Instructors' Certificates. As Cathy was a committed professional and Steve was in charge of RAF Kinloss Mountain Rescue Team we talked rather than walked over the hills. We went up from Melgarve and skipped the vanishing zigzags up out of Corrie Yairack to follow the burn up to the pass. The pylons rather spoil the route. Fences and tracks led us up Corrieyairack Hill, which is not far short of Munro height (2,922 feet). A gate with no fence stands in the middle of nowhere. The walk, with plenty of ups and downs and yet another Geal Charn (876 m) led to Gairbeinn. The going is drier than further into the Monadh Liaths. A "royal" was sheltering in the lee of the cairn so we took the stag's nook for a snack. We seemed to scatter stags all the way down south to the car at Melgarve. The last time I crossed the pass was with Tony on UC 81. Corrieyairack Hill was enough. The weather was not at its best, which is not unusual here. I feel sorry for the poor soldiers under Wade who had to make the "New Road" (Neil Munro's classic story is so called from the Corrieyairack).

If you believe that miles are easier than feet of ascent, then this day's walking can be prolonged eastwards to reach Meall na h-Aisre (9:9). On the map, things like Dubh Lochan (*black loch*) and areas of marsh-symbol hint, quite correctly, that the going is more typical of the range. You are on to the flat palm of plateau rather than the knobbly knuckles of Corrieyairack–Gairbeinn. There is not much to say about the route. A friend called it "a slaistery slog". The descent, down Leathad Gaothach, is firmer underfoot and the path down to Garva Bridge can be picked up. This is the obvious line of ascent if doing just this Corbett on its own. Coire Iain Oig is a bit watery to be a route. I've linked on to Geal Charn, the Munro, and you have another Dubh Loch on that side. There is not much you can do about the *dubhs* of the Monadh Liath — except enjoy them!

Section 9:   8. CARN A' CHUILINN   816 m   OS 34   416034
              Cairn of the holly

The vagaries of the *Tables* (blame the OS) demoted Carn Easgann
Bana to the north east of Carn a'Chuilinn from being a Corbett,
which is a pity for the 6 miles (which feel like 60) linking them are in
a class of their own for roughness. My round of the then brace of
Corbetts took 1½ hours longer than expected, though it included
falling asleep for half an hour at one of the lochs.

This was a walk which emphasised what I'd said earlier about the
richness of Monadh Liath wildlife. Apart from a few stalkers' cairns
and rotting fences there was no sign of man. A fox charged across
our route, there were many parcels of hinds, the flora was varied and
the bird life a constant pleasure with pipits pipitting all day, some
very vocal golden plovers, besides snipe, curlew, dunlin, sandpiper,
lark and wheatear. Some grouse gave the dog a fine distraction
display. Common gulls nested on Loch Tarff where we started and
finished the circuit. I'd still start there to enjoy an aesthetic day rather
than just nobbling the Corbett.

The quickest and easiest way is up the estate road of Glen Doe,
and the pony path onwards, in direct line to Carn a' Chuilinn —
but keep this for the return. Start up the footpath from Loch Tarff
(on the B862 two miles further east) to the Dubh Lochan and on in
the same line to Lochan a' Choire Ghlais, then head along the crest
for the Corbett. This is not easy walking. Even the new map cannot convey the bumpy roughness or the peat hags and tussock
grass. The old One Inch was depressingly inadequate: one lochan
had a contour line across it. This is high-quality wilderness, however, and Carn a' Chuilinn looks its best from this approach: a
moated castle of crag with a sweeping view of the western Highlands from its battlements.

The head of Glen Tarff is a spectacular corner and those crossing
the Corrieyairack Pass for the *n*th time could gain a reward by
diverting over Corrieyairack Hill and Bac nam Fuaran to explore
here, add Carn a' Chuilinn and descend by Glen Doe to Fort
Augustus. Carn a' Chuilinn is the best of all the Monadh Liath
Corbetts, perhaps best of all the summits of whatever height.

Section 9:   9. MEALL NA H-AISRE   862 m   OS 35   515000
             Hill of the defile

To avoid repetition this hill is described in the final paragraph of 9:6 and 7 with which it is sometimes combined on a good day's tramp. All face the upper reaches of the Spey above the Corrieyairack Pass.

Section 9:   10. CARN NA SAOBHAIDHE   811 m   OS 35   600145
             Cairn of the den (fox lair) (suv-eh)

Carn na Saobhaidhe and Carn na Laraiche Maoile (3 miles to the south west) were both Corbetts when I first came this way. They were unusual in being of equal height. The new mapping left Carn na Saobhaidhe higher, so we lost this anomaly though, strangely, it still exists not far away where Corrieyairack Hill was given the same height as Gairbeinn. There are some geo-mathematical quirks in the Corbett game.

This Corbett and Carn an Fhreiceadain (9:11) were done at a weekend. The logistics were complicated but, as Lorna, Mike and I were staying in our vehicles up Strath Dearn, we approached Carn na Saobhaidhe from the upper Findhorn. Mike and I had cycles which the three of us shared to speed us up to Dalbeg. Though it had been a wild night we were determined to visit this hill while in the area. It is not exactly situated for casual access. We had five miles of cycling to Dalbeg and then headed up a stalkers' path by the Allt Creagach which becomes the Allt Odhar. There is a steep-sided glen at the start and some small, whisky-tinted waterfalls. The red deer were very pale in colour. The day before, east of the Findhorn, we'd seen "white" deer, something I've only seen perhaps half a dozen times in my life. We saw a ptarmigan down in the valley and grouse near the summit, which was all wrong. The Allt Odhar runs through some prime bog country, bleak and open as some Andean *altiplano* with rimming snowy *cordilleras*. And as cold. We huddled on top of the Corbett under a bivvy bag for a brief snack. We found it very difficult to pick out features or peaks. As the next lashing of hail came in we tailed southwards for the other (now demoted) Corbett and on to the head of Glen Markie, a remarkable trench. We returned to the bikes down the Eskin River, which completed an enjoyable circular walk. We were back in our homes in Inverness, Nairn and Fife a few hours later.

On the UC 87 several of us shared the cost of a ferry across Loch

Ness, from Drumnadrochit to Inverfarigaig. The day began in dismal fashion but cleared steadily to give a splendid crossing to the Findhorn, via Carn na Saobhaidhe. We walked round the north end of Loch Mhor, cutting corners to gain a new bulldozed track above Farraline Farm. Janet had gone ahead by the farm and was puzzled to find us ahead on the track. We left the track to cut over to Loch Conagleann (trackless, whatever the map says) and had a sunny lunch and paddle in this sheltered nook. The trees had taken a battering, the result of a March gale a keeper informed us. With a car it would have been less effort to come in via Dunmaglass Lodge or from the south end of Loch Mhor by the estate road up the River E (*sic*). With no cars we had the advantage of a long traverse.

A good estate road took us up the Allt Uisg an t-Sidhean and a fork then led to the Aberchalder Burn which was followed to one of its sources on the col east of the Corbett. The track goes on further than shown but the bogs win in the end. Bob, Ray and Cynthia continued more directly for the Findhorn while Janet and Dave (from Philadelphia) sturdily plodded on up the diminishing burn, good 1 mph country, for the Corbett. The view, even with perfect clarity, was still difficult to fit into place. All the west appeared end-on and the big hills southwards seemed to be back-to-front. The Cairngorms glittered along the eastern horizon. As the highest point between the Corrieyairack and the A9, and Affaric and Aviemore, Carn na Saobhaidhe commands a huge panorama, even by Corbett standards.

We made a slow wending descent of the Allt Odhar ("Oh dear" weary Dave suggested) and where it joined the Allt Creagach we found the old stalkers' track had now been harshly bulldozed. The trio had tea and drams waiting at Dalbeg. Janet camped there but we had to walk down to Coignafearn where I'd previously cached some supplies by cycle. The deer grazed across the river from our camp and sandpipers called all night. We went out to Aviemore by the Dulnain and Geall-Charn Mor (9:12). The dreaded Monadh Liath are seldom so kind to visitors.

Section 9:   11. Carn an Fhreiceadain   878 m   OS 35   726071
Cairn of the watcher

Carn an Fhreiceadain watches over Kingussie, though I suspect the name may have derived from it being used by human watchers to keep out wanderers in the stalking season. The hill lies just off an old road (on Roy's map of 1755) up the Allt Mor and on by Bruach nan-Imirichean to descend the Allt Glas a' Charbaid to the Findhorn's upper reaches — quite populated at one time. Now I suspect a few walkers and stalkers are the only visitors. Note how cairns on the Corbett and Beinn Bhreac are positioned on the edge of the flat summits where they are well seen from lower down. This Corbett gives a mere stroll and the two estate roads (by Meall Unaig and Bad Each) can be linked by a traverse of Fhreiceadain and Beinn Bhreac.

One Friday in May, Lorna came from Nairn, Mike from Inverness and I arrived from Fife. We went up and left their two cars by the golf course above Kingussie, then drove round to Tomatin and the road up Strathdearn, the valley of the forgotten Findhorn River, to spend the night in my Dormobile. In the morning we drove on up to Coignafearn Old Lodge and, despite the attentions of curious garrons, set off early to walk on to the smart modern lodge. (Post bus runs to here, weekdays.) We crossed the Findhorn to follow a good path up the Elrick Burn, which ran down a deep glen and was the first of endless pleasing places we were to find that weekend. The burns were always a delight.

At a bothy we had a brew then zigzagged up to a vague watershed and down to another bothy at the head of the Dulnain River. It was a desolate pass with bog and snow booby-traps for the unwary. We lunched by the stream, enjoying brief sunny shafts that broke through the scudding clouds. After climbing out of the burn, a long, boggy moor led to the Corbett. Sleet showers had been swiping at the summits all day, so we carried on down Meall Unaig to pick up the track to Kingussie. Sunny and windless, the Allt Mor seemed a different world from the high hinterland. Carn an Fhreiceadain had proved a typical Monadh Liath hill.

We piled into Mike's Mini and drove back up the Findhorn, hoping for Carn na Saobhaidhe as well, but the cheery day went sulking to bed and a storm left us pessimistic for the Sunday that has already been described (9:10). It only remained for me to drop Lorna off at Kingussie on my way back down the A9.

Section 9:   12. GEAL-CHARN MOR   824 m   OS 35   837124
       Big white cairn

This is a very easy ascent which is nearly always made by walking up the estate road that crosses the Corbett's NE shoulder as it heads for the River Dulnain. Lynwilg, the start, has plenty of parking places and a pleasant hotel.

Having gone that way before with Kitchy, this time Storm and I set out from Aviemore after lunch one February day, first wending up Craigellachie by the Nature Trail. This gives a good view (over the mess of Aviemore) to the Loch Morlich basin and the wave-crest ridge of Meall a' Bhuachaille. I'd brought overnight gear and planned to stay at a bothy near the Corbett and then walk out down the River Dulnain back to the A9. These empty hills have an atmosphere all of their own, a crying sort of beauty and a sad desolation, as if abandoned by both man and God.

We met roe deer, red deer, hares and grouse in plenty as we skirted (rather a boggy route) along by Lochan Dubh and on by Creag na h-Iolaire (no eagles) to Carn Dearg Mor which greeted us with a salvo of hail.

I left my rucksack at the highest point on the road, itself about 660 m, with the summit just a kilometre away. Being above the level of deep heather the ascent is a pleasant stroll and no more, though in a rising wind there was a touch more effort required. As I wandered back and forwards the view changed from the array of the Glen Feshie side of the Cairngorms, across Speyside, to the nearer brooding Monadh Liaths across the Dulnain. Too cold to linger I circuited the trig point, an aberrant acolyte at an altar to strange gods, and romped back to the road in a blatter of horizontal snow and down northwards to the bothy — only there wasn't a bothy or, rather, the bothy wasn't.

My informant obviously had not been there for a long time and his "perfectly usable shelter" was now a doorless, windowless wreck, with parts of walls, floor and roof missing. Being dusk I decided that this inadequate shelter would have to do and we cringed over the stove in a corner to make a meal and then spread the sleeping bag on a drier area of creaky boards. The wind (which kept blowing out the candle) had been slowly rising all the while, and before midnight it became a considerable gale. Big winds like that almost invariably end in big "wets" and if a deluge caught me there I'd be soaked. There was also the possibility of the tin shack disintegrating in the storm. A section of wall blew out just at the time I was playing my torch-beam over the interior in a pessimistic survey. Somehow you feel singularly vulnerable lying in a sleeping bag. Hiding my panic I lit the stove for a brew, packed everything up, downed the warming tea — and fled. (On UC 87 we found the bothy looking exactly as it had done a decade earlier — and there must have been a few gales in that time.)

There was a half moon which lit the sky enough to see the splendid turmoil of clouds and I had a torch. Walking out was therefore no problem. The wind bullied me up the short distance to the top of the road, and then I had it downhill all the way to Lynwilg. There is an exhilaration at being out in a wild night and I was let off lightly with a few snow showers. The rain came rattling down just two hundred yards short of the welcoming Dormobile.

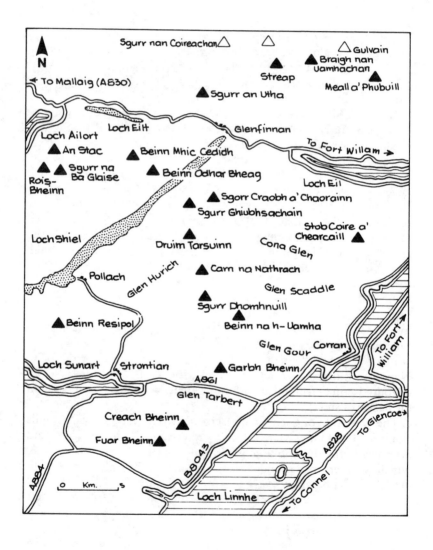

THE WEST, SOUTH OF LOCH ARKAIG

Section 10:   1. FUAR BHEINN   766 m   OS 49   853564
Cold hill (foor)

Section 10:   2. CREACH BHEINN   853 m   OS 49   871577
Mountain of spoil

THE CORBETTS OF Ardgour and Morven, climbed on one extended visit, gave days of ever-increasing heat. They are detailed later; but, briefly, I traversed from Strontian northwards with one camp, then cycled down Loch Shiel, traversed Resipol, added Garbh Bheinn and had a chilly night of frost in the Dormobile in Glen Tarbert. A meeting at Bridge of Orchy the next evening left me with the chance of adding these peaks only if I did "a quickie" ascent rather than the obviously classic circuit of Glen Galmadale.

To avoid the grilling I was up at a frosty 4 a.m. and off an hour later so, by the time the sun had glared up the sky, we were high enough to have a salvation breeze. There was no problem crossing the Carnoch River in Glen Tarbert. We cut up Coire Frithalt on to the bulging ridge of Meall a' Bhainaiche, for once avoiding all opportunities of "burning up" or scrambling on exposed rock. (My finger-tips were already worn smooth and rather sensitive.) The going was rough enough, anyway, and this, a rather scrappy ascent line, led almost on to Maol Odhar before suddenly producing the view down Glen Galmadale, a view like the proverbial gun-barrel with the sprawl of Lismore the target. Could the upper recess of Glen Galmadale (a hybrid Gaelic–Viking name) be where the *creach* spoils were hidden? On the way up the good ridge to Creach Bheinn there is an enclosure which looks a bit like an old fort but is reputedly a watch post dating to Napoleonic times. We had the only rest of the day on top, and devoured a tin of fruit salad with enjoyment. The Glen Coe hills lay in the dazzle of sun.

The west side of Glen Galmadale rather reminded me of the hills along from the Grey Mare's Tail: a succession of bold buttresses and deep-cut burns overlooking a fine valley. Here the rock is granite, which weathers into rounded shapes, while the burns have cut down in to the softer basalt dykes. There was a mile down to the col, the Cul Mham, before Fuar Bheinn, rather dull from that side. I left everything on the pass and pushed on in pants alone. Fuar Bheinn was hardly living up to its name.

South of Fuar Bheinn is Beinn na Cille, hill of the cell, which indicates a long gone religious settlement. Perhaps it was those Vikings again. *Gall* is stranger (Gaelic), *dal* or *dale* is valley (Norse).

The finest day on these hills is to walk anticlockwise round the rim of all the peaks surrounding Glen Galmadale. The morning sun will be at its best for the steep slopes above Loch Linnhe; you look across at the pap of Fuar Bheinn above the ranks of buttresses, you can dine on Creach Bheinn, and descend with the sun, off Fuar Bheinn or Beinn na Cille. One bonus for this route is the drive down Loch Linnhe on the B8043 under that riven chaos of red rock and green gullies. I can't think of anything like it except west of Dingle in Kerry.

I, perforce, returned to the Cul Mham (*the pass of the recess*) from where I contoured round and down. The cliffs of Choire Dhuibh are not as dramatic as the map suggests and I cut down them to follow the stream back to the valley. The heat and the heather increased with the loss of height. The conditions made me agree with one of my pupils who once declared, on top of Schiehallion, "If there's one thing I don't like about climbing hills it's going down again." A cuckoo belted along the hillside, making for the woods to the west, chased by several irate pipits, flying, you might say, hell for feather.

This half day brought to an end a May week of Corbetts and fine trekking which I thought would never be equalled. With only 40 Corbetts to go, the following summer brought eleven days of even hotter weather, which is why, when I think of Ardgour (or Arkle) the memories are such sunny ones. Just occasionally you are spoilt, and go spoiling. Ardgour had given a good *creach* of Corbetts.

Section 10:   3. GARBH BHEINN   885 m   OS 40   904622
              Rough hill (garven)

From the Ballachulish crossing the sunset hills across Loch Linnhe often look dramatic and, like a Victorian silhouette, the features of a head lying back among pillows can be made out. This is "the sleeping giant" which, on checking, proves to be Garbh Beinn of Ardgour, an eminently suitable peak to bear that title.

Everyone who writes of Garbh Bheinn goes into raptures about the hill and its setting. After two viewless ascents and a score of times refusing to add a third disappointment I'm prepared to go along with the roughness and the drama; the "astonishing views" and "the best mainland rock for climbing in the west" I'll take on trust. Some day, instead of planning Garbh Bheinn, and calling off at Corran Ferry as another depression sweeps the west, I'll go off proclaiming quite different intentions and, when the sun shines, I'll quickly sneak into Ardgour instead.

Donald Bennet's *Scottish Mountain Climbs* has a chapter on Garbh Bheinn which, in text and photographs, shows the nature of the hill. It very much lives up to its name. Bell and Brown, who made the first mountaineering approach to the hill in 1897, took the still popular route up Coire an Iubhair (yoo-ir, *yew*), probably a less muddy track then, and commented, as generations have done since, how "bit by bit Garbh Bheinn creeps into view, forming by the gradual addition of ridge to corrie and crag to buttress one of the boldest pictures of mountain grandeur to be seen on mainland Scotland". They climbed to the summit by the Great Ridge, the great tongue of rock facing east below the top, well demarcated to the right by Great Gully. Haskett Smith and Hastings tried the gully — unsuccessfully — just two days later. The first ascent was made by W. H. Murray and D. Scott in 1946. The attraction of the peak is mirrored in the long list of notables who have made new routes but, though that story deserves telling, I'd better stick to the easier lines for walkers. The hill relents in places.

Probably the easiest way up Garbh Bheinn is by Coire a' Chothruim, which drains the western flanks of the hill southwards to the Glen Tarbert road. This is an almighty slog as the whole height is gained in little over a mile. There are better ways. Coire an Iubhair is the favourite route, and deservedly so.

Inglis Clark in 1904 described the glen as being "swampy ground alternating with bog", and the thousands of tramping feet since have hardly improved the path. The walk starts through a landscape with the soft greens of an old kilt or the dun sett of last year's grass but the slopes are soon pleated with rocks and water. Boiler-plate slabs break through the thin texture of vegetation and after a couple of miles the stream junction below the summit corrie is reached. The old dog and I sat there with the clouds masking everything above. Up in the mists a lark was unwrapping a parcel of song and the burns were cheery company, vigorous with April showers. We went up into the corrie and swung right to puff and scramble to the crest of the mountain. There are crags on crags and summits on summits. We visited all the bumps to make sure of claiming the Corbett.

The best route up keeps more to the burn draining the corrie, and then moves left to the obvious col south of and below the summit mass. The long ridge of Sron a' Gharbh Choire Bhig is the alternative skyline approach and these two routes combined, in one direction or the other, are what I'd recommend for normal walkers. Those who are fit, fast and at home on the Cuillin crests could "make a day of it" and traverse Druim an Iubhair, Sgorr Mhic Eacharna and Beinn Beag to the pass at the head of the glen. This route gives a magnificent circuit; some day I still hope to claim its reward — the most impressive of all views of Garbh Bheinn. From Lochan Coire an Iubhair in the Bealach Feith n' Amean the northern bastions of Garbh Bheinn have to be tackled. This needs some competence in route finding and scrambling so "caw canny" as they say.

Garbh Bheinn being, in Donald's view, one of the half dozen grandest mountains in the West Highlands and, for rock-climbers, the finest, the investment in the 1:25,000 map is recommended. (Sheet NM 86/96 Strontian and Ardgour.) The starting point for all the recommended routes begins near the bridges (old and new, plenty of parking space) over the river of Coire an Iubhair, one kilometre past Inversanda the estate hamlet with the buildings seen after the road turns inland from Loch Linnhe. I give this description of the start, for the 1:50,000 Sheet 40 ends just north of these features; they are on Sheet 49. Coire an Iubhair is stalking country so check at Inversanda for access during late summer–autumn days. In winter conditions Garbh Bheinn becomes a peak for the experts only.

Section 10: 4. BEINN RESIPOL 845 m OS 40 766655
             Horse stead (ON *hross-bolstatr*, from the farm)

Beinn Resipol commands the heart of Sunart and as it rises in rough isolation it has a panoramic view which is hard to equal. An ascent just has to be kept for a clear day. I've had two such days and certainly endorse all the praise Resipol is given. Ardgour and Moidart are unusually wild areas, with a great jumble of peaks and ridges filling much of the near view but allowing distant views of ranges from Skye to Ben Nevis while, south, lies the graceful sprawl of Mull and, west, the magical margin of the island-studded sea.

My first visit was in a May 1975 Corbett blitz — the only such spell I've had, my excuse being that completing the list lay not so far ahead and some impatience was intruding into a game which had been going on for 22 years. I see a certain analytical note in my log which I'm sure others will recognise: "Only once 4 Corbetts in a day (Auch), 3 just a few times (Ardgour and Glenfinnan in the last few days, Moidart, Arkle, Merrick) and the rest in ones or twos. You have to work harder for the Corbetts than you do for the Munros."

I'd abandoned the car to walk over Ardgour's hills to Glenfinnan where I'd left my folding cycle, and I used it down Loch Shiel (forestry road) to camp at Polloch from whence, on a frost-crisp morning, I set off for Resipol by the old miners' track across its east ridge. The path was hard to find — a quarry had bitten into it — then it was very wet and heavy going up into Coire an t-Suidhe. After looking about the site of an old lead mine I angled up to reach Meall an t-Slugain, the saddle east of Beinn Resipol. The path bears off and drops down to Strontian and is quite often used as an approach to the hill. Strontian, an attractive village, gave its name to Strontium and up near the top of the public motor road to Polloch there has been some recent working again of the old mines. Having descended off Resipol, more or less by the same route, I had to cycle over that pass — a 342-m "pech" up and a wrist-straining braking down to Strontian. The dog had no difficulty keeping up but went in the rucksack for the A861 run along to Garbh Bheinn and then back to the Dormobile at Corran — a logistical exercise in itself.

The second ascent was exercise of another sort for I took in Resipol on a day's tramp from Acharacle to Corran Ferry, part of my UC from Ardnamurchan Point to Buchan Ness. (Once across Corran Ferry it rained every single day.) I didn't want to walk along the tarred A861 road so cut off at the end of the hamlet hoping to make an approach between the dreaded Claish Moss and the heathery lower hills. We ran into new plantings which were not on the map and wasted hours teasing a way through to the Allt Mhic Chiarain which is probably the most used line of ascent — but coming up it, sensibly, from Resipole Farm on Loch Sunart. The woods along the loch are oak and the walk up from Resipole uses a track on the Chiarain's south/left bank. The burn has quite a deep-set gorge, even above the tree line, but such a gorge usually ensures traces of deer or sheep tracks on its banks. I followed the pleasing stream up to Lochan Bac an Lochain (which would have been a scenic camp site) and left the rucker there to wander up the craggy slopes of Resipol carrying nothing but my cameras.

The view was as sweeping as ever and I scribbled down a few of the places I recognised: "Mull, Jura, Scarba, Arran, Cobbler hills, Argyll's Buidhe, Cruachan, Chocuill, Lui, Staravs, Clachlet, Sgulaird, Bidean, Vair pair, Aonach Eagach, Loch Leven's Corbetts bracketing far Schiehallion, Mamores, Nevis, Creag Mheagaidh ranges, Corbetts on both flanks of the Great Glen, Gulvain, Streaps, Thuilm, Gleouraich, Cluanie Ridge, Sgurr Mor, Ciche, all Knoydart, Sgriol, Applecross, Torridon, the Cuillin, Rhum, Eigg, Muck, the Outer Hebrides and then the great jumble from Moidart through to Loch Linnhe; a score of Corbetts and I'm sitting on the best perhaps."

John Leyden, that extraordinary genius from the Borders, who died young in the Orient where he collected languages quicker than most of us acquire Corbetts, made an ascent of Resipol in 1800, both to enjoy the setting and to search for good samples of garnets which can spot some of the rocks in great numbers. He so enjoyed cataloguing the view that he failed to notice darkness approaching and then tried to take a short cut down off the rocky peak, thereby landing in all sorts of trouble, scaring himself thoroughly and reaching Polloch in pitch dark where everyone had given him up for lost.

After lunching back at the loch I made a flanking traverse to the Meall an t-Slugain col and followed the crest eastwards to pick up a path down through all the mining sites to Bellsgrove Loch and so through to Glen Gour and eventually out to Corran Ferry and a good night at the Ardgour Hotel. Any benefit of using a car to the top of the road is lost by the heavy going thereafter. The best route is up from Resipole and down to Strontian — and a very good best it is.

Section 10:   5. BEINN NA H-UAMHA   762 m   OS 40   918665
          Hill of the cave (na hoo-ah)

Section 10:   6. SGURR DHOMHNUILL   888 m   OS 40   889679
          Donald's peak

Section 10:   7. CARN NA NATHRACH   786 m   OS 40   887699
          Cairn of the adders/serpents

There is the feel of an island to Ardgour: it is *nearly* surrounded by water and reached, as like as not, by ferry. Ardgour, ruggedly hilly, reminds me of Mull or Rhum or even Skye, except it is more complex and wooded than any of those genuine islands.

As well as the array of demanding peaks and ridges, Ardgour offers some of the best glens in the west for tramping through on backpacking trips. Willy nilly the glens will be explored in garnering the Corbetts. Glen Gour is the natural approach for Beinn na h-Uamha and Glen Scaddle for the other two. Uamha was discovered only with the metric revisions. I did it after the others.

Fortuitously I had been lecturing at Loch Ailort one January and next day drove round the Ardgour side of Loch Eil and Loch Linnhe to Sallachan at the foot of Glen Gour. Conditions were doubtful with a strong east wind, which I made full use of, but a dank, black thaw held some menace. The path up the glen was wet, with ice underneath; wellies with skates would have been useful. On the May Ardnamurchan to Buchan Ness walk, the day from Acharacle to Corran Ferry over Resipol took in a descent of lonely Glen Gour. The loch then was noisy with stonechats, wheatears, redshanks and a bedlam of curlews, today it was noisy with wind and waves, the only birds being a pair of communicative whoopers out in the middle of the loch. The path more or less disappears after a pleasant two miles, leaving one on bare tawny levels with Beinn na h-Uamha wrinkling down north of the strath. The river could be difficult in spate conditions but we crossed with no problems. Deer splashed over ahead of us. The dog found a very dead deer and I just caught him in time to prevent him rolling on the carcase.

We went up the SE Ridge of the Corbett, which was rather an infuriating route for someone in a hurry as there are endless bumps and crags entailing descents and diversions. The hurry was to try and beat the big bang promised by the black sky. The wind gave a good push, sometimes erratically, and the snow became sugary firm, perfect for making steps without needing crampons. We were soon up, cringed on top for a moment only, and we baled off more directly into Glen Gour, an easier, quicker but less interesting line.

The peak could as easily be climbed from Glen Scaddle, if based there for the other Corbetts, but linking it with Sgurr Dhomhnuill and Carn na Nathrach would be a real marathon of rough-stuff ridge-walking. I just managed across Corran and Ballachulish ferries before the rain began but, as everyone knows, all Scotland's weather is first distilled in Glen Coe.

Sgurr Dhomhnuill, highest of Ardgour's summits (just), and Carn na Nathrach, by the east-west nature of the glens, can be tackled from either east or west, or done in the course of a tramp through the glens. I'll describe both briefly for these hills merit exploration.

From Strontian I drove up the narrow road that crosses east of Resipol to reach the shores of Loch Shiel and parked near the old mine-workings above Bellsgrove. The hills are such a jumble that I took some time with the map to work out what was what. We then cut down by Bellsgrove Loch to the end of the Strontian woods (the attractive natural forest of the Ariundle Reserve) and on to a further area of old mine-workings. The Strontian River curves east and leads through a splendid pass to Glen Gour while a higher offset stream, the Feith Dhomhnuill, drains the Sgurr Dhomhnuill *cirque*. The last shaft at the mines was dry enough to enter but I had no torch so soon came out, to the relief of the dog who was rushing about trying to find me. This day in May was icy with a blasting wind and my Berghaus Goretex jacket earned its keep. My shoulder, increasingly in agony from cold like that, became bad enough to seek medical advice. Our local village GP tried acupuncture — and it worked. He retired not long afterwards and our new doctor, of Chinese descent, has never tried acupuncture. It's an ill wind . . .

We cut up the valley to gain the col south of the big peak which lies not far above, with just one bump on the way. The extra height of Sgurr Dhomhnuill ensured the summit kept a cloud streamer all day, but it was too like being in a wind tunnel to stay by the trig point, the only one on any of the Ardgour Corbetts, which is perhaps indicative of the general roughness and of this peak's dominance. Druim Garbh, the equally steep twin, which completes the western-facing horse-shoe, has been demoted as a Corbett (the cols don't have a 500 foot drop) but would be worth climbing, anyway, and will be by those traversing to Carn na Nathrach. The name Druim Garbh (*rough ridge*) applies strictly to the contorted ridge leading west to the summit of the Strontian–Loch Shiel road with its scores of lochans, a good way back if just circuiting Dhomhnuill.

While sheltering out of the wind on Druim Garbh the cloud lifted and the sun shone a shaft of light on Resipol. Rhum and Skye were sun-touched too, but Mull and the south stayed grey. The grim east was not studied at all; my eyes were streaming with the wind's assault. We started our descent on the west flank to keep out of the wind, but this was steep and craggy and we crept back on to the crest which still had plenty of rocky slabs and domes. For variety, the col had a peat bog. We went up a rib and then allowed the wind to bustle us up a rake on to the west ridge of Carn na Nathrach where I was thankful to leave my rucksack before wending up to the summit, a fine perch of a cairn following some scrambling on slabs and walls. The huge length of Glen Scaddle showed well from the top.

Having picked up my rucksack (ballast) we turned down the north flank, easy going if steep, to pitch the tent on the Mam Beathaig. The leeside of the hill was sunny and warm though there was a sharp enough frost overnight to form a skin of ice on my dixie of water. I'd envisaged being blasted off the col and needing to shelter among the trees of Glen Hurich. Resourie, just a mile away, was not yet a bothy but when the building was about to be restored I took the chance of doing the big traverse without having to carry a tent.

Two of us with our vehicles crossed the Corran Ferry on Saturday morning and, after leaving my Dormobile at the foot of Glen Scaddle, we drove in Sandy's car to Strontian and the familiar hill road over to Loch Doilet where we parked and walked up Glen Hurich to Resourie which the MBA had just adopted. The rest of the day was spent clearing back the brash, boulders, brambles and junk from the bothy walls, opening the back ditch and damming the burn for a spout of water, a much harder day than climbing Corbetts. The surrounding area had been felled and was smothered in foxglove spires, mostly pink but with a few white flowers as well.

The Mam Beathaig is rather like Knoydart's Mam na Cloiche

Airde. Sandy, Storm and I crossed the pass early, descending to a "Lost Valley" where the path ended. Round a corner we suddenly came on Loch Dubh and a two mile tramp beyond led to the great junction area, the classic pass behind, open Glen Scaddle ahead. We'd come down Gleann an Lochain Duibh and now went up Gleann na Cloiche Sgoilte, traversed Druim Garbh to Sgurr Dhomhnuill, and descended Gleann Mhic Phail — thus exploring all three of the triple glens. The walk down Glen Scaddle was most enjoyable: we had one long brew stop, and one delectable swim in a big pool. On reaching the Dormobile I found I'd left my watch at the pool so, while Sandy cooked supper, I took the dog up the glen again, making a 20-mile day.

We slept the night in the Dormobile with the intention of driving along to Loch Sunart and traversing Resipol back to Sandy's car but the weather changed for the worse. We merely collected Sandy's car and drove home. I was luckier on the camping trip. From the Mam Beathaig pitch I was to traverse northwards to Glenfinnan over the even tougher trio of 10:13, 14 and 15, where the day is described.

Section 10:   8. Rois-Bheinn   882 m   OS 40   756778
    Hill of showers (= Froisbheinn)

Section 10:   9. Sgurr na Ba Glaise   874 m   OS 40   770777
    Peak of the grey cow

Section 10:   10. An Stac   814 m   OS 40   763793
    The stack

Section 10:   11. Beinn Mhic Cedidh   783 m   OS 40   829788

Section 10:   12. Beinn Odhar Bheag   882 m   OS 40   846778
    The small tawny hill

Munroists acquainted with the sandpapered landscape of Knoydart will find a similar set of hills in the Corbetts of Moidart. Comparisons are arduous but the Corbetts are in no way inferior to the Munros and both areas have a parcelled completeness, a geographical and historical individuality. They are of the west, however, and take all that the Atlantic cares to throw at them. They are worth a visit in clear, settled conditions, even if you have to stalk them for weeks or months.

The Corbetts of Moidart are unique in offering a clutch of Corbetts all laid out along a single high-level walk. Only on the other side of Loch Shiel or north of Tyndrum might you cull five Corbetts on a single walk, and they are jumbles of peaks rather than anything else.

So make the most of Moidart. Not for nothing does Richard Gilbert include this traverse in his book *The Big Walks*. Had these hills been just a bit higher (i.e. Munros) or sited above Windermere they would be swarming with walkers. As it is they are "magnificent but unfashionable".

Before the road through Glenuig was opened Moidart could not be circled by car and even now there is a feeling of extraordinary remoteness to the area. That perimeter is worth careful exploration: from Castle Tiorim to Glenfinnan it offers varied scenery and a history still marked by the Forty Five. The mountainous interior is unpeopled and untracked, with some of the steepest corries and mountain flanks in Scotland. The going is tough and one advantage of the long traverse is that it minimises the physical demands. The day gives a long, hard traverse, certainly, but that is easier than the alternative of several medium-long, equally hard expeditions. I say this with feeling, having been blasted off several efforts at a complete traverse. Nor was I helped by the table revisions which added Beinn Mhic Cedidh, demoted Druim Fiaclach and promoted Sgurr na Ba Glaise. These map alterations are themselves an indication of the rough terrain and, as for certain Munro sections, only modern surveying methods finally covered the area adequately.

With my parents I'd sailed down from Kyle to Mallaig on the *Iona* and while they stayed at Morar I left the train at Glenfinnan with the plan that we all meet again on the homeward train two days later. "Just time for the Moidart Hills."

I had a Zarsky bivvy and minimal food. The normal direct assault from Glenfinnan to the Beinn Odhar peaks had always struck me as being an unduly complex and rough line so I backtracked westwards (sitting out a deluge under a railway bridge) and headed up Doire Dhamh. As I climbed, the weather leaked down, and a day of showers simply turned into sweaty clag. I took most of my clothes off in order to have them dry at the end of the day, and puffed up in my own steam tent of waterproofs. Moidart wetness has the touch of long practice. The ground was sodden and there was plenty of tussocky grass.

I gained the north ridge of Coire Odhar just as the cloud blotted out the view but a rising rim of steps led easily enough round and up to the trig point on Beinn Odhar Mhor (870 m). "Big" here presumably was the overall impression when viewed from below as Beinn Odhar Bheag is higher (882 m) — now equal highest, with Rois-Bheinn, of all the Moidart summits. The ridge between is corrie-bitten and complex but by careful compass work and dead reckoning I teased away at it. Well washed slabs gave the last pull to the Corbett. "Very windy, very wet, and no visibility" my log complained. I followed a dogged compass line down to the Bealach a' Choire Bhuidhe and baled off into *the yellow corrie*. (*A yellow corrie* is often so because the ground is grassy and will give a reasonable route — though Moidart grass is sometimes unreasonable. *Garbh choire*, rough corrie, would, conversely, be a warning of potentially bad walking conditions.)

Richard Gilbert had an almost identical experience when wind and rain lashed his party. They beat a hasty retreat by this same route. I cut through the gap behind Sgurr na Paite, the viewpoint bump above Loch Eilt, in a scattering of deer and a scattering of cloud. I felt relief in seeing the landscape was where it should have been after the hours of groping blindfold in the clouds. Bluebell banks and tumbling waters led me down to Essan which I'd spotted from the train as a possible emergency shelter. Since restored, at that time it had long been open to sheep and cows. Deluge or not, I passed by and spent the night in a wooden shack further on. Two pints of tea was the first priority for I was dehydrated. The last of my Martigny-brought *Reddy* (muesli) was all I had to eat. I was in bed before nine, coffee in hands, eyes closed, listening to the sounds of solitude. My waterproofs dripped like a ticking clock (to form puddles on the floor), the rain rattled on the roof and those bright summer-birds of the Highlands, the sandpipers, reeled and flitted along the margin of the loch. If sunset on top of the hills had been ruled out I was perfectly content with my low-level substitute.

The next day I set off up the Allt Easain. There were plenty of deer then and throughout the day. I gave myself some fun to gain wild Coire nan Gall. I had to skirt crags and then found the Allt Easain had cut a deep gorge, crossing which would mean quite a downward detour; however, I managed to fight down a rake in the corner with the hope of climbing up to the right of the waterfall. This line was dangerously loose, so after a good look at the fall I climbed straight up it in waterproofs only. Midsummer or not my fingers were frozen. Coire nan Gall was crossed regardless of surface water and I went for Druim Fiaclach *en face* only to find another small corrie tucked in its side. "Chinese boxes of corries" I noted at the time.

Before gaining the ridge I had a meal stop and the day's third long shower went over, but as soon as I gained the ridge the grim quality vanished: the rain stopped, the clouds broke and the sun shone. My yell of glee on the summit might have raised Corbett himself. I grudge having had Druim Fiaclach, *the toothed ridge*, demoted.

The toothed ridge runs eastwards but my way on, south and west, also gave ridge-traversing of great character. Coire Reidhe, which is circled, is ferociously steep and rimmed with precipice, and the bumpy crest of Slat-Bheinn leading to Sgurr na Ba Glaise is a delightful ridge between vast corries: Glen Moidart to the south and Coire a' Bhuiridh to the north. The col, Bealach an Fhiona, beyond Sgurr na Ba Glaise, is an old right of way linking the heads of Loch Moidart and Loch Ailort, a worthwhile walk.

At that time Sgurr na Ba Glaise had a special mention in the introduction to the Corbetts Table, suggesting it should be in the list. Now it is, but Fiaclach has gone. Always do everything is a good plan though, hopefully, the OS will leave things alone for the forseeable future. The biggest crags of the area flank *the peak of the grey cow*. (How did it come by that name?) Life seemed too good to be true as I lay in the lee of the cairn in warm sunshine. Plans to hitch along to join the parental comforts at Morar evaporated with the clouds. We could surely squeeze in Sgurr an Utha the next day and still catch the train, which is what happened (see 10:16).

I trotted down to the Bealach an Fhiona and was blown up beside the dyke that leads to and along double-headed Rois-Bheinn. From a distance the trig pillar had looked like a figure. The heads of thrift were dancing in the wind. The pillar is on the higher, eastern summit but the west top has the greater view, one even finer than Resipol's for Rhum and Skye are nearer and Sgurr na Ciche and other giants straddle the north view. Who needs a peak in Darien? Tir nan Og is just over yonder!

An Stac still remained, a Stob Ban to Rois-Bheinn's Claurigh, and was reached by returning almost to the Bealach Fhiona and then off to a lower col from which An Stac rose sharply. An Stac's clear shape is instantly recognisable from many directions. As the weather looked like changing for the worse I juddered directly down to Alisary on the Lochailort road rather than making for Inverailort by the crest or the Allt a' Bhuiridh. After sheltering for half an hour among birch trees I walked and read my way up to Lochailort. Too late for the train I read and thumbed and eventually had a lift up and over the watershed for a night in a bothy, another which has long disappeared.

Naturally, having omitted Beinn Mhic Cedidh, it was later promoted to Corbett status. A lecture tour one mid-January gave the chance of climbing this isolated peak, though I was lucky to win west as the A9 was blocked by snow soon afterwards. I had a night in the van near Glenfinnan, where a full moon hung like a Chinese lantern over the Beinn Odhar peaks, a view seen through the dark, bonsai-shaped pines clinging to the crags above Loch Shiel. At first light the mountain tops glowed pink. The weather was obviously settled and an unhurried start was pleasant. I drove along to the watershed and, with the dog, set off for the sneck behind the bump above the east end of Loch Eilt, leaving a tawny trail across the white-washed slopes. A long traverse led us into Coire Buidhe and the col where I had abandoned our traverse a decade earlier.

The east ridge up to the new Corbett required crampons as the ground was sheeted with ice, probably from rain which had then frozen. Every boulder and pebble and blade of grass was sheathed in ice. Storm had a difficult time slithering along at my heels. In the blaze of golden January sun the hill was a superlative viewpoint. Ben Nevis lay between the two Odhars; Ardgour, normally so dark, gleamed silver; Loch Shiel glittered; the Streaps pass and Knoydart were familiar shapes and, up Coire Reidh, the heart of Moidart was a bold, steep jumble of white mountains. The Cuillin Hills, rising from a plum-coloured haze, were an array of bright fangs.

We went down the narrow north ridge and I carried the dog till we were on snow again. I had quite a flounder thereafter. Storm found a blood track from a wounded deer and, later, appeared carrying the hoof of another beast. (The culling of hinds by estate keepers after the autumn stalking is over can go on into January or even February.) We drove fast to Lochailortside but were just too late to watch the sunset beyond the Sgurr of Eigg. My lecture at Lochailort Castle (on Morocco) was delayed a bit as the sky was full of the "northern dancers", one of the best displays of northern lights I've seen in Scotland. If all new Corbetts could give days like that, the OS are welcome to keep adding them indefinitely!

Section 10:   13. DRUIM TARSUINN   770 m   OS 40   875727
             The transverse ridge

Section 10:   14. SGURR GHIUBHSACHAIN   849 m   OS 40   876751
             Peak of the fir wood (goosachan)

Section 10:   15. SGORR CRAOBH A' CHAORAINN   775 m
             OS 40   895758
             Rowantree peak (cruv-a-*chae*ran)

"The Callop Corbetts" has long been the collective name I've used for these three scabrous summits. They catch the eye as one motors west from Loch Eil, and Callop gives the easiest access. They are a clan of steep, craggy and tough hills.

They are worth more than just a quick visit from Callop, however, and besides the day described below, another fine expedition is to make a two-day through trip using the Cona Glen, from Glenfinnan to Corran Ferry, doing these three on the first day, camping in Cona Glen, walking down it, adding Stob Coire a' Chearcaill (10:19) and so on to Corran. This grand walk gives varied scenery of the highest order.

As described in 10:6, 7 I'd started at Strontian and traversed the Sgurr Dhomhnuill hills to camp on the Mam Beathaig between Glen Hurich and Glen Scaddle. The site was also between Carn na Nathrach and Druim Tarsuinn so there wasn't far to go to begin the day's effort. I was off at 6 a.m. for, frosty or not, the sun was going to smite later in the day. Right opposite, a long buttress led upwards, and this gave 1,000 feet of scrambling on rough, solid rock which was quite exposed on the flank. (The rock could all be avoided by going up Coire an t-Searraich.) There was a bump or two and a tiny lochan before we could traverse across to the Bealach an Sgriodain below the shapely summit of the Corbett, called Druim Tarsuinn in sloppy *Tables* fashion, though Druim Tarsuinn is clearly shown as the knobbly ridge running away from the other side of the bealach. The Corbett name is perhaps Sgriodain. That so much is named is indicative of past use. Loch Shiel, now so quiet, probably had quite a population dwelling on its shores.

A derelict gate on the col was useful to hang the tent on and while it was drying we scrambled up the Corbett. Some deer were on top when we arrived. There was a sudden view downwards, and out along the silver-glittering Loch Dubh and Glen Scaddle to big Ben Nevis. Druim Tarsuinn, the ridge, dropped down to a boggy col from where a long, slowly ascending traverse led towards Sgurr Ghiubhsachain. A rocky buttress proved irresistible; I left the sack and had a 400-foot climb. This led nowhere near the summit as I'd hoped, so, after going over to look down the forsaken Loch Shiel corries, I returned to my burden. After another long traverse, with one nasty quartz band, I tried again. The best climb of the day ended right at the big cairn of the day's biggest peak, a fine rocky perch overlooking Loch Shiel.

We tend sometimes to think we are being original or doing something special but the Scottish hills have a long tradition of unconventional enjoyment. Back in 1893 the artist Colin Phillip set out to climb Ghiubhsachain at midnight, to avoid the oppressive heat of summer. He came up from Callop (then a watcher's cottage) to the head of the glen and made a rising traverse across the grassy slopes to the Corbett, scrambling up the rock to the top just in time for dawn breaking. He returned over the second Corbett and was back at base in time for breakfast.

When did you last make a night expedition?

I was loath to leave that splendid summit but the heat was oppressive and the day would become hotter yet. We dandered down to the gentle col to the east and set off a large herd of very dark-coloured deer. They trotted along the flank of Glac Gharbh; we followed, catching them up on the rough ridge that dropped to the head of the Callop glen. They turned downhill and, after leaving the rucksack again, we turned uphill, almost immediately startling a fox into flight up a rake. The rock was slabbier but we kept to it as much as possible, to the top of Sgor Craobh a' Chaorainn, which can look even rockier than Ghiubhsachain; and while there is plenty of rock on these hills it is not continuous enough for real climbing, but can give a day with constant scrambling options, which I was ready to take up.

The views had vanished in haze and I was glad to zigzag down the rakes and, at the first burn, after collecting the rucksack, have a longer stop. Nothing quite beats fresh tea under such circumstances. The time was only 2 p.m. but felt like evening. On reaching the col we put up our herd of deer for the third time. Colin Phillip saw some feral goats on his descent.

The glen down to Callop is wild but, in places, gives a superb mix of old forest: Scots pines, birch, hazel, alder and so on. I walked down with my mind away in daydreams, with the dog panting after. At the foot of the glen, a few days before, I'd left my folding bike which I bolted together for the long run down Loch Shiel. The bonus for the day was discovering the lochside forestry road was tarred all the way. A locked gate keeps the public out, of course, even though public money built the road, but as an old right of way they can't stop you walking, or cycling, and a push bike is often a useful "aid to pedestrianism".

The run down the loch gave a hot eleven miles but we had a delectable camp to end the day. Dog-tired would well describe my companion — even if he had journeyed down the loch in my rucksack. I'm glad he is not a St Bernard. The next day we traversed Resipol to the car, returned for the bike, and also went up Garbh Bheinn. You don't waste sunny days in Ardgour.

Section 10:   16. SGURR AN UTHA   796 m   OS 40   885839
           Peak of the udder

A bothy, no longer in existence, allowed a 7 o'clock departure for Sgurr an Utha. I was back at the Mallaig–Glenfinnan road by 10.30 and had time for coffee in the Stage House before catching the afternoon train home.

The start from the A830 is obvious, a path leaving the road just east of the "cross" shown on the map. The path crosses the Allt an Utha by a bridge (not shown) but is in a poor state thereafter. I simply followed the riverbank, the clear water racing down through a succession of pools and deep guts beside me, and then took a north fork, direct to the summit: "a pile of toast-filled racks of mica schist like some Lewis Carroll creation." The burns and pools I'd passed would have given any number of fine camp sites — I begrudged my night under a roof. The arrival on top is dramatic or perhaps instamatic, certainly photographic.

I came up and, bang, there, straight ahead, was the great pass to Loch Arkaig between Sgurr Thuilm and the Streaps. Below Utha, to the north, was another grassy trench of a pass (with a zip of path up the slope beyond) leading the eye westwards to the dark, spilt-ink length of Loch Beoraid. The Moidart hills lay to the south, northwards I looked over Carn Mor and Sgurr na h-Aide into Knoydart. The looking took half an hour, till I grew chilled and had to move. I cut all the corners running back down to the path. A shepherd and his dogs found me brewing at a pool above the road. One of the dogs cocked a leg over my rucksack. My yell of "Hey! Piss off you!" struck the shepherd as hilarious and he went on his way chuckling. I only noticed the choice of words later. By then I was in the hotel at Glenfinnan with the rain playing Gilbert and Sullivan on the west window-panes.

With a pack left below the hill my route was more or less dictated by necessity, better would have been to follow the path up and traversed everything from Sidhean Mor to Fraoch-bheinn and then down direct to Glenfinnan. "Next time", I promise, for this is one of the very best Corbett viewpoints — or any kind of viewpoint. At the west end of Loch Beoraid is a cave used by Prince Charlie on his post-Culloden wanderings, and he finally sailed away from Loch nan Uamh, a few miles beyond. On a Clan Map I noticed the name "Corbett" printed across the landscape between Sgurr an Utha and Loch Nevis. It seemed both symbolic and appropriate.

Section 10:   17. STREAP   909 m   OS 40   946863
               Climbing hill

Section 10:   18. BRAIGH NAN UAMHACHAN   765 m
               OS 40   975867
               The slope of the caves (brae-nan-oo-achan)

The Streaps were such a lure that Joe and I traversed them long before Corbetts became an interest. They have an eye-smacking boldness that provokes response. The pass between Streap and Sgurr Thuilm must have some of the steepest flanks of any in Scotland. Seen from Strathan at the west end of Loch Arkaig, or from Sgurr an Utha, or the hills west of Loch Shiel the pass is a much photographed feature, classic U-shaped, honed in glacial times and guarded by jagged, rough mountains. On Sgurr Thuilm Bonnie Prince Charlie skulked for a day before breaking through the redcoat cordon to the safety of the north. That pass is still a vital link to all sorts of mountain treks, climbs, Munros and Corbetts.

Joe and I traversed the Streaps (which are nearly Munros) on Christmas Eve 1961, the coldest Christmas for 40 years the radio reported. We believed it. Prunes left soaking overnight were encased in a cylinder of ice and our eggs froze solid inside the tent. On Boxing Day we took a lift to the Fort on the back of a lorry and ended up closer to hypothermia than ever I have been on a mountain.

Glenfinnan was unplanted then and very lonely. We wandered up to Corryhully and up on to point 844, Meall an Uillt Chaoil, to traverse all the ridge of many bumps to Streap. Stob Coire nan Ceare, *the peak of the hen's comb*, is a fine summit in its own right and gave a good view of Thuilm–Coireachan, the major objective of the day and the completion of a circuit that is the best for doing those Munros. Streap is no easy addition. I called it "a most impressive peak of narrow ridges and shattered corries, with unremittingly steep slopes". A glissade on firm snow shot us down to the pass.

Streap has an eastern Top, Streap Comhlaidh, reached by a fine ridge, this pair forming corries facing both north and south, a big H of ridges, all dropping down to give practical ascent or descent routes to the good access at lower levels. The crest between Streap Comhlaidh and its own SE toplet is a narrow crest, with steep grass precipices on the flanks.

Over the years I've tried most routes. The best of Streap is the ragged crest Joe and I followed. Beinn an Tuim is worth adding and can be approached by a forestry road on the east of Glenfinnan which has a branch ascending on the north side of the big gully draining Beinn an Tuim to the south west. Having travelled to Glenfinnan by train Joe and I spent the rest of the day cutting steps up this gully. Tuim, a Corbett, though we knew it not, was recently demoted as not having quite 500 feet of re-ascent on all sides.

Beinn an Tuim is a good climb from the east, too; from the Gleann Dubh Lighe I'd recommend finishing the traverse of Streap and Streap Comhlaidh by dropping down the green and gentle south ridge of the latter to take this forgotten glen out to the Glenfinnan–Fort William road. An even grander circuit is to do the complete skyline of the Gleann Dubh Lighe peaks. There are two Corbetts available, after all.

I've not actually done that, for, always being in Munro-dominated parties, Braigh nan Uamhachan has usually had to be combined with Gulvain, its neighbour to the east. So it is the circuit of Gleann

Fionnlighe I've more often done, often enough ending on my own, abandoned by Munros-only companions. As there is a long walk to this Corbett, the circuit of Streap and Uamhachan has much to recommend it. If the Gleann Dubh Lighe skyline walk was situated in the Lake District it would be a famous day's darg. I first did Braigh nan Uamhachan by its northern approaches. These are neither so illogical nor so rough as they look on the map. It was a route Tony and I repeated on UC 80, on a day that took us from Glen Pean bothy to the Loch Eil Centre near Corpach.

Gleann a' Chaorainn is the Strathan approach, a glen dominated by the Streaps, and we followed this till well past the lowest col on the ridge linking Leac na Carnaich to the Streaps before doubling back up to reach this col. You lose only a few hundred feet in angling down to near the head of Gleann Camgharaidh, and the Braigh is there on the other side of the valley. Usually, having heavy packs, we've made a rising round of its north end to dump things on the Gualann nan Osna col before tackling the Corbett and/or the Munro of Gulvain. It is a novel route out from expeditions into the Rough Bounds of Knoydart. Tony and I had a hot day and on UC 84 Claudia and Sandy, the two young nurses new to walking and to Scotland, had a full scale roasting. Having walked Loch Morar to Glen Pean the day before, we cut out the Braigh for an hour by (or in) Lochan a' Chomhlain (the deer were doing the same) and a dander down pretty Gleann Dubh Lighe where we spent a relaxing day and night. I don't recall much about the Corbett, in fact, but the fester hours with Tony or the girls are unforgettable. There are days when the best is *not* climbing hills! The traverse of Braigh nan Uamhachan, while not as spectacular as the Streaps–Tuim outing, is, as Donald Bennet writes, "a very interesting traverse which would undoubtedly be better known if the Braigh had the extra height to bring it to Munro status."

Needless to say the views from these hills are of the best. What a pity we have lost Beinn an Tuim, the best of all, with views out along, down along Loch Eil and Loch Shiel! Beinn an Tuim is more accurately Beinn an Tom, *hillocky hill*, which is a good general description of everything in the area.

Section 10:   19. Stob Coire a' Chearcaill   771 m
                       OS 41   017727
                       The spike of the circular corrie

This hill is more often observed than climbed. It is a Corbetteer's Corbett and few other walkers make the ascent. Like many isolated

Corbetts there is a panoramic view, with the big bad Ben bold in the east. The circle of corrie facing east is well seen from Fort William. Fort William, alas, is well seen from Stob Coire a' Chearcaill. Most spectacular is the sweep of country from Ardgour to Glenfinnan: as wild and dramatic as anything in Scotland — and not a Munro mugging that magnificence.

I feel a bit guilty about this Corbett as it was one which I did in that frantic period when suddenly completing the Corbetts became important. It was bagged, it was raided, it was raped. It was barely enjoyed. Some day I will make amends, wandering up Gleann Sron a' Chreagain and descending off Sgurr an Iubhair to the Cona Glen, the best combination. That will be in early summer, the trees will be in new leaf, the flowers at their best, the moors tangy with myrtle scent and the Ben a snowy glitter in the eye of the sun. There will be swims in the rivers and brews in solitary places. That landscape south of the Mallaig line and west of Loch Linnhe is one of the most varied and rewarding in Scotland. The hills are all malts. Drink slow and deep, my friends.

My ascent was made at the end of a long drive from Fife with several calls on the way. Coming out of the Locheil Centre I looked across the loch at the Corbett, looked at my watch, and quickly drove round the loch, past the Doire na Muice plantings to park by the Blaich crofts. I took to the hill with no great enthusiasm: the afternoon was too stuffily hot, I was too tired and a left calf muscle ached from rock climbing the day before. I took a book and read as I walked up the long, featureless slope. By Braigh Bhlaich the surface was too stony to read and walk. The view was disappointing as grey haze was overtaken by greyer dusk. Being April I was at least spared midges. Gaston Rebuffat once wrote of such a day, "the human animal was not happy". We all have off-days, I suppose, so, in this case, don't do as I did but do as I suggest.

Section 10:   20. MEALL A' PHUBUILL   774 m   OS 41   029854
         Hill of the tent

Poubelle is the French word for a dustbin and, perhaps justifiably, Meall a' Phubuill, to me, became linked with that word for, on my first visit, the hill treated me with the respect given to used tea leaves. I've had happy ascents since.

The normal route to Meall a' Phubuill is up Gleann Suileag from Fassfern, on the loop of old road by Loch Eil. An estate track runs up through the attractive forest to Glensulaig with a good path, not on the map, angling up to the Allt Fionn Diore col, above which stands the dumpling bulk of the Corbett. A poorer path also continues up the glen beyond Glensulaig and descends Glen Loy, becoming a seldom-used minor road, to reach the Great Glen. Beinn Bhan (12:1) above Glen Loy is a Corbett which could be linked on a pleasant two-day expedition. Meall a' Phubuill can also be reached via Glen Mallie, making a splendid high-level circuit, Monadh Beag–the Corbett–Druim Gleann Laoigh. The views *from* Phubuill make it memorable. The hill itself is less interesting.

Another good route to the Corbett is to combine Phubuill with the Munro Gulvain (Gaor Bheinn) by tramping up Gleann Fionnlighe, which is what led to my misadventures. I'd been trying to find the sailing schooner *Captain Scott* and eventually saw her anchored up Loch Eil and managed to get on board to meet her redoubtable skipper, Commander Victor Clark, a character in the Tilman class. The meeting was to lead to regular autumn months' instructing on the *Captain Scott* until financial necessity saw her sold to the Arabs where she now sails the Gulf as *Youth of Oman*. Nobody in Britain would pay the price of half a mile of motorway to save her. The trainees did a sort of sea and hills Outward Bound Course and when I was told they were off up Gleann Fionnlighe for a couple of nights with instructor David Osselton I decided to combine a visit to a wanted Munro and a wanted Corbett with seeing them operate in the field. I drove to the head of Loch Eil, packed and prepared, had supper and slept in the Dormobile.

I woke to that strange hush that means snow has fallen. The weight of snow nearly closed the roof down on to my bunk. I rose in self defence. Being a fair morning there would soon be a thaw so I made a dash west and back for photographs and only then set off, bare to the waist (in early March!) to try to track the others, a task which could be made difficult — or easy — by the new snow. Their first camp was spotted because of the beaten bracken where they'd commuted between tents and burn, and a good furrow of track in the new snow led on into the hills. We finally found their new site at 1,600 feet in Coire a' Chaorainn on the SE flank of Gulvain. One cripple was in a tent and he said the rest were up the hill. I'd just pitched and brewed when they returned. Soon there was a bustle of pitching tents and cooking, with the voices sinking into a murmur and finally silence. A slice of moon shone down on the pass under Meall a' Phubuill opposite. I read for a while by candle light and snuggled down in the new tent I'd just bought.

An hour later a howling gale and lashing rain were battering the camp. The new nylon tent rattled noisily and I had little sleep. Nearing dawn I realised the tent also leaked badly and my duvet, which I'd been lying on, was sodden, and much of the floor an inch deep in water. The sewn-in groundsheet was doing a fine job at not letting water out. The dog perched on top of me to keep out of the wet.

This was not one of my more cheerful camping experiences but I think the trainees (suffering a bit, too) rather enjoyed seeing one of the "experts" in the toils. David quoted bits of Gerard Manley Hopkins's "Inversnaid" to me as we retreated off the monsoon mountain.

A couple of days later I came back and cycled up the glen as far as possible then traversed Gulvain, an icy ridge and sodden flanks, before crossing, feet saturated, to climb Meall a' Phubuill. Such an effort for such a tame hill. The irony of its name was not lost on me.

Bonnie Prince Charlie, on his confident march from raising the standard at Glenfinnan, came by Fassfern, marching up Glen Suileag and through by Glen Loy to reach Invergarry. Sir John Cope retreated, and the rebel army went over the Corrieyairack to Edinburgh and the Battle of Prestonpans. Meall a' Phubuill had its moment of history. Since the killing times that followed that rebellion it has remained a forgotten, silent corner.

> "Where essential silence cheers and blesses
> And forever in the hill recesses
> Her more lovely music broods and dies."
> (Robert Louis Stevenson)

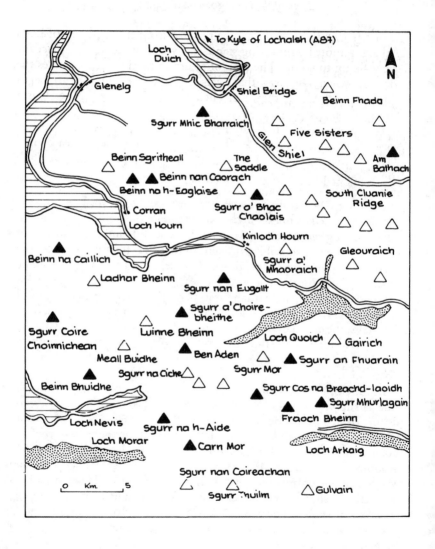

LOCH MORAR–LOCH ARKAIG TO GLEN SHIEL

Section 11: 1. CARN MOR   829 m   OS 40   903910
Big cairn

Section 11: 2. SGURR NA H-AIDE   867 m   OS 40   889931
Peak of the hat (sgoar na h'Atch)

USING A CAR these peaks can be reached from the west end of Loch Arkaig, remote by motoring standards, yet only the starting place for the walking to come. The fang of Sgurr na h-Aide so dominates the view up Glen Dessarry that walkers have been known to begin climbing it thinking they were heading up Sgurr na Ciche. It is a Hobson's choice which side of Glen Dessary one walks up. The glen is heavily planted. A' Chuil can make a good base, as can a tent pitched west of the massed forestry. The southern slopes of Sgurr na h-Aide have a straight trench of valley draining them; a fascinating through route, only tracked beyond Lochan Eanaiche, but worth using for interest as well as probably giving the easiest route to the Corbett.

Go along (very little *down*) to near the lochan and then turn up for the heartbreak steepness of the ascent. This toil cannot be avoided. The east ridge to Meall na Sroine is very rough and gives plenty of extra footage but so wild is the setting that the effort is repaid by the views. If adding Carn Mor, descend by the ascent line and follow the burn opposite more or less to the top of the second Corbett, then descend by Meall nan Spardan, or its flanking corries, back to the head of Glen Dessarry. This is a long day if done from a car. If done over two days, the alternative approach to Carn Mor by Glen Pean could be taken. Do not underestimate these Corbetts. They are as rough as anything in Knoydart and their flanks are among the steepest slopes in Scotland.

Beware of Lochan Leum an t-Sagairt. There is no path on the north side as shown, so pass by the south shore. (Note again the unusual feature of a contour line wandering through the loch.) Newcomers to Glen Pean should walk on over the watershed for the view down to Loch Morar then backtrack almost to Lochan Leum again before heading up the Corbett. If Glen Pean is a favourite western pass, Carn Mor is not one of my favourite ascents from this side. There are some unusual landslip fissures on the slopes above the loch, dangerous as crevasses in winter. The walk back along the crest to Monadh Gorm is grassier and easier than h-Aide's equivalent. The view stays fierce and rugged.

Two other access routes are used frequently. A train (or car) can be taken to Glenfinnan, and the pass between Sgurr Thuilm and the Streaps followed to Strathan at the west end of Loch Arkaig. Bothies in either Glen Pean or Glen Dessarry are alternatives to camping, and Sourlies, at the head of Loch Nevis, provides the same choice. Sailing in is perhaps the most satisfying approach to these hills. The mail boat from Mallaig will land you at Inverie with the Mam Meadail to be crossed to Sourlies (more Corbetts in Knoydart, or en route, if so desired) but a seldom-used alternative is to land at Tarbet and walk the south side of Loch Nevis to Sourlies. This is much more straight-forward than most books would suggest. They put me off trying this route for years but I now regard it as the easy way in; easy in Knoydart terms of course! There is nothing easy about Sgurr na h-Aide from Sourlies, or Finiskaig where I pitched camp on one occasion. (Sometimes, in summer, or if you book and pay for it, the boat will go up to land you at the head of Loch Nevis. Check the times etc. with Bruce Watt Cruises, the Pier, Mallaig, tel. 0687–2233.)

The dog and I had first called in to Camusrory, then an Outdoor Centre, before coming over to camp at Finiskaig. On a previous occasion there was a bitch on heat at the centre and Kitchy took off in the night. There was no bridge over the Carnoch at that time, which gave me several paddles to collect him. This time he was tied to the tent pole overnight.

We left Finiskaig in warm summer rain, I'd minimal clothing on under waterproofs and put my boots on over bare feet to keep my stockings dry. A Berghaus cover for my rucksack was pressed into service. On the way up Coire Dubh I made a point of inspecting the unusual feature of a burn shown as splitting into two but, sadly, it had stopped flowing off in two directions. A steady plod took us up to the so-called "pass" of the Bealach nan Daoine (680 m). Most of my gear was left there while I groped up Sgurr na h-Aide which has two tops, nearly a kilometre apart — and on a bit to make sure it really was the top. The cloud was thick as toffee, the air still — a grand evening for midges unless a salvation breeze could find us. The cloud peeled away as we descended the Leac Bhuidhe slopes and I was pleased to see we were actually descending to the right place.

Plans were altered in faith and, instead of aiming for the head of Loch Morar, we angled down to Gleann an Lochain Eanaiche, a descent which was hard on the knees. Gullies rather than crags drove us to the path below, which we followed up to Lochan Eanaiche, passed along its south shore and sweated up Carn Mor. We descended more directly and put both feet in the burn crossing back to the path. The walk to Loch Morar was like the River Carnach in character. We watched, with mixed feelings, as the clouds blew off our tops. (On h-Aide the wind had been southerly, on Carn Mor it was northerly.) At Kinlochmorar we met a cyclist heading from Glen Pean to Swordland. "Would you be Dave Norgate?" I asked. He was — and how had I guessed? "There are only half a dozen folks daft enough to take a bike along Loch Morar side, so it seemed likely." There is a certain satisfaction in meeting someone undoubtedly crazier than oneself! Rounding the head of the loch I gathered the accumulated driftwood before going on for a comfy night in the bothy. The wet tent was hung up to dry and five cups of tea began a well-earned binge. Our exit was made by Gleann Taodhail to Loch Beoraid and the train at Lochailort, a magnificently wild and lonely route out. This exploratory element is the greatest reward of Section 11 of the Corbetts.

It is interesting to see how things change — or don't change. A. E. Robertson (who, in 1901, was the first to complete a round of the Munros) visited this area in 1895. His party caught the morning mail-coach from Fort William as far as Glenfinnan and crossed to Loch Arkaig as I've mentioned (climbing Sgurr Tnuilm) then, "at Glendessarry, a farmhouse, we asked for and obtained accommodation. Next morning a very high hill in front, Sgurr na h-Aide, so attracted our attention by its sharp and narrow summit that we determined to set foot on it. Its appearance led us to expect some scrambling, and we were not disappointed. A very rugged descent brought us to the pass, the Mam na Cloich Airde . . . the keeper at Carnach put us up and his kindness will not be forgotten." They continued on over Sgurr na Ciche to a keeper's at Kinlochquoich (now *under* Loch Quoich) and out by Altbeithe and the Bealach Dubh Leac to Kintail.

Section 11:   3. SGURR COS NA BREACHD-LAOIDH   835 m
OS 33   948947
Peak of the cave of the bonny calf

Section 11:   4. FRAOCH BHEINN   858 m   OS 33   986940
Heather hill

Section 11:   5. SGURR MHURLAGAIN   880 m   OS 33   012944
Peak of the bag-shaped sea inlet

These three Corbetts are all lined up next to each other so are described together to avoid some repetition of practical information. Just how many are done in a day is up to the individual. I personally found each of them a useful half-day sortie going into or back from Knoydart or

Glen Kingie. They are all reached from the end of the tortuous public road along to the west end of Loch Arkaig. A private road, unsurfaced, continues up Glen Dessarry; they therefore have, for such a distant place, surprisingly easy access.

Sgurr Cos na Breachd-laoidh is rather meaningless. The *Tables* suggest the last word should be -laoigh (*cow*) but it is hardly the sort of place one would associate with cows. The erudite Rev. A. R. G. Burn (Munroist No. 2) in a 1917 *SMC Journal* suggests it is Sgurr Chois Breacaich, *the peak whose foot is speckled with stones*, which seems more reasonable. The whole peak is usually referred to as Druim a' Chuirn *the ridge of stones* rather than just its eastern summit, which is not a *druim*. This is the best of the three Corbetts but received scant attention until its promotion in the "Big Bang" changes of 1981. A party from our local club went up the hill a year earlier during a Western meet. We started with the Glen Kingie track from Glen Dessarry House and then moved on to the long SE Ridge up to the eastern top, Druim a' Chuirn. There is a mile-long crest along to the Corbett and this gives some scrambling. Half-way along a large flaky pinnacle sticks up, a feature which immediately distinguishes this hill when seen from other summits. Everyone scrambled up — even the dog — but an icy wind threatened to blow us off. The Glen Kingie flank is very craggy. The normal descent would be to the south but we dropped steeply down to the col to reach An Eag and traversed everything along to Sgurr Gairich, quite a long day, but midsummer encouraged a 10 p.m. return to Strathan. This Corbett could be combined with Sgurr nan Coireachan in a traverse of the crest of Coire nan Uth.

Fraoch Bheinn I took in on a March day after having gone through, by that same path to Glen Kingie, to climb Sgurr Mor. Deep snow and over-warm weather made a tiring day: Fraoch Bheinn was enough, rather than with Sgurr Mhurlagain as planned. There is very little heather on *heather hill* and the craggy buttresses can easily be bypassed. Using one or other of the flanking paths to gain as much height as possible before heading for the summits is a good plan. Kinbreack bothy in Glen Kingie is a good base for tackling these Corbetts by their more interesting NE Ridges. Fraoch Bheinn from the bothy looks like the Buachaille Etive Beag from Lagangarbh.

Sgurr Mhurlagain I took in while walking out from Kinbreack on another occasion. I tried to go up the gorge of the bothy burn but a big pool blocked the way so I just zigzagged up on to the Corbett's north ridge: walking with few clothes on and my umbrella up: one way with sweaty condensation in pre-Goretex days. All too soon I was into clouds, but the summit can hardly be missed as the cairn perches on the edge of a cliff-bitten corrie headwall. We descended the "interminable" SW Ridge as the car was parked by the Dearg Allt, but anywhere on the southern flank can be chosen if a quick and easy ascent is wanted. There is no telephone at Murlaggan — don't break a leg on running down those grassy slopes! The best of the descent is the view across to the Streaps and the scrum of peaks westwards.

> "Passing through,
> Stop for brew;
> Feel like new —
> Thanking you."
>   (Entry in Kinbreack Bothy Book)

Section 11:   6. SGURR AN FHUARAIN   901 m   OS 33   987980
        Oran's peak(?) (*ooaran*)

This hill, being twinned with Sgurr Mor, should have been done at the same time as "the big yin". If not, there is a long journey to penalise the original slackness. Even Rev. A. E. Robertson noted Sgurr Mor as being one of the remotest Munros and advocated, as have many writers since, taking in the peak as part of a cross-country tramp.

My most recent tramp was on an Ultimate Challenge: a long day that took us from A' Chuil bothy to Tomdoun Hotel; before that it was on a BFMC Meet based at Strathan when we traversed from Sgurr Cos na Breachd-laoidh to Sgurr an Fhuarain with one diehard adding Gairich; on my Munro marathon I'd camped above Loch Quoich, north of Sgurr Mor, and followed the ridge eastwards to the dam; earlier still my brother David had dropped Jim, Andrew, Kitchy and me off at Glenfinnan on a Friday night and picked us up at the Loch Quoich dam on Sunday — quite a weekend trip from the Lowlands. That was my first visit to this Corbett and the most memorable.

Saturday was spent traversing the hills south of Glen Pean and heading to A' Chuil for the night. On Sunday, we were off at six o'clock, grabbing the chance of shade for the steep haul up the Allt Coire nan Uth. Frogs were rather pathetically scrabbling about in the dried-out landscape while an eagle swung lazily overhead — even the thermals were up early. We thankfully left our packs on the col to go up Sgurr nan Coireachan. A clammy mist was fingering over the ridge and kept us cool but the signs were all of a scorcher to come. An Eag, with packs, set us on the start of the grand highway between tawny Glen Kingie and the out-of-bounds of Loch Quoich.

There is an abandoned stalkers' path of some character along the crest. High on Sgurr Mor it breaks into steps and swanks through the crags. We sat on Sgurr Beag, to brew, in an attempt to try and reduce the height of the tent-topped giant of Sgurr Mor. Our perch site was dotted with some freshly-made mole hills. I've never seen them so high. There were scores of deer, all high in search of some coolness, and we charged on over the Munro behind a herd of stags. Sgurr Mor is well named.

The heat was intense for the steep "down" and the long easy sweep up to Sgurr an Fhuarain. The landscape shimmered. After a few minutes by the trig point we set off down the east ridge to find water as soon as possible. The crags shown on the map are not so fierce as one would expect and the north ridge is equally easy for a continuation eastwards. (An ascent from the south is easy anywhere, just a matter of working up long grassy slopes.)

We found a delectable pool, drank half of it, swam in the rest and drip-dried over an hour-long lunch break. I'd draped all my clothes round me but the others had on only pants, and, by the day's end, they were glowing red. You could have fried eggs on their shoulders.

The stalkers' path up on to Gairich Beag is the steepest I've ever met, which made hard work for us, but we crossed the deer-busy "mountain of yelping" (Gairich) in good heart. The way off to the dam was well known and a "yoo-hoo" across the loch ensured there was tea ready for our arrival, 13½ hours from our A' Chuil departure. There was an element of unreality about work the next day and the glow was not just sunburn. We had experienced a majestic day; "smitten and addicted". I'm sure A.E.R. would have approved, even though it had been the sabbath. The sun shines on the just and the unjust — just like the rain.

Section 11:   7. BEN ADEN   887 m   OS 33   899986
             The hill of the face

Ben Aden is the forgotten peak of Knoydart. Being wedged between three of the roughest Munros in Scotland probably accounts for it being overlooked or ignored. The Carnach valley is dominated by Ben Aden and the peak stands over Lochan nam Breac, the secretive heart of the country of Knoydart. Be warned, though: the heaviest rainfall in Scotland is recorded at the west end of Loch Quoich.

The last time on these hills I canoed in along Loch Quoich with the loch wasted by summer drought and giving reflections of a clarity I've never seen equalled. You could turn slides upside down and nobody noticed. A camp by Lochan nam Breac is one of the classic experiences of the Scottish Highlands (like climbing the Inaccessible Pinnacle or traversing the Aonach Eagach by moonlight or seeing sunrise over the stacks of St Kilda) but Ben Aden is not the easiest of places to reach. The raising of Loch Quoich's waters destroyed some useful paths while almost all the rivers in these hills can quickly become impassable after heavy rain. Rain falls often and with lively exuberance and Lochan nam Breac can feel a long way from anywhere. Ben Aden and Druim Chosaidh which hem in the lochan are some of the least-climbed Corbetts. Corbettitis is usually well advanced before they are taken. Strong medicine.

There are no ambling routes up Ben Aden for the peak is one of the steepest, rockiest and roughest in Scotland. The rock is good — I am surprised climbs have not been recorded on the bolder cliff faces. Ben Aden doesn't hide its challenges, but is a peak best ascended on a clear day. Work out your line of ascent from the Carnach valley *before* rushing up into its complexities. I preach all this from the experience of having done none of these things.

Finiskaig used to be my original Knoydart base. This old building is a complete ruin now and Sourlies across the river is often over-crowded. In July 1973 a party of us sailed up Loch Nevis, landed at Camusrory and set up our tents at Finiskaig for several days before making an exit to Glenfinnan. We decided to combine Ben Aden with Sgurr na Ciche and do the Garbh Chiochs–Coireachan hills on the way out. I wonder if anyone has ever gone all the way from Ben Aden to Gairich in a day? It would give an incomparable traverse.

Some people complain that "Knoydart" should be used only of the country west of the Carnach but historically this was not so. The Cameron–Macdonnell march is at the head of Glen Dessarry, and Sgurr na Ciche and Ben Aden have always been part of the Knoydart Estate, centred on Inverie, at least until recent exercises in asset-stripping. Geologically these hills are Knoydart and Ben Aden is the roughest of all the Rough Bounds.

The path up the River Carnach is often more imaginary than accurate and you may not cross easily to reach the foot of Ben Aden. The tide was out when we set off on our grey summer morning, which enabled us to walk along the sands, wend through the saltings and on up the glen, keeping to the east bank. We resisted some fine pools at a rocky step. There were old walls and ruins where the Allt Achadh a' Ghlinne joined the Carnach. A solitary rowan had sprouted: a poignant memorial to the long-departed families who once lived in that lonely spot. We couldn't see much so tackled the hill *en face* (more or less what one does anyway). "Warm and muggy. Soon in a disgusting lather of sweat", I wrote later of that toil up into the mist. We ran against some crags which pushed us along into a gully. This required the use of our emergency abseil line and gave two pitches, first a backing-up exercise followed by a slabby wall and then a dank, black flue, down which a burn was pouring. The gloom was brightened by great clumps of roseroot and globeflower. Two hours were needed to land eight people, one dog and all our rucksacks at the top of the difficulties. The mist was really thick and we had some casting about among all the many rocky bumps to make sure of the summit.

The navigation after that was a complex business. We were aided by the line of lochans (something actually recognisable!) and a clearance on Meall a' Choire Dhuibh, where the general direction changes completely, was a welcome help. The clearance ended with rain sweeping in but by then all we had to do was to go upwards and, when there was no more up, that would be the top. Sgurr na Ciche's summit can always be recognised by its collection of shattered trig pillars. We weren't back at Finiskaig till 8 p.m.

The SW face of Aden is generally recognised as the easiest, but if you can't see a route up from below the best course would be to follow the Allt Achadh a' Ghlinne to where the map rather vaguely gives the name Bealach na h-Eangair. Head up the side stream which cuts the word "Bealach". This leads up to a gap, which is drained, on the NE side, by the Allt Coire na Cruaiche. This gap is a very definite pass (Bealach a' Chairn Deirg on 1:25,000), and as such could be found in mist, with not too difficult a ridge on up to the summit. The Allt Achadh a' Ghlinne descends from a wild corrie crowded with crags. The dip with the lochans is Bealach a' Choire Cruaidh (1:25,000), probably another old pass. From the north side, the Allt Coire na Cruaiche is the one relatively easy route. The rest of the north face is more suitable for climbing, rather than walking, not that the granite pegmatite has received much, if any, attention, from climbers. Ben Aden is worth an investment in a 1:25,000 map. (Sheet "NM89/99 Glen Dessarry")

I've just been reading some 1905 notes by the Rev. A. E. Robertson: "The best way to explore this region is probably to traverse it in several directions, carrying a rucksack with a few necessities, obtaining a night's shelter at some of the outlying shepherds' or keepers' houses in Glen Dessarry or Glen Kingie or by the shores of Loch Quoich. In fact this is the only way one can really see it, the distances from hotels being too great. A few days spent in this fashion will be a unique and charming experience; for this is one of the few districts not yet corrupted by the moneyed Sassenach, and the people in the glens are kind, courteous and hospitable." What would he make of today's desolation I wonder?

Section 11:   8. BEINN BHUIDHE   855 m   OS 33   822967
                   Yellow hill (boo-ee)

Section 11:   9. SGURR COIRE CHOINNICHEAN   796 m
                   OS 33   791011
                   Peak of the mossy corrie

Section 11:   10. BEINN NA CAILLICH   785 m   OS 33   796067
                   Old woman's hill

Section 11:   11. SGURR A' CHOIRE-BHEITHE   914 m
                   OS 33   895015
                   Peak of the birch corrie (corrie vey)

These are the Corbetts of Knoydart, an area renowned for its tough landscape, as the term "Rough Bounds" indicates. The Corbetts are up to expectation and are listed together here for descriptive convenience rather than with any idea of climbing them all at once. For that you would need several days. For Knoydart you will want many more days than you ever have available. Knoydart is a far country as well as a rough one.

The convenient ways in are few. Easiest is the mailboat from Mallaig to Inverie, the only hamlet in the area (farm bunkhouse/B & B accommodation) and the boat may also be chartered to take a party to the head of Loch Nevis. Sometimes it is possible to hire a boat from Corran to Barrisdale across Loch Hourn. I've also sailed and used a canoe to reach the near-island of Knoydart. There are no public roads reaching it, and only two, long, dead-end minor roads, by Loch Quoich to Kinloch Hourn and by Loch Arkaig to Glen Dessarry, come anywhere near.

At one time there were no bothies or bridges and Knoydart had a deserved reputation as a difficult and potentially dangerous place. Alas, it has been thoroughly tamed, and has lost greatly thereby. There is a constant, vociferous public demand to make things easier or safer which nibbles away at the glorious wildness of our mountains. Knoydart has suffered this aesthetical erosion and should be a lesson to all of us. We must learn, somehow, to leave things alone as much as possible. The safety arguments are fallacious for, however much you level the rough, there will always be someone who will stumble and hurt himself. Taken to its logical conclusion these people should bridge every single stream and level every mountain. It is time we stopped catering for the lowest human denominator and gave consideration to the landscape itself.

The Corbetts look as if they could be linked on to Munros easily enough, but such is the roughness of the ridges in Knoydart that this is often harder work than making two ascents from sea level. Sgurr a' Choire-bheithe (914 the OS now say) and Luinne Bheinn face each other across a high pass, Meall Buidhe and Beinn Bhuidhe do so as well, but less easily. As like as not, a first visit to Knoydart has been a Munro-bagging raid so linking Corbetts to Munros is not of particular interest. Time is what is most needed in Knoydart.

Even back in the bad old days when visitors were not welcomed to Knoydart we used to have school parties camping and trekking there, usually sailing in from Inverie and trekking out to Glenfinnan. As the kids were all hooked on Munros I had few chances of adding Corbetts. They had to be dealt with on later visits, but gave an excuse for making the most of Knoydart's best feature, the remarkable high-level traverses available.

The dog and I sailed from Mallaig in the familiar *Western Isles* and, as they were having to take a policeman up to Camusrory, I scrounged a lift as well. When a tiny inflatable came out to meet the *Western Isles* it could take only one other person, leaving me stranded on board till the bobby could finish his work (a tramp had broken into the outdoor centre there) and I could land with the Warden on his return trip. There is no good anchorage off Camusrory, and the skipper offered to put me ashore further along. The *Western Isles* was edged into the cliffs near Rubha Dubh a' Bhata and, from the bow, I placed the dog on a ledge and quickly stepped across myself. My rucksack was passed over and the boat drifted back. The landing took a few seconds: quite an impressive bit of seamanship.

I was tempted to go straight up Beinn Bhuidhe but I'd promised to call in at Camusrory. I set off along the coast, with stunning views of Ben Aden and Sgurr na Ciche at the head of the loch. The Warden had the kettle boiling when we arrived. This was a sad visit in some ways for the centre was on its penultimate course. Camusrory was just too remote and expensive to compete with the subsidised centres in the south. Tony Montgomery, the Warden, moved his ponies to Moray where he still offers real trekking rather than the gentle amble that passes for pony trekking. I miss meeting his ponies in the wild glens of Knoydart. The paths are drier, though!

The dog and I went up Glen Carnach and pitched our small tent a thousand feet up in Coire na Gaoithe, with Ben Aden just across the valley and a bold view up the Carnach River to the castellated wall of

Druim Chosaidh. There was plenty of dead wood. I lit a fire after supper and was relaxing in the delight of a pre-midge, perfect evening when two people descended on us — with mutual astonishment. The two students were camping at Carnoch and had traversed the Munros and our site was on their natural route back, but in those crags and folds and gullies to come upon the tent was quite a coincidence. They apologised! We sat and blethered over tea: they had a week and were wandering from Lochailort to Arnisdale.

We were up at five o'clock and carried the rucksack up to the loch before setting off on a long, intricate traverse for the Mam Unndalain and Sgurr a' Choire-bheithe. The gear had to be left in a spot with the utter certainty of finding it again. Aden and Ciche were damming back an eastern cloud sea. Stray streamers of cloud broke round to ebb and flow along Druim Chosaidh, the long, craggy, five mile ridge which runs from Sgurr a' Choire-bheithe to Loch Quoich. The shores of Loch Quoich offer another, difficult, approach walk in to Knoydart, one to be attempted only in reasonable weather as the Abhainn Chosaidh is impassable in spate.

Sgurr a' Choire-bheithe juts out as a bold, craggy step above the Mam Unndalain but this was easily outflanked to the right and the final bump gained. The whole east was under a starched cloud sheet but the ragged array of Ladhar Bheinn lay under a smiting sun. There are two superb big Corbett days to be had from Barrisdale. One is this hill, from the Mam Unndalain, followed by the scrambly traverse of Druim Chosaidh and back by the Gleann Cosaidh–Glen Barrisdale path, the other links this Corbett with Sgurr nan Eugallt over Slat-Bheinn. Barrisdale, green and with some remnants of natural woodland, is a delightful base. An estate bothy is available for walkers.

The Druim Chosaidh ridge was used by the Prince's party in escaping the Redcoat cordon strung up the western glens. The party came down Coire nan Gall having made a night escape from Glen Dessarry. From Druim Chosaidh they spied out the troops camped in the glen below and made another escape, over Eugallt's long crest, presumably to reach Coire Sgoireadail above Kinloch Hourn.

Luinne Bheinn, across the pass, felt an easier ascent. Though a Munro, it is not much higher than the Corbett which had enjoyed some months of prominence when there was speculation that it could be a new Munro — which would really have put the stoat among the widgeon. The Munro is double-headed, as were the two Bhuidhes to come. The cloud drifted on to us so I had to use map and compass back to the loch where my rucksack was waiting.

The traverse between the Munros is a complex one and I made slow progress carrying a pack and having to navigate. The cloud slowly began to break up and suddenly vanished as we neared the top to give a day of blazing sunshine thereafter. Meall Buidhe is a grand peak of ridges, crags and corries, and a central position gives it a panoramic view. Sgurr na Ciche and Garbh Chioch Mor jagged up dramatically in rough symmetry above the cloud sea.

We picked a careful way down to the Mam Meadail and lunched beyond its draughty cleft, continuing on in the same line to bypass Meall Bhasiter. Left leg muscles ached on the descent, right leg muscles felt the strain on the pull-up. We more or less ended on Meall Bhasiter, anyway. There was a big cairn beyond and, above the Mam Uchd, a tiny lochan acted as a reflecting pool for Sgurr na Ciche, now clear of cloud and soaring in all its glory. The rucksack was left on the Mam Uchd and, tired legs or not, I felt I was floating up the ridge. The summit looks well-defined on the map but the trig point, sticking up like a pinhead, lay on a second bump. Beinn Bhuidhe gave a more spacious panorama than Meall Buidhe, the Munro being a worthy addition to the scene.

Back at the rucksack I had a brew and sunbathed for an hour in a nook out of the chill east breeze. That breeze, blowing our scent ahead, had ensured we had seen very few deer during the traverse. When we descended north to Gleann Meadail we saw dozens. Twelve hours out and with over 6,000 feet of ascent (Knoydart miles and feet), I was glad to pitch the tent near the Dubh Lochan. The dog curled up in the bracken and only woke, briefly, for supper. Primroses, wild hyacinth, celandine and violets created a garden site. There was a perpetual cuckoo but I wrote in my log, "Even a crazy cuckoo won't keep me awake tonight."

We set off early again and, if the day before had steadily improved, this one did the opposite. A bright morning all too often means a wet afternoon. We left the tent standing and wended up the corrie above. This is a favourite deer calving site in June and best avoided then. Sgurr Coire Choinnichean is brutal by any standards — I was glad to be carrying only a day pack. This is the hill which so dominates the view as one sails in to Inverie but, as that aspect is craggy and planted low down, the Corbett is usually approached from the flanks: steep, craggy, demanding work. We aimed for the col east of the peak and then followed the crests up into gathering cloud. There was a top but, being suspicious, I continued — and found a higher. We came out of the cloud beyond that and could see all the way down to Inverie: no more summits.

After back-tracking to the col we descended to the north east, a knee-jarring descent which called for a laze by the pleasant Eas an

Fholaich before contouring round to some more waterfalls on the Abhain Bheag. While resting on the path up the burn a lizard ran over the dog's back and for the next half hour he kept twitching in reaction. On the way down I had a swim in a pool in the Abhain Bheag and took the chance of tick-hunting. I found a brace, in the usual place.

Beinn na Caillich was tackled from where all the burns join up, and it proved a disappointment. The wind had gone and the humid heat was very exhausting, besides which the hill was "a heap of rubbish, like the Sgriol Corbetts, greasy and loose, full of scree and boulders". The north side is fine, but seldom visited. Obviously a hill to go back to some day, perhaps by canoe across Loch Hourn as I've done twice for Ladhar Bheinn. An Arnisdale boatman once ferried A. E. Robertson across to Knoydart and was fascinated by his long ice-axe. He reported, once home, that the minister travelled "armed with a tomahawk".

The return trip was made round the flanks of Ladhar Bheinn and over the Mam Suidheig down to the Dubh Lochan. With only two sweets left I then had to cross the Mam Meadail in the rain to reach Camusrory where I'd left a stock of food. It rained all night (Sourlies Bothy did not exist) and I just wished I'd taken the boat out from Inverie. Knoydart rain is super rain.

That was a typical Knoydart Corbett-hunt, but you can take them a bit less frantically. I've been up some of the Corbetts again and still look forward to future visits while, on the periphery of Knoydart there are the equally tough Corbetts, Sgurr nan Eugallt, Ben Aden, Carn Mor and Sgurr na h-Aide. My escape from Knoydart after this assault was over Sgurr na h-Aide, already described in 11:2. Knoydart will never, ever, be other than a demanding proposition, an irresistible lure.

Section 11: 12. SGURR NAN EUGALLT 894 m OS 33 931045
Peak of death streams

"Dormobile dripping with condensation and drying clothes. Bloody rain. What a miserable April." So I wrote at my chosen spot by Loch Coire Shubh (*the loch of the raspberry corrie*) just above the steep descent to Kinloch Hourn. My frustration was that of a shopper finding so many goods on a shopping list "out of stock". Petrol costs the same whether one has days on the hill or not — so one tends to go regardless. I can laugh a bit, now, for my effort had gone into climbing Buidhe Bheinn, which has since been demoted as a Corbett. I'd rather given up Sgurr nan Eugallt (with a name like that!) when

there was a wobbling shimmer of light on the book I was reading. The
sun was shining through the puddle on the skylight.

At 3 p.m. we crossed the road and headed up bulbous crags to gain
the stalkers' path which runs up a long slot and then to a ridge joining
Sgurr Dubh. We lost the traverse line of the path under the snow but
just continued up Sgurr Dubh and along the ridge leading to Sgurr nan
Eugallt. There was more to the ridge than the map showed and we had
plenty of fun on small crags, finally reaching the summit up "a gem of
a chimney". Most of the time there was a dribbly, vertical rain, and,
when not using my hands, I used my umbrella — I am a confirmed
brolly boy, I loathe wearing waterproofs, even my luxury Berghaus
Goretex set.

Like The Saddle to the north, the trig point is not on the highest
point of the ridge. We arrived with a clearance in the weather. The
country to the south (the outer peaks of Knoydart) was very
impressive and I noted it then as "an area to explore valleys and ridges,
once the silly Corbetts are done", a promise I have kept. The bigger
hills stayed in the cloud and a Corbett was just right for the occasion.
Time, alas, forced me back down, but this is really a hill to be
traversed, end to end, or taken in with Sgurr a' Choire-bheithe. The
path up from Coire Shubh is a temptation to slackness.

Coire Shubh (*corrie hoo*) gave a long bumslide, after I'd put on my
waterproof trousers to reduce the coefficient of friction. The dog sat
on my lap and greatly enjoyed his ride. At the foot of the slope I found
a badly-mangled deer which I'm sure had been the victim of an
avalanche. The ground below the snowline was deeply frozen, hard
and also difficult to traverse back to the path. The lone monkey-
puzzle tree welcomed me home to the now hoar-covered Dormobile
— back to my book over a warming curry supper.

The bulbous, scoured nature of the *montagnes moutonnées* hereabouts
was noted by the early geologists, Geikie and Murchison, who
considered the pass from Glenquoich to Loch Hourn to be one of the
best examples of ice action to be found in Britain. Landseer also spent
many days here, drawing and painting.

Glenquoich Lodge is now under the waters of the raised Loch
Quoich. One of the proprietors, E. C. Ellice, last century wrote a
book, *Place Names of Glengarry and Glenquoich*, which is full of
interesting associations. This lonely road where I camped was once
the scene of a race from Loch Hourn to Invergarry. The chief,
Glengarry, one day drove home from Loch Hourn in four hours and
later rather boasted of this to Mr Green, the family tutor, who in turn
suggested he could do the journey as fast on foot. Glengarry bet £20 he
could not. A Glengarry man, Somerled Macdonell, was backed

against the Sassenach and Glenquoich wagered he could get "an old wife" off his farm to beat them both. Macdonell spurted ahead at the start but the ascent from Loch Hourn brought on a nose bleed and, while he was washing in a burn, the tutor went ahead. The highlander won, however, doing the 27 miles in 3 hours 40 minutes, but Mr Green won his wager by beating the 4 hours. The old wife lasted 7 miles but that was still up the brae from Loch Hourn and on to Glenquoich. Glengarry's wife received the successful pair with "bizzed porter on meal".

Section 11: 13. SGURR A' BHAC CHAOLAIS 885 m OS 33 958110
Peak of the hollow of the kyle (narrows)

This is one of the Corbetts which came in with the revisions of the 1981 *Tables*. As I had not been on it before, I had a good excuse for a Hogmanay visit when it could also lead on to Sgurr na Sgine by its seldom-climbed east face which had long been on my "wants" list. Seven Munros are arranged along the Cluanie ridge south of Glen Shiel; this Corbett, being tacked on at the west end of the seven, can be added to them at the cost of 500 feet of ascent rather than 2,500 feet if done later from the valley. There is some reward in careful planning — though few of us treat the game as tidily as we later wish we had. This Corbett has replaced Buidhe Bheinn which lies just over a mile to the south. Buidhe Bheinn, *the yellow hill*, towers above the head of Loch Hourn and is a superb hill which hardly deserved demotion. Good paths lead up it, and linking in with Chaolais and Sgine gives a magnificent "horseshoe" circuit from Kinloch Hourn.

Under a corona of frosty stars we set off from the roadside in Glen Shiel, heading up the path to the Bealach Duibh Leac, a pass which was used by Bonnie Prince Charlie after he'd escaped from the Rough Bounds further south. Largely due to his successful escape after Culloden, we now have Ordnance Survey maps. The locals who guided the prince knew the landscape, the government forces didn't, making a good case for producing proper maps.

We had a warm dawn plod up to the Allt Coire Toiteil, a good way of dealing with an overindulgence of seasonal fare. We paused there, to recover a bit and to admire Sgurr na Sgine at the head of the valley; it looked as grand as The Saddle in a rosy sunrise flush. We donned crampons, for the path was often icy or filled with hard snow. The surface promptly changed to granular snow — the crampons were not really needed. Ben's kept giving trouble. Ernst and I were on top of

Sgurr a' Bhac Chaolais an hour before him. Storm has built-in crampons and with twice the number of legs covers twice the ground.

In summer the path can be difficult to follow after crossing the Allt Coire Toiteil. Time and vegetation have largely obliterated the historic route's delineation. With everything covered in snow we angled up more directly for the summit, missing the small "mauvais pas" on the ridge up from the Bealach Duibh Leac. (Only on the descent does it really cause any delay.)

The summit is a large dome rather than a sharp point. Our view along the Cluanie Ridge was made dramatic by clearing clouds which spilled over the ridge in ever-changing shapes and colours: instant Henry Moore shapes which formed and melted in minutes before disappearing completely to give a day of pristine primary colours. The Glen Shiel ridges swept along like huge breakers caught as they prepared to topple over into surf. The best of the view however was westwards to the east face of Sgurr na Sgine, that secretive Munro which only looks its true best when seen from Knoydart. Quite a few casual plans to traverse from The Saddle to Sgurr na Sgine and on eastwards end with the aspirant peering down these eastern cliffs in surprise.

We went on to climb the face and, one way or another, having taken three different solo routes (with varied fortunes) lost most of the day before everyone was re-united on top. I'd left sandwiches on the main cairn for the others before going on to the West Top to drink in the view of The Saddle, and they failed to see them. A present for the ravens! Black clouds, shot with lurid red, rimmed the western view to the islands. We descended into Coire Toiteil fast and managed to reach our upward tracks before it became really dark. Two other walkers caught us up and, as so often, the number of torches present or working was less than the number of people. I pushed on ahead, following the white flag of Storm's tail, and when we all gathered at the Dormobile a hot brew and a glass of *Jura* was waiting to round off the day. Sgurr a' Bhac Chaolais is worth a winter visit.

There is no real hope of adding another summit to the Cluanie Ridge "seven" in midwinter; Sgurr a' Bhac Chaolais can conveniently be added to Sgurr na Sgine to make a fuller day. A descent can be made to Coire Toiteil from the col between Chaolais and Sgine, if a modest traverse of the Corbett alone is called for, or it can be taken in while following the old pass route between Loch Duich and Loch Quoich, a route which has royal precedents after all.

Section 11:   14. BEINN NA H-EAGLAISE   804 m   OS 33   854120
    The hill of the church (eglish)

Section 11:   15. BEINN NAN CAORACH   773 m   OS 33   871122
    The hill of the rowan berries (curuch)

One way to ensure good conditions in a period of doubtful weather is to forget, or decide not to take, a camera on the hill. Or you forget to carry a spare film. Under these circumstances the weather always clears up. When Charles and I set off for these hills on the penultimate day of 1986 there was no call for the camera, I thought. A couple of hours later I was cursing my laziness. Beinn Sgritheall (Sgriol), perhaps my favourite mainland Munro, was arrayed in all its winter glory.

We made our approach from Glen More, passing under the prehistoric fort of Torr Beag (splendid viewpoint) and Loch Iain Mhic Aonghais to the many junctions of Strath a' Chomair. Here we crossed a ford to a gate and a bad jeep track that swings round up the Allt Gleann Aoidhdailean, a route now milestoned with ugly pylons. This is a fine old right of way to Kinloch Hourn and was the route followed by the cattle which had swum across Kyle Rhea on the way to southern markets. We found the going messy, so crossed the stream to follow up the burn that drained the corrie between the northern spurs of the Corbetts. "Waterfall" on the map proved to be a whole series of little falls rather than any one leap, which made for an attractive line. The corner between the stream junctions has been planted; we cut into the corrie by walking along above the plantation fence.

The snow-line was half way up the corrie and rather wet — we were glad of our wellies. When the snow began to harden I walked up actually *in* the water, at one stage going through a tunnel of old snow which arched over the gash. Sgurr Dearg was a prominent tor to the east and we hit the ridge from it to Beinn nan Caorach after the angle eased, pleasant walking on the bands of old hard snow which were only slippery where clear of newer snow. The peaks of Sgriol and Eaglaise were dramatically arrayed.

On the ridge a knifing wind stabbed us. The east wind is always the executioner. We battered up the ridge to the summit for a brief visit. Knoydart was hidden in a black pall of cloud as was every Munro bar Sgriol but, away to the north west, Applecross was clear and the sky and sea shivered a lurid glow that promised nothing good.

A fence links the summits of the two Corbetts, which is worth knowing if caught by mist, but after following it for a while on the north ridge off Beinn nan Caorach we cut more directly down to the wide grassy saddle of the Bealach nam Bo. This seems a strange area to have so many *cow* names. The wind, whistling up Coire nam Bo to the south, had driven the grazing deer almost up to the pass. They were unconcerned at our presence. The wide saddle really leads to the Druim nan Bo, *the ridge of the cattle*, and this has quite a distinctive dip to a "sneck" before rearing up to Beinn na h-Eaglaise as a fine fin. We were lucky enough to find a wind-free spot on the Rosdail side and there changed out of our wellies into boots and gaiters.

The change was well judged for the route was iced up. In the end we banged our way along a swooping series of drifting crests to reach the summit as snow began to fall. Sgritheall had now vanished under the black blanket. We did not linger on Eaglaise in case there was any lightning about. It is a finer peak than Caorach. I've linked Eaglaise to Sgritheall, but the descent to the Bealach Arnisdail is steep, a mix of loose gullies and crags. The Corbett summit is only a mile back from Loch Hourn, and is really steep everywhere, but what an erne's viewpoint we have because of that! Sgritheall and these Corbetts form an overspill to the Rough Bounds of Knoydart.

My first visit linked the Corbetts to Sgritheall, from a camp at Corran where the public road to Arnisdale finally admits defeat at the roughness of the Loch Hourn slopes. We went up by the Allt Utha and Coire Dhruim nam Bo for Caorach first. There is now a bulldozed track up the east bank of the Allt Utha. The fall is an impressive one. While perhaps shorter in miles the approaches on the Loch Hourn side require a long drive in and then give brutally steep ascents. I'd recommend the approaches from either Glen More or Gleann Beag. The latter has the best-preserved brochs on the mainland (and other antiquities) so should be visited whatever one is doing in this magic area beyond Mam Ratagan.

Charles and I picked our careful way back to the gap on the ridge. The fence posts were icy pennants. Just before the dip the fence off Eaglaise makes a sharp turn right, downhill, but from the gap a line of smaller, more widely-spaced posts crosses the broad saddle and so up Caorach. After changing back into wellies we walked up to follow Druim nan Bo homewards rather than go down by wet Rosdail. The ridge is a long series of bumps and we wended along them in torrential rain. The burns were rising and we were very glad to reach our Glen More base. Friends who had been on Sgritheall came in several hours later.

Section 11:   16. SGURR MHIC BHARRAICH   781 m   OS 33   917174
Peak of the son of Maurice (Varrich)

With Beinn Sgritheall to the west, Sgurr Fhuarain to the east and The
Saddle to the south, Mhic Bharraich is perhaps rather junior in such a
family of brothers and sisters but the astute would recognise that the
hill must be a prime viewpoint. I'm biased for, on the first of January
1980, we were given one of the most magnificent days of deep
winter I've ever known in Scotland.

On my first visit I'd wandered up the Corbett with Kitchy from
Shiel Bridge via the Loch Coire nan Crogachan path on a manky day
when my friends nevertheless went off for The Saddle. The
Corbett's lesser height gave me some view, The Saddle yielded
none. On the last day of 1977 the hill was a bad-forecast alternative
and four of us went up the Allt Grannda to its lochan source, giving
ourselves fun on the snow-slobbery rocks of the gorge, then scrambling, where possible, to the summit and back by Loch Coire nan
Crogachan. The path down the Allt a' Ghleannain is not easy to
follow, now. Bealachasan is a ruin and the easiest line makes for the
Glenmore River forestry track. The whole hill is knobbly and rocky
but doesn't yield proper rock climbing. Part of its neglect is that the
side facing Loch Duich is intimidatingly steep and barred by forestry, but the Allt Undalain gives an easy-enough approach. Being
based in Glen More at Hogmanay we always went up from the west.

On the first of January 1979 two inches of new snow were lying
on the bothy when Martin, Anne, Ben, Storm and I set out.
Bealachasan we noted was rotting away fast. I found a newspaper
from 1950 which was full of rationing problems and gave an
obituary of Lord Wavell. Fashions and prices were a bit different
then, too. This time we scrambled up by visiting every lochan. We
had some good slides on them, whooping like schoolkids at play-
time. It was snowing on top and we were glad enough to escape
to the south *voie normal* and drop below the powder snow which was
all too often hiding ambushing ice. We put up a woodcock on the
pass, and a chatter of snow buntings had gone through while we
nibbled in lee of the cairn.

The Hallelujah start of the following year is the one that really
sings in the memory. I've never seen the west so white. We had
problems motoring over Mam Ratagan, and Glen More was choked
with snow. The bothy was snug enough and we'd carried in plenty
of logs, coal, festive food and appropriate libations. Some went to
bed, some were put to bed, but six of us and the dog made Mhic

Bharraich on the first day of 1980. Ben, Anne, Storm and I had been up exactly a year before. Ernst, Harry and Peter believed our good reports.

From Bealachasan we went straight up to break through the crags at the first gully. We sidled into the gully on thigh-deep drifts and the whole ascent was a furrow-ploughing slog, for all the world like fighting up some big peak in the Himalayas, but without the avalanche danger there. We used all the rock we could find but the climb was hard work in the blaze of sun. The day was bitterly cold. The snow on the flatter top levels had worked into glittering Lux flakes or Rice Krispie grains. The view to Sgritheall was Arctic rather than Himalayan, and the white went down to the sea waters of Loch Duich. Applecross and Torridon hardly showed any of their dark banding in this extravagance of whitewash. The Five Sisters were arrayed in a simplified geometry of triangles: sun-white on one side, plum-shadowy on the other.

The weather on the summit was Arctic too. We set off down at 2 p.m. Away on Sgritheall we could make out figures on one ridge: Donald and Charles, Munro-rivals, starting their final year of that game together. It was long after dark before they were back to the bothy fug. We collected and sawed wood and were just in before dark, having had a day as near perfection as we may ever know.

Browsing through the bothy book I noted one entry which said the bothy "was worked as a croft by my great uncle Donald Campbell, at the turn of this century before moving to Glenelg. Donald, a close relation of Sir Malcolm Campbell, lived until his 95th year." I'm sure Donald Campbell would have thoroughly approved of our gathering of the clans.

There were 24 of us (and 3 dogs) in his old house, which the Braes o' Fife had steadily renovated for several years to turn into a cosy bothy. Buildings as well as mountains can be much-loved places. Suardalan, *and* Mhic Bharraich, *and* Sgritheall; with such a combination our Hogmanay cup was filled to the brim and running over.

Section 11:   17. AM BATHACH   789 m   OS 33   073144
              The byre

"All very sleepy including the driver so we have a break before Loch Cluanie dam. Jim was feeling unwell. Andrew and I set off from the inn at about 9.30 a.m. Back at 6.30 p.m. after a lazy, blazing, marvellous day. Rather than go up either flanking glen with the views shut in we went straight up Am Bathach, seeking out the odd scramble, and with the cloud rolling up ahead of us, a prelude to all the hills from Ciste Dhubh to Saileag. Our route up gave a grassy crest and fine views back along the loch, over to A' Chralaig and across to the old road snaking down from Tomdoun way."

That was the first paragraph of my log note of a day on the Cluanie Hills which gave a first visit to Am Bathach. Most guidebooks suggest approaching an east-west walk along the north Cluanie ridge by either the Caorann Mor or the Caorann Beag valleys but, for the reason given above, the Corbett is the better way. I was unaware of its Corbett status on that occasion. It just happened to be in the right place for an approach to some Munros — and that is a bonus which is paid all too rarely. (The Cluanie Inn is another.) Ascended on its own I'd be tempted to go up one of the valleys and traverse back along the crest for the sake of being ambushed by the views. The southern panorama is a good excuse for resting on the descent of what is a steep nose of a hill.

The road coming over from the south is an old military road (but not built by Wade) which continues down Glen Shiel and over Mam Ratagan to Glenelg's Bernera Barracks and Skye. It was fifteen years in the making (1770–84) and Johnson and Boswell saw the work in 1773. They saw soldiers working on the road and called it a "dreariness of solitude".

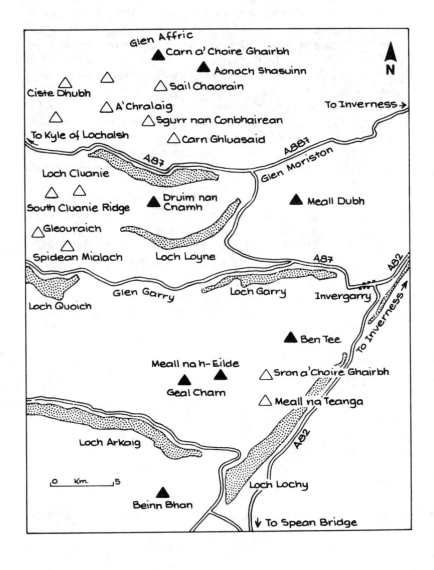

LOCH LOCHY & LOCH CLUANIE TO GLEN AFFRIC

Section 12:   1. BEINN BHAN   796 m   OS 34/41   141857
White hill (van)

THERE IS A perfectly easy way up Beinn Bhan from the south, but as nephew Colin, his mate Roddie and I were, ostensibly, canoeing up the Great Glen and just happened to be staying at Invermallie on Loch Arkaig, we climbed Beinn Bhan from the north. West of the Great Glen, northern slopes are often wickedly heathery low down — and this was no exception. A sticky hot day at the end of July was another drawback. The midges loved us.

To escape the swamping forestry we "burned up" into Coire Dubh right from the bothy, a long haul, indeed, but there was little water in the burn and we left its course only occasionally. Fallen tree-trunks frequently made good bridges and, as we sweated and puffed up, one of the lads commented that he felt like a cross between Tarzan and Richard Attenborough. We took the eastern stream in the corrie, which curved up to the summit edge, very welcome water. That was one benefit from our northern approach.

The best of Beinn Bhan's view is towards Ben Nevis and the Lochaber giants, and it was suddenly "opened to us" as we made our exit from corries almost at the trig point. We looked down on the Caledonian canal where we'd paddled up from Banavie the day before, a brilliant day which had turned on us after the portage from Clunes to Loch Arkaig, and gave the boys in their Canadian canoe "a new dimension of roughness" for the miles to Invermallie.

There was a breeze to chill our sweaty garments so we strode along over the two 771-m Tops to descend west of Coire Bhotrais. Horizontal deer tracks and red scars of "wash-outs" were frequent. Eventually the slope steepened for a midge infested, scrag and heather descent. Breaks in the trees were choked with bracken — and luscious clumps of blaeberry. I walked down the road stripping berries off their stems.

The normal approach which I'd used years before (and can remember very little about) is from Glen Loy. This has a minor motor-road up from the Banavie–Gairlochy B8004 which wiggles along linking Loch Linnhe and Loch Lochy. A couple of miles up the glen the road crosses the River Loy to its north bank. Walk up a side track to deserted Inverskilavulin and wander up the slopes above, east of Coire Mhuilinn, to the flat summit area. The circuit of Coire Mhuilinn would make an enjoyable high-level scenic promenade and vary the route as well. The ascent is still quite a slog.

If private transport can be arranged a good two day west–east tramp could be made from Fassfern on Loch Eil: day one being up to Glensulaig bothy and climbing Meall a' Phubuill and day two the long descent of Glen Loy and climbing Beinn Bhan on the way.

Section 12:   2. GEAL CHARN   804 m   OS 34   156943
              White hill

Section 12:   3. MEALL NA H-EILDE   838 m   OS 34   185946
              Hill of the hinds (eilid)

Maybe those who complain to me about changes in the *Tables* of Munros or Corbetts, as if it was my fault, will feel better if they knew that such changes can be as inconvenient to me as they are to them. These hills are a case in point.

With Kitchy, I traversed the then Corbett Meall Coire Saobhaidh and Geal Charn, our planned longer day over these hills being shortened by heavy snow conditions underfoot. I was not pleased when the first of these hills was struck off the register and replaced by Meall na h-Eilde next door, forcing a return, and yielding yet another dreich sort of day for the ascent, along with the newly acquired Storm.

Meall an Tagraidh, the hill east of Meall na h-Eilde, saw Bonnie Prince Charlie seeking refuge on it for several days and nights. Cameron of Clunes managed to take up some whisky and bread and cheese, and a fire was lit for half an hour. By day they lay on the summit, wrapped in plaids in the rain.

The first visit gave some views, at least, with only the Ben staying cloud-covered. The sun turned the considerable snow cover into porridge, however, and long before the path (now a bulldozed track) up the Allt Dubh ran out we abandoned all idea of circling everything up there with a descent by Gleann Cia-aig. That still waits for "next time" and there is also the temptation of Glas Bheinn which must be an even better viewpoint than Geal Charn for looking along Loch Arkaig, one of the west's most pleasing lochs.

Meall na h-Eilde was squeezed in with a work party visit to our local club's bothy near Glenelg. With several hundredweight of cement, tools and furniture in the Dormobile there was no way I could sleep in it, so I decided to spend the night at Invermallie Bothy on the south shore of Loch Arkaig. As I hadn't checked on the bothy I made a couple of mistakes: the first was cycling in — the road is a big dipper of wickedly sharp stones; the second was not checking Invermallie's exact location — I pedalled all the way up the glen to discover the bothy was a ruin. Dark by then, Storm and I survived a night tucked in under the rafters on the few feet of loft flooring that remained. I took the dog up Gulvain the next day and then we dropped down to the real Invermallie Bothy, superb in every way. A bird cherry hangs over the house, and seed from that tree has yielded me several small trees now flourishing in friends' gardens from Leicester to Aviemore. Howard Ashton, maintenance organiser of Invermallie, had a gang of us there to celebrate his last Munro, which was one way of acquiring a work party. I've a grand photo of Howard and Jim Cosgrove on top of Meall na Teanga in the rain.

As I still had to deliver my load to Suardalan Bothy I could only afford the morning for Meall na h-Eilde. I'm not really complaining but next time I want those hills by their northern approaches. I've had enough of the Allt Dubh. Perhaps they would make a good traverse at the start of a future Ultimate Challenge. Some of the routes put in for that event seem quite illogical and devious (days heading west, for instance), until you realise the motive is the linking of Munros and/or Corbetts.

There are some excellent stalkers' paths on the northern side, and wooded Loch Garry is as fine as Loch Arkaig while, westwards, the view into the country of Streap and the Rough Bounds is very grand indeed. These hills teem with deer and I've seen blackcock at their *lek*, others in the snow, and ospreys in their fastness. Perhaps the wildlife and emptiness are the special treats of this area but at what a price: a list of "vermin" destroyed in Glengarry early last century included "198 wild cats, 246 pine martins, 67 badgers, 48 otters, 78 merlins, 63 harriers, 27 white-tailed sea eagles, 18 ospreys, 63 goshawks, 371 rough-legged buzzards, 275 kites, 38 owls . . .'

Section 12: 4. BEN TEE 901 m OS 34 241972
The fairy hillock

Just what Ben Tee means is lost in the garbling of the original Gaelic. I've seen it given as coming from *tighe*, meaning "house" as well as *sidhean* meaning "fairy hillock". Both occur frequently in place names. I wonder if skiers rushing off up Glen *Shee* realise they're away with the fairies? The derivation has also been given as *di*, "the mountain of God". Whatever the name means, Ben Tee is one of the best of Corbetts, perhaps not to be bagged so much as potted.

In the sixties, when I used to have school parties climbing and canoeing from Loch Lochy Youth Hostel, we came to know the area quite well. Ben Tee's symmetrical cone became one of those instantly-recognisable summits, the Great Glen's answer to Schiehallion — which is another "fairy hill", of course, and backs up that derivation for Ben Tee. Because of the kids' endless Munro-bagging Meall na Teanga and Sron a' Choire Ghairbh received the brunt of youthful excursions. The only time the kids did Ben Tee I was laid low with flu so, while kindly Mrs Fraser nursed me, the boys went off on their own. The responsibility made a memorable day for them and I was regaled with their stories for months afterwards.

They'd made what is probably the standard approach, starting from Laggan Locks and rounding to the Kilfinnan Burn, seeing the falls, and then making a gradual rising line to reach the east ridge. There is some rough going on the lower moorland. Tidy-minded Munroists can also add the Corbett to their pair, continuing along Meall a' Choire Ghlais, down its north ridge, and straight up Ben Tee (a steep haul) to descend by this easiest-of-all route. A decade after our regular hostel parties I was rewarded by an ascent of the hill.

I escaped from Fife after a frustrating morning in the office and drove up to the Great Glen and set off at 5 p.m. This was on 20 June, one day off the longest day. I wanted to see the Kilfinnan Falls (a small bridal veil) so didn't keep high above the east bank which is the easiest line; but then I was lured on to follow up the gorge above the falls. Forcing the gorge took extra hours, was good fun, and I had a couple of intentional dips and one which was not planned. Luckily I was scrambling along wearing only shorts. It was 7.30 before I emerged at the top of the wood. I steamed up Ben Tee, keeping my eyes firmly on the ground until the summit was reached and then drinking deep of the 360-degree panorama.

The view was tonal rather than colourful, my perch utterly restful and quiet, after the uphill labour, a visual, spiritual counterpart to Beethoven's 6th symphony after the thunderstorm. Sgurr na Ciche was the most eye-catching of the sprawl of peaks to the west. Ben Nevis was a familiar cut-out shape, only in mirror-image, being more often seen from the south. Ben Tee is a particularly fine viewpoint as there is such a mighty outlook to the west. The converse also holds true, and from peaks like the Streaps, or those round Glen Kingie or Loch Quoich, the cone of Ben Tee is always a notable feature. From Faichem, or from along the shores of Loch Garry, Ben Tee rises in bold symmetry. Its colourful woodland must have attracted thousands of photographers without the viewer knowing what he is looking at. The name, for once, is easy to remember, Ben Tee being easier on the tongue of memory than Meallan Liath Coire Mhic Dhughaill or Sgurr Cos na Breachd-laoidh. The summit of Ben Tee was, anciently, known as Glengarry's Bowling Green. A local belief had it that Glengarry Castle was built of stone from the brow of Ben Tee, the rocks being passed, man to man, the seven miles down the hill. Pochin Mould in *Roads from the Isles* (the best book on old drove roads and tracks) singles out Ben Tee as being an exceptional viewpoint.

I descended by reedy Lochan Diota with the hills to the east of the Great Glen putting on nightcap clouds and the view up to lonely Coire Glas streaked with shafts of primrose light from the setting sun, calling to mind the primroses which had been flowering right up to the 2,000-foot level. The evening walk was rich in flora, from creeping azalea on high, through cloudberry moors with lousewort, cudweed, tormentil, milkwort, ladies' mantles, to the hyacinth-scented woods below. I squelched across the moor and down to the locks in the gloaming.

The other obvious approach to Ben Tee I took in May 1977 when walking from Sgurr na Banachdich to Mount Keen. The day was so appallingly hot that the two Munros were left well alone. I'd slept out in the heather the night before and started brewing at four o'clock in the first tweek of day, amid the hubbub of a blackcock *lek*, so had to watch that weird dance for a bit before wandering off along to Greenfield and the right-of-way up the Allt Ladaidh. By eight o'clock I was sweltering up to the Bealach Easan. The most notable object seen from the summit was a cloud. The OS is a bit over-generous with the marsh symbols. There are some peat hags but nothing very unusual. I cut corners to drop down to the locks quickly. The tea-room produced three Cokes and a pot of tea while I sat outside watching the idyllic *Wind in the Willows* life on the canal. I then crawled into the shade and slept for three hours till hostel-opening time.

Section 12 5. MEALL DUBH 788 m OS 34 245078
Black hill (myowl-doo)

Just how slavishly we are held by the bigger hills is shown by the fact that this hill and the next, Druim nan Cnamh, do not receive even a passing mention in the latest SMC district guide. Apparently there is nothing of note from Cluanie to the Great Glen, which is ridiculous: these two Corbetts have given me memorable days, and Meall Dubh has one of the country's finest summit views.

These two and Ben Tee, equally fine, were done one June when my real activity was canoeing in the west, a month of broiling heat and periodic storms. Some rams bumping the Dormobile woke me and we set off from the car park near the dam of Loch Loyne, back of eight.

Garbh Dhoire (*rough wood*) was all too apt but, by a mix of fresh track, a burn, and crawling under a deer fence, old Kitchy and I reached the moors. The cairn has a double view: through Garry–Kingie way and through to Cluanie. The Streaps, Gairich, Sgurr-Mor, Sgurr na Ciche, Spidean-Gleouraich, the South Shiel Ridge, the North Shiel Ridge, the Conbhairean hills, Affric, Farrar hills were all displayed. Meallfuarvonie, the impossible country east of Loch Ness, the pylons of the Corrieyairack, Glen Spean hills, Grey Corries, Ben Nevis, Ben Tee and its Munros, the Arkaig Corbetts, Gulvain, far Ardgour complete the circle. Wyvis was the most distant recognisable peak. That is not a bad selection.

We lingered by the cairn for an hour and then ambled west through a scattering of lochans before regretfully turning down to the car. There was some lively Scottish dance music on the radio and my delight obviously had the better of me. I performed a sword dance over imaginary weapons beside the car. When I collapsed, out of breath, there was polite applause. I looked up the bank to see two car-loads of German tourists.

That rough western approach is the obvious one but I was determined to revisit "Dubh of the View", as I'll always think of the hill, as soon as possible and to traverse it "properly". ASAP turned out to be a wait from 1973 to 1986, when I linked it to Druim nan Cnamh, the next Corbett. They were both traversed in one day, from Cluanie Inn to Loch Oich.

Section 12: 6. DRUIM NAN CNAMH 790 m OS 34 131077
Bony ridge (krav)

This hill was earmarked for a possible canoe-assault long before I had the motivation of Corbetting. When a gang of us were based on a Lundie camp for a few days I was able to make my "raid". There was only a mile to paddle across and I climbed up Coire Beithe, reduced to boots and pants, to keep near water. I came down the corrie's western arm and then cut in to enjoy a long swim in a pool I'd passed going up. A squall on the way back churned the loch to foam and this proved the start of another weather tantrum. A canoe was a most useful aid for this Corbett for, otherwise, access yields a certain frustration.

Thirteen years passed before I returned to Cnamh. I had started in Glenelg and had a very flexible first few days as we hoped to go high and stay high all the way from Sgurr Mhic Bharraich to the Great Glen (after all, several people had suffered heat stroke on the Cluanie Ridge the year before). The rain belted down, all day and for days on end.

We sneaked over Mam Ratagan and plodded up to the Cluanie Inn, that ancient haven of drovers' days, which took in Challengers like boat-people. As Tony and I had booked a B & B by Loch Oich for the next night, and were meeting friends in Glen Roy the day after (see 9:4, 5), we were concerned in case we could not proceed — there are limits. The next day, however, was "only raining" so, well fed, we set off for Cnamh on what is probably the easiest pedestrian route.

After an hour of steady plodding we reached the top of the old Road to the Isles. In very dry summers the old bridge over the River Loyne rises out of the water of the loch in a weird resurrection. Not today, though. At the pass we were able to take off our waterproofs and, after honey sandwiches, we plunged into the peat bog and river braes that defend the mountain.

Druim means ridge and Druim nan Cnamh strictly speaking is misappropriated as a name for the summit. As we toiled up the slopes we set off deer, golden plovers, a hare and then ptarmigan, the last whirred away with rude noises into the gathering clouds. We cringed below the stark, round, trig point only long enough to force in some food and check the compass bearing, then we fled as fast as the rough going would allow.

On a half-decent day it would be best to stay high and traverse Beinn Loinne, the real centre of these hills between Loch Cluanie and Loch Loyne, but we were glad to slither down poggy snow beneath the peak and skirt round to descend the Allt Coire na Creadha. This took us below the level of cloud and rain. We crossed the river high up (in case it was impassable lower down) and just linked odd deer tracks in a long, gradually descending traverse line to reach the Loch Loyne dam. We saw only one stag — which cantered off in a great splashy run across the sodden slopes.

Given helpful transport this traverse, in either direction, would make a good walk. Perhaps east-west would be better as the craggy eastern end of the ridge is then taken in ascent. The day gives ten rough miles. The rain was following us down. We therefore passed below the dam and took shelter *under* the A87 which crosses the Allt Garbh-dhoire on high stilts, a dry but draughty howff. We brewed, had hot apple flakes, Alpen and other goodies and at 2.30 p.m. set off on another day's walking, for Meall Dubh (12:5). After five minutes we had to stop and don all our waterproofs. I had my brolly which, with a back wind, allowed me to walk with my top half open. Once the clawing heather level was passed the going was quite good, though with sopping feet we were not very fussy. We made a steady rising line all the way. The last bit was on that "dead" ground which had just lost its winter snow covering. There is a second big cairn along from the highest one. The summit area is all rather knobbly and, as soon as we arrived, the weather really let rip.

My fingers holding the compass went numb as we navigated over a succession of mist-exaggerated bumps, and there was a certain relief in finding that an ancient fence and a boundary on the map were in agreement. We scurried down the rocky eastern ridge to a col. The cloud cleared a bit and we could see the Great Glen at last, with the distinctive shape of Ben Tee thrusting up out of boiling blackness. We descended, waterproofs off again, on another gentle traverse which took us to the Allt Lundie. This was another feature which had caught the eye years before. In about a mile of river the map has nine strokes and three verbal indications of waterfall. Ours was an excellent day for visiting waterfalls.

After the roar and clamour of the impressive riverside descent, mirror-still Loch Lundie was quite a contrast. The trees and green verges were reflected in its *dubh* waters. There were two possible tracks down to the Great Glen; we took the northern sweep by the Invervigar Burn to avoid any A82 walking and in just over an hour we reached the northern end of Loch Oich. It was 9 p.m. We'd been out for 13 hours. Before the UC walk I'd left an evening meal there as I was not sure just what accommodation we'd be using, or if an evening meal would be possible for our late arrival. We ate before doing the last mile to the B & B. The brolly proved quite useful again as we huddled underneath it waiting for our haggis to heat on a slowly-dying gaz stove . . .

Section 12:   7. CARN A' CHOIRE GHAIRBH   863 m
OS 34 & 25   137189
The cairn of the rough corrie (garve)

Section 12:   8. AONACH SHASUINN   889 m   OS 34 & 25   173180
The height of the Englishman (onach sassun)

I've linked these two together because they can be done in combination quite reasonably from the Glen Affric side, a walk giving varied and majestic scenery. The public motor road ends at the car park by Loch Beinn a' Mheadhoin (Benevian) as shown on Sheet 25. Walk west, then cross to the south side of the glen to take the path up the Allt Garbh, which rises about 450 m to a junction, joining what is now a Land Rover track for the continuation up the glen. Aonach Shasuinn can be climbed thereafter and the ridge followed over An Elric and Carn a' Choire Ghuirm to Carn a' Choire Ghairbh. Descend by the stalkers' path west of Coire Crom to the end of Loch Affric or the one off Cnapain back to the Allt Garbh.

Carn a' Choire Ghairbh was one of the Corbetts that was netted with my Munros-in-one haul. I was staying at Glen Affric Youth Hostel (Alltbeithe) and made the strenuous round of the Mullach–A' Chralaig–Conbhairean Munros, five of them, with Tigh Mor na Seilge then still the Munro before Sail Chaorainn superseded it. Carn a' Choire Ghairbh was simply a continuation of the circuit. I'd been on Aonach Shasuinn the year before so omitted it on this occasion. Little Loch a' Choinich had dried out into a black smudge with the heat. Looking up to Carn a' Choire Ghairbh from below there was a big cairn visible, but this is not the summit which is further on, on the more northerly of the two bumps. The lie of the land led me down westwards — into plantings which were not on the map. They are, now; and a line can be made to the gap which leads to the estate road down Gleann na Ciche to Loch Affric. With the bogs so dry I cut all the corners to gain the hostel track as soon as possible. If based on the hostel I'd prefer to climb up by the path at the west end of Loch Affric and, after linking the Corbetts, drop directly into Gleann na Ciche from Loch a' Choinich to avoid the plantings altogether.

Aonach Shasuinn had also been climbed on a hot day, with a party of friends from Inverness, Aberfeldy, Edinburgh and Adelaide! This was a round of the Conbhairean Munros for some and a Prince Charlie's Cave hunt as well. We left Mike's car at the Ceannacroc road-end and drove along to Lundie for the good track that twists up on to Ghluasaid. Even at the end of May there were big rims of snow along from Conbhairean to Tigh Mor. The Munroists went Top-bagging while three of us went down to look for the cave — which is really a boulder-shelter. By plugging the gap and laying heather on the floor we made quite a snug howff. Historically the Prince stayed for a week in a cave or caves in this area, but there are several contenders for the site besides the one shown on the map.

The next day the Munroists set off for A' Chralaig and the Mullach, to be met at Cluanie Inn, while the rest of us wandered up to Beinn an Iomaire to study the corrie for other cave possibilities and then skirted in and out to the top of Gleann Fada. From the col at its head easy walking led up Aonach Shasuinn. We had a noble view of all the big Affric hills, and Ben Nevis stood boldly to the south. The day was hot with blue skies and blue hills. We went on over Carn a' Choire Bhuidhe and down into Coire Dho. Conbhairean opposite was a snow-flanked cone, the centre of a big, balanced panorama. We had the first swim of the year before walking down to the car on the Glen Moriston road.

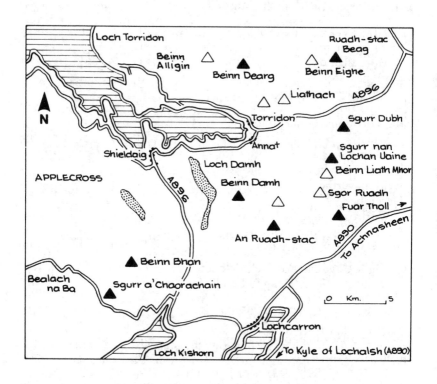

APPLECROSS & TORRIDON

Section 13: 1. SGURR A' CHAORACHAIN   792 m   OS 24   797417
Peak of the little field of berries

Section 13: 2. BEINN BHAN   896 m   OS 24   804450
White hill

"IT HAS EVERY attribute of hell except its warmth", was one climber's first reaction to seeing Beinn Bhan on a wild winter's day.

More than one "off day" from Gerry's hostel in Glen Carron (see p. 7) has seen a group of us motoring round Applecross. This secretive western corner often stays dry or showery while the Atlantic weather pours in overhead to let loose on the big Applecross hills or the Torridons. Good rainbow country is Applecross.

When we had climbed all the local Munros or Corbetts, Dave, Jim and I, regulars at Gerry's towards the end of the year, were more or less forced to head for Applecross. The weather was unsettled but we went nevertheless. And we went early — no mean feat on 31 December.

We drove round by Kishorn to park at Tornapress at the head of the loch, usually noisy with oystercatchers and covered with nodding heads of thrift, rather forlorn this grey dawn. From Kishorn on up the road past the Rassal oakwood there are spectacular views of the stratified cliff-faces and corries that make Applecross special. The cliffs are so ferocious that there are still only a few winter climbs recorded. Even the Torridons don't produce such vertical walls. Being salvationists we had no intention of climbing anything serious but we still wanted to nose about the corries of Beinn Bhan. We set off from the head of the loch up the stalkers' path shown on Sheet 24.

There is a whole array of corries: Coire Each, *horse corrie*; Coire na Feola, *corrie of blood*; Coire na Poite (with its twin lochans), *corrie of the pot*; Coire an Fhamhair, *the giants' corrie*; Coire Toll a' Bhein, *corrie of the hole in the skin*; Coire Gorm Beag, *little blue corrie*. Corrie na Feola is the first steep, deep one, with the prow of Beinn Bhan's A' Chioch (*nose*) jutting out as its north arm. We cut round under it (looking down on Lochan Coire na Poite) after investigating a bifurcation of streams low on the burn from Coire Each. This split in the stream is shown accurately on the map, unlike others I've checked. The most accessible of such features is on the northern slopes of Chno Dearg by Loch Treig and there's another at the west end of Loch Quoich — anything but accessible.

Coire na Poite is a deep rock cauldron. Oddly one of its lochans was completely frozen over while the other remained clear. Could there be warm springs or was it some freak chance? The head of the corrie soared up, featureless and ice-draped, into cloud while the sweep out to A' Chioch presented a series of buttresses and gullies: routes galore. On the other (north) side the lower prow of A' Poite had a level ridge connecting with a stepped ridge vanishing towards the plateau above. We continued on steep but firm snow, half hoping it would allow us up easily. Being a grade IV climb we did not go further. We also went to the A' Chioch col. The ridge from there to the top was first climbed in winter by Tom Patey and Joe Brown. We crept round to Coire an Fhamhair.

The NW corner of this corrie is free of cliffs and, apart from some icy slabs, we ascended quickly. The upper part of the A' Poite ridge drops in bold perpendicular fashion, a superwall with no chinks in its armour. (One can appreciate such features fully when there is no risk of having to try to climb them.) Before exiting on to the plateau we ate and muffled up in extra layers. We could just see the corniced edge so followed this rim along to Beinn Bhan, the highest summit in Applecross.

We carefully took bearings, counted steps, recorded time, etc., to steer accurately down to the Bealach nan Arr, the fine pass which separates the sprawling Corbetts. Coire Attadale to the north is a deer sanctuary: loch-splattered and defended by miles of cliff. Coire nan Arr to the south runs down to the sea at the oil-rig construction yard, now closed, but the site still waiting to be returned to the original state as agreed when it was opened.

Applecross was a human sanctuary in pre-Reformation times and was the site of one of the earliest Christian settlements, founded by St Maelrubha in 672. The crofts on the coast and the empty hinterland are the result of more modern Clearances. The link road along the north coast has done something to alleviate the isolation. As we'd discovered often enough, the Bealach na Ba can frequently be closed in winter, being over 2,000 feet in height. The road was originally planned to reach Toscaig by the coast but the elderly ladies who owned the land refused to allow this easy route.

Corbett, writing of a winter visit in the Thirties, commented that Applecross was an easy place to reach but not so easy to escape from. A boat from Kyle to Stornoway dropped him off into a rowing boat in the afternoon and he was told the exit was the same boat, same schedule, i.e., Kyle via Stornoway! Or he "rode St Francis' pony" over the Bealach na Ba. There were only Gaelic services held in the church. His first hill had a name he could not pronounce and the locals could not write, so it goes unrecorded. Sgurr a' Chaorachain became *Scoor a Hurricane*. Even Corbett had to work for his Corbetts.

We were tempted just to turn down Coire nan Arr, but there was also a certain pleasure in the navigational challenge, and there was a Corbett to be claimed. Both hills have long plateaux of very broken sandstone, sometimes detached blocks from areas of paving, but always unusually rough and reducing our speed. Why a *white hill* is made of *red* sandstone is a puzzle. Cairns led down to the col but we preferred to trust our own navigation (the cairns could go anywhere). The white flat area marking the lochan before the final pull up Sgurr a' Chaorachain gave us one certain position and from it a careful bearing led to the North Summit. A piece of linoleum sticking out the snow was an oddity — and then we found the top had some communications structures on top. They rather spoilt the polar exploration atmosphere.

Chaorachain (the OS spelling is a printing error) has a deep cauldron corrie facing east, with a minute tarn embedded in it, but the best-known feature is the terminal prow of its northern arm, A' Chioch. Norman Collie was the first to climb it, followed by Slingsby, Ling and Glover, J. H. B. Bell and others, but it is the "Cioch Nose" (Patey and Bonington, 1961) which has become one of the great sandstone classics. The southern spur of the corrie bulges out as a huge, obese buttress and has the Corbett on top of it, reached by a crest full of ups and downs which we found very tiring in the mixture of softening snow and the ambushing ice under it. Dave slipped and nearly knocked himself out and Jim left a blood spoor from a nose bleed, quite a useful help in backtracking from the summit cairn. We saw nothing and were still on compass bearings when we hit the Bealach na Ba road. "God help the poor cows", someone muttered.

The time was 4.15 and we quickly cut the corners of the 1-in-3 hairpin bends to tramp down in the cloudy gloom. Deer, like shadows, crossed the road, and the dark edge of Meall Gorm was stark against the satiny shimmer of Loch Kishorn. We were sitting round the fire, well fed, malts in hand, dreaming the year away when Dave looked up from the MacInnes walks guide to quote: "It should be noted that in the event of snow, or high winds, these high routes should be avoided."

Section 13: 3. BEINN DAMH 902m OS 24/25 893502
Hill of the stag (dav)

After a fairly cheerless day on Beinn Dearg (Just a few miles away) Beinn Damh gave me "a day among thousands" which I almost missed by sleeping-in at our comfy base at Glen Cottage under Liathach. I set off alone from the Beinn Damh Hotel by Loch Torridon.

A gate just west of the Allt Coire Roill bridge led to a path up through some splendid Torridonian forest. The track was well constructed for the tramp right up Coire Roill to the tiny lochan on the Drochaid Coire Roill, the col at the head of the valley.

Most guidebooks suggest ascending Beinn Damh by a branch path not far above the tree-line, and so along the ridge, but this then presents some awkward choices for the descent, assuming one is going to make a traverse and not just backtrack.

It is much more practical to go the other way round. The walk up Coire Roill gives a grand view of the tiered Torridonian cliffs of the east face, there is a sudden opening of the view from the col, and the route up to the summit can be studied from below a great deal more easily than trying to wiggle a route down such a maze of ledges, walls and screes. The way up looks impressive, too, especially once up the first spur above the col, for this spur leads to a corrie, not a ridge as one would expect. The two arms of the corrie are rocky prows, the northern angled across the spur down to the col. My log recorded: "Nice easy scrambling compared to yesterday [Beinn Dearg (13:4)] but equally a 'summer' ascent even if early January. Sandstone gave way to quartzite on the summit crag."

Being aware of what was happening weather-wise I carefully refrained from looking at the view. Picking a scrambling line up made that fairly easy, of course. At the summit I lifted my eyes to the hills. Fantastic! Beinn Damh was the bastion holding back a white, surging sea of cloud which stretched away over the eastern horizon and onto which a sun of molten magnificence set the blaze of white into spectrum brilliance. I sat on the cairn for over an hour, spellbound. All the hills to the east rose like dark islands out of the cloud-sea. Strangely, Torridon was clear and its giant hills stood pale and flat. Even as I watched the cliffs of Applecross were attacked by waves of vapour and slowly these overwhelmed the bluffs like a rising tide.

If driving round from Lochcarron village, have a look from Loch an Loin and you'll see why the map names the "Stirrup Mark" just below the summit. Loch an Loin is a pleasant alternative start/finish to a traverse of the Corbett, using the path up Strath a' Bhathaich, while a low-level-bad-weather-alternative of interest is to circumnavigate the hill: hotel, Coire Roill, Strath a' Bhathaich, Doire Damh, hotel — naturally ending back at the hotel. Thoughts of refreshment *in* the Beinn Damh stirred me from my sun-smitten perch *on* Beinn Damh.

I took some pleasure in kicking down a line of fatuous cairns along the perfectly obvious ridge. (Cairnomaniacs are leaving their mark all over Torridon.) Two figures were coming up the steep ascent and gave good scale to the clouds behind, already licking over the double col to Sgurr na Bana Mhoraire, the end top of Beinn Damh above Loch Torridon. On the col there was a flitting glimpse of a brocken spectre before the milky coldness of the inversion obliterated the magic. After picking up the path I danced back down to the Dormobile, quickly re-loaded the cameras, and drove round till dark, making the most of the glory given. Sunset lit Slioch like a torch and then plunged the peak into the black waters of night.

Section 13: 4. BEINN DEARG 914 m OS 19/24 895608
The red hill (jarrak)

Beinn Dearg had the misfortune, in prehistoric measurements, to be 2,998 feet and, in the change over to the sloppier metres, there was a great searching of decimals before it was finally allowed to rest as a Corbett. Quite a few Munroists climb it "just in case". As Beinn Teallach showed, promotion to Munro status has the same effect as throwing a bone to a pack of hounds. Beinn Dearg had a near escape so can now, hopefully, return to its shadowy "fourth man" position, hidden behind the big bad boys of Beinn Eighe, Liathach and Beinn Alligin. The SMC will — eventually — tidy the awkwardnesses and anomalies in the Corbett list.

The peak is split awkwardly between 1:50,000 sheets numbers 19 and 24 but because of its complex and serious nature it would be worth obtaining the 1:25,000 Outdoor Leisure Map "The Cuillin and Torridon Hills", which will also be useful for the other local Corbetts (see 15:1–4) and also for the Skye pair. For no obvious reason the *Tables* separate Beinn Dearg from other nearby Corbetts and, as some points will apply "equally to all", the following notes could be helpful.

A traverse of Beinn Dearg has something of the feel of traversing the two Munros of Liathach except Dearg has rough red sandstone rather than cold grey quartzite. The Corbett, too, is a peak demanding a head for heights. It is most easily approached by the Coire Mhic Nobuil path, and from that route the peak fills the view ahead, its many-tiered defences giving the more sedate walker some concern. This comes out in all accounts I've read of the peak. Even the restrained SMC district guide states, "The south and west sides rise in a continuous precipitous escarpment which at first glance seems impregnable", but quickly adds, "Fortunately, the walls are breached in several places by rock gullies and, while these offer a way on to the summit ridge with varying degrees of difficulty, caution should be exercised at all times . . . in adverse weather (or winter) this is not a hill for an inexperienced party." My one and only ascent was made one January through thick cloud when I was occasionally quite glad not to be seeing too much.

Like most of these hills of Torridonian sandstone a view uphill makes the slope appear all rock, while the view down appears all grass or heather — the basic cause of many troubles, especially in descent when only the horizontal terraces show and the vertical bands of rock are hidden. Worked into this horizontal world of wall and terrace are plenty of vertical lines of weakness caused by the eroding streams. A route will usually "go" by using a gully for much of the time but period-ically moving out on to the terraces. Safety lies in choosing a line suitable for one's capabilities. On both sides of the barrel-shaped bulk facing Coire Mhic Nobuil there are plenty of gullies to choose from, but I'd use the bridge and go up the Bealach a' Chomhla path to where it crosses the Allt a' Bhealaich and then continue on the *east* bank, taking any one of the tributaries to its gully source on Beinn Dearg. The steep teasing-up of a route then follows, the angle eventually falling back on to a relatively bare summit area. There is a big cairn, as if someone were determined the hill must pass the 3,000-foot barrier.

During the walk in, have a good look at the possibilities and also note the rocky prow that juts out to the right below the summit dome. This is the hang gliders' route off. Plenty of walkers stray on to it but the real way crosses a pinnacle more to the north — the line is shown on the map by the NTS boundary — and this is the only scrambly bit on the traverse eastwards. Stuc Loch na Cabhaig and Carn na Feola are both worth a visit for they are great prows thrusting into the Empty Quarter northwards. Oddly, I've met no descriptions of ascents from the north, and if a cross-country Corbett expedition is being made on that side, as suggested in 15:1–4, then that is the time and place to add Beinn Dearg. The Stuc is far more accessible on its eastern flank, and a south–north line down into Coire Beag from the lowest point on the ridge would be a simple descent by Torridon standards. To descend to the south, return to this lowest point and head just south of east, and the dip of the rocks will lead you down quite naturally. The gullies falling south from the main summit are sometimes suggested as descent routes but they are better left for the more experienced, being steep and tricky at times. Glen Torridon can be gained by finishing off the "circumnavigation" of Liathach by the Coire Dubh path.

Brenda Macrow, who lived in Torridon for some years, wrote a book *Torridon Highlands* which perfectly captures the feel of the area in the early 1950s, when corned beef and "Pom" in Inveralligin Hostel, reached after a sail from Shieldaig, would be the prelude to a good going sing-song round the fire. She and some friends climbed Beinn Dearg and their story is worth reading both for some practical information and to capture the special atmosphere of this mountain. They gained the summit from the east and commented how, glancing back, they were amazed at the wild beauty and seeming difficulty of the ridge they had traversed. This mix of threat and treat really sets Beinn Dearg aside as a Corbett for the more experienced walker. The Macrow day ended with a typical Torridon escapade: descending to the Bealach a' Chomhla.

"The gully was thick with wet grass, and we slid for a while beside the course of a stream. Then outcrops of rock appeared — the stream cascaded through a deepening chasm, and we ran into a little difficulty which was increased by the unbalancing tendency displayed by our rucksacks. A loose stone started a landslide just in front of us. It went with a terrific roar down the gully, drowning the rush of the waterfall. With one accord, we forsook our chimney and scrambled on to the left-hand spur, where we rested and 'recovered' before completing the last, and easiest, stage of the descent. Looking up from the bottom, we could hardly believe that we had managed it without mishap, for it looked almost perpendicular."

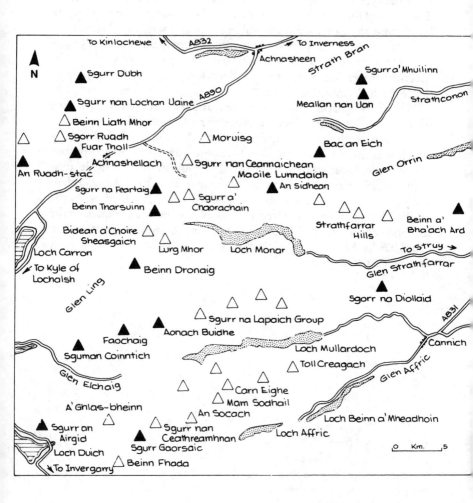

LOCH DUICH–GLEN AFFRIC NORTH TO STRATH BRAN

Section 14: 1. SGURR GAORSAIC   *c.*838 m   OS 33   036219
Peak of the thrill or horror (goresac)

SEVERAL TIMES I'VE approached, or descended from, Sgurr nan Ceathreamhnan without going up Sgurr Gaorsaic. I always meant to, even before this dome became a Corbett in the new listings, but either I'd run out of time, or steam, or the weather would pack in. When I finally climbed Sgurr Gaorsaic it was on a foul day, from Loch Duich, and the rewards were few. I missed out Gaorsaic again, even as I was compiling these Corbett accounts. In mid-May 1987, during the Ultimate Challenge, I had a grand solo day over An Socach, Mullach na Dheiragain and Sgurr nan Ceathreamhnan and had every intention of adding Sgurr Gaorsaic but, perched on the Alpamayo-like snow peak of Ceathreamhnan, one look at the West Top ruled out any hope of the Corbett beyond. Cornices and big snow sweeps made it far too risky without an ice-axe.

At the Alltbeithe hostel that night I raved about the view and then, just a few minutes later, someone else, quite independently, praised the view from Sgurr Gaorsaic. Everyone expects mighty Ceathreamhnan to have a view. Only those who ken the Corbetts know they always, well nearly always, are good viewpoints as well. I was pleased to have such a confirmation. The current SMC guidebook only mentions the Corbett in suggesting the best way round it to reach Ceathreamhnan.

My favourite way to Gaorsaic is an evening "descent" to it from the big Munro, which an earlier SMC guide highly recommends. The view then is quite something with Skye and Sgriol and all manner of good things showing boldly in the golden west. Some day, *Insh 'Allah*, I'd like to camp — or bivvy — by the summit tarn and see the sun go down from that high place. And the flat summit would be the perfect spot for a hockey match.

This Corbett is a strangely symmetrical bump, tacked on to a big neighbour, and jutting out into the furthest west end of Glen Affaric, as Glen Affric is known locally. At one time you could obtain permission to drive up Glen Elchaig to the A. E. Robertson memorial bridge and approach via the Falls of Glomach and the Abhainn Gaorsaic, but the foreign owners have forbidden this of late. There is still a good alternative expedition from Dorusduain, situated in from the head of Loch Duich. The Belach an Sgairne (Gates of Affric) is fine in its own right as well as for what it leads to. One winter I was greatly assisted by having Loch a' Bhealaich frozen and I walked over the ice as an easy option to floundering round. Gleann Gaorsaic tends to be peaty. The Corbett can be ascended from any direction, really. After traversing Sgurr Gaorsaic, the Falls of Glomach can be visited and a return made over the Bealach na Sroine. Good paths in and out make up for Gleann Gaorsaic. The Corbett could also be combined with as many local Munros as heroes care to add or it could be taken in on the way to, or from, Alltbeithe, the "iron lodge" that is one of Scotland's genuine, old-fashioned, primitive hostels (the hostel is left open out of season). As only those who have walked will be staying there, good company is normal.

Section 14:   2. Sgurr an Airgid   841 m   OS 25/33   940227
The silver peak

This is a quick and easy Corbett, but that does not make the hill any less of a "good thing". Airgid is another of my Hogmanay hills and the last time I climbed it was typical of the chancy nature of the Hogmanay mountain game. We set off from our Glenelg bothy base to climb Ciste Dhubh north of the Cluanie Inn and, instead, went up this hill above Loch Duich. No doubt many other gangs moderated their plans that day, at least those in a condition to be summit-bound on the first of January. As Byron said:

> "Let us have wine and women, mirth and laughter,
> Sermons and soda-water the day after."

It was our day after!

We had had rain on top of rain for days and days. The ground was sodden and we were weary of splashing about in our wellies. Kintail doesn't have a climate so much as a roulette wheel of various weathers. The tail-end of the 7.55 a.m. forecast told of blizzards sweeping in from the east — which was the end of plans for the bigger hills. They were too far away, too high, and bad in east winds. The neglected cars (and dogs), however, needed some exercise. We decided to chance Mam Ratagan and nip up Sgurr an Airgid, the near but neglected cousin of Kintail.

A pause on top of the Mam showed the peak well, but the Five Sisters were smothered in cloud and the glower of snow shone down the glens under the mantle of the dark. There was no time to waste. From a road verge in Glen Croe we set off up the hill direct, soon joining the pony track that wends back and forth on the steep south side before eventually leading off to the next hill to the east. The path was a good aid for gaining height fast.

The Professor, Martin and Alice had come up from London, Dave, Tim and I were more local, which perhaps accounted for our being three Munroists, as was my dog Storm, while Tim's Zoë (named after Joe Brown's daughter) was just starting her youthful career. Sgritheall two days earlier had been Alice's first Munro, a wild and wintry one. Three of the party had poor eyesight (contact lenses or essential spectacles) and I'd just recovered from several stitches in an eyeball. No recruiting officer would have looked at this mix of the halt, lame and half-blind but it was a cheery-enough platoon that plodded up into the rising wind. The days of wet had filled a bellyfold of hill with crystal-clear water and Zoë danced along its rim trying to catch the splashes from the stones we threw in. The pool was grassy right to the bottom so was obviously a temporary feature. It reminded me of Loch a' Chuirn Deirg on the steep flank of Ben Attow above Glen Lichd where I'd once had a winter camp. It is held by a similar slip of the slope. You also find this on the Five Sisters, the Grey Corries and other schisty areas.

Our only pause was at the gate in the deer fence which girdles the hill. Above, we were on to snow which had the dogs dashing back and forth in excitement. Zoë climbed the hill six times over as she chased every kicked-up piece of snow. Storm is more sedate, his chief joys being olfactory (he sniffs out mice with all the enthusiasm of a truffle hunter). He kept wrinkling his nose into the east wind, which usually indicated deer. We saw none as the icy blast made looking for them too unpleasant.

When the path veered off we had a last pause to don our full protective panoply of winter clothing. I changed from light wellies into boots and Yeti gaiters. Pockets were stuffed with food. Ice-axes in hand we angled up to the col. The clouds came down on us and the spindrift hungrily hunted over the frozen drifts. The change from a casual walk up a path to a serious fight on an Arctic mountain took only a few minutes. It was what we wanted, of course, the fun of the fight to hansel in the year, but it was treading, Agag-like, with a respect frosted with awe. A Scottish mountain can be a fearsome place.

The east ridge was a double one and the hollow between was a white road of hard snow which gave easy walking, if walking is the word to describe our wind-buffeted, drunken course. A bank of steep snow tempted us to cut steps up its wall — only a few metres but retrieving rusty rhythms and techniques. Sometimes we had to cut steps on almost level ground for the wind had planed the old snow hard as glass. Tim managed to cut a step in his dog's tail making a brief blood spoor for the laggards to follow. (Zoë constantly dived at one's feet trying to catch flying bits of snow.) Storm donned an additional pullover of white, his eyes staring out from a balaclava of snow.

Alice enjoyed her second winter-battering. She was a robust young lass who went home from Kintail to face trials for a place in the English rugby team. Often guile, not brute strength, counts most in these situations. Being aware of cause and effect, or sensing dangers (like rocks being suddenly coated in invisible ice) is something that comes from imagination as much as from direct instruction. I enjoyed seeing someone so at home, at once, in such a savage environment. Those with poor eyesight had the greatest problems. Long before the summit I realised we would not be able to retrace our upward route: the gravel-sharp searing of the storm on any bare skin would see to that.

Battling *into* storms or refusing to modify plans has led to some sad tragedies in the hills. I remember hearing a keeper commenting on the Cairngorm school kids' disaster with, "Aye, they should hae gone *with the wind*. It widna matter where as long as it wis doon. You can aye win roon when you canna gang ower."

After a scrum-down at the ice-sheathed trig point we blew on westwards. A first attempt at flanking off landed me thigh deep in drift — Tim had to yank me out on to the rocks again. The rock strata dipped conveniently to the south east and we angled down-along, out-along these gentle ramps in turn, to come out suddenly below the clouds. Through the thickly falling snow we could see the dark waters of the loch with the A87 curving across on its causeway. The storm had lowered the snow line by several hundred feet and it was with regret we came down below the dry (if wild) freezing level. I changed back into my wellies, and we made a fast contouring descent to the cars to escape this ambushing, lower wetness. A wild and rainy day followed at bothy level — once we'd slithered over the snow carpeting the Mam.

Next day the radio reported one climber killed in Torridon and one air-lifted from the Nevis cliffs. Now, I don't know the details, but I do wonder why they risked such big brutes of hills with such a forecast. Maybe they did not listen to a forecast. All I know is that we cowards had a grand day when we exchanged the big devil of Ciste Dhuibh (the black chest or coffin) for the safer stimulation of Sgurr na Airgid (the silver peak). Happiness is a hill successfully climbed at Hogmanay.

> "Only a hill: earth set a little higher
> above the face of the earth . . .

Only a hill; but all of life to me,
up there between the sunset and the sea."
(Geoffrey Winthrop Young)

Section 14: 3. SGUMAN COINNTICH 879 m OS 25 977304
Mossy peak

Section 14: 4. FAOCHAIG 868 m OS 25 022317
The whelk

Section 14: 5. AONACH BUIDHE 899 m OS 25 058324
Yellow ridge or height (oenach boo-ee)

These three hills stand in a remarkably moated block of wild country, circled by the waters of the River Ling and the River Elchaig. Loch Mhoicean, however, does not have a river flowing from its NE end even though the loch sits on a sprawling watershed whose escaping waters soon flow off to encircle this hilly area. The hills are bulky rather than beautiful and their rather chaotic nature is reflected in the summit panoramas which offer a confused view of other summits near and far. With Glen Shiel and Affaric on one side and Torridon on the other the scenery is a bit overwhelming.

Beinn Dronaig (see 14:7) had been climbed on a New Year raid that whetted the appetite for a return visit, which came the following Boxing Day, motoring to Killilan (where we were set on by a pack of enthusiastic dogs — Yorkshire terriers luckily), visiting the Falls of Glomach and, after a social call at Iron Lodge (a lot of the buildings were originally clad in corrugated iron), taking the good path up the Crom-Allt. Above Iron Lodge the steep path east has been bulldozed. Our route, however, lay northwards. A steeper pull led to a ruin topping the pass and, suddenly, we were looking to Beinn Dronaig, Bidean and Lurg Mhor. We sang down to Maol-bhuidhe where a cheery fire led to a pleasant bothy evening. Bright moonlight illuminated the deer meadows.

An early look out was discouraging but we set off later, six of us, back on the path to the watershed. We went up by the waterfall into the inner recesses of the hill in a vain hope of finding good snow for practising winter techniques. In the end we climbed the crags on to the stepped ridge and crossed the plateau to the summit of Faochaig. Unlike the peak next to The Saddle in Glen Shiel this *whelk* hill gave no hint as to why it should be so named. Carn nan Searrach, the west top above Coire Dubh, looked as high so we went over to climb it just in case the OS, aided and abetted by Jim Donaldson, should ever change the order of precedence. Sguman Coinntich appears as a huge, corrie-edged sprawl from here. The clouds had been building up and we were glad to take the path down to the col again and head for the car at Iron Lodge. We reached it just in time.

Aonach Buidhe had also been on the programme for that day, but our "winter" course was keener on avoiding a soaking than staying on the tops, a pity as the members were beginning to go well. I'd long ago learnt that the average hillman from the south is often content with a low level of challenge and achievement. If I'd paid for a course I'd want to be out 25 hours each day! I was back there in April with a younger group of three, two friends, and the dog. We returned to Maol-bhuidhe as before. This time there was a clear winter tideline on the hills and the sky was spilling over with frosty stars.

We wandered south up the river that passes the bothy. This came down over swelling slopes of bog, north of the ridges and corries of Aonach Buidhe. Our stream descended in a thin fall from the west corrie. We had been practising techniques, which took us up to the western spur, but the crisp morning had been slipping away as the temperature rose and the clouds fell. Helen had not been feeling too well. Later I read a long account of hers which was amusing in its innocence. She thought the Falls of Glomach visit was the end of the previous day's activities so was horrified to be faced with the night walk to the bothy. "Hamish did this deliberately," she had to explain. "I expected a meal ready, as in the huts in Austria, but the place was cold and dark and we had to do our own cooking. Hamish cheered me up by telling me there were mice, the reason for hanging up our food." And on the hill (ice-axe work): "I was extremely frightened. Hamish just threw himself down this slope, talking as he did, to demonstrate, then told us to do it. . . . Worse was to come, we had to fall head-first on our tums. On the summit it began to snow heavily."

My log doesn't even mention snow falling. We traversed the fine corrie to An Creacha Beag before baling off down the middle of the three northern spurs. After lunch by the river Dave took Helen down to the bothy. "I just went into my sleeping bag while Dave filled all the dixies and even got a lovely fire going." We were not far behind as the ice, for climbing practice, was simply peeling off with the rise in temperature. We shared our bedtime brew with a couple, Roger and Anne, who had come through from Glen Affaric. By then it was a wild, wet night and our exit next day, put off till noon, was into the face of a blizzard.

On the col we found some sheep in trouble, we saw an eagle (huge in the mist), and snow buntings went cheepering past. Helen wrote quite enthusiastically of the plod out. One adjusts surprisingly quickly. The car radio reported someone missing in the Cairngorms. "It was too wild to camp so we went to a hostel at Achnashellach run by a nice guy called Gerry. There was a bath and a real loo." A couple of days were spent at Gerry's, then we tramped and climbed in Glen Affaric before everyone departed from Kyle by train, "a glorious day just when I have to go back home. Please can I stay, Hamish?" Having seen Helen and the others off I felt a bit guilty at driving straight along to Ardelve and Killilan again. I had a dry but dreich day for Sguman Coinntich.

Just as Aonach Buidhe thrusts ridges and corries northwards this hill does so to the west, a whole fistful of ridges slanting off from the long crest that links Sguman Coinntich with Faochaig. Nearly every glen has a stalkers' path but the Allt a' Choire Mhoir, descending to Killilan, is the longest and most direct for the Corbett. Kitchy and I sweated up this path till it vanished under the poggy remains of snow under the Bealach Mhic Bheathain. Bidean a' Choire Sheasgaich appeared again, a sharp cone from this angle, framed by an arch of white clouds against the well-washed blue sky. This is the best viewpoint of the three Corbetts and, having gained them one by one, with a certain amount of struggle, I looked east and promised myself a return one day, a kindly day of early summer when "the dew is on the season", to traverse them all in a single walk. But that is another story. . . .

Most recently Charlie, on a trip north, and Storm the dog outvoted me and another raid was made on these hills. I'd been in Morven, Charlie on Jura, but we met up at a roadside rendezvous at the head of Loch Long.

Loch Long is the *loch of the longboat*, the boat being a galley which brought home the body of St Fillan for burial. This is probably not the more famous St Fillan but a local saint. In fact some of the legends here go back far beyond Christianity. When St Fillan was travelling in France he always carried a hazel-staff from Kintail. One day he met an alchemist who asked him to go back and catch the white serpent which had its hole under the root of the tree on which the staff had grown, at the north-east end of Loch Long. St Fillan went back and put out a pail of honey. Out came the serpent, and crawled into it. St Fillan had to cross seven streams with the pail before he was safe from all the other serpents. The Elchaig was one of these. When he had returned to France the alchemist put the pail on a fire to boil and told the saint not to touch any bubbles which rose to the surface. Unthinkingly, St Fillan burst the first bubble, put his scalded finger in his mouth, and was thereafter possessed of magical powers of healing. He then returned to Kintail, where he became renowned as a great physician.

Killilan is named after the saint and so is Ben Killilan which, with Sguman Coinntich, dominates the estate hamlet. Charles had done Sguman Coinntich. We cycled the eight miles up to Iron Lodge (now empty), quite an effort as I could not raise my saddle enough to pedal with any power and Charles's rucksack weight caused his carrier to disintegrate and the metal to dig huge chunks out of the tyre. We walked over the familiar path to Maol-bhuidhe. I made one diversion to check on the stream bifurcation shown on a stream descending to the col. This was more a braiding of trickles (like an estuary) being set in an alluvial fan. We did Beinn Dronaig that afternoon.

The next day, in rather sad conditions we squelched up to the pass and, free of rucksacks, did Faochaig (by the splendid, if steep path) and Aonach Buidhe (up *in* the big burn, a mix of climbing and botanising). The range of flowers was greater than usual in the west. Even the ruin on the col hosted six different fern species. I was collecting frogs for the bog-garden pond at home and Charles commented on the odd sight of myself on Aonach Buidhe, striding through the mist in shorts, brolly in one hand, a bag of frogs in the other.

Tea was brewed before cycling down the glen. Charles was lucky and did not have a blow out. Storm was lucky — he did most of the journey in a rucker on my back. After soup at the car Charles departed to try and make the Corran Ferry into Morven for the night and the first ferry to Mull for its Corbetts the next day. Even Storm drew a line at such fanaticism. We stayed where we were and did Sguman Coinntich the next morning, curving up out of the corrie to miss the crags in the mist, rain and wind. A few days later at home I unpacked Sheet 25 of the trip and from it came a tingling smell of wood smoke and wetness.

Section 14:   6. Sgorr na Diollaid   818 m   OS 25   282363
            Peak of the saddle (sgoor na jee ulij)

Sgorr na Diollaid has a hook-shaped summit which makes it easily recognisable from other hills. A knobbly crest rising to the highest point at the NW end is responsible for this individuality and a bit of (optional) fun can be had scrambling up the rocks. As there is the inconvenience of obtaining clearance to drive up Strathfarrar most people climb Sgurr na Diollaid from Glen Cannich to the south, which is probably the easier way anyway. Northern slopes in the western glens tend to be much more heathery (low down) and craggy (high up) compared to their gentler southern aspects. Dave, Kitchy and I went up from Glen Cannich one Boxing Day.

We started at Loch Carrie and wandered up in a chilled cocktail of weathers. We sat out some blatters in the recesses of the hill, or just contoured with the blast on our backs and then worked upwards in the dry spells. The slopes were a rich ochrous colour; apart from some bog, heather and crag, we had a very casual ascent. There were plenty of deer and as we approached the last bumps thirteen ptarmigan whirred off. We climbed the peaklets but had our snack in the lee of the crest.

A decade later (on 1 January) with Charles, Belinda, Ernst and Storm, we set off up the Allt Charaich again. This was entirely Charles's fault. The day before we had been grounded by amazing rain, some of the deluge that washed away roads all down the west. We were staying at Cozac Lodge beside the original outflow of Loch Mullardoch (now raised 110 feet by the big dam) and, simply to experience the wetness, we walked along the loch a bit. The waves were crashing and spraying over the dam and the Allt Mullardoch was a fearsome sight, full to the brim, roaring in spate, and grumbling its boulders down into the brim-full loch. Salmon, venison and Danish specialities made a memorable dinner that night. The year was well and truly washed away.

Corbett-bagging Charles demanded the scalp of Sgorr na Diollaid before we headed south the next day. We had reached the level area (630 m) just below the last bulk of hill when a ferocious blizzard swept in. Ernst and Storm found this sufficiently unfriendly to opt for a retreat. Charles and Belinda battled on up to the summit. A mere blizzard was not going to deprive Charles of the pleasure of the first new Corbett of the year. A dedicated lad is our Charles.

Section 14:   7. BEINN DRONAIG   797 m   OS 25   037382
Hill of the knoll or *Ragged hill*

Dave, the two Jims and I set off early from Strathcarron, taking the path from Achintee over the moors (fine views to the dawn-flushed Applecross Corbetts) and on up to the Bealach Alltan Ruairidh. Once down from the pass we briefly used the estate road to Bendronaig Lodge, as far as the bridge over the Uisge Dubh, an arch of iron fretwork with stone supports at the ends, a real period piece. We followed downstream and then began to cut round to join the eastern branch of the remote River Ling. Deer moved ahead of us and a buzzard circled above. Dave compared the country to Norway, where we'd been the summer before.

The scene was certainly as wild and the going was as difficult:

waterfalls, an awkward crag, some steep bits, then endless bogs and braes as we followed the many wendings of the river. In two hours of effort we passed only two places which had names on the map, *the speckled plain* and *the crooked bend*. The river was unusually low (for 2 January) so we could swap banks periodically. Dry feet were also a welcome change in that part of the world. An Cruachan, a 706-m cone north of An Socach, dominated our view along the valley. The peak never seemed to come any nearer; there was almost a feeling of surprise when we came on Loch Cruoshie and the bothy. We paddled across and a herd of deer grudgingly moved aside for us. Few bothies have such a setting of wide open spaciousness, an emptiness that made our haven feel snug and friendly. We had a brew and, at 1.30 p.m., set off again for the hill.

In normal — wet — conditions the river of that whole valley, from An Cruachan away down to the River Ling, can be difficult to cross. East of Loch Cruoshie the waters run slow, but deep; west of the loch they rush off down the glen in potentially dangerous spate. Over the years that moat has given us plenty of river-crossing experience. There is sometimes a reasonable crossing a mile east of the bothy but the easiest place, which we used on this occasion, is on the reach between the exit from the loch and the Allt na Sean-luibe junction. The river can change in character but we have nearly always managed across here. In real spate it would be safer crossing east of the loch — or even *in* it — as all one's belongings can go in a bivvy bag which can then act as a buoyancy aid for swimming over. A brief swim is a safer option (assuming you can swim) than perhaps being swept away downstream.

All my log recorded after we'd paddled over was "a gentle amble up Beinn Dronaig, another Corbett of smart views. Bidean was an angular pap and Lurg Mhor a bulk beached on Loch Monar. The barrier hills west [which we'd crossed] were overtopped by the paired pyramids of Maol Chean-dearg and An Ruadh Stac. The Corbetts in the south [14:3–5] deserve some attention soon." Beinn Dronaig is a plain, lumpy hill and easy enough, once you reach it. Loch Calavie and the pass to the north give the only features.

Just how remote this area is we saw from the entries in the bothy book or, rather, the absence of entries. The last party had been there in September, and the year before the first visitor of the year had been John Hinde on 27 January.

We had walked barefoot up the grassy meadow after our return paddle, then sat outside for a cup of tea. The mildness disappeared with the light and our paddle at dawn the next day was distinctly chilly. We made our exit over Lurg Mhor and Bidean a' Choire

Sheasgaich. Beinn Dronaig, I felt, had rather been a sop for my Corbetting hopes. Interestingly, though, Dave (Munros done) is now ticking off the Corbetts. I'd hazard he is glad to have Beinn Dronaig safely gathered in — and no more rivers to cross.

The bothy book had a note on previous residents. At the turn of the century there was a family of ten Renwicks, descended from Covenanting stock. One son, Alexander, went on to become a Professor of Divinity and Moderator of the Free Church. The last family there were the Burnetts who left in 1916. They shared a teacher with the children at Pait Lodge, seven miles along the glen. Pait is still occupied, perhaps the loneliest house in the Highlands, served only by the chancy miles of Loch Monar, which is the end of long, lonely Glen Strathfarrar.

On the recent July raid from Glen Elchaig with Charles there was no difficulty crossing the river at the loch's outflow. We went right up the Allt a' Choire Odhar which rises on the east ridge only five minutes off the summit. With a stiff wind in our faces we kept coming on browsing deer. One stag was even "doing a Landseer" by the tall trig-pillar. Charles raved about the view — the only one in a very wet week — and told me this was a marked feature of Corbetts!

We had walked in with the cloud down on the tops but, as we climbed, so did the cloud. We had our views then, as we descended, again with the cloud. That night gave one moment of magic. I went out in the dark, and in the midnight range of blacks, greys and silvers there was a window in the clouds, and there, right over Beinn Dronaig, was the friendly outline of the Plough.

Section 14: 8. BEINN THARSUINN 863 m OS 25 055433
           Transverse hill (tarshin)

This is certainly a Corbett which should have been done (or should be done) with the Munros Bidean a' Choire Sheasgaich and Lurg Mhor. If still "outstanding" you can easily combine it with the next peak in the list, Sgurr na Feartaig (14:9), as they both rise from the unusual *triple* col of the Bealach Bhearnais.

The usual, and most practical, approach is from Craig in Glen Carron. I'd like to hazard that Gerry Howkins' private hostel (always open) is likely to be the base from which most people set off into these remote parts. At Craig an estate road crosses the railway at a level-crossing, then bridges the River Carron and pulls up through the forest to end eventually at Glenuaig Lodge. Before the levels of Pollan Buidhe a pony track crosses the Allt a' Chonnais and makes a wet way up to the Bealach Bhearnais. If the river is in spate there is a footbridge downstream a bit (not immediately obvious on the ground). From the triple col Beinn Tharsuinn rises in a series of knobbly bumps, the summit giving a grand view to the sharp peak of Bidean a' Choire Sheasgaich. This Corbett, which acts as a stepping stone to that Munro and its very different twin, Lurg Mhor, is often the one Corbett a Munroist will have done, knowingly or otherwise.

Unless adding the Munros, or going on into the uninhabited hinterland, the easy option is to return to the Bealach Bhearnais. From the col a path, not on the map, makes a rising traverse on to the Sgurr na Feartaig ridge above Coire nan Each, which makes Feartaig an easy addition. The paths off Feartaig to Lair, or to the Allt a' Chonnais, are pleasant alternatives for the homeward journey.

Beinn Tharsuinn the Corbett, like Beinn Tarsuinn the Munro, is a slightly irritating hill in being positioned in the way of more desirable objectives. All Tarsuinns seem to have this habit, living up to their name, and invariably being long, rough, craggy, lumpy hills which are better traversed than flanked.

Section 14:   9. Sgurr na Feartaig   862 m   OS 25   055454
              The peak of thrift (i.e. sea pink, *Armeria maritima*)

Strange, how thrift (*feartaig*) thrives in the wilds only on the inhospitable summits or on the edges of the sea. Sgurr Fhuar-thuill, one of the Strathfarrar Munros, has a Top with the same name. Thrift can be found on most of the hills east of Glen Carron. The Corbett is the long skyline above Achnashellach, a cliff-topped array of corries rising above the massed forests. Gerry's hostel at Craig looks up to Feartaig and, not surprisingly, the Corbett is a popular easy day's walk from there. It is also a useful Corbett to take in while going into (or coming out from) the remote country further east.

During several Christmas holiday periods I used to run winter courses based on Gerry's and I always had a day beforehand laying out markers for a big map and compass exercise. Feartaig was first traversed and studied between laying markers in Golden Valley and at Pollan Buidhe under Ceannaichean. The obvious path traversing between these spots gives the best of walks on Feartaig, one that I never grow tired of repeating.

If the River Carron is low, paddle across the shallows and shingles opposite Lair. The bridge shown is simply two wires suspended over the river, and most people find it as off-putting as a high wire act in a circus, with the River Carron substituting for a safety net. Golden

Valley has some mature trees and once gave us a green-glowing, secretive camp site which felt like being in the foothills of the Himalayas. On that first visit I left my orienteering-type marker at the burn junction and walked on up the hills to the deer fence. The gate somehow managed to slam into my face and I was left sprawled on the path half unconscious!

The path flanks up Coire Leiridh (which has some good winter gullies in the headwall) and then wiggles successfully up to a wide plateau-like mossy col. Bidean a' Choire Sheasgaich is an impressive spike and Fuar Tholl, with its "white spider", dominates the jostle of Coulin and Torridon hills. There was hardly any snow, even with Christmas three days off, but at least there was no rain. I gave up "winter" courses eventually — they probably contravened the Trade Descriptions Act.

This sweeping saddle with its confusion of lochans and a path junction can be a tricky place in poor visibility. One path drops southwards to Bearnais and the uninhabited wilderness beyond, but a left fork zigzags up a flank to the offset western top of Sgurr nan Feartaig before wending along above the cliffs to the large cairn of the eastern, highest top, at 862 m. Deer down in Coire nan Each were grunting, sounding just like guinea pigs. Liathach and Beinn Eighe towered over the nearer hills while Skye and Sgriol and other favourite spots were all blowing out streamers of cloud. Sgurr nan Ceannaichean across the valley was long ago promoted to a Munro, to the chagrin of those who had "bagged" only Moruisg. This is poetic justice (as with most of the additions), in that, if the aesthetic *traverse* had been followed, the "new" would already have been done.

The path skirts the final bump to descend over several more bumps (grand walking) down to the Allt a' Chonais where there is an interesting bridge just above the tree line and a bit of spectacular gorge. Another path (not shown on the map) breaks off, right, before the final bump and angles down to the Bealach Bhearnais. Beinn Tharsuinn, if not climbed on a Bidean–Lurg Mhor traverse, can easily be done from here, and the rather wet path taken down to Pollan Buidhe. The path fords the river, but in spate the footbridge downstream (not easily seen) should be used. This day can be extended by starting further down Strathcarron at Arinckaig (south of Loch Dughaill). A path (not shown) breaks off the main one to head up towards Loch nan Gobhar.

Section 14:   10. AN RUADH-STAC   892 m   OS 25   922481
The red peak (roo-ah stac)

Dawn was just yawning when we parked at the foot of the Coulags Glen and set off up the footpath northwards. Long-tailed tits were busy in the riverside trees and the puddles on the path crackled their ice-plates underfoot. The year 1969 had two days left.

After a steeper pull the path crosses to the west bank, by a good bridge, mercifully, for the yellow water was high and the exposed boulders were bosses of ice. Half a mile further on we came to a lonely cottage (shut up and sad then, the building has now been restored as a bothy). We had our first pause at the isolated stone, Clach nan Con-Fionn, *the stone of Fingal's hound* Bran, traditionally tethered there during a stag-hunt.

Ten minutes up the glen the path forks and we took the steeper track left which heads to the col between Meall nan Ceapairean and Maol Chean-dearg. Andy opted out of proceedings as his boots were torturing him. Before reaching the windy col David, Jim, Kitchy and I traversed along to the line of crags on the east side of the long SE Ridge of the Munro. We took the left-most of the two biggest buttresses and enjoyed a modest 400-foot climb: a series of small quartz walls between which we rushed to restore life to freezing fingers till, higher, we were able to move together. The dog was patiently waiting at the top so we called our climb Ketchil Buttress (pronounced Kitchy). There was a cairn on top of the right buttress.

Maol Chean-dearg gave quite a tussle in the gale and we fought our way down again to bale off the ridge to the frozen lochan at the start of An Ruadh-stac's east ridge. The path from Coulags Glen is shown crossing the col but in fact ends on the col while the one from Torridon, skirting below the Munro, goes on a bit further than shown, to the Ceapairean spur leading to the col with An Ruadh-stac. Meall nan Ceapairean, 2,150 feet in old money, is worth climbing for its view — not that we had much today. An Ruadh-stac is worth seeing, however mis-named.

Ruadh is *red*, but An Ruadh-stac is a *grey* hill, sometimes touched white by the sun, but never red like its ruddy, bald-headed neighbour. We were at once struck by the grim north face looking down on Loch Coire an Ruadh-stac: two steep tiers and a broken one below them; and were not surprised to see that Patey and Bonington had put up a 600-foot route in 1960. Why such neglect since? Our delight was to find not quartz scree, but acres of ice-polished slabs on the south-east flank. David compared them to the Dubhs, even if the coefficient of friction is a bit different. We took to the slabs and romped about on them as we gained height. The route higher up became scraggy (crag/scree mixed) but soon landed us by the big cairn, and a big, if brief, view. Skye was wedged between silver sea-glitter and black, fingering clouds.

We had discovered An Ruadh-stac to be one of the roughest hills in an area of rugged hills; the paths are godsends. The east ridge is probably the most ascended route up and, whether coming from the Coulags Glen and Strath Carron, or by the path from Annat at the head of Loch Torridon, there is, successively, a good first view of the peak, the rousing scramble up and then the wide view from the summit. You cannot really ask for more of any mountain.

On one of the many Christmas days on the hills round here we climbed An Ruadh-stac from the Kishorn–Sheildaig road (sheet 24: 853445), skirting Loch an Loin to Glasnock and following up the secretive Allt a' Ghiubhais and the Allt Eisg which has a succession of small falls on its sandstone steps. This is a variation I'd recommend if two cars can be organised in the party.

Just to be different we descended the south ridge. This was rough, too, but the main memory is the desperate effort required to make headway into the gale. We were glad to turn off across the moors to pick up the burn draining Loch Moin a' Chriathar, the loch that keeps wicket below the An Ruadh-stac slabs. The burn sidled along the sandstone strata to drop into the gorge below. We cut across to the bridge and reached the car at dusk, yawning our heads off from a day of windy walking.

Section 14: 11. FUAR THOLL 907 m OS 25 975489
The cold hole

There is some lack of clarity as to which corrie of this grand hill is responsible for the name but my money would go on that grim, cliff-held eastern hollow which is *the* feature of the peak seen from Glen Carron. Names were usually given from below, of the most obvious characteristics, and that shadowy corrie certainly can be gruey even in summer and an icy cauldron in winter. Fuar Tholl, to me, is a winter mountain. I am past the age of being tempted by its considerable cliffs and being there at the back end of the year anyway, means my many visits have all been snowy ones. I've climbed the hill on Christmas Day, on Boxing Day and on the first of January, besides less-noted days.

Almost invariably we've been staying at Gerry's hostel at Craig (see

p. 7) for we like our comforts and freedom and good company, and Gerry's is the right accommodation in the right place for a good number of fine hills and as a link in some f the best trekking available in Britain. Fuar Tholl is the nearest notable peak on the western side of Glen Carron, very visible as it scowls down on Craig.

My attachment to the glen pre-dates the hostel: for several Christmas holidays we camped there, always in conditions of massive snowfall. On one occasion we bivouacked in the shelter at the old Glencarron Halt (built to serve the Lodge above) and, to ensure the morning train stopped, we climbed up to bring down the signal lantern which we filled with paraffin from our stoves and then set at red. This worked, but the following year lantern, signal and station had gone, and even Achnashellach Station was reduced to a pathetic hut lit by time switch, which assumed the train would always be on time. As it seldom is, arriving at Achnashellach can be fun. One friend I was meeting assumed the platform was as long as the train and stepped down with his heavy rucksack. Long after the train had proceeded we found him down the bank, on his back, caught in the rhododendron bushes, thrashing about like a stricken stag.

Achnashellach Station is the starting point for Fuar Tholl and the other hills surrounding Coire Lair. Fuar Tholl should have been done when traversing the Munros, Beinn Liath Mhor and Sgorr Ruadh. However, in winter Fuar Tholl is sometimes quite enough by itself. The path starts on the north side of the railway line near a cottage enclosed in high fencing. The fence has kept the devouring deer out and allowed the creation of a beautiful Highland garden — well worth a look. The estate road heads off on a long traverse to the Coulin (Cow-lin) Pass while the footpath wends up through fine woodlands and massive old pines beside the River Lair. This river flows in a deep ravine and is virtually impassable, while any approach to Fuar Tholl across it, or up its west bank, will be hampered by deep heather and rock. The path is an aid not to be scorned. Follow it up to Coire Lair.

On gaining the corrie the path splits into three and the left branch is taken to ford the river. You won't manage across in really wet weather. The path goes up and over the col, "the big pass", that separates Fuar Tholl from Sgorr Ruadh, the highest peak of the area, rising under several buttresses which give some of the longest, hardest and best sandstone climbs in the country. In 1870 the Prince of Wales (later Edward VII), a crack shot and fanatic sportsman, took part in a deer drive up here and nearly lost his life in a big rockfall.

You can pick a way up between the cliffs or follow the ridge up from the highest point of the path, keeping on the Coulags Glen side. The Coulags Glen flank is recommended by one guide as an easy way up but my wording of that line would be "purgatorial", which is being polite. The col itself holds an array of bumps and hollows and lochans which on one occasion gave me a very frustrating time.

Being a rather unpleasant winter day, and being alone, I followed this *voie normale*, perfectly straightforward even in the cloud and falling snow. Back at the col, and set on adding Sgorr Ruadh, I found my compass was missing, thanks to a hole in my pocket. (It turned up in Gerry's garden.) Now, on the map, Sgorr Ruadh looks a big enough target and is definite enough in shape that, once on its slopes, going uphill would inevitably lead to the summit while my track in the snow could be followed down again. I set off. After a while, following along one of the elongated bumps, I came on other footprints, which of course were not other footprints but my own footprints, all too recognisable by a distinctive tread. I'd gone in a circle, not the imagined straight line.

A long wait did not produce any clearance so I tried again. I ended making a second circle! In the mist, snow hollows and snow-covered lochans could not be told apart. I went through into water once. I tried every dodge. In the end a clearance allowed me to see down into Coire Lair and I quickly marked the snow in the assumed direction of Sgorr Ruadh. By carefully looking back, I made a slow but straighter line, which almost landed me in a bigger loch. It could only be the one immediately under the desired peak. Ironically, I'd traversed the Ben in mist the week previously and never used a compass though I found I'd accumulated *three* in my pockets and rucksack.

Perhaps my best-ever climb of Fuar Tholl was the Boxing Day one. Over the years I'd steadily been trying routes up and down all round the peak and had already come to regard the east ridge as favourite. This is the right boundary of the Cold Hole as you look up from the glen. There is one spot, high up, where the ridge becomes narrow, steep and exposed. On this day the route was very snowy and corniced, but compressed drift snow gave us a good climb and, at the neck, I was able to throw the rope down for each of the party to follow. That spot was like something in the Alps, for the cliffs of the corrie were draped in snow and ice and rimmed with cornices, a world of startling white that contrasted with the black depths of the forested glen. Two ropes' lengths were used as a hand-rail to gain easier ground and we edged round to the cairn. (One of the illustrations shows this route.)

There a vicious storm hit us, so we stomped and slid down the gully under the 500-foot Mainreachan Buttress and followed a burn down to Loch Coire Lair. We tracked wildcat prints across its frozen surface and had a memorable tussle through the pass to the Ling Hut in Glen Torridon: a ten hour expedition. We returned to Gerry's the next day over the classic Coulin Pass, using the old footpath that can still be traced down from the elbow on the road (at 024496) to reach the A890 just west of Craig.

There's a special warm spot in my affections for the Cold Hole, tenth highest in the Corbett hierarchy.

Section 14:   12. SGURR NAN LOCHAN UAINE   873 m
              OS 25   969531
              The peak of the green loch

Section 14:   13. SGURR DUBH   782 m   OS 25   979558
              The black peak

This is a pair of surprisingly neglected peaks; or maybe not so surprising as they look across Glen Torridon to Beinn Eighe and Liathach and for most visitors the giants will claim precedence. I know I'd been up the Big Three many times before I realised there were other good hills nearby, sometimes climbing them for the views of the big ones, sometimes to escape bad weather on high and sometimes, dare I confess, to avoid "yet another slog" up Liathach's 3,456 feet.

For a quarter of a century I've usually had a week in Strathcarron or Torridon during the Christmas break and this has equally given fabulous days and dreadful days out on the hill. On Christmas Days we always tried to climb something worthy. Christmas Day 1979 gave us two crackers: Sgurr nan Lochan Uaine and Sgurr Dubh.

We drove round to Glen Torridon in Dave's car and set off up the track past the Ling Hut, which sits below an extraordinary area of hundreds of small moraine bumps — a good start to a day of considerable geological interest. In Torridon you feel very close to the raw beginnings of life. The bare hills are scoured by glacial Brillopads. Some of the hills have even been stood on their heads — literally. Such forces are mercifully subdued now, but the evidence remains stark and clear. Torridon is not a tame part of the country.

The path goes on to join the one through to Coire Lair and Achnashellach, though the map shows it stopping. There was a south gale blowing so we followed the path into the wind to gain the maximum useful altitude with the least effort, then cut up to scramble on the sandstone chaos to the summit of Sgurr nan Lochan Uaine. We had a picnic before the top where we were partly sheltered and could look down on the lochans that give the peak its name. They were frozen over but patterned with cracks. A raven croaked through the pass. Dave and I recalled our camp there on a Christmas Day/Night seven years before. We'd carried up to camp below the lochans and climbed Beinn Liath Mhor; quite a worthy day. The wind blew big guns on that occasion as well, and the camp, on snow at dusk, was clear of snow by dawn. Our tent doors looked out to the high battlements of Liathach. While Dave and Stephen circuited Beinn Liath Mhor on the east to descend Coire Lair to Gerry's, I nipped up Sgurr nan Lochan Uaine being, by then, keen on Corbetts, and descended to collect my car in Glen Torridon. Today was Dave's turn for the Corbetts. Stephen, sadly, had been killed in a motoring accident not long after that Christmas visit.

When we set off to descend the NE Ridge I was at once in trouble. I'd worn Bogtrotters, seeing it was a "soft" day, but that exposed side of the peak was iced-up and I ended chipping steps to link every rock that managed to break through the glassy surface: nervy work that had the adrenalin going. On An Teallach once we had something similar and I cheerfully warned a friend, as we crept up from pebble to pebble, "Don't slip or you're dead." That was his first winter Munro — and his last.

The ice slope eased off eventually and on the col I put my boots on for Sgurr Dubh, which then presented nothing but soft snow. (In winter I keep my boots for use above the freezing level so that they never become wet, and last indefinitely, while, below that level, I use Bogtrotters or wellies so that my feet never become wet.) Fionn Bheinn was an impressive cone and the "Conon Corbetts" looked good. Slioch and the Fannichs and the near giants of Torridon were all arrayed in plain monochrome, from blackest rocks to brightest snow. Sgurr Dubh, like its namesake between Loch Garry and Glen Moriston, is a "Dubh with a view". (On the last day of 1987, we wandered on to the lower summit overlooking Glen Torridon to find the ground ruptured, and boulders tossed aside, by a recent lightning strike.)

Dave and I descended by the array of lochans shown on the map. They had decided the line of my first ascent, with Stephen, those seven years before, and on subsequent occasions. They were as interesting as expected and the burn flowing from them breaks down by a fine ravine up which we had climbed by rock or ice till its fierceness always forced us out. That is the way up I'd recommend, for the ground features will keep the interest going and on the final cone you can play the old game of not lifting eyes until the summit is reached. There is a similar landscape of knolls and lochans on the col between Fuar Tholl and Sgorr Ruadh. The Dubh of Sgurr Dubh is probably from the summit cone being grey quartz rather than the warm-coloured Torridonian sandstone.

We made some fun out of the descent, at one stage penguin-sliding on our bellies down a snow gully while a parcel of stags stood landseering at us. Sgurr Dubh is high enough for ptarmigan to mock one on top, while the heathery lower slopes have go-backing grouse. Nature is very conservative. We cut some holly berries to take back to the hostel.

Fourteen of us sat down for Christmas dinner that night in Gerry's, a royal feast. I'd saved some exotic wine for the occasion (and a box of Turkish Delight bought in Bodrum). I doubt if Torridon hills have been toasted very often in Turkish wine, but we'd had a worthy day so earned the treat. *Sliante!* — to the Green and the Black.

Section 14:   14. An Sidhean   814 m   OS 25   171454
                          Fairy hill (shee)

Section 14:   15. Bac an Eich   849 m   OS 25   222489
                          Bank/ridge of the horse

Strathconon gives the easiest access to these hills, though An Sidhean is also within reasonable range of the Monar dam at the head of Glen Strathfarrar. Strathconon can be motored up as far as the west end of Loch Beannacharain where there is a small car-parking area. This route, also applicable to 14:16, 17, is on Sheet 26.

The A832 Muir of Ord–Achnasheen road is left at Marybank for the 11 miles up to Scardroy. If one has crossed the bridge avoiding Inverness and on across the Black Isle, turn off at Moy Bridge, a mile across from Marybank. The road from beyond Contin via Loch Achilty is private after some miles so is not a motoring route into Strathconon.

One or both these Corbetts can be done from Scardroy with little difficulty, the area being liberally supplied with pony tracks. Gleann Fhiodhaig with its dominant Creag na h-Iolair is followed for about five miles, then the path up the Allt an Amise. The River Meig can be impassable in wet conditions, so plan accordingly. From near the watershed a stalkers' path wends high up on to An Sidhean. On the other side, note the unusual feature, below Loch a' Chlaidheim (*loch of the sword*), of a burn which splits and later rejoins.

An Sidhean is too hemmed-in to be a great viewpoint but at least it is not an over-populated summit. I'd several times walked through the glens round the Corbett before actually going to the summit — an expedition made from the less convenient starting point of the Loch Monar dam. Glen Strathfarrar has a locked gate at its foot, and a key has to be obtained (from the gatehouse) to drive up for the day, which can rather inhibit lengthy walks or multi-day visits unless one makes appropriate logistical plans or has a helpful driver. Information is on the gate, so check at the time as arrangements change periodically (tel: 046–376260).

Fortunately I was staying up the glen and was able to squeeze An Sidhean into a winter day from the Loch Monar side. The only problems, driving up, were the stags lying on the tarmac. The path along the north shore of Loch Monar is a fine one but we caught the westerly wind and had a foul day on top. I abandoned the poorer path up the hill to ascend the south ridge (Mullach a' Gharbh-leathaid) but came down by the burn so as not to need to use the compass — hands were warmer in pockets.

A high-level route over Sgurr Coire nan Eun can lead one to Bac an Eich or down by Coire Mhoraigein, which is also the best wet-weather approach to An Sidhean. Alternatively, descend An Sidhean east of south to the watershed to pick up the poor path on the infant River Orrin and out to Inverchoran. This is a more interesting approach if just doing An Sidhean. Gleann Chorainn or Coire Mhoraigein are equally easy ways to gain height for climbing Bac an Eich. I wandered on to Meall Buidhe for the view down to the loch and then descended the west ridge to Corriefeol — quite a pleasant way off, if steep.

Gleann Fhiodhaig is an old track through to Glen Carron, and another old way linked Scardroy westwards to Achnasheen, both useful routes if using trains and then backpacking into the area. A Post bus operates up Glen Conon from Muir of Ord.

Section 14:   16. MEALLAN NAN UAN   840 m   OS 25   264545
              Little hill of the lambs

Section 14:   17. SGURR A' MHUILINN   879 m   OS 25   265558
              Peak of the mill (voo-lin)

These are extraordinarily shy hills which manage to stay hidden from most directions. Even from the A832 Dingwall to Achnasheen road along Strath Bran what we see are strictly speaking their outliers. Nor are the approaches from Strath Bran worth contemplating unless one has a fetish for flogging over miles of peaty moorland. Admire from Strath Bran and approach up Strath Conon — as for 14:14, 15.

Strathanmore is the obvious starting point but I have preferred to go on slightly to the church shown (292538) which is one of the thirty or so built by Thomas Telford, a side of his work not as well known as the

Caledonian Canal, for instance. His churches are instantly recognisable: all have four door or window settings along the side of their simple design and a small belfry atop one gable. (There is a Telford church by Loch Luichart on the A832 at 334634.) Visit the Telford church, anyway, wherever you start.

Simply angle up the slopes behind Strathanmore or the church to gain the NE Ridge up to Creag Ruadh. These have some bracken in the summer, and heather higher up, which can give the group a rather dark appearance. Meallan nan Uan sticks out as a sharp cone, and a grand highway leads along to its double top with unusual views of many ranges. I've only once made the circuit and was nearly blasted off this traverse by batterings of hail and sleet. The Torridons to the west had begun the day as black spikes. By the time I'd wended down and up Sgurr a' Mhuilinn they glittered like white teeth. I've seldom been so cold on a hill. Some wheatears looked as if they wished they'd stayed in Africa.

On another occasion I cycled up Gleann Meinich, an easy-angled forestry track, on a spanking January day (for which there had been a dismal forecast). Creag Ghlas is a very rocky top and the whole north side of the glen is steep and rough. I went up by the burn just beyond the ruin (254537). There was a cheery fall and an awkward fence. It was a joy to leave the heather for firm snow. There seemed to be snow buntings about all day — a day among millions — and on Sgurr a' Ghlas Leathaid of the two peaks I sat and wrote out a catalogue of the view. As it is a page long I won't repeat it. "As fine a view as possible", I summed up. (The second peak, not named on the map, is Sgurr a' Choire Rainich.)

Sgurr a' Mhuilinn was very snow-plastered on the day of my late-April circuit. I came down the SE Ridge then bore over, eastwards, to avoid the great bog-hollow below, not that the bare moor was much easier with the paring wind out of the east. I crossed the Allt an t-Strathain Mhoir high up to make my way back down to Stratheonon church.

Given time it is well worth adding Sgurr a' Ghlas Leathaid to the round. (The Gleann Meinich approach is best.) This is the peak that dominates the view from Strath Bran and is, itself, the finest viewpoint of this juggle of peaks. Watching sunset over Torridon from up there is a breathtaking experience, and to north and south there is a great huddle of hills which can be difficult to recognise from this angle. Loch Coire a' Mhuilinn is a lonely spot (frozen, and cracked all over like a jigsaw, on the January trip). What a place for a camp! The *mill* is probably a reference to the racing river rather than to any building, just as the similar brawling burn from the CIC Hut on

Nevis is the Allt a' Mhuillin. This round gives enough rough walking throughout to ensure you will grind slowly.

Section 14:   18. BEINN A' BHA'ACH ARD   862 m   OS 26   361435
  Hill of the high byre(?) (Vaichart)

This hill, at the eastern end of Glen Strathfarrar, is not a very striking summit but its isolated height ensures good views to the Lapaichs, Sgurr a' Mhuilinn, Ben Wyvis and even the far Cairngorms. Motoring up the glen is restricted so a cycle might be worth taking for the odd mile of road along to the power station, as it is for the Munros further up the glen. (Munro himself took a day off stalking to cycle up for these hills.) For the initial approach the 1:50,000 First Edition map leaves much to be desired.

Last winter, returning from the north, I turned aside to let the dog have a shot at the Corbett, but we had only just reached the locked gate at Leishmore when the snow began to fall. I'd half thought of trying the road to Dunmaglass on the south of the Farrar River, but the bridge shown at the Culligram Falls does not exist. You could not cross the gorge. On the north bank are various Hydro works and the estate road (not path) up the Neaty Burn starts beside an underground power station. By the time I'd had a look at these changes the snow was pillowing down and there was no hope of going high. The dog arrived back at the car with a saddle of new snow on his back. Cars were slewed all over the road on the Aigas Brae and we had a hairy crossing of the Slochd before giving up the battle against the snow at Aviemore.

On the only other visit I'd been up seeing the keeper at Loch Monar and had also hidden a parcel for the Munro trip which started a few weeks later. Because of this latter, my One Inch maps were not available (all being packed for picking up along the way) and my Half-Inch Bartholomews were with my brother who was to keep tabs on my progress. All I could muster was a Six Inch to One Mile map. I therefore set off too soon and had a bit of wood-and-crag thrashing on a direct assault up the Corbett, whereas there was a helpful path up the Neaty Burn which gives easy access to the Corbett's west ridge. I used the snowier east corrie for starting off down (a good slide) and came out to Culligran. The lower slopes have pine and birch forests which make for attractive scenery compared to what lies at the head of Glen Strathfarrar. With views out to the Black Isle this Corbett has a strange feeling of being perched between "the desert and the sown".

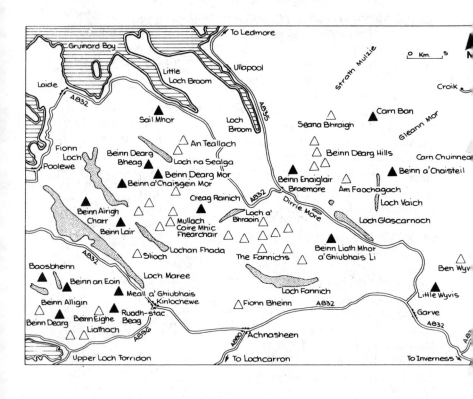

WESTER & EASTER ROSS

Section 15:   1. BAOSBHEINN   875 m   OS 19/24   871654
   The wizard's hill (bus-ven)

Section 15:   2. BEINN AN EOIN   855 m   OS 19   905646
   The hill of the bird (bin-in-eeon)

Section 15:   3. RUADH-STAC BEAG   896 m   OS 19   973614
   The small red spike

Section 15:   4. MEALL A' GHIUBHAIS   *c.*880 m   OS 19   976634
   Fir tree hill (meyoul a huish)

FOR THIS CLUSTER of Corbetts I'd advise using the 1:25,000 Map "The Cuillin and Torridon Hills" as they are set in an unusually rugged bit of country for which increased detail will be needed when trying to walk through the wilder parts.

Baosbheinn occupies a unique place in my affections, being my last Corbett back in 1976. You can never have another last Corbett, though there has been a sort of altitude musical chairs over the years since. If Munroists thought they had grievances with the 1981 map revisions theirs was a mild inconvenience compared to the poor Corbetteers who had to ride forth for up to nineteen more scalps, scattered at a maximum range and sited in the most inconvenient places. I still regard Baosbheinn as my last.

Flowerdale and Torridon (as in the SMC district guide) form an entity, and a glorious multi-day trek can take in these Corbetts in several possible combinations. You could start at Kinlochewe and take the path west from near the Anancaun NCC Centre over the col between Ruadh-stac and Meall a' Ghiubhais, from where those Corbetts can be tackled, before going on to camp further west. Similarly, on the second day, Beinn an Eoin may be added and, on the third day, Baosbheinn, exiting thereafter on the same or the following day. The pass between Beinn Alligin and Beinn Dearg is the easiest way out. The path shown coming through the Bealach a' Chomhla continues right on under Alligin's east face to end in Toll nam Biast. A bridge links to the Coire Mhic Nobuil track. Check, beforehand, the time of the Post bus for the return up Glen Torridon to Kinlochewe. Beinn Dearg, of course, could also be included in this quality Corbett-bagging. An alternative entry could be made up Glen Grudie and alternative exits could lead out, north west to the Gair Loch or, west, to the lonely walkers' hostel at Craig; neither being an easy option.

While I've criss-crossed this area in all sorts of combinations I've not actually made the long Corbett-traverse I've advocated; for my Corbetts, like my Munros, and like most people's peaks, were never done with any tidy planning or execution. Ruadh-stac Beag was reached with three friends on a full traverse of all Beinn Eighe's ridges; Beinn Dearg on the fourth day of January was quite sufficient unto that day on its own; Beinn an Eoin was grabbed during a course, after a thrashing while camped by Loch na Cabhaig; Meall a' Ghiubhais was chosen to fill a half-day in early January, and Baosbheinn was an autumn sortie that saw camps in Coire Mhic Fhearchair and by Loch Toll nam Biast with several Munros and Corbetts culled in between.

Those were just the first visits. This is an area of such tough character that one to keep returning. It is so tough and remote that few people other than dedicated Corbetteers stray far from the paths shown — and these should be fully utilised, for vast areas are a mix of scoured sandstone and endless bog and water holes or, as nowhere else in the country, a spreading of chaotic boulders. One mile an hour is good going, out in its centre, an area I once described as a "Piccadilly of peaks and passes". Rather than retell too many tales, I'll give a brief practical summary of the Corbetts in turn, then finish with the story of our wanderings that led to Baosbheinn as the last Corbett.

Ruadh-stac Beag is not usually included in the traverse of Beinn Eighe, but as the Corbett is hardly more "out on a limb" than the Munro of Ruadh-Stac Mor it would be logical to add it to such a day. The traverse is a major undertaking and therefore a recommendation for the fit and experienced. In winter all these hills, Munros and Corbetts, are demanding climbs rather than walks and should only be attempted by those qualified to tackle winter challenges. A rescue on Baosbheinn hardly bears thinking about!

Lochain Uaine, *the green loch*, on the col between the Corbett and the rest of Beinn Eighe is at about 710 m. If Beinn Eighe has not caused problems the descent to the lochan will "go" quite easily. Coming up from Anancaun leave the track on the col to head south and then south west to reach the Corbett without losing precious height. There is pleasant walking up to the lochan; then the ridge should be tackled from there, turning crags on the right. The Corbett's north side is not advisable and the worst of the screes should be avoided. There is no problem dropping down into Coire Ruadh-staca and by traversing under Ruadh-stac Mor the Maol Cheannan shambles can be circumvented. Meall a' Ghiubhais presents no real problems from the top of the Anancaun track. Note the

Corbett is the south-westerly of the two summit bumps (not given a height on the 1:50,000; 886 m on the 1:25,000) but the *lower* 878 m bump is indicated. There is a fine aerial view over Loch Maree to Slioch from the lower top.

The 1:50,000 cannot hope to indicate the complexities of the central "Concordia" that lies surrounded by these Corbetts and Munros, while what the 1:25,000 shows is probably discouraging. On my first venture we had just reached Loch na Cabhaig (over the western watershed) when a storm hit us. We had a wild pitching of tents, and cringed inside for the rest of the day as an endless succession of blasts battered the site. At dusk a watery sunshine lit Loch a' Bhealaich, our view down along, out along, west, while Carn an Feola and Sail Mhor were like the bows of big liners churning through bow-waves of cloud. Torrents were pouring off Beinn Dearg. After survival camping that night the weather cleared up in the morning. Our shocked systems needed some time to return to Corbett tuning.

"Lumpy" was someone's description of the landscape over to Loch na h-Oidhche (*loch of night*, often meaning good night fishing), and from Pocca Buidhe we wandered up to arrive right at the trig point on top of Beinn an Eoin (*the hill of the bird*, usually meaning eagle, of which this area has several). The track along the loch is now an estate road rather than a pony path. Given the choice of walking along the crest or exploring down the rockier southern prow of the hill we chose the latter — and had the fun we wanted, finally traversing off on some exposed sandstone slabs. Two people were fishing in "our" loch and fourteen orange dots could be seen descending from Beinn Dearg — probably innocent trainees off the *Captain Scott* which we'd seen anchored in Loch Torridon. We packed tents and Naismith and began wandering east. Some hours later we pitched our tents on the promontory in Loch nan Cabar (*antler loch*), an apron stage, with Liathach a surrealist backcloth.

Both Beinn an Eoin and Baosbheinn can be climbed, fairly unadventurously, from Loch na h-Oidhche, which can be reached by the estate road that breaks off the A832 Loch Maree–Gairloch road near Loch Bad an Sgalaig (857720) but this approach removes the special quality of the southern approaches. The Talladale–Strath Lungard glen is tracked on the west bank to the end of the trees but gives easier walking than might be expected.

The best tramp of all was the one that led to Baosbheinn. We started by going up to camp in Coire Mhic Fhearchair which is one of those special things one should do at least once in a lifetime. The landscape was lapped in the ochres, purples and silvers of early autumn. What an idyllic site! We could hardly tear ourselves away to make a traverse of the corrie top from Sail Mhor to Ruadh-stac Mor, then we could hardly bear to leave that seat in the gods to return to the tents: Ian and Mary in one, dog and myself in the other. A local stag serenaded us to sleep.

All next day the rutting of the stags echoed on the crags ("very Walter Scottish") and frequently the beasts would be charging about, so involved with themselves that they paid little heed to us. The end peaks of Beinn Dearg took on bold shapes, in turn, as we slowly wended west over the watershed, passing Loch na Cabhaig, as every journey seems to do, and eventually ascending by a brawling burn and through a slotted rock gateway into Toll nam Biast (*the hollow of the beast*). A snooker table of grass among the sandstone pavements made a comfy site — as long as the river did not rise more than two feet. The rest of the day was spent on a traverse of Beinn Alligin and the Horns and we returned to camp as the rain came on for the day/week/month/ for ever. . . . Our earlier jokes about the river rising sounded a bit misplaced as we listened to the increasing roar. My log of the day ended, "The world reduced to a mad wetness. Sealed into the tent like a hornbill in its hole. A small tunnel of security a mere skin of nylon in thickness. What about Baosbheinn now?"

The barometer rather than the cloudy view gave us the faith to move for mountains the next day. We skirted the corrie below Loch na Cabhaig (an area of black gabbro rocks) to reach the ridge leading to Baosbheinn, flanked Ceanna Beag, the 707-m top, and finally used deer tracks along to go directly up on to the highest top, Sgorr Dubh. As we arrived the clouds symbolically rolled back and we had a succession of brilliant brocken spectres — a magical way to finish the Corbett.

Section 15: 5. BEINN AIRIGH CHARR 791 m OS 19 930762
           The hill of the rough shieling (bin arry har)

Section 15: 6. BEINN LAIR 860 m OS 19 982732
           Hill of the mare

Beinn Lair is a long flat but broken ridge presenting on its south or Loch Maree side no outstanding features. To the north, however, for a distance of some 2½ miles it throws down what is possibly the grandest inland line of cliffs to be found in Scotland.

(H. T. Munro)

Ben Lair: graceful, solid, and broad.

(John Maccullough)

We spent a little time on the summit of Beinn Airigh Charr and agreed that hills do not rank by height alone.

(G. T. Clover)

Mountaineers were long in discovering the spectacular nature of these Corbetts, for their grandest faces point northwards to one of Scotland's wildest empty quarters. Loch Maree did not have efficient roads till recent times. The post went on foot along the north shore, which sounds impossible, and boats were the main means of travel till well into the nineteenth century. Maccullough, writing in 1824, enthuses both about Loch Maree and the surrounding hills, at a time when hills were still generally regarded with horror. He is worth quoting in part for he was far ahead of his time. A cart and twelve men helped haul his ship's boat from the sea into Loch Maree, along which they rowed on a fair summer day.

Loch Maree's mountains present a greater diversity of form and character than any of the Scottish lakes. Ben Lair is the principal feature. The middle ground is splendid and wild: rock and wood, silvery clouds and the sun shedding a flood of light over the lake. Even the dark firs and the cold grey cliffs of Ben Lair seemed to rejoice in the bright sunshine, while the warm brown and purple of the heath tinged the nearer hills with that richness of colour known only to these mountainous regions. Every summit assumed a bluer tone till the last peaks emulated the misty azure of the sky into which they melted. It was a scene, as the Emperor Charles said of Florence, too beautiful to be looked at except on holidays. But such days are indeed the holidays of the Highlands, rare and precious and compensating for many previous ones of mist and rain, of weariness and disappointment.

It is not only that nature gives us a keener enjoyment of those gleams of happiness which break through the dreary atmosphere of life but, as if in compensation for the savage aspect of the mountains derived from bad weather, its hours of sunshine are hours which can be found nowhere else. No one can know the full value of summer who has not known it in a land of mountains, no one can feel, who has not felt it among the hills, the joy which can fill the mind, the sense of beauty, the bounding, exuberant happiness . . .

An even earlier traveller, James Hogg, the Ettrick Shepherd, came this way in 1803. Two locals "who, perceiving that my attention was much taken by the scenery, promised to lead me through some which I should not see equalled, and I believe they were as good as their word. Some parts are grand beyond measure, parts were named after Fingalian heroes, the chief being the Fion Loch."

Ling and Glover in 1909 made the first serious climbing sortie to these northern cliffs and half their account is taken up telling of their travel to reach the hills. As Ling said, "It is a far cry to Poolewe." The Munro quote at the head of this section, made in 1905, was the spur that sent them this way. They hired a charabanc at Achnasheen, somewhat taken aback at the fifteen-seater just for the two of them. Their "modest weight" was insufficient to keep the vehicle from bouncing into the loch so they "were obliged to carry some ballast in the shape of bags of corn". They walked along the north shore and up and across to the Bealach Rheinnidh (a route I too followed, in reverse) to come on "the appalling overhangs" of Beinn Lair's north face. They climbed a gully to reach the summit, had a snack where they could look down on Isle Maree and then returned to Poolewe. That would still be a long day's walk today.

The next day a keeper led them round to the north side of Beinn Airigh Charr. The great tower, north of the summit, is locally known as Martha's Peak. Martha was a legendary heroine who took her goats to pasture on the mountain and was reputed to have made the first and only traverse of the tower. Unfortunately she dropped her distaff and, in endeavouring to recover it, fell and was killed. Ling and Glover's day on Martha's Peak was sufficiently interesting for them to return the following year with some other climbers. Several new routes were climbed. This sort of chance discovery and enthusiastic follow up has marked climbing on these two mountains ever since. Often on a first visit people had not been equipped for climbing such unexpectedly huge cliffs so felt compelled to return. Students, with longer holidays, have often been the winners in this game. If today's colourful ballerinas could manage the walk they'd find rock beyond their dreams. Thankfully this is not country for psychedelic egos so much as for those with a touch of the Maccullough enthusiasm.

Having read about the area, and made some long tramps through it, when I came seeking the Corbetts I did so across Loch Maree — as did Ling, Glover *et al* in 1910 — as did Maccullough before them in 1824. I was to enjoy Maccullough's weather, too, the start of a long summer heatwave such as I have never met before or since while actively seeking Corbetts. I'd been canoeing further down the west coast and when I drove north I felt I was blundering into the Sahara. I did not launch on Loch Maree until 7.30 in the evening and the day was still monstrous hot. I paddled out on an oily swell to the choke of islands and had some interesting navigation through their jungly, chunky sandstone chaos as my maps disagreed with each other and with the reality. A startled deer on one island careered off along the shore and right round to come back almost on top of me again. The number of islands on Loch Maree varies according to the level of the water but Eilean Subhainn is the biggest, and has a loch in it, obviously higher than Loch Maree, yet 64 feet deep, 30 feet deeper than Loch Maree. On the original bathymetrical survey, no boat could be carried to the loch; soundings were taken by a member of the team swimming about in the water. I rounded Eilean Subhainn and, accompanied by a noisy diver, moved on towards Isle Maree, where I landed.

The old walled graveyard on Isle Maree had all but vanished and the carvings on the few old stones were weathered beyond reading. St Maelrubha's well, scene of ancient bull sacrifices and many hoped-for cures for insanity, had also disappeared but I found the penny tree, a real oddity. The original tree has died (copper poisoning?) and bits and pieces, embedded with a scaling of coins, lay about among the deep litter of pennies going back over generations. Queen Victoria visited this older tree but now a new oak has taken over and already its trunk has the scaly appearance of an armadillo hide. Pure superstition sees modern man enact this custom of hammering a penny into the tree, for the allied hope of a cure from the well has long gone. The well supposedly went dry after someone dipped a mad dog into it. (The book *Sacred Waters*, by Janet and Colin Bord, is a good introduction to the topic of wells in Britain.)

The midges rather curtailed my explorations and I paddled across to the north shore. Maccullough again: "The northern margin presents rocky, wooded bays and creeks rising into noble overhanging cliffs and mountains. The effect of Sleugach [Slioch, *a spear*] is perhaps more striking than of any mountain in Scotland. Where the skirts of Ben Lair descend into water the remains of a forest are almost incredible, producing a landscape that might be expected in the Alps rather than the tamer arrangements of Scottish mountains.

"The long shadows of evening gave a repose to the scene so that even the liquid sound which followed the dip of the oars seemed an intrusion on the hush of nature. The last crimson at length vanished from the summits and all became alike wrapped in one gentle hue of tranquil grey marking the summer twilight of a northern July."

Maccullough had fun navigating the islands, in the gloaming, back to the western end of the loch. Even at midnight he recorded the temperature was up over 70°F. I pulled my canoe on to a slope of bracken and camped on a knoll 200 feet up among the oak, birch, alder and holly: a world of grey verticalities and vegetative advance, the hornblende schists and the most northerly outposts of the old wood of Caledonia. "Camping" was lying stickily inside a sheet bag on top of my rucksack in the heather. There were a lot of wee beasties making scratchy noises and a roding woodcock went round and round on his clockwork flight.

"Ben Lair will well repay the toil to its summit. The height exceeds 3,000 feet [mercifully, it is only 2,817 feet] and though it produces few alpine plants there is perhaps the greatest variety of quartz in the world, ranging from jet black to snow white. The great attraction is the view, and chiefly to the north over the wildest mountains of Ross. It is usual to speak of rocks and precipices, whether present or not, but here they exist with no need of exaggeration. Here are mountains which show the very skeleton of the earth. Everything is gigantic and fearsome, wild and strange and new." (Maccullough)

Hogg was equally impressed. Of the Black Rock (the East Top of Beinn Lair is still Sgurr Dubh) he considered its spectacle far out of reach of comparison with anything else he'd ever seen: "It extends a whole English mile, along which nothing may pass, and is so appropriately termed black that it appears stained with ink, its face everywhere distorted by dark slits, gaping chasms and a most awful deformity."

At 6.30 a.m. I was teasing my way up the steep mix of crag and forest which is so typical of this shore of Loch Maree. Slioch had an edging of sunrise brightness and the day soon pulsed and shimmered in heat haze. The Torridons stood on their heads in the loch below, the reflection and the reality identical. I was not lucky enough to see a sea eagle as did Maccullough. (Next time maybe, for, since his day, they have become extinct, and reintroduced.) The gorge of the Allt na Cloich-bheith led to grassier slopes and my devil's halo of flies slowly faded. The flora was quite rich and varied with quiet banks of avens and campion and louder shouts of tormentil and thyme. A wild rose had glowed a ghostly exuberance against the dark trees when I'd landed the night before. The day was too hot to botanise properly. I didn't perspire so much as run with salt water. Long before the top my swimming shorts were as wet as if I'd been in the Loch.

Approaching Meall a' Choire Ghlais I set off some goats (the descendants of Martha's flock perhaps?), but all the deer just lay and let me past. The view all round had largely vanished into haze so when I finally stepped on to the summit of Beinn Airigh Charr the view *downwards* came as a shock. A knoll beyond made a fine perch. A score of goats were lying on the ridge out to Martha's Peak. A tiny tent, obtrusively orange, down by one of the lochans, gave scale to that lonely country, surely one without equal in Scotland for sheer wildness.

Eventually I went on, down to the Strathan Buidhe pass and up *the*

Middle Hill, Meall Mheinnidh (where a rabbit scampered off on the summit), and down again to the Bealach Mheinnidh where a short traverse led to welcome water and two pints of tea. I angled up — for ever, it felt — to a notch above the cliffs and then wended to a cairn on the edge of the summit dome. Gleann Tulacha, between the cliffs of Beinn Lair and those of A' Mhaighdean, can have no rivals for dramatic grandeur. Superlatives falter here. They are superfluous in such elemental simplicity.

The summit cairn was reached at 11 a.m. When a small breeze blew, the heat was like the opening of an oven door. I descended on a long, falling traverse line that bisected both the paths over the hills (Ling and Glover reached Beinn Lair doing the opposite) and having collected my buzz of flies, launched the canoe at once. I passed Isle Maree again and, the circumnavigation of Eilean Subhainn completed, landed below the main road at 3 p.m.

I've never sweated so while canoeing, and before driving off I waded out into Loch Maree with a bar of soap for a tepid bath, to the amusement of some tourists. The canoe was left that night at Garve and the next day I was off for the Lewisian gneiss of the far north: Hee, Arkle, Quinag — all in beating sunshine — described later on.

With hindsight, I'm amazed at my dedication but then, given our normal weather conditions, who would not push things a bit? After Beinn Airigh Charr and Beinn Lair I tended to call such heat "Maccullough conditions" — then I read further and found him complaining because his champagne was skimmed with ice by the freezing blast on top of Ben More in Mull. We were both just lucky on these singeing summits above Loch Maree.

A boat might be hired at the Loch Maree Hotel, popular with fishermen, otherwise the approaches to these Corbetts are long tramps from either end of the loch. The paths shown are all good pony tracks. With permission a car can be taken to Inveran or Kernsary but the road is a rough one. Carnmore has limited bothy accommodation, otherwise the country to the north offers no shelter. This utter remoteness, which has not changed at all since the days of Maccullough, or of Ling and Glover, combined with the sheer scale and drama of the landscape, makes it altogether a special place. Walk gently in this wilderness.

Section 15: 7. CREAG RAINICH 807 m OS 19/20 097751
         Bracken crag

Wanderings in the Fannichs and through between Loch Maree and Dundonnell had kept showing me new, good prospective expeditions, for this is tremendous country for trekking — and the hills are not so bad either!

Creag Rainich became a summit which was long-intended but somehow never ascended. Eventually I made a special trip to the Corbett at the tail end of the scorching days which began on Loch Maree and marked ascents of Arkle and Quinag in the north. I found a quiet spot off Destitution Road (A832) for the Dormobile and, by burning smoke coils, I could sleep with the door open. Big green-eyed flies were the main pest. The only car that pulled in, briefly, disturbed a pair of common gulls who were putting on a fascinating courtship display outside my mobile hide. I was away by 6.30 a.m. A rolling mass of clouds was being held back on the Dirrie More by a cordon of Fannichs. A streamer broke forth every now and then only to evaporate into nothingness.

I'd walked a mile up Destitution Road (built in the 19th century to provide work for the hard-hit local population) towards Fain, the now derelict inn/staging post of those days and crossed to a nettle-covered ruin to utilise a path up on to the moors. Though only about four miles from road to summit, I needed three hours to tease a way over the bogs and braes. On the broad saddle below the Corbett I left my heavy rucksack, a line of fence poles clearly marking the place. (Losing a rucksack is rather embarrassing.)

The NE Ridge gave an enjoyable ascent but I was beginning to long for water. Even the Allt na Faine, draining the big eastern corrie, had nearly dried out. There were 200 noisy deer on the slope across the burn: plenty of grunting, the odd bellow and the bubble and squeak of the calves. The clegs were making life miserable for the sheep — but at least they seemed to prefer the sheep rather than the stray human. The view round the ring of Fannichs, Deargs, An Teallach and Torridon was a mighty one (as expected) but conditions were hazy, a milky haze which I did not like the look of at all. I was not long on the summit.

The lochan in the first dip, as I retraced the route up, was bubbling with tadpoles and the water felt tepid. The air reeked of drying bogs, sheep and deer, for the big herd had crossed the corrie and the deer were streaming down and along, past where my rucker lay, to wallow in any small pools they could find. They were not keen to move when I, with rucker again, began to descend westwards off the saddle but I was not very keen to move either when at last I found some clear, flowing water. Down, nearer the Eas Ban, I peeled off my clingfilm clothing for a delicious dook and a brew.

The gash of a side burn forced a detour to the west bank of the river which tumbled lethargically from pool to pool then fell, as the Eas Ban (White Falls), into another big gash. I couldn't really see the fall from above but the view over the strath to the many spires of An Teallach was rewarding. The woods were strangely silent. The fall must be one of the country's most impressive. Only the top half shows from the valley below and, even with the severe drought, was spraying up daintily. I crossed below the fall but was forced on to the bed rocks by another side gorge. Out into the valley, golden with sweet gale, the clegs decided I was worthy prey after all. Perhaps I hadn't cooked enough till then.

I followed the strath past Achneigie to Shenavall where I had a couple of nights and climbed the Deargs (15:9, 10) before heading out. My armful of firewood had to be abandoned as I needed my hands to slaughter the pernicious clegs. I cleared seven sacks of rubbish (mostly empty whisky bottles) out of the bothy and was brewing when a lady, with a posse of terriers, arrived from a boat on the loch. We chatted and it turned out that she and her brothers owned Camusunary in Skye. They were wondering what to do with the old Celtic Lodge by the shore there, so I suggested the MBA might be interested. Who knows, that cup of tea for the visitor could have been a crucial influence?

The barometer had been falling all day and the stifling heat finally exploded into a (for once) welcome deluge. I felt like going out to dance in it — then I remembered I'd left the skylights of the Dormobile wide open! I went out from Shenavall over the moors to the A832 at the head of the Dundonnell River's steep setting. In dry conditions reaching Shenavall this way is less toilsome than the tramp up the stony road from Corrie Hallie.

This was quite an interesting round-route for Creag Rainich (if having to return to a parked vehicle) but, if a kindly driver could help, it is easier to walk along the path north of Loch a' Bhraoin, *the loch of the showers*, and start the traverse from there. The hill is also perfectly possible in a day from Corrie Hallie. By whatever route the Eas Ban should not be missed: not every good Corbett is twinned with a splendid waterfall.

Section 15:　8. Beinn a' Chaisgein Mor　857 m　OS 19　983785
　　　　　　　　The big forbidding hill

Being neighbour to A' Mhaighdean, this hill is a contender for the title, "remotest Corbett". We had dealt with the remoteness problem by basing ourselves at Shenavall for several days. At that time Corbetts were not specifically being chased, just "good things", so this hill was done for its own sake, as was Beinn a' Chlaidheim which later escaped to Munro status, and we went out via Loch a' Bhraoin, unaware of Corbett Creag Rainich above. Since then Shenavall has become so busy that I tend to camp in order to keep the element of solitude which this magnificent area demands.

Beinn a' Chaisgein Mor is a two-faced hill: to north and east a big dome, utterly unpretentious, but from south and west every bit the big, forbidding hill. Above Carnmore rise blocks of cliff with some of the longest and best rock-climbing routes in the north. Carnmore has a barn howff which could be a useful overnight stop if Beinn Lair and Beinn Airigh Charr are also planned. They are a little too distant from a base at Shenavall.

There was quite a gang of us: Dave and Stuart (local friends), and newcomers David, Louise and Glyn. A first look through the skylight showed misty tops but nothing to delay setting out. "Just another ordinary sort of day", someone suggested. Soft-boiled eggs were an interesting breakfast game. We walked down to the river in bare feet, paddled across and edged the bogs to Larachantivore. There was a bridge then, one which tended to come and go (now definitely gone), which enabled us to keep moving, essential with a clout of clegs giving us their undivided attention. We scurried up Gleann na Muice and Gleann na Muice Beag until the path, curling over the head of the glen, brought our pace down. At the scattering of lochs on the watershed we had a coffee break and were caught up by a keeper with five terriers, a bag of fish and a pony. He was returning to Letterewe but was happy to pause for a chat and a drink.

A long grassy brae took us up to the top of the Corbett. We found the remains of a meteorological balloon and also the remains of a stag. Dave wanted to collect the antlers but they were attached to the skull, not being cast, and were full of putrified goo with the most revolting smell. Dave had to walk downwind from us for the rest of the day. We found one of our daintiest mountain flowers, dwarf cornel, whose white "petals" are bracts and the dark centre is the real flower.

We sat for a long time on top, with the Fionn Loch below, and all the southern hills wrapped in a fur of cloud (ermine round their shoulders, like a duchess) then slowly followed the cliffs round before returning to the path where we'd left our rucksacks. We pitched tents by the Fuar Loch Mor, then headed off for A' Mhaighdean which was reflected in the black waters: a world of reds and greys, sandstone and gneiss. We went up the NW Ridge, and the evening became one of sheer splendour.

The clouds largely vanished and a lit pathway of watery brilliance led the eye west over lochs and sea to the Outer Hebrides. The thirty buttresses of Beinn Lair faced us, with Slioch and the Torridon giants beyond. The Mullach group looked like snow-capped active volcanoes, and northwards lay the mighty Deargs and mightier An Teallach. Between good scrambling on sandstone towers and gazing at this incomparable view sunset was near when we reached the summit. We raced down to the Fuar Loch which burned red as the sun was setting beyond the Carn Mor crags of Beinn a' Chaisgein Mor. One could almost hear the frost sliding off the stars, and the breathy silence was broken only by one tingling, echoing cry from a loon. In the ghostly moonlight the cloud re-formed and rose up the face of those crags, churning and towering high into the sky above the Corbett. We may have started on an ordinary sort of day. We ended on one with awe, an almost mystical splendour.

Section 15:   9. BEINN DEARG MOR   908 m   OS 19   032799
  Big red hill

Section 15:   10. BEINN DEARG BHEAG   818 m   OS 19   020811
  Small red hill

Sir Hugh Munro described Beinn Dearg Mor as being "a long way from anywhere", a base at Shenavall was therefore a help in making the first sortie to these Corbetts. They are well worth the effort but I suspect they are more often admired (from An Teallach opposite or from the Fannichs to the east) than they are climbed. I'd reached Shenavall over Craig Rainich (see 15:7) on a day that saw a long heatwave finally crash out with rain and storm. An early visit outside next morning showed that it was still raining, but later the barometer rose and so did the cloud.

   When I set off, the red peaks of Beinn Dearg Mor were lancing the clouds and the strath glittered as if newly painted in silver and green. The rain had been refreshing and the hot world had drunk deep of it: all was crisp, sharp and wondrous clear again. Even the pestilential clegs had vanished.

   I criss-crossed the plenteous rivers and bogs of Strath na Sealga and eventually pulled up into the NE Corrie, the mountain's great feature, via a gurgly underground burn. Asphodel spears and heather bells were colourful and the first blaeberries of the year (in July) an unexpected bonus. From the corrie lip I went up a sizeable split-rock deposit and then took to the rocks: odd wee steps that became quite good walls which were skirted or climbed and, as so often, gave more sport than was envisaged. I was experimenting with a pack frame and it proved a great inconvenience. At one stage I had to lower it before being able to climb down a crack and then I was forced right under chimneys and ribs till these were more climbable. In a good old sweat I reached a subsidiary peaklet (*c*. 810 m) and was glad to rest awhile for the view was perhaps one of the Top Ten, as befits one of the top ten Corbetts for height.

After a small gap a short pull led to the grassy top with its substantial cairn. The NE Corrie (Corrie nan Clach), seamed with gullies and jutting prows of rock, looked very wild. One gully framed An Teallach. I ran out of film — and discovered the spare I'd brought was the used one I thought I'd left in the bothy. Ah well, the sky was steadily clouding over, so the loss was not too annoying. Beinn Dearg Bheag looked very small in the scale of that wild landscape. Strath Beinn Dearg and the water rushing down from the worn plateau of Lochan na Bearta reminded me vividly of Norway, a country which is in many ways a sort of super-Scotland. In either country one keeps making comparisons. It is quite different in my other stamping ground of Morocco; there it is the contrasts that startle and attract.

Two ptarmigan burped off as I descended to the col for the narrow ridge to the second Corbett. Loch Toll an Lochain, down to the right, was a text-book corrie lochan. Beinn Dearg Bheag I noted in my diary as being "about the easiest second Corbett ever" and, for all its startling appearance, Beinn Dearg Mor is easy enough if approached from the top of Gleann na Muice Beag and Loch Beinn Dearg or even the NE Ridge. I'd just been looking for fun by going into the corrie.

The second Corbett had a tiny cairn on its grassy summit. I went on along the broken crest for a while but, with rain threatening, I chose to turn down steeply on to an indeterminate east ridge. There were a few crags to avoid and on one the mossy surface had peeled away taking a rowan tree with it. I shoved the tree in my pack and it is now growing and flourishing outside the bothy. The strath had plenty of long-leaved sundew in flower and the lochside produced plenty of clean bogwood.

Two Glasgow lads had arrived and one yarned and drank with me (he drank Grouse and I drank tea) until he keeled over off the end of the bench. A while later they went off to "fish" and four Aberdonians arrived. After the two returned, a girl staggered in, wearing town shoes, and rather exhausted. She was given tea *with* whisky to drink, and became loquacious. With lack of discretion she asked the lads what they were up to. One quickly said, "Oh us, we're frae the department", and when pressed about which department added, "Oh, tourism an aw that. See you, we canna have the likes of you hirplin in here. We'll hae a proper motorway. An we'll hae a five star hotel an no this dump o a place. An you see yon [pointing to Beinn Dearg Mor], we're gonna shift yon bing."

My most memorable day on Beinn Dearg Mor was on a New Year's Day. We ploughed into the bothy through deep snow on the last day of the year and with song and drams saw it away in pleasant ease. John, on a last fling before going off to be a doctor in Bhutan, led Dave and Jim off for a likely line on the corrie face of the East Top. He gave them an unforgettable Hogmanay. Dave said he'd never been so scared for so long, ever! The other Dave, Duncan, Margaret, Stuart and Tommy and I went along the moraine, then had a flounder in deep snow before going over the gouged centre to the East Ridge. Its successive steps gave plenty of fun and I sent plenty of wind-compressed snow tumbling on their heads. We kept very much to the rock crests as the big snow slopes on the flanks had a slabby feel that threatened avalanches. We zigzagged up some ledges, climbed a corner, revelled in an icy gully and soon reached the East Top. The view was unbelievably white, blazing white, and the sun glittered the powder we kicked up into the freezing air. You could go a lifetime and not equal that view.

Young Duncan was pushed ahead to flog a trail from Top to Summit. We photographed him, with the drift blowing off against the blue sky, then plodded along behind. Cameras clicked madly. In that pristine winter array the scene was so intensely beautiful that I, for one, found it deeply moving. What a way to start a year!

After an almost ritualistic naming-off of every hill in sight we went on down to the col to Beinn Dearg Bheag, but it was already 1.30 p.m. so we cannily said "Enough!" and floundered off downwards, on the Loch Beinn Dearg side as it was still in the sun, to reach the Carnmore track. At Larachantivore a storm ambushed us out of nowhere and the bogs and the paddles across to the bothy reverted to their usual interesting state. You can never take liberties in that wild country. If they ever shift "yon bing" they can happily put it in my back garden.

Section 15:   11. SAIL MHOR   767 m   OS 19   033887
               The big heel

The last time I went up this superb hill was with a frisky octogenarian, Ivan, a borrowed black labrador, Widge, and my own Sheltie, Storm. If I thought I could gain a leisurely ascent I was soon disillusioned. Most of the time I seemed to be chasing Ivan (with Widge climbing the hill six times over as he dashed to and fro), for Ivan just never stopped while I took photos, ate lunch, plastered heels and enjoyed standing to stare. Beware energetic octogenarians!

Sail Mhor forms a sort of coda to the symphonic sprawl of
An Teallach. While the eastern corries of *The Forge* are famous there is
a huge complex of circling ridges facing north west, and one arm ends
in Sail Mhor, a tiered sandstone upthrust of grand character. All that
secretive land drains down by the Allt Airdessaidh; even in rare dry
conditions there is a brawling burn, which cuts down in a series of
falls, among the best in the country, to Ardessie, about 2½ miles along
Little Loch Broom from the Dundonnell Hotel where we were
staying. We set off up the east bank path on a morning of golden
spring sunshine.

There are waterfalls all the way. After several smaller shoots there is
a wide one falling into a pool with Sail Mhor as backcloth. The gorge
runs deep and straight, as you notice looking down, but the four main
cascades are out of sight, and need to be seen from the west bank.
There is no crossing the river, however. Even after we'd breasted the
slopes overlooking the sea loch and could see away up a high valley
with the jagged top of Sgurr Ruadh at its head (the westmost top of
An Teallach's west ridge) the river was just too deep to boulder-hop
across. The tributary draining from Sail Mhor was passed before we
managed to pick a way over. We then followed this side stream up
towards the col between Sail Mhor and Ruigh Mheallain, a bump on
the ridge leading to Sgurr Ruadh. Deer tiptoed over the skyline ahead
of us.

We turned to zigzag up to the prow above. The glory had gone
from the day and an icy wind made the jagged crags on the skyline a
first objective. There I found a lee to plaster feet and to eat. Ivan
stormed on. Widge commuted between us. We walked an erratic arc
round the south-facing hollow of Sail Mhor to the summit cairn. The
stone cairn-shelter, earlier, is the cairn visible from the A832 road to
Gruinard Bay, from which angle Sail Mhor is an inverted pudding-
bowl shape.

The view from the upper slopes is tremendous. An Teallach's great
circuit is near and bold and the Beinn Deargs — Mhor and Bheag —
thrust up in jagged array with all the jumbled country of rock and
water sprawled to the south giving perhaps the most dramatic
landscape in mainland Scotland. The Summer Isles, Coigach, Beinn
Ghobhlach make the north as interesting. Sail Mhor is a viewpoint
high even in the Corbett ratings.

We arrived at the summit with a touch of rain. Ivan was for going
on. He completed the ridge round and down to the col to Ruigh
Mheallain, to retrace his upward route (the only straightforward one),
but I lay out of the blatter hoping the sun would reappear for
photographs. After a cold and fruitless wait I returned to the lowest

point on the summit rim and made a direct descent to Ardessie, sneaking past a snow edge and down a steep gully to reach the moorland and on down the west bank of the stream.

My combination of routes would be possible in either direction, but the direct route is brutally steep on the upper slopes of the mountain. Most people, I think, would prefer Ivan's gentler return route. There is no recommended route off along to Sail Bheag and the only attractive addition needs a tame driver — descending south to the col, as Ivan did, but then going down west to Lochan Gaineamhaich for the path which leads down to Gruinard Bay; wild and lonely country.

Section 15:   12. BEINN LIATH MHOR A' GHIUBHAIS LI   766 m   OS
20   281713
Big grey hill of the colourful pines (bin lee-ah vor a goo-vus lee)

This is one of the less memorable of Corbetts and, having been brought in with the metric revisions, my memories are perhaps enhanced by doing the hill on my birthday (mid-August), a day which completed my topping-up of all the new Corbetts. Sadly, I had a dull grey day: the ascent was redeemed neither by the view nor by much in the way of wildlife or topographical interest. The Abhainn a' Ghiubhais Li probably preconditions Munroists against Beinn Liath Mhor. A big grey hill above big black bogs.

The Corbett can be climbed from anywhere along the A835 Dirrie More road. As my Dormobile was parked overnight towards the west end of Loch Glascarnoch I crossed the heathery moors to pick up the stream running down from Meall Daimh. This is *the hill of the hinds*, which was fair description, as the corrie was crowded with them. They were surprisingly vocal, their grunting and groaning being a sound the dog immediately recognises. I returned over Meall Daimh. The one place I would not go is that peat-riven valley west of the Corbett. Those who have approached the eastern Fannichs by that route will know why.

The view is restricted but varied: Fannichs close, Deargs with their Coire Lair trench *en face*, Am Faochagach (another unfavourite hill with many), and Wyvis away to the spacious east. I keep meaning to go back. Objectively, this must be a good hill on the right day. A stuffy, viewless, midsummer plod affected my judgment — but at least there were no midges.

Section 15:   13. BEINN ENAIGLAIR   889 m   OS 20   225805
                The hill of the timid birds

If anyone asked me for a typical Corbett I might suggest Beinn
Enaiglair. The hill has the sturdy individuality and superb view of so
many. The Beinn Dearg hills are sternly impressive yet, after a long
tramp in their fastness, the six of us who puffed up Beinn Enaiglair
agreed it was the best place we'd found on our ten-hour day.

We had started out early from Loch Droma on the Dirrie More and
taken the path over to the ruins near Loch a' Gharbhrain (not shown on
the map) to walk up the Long Corrie, then up through the Princess
Corrie to the scoured world of lonely Loch nan Eilean. After wending
along to Loch a' Choire Ghranda we had a good climb up to traverse
Cona Mheall, a very fine ridge indeed. By the time we were off the
boulders hunger cried lunchtime and we sat in the lee of the wall by the
tiny lochan on the col to Beinn Dearg. Though midsummer there were
still large snow patches on this big hill. We toiled up Dearg and followed
the wall which swooped along above deep Gleann na Sguaib. We then
went up the cone of Iorguill (*battle hill*) which gave a nasty descent until
we found ourselves on a path down to the col and up to join the one
(shown on the map) which circuits Beinn Enaiglair. We turned along it
and, by the stream of the Corbett's eastern corrie, found another non-
map path which took us up to the summit.

What a viewpoint we found! From the bouldery dome we looked at
near Fannichs and far Torridons and all the giants from there to
An Teallach to Beinn Ghobhlach between the Loch Brooms, where
we'd been the day before (it only just makes 2,000 feet but lacks nothing
else), to cloud-streaming Coigach, to distant Assynt and the big, bold
Deargs. The last two to arrive were given the bonus of seeing an eagle
gliding past.

A descent by the SE Ridge led us to the path which wanders on and on
along the heights before turning down to Lochdrum at the west end of
Loch Droma. The Allt Leachachain did not present an alternative,
being full of peat bogs; its waterfalls were later explored from below. In
this rough country everyone is only too happy to use paths when they
exist. Beinn Enaiglair is ringed by paths — take your pick — but finish
up the eastern corrie: the unmapped path goes up the burn's north bank
and then turns to zigzag up to the SE Ridge not far from the top.

If starting from Braemore (the lodge has gone but the path goes up by
the Home Loch) don't omit to visit the Corrieshalloch Gorge and its
falls (NTS). Lael Forest is full of hidden surprises and the views are on a
grand scale. The Cuileag Gorge is an interesting place too.

Section 15: 14. BEINN A' CHAISTEIL 787 m OS 20 370801
Castle hill

The six of us who had been on Beinn Enaiglair (15:13) the day before
went our various ways this day: some left from Braemore to Ullapool
for Lairg and the rest were dropped at Aultguish Inn to wait for the
Ullapool–Inverness bus. That evening I was meeting three other
friends off the Inverness–Ullapool bus at Braemore — the day was
mine and Beinn a' Chaisteil beckoned.

Beinn a' Chaisteil and Meall a' Ghrianain are the two rolling
summits east of Loch Vaich. They face that most massive of Munros,
Am Faochagach, which sprawls from west of Loch Vaich to the Allt
Lair boundary of the Beinn Dearg hills. Strath Vaich, a pretty strath,
drains to the south and is served by a private estate road leaving the
A835 two kilometres east of Aultguish Inn. I cycled up the road with
the dog trotting along, sometimes ahead, sometimes behind. He was a
bit puzzled at a black sheep with a black lamb. Being midsummer the
strath rang with the voices of oystercatchers, peewits, curlews and
sandpipers — and the ubiquitous cuckoo.

The good road goes up to Strathvaich Lodge but we were left with a
rough old road which put in a stiff brae above the dam of Loch Vaich.
The view is very much dominated by the hogsback of Meall
a' Ghrianain above and by the Tollomuick Forest crags and corries
across the water. Most hollows held dirty remnants of the winter
snows, even on hot midsummer's day.

At Lubachlaggan I was quite glad to dump the cycle. By going up
beside the burn (or in it) I was able to enjoy a breezy shade, and also
avoid some of the heather. It seemed a long haul up on to the
sprawling dome of a summit plateau. The view from the trig point
was very different from yesterday's on Enaiglair: that being of the
stark west, this the rolling, bovine bumps of the east. Wyvis rose large
and blue beyond Inchbae and Rannoch Forest, and Carn Chuinneag
was a very visible Corbett to the east. This is vast uninhabited deer-
forest country with long valley approaches. The track by Loch Vaich
goes through to Gleann Mor and Alladale: great country for bike and
hike, for bens and bothies and solitary exploration. All the water
drains out to Ardgay/Bonar Bridge and buses and trains make long
tramps through (even coast-to-coast) perfectly feasible — and more
rewarding.

The bike dictated my return route, but if I'd *walked* up by the loch
I'd have returned along the heights, over Meall a' Ghrianain. *Grianan*
is a sunny spot, or a peat-drying place or a lovers' meeting place. The

hill's long south ridge is eventually cut by an estate road that leads back down to Strath Vaich. An interesting variant would be to drop down the other side to Strath Rannoch which exits to the A835 a couple of kilometres nearer Garve, at Inchbae Lodge. I juddered down directly, west, to the head of the loch and back along the road, wheeled the bike over the dried-out bogs to the dam, crossed it, and so enjoyed the good road down by the lodge. Chickweed wintergreen grew near the wood and a hoodie crow was noisily objecting to the presence of a kestrel.

Shoving the bike into the Dormobile I gave my head such a crack I nearly passed out and by the time I'd recovered the Inverness–Ullapool bus, followed by a long tail of cars, had gone by. I drove all the way to Braemore Junction before overtaking everything, and a minute later Tony and Mike stepped off the bus. Tony, on his first visit to Scotland, was astonished at the emptiness. He had expected Braemore Junction to be a town at least, not just a junction of roads. But what roads and what Corbett country they led us to!

Section 15:   15. CARN BAN   845 m   OS 20   339876
White cairn

This must be a claimant for the remotest Corbett, being equidistant from nowhere. Tackling the hill on the last day of the year was perhaps unconventional, but Dave was Munro-bagging and keen to visit Seana Bhraigh, etc., so I managed to do a trade: a chance of Carn Ban for joining his Munro foray. (As he is now climbing Corbetts he is pleased not to need another expedition into the area.)

We went in over Am Faochagach from the Dirrie More and, abandoning camping ideas as the weather deteriorated, stayed in the private bothy at Glenbeg, next to an "iron lodge". Neither looks much used, being a long way from Inverlael, whose deer-forest extends down to here. We sealed ourselves in, made a fire of bogwood and cooked a festive meal, trying not to think of the weather — a wild night, with a violent wind eventually giving way to hours of torrential rain. The alarm clock was ignored.

At dawn we looked out on rushing torrents where the day before there had been minor streams. Most of the snow cover had been washed away. We set out only at ten o'clock when the floods had subsided a bit and managed to cross the river without difficulty. Some big crags overlook the glen; among the tumbled boulders below them there are several likely howffs. The stream down from Loch Sruban Mora was a dashing waterslide. We picked up a good stalkers' path which wiggled up to the loch. Water was sheeting off the surface and as the outflow was a deep torrent we, perforce, rounded the boggy west side to cross the inflow. A long rising line led us to the corner of Coire Mhor, a plunging glen, cliff-lined and wild. The clouds were down on the bigger hills but somehow we stayed just on the dry side of wet. We had a snack before sidling up and along a bump or two in the gale to the debatable top of Carn Ban.

I called the summit "debatable" in my log because we were not at all convinced that the highest point was as shown in relation to other features. We thought the summit somewhat further north. I dragged Dave over every possible claimant rise, before allowing him to hobble off down Coire Mhor. He'd collected as many blisters as Munros and/or Corbetts. The Corriemulzie shepherd was at the bothy and I had a crack with him till Dave limped in. We collected driftwood from the loch. Two whooper swans were bouncing on the waves.

The bothy was fairly primitive, with a concrete floor. After we'd dined we took to our sleeping bags for comfort, setting the alarm for 11.30 to hansel in the new year (1975). When the alarm went off the fire was out, the night was raw-cold, Dave was snoring, I turned over and went back to sleep; an eleven hour kip was a novel Hogmanay. The swans called on the loch and we went out to a golden crisp morning with a faint half flush along the jagged cliffs above. We had a grand two-day exit over all the Dearg Munros back to the Dirrie More. "Exit swimming", I wrote. Dave ended with more Munros than blisters so felt satisfied. And I'd collared Carn Ban.

If Carn Ban is tackled as a day walk many of the approach miles can be cycled. From the south the hydro road along Loch Vaich reaches into Gleann Beag and the path which we followed. From the east a car can be taken from Ardgay/Bonar Bridge to The Craigs in Strath Carron, then a cycle by Glencalvie Lodge, Alladale Lodge, along Gleann Mor to near Deanish Lodge, before rounding Meall Dionach to walk up the Allt Bheargais to Carn Ban.

From the north there is an estate road up Strath Mulzie to Loch a' Choire Mhoir which makes cycling possible from Oykell Bridge. This loch could also be reached from the west by Glen Achall and the Allt an Caorach (which now has an estate road too). Cycling to Loch an Daimh and making a long walking circuit up Glen Douchary of the many falls, Seana Bhraigh, Carn Ban, Coire Mor, Allt na Caorach would be my aesthetic recommendation.

Inverlael is also a possible — pedestrian — starting point. Enquire about using Glenbeg bothy from the keeper at Inverlael before leaving and reach it up Gleann na Squaib and exit over Coire an Lochain Sgeirich. Several Munros can be added *en route* on what is a three-day jaunt. The obvious southern trench of Loch Coire Lair–Loch Prille gives very heavy going and walking is easier over the pudding of Am Faochagach. Munroists will need little urging to make another foray into these hills for they are among the finest in the land.

Section 15: 16. CARN CHUINNEAG 838 m OS 20 484833
Cairn of the churn/buckets

This is the highest hill in the empty country north of Wyvis. The twin summits are often visible from a long way off and their identity can be puzzling. Carn Chuinneag is almost invariably climbed from Glen Calvie in the north.

I motored up Strath Carron one July from Ardgay/Bonar Bridge partly to climb this hill but also to see Croik church, remembered from the 1845 evictions. The people of Glen Calvie took shelter in the churchyard and scratched messages on the window panes. I remember the shock when I read of their being scratched *on the outside*. The church was barred to them in their need. "Glen Calvie. A wicked generation," they wrote. Having motored to Glencalvie Lodge, the end of the tarmac, I walked up Glen Calvie. There were no buildings visible, the bracken invades the in-fields and the heather creeps down. The silent emptiness was like Munch's "The Scream".

After an hour's walk up Glen Calvie the glen suddenly becomes Glen Diebidale, with Diebidale Lodge in Diebidale Deer Forest. The glen swings away west as a steep-flanked valley, and dominating this bend is Carn Chuinneag. A stalkers' path contorts a route up the western ridge of the Coire Cas-like corrie that runs down from between the two summits. As I set off up this path I was enveloped in a cloud of small whitish moths, which rose out of the deep heather. On the ridge the heather was closer cropped. Down in Glen Diebidale there were many deer grazing. I turned east at a junction of paths, using all the uphill help possible. All these tracks and paths make the Corbett a very easy ascent. The top path leads almost to the col between the summits.

The summit is a granite cone. Three stags were nearby and I managed to stalk them to about three feet. They were so stunned at finding me that they took a while to react and gallop off. Wheatears were active and ptarmigan flew round and round. Wyvis was the nearest big hill in view but black clouds on the Deargs sent me packing: down by Carn Maire and Loch Chuinneag to descend by estate road rather than the path I'd used in ascent: a modest expedition but an enjoyable one.

Section 15:   17. LITTLE WYVIS   764 m   OS 20   430645
         The little noble or high mountain (wi'vis)

Wyvis the Munro rather hides its nobility, the normal approach from Garbat showing rather bald features on top and a beard of forest below. Little Wyvis is even more surrounded by spruce but has plenty of interesting routes. Both hills, Munro and Corbett, have noble views. Seen from Inverness or the coast they certainly impress with their height. Little Wyvis looks tiny compared to the Munro.

I'd managed to park my Dormobile near the Black Water Bridge (22 December). The snow fell quite heavily that night. The scenery looked very Christmassy when I woke. (Bridge and road have since been re-aligned but adequate parking places are available.) Several tracks are shown on the map on the lower slopes of Wyvis and in reality there are more of these than indicated while the NW flank has substantial additions to the forest shown. The best track is the one that wanders up towards the Bealach Beag and then swings south west under Beinn a' Ghuilbein where it forks, one branch going on to Meall Ruighe an Fhirich and the other angling down into the forest. Before crossing the Bealach Beag stream, another branch turns left (north) for a bit and then zigzags to the top of the Corbett. There are not many Corbetts with a road to the top!

Not that the road was very useful in the deep powder snow. The view from the top was relished: ice cream Fannichs and Wyvis cassata, with a dark peppermint-cream tablecloth of forest below the panorama. The summit cairn was small (with an iron post stuck in it) so is probably seldom visited. Coming back down, a clump of rushes held the new snow on its seed heads, the cluster gleaming like a diamond tiara. Little Wyvis rose as a shapely cone behind. I cut all the corners descending this grassy hill and at the sheep fanks saw a group of strange beasts which later research showed to have been Andean guanacos (related to llamas). There were plenty of red deer, too, and hyperactive coal-tits and long-tailed tits.

This is the easiest way up Little Wyvis, but the hill could also be reached from the Bealach Mor in combination with Wyvis the Munro. A path continues up the Allt a' Bhealaich Mhoir to the col east of Tom na Caillich. They are hills worth saving for a fine winter's day and, if small is beautiful, then little is noble.

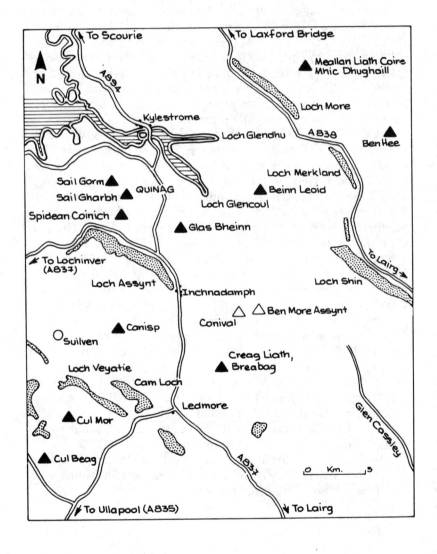

COIGACH & ASSYNT

Section 16:   1. Cul Beag   769 m   OS 15   140088
            Small back

Section 16:   2. Cul Mor   849 m   OS 15   162119
            Big back

"A LAND FOR young and eager and active" was how Inglis Clark described the North West in 1907, but, if good roads and cars have reduced the distances and isolation, it is still possible for us, as for the Clark family, to be "excited by tales of the ridges and precipices of Cul Beag and Cul Mor". These peaks now stand in and dominate the Inverpolly National Nature Reserve. They are thus officially designated as worthy by man as well as God.

Both peaks have surprisingly easy access for such grand-looking mountains, but their wilder, remoter corners deserve exploration. A tramp through the area, looking at these peaks, is as rewarding as climbing them. Every view seems to have a loch in the foreground and, as if these two were not sufficient, there is the bonus of little Stac Polly. I was a gangly schoolboy on a bike when I first came this way: young, eager and active, indeed. The lure has lasted and, when I wandered from Duncansby Head to Cape Wrath and southwards to Land's End, I stravaiged by Canisp and Suilven and out again by charming Gleann Laoigh between Cul Mor and Cul Beag. Several people reading the account in *Hamish's Groats End Walk* have commented, "It is easy to see which part of Britain you love best."

On another occasion we boldly attacked Cul Beag from Loch Lurgain, setting off in thick mist; perhaps we did not know what lay above, but then we wanted some sport, not a plod. As loch to summit is only a mile the hill is steep and we had the fun we wanted, following up gullies and tackling trim crags and heather ledges to break out eventually on the upper grassier slopes. Danni and Kathy had never scrambled before and Dave and Alex were no tigers. The dog chose his own line and was usually grinning down at our escapades. There were some adventurous frogs, and a wren family which churred loudly at our intrusion. Our clothes were silvered by the mist on the summit and after half an hour we gave up hoping for a view and found another exciting route down the cliffs. Saner walkers will not scale Cul Beag by these western cliffs. Both hills are normally approached from the east.

Oddly enough, the same off-beat approach occurred on Cul Mor.

My Watch from the *Captain Scott* was camping between Suilven and Cul Mor so, perforce, our approach was from the north, thereby discovering the grandeur of Coire Gorm. This is so deeply gouged out that one would expect there to be a lochan. The corrie is crowned with a circle of crags, and it teemed with deer (new to most of the English trainees). We swung up, right, to the Pinnacled Ridge, and steep scrambling among weird shapes led to Cul Mor's NW Top and a sudden revelation of Suilven, Stac Polly, Cul Beag and Coigach above an extravagant water world. One pinnacle looks exactly like the knight from a set of chessmen. There is a sudden change from Torridonian sandstone to the capping quartzite: purply-red to stark grey in a few strides. Our half-hour on top had heaven itself in the view. We descended north eastwards until able to cut down into Coire Gorm again. After a brew, camp was struck and we packed round Suilven ready for Canisp the next day. Ah yes, they were young and active. I'm not so sure about the eager.

The same year I ascended Cul Mor from the east, with Tony, Mike and Peter, setting out along the path heading north from near the Knockan centre and then on by Meallan Diomhain and the final cone —a route with unnecessary cairning. The reward of the North is that so many peaks stand clear in the view. Suilven, Canisp, Quinag, Assynt, Arkle, Hope, Klibreck, Seana Bhraigh, Beinn Dearg, The Fannichs, An Teallach, Coigach is quite a roll call. We made the circuit over Creag nan Calman, which can look the highest point from some angles, putting up a family of ptarmigan, the young only just able to fly and scattering in a great flurry. "How do they find each other again?" Tony asked.

Cul Beag has the same sort of feel from the east, setting out on a path from just south of the Knockan centre before wandering up the long, easy-angled Creag Dhubh Ridge to Meall Dearg and then the steep, boulder-capped cone of Cul Beag itself. Both hills are double-headed, prows to west, cliff-ringed and with long, gentle angles to the east. Cul Beag can equally well be approached from the Drumrunie–Loch Lurgain road or, for burn-followers, by the stream that drains the eastern corrie. The eastern approaches keep views hidden, then yield summit revelations. Ah well, I may not be so young, nor so active, now, but I'm as eager as ever to return to these Tweedle Dum and Tweedle Dee Corbetts. Norman MacCaig who knows the area well referred to the peaks here as his "mountains of mountains".

Section 16: 3. CANISP 846 m OS 15 203187
White mountain

Canisp exemplifies that big is not necessarily best. In most minds Canisp is completely overshadowed by neighbouring Suilven, which does not even make the Corbett altitude. Canisp's great merit, however, is as a viewpoint — it stands in the centre of the huge rock-and-water wildness that is so typically "North West" and out of which rise the starkest and most dramatic peaks in Britain: Cul Mor, Stac Polly, Suilven, Quinag, Conival, to name the nearest and clearest. These are names that can whistle a fresh wind into Southern hearts. Nowhere else is height so unimportant, but Canisp is a Corbett, for all that, built on some of the oldest rocks in the world.

One June day in 1967 saw my first visit to Canisp. Ann and two boys, both Davids, went Munro-ing east of the A837 while James (aged 15) and I set off to traverse Canisp and Suilven, Ann to collect us from Lochinver in the evening. The A837 (Ledmore Junction–Inchnadamph) is the obvious start and, unless the river is in spate, you can leave the road at any point. (There are bridges over the River Loanan at the Loch Awe outflow and near Stronchrubie.) There is little in the way of vegetation and the grey skeleton of the world surfaces in shattered layers of Lewisian gneiss, pleasantly dry underfoot. Following up the Allt Mhic Mhurchaidh Gheir to the lochan below Meall Diamhain is pleasant, the stream is a succession of stepped falls and pools. The lochan made a good reflecting pool (two Canisps for the price of one). A circling uphill sweep leads to the final cone and the summit cairn which perches on the edge of a bite of corrie. We may have looked down on Suilven but it was still big, black and monumental — and gave us the exciting traverse we'd expected. In the pub I ordered a Guinness and a Coke. James had the Guinness and I had the Coke. He was a hefty farmer's son, a talented mechanic, theatrical stage manager and climber; when he was killed in a tractor accident a year later, he was much missed.

Our walk through to Lochinver hit off the right way to visit Canisp. The peak, and the crying wilderness from which Canisp soars, are an indivisible whole, giving a rounded experience; merely to nip up and down Canisp from the A837 would be an unworthy effort. I've been back many times since, and always spending a night or two in that fastness. All the paths shown are well-made pony tracks, allowing easy if long approaches. Even the widest river-crossings seldom give problems. The heartland is too flat to create ferocious spates (those are on the perimeter), and the quality of tramping is hard to beat anywhere.

Canisp was an introduction to the wilds for one group of trainees from the schooner *Captain Scott* and they had two overnight camps, and three days of hill exploration in riotous October colouring. We climbed Canisp via the path that rises from Loch na Gainimh to its NW Ridge, perhaps the most pleasing way up the Corbett. The view down from Canisp has a map-like quality which is peculiar to the far North. Canisp means *white* mountain, which is accurate enough when sunshine beats off the grey rock. Suilven (*the pillar*) is always dark in contrast.

An even more memorable camp was during a May visit on my *Groats End Walk*. I had camped above the salmon hatchery on the Allt nan Uamh so made a fairly standard ascent from the east (two hours from the road). I had snow on top of Canisp and next morning the snow was down to my camp by Loch nan Rac under Suilven. The SW flank of Canisp is craggy and/or scree but there is no difficulty descending to Lochan Fada from the foot of the SE Ridge as I'd done. I came up to the SE Ridge at the start of a 1985 trek from Lochinver to Berriedale — my "most impressive ever" coast-to-coast tramp.

From half way along Loch Fada we made a rising line to a waterfall spouting off the lower band of crag. Once we'd tiptoed up to the lip of the fall we entered a more spacious world. Suilven's fangs dominated the backward view. The layered hollows led on for Canisp. Storm was led off by a grouse doing a broken wing act, several deer trickled over the skyline and a fleeting shadow on the crags suddenly resolved itself into a swooping golden eagle, just a hundred yards off.

Section 16:   4. CREAG LIATH, BREABAG   814 m   OS 15   287158
The grey crag

My last visit to Creag Liath's summit was on 20 December 1975 when hill, sky and human were all pretty *liath*. I had a streaming cold with a strangling sore throat and even the completion of a fifth round of the Munros on Ben More Assynt did not cheer me. There weren't even decent winter conditions.

Kitchy and I had travelled north in foul conditions and had spent the previous day cooped up in the Dormobile, so desperation as much as anything else drove us out. We set off up the Allt nan Uamh, three miles south of Inchnadamph (where the salmony hatchery has been built since), a river with plenty of surprises. There was a charming fall to start with, then a gush of water spouted out of the left bank while the main stream disappeared. Up on the right there were caves, with green aprons below them, like overgrown shearwater burrows, which once yielded the archaeologist stacks of bones of long-extinct animals. This whole area is riddled with vanishing rivers, resurgences, caves and a rich flora, for here the Moine thrust is at work with limestone, rare in Scotland, providing the material for centuries of work by aquatic Henry Moores — a unique area. Walking routes should be planned so as to explore some of the peculiar sites.

We took to a side burn to avoid the heather and as we climbed the view back down began to open up, allowing us to see Canisp and Suilven to the west. We went up into the clouds by a small waterfall just north of the slabby barrier. The landscape resembled nothing so much as an open-cast coal-mine with broken rocky pavements and banks of dirty snow. I needed a cast or two before catching the Corbett's summit. There were two cairns with a shelter where we cringed out of the icy blast.

Creag Liath is strictly speaking the crag at the 650 contour and Breabag on the map is strictly speaking the slope up to the 715 top to the north, but I don't believe the summit is nameless, only that the OS haven't found or given us a name. Most books compromise with Creag Liath, Breabag as did the *Tables* until now. Mind you, Breabag is not accurate. The name is probably *brae* and *beg*, meaning the *little slope*.

The walk along Breabag is very rough in places and on the eastern, Glen Oykel, side, a line of ragged cliffs should provide climbing routes, though I know of none. There are odd little pools perched above the Glas Choire Mor headwall and on Breabag there is a deep slot across the ridge. As a lad I had thought it would make a grand murder hole, or perhaps one worth abseiling into to see what had fallen in over the ages — maybe a Victorian mountaineer with a pocket full of sovereigns! (There are something like 60 cases of unaccounted-for disappearances in the Highlands.)

Kitchy and I went along and down over Breabag Tarsuinn to the well-defined pass under Conival and then traversed the Munros. Oddly, Ben More had also been my last Munro of round four. Sgurr na Ciche had happily been that of the first, Sgurr Gairich of the second, A' Chralaig of the third, Ben Lomond of the sixth and new Beinn Teallach of the seventh. This was the least enjoyed of endings for the weather became pernicious and I was creaky with a cold. Adding the Munros certainly makes for a good testing day, and with Glas Bheinn, another Corbett, away north of them, a very big, very demanding and quite magnificent traverse is possible.

For simply climbing the Corbett I'd come up as described, traverse to the col under Conival (the Bealach Traligill) to enjoy the contrasting geology and the allied flora and wander down the Allt

a' Bhealaich for half a mile before swinging round and down into Cuil
Dhuibh, the well-named *black hollow*. Several burns join to wiggle
across the boggy flat as a juvenile river which then suddenly runs up
against a clasp of crag — and vanishes. Perhaps it is the source of the
gush of stream into the Allt nan Uamh, perhaps it heads to one of the
resurgences in Gleann Dubh. If transport can be arranged, or an hour's
tramp up the road does not appeal, take the path from Loch
Mhaolach-coire down into Gleann Dubh to Inchnadamph, otherwise
beat across the moors back to the salmon hatchery. On this day of
mine I had to tackle these miles in the dark. As the moor is amply
supplied with sink holes it was a nervy crossing, even with a torch.
Ducks taking off from one lochan nearly gave me a heart attack.

Altnacealgach Hotel is sometimes suggested as a starting point, but
this merely gives many more moorland miles for much less interest.
Cycling up Glen Oykel would be interesting, and the whole
horseshoe of Creag Liath, Breabag, Conival, Ben More and Carn nan
Conbhairean is another traverse of northern austerity, grandeur, and
rewarding exertion, though not a circuit for novices. Easy miles don't
exist in Assynt.

Section 16: 5. GLAS BHEINN 776 m OS 15 255265
The grey hill (glashven)

Glas Bheinn lies just a couple of miles east of the Inchnadamph–
Kylesku road. Despite its rough gneiss defences it is an easy Corbett
by northern standards. There was logic, however, in our climb of the
hill from the east — which cannot occur very often.

Dave, Danni, Kath, Alec, Kitchy and I had been on a short camping
visit to that good Badlands country east of the Assynt barrier, making
the most of two cars to wander effectively. We made our exit over
Glas Bheinn from a camp by Loch Beag, as the head of Loch Glencoul
is called, and walked out to Alec's car at Inchnadamph, from where I'd
be run up to my own vehicle at our entry point at Loch na Gainmhich
(*sandy loch*). The others would no doubt replace sweat with something
from the Inchnadamph bar.

We had come out from the wilds on the first of August and close,
muggy weather made uphill effort a drip-drag affair, the only real spur
being the need to keep moving to avoid the midges. We had departed
sometime after 8 a.m. "Pack and off up the wet, dripping, infested
jungle", was my logbook description. Lower slopes in the North
often give the harder walking, the going being pleasanter once the
clawing heather is left behind. We worked our way up to the lochan

above the Leitir Dhubh and quickly erected a flysheet when heavy rain started. By the time we'd scoffed a brew the shower had gone past. There is quite a maze of paths in this complex world of bumps and gashes but all we did was take the one that runs south east towards Gorm Loch Mor and then branched off it to double back on another which led up to the col between Glas Bheinn and Beinn Uidhe, quite a bonus as the pass is 2,000 feet. The summit stands on a wide, flat, mossy green, but the ridge up is quite narrow. Glas Bheinn gives a full-frontal view across to Quinag, and Suilven is splendidly arrayed. We returned to our rucksacks on the col when the warm cloud closed in.

The favourite ways up Glas Bheinn are, I suspect, from the north, using the maximum height-gain possible on the Kylesku road. Make for either the NW or the NE ridge of the Corbett, but which burn and/ or corrie you follow from Loch na Gainmhich is a matter of personal choice. Up one ridge and down the other is a good circuit. The long western flank is not recommended. If two cars can be arranged the path down to Inchnadamph completes a fine traverse. In fact traversing can be taken to almost any length; what about Glas Bheinn to Creag Liath (as suggested in 16:4)?

We followed the path down under the barren slopes to Loch Fleodach Coire and an hour later reached the road and Alec's car at Inchnadamph. There we found a great clutter of vehicles: the RAF Kinloss team, police, and press vultures. Folk camping on Conival reported hearing shouts in the night and an enthusiastic local rescue lad put two and two together with Alec's car and made a wrong number. They were looking for us!

We found it embarrassing to be "rescued" unexpectedly but the police were very nice and we soon tumbled into the hotel with the Kinloss lads for some "area familiarisation". I had to climb into the police car to be able to speak with those in charge free of harassment from the photographers. They were most upset at the complete lack of blood and drama but made such ridiculous copy of the non-event that some of our party wondered whether they should sue one paper.

As Dave and I had recently been involved in a horrific rescue following a gaz-stove explosion, when a photographer had barged into the rescue helicopter to get a picture of a schoolboy with his face melted (which the paper actually used!) we had a job not to let rip and give them real copy. The police had been aware of both cars and were not concerned. They agreed that leaving notes in cars is more an invitation to robbery than any help.

We had a midgey camp by Loch Assynt and I wrote in my log that here was country for exploring on a through-expedition; but thirteen years passed before I made the walk through from Lochinver to

Berriedale, a story told in my book *Travels*. That gave Storm new Corbetts: Canisp, Beinn Leoid and Ben Hee.

Section 16:　6. QUINAG: SPIDEAN COINICH　764 m　OS 15
　　　　　　　　205278
　　　　　　　　Mossy peak

Section 16:　7. QUINAG: SAIL GHARBH　808 m　OS 15　209292
　　　　　　　　Rough heel

Section 16:　8. QUINAG: SAIL GORM　776 m　OS 15　198304
　　　　　　　　Blue heel (Quinag is *Cuinneag* (coon-yag), Gaelic for
　　　　　　　　a *bucket* or perhaps, *water stoup*)

Unlike the Munros, it is not easy to scale three Corbetts in a day, so three Corbetts sited on one mountain, or mountain group, is quite a cause for rejoicing. Quinag, being the sum of its superb parts, rather defeats glib description. This is a mountain among mountains, even in the north of Scotland where superlatives are scattered as liberally as the lochs. "There is no mountain to equal it in Sutherland, not even Suilven", declares Gwen Moffat, writing of Quinag.

From below, Quinag can look quite intimidating, its gully-riven, barrel buttresses and jutting prows of bare rock hopelessly steep, yet my memory is of greenness, which photographs confirm. The horizontal lines of crag support green terraces and there is a majestic openness to the walking. The only complaint is that "Quinag is all ups and downs", not only on the three Corbetts but over the intervening lesser heights. The group takes the form of a rather squashed E; the three Corbetts at the ends of the prongs add a certain amount of out-and-back to the ups-and-downs.

Quinag owes its features to the familiar north western pattern of Torridonian sandstone cake on a gneiss platter with an icing of quartzite. It is worth circumnavigating the group by car so that the peak can be seen over a diversity of foregrounds. The road from Lochinver to Loch Assynt gives a view of the hill's backbone (with all the ups-and-downs linked like vertebrae), while from Kylesku there is the dramatic view of the prows and buttresses. These prows and buttresses are every bit as fierce as they look but most of the saddles and corrie slopes are relatively easy, however steep. The path over the Bealach Leireag from Loch Assynt to Loch Nedd is a recommended extra. Sail Gorm is a new Corbett, following recent map revisions — those who failed to traverse everything previously will have to make a return visit.

I set off from near the top of the Kylesku–Loch Assynt road early one summer morning. The stalkers' path, which goes off in the wrong direction, was abandoned for the East Ridge. The quartzite strata makes for easy walking and the ridge, being well edged on the right with crags, is an easy line so I was a bit disappointed to find cairns all the way up. There must be some quirk, some lack in *homo sapiens* that he cannot let the natural world be; he has to leave his mark — figurative or literal turds in the wilderness. There is a long steady rise, a small dip and then the castle-edged, table-top summit of Spidean Coinich is reached. Suilven, which is akin to Quinag, sits boldly out on the moor to the south, westwards lies country as much water as land, leading the eye to the Minch and the Hebrides, north is the queue of good things to come. I sat there for an hour while ravens dived and called in the corrie below: black birds that glittered silver as they spun in the morning sunlight.

The biggest descent of the day followed with the drop down to the Bealach a' Chornaidh. From above I could spot deer, the young ones just sprawling on the ground, and by using the ledges made several successful stalks to within mere yards. The camera clicking usually frightened them more than the human presence. I watched other deer tip-toe through the shallows by the sand spit of Lochan Bealach Cornaidh and envied them their cool water. I had to traverse along under the 745 m Centre Top to find a trickle of water. A gentle-angled walk led out to Sail Gharbh, the highest point of the group. Thyme, alpine lady's-mantle and bedstraw made attractive carpets. Sail Gharbh, strictly speaking, applies to the gully-divided prow with the climbers' Barrel Buttress on it, but the name has been hijacked for convenience for the Corbett.

There were more towers and rises along to Sail Gorm (not yet a Corbett) where I had "lunch". The view had become hazy with the heat and, as on Arkle the day before, I was down to boots and pants. (On the next visit I was blasted off Quinag before even reaching the crest.) My car being at the pass, I threaded my way back and dropped down into the corrie to join the deer in the loch. They promptly fled. The corrie between the two *Sails* can be descended equally easily. It is deeper and narrow but lacks a loch. Bhatchaich is *barn*. Cairns marked my route down to the loch and across to the stalkers' path — quite uncalled-for. There were cars parked along from mine and tiny dots on the long ridge up to the Spidean. Being midday, with the day just warming up, I did not envy them their grilling ahead. Most of the afternoon I spent near Ardvreck Castle — in and out the loch — before going on to the charming Achiltibuie hostel with its sea view — and no clegs or midges. Heat and insects came up a great deal in conversation. An early start *always* pays off. I don't really want to do Quinag again. How can you improve on the perfect day?

Quinag is covered in W. A. Poucher's *The Scottish Peaks*. This idiosyncratic book provides plenty of illustrations, not only of Quinag but of Foinaven 17:1, 3, Ben Loyal 17:6, Cul Mor and Cul Beag 16:1, 2, Applecross 13:1, 2, Garbh Behinn 10:3, The Cobbler 2:4, and the Arran hills 18:9–12.

Section 16:   9. BEINN LEOID   792 m   OS 15   320295
           The sloping hill

Even without Beinn Leoid as bait, the "behind the ranges" area of Assynt is one which draws again and again. This is really wild and spectacular country with a feeling of remoteness seldom known anywhere else. The area's problems are more imagined than real. Beinn Leoid can be reached from several directions as a day outing, but it is worth combining several good things in Assynt and making a through-trek over several days. A mountain takes on a special quality when you sleep on it.

Though I've followed every coastline and track shown in the area, I've been to the summit only twice and both times were on multi-day adventuring. Once was on the Lochinver to Berriedale coast-to-coast. After crossing Conival and Ben More we (Storm and I) descended into the cloudy, wet wilderness of the upper Cassley and were delighted to find the waters low enough to cross between Gorm Loch Mor and Fionn Loch Mor. We camped finally a mile up, on a stream-side sward by the Fionn Allt which drains the southern slopes of Beinn Leoid. While that approach is really the least practicable, the descent and exit took what could be termed "the line of least resistance", yet I have not seen that line suggested anywhere.

If you take the A838 from Lairg to Laxford Bridge you pass a watershed just beyond Loch Merkland and then, shortly after, there is a good path which heads up south from the road through a gap in the trees. This is right on the edge of sheet 15 (356333) which is convenient. The track is good and the initial steep slog up is rewarded by a big view over Loch More to the Reay Forest (Arkle mountains) and other giants. Ben Hee is well seen, too. The path ends on the Meall na Leitreach saddle from which one angles down to pick up the Strath nan Aisinnin track, from Lochmore, that leads past Loch Dubh to the col east of Beinn Leoid, a very easy ascent up grassy slopes with a few rockier bands. The summit would make a pleasing bivvy spot. There was a vivid clump of white moss-campion by the stone circle round the cairn. With neighbours such as Quinag, Ben Stack, Arkle and Ben More Assynt, the view is first-class. That route is the simplest, but is just one of many variations. The most satisfying approaches are from the west, from the sea.

Loch Glendhu and Loch Glencoul are arms of a *fjord*, their joint exit narrow and blocked by islands and reefs, and now spanned by the bridge which replaced the old Kylesku Ferry. At Kylestrome or, better, Unapool one can usually arrange to hire a boat up Loch Glencoul, to the landing at Glencoul, where a good track leads up under the Stack to Loch an Eircill and the soft, southern underbelly of Beinn Leoid. A return could be made northwards to descend Gleann Dubh, which has a large waterslide, and out along the north shore of Loch Glendhu to Kylestrome or, from Glencoul, round the peninsula of Aird da Loch (*point between the lochs*) for the same exit. There is a path gradually descending to Loch Glendhu along the top of the crags from near the 205 spot height.

On our first visit we wanted to see the Eas a' Chual Aluinn, Britain's highest waterfall, so we went in over the gneiss-knobbly miles from Loch na Gainmhich on the Loch Assynt–Loch Glencoul watershed and managed to break down the steep Leitir Dhubh slopes to camp near the head of the loch, a day of calling divers, as I remember it. The river at some time has completely altered its course down the valley. We strolled up to see the fall. As it plunges and splatters down the crags in full view it can be wholly appreciated. The evening was spent huddled round a seaweed-driftwood bonfire trying to smoke some sanity into midsummer midge madness.

We climbed steeply up to the Stack of Glencoul, wending under its prow of cliffs and setting off a ptarmigan family and an eagle which rose just twenty yards away and drifted south along Loch nan Caorach. The natural rock sequence has been upended, the gneiss lying on top of the Cambrian layer. The whole area is one of knobbles and hollows, of naked bulges and loch-filled navels. Looking south from Leoid later we could see that the strata of the hill north of Conival were so contorted that it looked like a petrified jam roll. Loch Shin was so big that it gave the impression of cutting the North in half. Our summit picnic on Leoid was spoilt by a persistent drizzle but after we'd wandered back down Glen Coul we enjoyed a swim and sunbathe at the camp. The tide was out. When the flow started, some areas bubbled furiously. We decided the shore must be porous and that the ebb-made air pockets were being recaptured by the sea. Our exit, and what befell us, is told under Glas Bheinn (16:5) but do, when it comes to visiting this area, make an expedition worthy of a landscape rich in serendipity.

Section 16:   10. MEALLAN LIATH COIRE MHIC DHUGHAILL
801 m   OS 15   357392
The grey hill of Macdougall's corrie

The Reay (Ray) Forest, with such spectacular summits as Arkle and Foinaven and with an abundance of climbable rock and long cross-country tracks, still has neglected corners. Even graceful Ben Stack is more often admired than ascended while Meallan Liath Coire Mhic Dhughaill might as well not exist for all the notice the hill receives in the books I've consulted.

Combining this peak with Ben Hee on a hot summer's day left me with no great impression of either and my approach by the Allt Beithe was mostly enjoyed for a prolonged swim in one of the pools on the way down. The sensible route is from the Kinloch–Aultanrynie estate road using one — or both — of the stalking paths shown on the map. This is deer-forest country. The hill is to be avoided from mid August to mid October, no great sacrifice as that is also the midges' open season for humans, and the midges of Reay are man-eaters.

I'd be inclined to slant up the track above Loch More and curve round to take the Corbett by its bold western ridge (no real problems) and then descend the south ridge on to the Meall Reinidh plateau, cross the Allt an Reinidh and pick up the other path down to Aultanrynie. The walking is rough off the tracks (everywhere in the far north, not just here) so where paths exist they are worth using. They are there to allow pony access to retrieve the stags or hinds which have been shot, rather than for the convenience of hill-walkers or Corbett poachers — so be grateful.

Being the Cinderella of the Reay country this Corbett is worth doing *before* its northern neighbours. It will make quite an impression then, but if you do Arkle and Foinaven first, well, you may consider you've gone from the sublime to the ridiculous. And Meallan Liath Coire Mhic Dhughaill is not ridiculous. An eagle soared above the summit, I saw plenty of deer on knobbly Meallan Liath Beag and the long pull up was made amid a constant crying of golden plovers — a sound that suits the savage nature of the northern wilderness. Past sins have made this perhaps the emptiest landscape in the country. No wonder the plovers' voices are so sad.

Section 16:   11. BEN HEE   873 m   OS 16   426339
            The fairy hill (from *Shidh*)

This hill was climbed right after its mouthful of a neighbour during a
1976 summer blitz of Corbetts in the far north, with the result that I
can recall little of the day except the heat which boiled over into a
storm on Ben Hee, interrupting the prolonged heatwave. Near the
summit I had to duck fast to avoid being hit by a cuckoo which was
being chased by an irate pipit. I had gone up and down the Allt
Coir' a' Chruiter stalking path, which is the quickest and easiest
route, but was determined to revisit the area for a more protracted
stay. This came during the 1985 crossing of Sutherland and Caithness which gave a rich haul of Corbetts.

The day began camping west of Bein Leoid and ended camping to
the north east of Ben Hee. The whole crossing is described in *Travels*
and I'm now sure the most enjoyable Munroing and/or Corbetting
experiences are those done as part of a big journey. The travelling is
the thing, the ascents are just the plums in the pudding. My entrance
to Ben Hee was still from the north end of Loch Merkland, that
lonely loch left between huge Loch Shin and the lochs which are
backed by the shining peaks of Arkle and his kin. The Bealach nam
Meirleach which separates the Reay Forest from Ben Hee is an old
drovers' route, leading through to Loch Hope and the north coast.
The name means *the pass of the robbers* but if these are specific, the
story is lost. The right-of-way track is also a private estate road,
useful, but hard on the feet. The atmosphere is rather bleak.

The footpath shown cutting across the neck between the lochs was
my point of leaving the road. The path led up on to the hillside, and
from there I made a circuiting traverse to drop down to Loch Coire
na Saidhe Duibhe, *the loch of the corrie of the black hay*, which sounds
daft. Probably the word is Saidh which is a *bitch* or the *prow* of a ship.
The loch was rough, and for shelter I pitched in the lee of a peat
bank, a strip so narrow that my port guylines were anchored to
boulders in the loch. I hoped the wind would not change direction! It
was a superbly empty spot — I'd walked for four days without
speaking to another person. I looked out from the end of the loch
over a huge moorland (the OS goes daft with bog symbols) to the
sprawling bulk of Ben Klibreck and the distant Griams, still three
days of walking away. The hills of the north rise from such a vast
lower platform that they are unusually visible from each other.
Later, on Morven, the last peak of the crossing (not even of Corbett
height), I could see all my hills right back to Suilven. Ben Hee may

be a schisty dome compared to some of the other giants but it shares this special, spacious splendour.

The path coming in from the Altnahara–Loch Hope road shies off at the loch and heads up towards a bold buttress. I took it, and then angled up across the crags looking down on the loch, to end eventually on the secondary, NE peak, Ben Hee being double-headed. Coire Gorm was living up to its name as we rounded to the trig point of Ben Hee proper. Gorm is *blue* and the shadowy depths were a deep violet-blue with a jutting crag which might yield some sporting climbing lines in winter. I would have liked to have descended southwards to return under that wild eastern profile with its lonely lochs, but I had a long way to travel (to and over Klibreck that same day) so returned more or less as I'd ascended.

The path out to the Altnahara–Loch Hope road was my continuation, and that is the route of approach I'd recommend for Ben Hee, a long route but one leading to all the good things of the mountain. Walk in, traverse Ben Hee from north to south, and exit by the lochans again. The only comparable route would be the same way to the summit and then out to Loch Merkland by the easy route first mentioned.

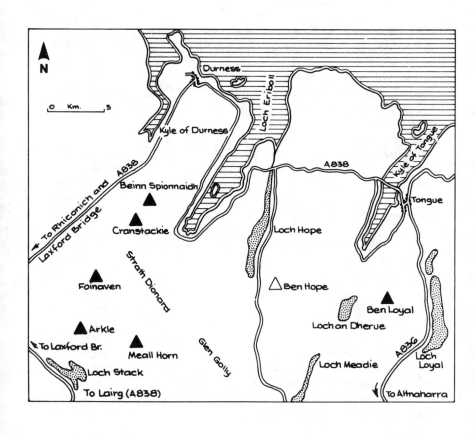

SECTION SEVENTEEN

THE FAR NORTH

Section 17: 1. ARKLE (ARCUIL) 787 m OS 9 303462
Ark-fjell from the Norse?

Section 17: 2. MEALL HORN 777 m OS 9 353449
Hill of the cairn

Section 17: 3. FOINAVEN 908 m OS 9 317507
The white hill

THE REVEREND A. E. ROBERTSON, writing in 1907, suggested that Arkle (Arcuil) "may be somewhat profanely likened to a vast shale heap, and the individual who essays to scale 'the ghastly cheek of Arkle' will have an experience in rough walking he will not easily forget". You have been warned. If it is as bad as that it must be good.

Foinaven and Arkle are jagged heaps of Cambrian quartzite rather than douce shale. Meall Horn is into an area of schistose rocks, gentler in appearance. Appearance is the one thing all these hills enjoy — the drive along Loch Stack would surely tempt anyone into Corbett-bagging. Ben Stack (718 m) may fail to reach even Corbett status but should not be omitted. Every step yields a view and the summit panorama is one of the best in Scotland. I've enjoyed several visits to the area, either climbing on cliffs, wandering the rough ridges or criss-crossing the fine glens and passes that define it. The stalkers' paths are vital for access and any day's plan should utilise them. All Reay is prime deer forest. The estate office is at the hamlet of Achfarry at the head of Loch More.

Anciently the Lords of Reay were chiefs of clan Mackay but they sold out in 1829 to the Sutherland-gobbling Lord Stafford, later Duke of Sutherland, the man responsible for the "improvements" that have left Sutherland the desert we see today. The hills are now part of the Westminster Estates, one of Britain's largest land conglomerates. Contrary to what I've heard suggested more than once, the famous racehorses were named after the hills and not vice versa. On the radio I once heard a sports commentator say, "Lochnagar is a fine horse too. Like Foinaven and Arkle, this is another peak found in the north of Scotland."

In fact, A. E. Robertson's warning should be heeded. The going is rough and the quartz crests can be precipitous and tricky in poor visibility. It is not country for the inexperienced. Assuming visitors will be competent I can perhaps give less detail. Really wild country gains by not being over-described. Part of the experience should be exploratory. In big, bold country like this more than one visit is desirable and, once visited, is desired. Sometime, one has to walk through by Glen Golly and Strath Dionard or reach Arkle-foot by that loch-scattered region cutting south from Rhiconich or traverse the Bealach na Feithe, the southern boundary of these peaks. Some of this is described in my *Hamish's Groats End Walk*; musing over the map of the area makes me want to go off and do this circuit. There is quite good access, too, from the head of Loch Eriboll over the Bealach a' Chonnaidh to Loch Dionard, and a path, not on the map, runs up the west bank of the Allt an Easain Ghil to join the Glen Golly–Lone path. Strath Dionard, even with its track, is infamously boggy and is having a vehicle road built along its length. Those climbers willing to walk have found bold routes on remote cliffs here. Ling — Weir — Tranter — Patey — Nisbet were, or are, some of the pioneers.

I've only once done all three Corbetts in one day. It was 12½ hours, car to car; with 10½ hours on the hill. At 5.30 a.m. larks, divers and greenshanks were calling as I cut across from the Rhiconich–Durness A838 road to reach the northern battlements of Foinaven. This was easier going than guidebooks had suggested. It was such a broiling day that when I began the steep assault I soon took to going in my birthday suit, sneaking up by the burn in the cleft of the northern corrie, dipping in every wee fall and hugging all the shade possible. The Ceann Garbh (*rough head*) summit was reached at 8.30 and a salvation breeze dried the sweat. Perched on a block on the cliff edge I found I was looking down on seven tents in upper Coire Duail — probably one of John Ridgway's gangs, I thought, his centre at Ardmore being not so far away.

A narrow crest led along to Ganu Mor (*big head*), Foinaven's highest point, 2,980 feet in the old currency, and a mere 600 feet more would have allowed it to overtop Ben Hope as higher than anything else in the far north. The grass (and thrift) ceased on the crest and for much of the day naked rock would give rugged going. Sadly, there were no more layers I could take off for the hot march along the cliffs and screes. Such blinding screes. They would look quite at home in the Jbel Sahro. The A' Cheir Ghorm ridge is worth a diversion. Coire na Lice with its tiny lochan is impressive. At the head of the corrie is Lord Reay's Seat, not quite up to Lord Berkeley's; the next rise gave me some scrambling. Meall Horn and the Corbetts to the south were inverted pudding-bowl shapes. There was a good earthy smell from the rocky crest. Eventually I skirted round Coir a' Chruiteir, one of the many corries-off-the-corrie holding Loch an Easain Uaine. (The 778-m trig point is Creag Dionard.) A grassy rake, and then grassy slopes, led down to the col with the bliss of water at the first burn available. Dwarf cornel, cow-wheat and thrift adorned its banks.

My rucksack was left by the path and, clad only with a camera, I tackled the scrag up on to Creagan Meall Horn then, after a banded saddle, Meall Horn, the Corbett. Deer were grunting and I could see them just down a bit on the northern flanks. They were finding little coolness even on the heights. Back at my rucker a spotty calf ambled past twenty yards away. The prospect of a dip had me romping off and I left a precious knife behind. The topmost lochan (count them down to Loch Inchard) gave a fabulous swim, and I kept going in again and again. The tadpoles in the shallows were, I'm sure, slowly cooking. A tin of chicken I'd brought smelt foul and my bar of chocolate had run over everything else in the lunch bag. I didn't even put on my boots after eating, and had a prickly walk up to Lochan na Faoileige for another swim: diving in off the east corner crags and swimming right round the lochan. While drying off I realised how pink I was becoming and (too late) covered up flesh rather than exposing it any further. That night I suffered.

Foinaven looked very grand from Meall Aonghais. I went over to the white blaze of the dried-up burn which led to the plateau-like south top of Arkle. The highest summit lies a mile on round a scalloped corrie, facetiously called The Barn (*Am Bathaich*). Scree led down to a col and there was one intermediate bump. The Corbett was reached at 3 p.m. I'd had a good look at the western flanks the day before when motoring north so was able to make a fairly direct descent to where the stalkers' path bends at right angles to pass between two lochs. I swam in only one of them.

The easier and safer descent is down to the north west (Sail Mhor) to pick up this track. From then onwards the day produced a few nasty experiences. The sun was butchering me but I had to rush off down the path to evade some of the clegs, and in the two miles down to Lochstack Lodge and the A838 I killed over 100 of the devils. There was also a multicoloured fly of an unknown species whose bite became all too well known. The road was reached at 4.30. I'd left my folding cycle in the heather and raced off to escape these insect attacks. The sea at Laxford Bridge stank and the brae beyond nearly killed me. The tired tyres made a zipping sound in the melted tar. At Rhiconich the shop was on the point of closing. I drank two cans and ate two ice-creams, which made the run up to the car just bearable. Its locked oven interior was registering 120°F. Most of my food had gone bad. At 8 p.m. the thermometer still registered over 90°F, even with windows open — but netted to keep out the clegs. At 10 p.m. it felt quite cool: down to 70°F. My thighs looked like well grilled gammon.

Lone–Arkle via Meall Aonghais–Meall Horn–Foinaven and out by Lochstack Lodge is probably the easiest round if having to start/finish at one place, but you can make all sorts of different routes. Arkle and Meall Horn from Lone and Foinaven via Strath Dionard would be a better two-day accumulation. You don't have to be a glutton for punishment, not that such a day of heat as I've described will stalk these hills very often. Do keep these hills for clear days. The views are spectacular, in every direction, westwards they are both spectacular and unusual, the eye being led over a landscape of scoured gneiss and scores of lochans to the shimmer of the western seaboard. This is eagle country and, if you believe one seventeenth-century writer (Sir Robert Gordon), the Reay deer can be told from all others because they have forked tails.

Section 17: 4. CRANSTACKIE 800 m OS 9 351556
    The rugged hill

Section 17: 5. BEINN SPIONNAIDH 772 m OS 9 362573
    Mountain of strength

There is a certain end-of-the-world feeling to walking the crests of these, the most northerly Corbetts. The sea lies near and visible both to the west and to the north. After the day over the Foinaven hills, already described, they gave a kindly walk, even if the heatwave continued.

The car was parked at Carbreck on the Rhiconich–Durness A838 road at 6.30 a.m. and the pebbly track taken over to Rhigolter. The bogs were dry and I filled two water-bottles low down in case there was none higher up; a wise move as it proved. The early start allowed me to zigzag up the steep western side in shade. This led to the marked NW spur of Beinn Spionnaidh and was followed to the summit trig point, bouldery in the end after being grassy nearly all the way. Unusually the lower of the two Corbetts has the trig point on it. These hills were obviously sheep country yet there were no sheep. Later I could hear a great bleating, but still no sheep visible. Eventually, from Cranstackie, I saw big flocks down near the A838. They were being gathered by the Gualin shepherd.

Cranstackie was reached by pleasant grassy walking, though I diverted at the band of crags to get some scrambling on the rather tottery rock. This led to the summit boulder-field with its cairn perched on the west. The haze was too thick for views and the descent was made directly to Rhigolter. It was interesting to see the vegetation change several times in the course of the descent. There were some brilliant patches of tormentil, the burn was edged with starry saxifrages; ring ouzel and dipper were resident and the air was loud with skylark song — becoming all too rare these days.

I was back at the car at 11.15 — under five hours was a very gentle day compared to that on Fionaven. Making Corbetts while the sun shone I drove south for a day on Quinag.

Section 17:   6. BEN LOYAL (LAOGHAL)   764 m   OS 10   578489

A long weekend beguiled us north of Inverness, quite a crowd in Ann's wee car, two adults and three lads. On the Sunday night we camped by lonely Loch Naver, a site made noisy with oystercatchers and sandpipers calling. The boys rescued some curlew chicks from the road. June is the best month for the north: at 4 a.m. there was sufficient light to read, and the early sun soon danced the dewdrops off the grasses. We sunbathed over breakfast tea and omelettes. This was almost too perfect a day to be spent on mountains and I only escaped being dragged off for Ben Hope by pleading a case for Ben Loyal. The Munroists still went to Ben Hope and I was dropped off on the tangy moors by Loch Hakel. "See you this evening," Ann grinned as she drove off with her crew of fanatics.

The normal route up Ben Loyal is from Tongue (the northern end) via Ribigill and Cunside, then sneaking up east of the rock prow of Sgor Chaonasaid to gain the weird heights. I was dropped off two miles further along the Kyle of Tongue road and was rewarded with the classic view of the long reach of mountain mirrored in Loch Hakel. The gorse was in flower and the blue loch complemented its golden extravagance. Ben Loyal has a succession of bold towers above lower slopes, which can be intimidating, and exaggerate the height. The highest tower scrapes over Corbett height by less than two metres. My choice of starting place allowed me to see the cup-and-ring marked stones by the southern corner of the loch. There is a prehistoric islet fort as well. It is a spot well worth a visit and, with the moor dry, there was no problem ambling on towards the black triangle of Sgor Chaonasaid, nor would there have been any problem angling up by the trees to gain the tops by the corrie between Sgor Chaonasaid and Sgor a' Bhatain. In fact I'd recommend this route, especially with hindsight. The way I went I would wish only on my best enemies. Ben Loyal, like Ben More and others, can have a distorting effect on a compass, the rock being magnetic in places.

Since that visit I've read several accounts of attempted and actual climbs on Ben Loyal's rocky towers and all indicate the decayed nature of the rock, the unadhesive quality of the vertical vegetation and the botanical bounty of the more aquatic flora. All this I can verify from the direct assault I made up Sgor Chaonasaid. I'd gone to the white scar of a stream hoping for a drink but there was no water and even the globe flowers were looking drouthy. I set off to scramble up the burn. My log account barely conceals my panic. "Slabs led to a corner which led to a 50-foot groove with a beast of a pull over a heather cornice . . . vegetation can't be so steep . . . the only handholds were into gravelly granite under the rolls of dusty moss . . . I stopped throwing down the loose rock for there soon wouldn't be anything left to climb up on . . . the sting in the tail left me lying gasping like a dying trout. Never again!" Aye, Sgor Chaonasaid is best outflanked. My only reward was finding a 60-year-old lemonade bottle after scrambling through a cave pitch — a Riley's patent screw-stoppered bottle with the beaver symbol of Walter Forbes and Co., Edinburgh.

On the top I was suddenly savaged by a fierce wind. Having climbed up in boots and Y-fronts I quickly dug out some clothes before wandering on to Sgor a' Bhatain by a scattering of tors, two quite big and many with completely round holes weathered into them. The same thing occurs on the summit tor of Ben Avon in the Cairngorms. (Wind and water erosion is the cause.) I noticed a dead ptarmigan that had its innards completely full of granite grit. On An Caisteal (the Castle — which it looks like from some angles) I overtook another walker. He had come up the proper route from Tongue. After a brief summit snack and a chat we descended a rift southwards and on to the 741 m top (Heddle's Top), where we separated, he to visit Sgor a' Chleirich and descend its corrie and so back along under the battlements to his starting point. I continued to Carn an Tionail, with its views of the moors to the south west, moors which are more water than land, before losing height over cloudberry slopes to Loch na Beiste (a low sun striking silver off the high waves) and a final top, Cnoc nan Cuilean, where I put up an eagle. A breast feather floated down as the bird flew off — and now adorns the pelmet over my bedroom window.

There is a curious legend attached to Ben Loyal, concerning the origin of fairies. When Eve was driven out of the Garden of Eden she had many more children, who were rather neglected by their distraught mother, to such an extent that the Lord God warned her that a department angel would visit her in a month and possibly take her brood into care. In a last-moment panic, Eve drove her children into the River Naver but had washed only half of them and their clothes when the angel (I almost said social worker) proclaimed his imminent arrival. Terrified, Eve drove the unwashed into a cave on Ben Loyal and took the clean ones to be shown to the authorities. The poor little dirty ones were forgotten and have been living underground ever since, only daring to come out at night.

As I descended to the road a pair of golden plovers did a marvellous distraction act, flapping and crying to lead me away from their nest. Ann's car appeared on the brae over from Altnaharra as I came in sight of the Inchkinloch bridge. We reached that rendezvous almost simultaneously. The boys were full of their day on Ben Hope, and for much of the evening Ann pored over her records and then yelled in glee that Ben Hope was her 100th Munro. Even the nineteenth-century New Statistical Account raved about Ben Loyal — as have hundreds of visitors in the century since. With a view embracing Orkney, Reay, Assynt, An Teallach, Hope and Klibreck, Morven of Caithness and the Cairngorms, how could it be otherwise?

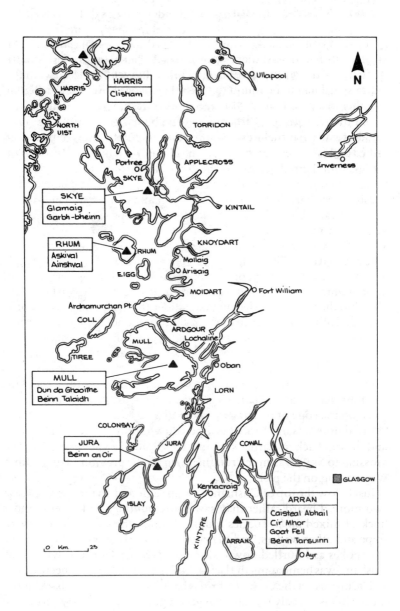

THE ISLANDS

Section 18 Harris: 1. CLISHAM 799 m OS 13 or 14 155073

THE WEATHER WAS so wild that the ferry was not operating at the Ballachulish narrows; there were curses and an extra drive round (the long legs of the bridge were being built this November day, 1973), then extra speed had to be found to catch the boat at Kyle. After installing Mother in a B & B at Uig I made another dash, with a laden cycle, to catch the *Hebrides* for Tarbet. The Minch behaved reasonably. Just a modest gale. All the crew, who outnumbered the passengers, were glued to the TV set watching Princess Anne's wedding. The boat more or less took herself across to the Outer Hebrides — that other, saner, uncluttered world where there are still sixty minutes in an hour and the fresh breezes are honey pure. I felt ashamed to be making a mere Corbett-raid, but guilt lay behind it. I was supposed to be giving my mother a tour of Skye.

I puffed westwards, against wind and brae, to set up my bivvy by the Skeaudale River. The shelter was swept periodically by the searchlight beams of passing cars, peppered by showers or glowing eerily in cold moonlight. The moonlight was so bright at 5.30 that I began breakfast, then hid the bivvy and sleeping bag under the bridge and cycled off. I cycled all of 50 yards only to push the bike for the next mile, up to a series of lochans at 600 feet. That was a quarter of Clisham climbed.

Clisham lies less than two miles north of this Tarbet–Stornoway road and by the direct route presents no difficulty. The summit cone rose white with new snow. Grass gave way to boulders and scree and the final approach was on a narrow crest to a trig point standing inside a big cairn on the edge of the crags. I wandered on to another cairn but my allotted time was up. Sadly I romped down through the falling snow, and the run back to Tarbet kept me just ahead of a vicious storm. The crossing to Skye was much rougher than on the previous day. Mother was waiting on the pier.

Just below the top of Clisham I saw an eagle and on the descent I saw two more. I heard rather than saw snow buntings and ravens, and a flock of mixed *turdus* species fought through the storm. There were snipe and other waders, and a curlew very nearly stuck its big beak in my spokes as I hurtled down to sea level. Seton Gordon, writing of Clisham, was bemoaning the lack of bird life, so I must have been lucky.

The highest of the Outer Hebrides has naturally lured me back since, for the hill is a lordly one and can give a grand, natural, day-circuit of about eight miles. There is a daily bus which helps with access but lifts are readily offered. It is probably worth starting, as I did that first time, at the highest point of the road, using the easy ascent to set up the more demanding circuit. The continuation west leads the eye off to an Atlantic horizon where, on a clear day, the sharks'-teeth stacks of St Kilda and the humps of the Flannan Isles can be observed.

The descent westwards from the summit is rocky down to the col then rears up to grassy An t-Isean (not named on the map) with its deep corries to south and north and a narrow ridge off before the steep pull up Mulla-fo-dheas (*lower south summit*, 743 m) where the horseshoe bends slowly to the north over Mulla-fo-thuath (*lower north summit*) and Mullach an Langa. Each step down gives gentler country but the bones are just below the surface. The walking is dry on the whole. Local legend recounts that when the Lord reached the end of the Sixth Day He simply dumped His surplus building material on the earth. The stones landed on the Long Island, and traversing the Clisham you could believe this: the world is very rough, very wild, very bleak. There has not been much change since the day of Creation. There are almost no trees and a limited vegetation; the beauty lies in textures and tones, colours and contrasts and the unique blend of sky, rock and sea.

Our Clisham circuit continues round the northern rim of the Scaladale basin to end on Creag Mo, from whence Ardvourlie can be reached down the east ridge. Creag Mo, like most areas showing crag, is steep cliff and has some rock climbs. Instead of swinging east to Creag Mo, I find it more interesting to skirt above Langadale north to the Bealach na h-Uamba (*Cave pass*) and descent by the impressive path to the A859 at Vigadale Bay. Bus or hitching ends the day. If one has to return to a starting point then Clisham–Mulla-fo-dheas–Mo Buidhe is a good minor circuit.

Harris and Lewis are not separate islands, as one might suppose. What separated them anciently was this barrier of mountains. The Clisham is the most easterly of four wave-crests of hills that seem to storm in from the Atlantic. For centuries no road linked Harris with Lewis. The ice ages feel like just yesterday's work and Creation an event of last week.

Section 18 Skye: 2. GLAMAIG   775 m   OS 32   514300
                    Greedy woman

Section 18 Skye: 3. GARBH-BHEINN   806 m   OS 32   531232
                    Rough hill (garven)

"I drew the blind on a still, lemon-coloured sky and a sight that made me gasp. Right in front of me a tremendous Vesuvius called Glamaig shot up in the air, a colossal cone, with grey-pink ravines searing his gigantic flanks. The rising sun covered him in a weird, reflected light, that hung over his vastness like gold dust. All round were other mountains, vague in morning mists, enormous shadows with white clouds steaming over their crests. Gentler moorlands, brown with heather, formed the reverse slope of that wild valley through which the ice-white stream tumbled beneath a stone bridge towards the waters of Loch Sligachan. No words can tell the strange atmosphere of this place, which is unlike Scotland, unlike Norway, unlike Switzerland, unlike anything else on earth."

Those were the rather rushed words of H. V. Morton, *In Search of Scotland*, but their general tenor is accurate enough. But to practicalities: the 1:25,000 Outdoor Leisure map "The Cuillin and Torridon Hills" is advised for these Skye Corbetts; though Glamaig and much of the crest to Garbh-bheinn is of Red Cuillin character the going is still complex and rough beyond anything on the mainland, while Garbh-bheinn is Black Cuillin in every way. The traverse to Garbh-bheinn from Blaven should only be tackled by rock climbers familiar with Skye ridges, being one of the more complex and technical parts of the Cuillin, and recommended as such. The description belongs in a climbers' rather than a walkers' guidebook so is not given here.

That, however, was the way I first reached Garbh-bheinn. Back in the sixties we often had camping meets by Loch an Athain, and the west faces of Blaven and Clach Glas were a regular playground. One day we did a route up Clach Glas and turned north to add the rest of the *black* hills: Sgurr nan Each, Garbh-bheinn and Belig, a day memorable for alpine flora (Skye is unusually rich, botanically) and for Danny coming out with a classic comment when struggling with one wall of gabbro: "More slack please, Hamish, I want to take a run at it." From Loch an Athain a long but uncomplicated pull leads up to the col south of Garbh-bheinn whence the Corbett can be ascended easily enough, turning any problems on the west. Clach Glas appears as a mini alpine tower from the col.

Loch an Athain is rather remote, and more practical approaches can be made from the north or east. From Loch Slapin head, the obvious Allt Aigeann corrie is boulder-strewn and gives tough going; an easier approach is to follow the path up the Allt na Dunaiche (beaten out as the normal way up Blaven) and then bear up Choire a' Caise to the north west. From the upper bowl of scree take the broad right-hand slope up to the western end of Sgurr nan Each from whence there are about 100 feet down to the col under Garbh-bheinn. Best of all is a circuit from Loch Ainort, which gave me a sparkling day one summer.

Start at the attractive Eas a' Bhradain (*Robbers' Fall*) and work southwards up to the Bealach na Beiste. At least two other falls can be taken in (waterfalls are another Skye speciality) and the walking is easy if a bit damp or heathery at times. Belig is a worthwhile diversion before heading up Garbh-bheinn. This NE Ridge of the Corbett is broad and easy for most of the way, then becomes interestingly rough before popping one out suddenly on to the summit. Descend the North Ridge, with big cliffs on the right, to Druim Eadar Da Choire (*the ridge between the corries*). This ridge can be followed, or Coire nam Bruadaran (*Dream Valley*) and, for the enthusiast, Marsco could also be climbed up and down by the SE Ridge. This is a very pleasant day out and gives something of the "Alternative Skye" which so few discover.

Skye all too often is an infatuation with the main Black Cuillin and the peaks, ridges and routes thereon. Skye generally is magnificent walkers' country and nothing exemplifies this better than a visit to the Red Hills of Glamaig–Marsco across Glen Sligachan. A traverse between the two gives a marvellous panorama of the Black Cuillin in a way you can never enjoy while *on* their cluttered complexities. Glamaig to Garbh-bheinn is even better: a long, hard day which is worth every scree-step of the way.

The screes of the Red Hills are notorious. Glamaig, from Sligachan, looks like a coal-bing of scree yet, by cunning and care, most of it can be avoided in ascent — and utilised in descent. Early this century a Gurkha soldier ran up and down from the hotel in under an hour. My first ascent took a modest three hours one November during my week on Skye holidaying with Mother. I had been up the Clisham two days earlier and then I'd taken her on a walk to the Quirang. Glamaig came as a bonus. At 3 a.m. I came down from the roof bunk in my Dormobile and lowered the roof for I was afraid the wind would tear it off. The storm wrote a new tide-line of snow on Glamaig.

The sheets of ice on the road were the day's main hazard, the heathery moors the day's main effort but they petered out on to grass which petered out on to the screes which were tamed by being glued into place by the new snow. The wind was terrific and the colours were a riot of wine and gold as the sun glittered in below the receding clouds. Glamaig's triangle of shadow lay across Loch Sligachan. The view was reminiscent of looking down on the Kingshouse and Rannoch Moor from the Buachaille. There was a slight easing of the angle and, fighting the wind, I could hardly breathe — the breath was just shoved down my throat again. The trig point of Sgurr Mhairi, the summit of Glamaig, gave a welcome wind-break. I made myself as trig-shaped as I could! Through watering eyes I took in the colossal panorama: An Teallach, Torridon, Applecross, Kintail, right down to Mull, peak upon snowy peak, lit by golden fire. Raasay, a favourite island, made a foreground to the seascape and then there was the uplifted, classic Sligachan view to the Gillean side of the bold Black Cuillin.

The ridge on to An Coilleach (the NE Top) was not to be resisted but I welcomed the chance to turn my back on the wind and angle down into Coire na h-Airidhe to hit the road at the last house of Sconser, a quick romp for the scree was either drifted over with snow or stood brittle on crystals of frozen soil, both giving an efficient scree-running surface. A few years later came our Glamaig–Marsco traverse.

That day used up our full ration of superlatives and I'm glad Dave and Tony, two of my most constant companions, were along. As it was going to be a scorcher we set off at 6.30 a.m., and were back at our Sligachan camp at 3.15 p.m. My earlier comments on playing the screes with cunning were borne out by our experiences. I doubt if we had fifty feet of real rubbish all day. The early start allowed us to make the initial ascent in shadow. The Bealach na Sgairde had had cloud teasing over and when we reached it we gasped with astonishment. Eastwards, as far as the eye could see, was a blazing white sea of cloud. The Red Hills alone seemed to be holding back the flood. Every now and then a stray wisp would sneak through a col but all day we walked with this white wasteland on the left hand and the sun-delineated Black Cuillin on the right.

We zigzagged up grass to reach Glamaig by a right-flanking route. We bombed down to the bealach on the screes. This pattern was repeated over the big, middling and smaller Beinn Deargs that led ever-southwards. The last descent to the Mam a' Phobuill was the worst. The waterfall was reduced to a mere spout but we lunched and paddled in the burn and filled our hats with water. The banks were yellow with huge primroses, tormentil, rose-root and globeflower. A ridge of crack-shattered rocks, reminiscent of Rhum, led right to the summit. "Poucherseque", was Dave's comment on the view but I quickly retorted that Poucher had dismissed the Red Hills in a mere two lines in his *Magic of Skye*. I've also noted that neither that book, nor his *The Scottish Peaks*, makes any mention of midges!

Section 18 Rhum: 4. ASKIVAL   812 m   OS 39   393952
                      Hill of ash trees

Section 18 Rhum: 5. AINSHVAL   781 m   OS 39   379944
                      Hill of strongholds?

Sir Hugh Munro had a high regard for the Rhum Cuillin and in the
first volume of the *Journal* (1891) put his case: "Only four hills exceed
2,000 feet and these lie in the south east corner which for ruggedness
of mountain outline and boldness of shape, as well as variety and
beauty of distant views, is probably unequalled in Scotland except in
the neighbouring Cuchullins."

Munro ran into the usual Rhum weather mix. "The 4th was not
tempting for climbing so I went out to try for woodcock, accompanied by a keeper with a broad Lancashire accent." (Mr Bullough had,
after all, placed all the resources of the island at his disposal.) The 5th
was a washout but on the next day he had a day which is perhaps so
typical of many people's doings that it is worth quoting in part.

On the 6th, having waited about until 10.30, I determined to profit
by a slight weather improvement, and at any rate climb Allival. I
ascended Coire Dubh in the direction of Barkeval, a fine-shaped
rocky mountain. A very easy ascent led to a flattish ridge between it
and Allival at a height of about 1,500 feet. I was puzzled by the
distance the island appeared to extend but found I was looking at
Canna, the intervening sound being hidden. A quarter of a mile led
to the north west arête of Allival, which although steep, and
continually requiring the use of hands, is not difficult. Reached the
summit at twelve. The top was entirely clear of mist and the views
lovely though, as on the 4th, the summits of the mainland hills were
hidden in cloud.

The ridge connecting this mountain with Askival runs south. It
descends to a col, which falls away steeply both east and west, and
then rises by a very narrow arête to Askival, the summit of which
was now entirely clear of mist. Viewed from Allival, this arête
looked practicable for about half-way up, where a veritable
gendarme appeared entirely to block the way. Both the east and
west faces of the mountain looked inaccessible, and two smaller
blocks within a few feet of the summit seemed insurmountable.
Anyhow, I was only out for a stroll, fully intending to have another
day on these hills; and we all know that although snow slopes are
generally found to be far more formidable than what they appear at

a distance, rocks, on the contrary, which even from a short way off seem inaccessible are often found easy when attacked. It proved so in this case.

I struck an easy way to the col, and a few minutes' ascent by the narrow ridge brought me face to face with the gendarme, which, as anticipated, was quite perpendicular and probably one hundred feet high. The east face, however, though steep presented no particular difficulty. Several attempts to regain the ridge proved abortive, I therefore kept to the face, reaching the summit almost without knowing it at 1.5 p.m.

The clouds had clung persistently to Ainshval and Sgurr nan Gillean, although neither are quite as high as Askival. However, I had plenty of time before me, so determined to descend to the head of Glen Dibidil, the easiest way down from Askival. Reaching Bealach an Oir, I thought I would at least go to the base of Ainshval and have a look, so I skirted the base of Trallval to Bealach an Fhuarain [*the pass of the springs*] between Trallval and Ainshval. There is a very pretty view down a narrow glen and over Loch Fiadh-innis to the sea.

After striking upwards across some uncomfortably steep screes on the north west face, and ascending by a nice bit of real rock-climbing with some rather awkward smooth slabs of rock, I found the slope eased off for the last couple of hundred feet, and the top was reached at 2.50. The last two hundred feet or so had been in thick mist, which now got worse. From here to the top of Sgurr nan Gillean (2,503 feet) is an easy twenty-five minutes' walk along a broad, almost level, and often grassy ridge, with fine corries to the left, which today had some good cornices of snow.

I had been told that Sgurr nan Gillean was anywhere easy on this side; if so, I was unlucky in the mist in striking the one difficult place. I managed to get down into the almost dry bed of a small burn, between cliffs sometimes so close that I could touch them on each side. I had lowered myself down on to a ledge and could not re-ascend, and for half an hour had as steep and disagreeable a piece of climbing as I wish to experience alone; sometimes on rocks at the side, sometimes on loose boulders in the bed of the burn.

I emerged from this gully and from the mist at the same time, at a height of about 1,600 feet, and in half an hour, at 4.30 p.m., reached the track from Loch Scresort, at the foot of Glen Dibidil. This glen, though only a mile and a half long, vies with Glencoe in rugged grandeur, while in its contrasts of glorious sea views it far surpasses it. Right at the head of the glen Trallval stands boldly out; Beinn nan Stac and Askival on the right, Sgurr nan Gillean and

Ainshval on the left. The glen faces to the Sgurr of Eigg and the low-lying green island of Muck. Over this is the long promontory of Ardnamurchan, the westernmost point on the mainland of Britain and behind it again the mountains of Mull, faintly seen in the haze. Towards the mainland there is a grand panorama of sea and mountains.

The distance from Glen Dibidil to the lodge is six miles. The track rises above the sea, with grand cliffs of dark rock, fringed with foam. White-winged gulls float on the waters or a solitary scart skims over them in arrowy flight. As the track rises grand views of Skye, over Soay, open out, then the track descends to Kinloch and Loch Scresort.

The following day it poured in torrents, and on the 8th, profiting by a slight wind and an unlooked-for opportunity, I sailed over in a small open boat to Arisaig. The day was absolutely perfect, without a cloud and I cast many a regretful glance back at the glorious peaks of Rhum.

There is little one need to add to that for, though the island has seen plenty of changes, the hills remain the same. Being an island, however, does present certain logistical problems. The easy answer is to buy a copy of the guidebook to Rhum; as its author I am all for boosting sales! Seriously, the guide provides all the information, not only on the prosaic practical points, but on the lore and history of an unusually interesting island, which is a unique National Nature Reserve. The history of research since the Nature Conservancy Council bought Rhum is fascinating — into red deer, re-afforestation, shearwaters, sea-eagles, archaeology and all sorts of things. Rhum is an island worth some *time*, not just a Corbett raid. Allow a week at least for a first visit.

Being such a special place, access is regulated. You can't just land and bomb off for Askival. For permission write to the Chief Warden, White House, Rhum by Mallaig, or give him a ring: 0687–2026. The staff are very friendly and helpful and contribute much to any visit. Most people camp by Loch Scresort but there is some estate bothy accommodation and a range of residential facilities in Kinloch Castle, the ludicrous mansion of the Bulloughs, and one or two cottagers do B & B. In high summer midges and clegs abound.

Rhum is usually reached by boat from Mallaig, which is the end of the West Highland railway line, and as the *Lochmor* also takes in Eigg, Muck and Canna going, or returning, you have quite a Hebridean sail as well. The views to Rhum and Eigg from the west coast are classic but how few who gaze west over sea actually sail to the Parish of the

Small Isles. Askival is less than 1½ miles from the coast and Sgurr nan Gillean, a Top of Ainshval, is likewise less than a mile. On Bloodstone Hill you feel you could parachute into the waves. The views *from* Rhum are spacious and grand — Sir Hugh has already said so. Munro does not overstate Rhum's excellence, but you can find the many reasons in the guidebook (*The Island of Rhum*, Cicerone Press). Not many Corbetts are given such extensive background description. Maybe Arran. And that is another island. When you have done all the Corbetts you can start collecting Scottish islands.

Section 18 Mull: 6. BEINN TALAIDH   762 m   OS 49   625347
                      The hill of happiness (cf. Valhalla) or *Hill of good pastures (talla)*

The Island of Mull, third largest of the Hebrides, is an island of inexhaustible attractions. It has something of everything, including a bonus of satellite islands, gems such as Iona and Staffa. Mull is rich in history and lore, is a geologist's and naturalist's paradise, the seaman's delight and the hillgoer's valhalla; indeed, with one Munro, two Corbetts (Talaidh promoted in 1981) and plenty of other hills as well, it is one of the best places in Scotland for walking through glens and round coasts, enough for days on end. We grabbed a bit of everything last time, gluttony perhaps, but we did not suffer indigestion.

"We" were nephew Colin on his Easter holiday, Storm and myself. Our route was worked out in the caravan Mother had taken for the week. We motored round to Glen More (the eastern Glen More) and when the road broke out above the plantings of the Lussa River, Bein Talaidh rose straight ahead in simple symmetry, a cone-shape that is instantly recognisable from as far away as Barra. The peak gives the impression of being much higher than 762 m. At the crook of the road we parked the car and waited for the Craignure–Iona bus.

This corner would give the most direct and quickest ascent of Talaidh but we wanted to approach the peak more graciously. A drift of sheep came out from the low watershed to Glen Forsa, the glen that cuts off the Talaidh–Ben More complex of hills from Dun da Ghaoithe and the Sound of Mull. The road west up Glen More cuts off Ben Buie and Lochbhui to the south — one of the many corners that repay exploration. The early light had fallen well down on Talaidh when the bus came and bore us over that watershed to descend Glen More (the western one). We were dropped off at the bridge over the Allt Teanga Brideig, a couple of miles from Loch Scridain, and wandered upstream to pitch our tents and pass the rest of the day on a leisurely ascent of Ben More. After supper I half-climbed Corra-bheinn, while trying to read a book, as the cold shadow of evening kept chasing me up the hill every few minutes.

In the morning we traversed to find a hollow where we left the tents and then set off up Coir' a Mhaim to a col between two haunches of hill, passing through hind country with beasts grazing on all sides. The Mam Breapadail was a surprise: our long, slow sweat up suddenly led to deep-cut Coire Mor which was a bit like the Devil's Beef Tub near Moffat, which meant a brutal descent; where several burns met we had a break. The sky had clouded over and strange clouds were billowing through the passes but when we smelt them we realised the cloud was the smoke of moor-burning.

We passed a ruined burial ground and a 1910 footbridge which was reduced to two beams. Storm preferred to paddle across. Ben More must have been well alight for smoke was pouring over the hills and when we tramped through to Tomsleibhe above Glen Forsa we found that glen in flames and the shepherds busy taking the beasts down. The circles of flame were still bright in the dark when we had a last look out from the bothy. Our morning's walk placed us at the northern end of Beinn Talaidh. The hill has a gabbro satellite top from whose col a burn, the Allt nam Clar, runs in a deep, straight line down to Glen Forsa. We set off up the burn after lunch. Almost at once we found a piece of twisted metal.

By burning up we eventually came on the main wreckage of an aircraft, the remains of a wartime accident following which the epic winter search and rescue led to several awards. (Quite by chance we learnt something of the story when visiting the church in Salen.) We had to escape as the gorge became too deep-cut, so we zigzagged up the steep east flank to the summit screes. Here a sheep path led along and up on to the North Ridge and we plodded to the summit, which lies 25 yards to the south west of the trig point. The whole island seemed to be on fire, the views hazy, tones upon tones of grey, but a fantastic view, better even than Ben More's because Ben More was part of this panorama that ran from Arran to Skye and from Outer Hebrides to Ben Nevis.

A few flakes of snow fell on top so we didn't linger. By keeping to the grass on the western edge we were able to chunter down the North Ridge easily enough. There were large areas of frost-combing. (The south-east approaches may be shorter but they are steeper and give some crags and roughness. We were in at six. Colin filled some plastic bags with dry grass and we lay on them under the skylight till too dark to read. Storm kept an eye on the hares, hinds and ewes that wandered about outside. I've never seen so many dead sheep on the hills. Quite a few were in the Allt nam Clar — protein enrichment for our water supply.

We walked out along Glen Forsa under our Corbett and arrived at the car with our lower parts filthy with wet, clinging soot from the burnings. Storm had changed from bracken-colour to a uniform black. David Balfour in *Kidnapped* came this way, though his precise route is infuriatingly vague. He, of course, had suffered shipwreck rather than fire.

When we drove over to collect our hidden tents we were horrified to see the whole hillside had been burnt. Burnt too was the flysheet of my Ultimate Tramp but at least its sacrifice had saved the other tent below it. Tents, people and dogs took quite a bit of cleaning. Beinn Talaidh, for us, will always be associated with fire and smoke. Necklaces of flame had been our last view out the bothy skylight, and weeks passed before the lingering smell vanished from our belongings or the car.

Section 18 Mull: 7. DUN DA GHAOITHE   766 m   OS 49   672362
Fort of the wind. The castle of the two winds (goe-ee)

Dun da Ghaoithe dominates the Sound of Mull and is the largest hill to be seen when sailing to Craignure from Oban, the most usual approach to Mull. A cheaper car ferry also operates from Lochaline in Morven, crossing to Fishnish. Quite often the impecunious walker compromises by bringing a cycle rather than a car (I've done it myself) but Mull deserves a week and a car simply to begin exploring the island. The magnet of Iona also means that there are buses which can be used if one comes without any means of self-propulsion.

So, from Craignure take the Iona bus round to Torness (ruin) in Glen More and head up, traversing rocky Sgurr Dearg to Mainnir nam Fiadh (*the field of the deer*) and Dun da Ghaoithe, descending by the east ridge to Maol nan Uan with its TV station service road down to the A849 at Torosay Castle. This castle has attractive gardens and, in season, there is a miniature railway to take you back to Craignure. Duart Castle is older and set in a commanding site overlooking the Sound of Mull. There is time to enjoy both the hill and the castles on a summer's outing. Another day of high walking can be had by taking the Tobermory bus to Fishnish Bay, wandering up Maol Buide, then along by the Beinn Chreagachs and Beinn Mheadhon to reach the Corbett. Or you could traverse the lot — but that is not so easily fitted in to a day trip from Oban! A simple circuit from Craignure is probably the most popular expedition, if popular is the right word for the uncrowded hills of Mull. At least I've met accounts of Dun da Ghaoithe; Beinn Talaidh seems to lie under a strange moratorium.

Campbell Steven's *The Island Hills* has a description of Dun da Ghaoithe and, as the book takes in Arran, Jura, Rhum and Skye as well as Mull (plus plenty of islands without Corbetts), those bent on the Corbett quest would enjoy reading it. Campbell Steven describes two ascents of the hill, both from the Craignure side, circuits similar to one I made on a frantic Corbetts tour during a Sabbatical year spent in mountains all round the world. My notes were a bit sparse but they can recapture the day in a way unaided memory cannot do. The briefest of hill logs is better than none.

28.6.72 Dun da Ghaoithe. Crazy pace still. A week ago in the Alps, then the flight to Benbecula unable to land so this week of unplanned Corbett-bagging instead. Up at 4 a.m. to do Leum Uilleim before morning train to Glasgow, collect the car from the airport, collect the dog from Dollar and motor to Oban and a night in the Dormobile by Loch Nell. Body not keen on rising today. Just a cuppa and in for 6.30 sailing to Craignure. Breakfast on *Columba* till out to watch Duart Castle. Motor a couple of miles along to Scallastle Bay. Skirt bracken bump of Cnoc Bhacain and then curling ridge to the summit, overlooking Coire na Circe. Neat shelter for one shower: laid two posts against the fence and roofed it with space blanket. Regular outbursts and then into cloud for the last gravelly steps. Slaggy corries of grey. And a big cairn. Pause naturally, and it cleared, instantly. Great. Romp round the rim of Coire Mor to the peakier pap of Mainnir nam Fiadh. Sgurr Dearg an attractive peak, too. West of it all was blotted out in cloud. As so often the view *down* rewarding on islands. Clutch of islands' Corbetts too. Continue on down the curve of east ridge: chips laid down in regular stripes like a patterned carpet. Bale off into Coire nan Dearc but come on a deer fence for new tree planting. The Scallastle River a succession of falls and pools. Mull rivers are made for swimming. Not today though. Cut across before house to the Dormobile. Lunch of toasted cheese. Road works but fine tarred surface (silver straight after rain) up Glen More. Time to relax. Corbetts will take a long time yet — but a pleasing prospect with more islands and breaking new ground; the delights of discovery. Ben More cleared but last memory of the calling curlews, oyster catchers and snipe, the Mull magic.

Section 18 Jura: 8. BEINN AN OIR   784 m   OS 61   498749
                   Hill of Gold

We had come to know the north end of Jura from several school visits,
an exciting coast with huge caves and the great Sound of Corrie-
vreckan, but we had always sailed there from Loch Craignish. The
three Paps of Jura (such odd symmetrical cones) were at the other end
of the island, alluring but out of reach. They became "someday hills".
The Outer Hebrides and western seaboard had been keeping me
occupied. Regretfully the time came to return home but as I sailed
from Mull back to Oban I decided the west could have one more fling:
we'd end with the Hill of Gold on Jura. The 4.30 p.m. ferry took us to
Port Askaig and ten minutes later the "landing-craft" ferry was slap-
slapping into the waves across the Sound of Islay to Feolin on Jura. A
stuffy south wind rose in the night; it was almost a pleasure to set off
early.

   All I knew of Beinn an Oir was its reputation of being a pile of
"loose and shifty", boot-destroying quartzite, so I wore my oldest
pair and decided feet could just become wet. The walk up the Corran
River therefore came as a pleasant surprise, the wind had dried the
grass and the going, by the burn, was pleasant. My only excitement
was when a big boulder supporting the bank gave way when I stood
on it. The dog's excitement was the large number of deer all day. A
cuckoo, down to one syllable, "cucked" at us regularly on the way up
to Loch an t-Siob under Beinn Shiantaich. I was thinking the loch
would be a likely place for divers when a pair started cackling on its
wind-whipped surface. The heat was boiling up for a storm and
streamers were already touching the grey peaks. Thoughts of a long
day over the three Paps vanished and I had to race to win the summit of
Jura.

   The cloud was down to the beallach by the time we had been blown
up to it. I started up right and a brief break showed a stormy sea round
Rhuvaal light at the northern end of Islay. Bad quartz was not good in
those conditions. Gusts were apt to throw me off balance and the
greasy rock caused several slithers. The dog, as ever, seemed quite
unaffected. A lot of the scree could not be dodged and we ended on a
surprisingly narrow crest. I left the odd wee marker cairn as I went so
that I could backtrack quickly without the rigmarole of compass
work. A final rocky cone landed us beside the trig point. We were
there just long enough to eat some chocolate before retreating as we'd
come. We kept higher across the moors, cut corners, and had a great
tussle with the wind. We crossed back to Islay all right, but the ferry to

the mainland was hours late. The deluge began on the crossing. I suppose I had been lucky.

Jura's hills are not climbed very often I'm sure, but the unusual nature of the peaks seems to drive ascensionists into print. One of the few *Journal* notes by J. Rooke Corbett was about his visit to the Paps in 1931. The ferry crossing cost him six shillings return, then he took the direct route from the ferry to the Paps over the moors, rounded Beinn a' Chaolais (*the hill of the sound*) to ascend Beinn an Oir by its easiest, most vegetated line, the NW Ridge. The NW side of Beinn Shiantaidh (*the consecrated hill*) is also its easiest, grassiest; he went up and down it that way. Beinn a' Chaolais was tackled by its East Ridge and, as in my case, Corbett lost a race to have the summit clear. Quite a few accounts I've read tell of these sudden changes of weather. The Paps seem to cull clouds out of any sky. On their tops you certainly "stumble between the immensities".

A new bulldozed track heading northwards from the ferry helps the direct moorland approach. Charles, on an appalling day, was glad to use the footpath to Glen Batrick for easy access. Charles also pointed out to me that both sheets 60 and 61 have Beinn an Oir on them but each gives a different height. The Islay sheet gives 785 m.

Corbett, on Beinn an Oir, commented about two huts in a dip to the north of the summit with a causeway leading to the top, and Inkson McConnochie (1914) described a hut by the lochan north east of the hill. The summit had a huge survey cairn. Recent visitors have sometimes mentioned the causeway, an odd man–made intrusion into the stark, bony landscape, and these remains point back to the Ordnance Survey's original great triangulation of the country. They pinpointed peaks as far distant as Slieve Snacht in Donegal, Beinn Mhor in South Uist, Ben Nevis, Lawers and The Merrick.

The Paps are often mentioned by the early "tourers": Pennant, Grierson, Maccullough and others. The last, usually a loquacious enthusiast, girned, "Intimate as I am with Jura, I have little to say of it, and much less to say in its favour." However, commenting on the striking, and unique, appearance of the symmetrical Paps and, of the view from the top, he recorded, "the skeleton and structure of Jura, which seems atomized to its very foundations". Grierson found the ascent "very abrupt" and commented on "loose blocks so trouble-some that much care was required to escape broken bones", yet there were "blaeberries, crawberries, junipers and braelics". Several people note the thrift which grows as happily on the rocks by the sea as on the rocks on the barren heights. Thomas Pennant, who was no mountain man, scaled Beinn an Oir on his 1772 tour, "a task of much labour and difficulty". He, at least, had a view:

Find our fatigues fully recompenced by the prospect from this sublime spot: *Jura* itself afforded a stupendous scene of rock, varied with little lakes innumerable. The depth below was tremendous on every side.

To the South appeared *Ilay*, extended like a map beneath us; and beyond that, the North of *Ireland*; to the East, *Gigha* and *Cara*, *Cantyre* and *Arran*, and the Firth of *Clyde*, bounded by *Airshire*; an amazing tract of mountains to the north east as far as *Ben-lomond*; *Skarba* finished the Northern view; and over the Western ocean were scattered *Colonsay* and *Oransay*, *Mull*, *Iona* and still further the long extents of *Tirey* and *Col* just apparent.

On the summit are several lofty *cairns*, the work of idle herds, or curious travellers. A hind passed along the sides full speed, and a brace of *Ptarmigans* often favored us. The other *paps* are seen very distinctly; all of the same figure, perfectly mamillary.

An Englishman, a Scotsman and an Irishman had been marooned in the hut on Beinn an Oir one long day of storm when one of them noticed an old bottle lying in the debris on the floor. He picked up the bottle and began rubbing the dirt off, then uncorked it to have a sniff only to recoil as a cloud poured out and quickly took the form of a genie. The genie offered them a wish each. The Englishman, who had been thinking of home comforts in soft Sussex, at once blurted out, "I wish I was back home" — and promptly vanished. The others goggled, then the Scotsman half-suggested, "I wish I was comfy and dry in the *Ranger's Rest* in Glasgow with a *Jura* in my hand." He too vanished. The Irishman looked at the blowing rain and cloud outside and shuddered. What a miserable place! "Bejabers this is a desolate place. I wish me two friends were back here with me now."

Section 18 Arran: 9. GOAT FELL 874 m OS 69 991415
Hill of the wind

"Arran is magic", was the reaction of one lad I spoke to recently. He had taken his cycle over and explored the island thoroughly by road, by tramping and camping the glens and ridges and enjoying several rock climbs. Few places can give such a variety of good things; and my own list would add prehistoric monuments, wildlife, seashore and garden interests. That lad had, unprompted, commented on the "bonny bright bushes" at Brodick Castle — having been there at rhododendron time. The moment one lands on the pier at Brodick, Goat Fell catches the eye; the peak rises behind the castle across the bay as gracefully as Fuji Yama and, as Pennant said of Lochranza, "the whole is environed with a theatre of mountains."

All the Corbetts can be traversed in a day, something of a marathon; but Arran should be savoured, selectively and sensitively, rather than gulped down, a whole menu in one binge. The peaks break down into two logical and immensely enjoyable expeditions: you can have your cake and eat it.

Glen Rosa and Glen Sannox reach into the big granite hills as if they were trying to remove Goat Fell from the rest of the peaks. Goat Fell is really a solitary summit and, being the highest, both dominates the scenery from Brodick Bay and gives a huge view from its trig point. I can still remember the thrill of reaching the top the first time, as a boy, and seeing the Clyde glittering in the sun, and Tarsuinn, Cir Mhor and Caisteal Abhail ranged raggedly against the sunset colours.

Arran attracted me first as an island. I had never heard of Corbetts or Munros though the visit was to double my tally of the former. Arran was reached by cycling from home in Dollar and staying in Brodick Youth Hostel (a bad gap now without a hostel) and, like the youth I was speaking to thirty years on, I explored thoroughly, besides traversing all the ridges and getting gripped on the granite crags. Arran was magic, all right. Some things don't change.

There is a well marked path for Goat Fell from Brodick, leaving the lushness of the castle grounds up by the Cnocan Burn. On the moors the map shows this burn splitting into two and I remember going to inspect it and being disappointed to find the split was caused by an old mill dam. The path curves up from the SE corrie to reach the summit via the East Ridge. The panoramic view is "One of the most entrancing in Scotland" (Poucher). "A marvellous combination of fantastic mountain scenery so near, sunlit seas far below, and the isles away to the west makes this prospect unique."

One of the few mountain books I have read over and over again is Janet Adam Smith's *Mountain Holidays*. The book opens with a chapter on Arran, where she climbed Goat Fell at the age of nine, having been blasted off the East Ridge the year before. Those were family holiday visits, under the care of the poet and mountaineer W. P. Ker (whose telling influence is gently described), and they led to many of the participants going on to climb and explore in other parts of the world. The book continues with Alpine holidays and I found it quite infectious. Even the Alps could be fun, as Goat Fell was fun. A fun based on acquired skills, but still fun. Where grim-faced Whymper had left me gasping, Janet Adam Smith beguiled me to the Alps — and beyond.

I'd already read about Arran's ridges, for Dollar was the home of W. K. Holmes and his sister, who were kind to the maverick youth who already ran wild on the Ochils. W.K.H.'s modest book *Tramping Scottish Hills* has a chapter on the Goat Fell Horseshoe. That book I knew almost by heart. W.K.H. and W.P.K. I suspect were very alike in many ways. Their quiet, solid, yet visionary approach to the hills I feel is sadly lacking today when big egos seem to want instant trips. Thank God we have had these peers, these poets and philosophers whose love is of the hills themselves, for themselves. Read them, friends, and also read Tom Weir and W. H. Murray and Seton Gordon. Arran was special for all of them.

Arran has a mention in just about every general book on the Scottish hills, and scores of entries in journals and magazines. Hamish MacInnes's *West Highland Walks*, Vol. 3, gives a good general coverage of the island while Poucher's *The Scottish Peaks* and Bennet's *Scottish Mountain Climbs* have interesting photographs of its mountains.

I cannot remember how I descended on that first visit — it was probably by the "tourist path" I'd ascended — but I can recall the next descent, to Sannox, and this, with the ascent from Brodick, is the classic traverse. From the trig point head north along the castellated ridge of the Stacach to North Goat Fell which is the real hub of the mountain with ridges radiating in three directions, that to the north west dropping to the Saddle linking Goat Fell with the other granite giants while the NE Ridge is the continuation of the traverse, edging down along the cliffs of Coire nam Fuaran. (In 1889 a young man was murdered and his body found below these cliffs.) The ridge levels off over Mullach Buidhe (819 m) then becomes a rocky crest, sheer on the east (Coire na Ciche) side and super-steep above Glen Sannox. Cioch na h-Oighe (*the Maiden's breast*) is 661 m. There is a path all the way, now, down into Glen Sannox. For a young lad on his own this descent was quite exciting: a first taste of exposure and the friendly adhesiveness of granite.

During the early to mid 1970s I was to see plenty of young men react to Arran's hills: we went there several times with trainees from the *Captain Scott* and had a survival camp in Glen Rosa on one occasion. Some of the townies found the wind on Goat Fell quite frightening, it periodically knocked whole groups to the ground at once. On another occasion we backpacked over Goat Fell to camp on the Saddle with a view down Glen Rosa and the wind and cloud racing harmlessly up Cir Mhor from Glen Sannox. Those winter months on a tall ship are an unforgettable experience — and what an approach to the hills!

Section 18 Arran: 10. BEINN TARSUINN   825 m   OS 69   959412
                         Transverse hill

Section 18 Arran: 11. CIR MHOR   798 m   OS 69   973432
                         Big comb (keer vor)

Section 18 Arran: 12. CAISTEAL ABHAIL   859 m   OS 69   969444
                         Ptarmigan stronghold (cash-tyal-avil)

W. Douglas, of Douglas Boulder fame, produced the first SMC *Journal* article on Arran in 1896. He extensively quotes Alexander Nicolson, the Skye enthusiast who, nevertheless, had much to say about Arran which he considered the most beautiful island in Scotland. He in turn quotes someone else in describing the view of these hills from Goat Fell: a "terrible congregation of jagged ridges and fantastic peaks". Douglas delves back with several quotations, which mirror the changing view people had of mountains.

In 1628 "Lugless Willie Lithgow" commented on "Goatfield which, with wide eyes, overlooketh the western continent and the northern country of Ireland, the Isle of Man and the higher coast of Cumberland. A larger prospect no mountain in the world can show, pointing out three kingdoms at one sight; neither is there any isle like it for brave gentry, good archers, and hill hovering hunters."

Maccullough (1811) found the "high and serrated forms peculiarly striking, presenting a rugged mountainous character unequalled in Scotland except by the Cuchullin in Sky". He was a geologist, of course, and keen on all sorts of studies. Science was becoming *the* reason for climbing hills at home, or abroad, so he was at a loss over the ascent by a minister who, having climbed up, "just went down again". I suspect more people made ascents for fun, even in those days. No one wrote about them, that's all.

The Rev. Thomas Grierson in his *Autumnal Rambles among the Scottish Mountains* (1850) is delightful with his "thrills of horror", Lord Cockburn broke into his "Circuit Journeys" to climb Goat Fell (a $5\frac{1}{2}$-hour round trip), Hugh M'cullough looks at these hills as "such a wild storm of mountains" and is tempted to quote a Paisley weaver on top of Ben Lomond turning to a friend with, "Man, Jock, are the works of God no devilish?"

Walkers are sometimes put off the Arran hills by reports of difficulties, of unavoidable climbing, of Bad Steps, of cyclopean rocks and boiler-plate slabs, which is a pity: Arran is a great place for walkers and for backpacking. The young *Captain Scott* trainees quite happily carried their gear over Goat Fell to that camp on the Saddle and the next day traversed Cir Mhor and Caisteal Abhail to camp by Loch Tanna west of Glen Iorsa before climbing Beinn Bharran above the west coast and rejoining ship off Lochranza Castle. Distances are not great in the Arran hills, there are many paths and plenty of grassy slopes and easy valleys, besides the dramatic upsurge of peaks. The traverse of these peaks is a classic expedition.

The walk begins from Glen Rosa and follows up the Garbh Allt (*rough burn*) which drains Coire a' Bhradain to gain Beinn Nuis (*face hill*) from the south east, an easy tramp with a final steep pull. The walk north to Beinn Tarsuinn presents no difficulty though the east face is an amazing world of granite slabs and pinnacles. Tarsuinn has perhaps the best panoramic view for it includes Goat Fell soaring over its scoured, rocky base. Rock, heather and boulders quickly lead down to the Bowmen's Pass, Bealach an Fhir-bhogha, where decisions have to be made, for the A' Chir Ridge lies ahead. This can be outflanked on the west below the overlapping rocks, and both the Coire a' Bhradain and Glen Iorsa sides of the pass can be descended, but the crest is not as difficult as appearances suggest and it is worth "having a look". Most of the day's route has been worn into a path, and even on the rocks the way is usually visible from the marks of passing feet. A rising line up the slabs on the west side leads to the crest.

Exposed but easy scrambling leads along to the summit of A' Chir (*The comb*: Ah keer), the top being a large, undercut boulder which is a minor challenge in itself. Beyond the summit, on the descent, lies the notorious *mauvais pas*, which is basically unavoidable so has to be faced. The exposure rather than any technical difficulty gives the Bad Step its reputation. A cairn shows where the ridge has to be left to descend a twelve-foot wall on the east face to a ledge angling along to easier ground. Some people claim this is not the actual Bad Step but just a difficult section of ridge. That name they would keep for a feature met not long before, at the foot of the initial descent off A' Chir, where a foot-wide col (the narrowest part of the whole ridge) is cleft through so that you have to make "a step across space", so to speak. You can allocate the name as you choose.

Beyond these adrenalin-boosting spots there is one further granite tower and then easy grass slopes which lead up to Cir Mhor, famous for the Rosa Pinnacle, a soaring, curving buttress of granite on the right. (The best view of the pinnacle is from the Fionn Choire, reached by walking up Glen Rosa.) The summit of this *aiguille*-like peak is a superb situation for such an easy ascent, the central position giving views in all directions, both down the glens and to the other peaks, but my favourite view is from Caisteal Abhail. There, the view takes in Cir Mhor as well. The crest from Cir Mhor to Caisteal Abhail is easy.

There is a welcome spring on the shoulder, as one pulls up to the *Ptarmigan's castles*, which is a good resting place. Cir Mhor appears to lean over into Glen Sannox and its jagged shape is echoed in Goat Fell behind and, distantly, in the thrust of Holy Island opposite Lamlash. The Castles are a collection of summit boulders and tors, as is the route's continuation eastwards for the next mile. Careful navigation is required not to stray on to secondary ridges — and then there is the Witch's Step, the Carlin's Leap, Ceum na Caillich.

These are either the deep gash in the ridge caused by the weathering away of a whin dyke, or the tricky exit up the far side — opinion again does not agree — but everything can be avoided by descending a short way from the gap and traversing along the northern flanks. (Sheep have long ago worn paths under all the crags, and these are usually clear.) The far side of the gap appears intimidating but "goes" with just one awkward place — the sloping slab from which a bulge of granite tries to push you off. This leads to a gully which runs up to easier ground, the top being another claimant for the actual title of the Witch's Step. I reckon the Step names, on both hills, belong to the gaps where there is a step across. (The name Ceum na Caillich on the 1:50,000 map is much misplaced.)

The ridge runs out over a rise (634 m) to the prow of Suidhe Fhearghas (Soo-ee Fergus, *Fergus's Seat*) from which the descent can be made to the nineteenth hole of the Sannox Golf Course. Fergus was the bard of the Fiana, who often hunted in Arran according to Irish legends. Or Fergus was the king who came up here to survey his domains. Again, take your pick.

If simply seeking the Corbetts and wishing to avoid the Bad Insteps, Witches' Hiccups and so on I'd recommend the following. Reach Beinn Tarsuinn as above and then, from the Bealach an Fhirbhogha, take the pavement-like crest of Beinn a' Chiabhain to descend by Crioc Breac back to Glen Rosa. For Cir Mhor walk up Glen Rosa and gain the A' Chir–Cir Mhor saddle. Perhaps add Caisteal Abhail and return the same way or cross the Saddle to descend Glen Sannox; or, best of all, from the castles, head for Loch na Davie and Lochranza.

When I took the dog to Arran for his Corbetts we did the three together by going up by Beinn a' Chiabhain, adding Tarsuinn, along A' Chir, out to Caisteal Abhail, back to Cir Mhor and down Fionn Choire to Glen Rosa. The dog's exuberance was rather alarming. On the tricky wall I tied clothes together to make a rope to lower Storm in the rucksack, but he decided to jump out half-way down. As often as not when I was struggling he'd be peering down at me, mocking my incompetence. He's very hard to live up to.

On Goat Fell there is a good path off Meall Breac down to Corrie, giving a traverse that can be made without difficulty. These are all recommendable routes. Perhaps they will help bring you back to Arran again. Once you have got the Corbetts out of your system you still have to do something. As Robert Louis Stevenson said: ". . . where we have discovered a continent or crossed a chain of mountains [or done the Corbetts] it is only to find another ocean or another plain upon the farther side. Even in one corner the weather and the seasons keep so deftly changing that, though we walk there for a lifetime, there will be always something new to startle and delight. Little do you know your blessedness; for to travel hopefully is a better thing than to arrive . . .

"You lean from the window, your last pipe reeking whitely into the darkness, your body full of delicious pains, your mind enthroned in the seventh circle of content; when suddenly the mood changes, the weathercock goes about, and you ask yourself one question more: whether [Corbetts done] you have been wise, or the most egregious of donkeys? But at least you have had a fine moment, and looked down upon all the kingdoms of the earth. And whether it was wise or foolish, tomorrow's travel will carry you body, and mind, into some different parish of the infinite."

APPENDICES

BIBLIOGRAPHICAL NOTES

SOME BOOKS MENTIONED IN THE TEXT

Bennet, Donald, *Scottish Mountain Climbs*, Batsford 1979
Bord, Janet & Colin, *Sacred Waters*, Granada 1985
Borthwick, Alistair, *Always a Little Further*, Faber 1939, repr. Diadem 1983
Brown, Hamish M., *Hamish's Mountain Walk*, Gollancz 1978, paperback Paladin 1980
—— *Hamish's Groats End Walk*, Gollancz 1981, paperback Paladin 1983
—— *The Island of Rhum*, Milnthorpe, Cicerone Press 1988
—— *Travels*, Edinburgh, The Scotsman 1986
Corbett, J. Rooke, see *SMC Journal*
Crockett, S. R., *The Raiders*, T. Fisher Unwin 1894, repr. Ernest Benn 1947
Ellice, E. C., *Place Names of Glengarry and Glenquoich*, Routledge 1931
Firsoff, V. A., *In the Hills of Breadalbane*, Hale 1954
Grierson, Rev. Thomas, *Autumnal Rambles among the Scottish Mountains*, Edinburgh, Paton & Ritchie 1850
Hall, Rev. James, *Travels in Scotland*, London, J. Johnson 1807
Hogg, James, *A Tour in the Highlands in 1803*, Paisley, A. Gardner 1888
Holmes, W. K., *Tramping Scottish Hills*, Stirling, Eneas Mackay 1946, repr. as *On Scottish Hills*, Oliver & Boyde 1962
Jeffrey, Alan, *Scotland Underground*, A. Oldham, Rhychydwr, Crymych, Dyfed
Maccullough, J., *A Description of the Western Islands (1811–21)* extracted in *SMC Journal*
—— *Highlands and Western Islands of Scotland* extracted in *SMC Journal*
McGill, Patrick, *Children of the Dead End*, Herbert Jenkins 1914, paperback Caliban Books 1985

MacInnes, Hamish, *West Highlands Walks*, 3 vols. Hodder 1979–84
McOwan, Rennie, *Walks in the Trossachs and Rob Roy Country*, Edinburgh, The Saint Andrew Press 1983
Macrow, Brenda, *Torridon Highlands*, Hale 1950
Miles, Hamish, *Fair Perthshire*, Bodley Head 1930
Morton, H. V., *In Search of Scotland*, Methuen 1930, paperback Methuen 1984
Mould, D. D. C. Pochin, *Roads from the Isles*, Oliver & Boyd 1950
Munro's Tables and other Tables of Lesser Heights, Edinburgh, SMC 1984 edit.
Munro, H., see also *SMC Journal*
Plumb, Charles, *Walking in the Grampians*, A. Maclehose 1935
Poucher, W. A., *The Scottish Peaks*, Constable 1965, 6th ed. 1982
——*The Magic of Skye*, Constable 1949
Robertson, Rev. A. E., see *SMC Journal*
Smith, Janet Adam, *Mountain Holidays*, Dent 1946
Smith, Robert, *Grampian Ways*, Melven Press 1980
Steven, Campbell, *The Island Hills*, Hurst & Blackett 1955
Stevenson, Robert Louis, "El Dorado" in *Virginibus Puerisque*, Kegan Paul 1881, paperback Penguin 1946
Stott, Louis, *Waterfalls of Scotland*, Aberdeen University Press 1987
Victoria, Queen, *More Leaves from the Journal of a Life in the Highlands*, Smith, Elder & Co. 1884, extracted in *Our Life in the Highlands*, Wm Kimber 1968
Wilson, Ken, and Gilbert, Richard, *The Big Walks*, Diadem 1980
——*Classic Walks*, Diadem 1982
Young, Geoffrey Winthrop, *Collected Poems*, Methuen 1936

JOURNALS AND GUIDES

Cairngorm Club *Journal*
Getting Around the Highlands and Islands, F. H. G. Publications, Abbey Mill Centre, Seedhill, Paisley PA1 1JN (or from Tourist Offices)
Grampian Club *Bulletin*
SMC District Guides
SMC Journal
Scottish Postbus Timetable (can be ordered from any Post Office)

MUNROS WITH ADJACENT CORBETTS

Munro Section & Number	Munro Name	Corbett Section & Number	Corbett Name
1: 2	Beinn Narnain and	2: 4	The Cobbler and
1: 3	Beinn Ime	2: 5	Beinn Luibhean, & others
1: 7	Beinn Bhuidhe	2: 8	Meall an Fhudair
1: 9	Ben Lui	3: 2	Beinn Chuirn
1:24	Ben Vorlich and	2:15	Meall na Fearna and
1:25	Stuc a' Chroin	2:14	Beinn Each
1:26	Ben Chonzie	4:13	Auchnafree Hill
2: 8	Carn Gorm	4:12	Beinn Dearg
2: 9	Stuchd an Lochain	4: 9, 10	Sron a' Choire Chnapanich & Meall Buidhe
2:11	Meall Buidhe	4:11	Cam Chreag
2:19	Meall a' Choire Leith	4: 6	Meall Luaidhe
2:20	Meall nan Tarmachan	4: 7	Beinn nan Oighreag
2:24	Meall Ghaordie	4: 7	Beinn nan Oighreag
	and	4: 8	Meall nan Subh
2:26	Creag Mhor	3: 8	Cam Chreag
2:28	Ben Challum	3: 8	Cam Chreag
	and	3: 7	Beinn Chaorach
2:30	Meall Glas	4: 1	Beinn nan Imirean
2:40	Beinn Mhanach	3:10	Beinn nam Fuaran
3: 5	Stob Diamh, Cruachan	3: 1	Beinn a' Bhuiridh
3:16	Meall nan Eun	3:13	Stob Dubh, Beinn Ceitlein
3:23	Creise	5: 4	Beinn Mhic Chasgaig
3:33	Bidean nam Bian	5: 3	Beinn Maol Chaluim
3:41	Meall Dearg	5: 6	Garbh Bheinn
3:43	Sgorr na h-Ulaidh	5: 2	Meall Ligiche
3:46	Beinn Sgulaird	3:11	Creach Bheinn
4:40	Stob Ban	5:10, 11	Sgurr Innse, Cruach Innse
4:41	Stob Coire Easain	5:10, 11	Sgurr Innse, Cruach Innse
4:47	Beinn na Lap	5: 9	Leum Uilleim
4:48	Carn Dearg	6: 1	Meall na Meoig
5: 1	Sgairneach Mhor	6: 6	Sow of Atholl
5: 6	Carn na Caim	6: 8	An Dun
6: 1	Carn an Fhidhleir	7: 6	Beinn Bhreac
6: 3	Beinn Dearg	7: 5	Beinn Mheadhonach
	or	7: 6	Beinn Bhreac
6: 4	Carn a' Chlamain	7: 5	Beinn Mheadhonach
7:20	Lochnagar	7:11	Conachraig
8:29	Bynach More	8: 1	Creag Mhor
8:41	Beinn a' Chaorainn	8: 1	Creag Mhor

THE CORBETTS IN ORDER OF ALTITUDE

862   Cam Chreag (Glen Lyon 4:11)
      Beinn Mhic Chasgaig
      Meall na h-Aisre
      Sgurr na Feartaig
      Creag an Dail Bheag (Carn Liath)
      Beinn a' Bha'ach Ard

860   Beinn Lair

859   Morrone
      Caisteal Abhail

858   Beinn Luibhean
      Fraoch Bheinn

857   Beinn a' Chrulaiste
      Cruach Innse
      Carn Dearg Mor
      Beinn a' Chaisgein Mor

855   Stob an Aonaich Mhoir
      Beinn Bhuidhe
      Beinn an Eoin

853   Creach Bheinn (Ardgour 10:2)

852   Meall an t-Seallaidh

849   Cul Mor
      Bac an Eich
      Sgurr Ghiubhsachain

847   Ben Donich

846   Canisp

845   Carn Ban
      Beinn Resipol

844   Beinn nan Imirean

843   The Merrick

841   Sgurr an Airgid
      Ben Vrackie
      Beinn Mholach

840   Broad Law
      Meallan nan Uan
      Ben Rinnes
      Beinn Udlaidh

c.840   Beinn Trilleachan

838   Carn Chuinneag
      Meall na h-Eilde

c.838   Sgurr Gaorsaic

837   Sron a' Choire Chnapanich

835   Sgurr Cos na Breachd-laoidh

834   Creag nan Gabhar

830   Beinn Dearg (Glen Lyon 4:12)
      Carn Dearg (S of Glen Roy 9:2)

829   Brown Cow Hill
      Carn Mor (Glen Pean 11:1)

827   An Dun

825   Beinn Tarsuinn (Arran 18:10)

824   Geal-charn Mor

822   White Coomb

821   Geal Charn (Caiplich 8:3)
      Benvane

818   Beinn Chaorach
      Carn na Drochaide
      Sgorr na Diollaid
      Beinn Dearg Bheag

817   Binnein an Fhidhleir

816   Carn a' Chuilinn

815   Carn Dearg (N of Gleann Eachach
      9:5)

814   Corserine
      An Stac
      An Sidhean
      Creag Liath, Breabag

813   Beinn Each
      Sgor Mor

812   Askival

811   Carn na Saobhaidhe

810   Creach Bheinn (Loch Creran 3:11)
      Meall a' Bhuachaille

809   Creag MacRanaich
      Meall na Fearna

808   Sail Gharbh, Quinag
      Sgurr Innse
      Hart Fell

807   Beinn nam Fuaran
      Craig Rainich
      Monamenach

806   Ben Gulabin
      Garbh-bheinn (Skye 18:3)

804   Geal Charn (Arkaig 12:2)
      Beinn na h-Eaglaise
      Carn Mor (Ladder Hills 8:5)
      Meall nan Subh

803   The Sow of Atholl
      Beinn Bhreach-liath

CORBETT INDEX